µC/OS-III™
The Real-Time Kernel

Jean J. Labrosse

Micriµm
Press

Weston, FL 33326

Micriµm Press
1290 Weston Road, Suite 306
Weston, FL 33326
USA
www.micrium.com

Library of Congress Control Number: 2010922732

Library of Congress subject headings:

1. Embedded computer systems
2. Real-time data processing
3. Computer software - Development

For bulk orders, please contact Micrium Press at: +1 954 217 2036

100-uCOS-III-Renesas-RX62N-001

ISBN: 978-0-9823375-7-8

*To my loving and caring wife, Manon,
and our two children James and Sabrina.*

Table of Contents

Part I: µC/OS-III – The Real-Time Kernel

Part II: µC/OS-III and the Renesas RX62N

Foreword to μC/OS-III — by Jack Ganssle

Your system has to read a keyboard and update the display. That's pretty easy to handle in a simple loop.

Oh, wait, then there's the A/D converter which needs service once a millisecond. The data is noisy so ten samples must be averaged and the result fed into a computation which is sent to the display. But you can't do the math till the results of the encoder become available, and that can only be read on 20 msec intervals.

But don't forget to monitor the radiation source; if it goes out of limits a safety protocol has to be invoked to avoid harming users. That has to be monitored every 250 milliseconds.

How would one write this code? Sure, it's possible to write an interrupt handler that takes clock ticks and then, via a number of tortured loops, sequences off the proper activities. It'll be tough to debug and harder to maintain. You can be sure the boss will come in, red-faced, wondering why the heck the system only looks at safety parameters every quarter second when any idiot knows the rate should be 0.230 sec, no matter how he wrote the spec. The loops grow more complex and the program ever more convoluted.

This is a very old problem, one solved by the use of a Real-Time Operating System (RTOS). Write each activity as a separate task. The code is simple, crystal clear, and easy to change.

An old problem, yes. But there's surprisingly little written about the use of an RTOS. Jean Labrosse wrote one of the first and best books on the subject: the first edition of this volume. I'm told the first edition, and the subsequent second edition, are the best selling books ever published about embedded systems, and I'm not surprised. Extremely-well written, they covered the subject in depth and with finesse. He wrote using the μC/OS and μC/OS-II RTOSes as examples.

Now Jean and the crew at Micrium have a new and hugely improved version of that RTOS: µC/OS-III. Where µC/OS-II is a commercial quality product, one that even meets the highest safety-critical requirements, µC/OS-III takes that quality and reliability level to even the most demanding applications.

Jean has supplemented the new RTOS with this book. It's much weightier than his previous RTOS books as this volume goes in depth into the nuances of using an operating system in real applications. µC/OS-III lays out the rationale behind an RTOS, and then in a very logical fashion presents each of the resources provided by an RTOS and how one goes about using those features in a product. Though µC/OS-III is used as an example, it is not presented as the canonical RTOS, and users of any real-time operating system will find this material immensely useable.

I have long counted Jean a friend, and have great respect for his perfectionism. That is clear when reading the µC/OS source code, which is probably the most beautiful code I have read, and, since it has been used in products certified to DO-178B level A, also works!

That perfectionism also manifests itself in this book, in which it's clear he has taken pains to get every fact right, every drawing clear, all while maintaining a very consistent style.

This is a book by an engineer, for engineers (including engineering students). Devoid of fluff, it's packed with information about using an RTOS in a real system… today. What do I need to do to get started? What are all those files? Where is the information I need located?

Are you using an RTOS? If so, read this book. If you're not using one, read this book; not every embedded system needs an operating system, but there are too many that have been cobbled together through the painful use of ad hoc loops that an RTOS would vastly improve.

Preface

µC/OS-III (pronounced "Micro C O S Three) is a scalable, ROMable, preemptive real-time kernel that manages an unlimited number of tasks. µC/OS-III is a third-generation kernel and offers all of the services expected from a modern real-time kernel, such as resource management, synchronization, inter-task communications, and more. However, µC/OS-III offers many unique features not found in other real-time kernels, such as the ability to complete performance measurements at run-time, to directly signal or send messages to tasks, achieve pending on multiple kernel objects, and more.

WHY A NEW µC/OS VERSION?

The µC/OS series, first introduced in 1992, has undergone a number of changes over the years based on feedback from thousands of people using and deploying its evolving versions.

µC/OS-III is the sum of this feedback and experience. Rarely used µC/OS-II features were eliminated and newer, more efficient features and services, were added. Probably the most common request was to add round robin scheduling, which was not possible for µC/OS-II, but is now a feature of µC/OS-III.

µC/OS-III also provides additional features that better exploit the capabilities of today's newer processors. Specifically, µC/OS-III was designed with 32-bit processors in mind, although it certainly works well with 16- and even several 8-bit processors.

µC/OS-III GOALS

The main goal of µC/OS-III is to provide a best-in-class real-time kernel that literally shaves months of development time from an embedded-product schedule. Using a commercial real-time kernel such as µC/OS-III provides a solid foundation and framework to the design engineer dealing with the growing complexity of embedded designs.

Another goal for µC/OS-III, and therefore this book, is to explain inner workings of a commercial-grade kernel. This understanding will assist the reader in making logical design decisions and informed tradeoffs between hardware and software that make sense.

Chapter

1

Introduction

Real-time systems are systems whereby the correctness of the computed values and their timeliness are at the forefront. There are two types of real-time systems, hard and soft real time.

What differentiates hard and soft real-time systems is their tolerance to missing deadlines and the consequences associated with those misses. Correctly computed values after a deadline has passed are often useless.

For hard real-time systems, missing deadlines is not an option. In fact, in many cases, missing a deadline often results in catastrophe, which may involve human lives. For soft real-time systems, however, missing deadlines is generally not as critical.

Real-time applications cover a wide range, but many real-time systems are embedded. An embedded system is a computer built into a system and not acknowledged by the user as being a computer. The following list shows just a few examples of embedded systems:

Aerospace
- Flight management systems
- Jet engine controls
- Weapons systems

Audio
- MP3 players
- Amplifiers and tuners

Automotive
- Antilock braking systems
- Climate control
- Engine controls
- Navigation systems (GPS)

Communications
- Routers
- Switches
- Cell phones

Computer peripherals
- Printers
- Scanners

Domestic
- Air conditioning units
- Thermostats
- White goods

Office automation
- FAX machines / copiers

Process control
- Chemical plants
- Factory automation
- Food processing

Robots

Video
- Broadcasting equipment
- HD Televisions

And many more

Real-time systems are typically more complicated to design, debug, and deploy than non-real-time systems.

1-1 FOREGROUND/BACKGROUND SYSTEMS

Small systems of low complexity are typically designed as foreground/background systems or super-loops. An application consists of an infinite loop that calls modules (i.e., tasks) to perform the desired operations (background). Interrupt Service Routines (ISRs) handle asynchronous events (foreground). Foreground is also called interrupt level; background is called task level.

Critical operations that should be performed at the task level must unfortunately be handled by the ISRs to ensure that they are dealt with in a timely fashion. This causes ISRs to take longer than they should. Also, information for a background module that an ISR makes available is not processed until the background routine gets its turn to execute, which is called the task-level response. The worst-case task-level response time depends on how long a background loop takes to execute since the execution time of typical code is not constant, the time for successive passes through a portion of the loop is nondeterministic. Furthermore, if a code change is made, the timing of the loop is affected.

Most high-volume and low-cost microcontroller-based applications (e.g., microwave ovens, telephones, toys, etc.) are designed as foreground/background systems.

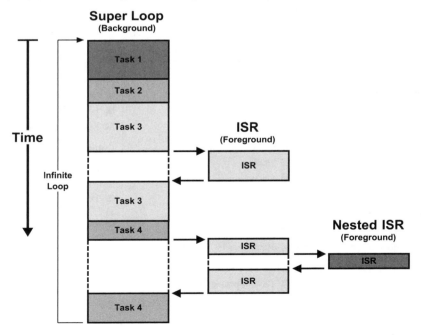

Figure 1-1 **Foreground/Background (SuperLoops) systems**

1-2 REAL-TIME KERNELS

A real-time kernel is software that manages the time and resources of a microprocessor, microcontroller or Digital Signal Processor (DSP).

The design process of a real-time application involves splitting the work into tasks, each responsible for a portion of the job. A task (also called a thread) is a simple program that thinks it has the Central Processing Unit (CPU) completely to itself. On a single CPU, only one task executes at any given time.

The kernel is responsible for the management of tasks. This is called multitasking. Multitasking is the process of scheduling and switching the CPU between several tasks. The CPU switches its attention between several sequential tasks. Multitasking provides the illusion of having multiple CPUs and maximizes the use of the CPU. Multitasking also helps in the creation of modular applications. One of the most important aspects of multitasking is that it allows the application programmer to manage the complexity inherent in real-time applications. Application programs are easier to design and maintain when multitasking is used.

μC/OS-III is a preemptive kernel, which means that μC/OS-III always runs the most important task that is ready to run as shown in Figure 1-2.

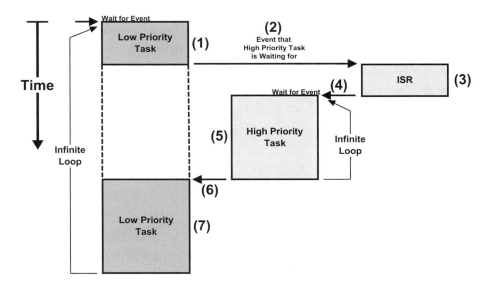

Figure 1-2 **μC/OS-III is a preemptive kernel**

FI-2(1)   A low-priority task is executing.

FI-2(2)   An interrupt occurs, and the CPU vectors to the ISR responsible for servicing the interrupting device.

FI-2(3)   The ISR services the interrupt device, but actually does very little work. The ISR will signal or send a message to a higher-priority task that will be responsible for most of the processing of the interrupting device. For example, if the interrupt comes from an Ethernet controller, the ISR simply signals a task, which will process the received packet.

FI-2(4)   When the ISR finishes, µC/OS-III notices that a more important task has been made ready to run by the ISR and will not return to the interrupted task, but instead context switch to the more important task.

FI-2(5)   The higher-priority task executes and performs the necessary processing in response to the interrupt device.

FI-2(6)   When the higher-priority task completes its work, it loops back to the beginning of the task code and makes a µC/OS-III function call to wait for the next interrupt from the device.

FI-2(7)   The low-priority task resumes exactly at the point where it was interrupted, not knowing what happened.

Kernels such as µC/OS-III are also responsible for managing communication between tasks, and managing system resources (memory and I/O devices).

A kernel adds overhead to a system because the services provided by the kernel require time to execute. The amount of overhead depends on how often these services are invoked. In a well-designed application, a kernel uses between 2% and 4% of a CPU's time. And, since µC/OS-III is software that is added to an application, it requires extra ROM (code space) and RAM (data space).

Low-end single-chip microcontrollers are generally not able to run a real-time kernel such as µC/OS-III since they have access to very little RAM. µC/OS-III requires between 1 Kbyte and 4 Kbytes of RAM, plus each task requires its own stack space. It is possible for µC/OS-III to work on processors having as little as 4 Kbytes of RAM.

Finally, µC/OS-III allows for better use of the CPU by providing approximately 70 indispensable services. After designing a system using a real-time kernel such as µC/OS-III, you will not return to designing a foreground/background system.

1-3 RTOS (REAL-TIME OPERATING SYSTEM)

A Real Time Operating System generally contains a real-time kernel and other higher-level services such as file management, protocol stacks, a Graphical User Interface (GUI), and other components. Most additional services revolve around I/O devices.

Micriµm offers a complete suite of RTOS components including: µC/FS (an Embedded File System), µC/TCP-IP (a TCP/IP stack), µC/GUI (a Graphical User Interface), µC/USB (a USB device, host and OTG stack), and more. Most of these components are designed to work standalone. Except for µC/TCP-IP, a real-time kernel is not required to use the components in an application. In fact, users can pick and choose only the components required for the application. Contact Micriµm (www.micrium.com) for additional details and pricing.

1-4 µC/OS-III

µC/OS-III is a scalable, ROMable, preemptive real-time kernel that manages an unlimited number of tasks. µC/OS-III is a third-generation kernel, offering all of the services expected from a modern real-time kernel including resource management, synchronization, inter-task communication, and more. However, µC/OS-III also offers many unique features not found in other real-time kernels, such as the ability to perform performance measurements at run time, directly signal or send messages to tasks, and pending (i.e., waiting) on such multiple kernel objects as semaphores and message queues.

Here is a list of features provided by µC/OS-III:

Source Code: µC/OS-III is provided in ANSI-C source form to licensees. The source code for µC/OS-III is arguably the cleanest and most consistent kernel code available. Clean source is part of the corporate culture at Micriµm. Although many commercial kernel vendors provide source code for their products, unless the code follows strict coding standards and is accompanied by complete documentation with examples to show how the code works, these products may be cumbersome and difficult to harness. With this book, you will gain a deep understanding of the inner workings of µC/OS-III, which will protect your investment.

Intuitive Application Programming Interface (API): µC/OS-III is highly intuitive. Once familiar with the consistent coding conventions used, it is simple to predict the functions to call for the services required, and even predict which arguments are needed. For example, a pointer to an object is always the first argument, and a pointer to an error code is always the last one.

Preemptive multitasking: µC/OS-III is a preemptive multi-tasking kernel and therefore, µC/OS-III always runs the most important ready-to-run task.

Round robin scheduling of tasks at equal priority: µC/OS-III allows multiple tasks to run at the same priority level. When multiple tasks at the same priority are ready to run, and that priority level is the most important level, µC/OS-III runs each task for a user-specified time called a time quanta. Each task can define its own time quanta, and a task can also give up the CPU to another task at the same priority if it does not require the full time quanta.

Low interrupt disable time: µC/OS-III has a number of internal data structures and variables that it needs to access atomically. To ensure this, µC/OS-III is able to protect these critical regions by locking the scheduler instead of disabling interrupts. Interrupts are therefore disabled for very little time. This ensures that µC/OS-III is able to respond to some of the fastest interrupt sources.

Deterministic: Interrupt response with µC/OS-III is deterministic. Also, execution times of most services provided by µC/OS-III are deterministic.

Scalable: The footprint (both code and data) can be adjusted based on the requirements of the application. This assumes access to the source code for µC/OS-III since adding and removing features (i.e., services) is performed at compile time through approximately 40 **#defines** (see **OS_CFG.H**). µC/OS-III also performs a number of run-time checks on arguments passed to µC/OS-III services. Specifically, µC/OS-III verifies that the user is not passing **NULL** pointers, not calling task level services from ISRs, that arguments are within allowable range, and options specified are valid, etc.. These checks can be disabled (at compile time) to further reduce the code footprint and improve performance. The fact that µC/OS-III is scalable allows it to be used in a wide range of applications and projects.

Portable: µC/OS-III can be ported to a large number of CPU architectures. Most µC/OS-II ports are easily converted to work on µC/OS-III with minimal changes in just a matter of minutes and therefore benefit from more than 45 CPU architectures already supported by µC/OS-II.

ROMable: µC/OS-III was designed especially for embedded systems and can be ROMed along with the application code.

Run-time configurable: µC/OS-III allows the user to configure the kernel at run time. Specifically, all kernel objects such as tasks, stacks, semaphores, event-flag groups, message queues, number of messages, mutual exclusion semaphores, memory partitions and timers, are allocated by the user at run time. This prevents over-allocating resources at compile time.

Unlimited number of tasks: µC/OS-III supports an unlimited number of tasks. From a practical standpoint, however, the number of tasks is actually limited by the amount of memory (both code and data space) that the processor has access to. Each task requires its own stack space and, µC/OS-III provides features to allow stack growth of the tasks to be monitored at run-time.

µC/OS-III does not impose any limitations on the size of each task, except that there be a minimum size based on the CPU used.

Unlimited number of priorities: µC/OS-III supports an unlimited number of priority levels. However, configuring µC/OS-III for between 32 and 256 different priority levels is more than adequate for most applications.

Unlimited number of kernel objects: µC/OS-III allows for any number of tasks, semaphores, mutual exclusion semaphores, event flags, message queues, timers, and memory partitions. The user at run-time allocates all kernel objects.

Services: µC/OS-III provides all the services expected from a high-end real-time kernel, such as task management, time management, semaphores, event flags, mutexes, message queues, software timers, fixed-size memory pools, etc.

Mutual Exclusion Semaphores (Mutexes): Mutexes are provided for resource management. Mutexes are special types of semaphores that have built-in priority inheritance, which eliminate unbounded priority inversions. Accesses to a mutex can be nested and therefore, a task can acquire the same mutex up to 250 times. Of course, the mutex owner needs to release the mutex an equal number of times.

Nested task suspension: µC/OS-III allows a task to suspend itself or another task. Suspending a task means that the task will not be allowed to execute until the task is resumed by another task. Suspension can be nested up to 250 levels deep. In other words, a task can suspend another task up to 250 times. Of course, the task must be resumed an equal number of times for it to become eligible to run on the CPU.

Software timers: Define any number of "one-shot" and/or "periodic" timers. Timers are countdown counters that perform a user-definable action upon counting down to 0. Each timer can have its own action and, if a timer is periodic, the timer is automatically reloaded and the action is executed every time the countdown reaches zero.

Pend on multiple objects: µC/OS-III allows an application to wait (i.e., pend) on multiple events at the same time. Specifically, a task can wait on multiple semaphores and/or message queues to be posted. The waiting task wakes up as soon as one of the events occurs.

Task Signals: µC/OS-III allows an ISR or task to directly signal a task. This avoids having to create an intermediate kernel object such as a semaphore or event flag just to signal a task, and results in better performance.

Task Messages: µC/OS-III allows an ISR or a task to send messages directly to a task. This avoids having to create and use a message queue, and also results in better performance.

Task registers: Each task can have a user-definable number of "task registers." Task registers are different than CPU registers. Task registers can be used to hold "errno" type variable, IDs, interrupt disable time measurement on a per-task basis, and more.

Error checking: µC/OS-III verifies that `NULL` pointers are not passed, that the user is not calling task-level services from ISRs, that arguments are within allowable range, that options specified are valid, that a handler is passed to the proper object as part of the arguments to services that manipulate the desired object, and more. Each µC/OS-III API function returns an error code concerning the outcome of the function call.

Built-in performance measurements: µC/OS-III has built-in features to measure the execution time of each task, stack usage of each task, number of times a task executes, CPU usage, ISR-to-task and task-to-task response time, peak number of entries in certain lists, interrupt disable and scheduler lock time on a per-task basis, and more.

Can easily be optimized: µC/OS-III was designed so that it could easily be optimized based on the CPU architecture. Most data types used in µC/OS-III can be changed to make better use of the CPU's natural word size. Also, the priority resolution algorithm can easily be written in assembly language to benefit from special instructions such as bit set and clear, as well as count-leading-zeros (CLZ), or find-first-one (FF1) instructions.

Deadlock prevention: All of the µC/OS-III "pend" services include timeouts, which help avoid deadlocks.

Tick handling at task level: The clock tick manager in µC/OS-III is accomplished by a task that receives a trigger from an ISR. Handling delays and timeouts by a task greatly reduces interrupt latency. Also, µC/OS-III uses a hashed delta list mechanism, which further reduces the amount of overhead in processing delays and timeouts of tasks.

User definable hooks: µC/OS-III allows the port and application programmer to define "hook" functions, which are called by µC/OS-III. A hook is simply a defined function that allows the user to extend the functionality of µC/OS-III. One such hook is called during a context switch, another when a task is created, yet another when a task is deleted, etc.

Timestamps: For time measurements, µC/OS-III requires that a 16-bit or 32-bit free running counter be made available. This counter can be read at run time to make time measurements of certain events. For example, when an ISR posts a message to a task, the timestamp counter is automatically read and saved as part of the message posted. When the recipient receives the message, the timestamp is provided to the recipient, and by reading the current timestamp, the time it took for the message to be received can be determined.

Built-in support for Kernel Awareness debuggers: This feature allows kernel awareness debuggers to examine and display µC/OS-III variables and data structures in a user-friendly way, but only when the debugger hits a breakpoint. Instead of a static view of the environment the kernel awareness support in µC/OS-III is also used by µC/Probe to display the same information at run-time.

Object names: Each µC/OS-III kernel object can have a name associated with it. This makes it easy to recognize what the object is assigned to. Assign an ASCII name to a task, a semaphore, a mutex, an event flag group, a message queue, a memory partition, and a timer. The object name can have any length, but must be NUL terminated.

1-5 µC/OS, µC/OS-II AND µC/OS-III FEATURES COMPARISON

Table 1-1 shows the evolution of µC/OS over the years, comparing the features available in each version.

Feature	µC/OS	µC/OS-II	µC/OS-III
Year introduced	1992	1998	2009
Book	Yes	Yes	Yes
Source code available	Yes	Yes	Yes (Licensees only)
Preemptive Multitasking	Yes	Yes	Yes
Maximum number of tasks	64	255	Unlimited
Number of tasks at each priority level	1	1	Unlimited
Round Robin Scheduling	No	No	Yes
Semaphores	Yes	Yes	Yes
Mutual Exclusion Semaphores	No	Yes	Yes (Nestable)
Event Flags	No	Yes	Yes
Message Mailboxes	Yes	Yes	No (not needed)
Message Queues	Yes	Yes	Yes
Fixed Sized Memory Management	No	Yes	Yes
Signal a task without requiring a semaphore	No	No	Yes
Send messages to a task without requiring a message queue	No	No	Yes
Software Timers	No	Yes	Yes
Task suspend/resume	No	Yes	Yes (Nestable)
Deadlock prevention	Yes	Yes	Yes
Scalable	Yes	Yes	Yes
Code Footprint	3K to 8K	6K to 26K	6K to 20K
Data Footprint	1K+	1K+	1K+
ROMable	Yes	Yes	Yes

Feature	µC/OS	µC/OS-II	µC/OS-III
Run-time configurable	No	No	Yes
Compile-time configurable	Yes	Yes	Yes
ASCII names for each kernel object	No	Yes	Yes
Pend on multiple objects	No	Yes	Yes
Task registers	No	Yes	Yes
Built-in performance measurements	No	Limited	Extensive
User definable hook functions	No	Yes	Yes
Time stamps on posts	No	No	Yes
Built-in Kernel Awareness support	No	Yes	Yes
Optimizable Scheduler in assembly language	No	No	Yes
Tick handling at task level	No	No	Yes
Source code available	Yes	Yes	Yes
Number of services	~20	~90	~70
MISRA-C:1998	No	Yes (except 10 rules)	N/A
MISRA-C:2004	No	No	Yes (except 7 rules)
DO178B Level A and EUROCAE ED-12B	No	Yes	In progress
Medical FDA pre-market notification (510(k)) and pre-market approval (PMA)	No	Yes	In progress
SIL3/SIL4 IEC for transportation and nuclear systems	No	Yes	In progress
IEC-61508	No	Yes	In progress

Table 1-1 **µC/OS-II and µC/OS-III Features Comparison Chart**

1-6 HOW THE BOOK IS ORGANIZED

This book consists of two books in one.

Part I describes µC/OS-III and is not tied to any specific CPU architecture. Here, the reader will learn about real-time kernels through µC/OS-III. Specifically, critical sections, task management, the ready list, scheduling, context switching, interrupt management, wait lists, time management, timers, resource management, synchronization, memory management, how to use µC/OS-III's API, how to configure µC/OS-III, and how to port µC/OS-III to different CPU architectures, are all covered.

Part II describes the port of a popular CPU architecture. Here, learn about this CPU architecture and how µC/OS-III gets the most out of the CPU. Examples are provided to actually run code on the evaluation board that is available with this book.

As I just mentioned, this book assumes the presence of an evaluation board that allows the user to experiment with the wonderful world of real-time kernels, and specifically µC/OS-III. The book and board are complemented by a full set of tools that are provided free of charge either in a companion CD/DVD, or downloadable through the Internet. The tools and the use of µC/OS-III are free as long as they are used with the evaluation board, and there is no commercial intent to use them on a project. In other words, there is no additional charge except for the initial cost of the book, evaluation board and tools, as long as they are used for educational purposes.

The book also comes with a trial version of an award-winning tool from Micriµm called µC/Probe. The trial version allows the user to monitor and change up to five variables in a target system.

1-7 µC/PROBE

µC/Probe is a Microsoft Windows™ based application that enables the user to visualize variables in a target at run time. Specifically, display or change the value of any variable in a system while the target is running. These variables can be displayed using such graphical elements as gauges, meters, bar graphs, virtual LEDs, numeric indicators, and many more. Sliders, switches, and buttons can be used to change variables. This is accomplished without the user writing a single line of code!

µC/Probe interfaces to any target (8-, 16-, 32-, 64-bit, or even DSPs) through one of the many interfaces supported (J-Tag, RS-232C, USB, Ethernet, etc.). µC/Probe displays or changes any variable (as long as they are global) in the application, including µC/OS-III's internal variables.

µC/Probe works with any compiler/assembler/linker able to generate an ELF/DWARF or IEEE695 file. This is the exact same file that the user will download to the evaluation board or a final target. From this file, µC/Probe is able to extract symbolic information about variables, and determine where variables are stored in RAM or ROM.

µC/Probe also allows users to log the data displayed into a file for analysis of the collected data at a later time. µC/Probe also provides µC/OS-III kernel awareness as a built-in feature.

The trial version that accompanies the book is limited to the display or change of up to five variables.

µC/Probe is a tool that serious embedded software engineers should have in their toolbox. The full version of µC/Probe is included when licensing µC/OS-III. See www.micrium.com for more details.

1-8 CONVENTIONS

There are a number of conventions in this book.

First, notice that when a specific element in a figure is referenced, the element has a number next to it in parenthesis. A description of this element follows the figure and in this case, the letter "F" followed by the figure number, and then the number in parenthesis. For example, F3-4(2) indicates that this description refers to Figure 3-4 and the element (2) in that figure. This convention also applies to listings (starts with an "L") and tables (starts with a "T").

Second, notice that sections and listings are started where it makes sense. Specifically, do not be surprised to see the bottom half of a page empty. New sections begin on a new page, and listings are found on a single page, instead of breaking listings on two pages.

Third, code quality is something I've been avidly promoting throughout my whole career. At Micrium, we pride ourselves in having the cleanest code in the industry. Examples of this are seen in this book. I created and published a coding standard in 1992 that was published in the original µC/OS book. This standard has evolved over the years, but the spirit of the standard has been maintained throughout. The Micriµm coding standard is available for download from the Micriµm website, www.micrium.com

One of the conventions used is that all functions, variables, macros and **#define** constants are prefixed by "OS" (which stands for Operating System) followed by the acronym of the module (e.g., **Sem**), and then the operation performed by the function. For example **OSSemPost()** indicates that the function belongs to the OS (µC/OS-III), that it is part of the Semaphore services, and specifically that the function performs a **Post** (i.e., signal) operation. This allows all related functions to be grouped together in the reference manual, and makes those services intuitive to use.

Notice that signaling or sending a message to a task is called posting, and waiting for a signal or a message is called pending. In other words, an ISR or a task signals or sends a message to another task by using **OS???Post()**, where **???** is the type of service: **Sem**, **TaskSem**, **Flag**, **Mutex**, **Q**, and **TaskQ**. Similarly, a task can wait for a signal or a message by calling **OS???Pend()**.

1-9 CHAPTER CONTENTS

Figure 1-3 shows the layout and flow of Part I of the book. This diagram should be useful to understand the relationship between chapters. The first column on the left indicates chapters that should be read in order to understand µC/OS-III's structure. The second column shows chapters that are related to additional services provided by µC/OS-III. The third column relates to chapters that will help port µC/OS-III to different CPU architectures. The top of the fourth column explains how to obtain valuable run-time and compile-time statistics from µC/OS-III. This is especially useful if developing a kernel awareness plug-in for a debugger, or using µC/Probe. The middle of column four contains the µC/OS-III API and configuration manuals. Reference these sections regularly when designing a product using µC/OS-III. Finally, the bottom of the last column contains miscellaneous appendices.

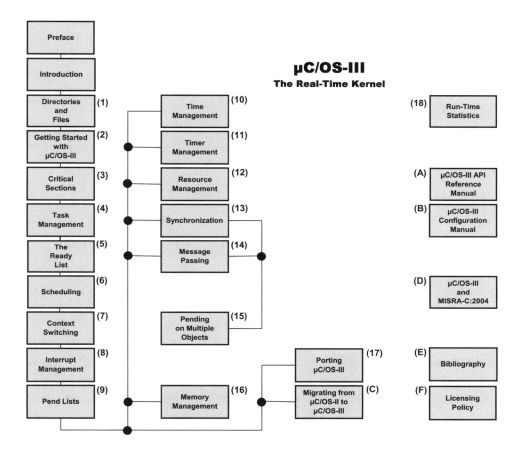

Figure 1-3 **µC/OS-III Book Layout**

Chapter 1, Directories and Files. This chapter explains the directory structure and files needed to build a µC/OS-III-based application. Learn about the files that are needed, where they should be placed, which module does what, and more.

Chapter 2, Getting Started with µC/OS-III. In this chapter, learn how to properly initialize and start a µC/OS-III-based application.

Chapter 3, Critical Sections. This chapter explains what critical sections are, and how they are protected.

Chapter 4, Task Management. This chapter is an introduction to one of the most important aspects of a real-time kernel, the management of tasks in a multitasking environment.

Chapter 5, The Ready List. In this chapter, learn how µC/OS-III efficiently keeps track of all of the tasks that are waiting to execute on the CPU.

Chapter 6, Scheduling. This chapter explains the scheduling algorithms used by µC/OS-III, and how it decides which task will run next.

Chapter 7, Context Switching. This chapter explains what a context switch is, and describes the process of suspending execution of a task and resuming execution of a higher-priority task.

Chapter 8, Interrupt Management. Here is how µC/OS-III deals with interrupts and an overview of services that are available from Interrupt Service Routines (ISRs). Learn how µC/OS-III supports nearly any interrupt controller.

Chapter 9, Pend Lists (or Wait Lists). Tasks that are not able to run are most likely blocked waiting for specific events to occur. Pend Lists (or wait lists), are used to keep track of tasks that are waiting for a resource or event. This chapter describes how µC/OS-III maintains these lists.

Chapter 10, Time Management. In this chapter, learn about µC/OS-III's services that allow users to suspend a task until some time expires. With µC/OS-III, specify to delay execution of a task for an integral number of clock ticks or until the clock-tick counter reaches a certain value. The chapter will also show how a delayed task can be resumed, and describe how to get the current value of the clock tick counter, or set this counter, if needed.

Chapter 11, Timer Management. µC/OS-III allows users to define any number of software timers. When a timer expires, a function can be called to perform some action. Timers can be configured to be either periodic or one-shot. This chapter also explains how the timer-management module works.

Chapter 12, Resource Management. In this chapter, learn different techniques so that tasks share resources. Each of these techniques has advantages and disadvantages that will be discussed. This chapter also explains the internals of semaphores, and mutual exclusion semaphore management.

Chapter 13, Synchronization. µC/OS-III provides two types of services for synchronization: semaphores and event flags and these are explained in this chapter, as well as what happens when calling specific services provided in this module.

Chapter 14, Message Passing. µC/OS-III allows a task or an ISR to send messages to a task. This chapter describes some of the services provided by the message queue management module.

Chapter 15, Pending on multiple objects. In this chapter, see how µC/OS-III allows an application to pend (or wait) on multiple kernel objects (semaphores or message queues) at the same time. This feature makes the waiting task ready to run as soon as any one of the objects is posted (i.e., OR condition), or a timeout occurs.

Chapter 16, Memory Management. Here is how µC/OS-III's fixed-size memory partition manager can be used to allocate and deallocate dynamic memory.

Chapter 17, Porting µC/OS-III. This chapter explains, in generic terms, how to port µC/OS-III to any CPU architecture.

Chapter 18, Run-Time Statistics. µC/OS-III provides a wealth of information about the run-time environment, such as number of context switches, CPU usage (as a percentage), stack usage on a per-task basis, µC/OS-III RAM usage, maximum interrupt disable time, maximum scheduler lock time, and more.

Appendix A, µC/OS-III API Reference Manual. This appendix provides a alphabetical reference for all user-available services provided by µC/OS-III.

Appendix B, µC/OS-III Configuration Manual. This appendix describes how to configure a µC/OS-III-based application. OS_CFG.H configures the µC/OS-III features (semaphores, queues, event flags, etc.), while OS_CFG_APP.H configures the run-time characteristics (tick rate, tick wheel size, stack size for the idle task, etc.).

Appendix C, Migrating from µC/OS-II to µC/OS-III. µC/OS-III has its roots in µC/OS-II and, in fact, most of the µC/OS-II ports can be easily converted to µC/OS-III. However, most APIs have changed from µC/OS-II to µC/OS-III, and this appendix describes some of the differences.

Appendix D, MISRA-C:2004 rules and µC/OS-III. µC/OS-III follows most of the MISRA-C:2004, except for 7 of these rules.

Appendix E, Bibliography.

Appendix F, Licensing µC/OS-III.

1-10 LICENSING

This book contains μC/OS-III precompiled in linkable object form, an evaluation board, and tools (compiler/assembler/linker/debugger). Use μC/OS-III for free, as long as it is only used with the evaluation board that accompanies this book. You will need to purchase a license when using this code in a commercial project, where the intent is to make a profit. Users do not pay anything beyond the price of the book, evaluation board and tools, as long as they are used for educational purposes.

You will need to license μC/OS-III if you intend to use μC/OS-III in a commercial product where you intend to make a profit. You need to purchase this license when you make the decision to use μC/OS-III in a design, not when you are ready to go to production.

If you are unsure about whether you need to obtain a license for your application, please contact Micrium and discuss your use with a sales representative.

1-11 CONTACTING MICRIUM

Do not hesitate to contact Micrium should you have any licensing questions regarding μC/OS-III.

Micrium
1290 Weston Road, Suite 306
Weston, FL 33326

+1 954 217 2036
+1 954 217 2037 (FAX)

E-Mail: sales@micrium.com

Website: www.micrium.com

Directories and Files

µC/OS-III is fairly easy to use once it is understood exactly which source files are needed to make up a µC/OS-III-based application. This chapter will discuss the modules available for µC/OS-III and how everything fits together.

Figure 2-1 shows the µC/OS-III architecture and its relationship with hardware. Of course, in addition to the timer and interrupt controller, hardware would most likely contain such other devices as Universal Asynchronous Receiver Transmitters (UARTs), Analog to Digital Converters (ADCs), Ethernet controller(s) and more.

This chapter assumes development on a Windows®-based platform and makes references to typical Windows-type directory structures (also called Folder). However, since µC/OS-III is available in source form, it can also be used on Unix, Linux or other development platforms.

The names of the files are shown in upper case to make them "stand out". However, file names are actually lower case.

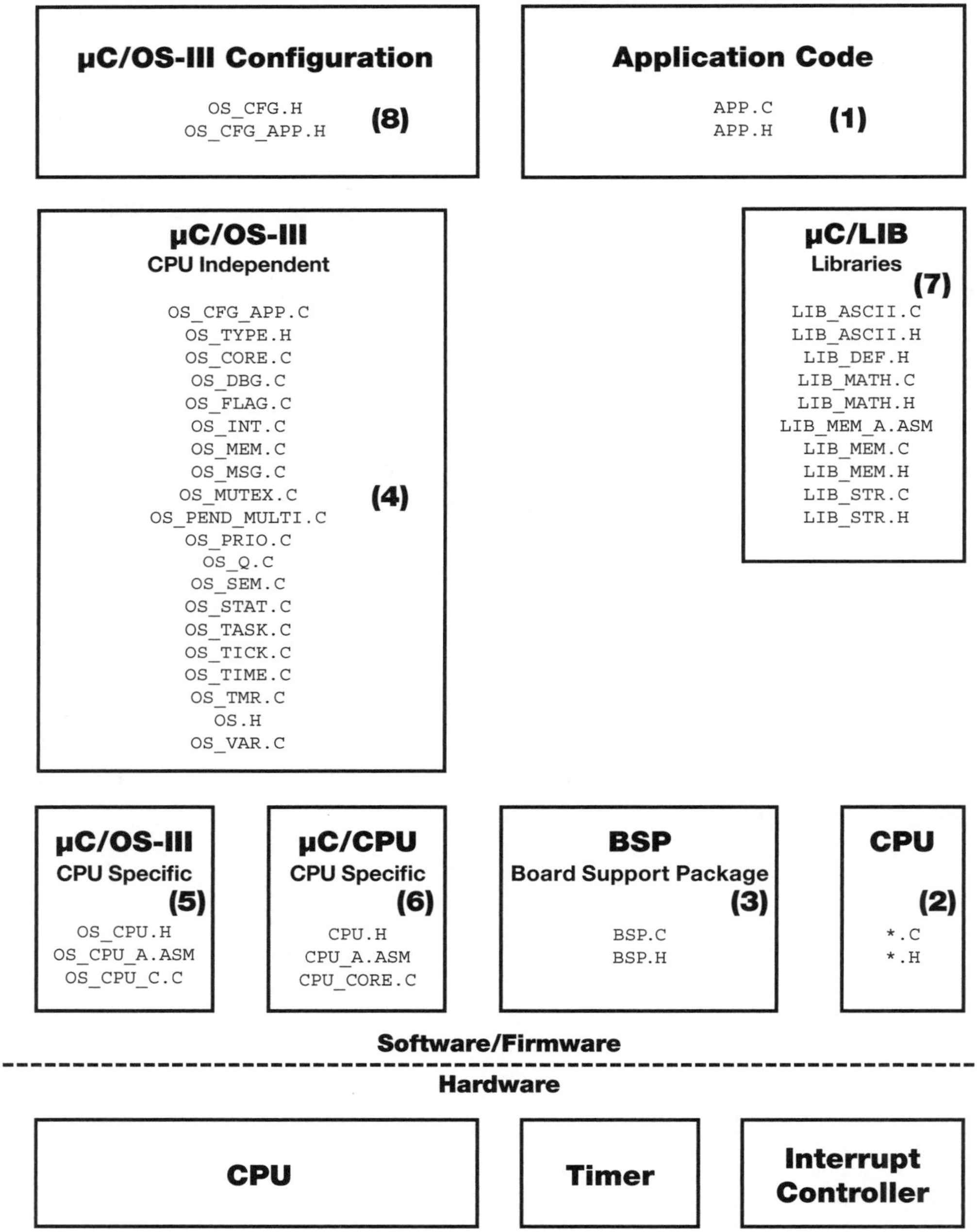

µC/OS-III Configuration		Application Code	
OS_CFG.H OS_CFG_APP.H	**(8)**	APP.C APP.H	**(1)**

µC/OS-III
CPU Independent

```
OS_CFG_APP.C
OS_TYPE.H
OS_CORE.C
OS_DBG.C
OS_FLAG.C
OS_INT.C
OS_MEM.C
OS_MSG.C
OS_MUTEX.C               (4)
OS_PEND_MULTI.C
OS_PRIO.C
OS_Q.C
OS_SEM.C
OS_STAT.C
OS_TASK.C
OS_TICK.C
OS_TIME.C
OS_TMR.C
OS.H
OS_VAR.C
```

µC/LIB
Libraries
(7)

```
LIB_ASCII.C
LIB_ASCII.H
LIB_DEF.H
LIB_MATH.C
LIB_MATH.H
LIB_MEM_A.ASM
LIB_MEM.C
LIB_MEM.H
LIB_STR.C
LIB_STR.H
```

µC/OS-III CPU Specific **(5)**	µC/CPU CPU Specific **(6)**	BSP Board Support Package **(3)**	CPU **(2)**
OS_CPU.H OS_CPU_A.ASM OS_CPU_C.C	CPU.H CPU_A.ASM CPU_CORE.C	BSP.C BSP.H	*.C *.H

Software/Firmware
- -
Hardware

CPU	Timer	Interrupt Controller

Figure 2-1 **µC/OS-III Architecture**

F2-1(1)   The application code consists of project or product files. For convenience, these are simply called **APP.C** and **APP.H**, however an application can contain any number of files that do not have to be called **APP.***. The application code is typically where one would find **main( )**.

F2-1(2)   Semiconductor manufacturers often provide library functions in source form for accessing the peripherals on their CPU or MCU. These libraries are quite useful and often save valuable time. Since there is no naming convention for these files, ***.C** and ***.H** are assumed.

F2-1(3)   The Board Support Package (BSP) is code that is typically written to interface to peripherals on a target board. For example such code can turn on and off Light Emitting Diodes (LEDs), turn on and off relays, or code to read switches, temperature sensors, and more.

F2-1(4)   This is the µC/OS-III processor-independent code. This code is written in highly portable ANSI C and is available to µC/OS-III licensees only.

F2-1(5)   This is the µC/OS-III code that is adapted to a specific CPU architecture and is called a port. µC/OS-III has its roots in µC/OS-II and benefits from being able to use most of the 45 or so ports available for µC/OS-II. µC/OS-II ports, however, will require small changes to work with µC/OS-III. These changes are described in Appendix C, "Migrating from µC/OS-II to µC/OS-III" on page 605.

F2-1(6)   At Micriµm, we like to encapsulate CPU functionality. These files define functions to disable and enable interrupts, **CPU_???** data types to be independent of the CPU and compiler used, and many more functions.

F2-1(7)   µC/LIB is of a series of source files that provide common functions such as memory copy, string, and ASCII-related functions. Some are occasionally used to replace **stdlib** functions provided by the compiler. The files are provided to ensure that they are fully portable from application to application and especially, from compiler to compiler. µC/OS-III does not use these files, but µC/CPU does.

F2-1(8)   µC/OS-III configuration files defines µC/OS-III features (**OS_CFG.H**) to include in the application, and specifies the size of certain variables and data structures expected by µC/OS-III (**OS_CFG_APP.H**), such as idle task stack size, tick rate, size of the message pool, etc.

2-1 APPLICATION CODE

When Micriμm provides example projects, they are placed in a directory structure shown below. Of course, a directory structure that suits a particular project/product can be used.

```
\Micrium
    \Software
        \EvalBoards
            \<manufacturer>
                \<board_name>
                    \<compiler>
                        \<project name>
                            \*.*
```

\Micrium
This is where we place all software components and projects provided by Micriμm. This directory generally starts from the root directory of the computer.

\Software
This sub-directory contains all software components and projects.

\EvalBoards
This sub-directory contains all projects related to evaluation boards supported by Micriμm.

\<manufacturer>
This is the name of the manufacturer of the evaluation board. The "<" and ">" are not part of the actual name.

\<board name>
This is the name of the evaluation board. A board from Micriμm will typically be called **uC-Eval-xxxx** where "**xxxx**" represents the CPU or MCU used on the board. The "<" and ">" are not part of the actual name.

\<compiler>
This is the name of the compiler or compiler manufacturer used to build the code for the evaluation board. The "<" and ">" are not part of the actual name.

\<project name>

The name of the project that will be demonstrated. For example, a simple µC/OS-III project might have a project name of "**OS-Ex1**". The "**-Ex1**" represents a project containing only µC/OS-III. The project name **OS-Probe-Ex1** contains µC/OS-III and µC/Probe.

.

These are the project source files. Main files can optionally be called **APP*.***. This directory also contains configuration files **OS_CFG.H**, **OS_CFG_APP.H** and other required source files.

2-2 CPU

The directory where you will find semiconductor manufacturer peripheral interface source files is shown below. Any directory structure that suits the project/product may be used.

```
\Micrium
    \Software
        \CPU
            \<manufacturer>
                \<architecture>
                    \*.*
```

\Micrium

The location of all software components and projects provided by Micriµm.

\Software

This sub-directory contains all software components and projects.

\CPU

This sub-directory is always called CPU.

\<manufacturer>

Is the name of the semiconductor manufacturer providing the peripheral library.

\<architecture>

The name of the specific library, generally associated with a CPU name or an architecture.

.

Indicates library source files. The semiconductor manufacturer names the files.

2-3 BOARD SUPPORT PACKAGE (BSP)

The Board Support Package (BSP) is generally found with the evaluation or target board as it is specific to that board. In fact, when well written, the BSP should be used for multiple projects.

```
\Micrium
    \Software
        \EvalBoards
            \<manufacturer>
                \<board name>
                    \<compiler>
                        \BSP
                            \*.*
```

\Micrium

Contains all software components and projects provided by Micriµm.

\Software

This sub-directory contains all software components and projects.

\EvalBoards

This sub-directory contains all projects related to evaluation boards.

\<manufacturer>

The name of the manufacturer of the evaluation board. The "<" and ">" are not part of the actual name.

\<board name>

The name of the evaluation board. A board from Micriµm will typically be called **uC-Eval-xxxx** where "**xxxx**" is the name of the CPU or MCU used on the evaluation board. The "<" and ">" are not part of the actual name.

\<compiler>

The name of the compiler or compiler manufacturer used to build code for the evaluation board. The "<" and ">" are not part of the actual name.

\BSP

This directory is always called BSP.

.

The source files of the BSP. Typically all of the file names start with BSP. It is therefore normal to find **BSP.C** and **BSP.H** in this directory. BSP code should contain such functions as LED control functions, initialization of timers, interface to Ethernet controllers and more.

2-4 µC/OS-III, CPU INDEPENDENT SOURCE CODE

The files in these directories are available to µC/OS-III licensees (see Appendix F, "Licensing Policy" on page 651).

```
\Micrium
    \Software
        \uCOS-III
            \Cfg\Template
                \OS_APP_HOOKS.C
                \OS_CFG.H
                \OS_CFG_APP.H
            \Source
                \OS_CFG_APP.C
                \OS_CORE.C
                \OS_DBG.C
                \OS_FLAG.C
                \OS_INT.C
                \OS_MEM.C
                \OS_MSG.C
                \OS_MUTEX.C
                \OS_PEND_MULTI.C
                \OS_PRIO.C
                \OS_Q.C
                \OS_SEM.C
                \OS_STAT.C
                \OS_TASK.C
                \OS_TICK.C
                \OS_TIME.C
```

\OS_TMR.C
\OS_VAR
\OS.H
\OS_TYPE.H

\Micrium
Contains all software components and projects provided by Micriµm.

\Software
This sub-directory contains all software components and projects.

\uCOS-III
This is the main µC/OS-III directory.

\Cfg\Template
This directory contains examples of configuration files to copy to the project directory. You will then modify these files to suit the needs of the application.

OS_APP_HOOKS.C shows how to write hook functions that are called by µC/OS-III. Specifically, this file contains eight empty functions.

OS_CFG.H specifies which features of µC/OS-III are available for an application. The file is typically copied into an application directory and edited based on which features are required from µC/OS-III. If µC/OS-III is provided in linkable object code format, this file will be provided to indicate features that are available in the object file. See Appendix B, "µC/OS-III Configuration Manual" on page 585.

OS_CFG_APP.H is a configuration file to be copied into an application directory and edited based on application requirements. This file enables the user to determine the size of the idle task stack, the tick rate, the number of messages available in the message pool and more. See Appendix B, "µC/OS-III Configuration Manual" on page 585.

\Source
The directory containing the CPU-independent source code for µC/OS-III. All files in this directory should be included in the build (assuming you have the source code). Features that are not required will be compiled out based on the value of **#define** constants in OS_CFG.H and OS_CFG_APP.H.

OS_CFG_APP.C declares variables and arrays based on the values in **OS_CFG_APP.H**.

OS_CORE.C contains core functionality for µC/OS-III such as **OSInit()** to initialize µC/OS-III, **OSSched()** for the task level scheduler, **OSIntExit()** for the interrupt level scheduler, pend list (or wait list) management (see Chapter 10, "Pend Lists (or Wait Lists)" on page 183), ready list management (see Chapter 6, "The Ready List" on page 129), and more.

OS_DBG.C contains declarations of constant variables used by a kernel aware debugger or µC/Probe.

OS_FLAG.C contains the code for event flag management. See Chapter 14, "Synchronization" on page 257 for details about event flags.

OS_INT.C contains code for the interrupt handler task, which is used when

OS_CFG_ISR_POST_DEFERRED_EN (see **OS_CFG.H**) is set to 1. See Chapter 9, "Interrupt Management" on page 163 for details regarding the interrupt handler task.

OS_MEM.C contains code for the µC/OS-III fixed-size memory manager, see Chapter 17, "Memory Management" on page 329.

OS_MSG.C contains code to handle messages. µC/OS-III provides message queues and task specific message queues. **OS_MSG.C** provides common code for these two services. See Chapter 15, "Message Passing" on page 295.

OS_MUTEX.C contains code to manage mutual exclusion semaphores, see Chapter 13, "Resource Management" on page 215.

OS_PEND_MULTI.C contains the code to allow code to pend on multiple semaphores or message queues. This is described in Chapter 16, "Pending On Multiple Objects" on page 319.

OS_PRIO.C contains the code to manage the bitmap table used to keep track of which tasks are ready to run, see Chapter 6, "The Ready List" on page 129. This file can be replaced by an assembly language equivalent to improve performance if the CPU used provides bit set, clear and test instructions, and a count leading zeros instruction.

OS_Q.C contains code to manage message queues. See Chapter 15, "Message Passing" on page 295.

OS_SEM.C contains code to manage semaphores used for resource management and/or synchronization. See Chapter 13, "Resource Management" on page 215 and Chapter 14, "Synchronization" on page 257.

OS_STAT.C contains code for the statistic task, which is used to compute the global CPU usage and the CPU usage of each of tasks. See Chapter 5, "Task Management" on page 81.

OS_TASK.C contains code for managing tasks using OSTaskCreate(), OSTaskDel(), OSTaskChangePrio(), and many more. See Chapter 5, "Task Management" on page 81.

OS_TICK.C contains code to manage tasks that have delayed themselves or that are pending on a kernel object with a timeout. See Chapter 5, "Task Management" on page 81.

OS_TIME.C contains code to allow a task to delay itself until some time expires. See Chapter 11, "Time Management" on page 189.

OS_TMR.C contains code to manage software timers. See Chapter 12, "Timer Management" on page 199.

OS_VAR.C contains the µC/OS-III global variables. These variables are for µC/OS-III to manage and should not be accessed by application code.

OS.H contains the main µC/OS-III header file, which declares constants, macros, µC/OS-III global variables (for use by µC/OS-III only), function prototypes, and more.

OS_TYPE.H contains declarations of µC/OS-III data types that can be changed by the port designed to make better use of the CPU architecture. In this case, the file would typically be copied to the port directory and then modified. µC/OS-III in linkable object library format provides this file to enable the user to know what each data type maps to. See Appendix B, "µC/OS-III Configuration Manual" on page 585.

2-5 μC/OS-III, CPU SPECIFIC SOURCE CODE

The μC/OS-III port developer provides these files. See also Chapter 18, "Porting μC/OS-III" on page 341.

```
\Micrium
    \Software
        \uCOS-III
            \Ports
                \<architecture>
                    \<compiler>
                        \OS_CPU.H
                        \OS_CPU_A.ASM
                        \OS_CPU_C.C
```

\Micrium
Contains all software components and projects provided by Micriμm.

\Software
This sub-directory contains all software components and projects.

\uCOS-III
The main μC/OS-III directory.

\Ports
The location of port files for the CPU architecture(s) to be used.

\<architecture>
This is the name of the CPU architecture that μC/OS-III was ported to. The "<" and ">" are not part of the actual name.

\<compiler>
The name of the compiler or compiler manufacturer used to build code for the port. The "<" and ">" are not part of the actual name.

The files in this directory contain the μC/OS-III port, see Chapter 18, "Porting μC/OS-III" on page 341 for details on the contents of these files.

OS_CPU.H contains a macro declaration for **OS_TASK_SW()**, as well as the function prototypes for at least the following functions: **OSCtxSw()**, **OSIntCtxSw()** and **OSStartHighRdy()**.

OS_CPU_A.ASM contains the assembly language functions to implement at least the following functions: **OSCtxSw()**, **OSIntCtxSw()** and **OSStartHighRdy()**.

OS_CPU_C.C contains the C code for the port specific hook functions and code to initialize the stack frame for a task when the task is created.

2-6 µC/CPU, CPU SPECIFIC SOURCE CODE

µC/CPU consists of files that encapsulate common CPU-specific functionality and CPU and compiler-specific data types. See Chapter 18, "Porting µC/OS-III" on page 341.

```
\Micrium
    \Software
        \uC-CPU
            \CPU_CORE.C
            \CPU_CORE.H
            \CPU_DEF.H
            \Cfg\Template
                \CPU_CFG.H
            \<architecture>
                \<compiler>
                    \CPU.H
                    \CPU_A.ASM
                    \CPU_C.C
```

\Micrium
Contains all software components and projects provided by Micriµm.

\Software
This sub-directory contains all software components and projects.

\uC-CPU

This is the main µC/CPU directory.

   CPU_CORE.C contains C code that is common to all CPU architectures. Specifically, this file contains functions to measure the interrupt disable time of the CPU_CRITICAL_ENTER() and CPU_CRITICAL_EXIT() macros, a function that emulates a count leading zeros instruction and a few other functions.

   CPU_CORE.H contains function prototypes for the functions provided in CPU_CORE.C and allocation of the variables used by the module to measure interrupt disable time.

   CPU_DEF.H contains miscellaneous #define constants used by the µC/CPU module.

\Cfg\Template

This directory contains a configuration template file (CPU_CFG.H) that must be copied to the application directory to configure the µC/CPU module based on application requirements.

CPU_CFG.H determines whether to enable measurement of the interrupt disable time, whether the CPU implements a count leading zeros instruction in assembly language, or whether it will be emulated in C, and more.

\<architecture>

The name of the CPU architecture that µC/CPU was ported to. The "<" and ">" are not part of the actual name.

\<compiler>

The name of the compiler or compiler manufacturer used to build code for the µC/CPU port. The "<" and ">" are not part of the actual name.

The files in this directory contain the µC/CPU port, see Chapter 18, "Porting µC/OS-III" on page 341 for details on the contents of these files.

   CPU.H contains type definitions to make µC/OS-III and other modules independent of the CPU and compiler word sizes. Specifically, one will find the declaration of the CPU_INT16U, CPU_INT32U, CPU_FP32 and many other data types. This file also specifies whether the CPU is a big or little endian machine, defines the CPU_STK data type used by µC/OS-III, defines the macros OS_CRITICAL_ENTER() and OS_CRITICAL_EXIT(), and contains function prototypes for functions specific to the CPU architecture, and more.

CPU_A.ASM contains the assembly language functions to implement code to disable and enable CPU interrupts, count leading zeros (if the CPU supports that instruction), and other CPU specific functions that can only be written in assembly language. This file may also contain code to enable caches, setup MPUs and MMU, and more. The functions provided in this file are accessible from C.

CPU_C.C contains C code of functions that are based on a specific CPU architecture but written in C for portability. As a general rule, if a function can be written in C then it should be, unless there is significant performance benefits available by writing it in assembly language.

2-7 µC/LIB, PORTABLE LIBRARY FUNCTIONS

µC/LIB consists of library functions meant to be highly portable and not tied to any specific compiler. This facilitates third-party certification of Micriµm products. µC/OS-III does not use any µC/LIB functions, however the µC/CPU assumes the presence of **LIB_DEF.H** for such definitions as: **DEF_YES, DEF_NO, DEF_TRUE, DEF_FALSE, DEF_ON, DEF_OFF** and more.

```
\Micrium
    \Software
        \uC-LIB
            \LIB_ASCII.C
            \LIB_ASCII.H
            \LIB_DEF.H
            \LIB_MATH.C
            \LIB_MATH.H
            \LIB_MEM.C
            \LIB_MEM.H
            \LIB_STR.C
            \LIB_STR.H
            \Cfg\Template
                \LIB_CFG.H
            \Ports
                \<architecture>
                    \<compiler>
                        \LIB_MEM_A.ASM
```

\Micrium

Contains all software components and projects provided by Micriµm.

\Software

This sub-directory contains all software components and projects.

\uC-LIB

This is the main µC/LIB directory.

\Cfg\Template

This directory contains a configuration template file (**LIB_CFG.H**) that are required to be copied to the application directory to configure the µC/LIB module based on application requirements.

LIB_CFG.H determines whether to enable assembly language optimization (assuming there is an assembly language file for the processor, i.e., **LIB_MEM_A.ASM**) and a few other #defines.

2-8 SUMMARY

Below is a summary of all directories and files involved in a µC/OS-III-based project. The "<-Cfg" on the far right indicates that these files are typically copied into the application (i.e., project) directory and edited based on the project requirements.

```
\Micrium
    \Software
        \EvalBoards
            \<manufacturer>
                \<board name>
                    \<compiler>
                        \<project name>
                            \APP.C
                            \APP.H
                            \other
        \CPU
            \<manufacturer>
                \<architecture>
                    \*.*
```

```
\uCOS-III
    \Cfg\Template
        \OS_APP_HOOKS.C
        \OS_CFG.H                        <-Cfg
        \OS_CFG_APP.H                     <-Cfg
    \Source
        \OS_CFG_APP.C
        \OS_CORE.C
        \OS_DBG.C
        \OS_FLAG.C
        \OS_INT.C
        \OS_MEM.C
        \OS_MSG.C
        \OS_MUTEX.C
        \OS_PEND_MULTI.C
        \OS_PRIO.C
        \OS_Q.C
        \OS_SEM.C
        \OS_STAT.C
        \OS_TASK.C
        \OS_TICK.C
        \OS_TIME.C
        \OS_TMR.C
        \OS_VAR.C
        \OS.H
        \OS_TYPE.H                        <-Cfg
    \Ports
        \<architecture>
            \<compiler>
                \OS_CPU.H
                \OS_CPU_A.ASM
                \OS_CPU_C.C
\uC-CPU
    \CPU_CORE.C
    \CPU_CORE.H
    \CPU_DEF.H
    \Cfg\Template
        \CPU_CFG.H                        <-Cfg
```

```
\<architecture>
    \<compiler>
        \CPU.H
        \CPU_A.ASM
        \CPU_C.C
\uC-LIB
    \LIB_ASCII.C
    \LIB_ASCII.H
    \LIB_DEF.H
    \LIB_MATH.C
    \LIB_MATH.H
    \LIB_MEM.C
    \LIB_MEM.H
    \LIB_STR.C
    \LIB_STR.H
    \Cfg\Template
        \LIB_CFG.H                    <-Cfg
    \Ports
        \<architecture>
            \<compiler>
                \LIB_MEM_A.ASM
```

3

Getting Started with µC/OS-III

µC/OS-III provides services to application code in the form of a set of functions that perform specific operations. µC/OS-III offers services to manage tasks, semaphores, message queues, mutual exclusion semaphores and more. As far as the application is concerned, it calls the µC/OS-III functions as if they were any other functions. In other words, the application now has access to a library of approximately 70 new functions.

In this chapter, the reader will appreciate how easy it is to start using µC/OS-III. Refer to Appendix A, "µC/OS-III API Reference Manual" on page 381, for the full description of several of the µC/OS-III services presented in this chapter.

It is assumed that the project setup (files and directories) is as described in the previous chapter, and that a C compiler exists for the target processor that is in use. However, this chapter makes no assumptions about the tools or the processor that is used.

3-1 SINGLE TASK APPLICATION

Listing 3-1 shows the top portion of a simple application file called **APP.C**.

```
/*
*********************************************************************************
*                               INCLUDE FILES
*********************************************************************************
*/
#include <app_cfg.h>                                                    (1)
#include <bsp.h>
#include <os.h>
/*
*********************************************************************************
*                           LOCAL GLOBAL VARIABLES
*********************************************************************************
*/
static  OS_TCB          AppTaskStartTCB;                                (2)
static  CPU_STK         AppTaskStartStk[APP_TASK_START_STK_SIZE];       (3)
/*
*********************************************************************************
*                           FUNCTION PROTOTYPES
*********************************************************************************
*/
static  void  AppTaskStart (void *p_arg);                               (4)
```

Listing 3-1 **APP.C (1st Part)**

L3-1(1)   As with any C programs, include the necessary headers to build the application.

APP_CFG.H is a header file that configures the application. For our example, **APP_CFG.H** contains **#define** constants to establish task priorities, stack sizes, and other application specifics.

BSP.H is the header file for the Board Support Package (BSP), which **defines** **#defines** and function prototypes, such as **BSP_Init()**, **BSP_LED_On()**, **OS_TS_GET()** and more.

OS.H is the main header file for μC/OS-III, and includes the following header files:

OS_CFG.H
CPU.H
CPU_CFG.H
CPU_CORE.H
OS_TYPE.H
OS_CPU.H

L3-1(2)   We will be creating an application task and it is necessary to allocate a task control block (**OS_TCB**) for this task.

L3-1(3)   Each task created requires its own stack. A stack must be declared using the **CPU_STK** data type. The stack can be allocated statically as shown here, or dynamically from the heap using **malloc()**. It should not be necessary to free the stack space, because the task should never be stopped, and the stack will always be used.

L3-1(4)   This is the function prototype of the task that we will create.

Most C applications start at **main()** as shown in Listing 3-2.

```
void  main (void)
{
    OS_ERR  err;

    BSP_IntDisAll();                                                        (1)
    OSInit(&err);                                                           (2)
    if (err != OS_ERR_NONE) {
        /* Something didn't get initialized correctly ...            */
        /* ... check OS.H for the meaning of the error code, see OS_ERR_xxxx */
    }
    OSTaskCreate((OS_TCB     *)&AppTaskStartTCB,                            (3)
                 (CPU_CHAR   *)"App Task Start",                           (4)
                 (OS_TASK_PTR )AppTaskStart,                               (5)
                 (void       *)0,                                          (6)
                 (OS_PRIO    )APP_TASK_START_PRIO,                         (7)
                 (CPU_STK    *)&AppTaskStartStk[0],                        (8)
                 (CPU_STK_SIZE)APP_TASK_START_STK_SIZE / 10,               (9)
                 (CPU_STK_SIZE)APP_TASK_START_STK_SIZE,                    (10)
                 (OS_MSG_QTY )0,
                 (OS_TICK    )0,
                 (void       *)0,
                 (OS_OPT     )(OS_OPT_TASK_STK_CHK | OS_OPT_TASK_STK_CLR), (11)
                 (OS_ERR     *)&err);                                      (12)
    if (err != OS_ERR_NONE) {
        /* The task didn't get created.  Lookup the value of the error code ... */
        /* ... in OS.H for the meaning of the error                   */
    }
    OSStart(&err);                                                         (13)
    if (err != OS_ERR_NONE) {
        /* Your code is NEVER supposed to come back to this point.     */
    }
}
```

Listing 3-2 **APP.C (2nd Part)**

L3-2(1)   Start **main()** by calling a BSP function that disables all interrupts. On most processors, interrupts are disabled at startup until explicitly enabled by application code. However, it is safer to turn off all peripheral interrupts during startup.

L3-2(2)   Call **OSInit()**, which is responsible for initializing µC/OS-III. **OSInit()** initializes internal variables and data structures, and also creates two (2) to five (5) internal tasks. At a minimum, µC/OS-III creates the idle task (**OS_IdleTask()**), which executes when no other task is ready to run. µC/OS-III also creates the tick task, which is responsible for keeping track of time.

Depending on the value of **#define** constants, µC/OS-III will create the statistic task (**OS_StatTask()**), the timer task (**OS_TmrTask()**), and the interrupt handler queue management task (**OS_IntQTask()**). Those are discussed in Chapter 5, "Task Management" on page 81.

Most of µC/OS-III's functions return an error code via a pointer to an **OS_ERR** variable, err in this case. If **OSInit()** was successful, err will be set to **OS_ERR_NONE**. If **OSInit()** encounters a problem during initialization, it will return immediately upon detecting the problem and set err accordingly. If this occurs, look up the error code value in **OS.H**. Specifically, all error codes start with **OS_ERR_**.

It is important to note that **OSInit()** must be called before any other µC/OS-III function.

L3-2(3)   Create a task by calling **OSTaskCreate()**. **OSTaskCreate()** requires 13 arguments. The first argument is the address of the **OS_TCB** that is declared for this task. Chapter 5, "Task Management" on page 81 provides additional information about tasks.

L3-2(4)   **OSTaskCreate()** allows a name to be assigned to each of the tasks. µC/OS-III stores a pointer to the task name inside the **OS_TCB** of the task. There is no limit on the number of ASCII characters used for the name.

L3-2(5)   The third argument is the address of the task code. A typical µC/OS-III task is implemented as an infinite loop as shown:

```
void  MyTask (void *p_arg)
{
    /* Do something with "p_arg".
    while (1) {
        /* Task body */
    }
}
```

The task receives an argument when it first starts. As far as the task is concerned, it looks like any other C function that can be called by the code. However, the code *must not* call **MyTask()**. The call is actually performed through µC/OS-III.

L3-2(6)   The fourth argument of **OSTaskCreate()** is the actual argument that the task receives when it first begins. In other words, the "**p_arg**" of **MyTask()**. In the example a **NULL** pointer is passed, and thus "**p_arg**" for **AppTaskStart()** will be a **NULL** pointer.

The argument passed to the task can actually be any pointer. For example, the user may pass a pointer to a data structure containing parameters for the task.

L3-2(7)   The next argument to **OSTaskCreate()** is the priority of the task. The priority establishes the relative importance of this task with respect to the other tasks in the application. A low-priority number indicates a high priority (or more important task). Set the priority of the task to any value between 1 and **OS_CFG_PRIO_MAX-2**, inclusively. Avoid using priority #0, and priority **OS_CFG_PRIO_MAX-1**, because these are reserved for µC/OS-III. **OS_CFG_PRIO_MAX** is a compile time configuration constant, which is declared in **OS_CFG.H**.

L3-2(8)   The sixth argument to **OSTaskCreate()** is the base address of the stack assigned to this task. The base address is always the lowest memory location of the stack.

L3-2(9)   The next argument specifies the location of a "watermark" in the task's stack that can be used to determine the allowable stack growth of the task. See Chapter 5, "Task Management" on page 81 for more details on using this feature. In the code above, the value represents the amount of stack space (in **CPU_STK** elements) before the stack is empty. In other words, in the example, the limit is reached when there is 10% of the stack left.

L3-2(10)   The eighth argument to **OSTaskCreate()** specifies the size of the task's stack in number of **CPU_STK** elements (not bytes). For example, if allocating 1 Kbyte of stack space for a task and the **CPU_STK** is a 32-bit word, then pass 256.

L3-2(11)   The next three arguments are skipped as they are not relevant for the current discussion. The next argument to **OSTaskCreate()** specifies options. In this example, we specify that the stack will be checked at run time (assuming the statistic task was enabled in **OS_CFG.H**), and that the contents of the stack will be cleared when the task is created.

L3-2(12)   The last argument of **OSTaskCreate()** is a pointer to a variable that will receive an error code. If **OSTaskCreate()** is successful, the error code will be **OS_ERR_NONE** otherwise, look up the value of the error code in **OS.H** (See **OS_ERR_xxxx**) to determine the problem with the call.

L3-2(13)   The final step in **main()** is to call **OSStart()**, which starts the multitasking process. Specifically, µC/OS-III will select the highest-priority task that was created before calling **OSStart()**. The highest-priority task is always **OS_IntQTask()** if that task is enabled in **OS_CFG.H** (through the **OS_CFG_ISR_POST_DEFERRED_EN** constant). If this is the case, **OS_IntQTask()** will perform some initialization of its own and then µC/OS-III will switch to the next most important task that was created.

A few important points are worth noting. For one thing, create as many tasks as you want before calling **OSStart()**. However, it is recommended to only create one task as shown in the example because, having a single application task allows µC/OS-III to determine how fast the CPU is, in order to determine the percentage of CPU usage at run-time. Also, if the application needs other kernel objects such as semaphores and message queues then it is recommended that these be created prior to calling **OSStart()**. Finally, notice that that interrupts are not enabled. This will be discussed next by examining the contents of **AppTaskStart()**, which is shown in Listing 3-3.

```
static  void  AppTaskStart (void *p_arg)                    (1)
{
    OS_ERR  err;


    p_arg = p_arg;
    BSP_Init();                                             (2)
    CPU_Init();                                             (3)
    BSP_Cfg_Tick();                                         (4)
    BSP_LED_Off(0);                                         (5)
    while (1) {                                             (6)
        BSP_LED_Toggle(0);                                 (7)
        OSTimeDlyHMSM((CPU_INT16U)  0,                     (8)
                      (CPU_INT16U)  0,
                      (CPU_INT16U)  0,
                      (CPU_INT32U)100,
                      (OS_OPT     )OS_OPT_TIME_HMSM_STRICT,
                      (OS_ERR    *)&err);
        /* Check for 'err' */
    }
}
```

Listing 3-3 **APP.C (3rd Part)**

L3-3(1)   As previously mentioned, a task looks like any other C function. The argument "p_arg" is passed to **AppTaskStart()** by **OSTaskCreate()**, as discussed in the previous listing description.

L3-3(2)   **BSP_Init()** is a Board Support Package (BSP) function that is responsible for initializing the hardware on an evaluation or target board. The evaluation board might have General Purpose Input Output (GPIO) lines that might need to be configured, relays, sensors and more. This function is found in a file called **BSP.C**.

L3-3(3)   **CPU_Init()** initializes the µC/CPU services. µC/CPU provides services to measure interrupt latency, receive time stamps, and provides emulation of the count leading zeros instruction if the processor used does not have that instruction and more.

L3-3(4)   **BSP_Cfg_Tick()** sets up the µC/OS-III tick interrupt. For this, the function needs to initialize one of the hardware timers to interrupt the CPU at a rate of: **OSCfg_TickRate_Hz**, which is defined in **OS_CFG_APP.H** (See **OS_CFG_TICK_RATE_HZ**).

L3-3(5)   **BSP_LED_Off()** is a function that will turn off all LEDs because the function is written so that a zero argument means all the LEDs.

L3-3(6)   Most µC/OS-III tasks will need to be written as an infinite loop.

L3-3(7)   This BSP function toggles the state of the specified LED. Again, a zero indicates that all the LEDs should be toggled on the evaluation board. Simply change the zero to 1 and this will cause LED #1 to toggle. Exactly which LED is LED #1? That depends on the BSP developer. Specifically, encapsulate access to LEDs through such functions as **BSP_LED_On()**, **BSP_LED_Off()** and **BSP_LED_Toggle()**. Also, we prefer to assign LEDs logical values (1, 2, 3, etc.) instead of specifying which port and which bit on each port.

L3-3(8)   Finally, each task in the application must call one of the µC/OS-III functions that will cause the task to "wait for an event." The task can wait for time to expire (by calling **OSTimeDly()**, or **OSTimeDlyHMSM()**), or wait for a signal or a message from an ISR or another task. Chapter 11, "Time Management" on page 189 provides additional information about time delays.

3-2 MULTIPLE TASKS APPLICATION WITH KERNEL OBJECTS

The code of Listing 3-4 through Listing 3-8 shows a more complete example and contains three tasks: a mutual exclusion, semaphore, and a message queue.

```
/*
*********************************************************************************
*                              INCLUDE FILES
*********************************************************************************
*/
#include <app_cfg.h>
#include <bsp.h>
#include <os.h>
/*
*********************************************************************************
*                           LOCAL GLOBAL VARIABLES
*********************************************************************************
*/
static  OS_TCB          AppTaskStartTCB;                            (1)
static  OS_TCB          AppTask1_TCB;
static  OS_TCB          AppTask2_TCB;
static  OS_MUTEX        AppMutex;                                   (2)
static  OS_Q            AppQ;                                       (3)
static  CPU_STK         AppTaskStartStk[APP_TASK_START_STK_SIZE];   (4)
static  CPU_STK         AppTask1_Stk[128];
static  CPU_STK         AppTask2_Stk[128];
/*
*********************************************************************************
*                            FUNCTION PROTOTYPES
*********************************************************************************
*/
static  void  AppTaskStart (void *p_arg);                          (5)
static  void  AppTask1     (void *p_arg);
static  void  AppTask2     (void *p_arg);
```

Listing 3-4 **APP.C (1st Part)**

L3-4(1)   Allocate storage for the **OS_TCB**s of each task.

L3-4(2)   A mutual exclusion semaphore (a.k.a. a mutex) is a kernel object (a data structure) that is used to protect a shared resource from being accessed by more than one task. A task that wants to access the shared resource must obtain the mutex before it is allowed to proceed. The owner of the resource relinquishes the mutex when it has finished accessing the resource. This process is demonstrated in this example.

L3-4(3)   A message queue is a kernel object through which Interrupt Service Routines (ISRs) and/or tasks send messages to other tasks. The sender "formulates" a message and sends it to the message queue. The task(s) wanting to receive these messages wait on the message queue for messages to arrive. If there are already messages in the message queue, the receiver immediately retrieves those messages. If there are no messages waiting in the message queue, then the receiver will be placed in a wait list associated with the message queue. This process will be demonstrated in this example.

L3-4(4)   Allocate a stack for each task.

L3-4(5)   The user must prototype the tasks.

Listing 3-5 shows the entry point for C, **main()**.

```
void  main (void)
{
   OS_ERR  err;

   BSP_IntDisAll();
   OSInit(&err);
   /* Check for 'err' */

   OSMutexCreate((OS_MUTEX  *)&AppMutex,                                     (1)
               (CPU_CHAR  *)"My App. Mutex",
               (OS_ERR    *)&err);
   /* Check for 'err' */


   OSQCreate   ((OS_Q      *)&AppQ,                                          (2)
               (CPU_CHAR  *)"My App Queue",
               (OS_MSG_QTY )10,
               (OS_ERR    *)&err);
   /* Check for 'err' */


   OSTaskCreate((OS_TCB     *)&AppTaskStartTCB,                              (3)
               (CPU_CHAR  *)"App Task Start",
               (OS_TASK_PTR )AppTaskStart,
               (void      *)0,
               (OS_PRIO   )APP_TASK_START_PRIO,
               (CPU_STK   *)&AppTaskStartStk[0],
               (CPU_STK_SIZE)APP_TASK_START_STK_SIZE / 10,
               (CPU_STK_SIZE)APP_TASK_START_STK_SIZE,
               (OS_MSG_QTY )0,
               (OS_TICK   )0,
               (void      *)0,
               (OS_OPT     )(OS_OPT_TASK_STK_CHK | OS_OPT_TASK_STK_CLR),
               (OS_ERR    *)&err);
   /* Check for 'err' */

   OSStart(&err);
   /* Check for 'err' */
}
```

Listing 3-5 **APP.C (2nd Part)**

L3-5(1)   Creating a mutex is simply a matter of calling **OSMutexCreate()**. Specify the address of the **OS_MUTEX** object that will be used for the mutex. Chapter 13, "Resource Management" on page 215 provides additional information about mutual exclusion semaphores.

You can assign an ASCII name to the mutex, which is useful when debugging.

L3-5(2)   Create the message queue by calling **OSQCreate()** and specifying the address of the **OS_Q** object. Chapter 15, "Message Passing" on page 295 provides additional information about message queues.

Assign an ASCII name to the message queue.

Specify how many messages the message queue is allowed to receive. This value must be greater than zero. If the sender sends messages faster than they can be consumed by the receiving task, messages will be lost. This can be corrected by either increasing the size of the message queue, or increasing the priority of the receiving task.

L3-5(3)   The first application task is created.

Listing 3-6 shows how to create other tasks once multitasking as started.

```
static  void  AppTaskStart (void *p_arg)
{
    OS_ERR  err;


    p_arg = p_arg;
    BSP_Init();
    CPU_Init();
    BSP_Cfg_Tick();
    OSTaskCreate((OS_TCB     *)&AppTask1_TCB,                                (1)
                 (CPU_CHAR   *)"App Task 1",
                 (OS_TASK_PTR )AppTask1,
                 (void       *)0,
                 (OS_PRIO     )5,
                 (CPU_STK    *)&AppTask1_Stk[0],
                 (CPU_STK_SIZE)0,
                 (CPU_STK_SIZE)128,
                 (OS_MSG_QTY  )0,
                 (OS_TICK     )0,
                 (void       *)0,
                 (OS_OPT      )(OS_OPT_TASK_STK_CHK | OS_OPT_TASK_STK_CLR),
                 (OS_ERR     *)&err);

    OSTaskCreate((OS_TCB     *)&AppTask2_TCB,                                (2)
                 (CPU_CHAR   *)"App Task 2",
                 (OS_TASK_PTR )AppTask2,
                 (void       *)0,
                 (OS_PRIO     )6,
                 (CPU_STK    *)&AppTask2_Stk[0],
                 (CPU_STK_SIZE)0,
                 (CPU_STK_SIZE)128,
                 (OS_MSG_QTY  )0,
                 (OS_TICK     )0,
                 (void       *)0,
                 (OS_OPT      )(OS_OPT_TASK_STK_CHK | OS_OPT_TASK_STK_CLR),
                 (OS_ERR     *)&err);
    BSP_LED_Off(0);
    while (1) {
        BSP_LED_Toggle(0);
        OSTimeDlyHMSM((CPU_INT16U)  0,
                      (CPU_INT16U)  0,
                      (CPU_INT16U)  0,
                      (CPU_INT32U)100,
                      (OS_OPT    )OS_OPT_TIME_HMSM_STRICT,
                      (OS_ERR   *)&err);
    }
}
```

Listing 3-6 **APP.C (3rd Part)**

L3-6(1)   Create Task #1 by calling **OSTaskCreate()**. If this task happens to have a higher priority than the task that creates it, µC/OS-III will immediately start Task #1. If the created task has a lower priority, **OSTaskCreate()** will return to **AppTaskStart()** and continue execution.

L3-6(2)   Task #2 is created and if it has a higher priority than **AppTaskStart()**, µC/OS-III will immediately switch to that task.

```
static  void  AppTask1 (void *p_arg)
{
    OS_ERR   err;
    CPU_TS   ts;


    p_arg = p_arg;
    while (1) {
        OSTimeDly ((OS_TICK    )1,                            (1)
                   (OS_OPT     )OS_OPT_TIME_DLY,
                   (OS_ERR    *)&err);
        OSQPost   ((OS_Q      *)&AppQ,                         (2)
                   (void      *)1;
                   (OS_MSG_SIZE)sizeof(void *),
                   (OS_OPT     )OS_OPT_POST_FIFO,
                   (OS_ERR    *)&err);
        OSMutexPend((OS_MUTEX  *)&AppMutex,                    (3)
                   (OS_TICK    )0,
                   (OS_OPT     )OS_OPT_PEND_BLOCKING;
                   (CPU_TS    *)&ts,
                   (OS_ERR    *)&err);
        /* Access shared resource */                          (4)
        OSMutexPost((OS_MUTEX  *)&AppMutex,                    (5)
                   (OS_OPT     )OS_OPT_POST_NONE,
                   (OS_ERR    *)&err);
    }
}
```

Listing 3-7 **APP.C (4th Part)**

L3-7(1)   The task starts by waiting for one tick to expire before it does anything useful. If the µC/OS-III tick rate is configured for 1000 Hz, the task will execute every millisecond.

L3-7(2)   The task then sends a message to another task using the message queue AppQ. In this case, the example shows a fixed message "1," but the message could have consisted of the address of a buffer, the address of a function, or whatever would need to be sent.

L3-7(3)   The task then waits on the mutual exclusion semaphore since it needs to access a shared resource with another task. If the resource is already owned by another task, **AppTask1()** will wait forever for the mutex to be released by its current owner. The forever wait is specified by passing 0 as the second argument of the call.

L3-7(4)   When **OSMutexPend()** returns, the task owns the resource and can therefore access the shared resource. The shared resource may be a variable, an array, a data structure, an I/O device, etc.

L3-7(5)   When the task is done with the shared resource, it must call **OSMutexPost()** to release the mutex.

```
static  void  AppTask2 (void *p_arg)
{
    OS_ERR       err;
    void         *p_msg;
    OS_MSG_SIZE  msg_size;
    CPU_TS       ts;
    CPU_TS       ts_delta;


    p_arg = p_arg;
    while (1) {
        p_msg = OSQPend((OS_Q          *)&AppQ,                       (1)
                        (OS_MSG_SIZE *)&msg_size,
                        (OS_TICK      )0,
                        (OS_OPT       )OS_OPT_PEND_BLOCKING,
                        (CPU_TS     *)&ts,
                        (OS_ERR     *)&err);
        ts_delta = OS_TS_GET() - ts;                                 (2)
        /* Process message received */                              (3)
    }
}
```

Listing 3-8 **APP.C (5th Part)**

L3-8(1)   Task #2 starts by waiting for messages to be sent through the message queue AppQ. The task waits forever for a message to be received because the third argument specifies an infinite timeout.

When the message is received **p_msg** will contain the message (i.e., a pointer to "something"). Both the sender and receiver must agree as to the meaning of the message. The size of the message received is saved in "**msg_size**". Note that "**p_msg**" could point to a buffer and "**msg_size**" would indicate the size of this buffer.

Also, when the message is received, "**ts**" will contain the timestamp of when the message was sent. A timestamp is the value read from a fairly fast free-running timer. The timestamp is typically an unsigned 32-bit (or more) value.

L3-8(2)   Knowing when the message was sent allows the user to determine how long it took this task to get the message. Reading the current timestamp and subtracting the timestamp of when the message was sent allows users to know how long it took for the message to be received. Note that the receiving task may not get the message immediately since ISRs or other higher-priority tasks might execute before the receiver gets to run.

L3-8(3)   Proceed with processing the received message.

4

Critical Sections

A critical section of code, also called a *critical region*, is code that needs to be treated indivisibly. There are many critical sections of code contained in µC/OS-III. If a critical section is accessible by an Interrupt Service Routine (ISR) and a task, then disabling interrupts is necessary to protect the critical region. If the critical section is only accessible by task level code, the critical section may be protected through the use of a *preemption lock*.

Within µC/OS-III, the critical section access method depends on which ISR post method is used by interrupts (see Chapter 9, "Interrupt Management" on page 163). If OS_CFG_ISR_POST_DEFERRED_EN is set to 0 (see OS_CFG.H) then µC/OS-III will disable interrupts when accessing internal critical sections. If OS_CFG_ISR_POST_DEFERRED_EN is set to 1 then µC/OS-III will lock the scheduler when accessing most of its internal critical sections.

Chapter 9, "Interrupt Management" on page 163 discusses how to select the method to use.

µC/OS-III defines one macro for entering a critical section and two macros for leaving:

    OS_CRITICAL_ENTER(),
    OS_CRITICAL_EXIT() and
    OS_CRITICAL_EXIT_NO_SCHED()

These macros are internal to µC/OS-III and must not be invoked by the application code. However, if you need to access critical sections in your application code, consult Chapter 13, "Resource Management" on page 215.

4

4-1 DISABLING INTERRUPTS

When setting OS_CFG_ISR_POST_DEFERRED_EN to 0, μC/OS-III will disable interrupts before entering a critical section and re-enable them when leaving the critical section.

OS_CRITICAL_ENTER() invokes the μC/CPU macro CPU_CRITICAL_ENTER() that, in turn, calls CPU_SR_Save(). CPU_SR_Save() is a function typically written in assembly language that saves the current interrupt disable status and then disables interrupts. The saved interrupt disable status is returned to the caller and in fact, it is stored onto the caller's stack in a variable called "cpu_sr".

OS_CRITICAL_EXIT() and OS_CRITICAL_EXIT_NO_SCHED() both invoke the μC/CPU macro CPU_CRITICAL_EXIT(), which maps to CPU_SR_Restore(). CPU_SR_Restore() is passed the value of the saved "cpu_sr" variable to re-establish interrupts the way they were prior to calling OS_CRITICAL_ENTER().

The typical code for the macros is shown in Listing 4-1.

```
#define  OS_CRITICAL_ENTER()          { CPU_CRITICAL_ENTER(); }
#define  OS_CRITICAL_EXIT()           { CPU_CRITICAL_EXIT(); }
#define  OS_CRITICAL_EXIT_NO_SCHED()  { CPU_CRITICAL_EXIT(); }
```

Listing 4-1 **Critical section code – Disabling interrupts**

4-1-1 MEASURING INTERRUPT DISABLE TIME

μC/CPU provides facilities to measure the amount of time interrupts are disabled. This is done by setting the configuration constant CPU_CFG_TIME_MEAS_INT_DIS_EN to 1 in CPU_CFG.H.

The measurement is started each time interrupts are disabled and ends when interrupts are re-enabled. The measurement keeps track of two values: a global interrupt disable time, and an interrupt disable time for each task. Therefore, it is possible to know how long a task disables interrupts, enabling the user to better optimize their code.

The per-task interrupt disable time is saved in the task's OS_TCB during a context switch (see OSTaskSwHook() in OS_CPU_C.C and described in Chapter 8, "Context Switching" on page 153).

The unit of measure for the measured time is in CPU_TS (timestamp) units. It is necessary to find out the resolution of the timer used to measure these timestamps. For example, if the timer used for the timestamp is incremented at 1 MHz then the resolution of **CPU_TS** is 1 microsecond.

Measuring the interrupt disable time obviously adds measurement artifacts and thus increases the amount of time the interrupts are disabled. However, as far as the measurement is concerned, measurement overhead is accounted for and the measured value represents the actual interrupt disable time as if the measurement was not present.

Interrupt disable time is obviously greatly affected by the speed at which the processor accesses instructions and thus, the memory access speed. In this case, the hardware designer might have introduced wait states to memory accesses, which affects overall performance of the system. This may show up as unusually long interrupt disable times.

4-2 LOCKING THE SCHEDULER

When setting **OS_CFG_ISR_POST_DEFERRED_EN** to 1, µC/OS-III locks the scheduler before entering a critical section and unlocks the scheduler when leaving the critical section.

OS_CRITICAL_ENTER() simply increments **OSSchedLockNestingCtr** to lock the scheduler. This is the variable the scheduler uses to determine whether or not the scheduler is locked. It is locked when the value is non-zero.

OS_CRITICAL_EXIT() decrements **OSSchedLockNestingCtr** and when the value reaches zero, invokes the scheduler.

OS_CRITICAL_EXIT_NO_SCHED() also decrements **OSSchedLockNestingCtr**, but does not invoke the scheduler when the value reaches zero.

The code for the macros is shown in Listing 4-2.

```
#define   OS_CRITICAL_ENTER()           {                                            \
                                        CPU_CRITICAL_ENTER();                        \
                                        OSSchedLockNestingCtr++;                     \
                                        CPU_CRITICAL_EXIT();                         \
                                        }
#define   OS_CRITICAL_EXIT()            {                                            \
                                        CPU_CRITICAL_ENTER();                        \
                                        OSSchedLockNestingCtr--;                     \
                                        if (OSSchedLockNestingCtr == (OS_NESTING_CTR)0) {  \
                                            CPU_CRITICAL_EXIT();                     \
                                            OSSched();                               \
                                        } else {                                     \
                                            CPU_CRITICAL_EXIT();                     \
                                        }                                            \
                                        }
#define   OS_CRITICAL_EXIT_NO_SCHED()   {                                            \
                                        CPU_CRITICAL_ENTER();                        \
                                        OSSchedLockNestingCtr--;                     \
                                        CPU_CRITICAL_EXIT();                         \
                                        }
```

Listing 4-2 **Critical section code – Locking the Scheduler**

4-2-1 MEASURING SCHEDULER LOCK TIME

µC/OS-III provides facilities to measure the amount of time the scheduler is locked. This is done by setting the configuration constant **OS_CFG_SCHED_LOCK_TIME_MEAS_EN** to 1 in **OS_CFG.H**.

The measurement is started each time the scheduler is locked and ends when the scheduler is unlocked. The measurement keeps track of two values: a global scheduler lock time, and a per-task scheduler lock time. It is therefore possible to know how long each task locks the scheduler allowing the user to better optimize code.

The per-task scheduler lock time is saved in the task's **OS_TCB** during a context switch (see **OSTaskSwHook()** in **OS_CPU_C.C** and described in Chapter 8, "Context Switching" on page 153).

The unit of measure for the measured time is in **CPU_TS** (timestamp) units so it is necessary to find the resolution of the timer used to measure the timestamps. For example, if the timer used for the timestamp is incremented at 1 MHz then the resolution of **CPU_TS** is 1 microsecond.

Measuring the scheduler lock time adds measurement artifacts and thus increases the amount of time the scheduler is actually locked. However, measurement overhead is accounted for and the measured value represents the actual scheduler lock time as if the measurement was not present.

4-3 µC/OS-III FEATURES WITH LONGER CRITICAL SECTIONS

Table 4-1 shows several µC/OS-III features that have potentially longer critical sections. Knowledge of these will help the user decide whether to direct µC/OS-III to use one critical section over another.

Feature	Reason
Multiple tasks at the same priority	Although this is an important feature of µC/OS-III, multiple tasks at the same priority create longer critical sections. However, if there are only a few tasks at the same priority, interrupt latency would be relatively small. If multiple tasks are not created at the same priority, use the interrupt disable method.
Event Flags Chapter 14, "Synchronization" on page 257	If multiple tasks are waiting on different events, going through all of the tasks waiting for events requires a fair amount of processing time, which means longer critical sections. If only a few tasks (approximately one to five) are waiting on an event flag group, the critical section would be short enough to use the interrupt disable method.
Pend on multiple objects Chapter 16, "Pending On Multiple Objects" on page 319	Pending on multiple objects is probably the most complex feature provided by µC/OS-III, requiring interrupts to be disabled for fairly long periods of time should the interrupt disable method be selected. If pending on multiple objects, it is highly recommended that the user select the scheduler-lock method. If the application does not use this feature, the interrupt disable method is an alternative.
Broadcast on Post calls See OSSemPost() and OSQPost() descriptions in Appendix A, "µC/OS-III API Reference Manual" on page 381.	µC/OS-III disables interrupts while processing a post to multiple tasks in a broadcast. When not using the broadcast option, you can use the interrupt disable method.

Table 4-1 **Disabling interrupts or locking the Scheduler**

4-4 SUMMARY

µC/OS-III needs to access critical sections of code, which it protects by either disabling interrupts (OS_CFG_ISR_POST_DEFERRED_EN set to 0 in OS_CFG.H), or locking the scheduler (OS_CFG_ISR_POST_DEFERRED_EN set to 1 in OS_CFG.H).

The application code must not use:

```
OS_CRITICAL_ENTER( )
OS_CRITICAL_EXIT( )
OS_CRITICAL_EXIT_NO_SCHED( )
```

When setting CPU_CFG_TIME_MEAS_INT_DIS_EN in CPU_CFG.H, µC/CPU measures the maximum interrupt disable time. There are two values available, one for the global maximum and one for each task.

When setting OS_CFG_SCHED_LOCK_TIME_MEAS_EN to 1 in OS_CFG.H, µC/OS-III will measure the maximum scheduler lock time.

Chapter

5

Task Management

The design process of a real-time application generally involves splitting the work to be completed into tasks, each responsible for a portion of the problem. μC/OS-III makes it easy for an application programmer to adopt this paradigm. A task (also called a *thread*) is a simple program that thinks it has the Central Processing Unit (CPU) all to itself. On a single CPU, only one task can execute at any given time.

μC/OS-III supports multitasking and allows the application to have any number of tasks. The maximum number of task is actually only limited by the amount of memory (both code and data space) available to the processor. Multitasking is the process of *scheduling* and *switching* the CPU between several tasks (this will be expanded upon later). The CPU switches its attention between several *sequential* tasks. Multitasking provides the illusion of having multiple CPUs and, actually maximizes the use of the CPU. Multitasking also helps in the creation of modular applications. One of the most important aspects of multitasking is that it allows the application programmer to manage the complexity inherent in real-time applications. Application programs are typically easier to design and maintain when multitasking is used.

Tasks are used for such chores as monitoring inputs, updating outputs, performing computations, control loops, update one or more displays, reading buttons and keyboards, communicating with other systems, and more. One application may contain a handful of tasks while another application may require hundreds. The number of tasks does not establish how good or effective a design may be, it really depends on what the application (or product) needs to do. The amount of work a task performs also depends on the application. One task may have a few microseconds worth of work to perform while another task may require tens of milliseconds.

Tasks look like just any other C function except for a few small differences. There are two types of tasks: run-to-completion (Listing 5-1) and infinite loop (Listing 5-2). In most embedded systems, tasks typically take the form of an infinite loop. Also, no task is allowed to return as other C functions can. Given that a task is a regular C function, it can declare local variables.

5

When a μC/OS-III task begins executing, it is passed an argument, **p_arg**. This argument is a pointer to a **void**. The pointer is a universal vehicle used to pass your task the address of a variable, a structure, or even the address of a function, if necessary. With this pointer, it is possible to create many identical tasks, that all use the same code (or task body), but, with different run-time characteristics. For example, one may have four asynchronous serial ports that are each managed by their own task. However, the task code is actually identical. Instead of copying the code four times, create the code for a "generic" task that receives a pointer to a data structure, which contains the serial port's parameters (baud rate, I/O port addresses, interrupt vector number, etc.) as an argument. In other words, instantiate the same task code four times and pass it different data for each serial port that each instance will manage.

A run-to-completion task must *delete* itself by calling **OSTaskDel()**. The task starts, performs its function, and terminates. There would typically not be too many such tasks in the embedded system because of the overhead associated with "creating" and "deleting" tasks at run-time. In the task body, one can call most of μC/OS-III's functions to help perform the desired operation of the task.

```
void MyTask (void *p_arg)
{
    OS_ERR  err;
    /* Local variables                            */


    /* Do something with 'p_arg'                  */
    /* Task initialization                        */
    /* Task body ... do work!                     */
    OSTaskDel((OS_TCB *)0, &err);
}
```

Listing 5-1 **Run-To-Completion task**

With μC/OS-III, call either C or assembly language functions from a task. In fact, it is possible to call the same C function from different tasks as long as the functions are reentrant. A *reentrant* function is a function that does not use static or otherwise global variables unless they are protected (μC/OS-III provides mechanisms for this) from multiple access. If shared C functions only use local variables, they are generally reentrant (assuming that the compiler generates reentrant code). An example of a non-reentrant function is the famous strtok() provided by most C compilers as part of the standard library. This function is used to parse an ASCII string for "tokens." The first time you call this function, you specify the ASCII string to parse and what constitute tokens. As soon as the function finds the first token, it returns. The function "remembers" where it was last so when called again, it can extract additional tokens, which is clearly non-reentrant.

The use of an infinite loop is more common in embedded systems because of the repetitive work needed in such systems (reading inputs, updating displays, performing control operations, etc.). This is one aspect that makes a task different than a regular C function. Note that one could use a "while (1)" or "for (;;)" to implement the infinite loop, since both behave the same. The one used is simply a matter of personal preference. At Micrium, we like to use "while (DEF_ON)". The infinite loop **must** call a µC/OS-III service (i.e., function) that will cause the task to wait for an event to occur. It is important that each task wait for an event to occur, otherwise the task would be a true infinite loop and there would be no easy way for other tasks to execute. This concept will become clear as more is understood regarding µC/OS-III.

```c
void MyTask (void *p_arg)
{
    /* Local variables                                        */

    /* Do something with "p_arg"                              */
    /* Task initialization                                    */
    while (DEF_ON) {        /* Task body, as an infinite loop. */
        :
        /* Task body ... do work!                             */
        :
        /* Must call one of the following services:           */
        /*      OSFlagPend()                                   */
        /*      OSMutexPend()                                  */
        /*      OSPendMulti()                                  */
        /*      OSQPend()                                      */
        /*      OSSemPend()                                    */
        /*      OSTimeDly()                                    */
        /*      OSTimeDlyHMSM()                                */
        /*      OSTaskQPend()                                  */
        /*      OSTaskSemPend()                                */
        /*      OSTaskSuspend()     (Suspend self)             */
        /*      OSTaskDel()         (Delete  self)             */
        :
        /* Task body ... do work!                             */
        :
    }
}
```

Listing 5-2 **Infinite Loop task**

The event the task is waiting for may simply be the passage of time (when **OSTimeDly()** or **OSTimeDlyHMSM()** is called). For example, a design may need to scan a keyboard every 100 milliseconds. In this case, simply delay the task for 100 milliseconds then see if a key was pressed on the keyboard and, possibly perform some action based on which key was pressed. Typically, however, a keyboard scanning task should just buffer an "identifier" unique to the key pressed and use another task to decide what to do with the key(s) pressed.

Similarly, the event the task is waiting for could be the arrival of a packet from an Ethernet controller. In this case, the task would call one of the **OS???Pend()** calls (pend is synonymous with wait). The task will have nothing to do until the packet is received. Once the packet is received, the task processes the contents of the packet, and possibly moves the packet along a network stack.

It's important to note that when a task waits for an event, it does not consume CPU time.

Tasks must be created in order for μC/OS-III to know about tasks. Create a task by simply calling **OSTaskCreate()**. The function prototype for **OSTaskCreate()** is shown below:

```
void  OSTaskCreate (OS_TCB        *p_tcb,
                    OS_CHAR       *p_name,
                    OS_TASK_PTR   p_task,
                    void          *p_arg,
                    OS_PRIO       prio,
                    CPU_STK       *p_stk_base,
                    CPU_STK_SIZE  stk_limit,
                    CPU_STK_SIZE  stk_size,
                    OS_MSG_QTY    q_size,
                    OS_TICK       time_slice,
                    void          *p_ext,
                    OS_OPT        opt,
                    OS_ERR        *p_err)
```

A complete description of **OSTaskCreate()** and its arguments is provided in Appendix A, "μC/OS-III API Reference Manual" on page 381. However, it is important to understand that a task needs to be assigned a *Task Control Block* (i.e., TCB), a stack, a priority and a few other parameters which are initialized by **OSTaskCreate()**, as shown in Figure 5-1.

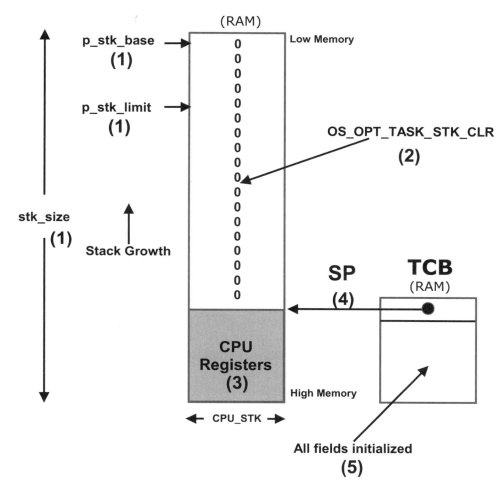

Figure 5-1 **OSTaskCreate() initializes the task's TCB and stack**

F5-1(1)   When calling **OSTaskCreate()**, one passes the base address of the stack (**p_stk_base**) that will be used by the task, the watermark limit for stack growth (**stk_limit**) which is expressed in number of **CPU_STK** entries before the stack is empty, and the size of that stack (**stk_size**), also in number of **CPU_STK** elements.

F5-1(2)   When specifying **OS_OPT_TASK_STK_CHK** + **OS_OPT_TASK_STK_CLR** in the opt argument of **OSTaskCreate()**, µC/OS-III initializes the task's stack with all zeros.

5

F5-1(3)   μC/OS-III then initializes the top of the task's stack with a copy of the CPU registers in the same stacking order as if they were all saved at the beginning of an ISR. This makes it easy to perform context switches as we will see when discussing the context switching process. For illustration purposes, the assumption is that the stack grows from high memory to low memory, but the same concept applies for CPUs that use the stack in the reverse order.

F5-1(4)   The new value of the stack pointer (SP) is saved in the TCB. Note that this is also called the **top-of-stack**.

F5-1(5)   The remaining fields of the TCB are initialized: task priority, task name, task state, internal message queue, internal semaphore, and many others.

Next, a call is made to a function that is defined in the CPU port, **OSTaskCreateHook()** (see **OS_CPU_C.C**). **OSTaskCreateHook()** is passed the pointer to the new TCB and this function allows you (or the port designer) to extend the functionality of **OSTaskCreate()**. For example, one could printout the contents of the fields of the newly created TCB onto a terminal for debugging purposes.

The task is then placed in the ready-list (see Chapter 6, "The Ready List" on page 129) and finally, if multitasking has started, μC/OS-III will invoke the scheduler to see if the created task is now the highest priority task and, if so, will context switch to this new task.

The body of the task can invoke other services provided by μC/OS-III. Specifically, a task can create another task (i.e., call **OSTaskCreate()**), suspend and resume other tasks (i.e., call **OSTaskSuspend()** and **OSTaskResume()** respectively), post signals or messages to other tasks (i.e., call **OS??Post()**), share resources with other tasks, and more. In other words, tasks are not limited to only make "wait for an event" function calls.

Figure 5-2 shows the resources with which a task typically interacts.

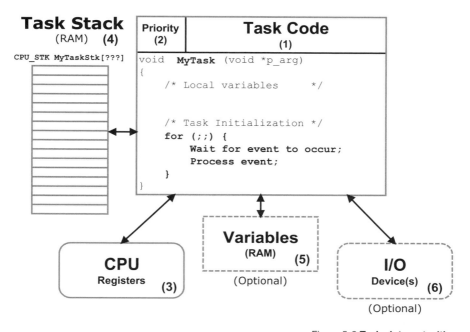

Figure 5-2 **Tasks interact with resources**

F5-2(1)   An important aspect of a task is its code. As previously mentioned, the code looks like any other C function, except that it is typically implemented as an infinite loop. Also, a task is not allowed to return.

F5-2(2)   Each task is assigned a priority based on its importance in the application. µC/OS-III's job is to decide which task will run on the CPU. The general rule is that µC/OS-III will run the most important *ready-to-run* task (highest priority).

    With µC/OS-III, a low priority number indicates a high priority. In other words, a task at priority 1 is more important than a task at priority 10.

    µC/OS-III supports a compile-time user configurable number of different priorities (see **OS_PRIO_MAX** in **OS_CFG.H**). Thus, µC/OS-III allows the user to determine the number of different priority levels the application is allowed to use. Also, µC/OS-III supports an unlimited number of tasks at the same priority. For example, µC/OS-III can be configured to have 64 different priority levels and one can assign dozens of tasks at each priority level.

    See section 5-1 "Assigning Task Priorities" on page 90.

F5-2(3)   A task has its own set of CPU registers. As far as a task is concerned, the task thinks it has the actual CPU all to itself.

F5-2(4)   Because µC/OS-III is a preemptive kernel, each task must have its own stack area. The stack always resides in RAM and is used to keep track of local variables, function calls, and possibly ISR (Interrupt Service Routine) nesting.

Stack space can be allocated either statically (at compile-time) or dynamically (at run-time). A static stack declaration is shown below. This declaration is made outside of a function.

```
static  CPU_STK MyTaskStk[???];
```

or,

```
CPU_STK MyTaskStk[???];
```

Note that "**???**" indicates that the size of the stack (and thus the array) depends on the task stack requirements. Stack space may be allocated dynamically by using the C compiler's heap management function (i.e., **malloc()**) as shown below. However, care must be taken with fragmentation. If creating and deleting tasks, the process of allocating memory might not be able to provide a stack for the task(s) because the heap will eventually become fragmented. For this reason, allocating stack space dynamically in an embedded system is typically allowed but, once allocated, stacks should not be deallocated. Said another way, it's fine to create a task's stack from the heap as long as you don't free the stack space back to the heap.

```
void SomeCode (void)
{
    CPU_STK *p_stk;
    :
    :
    p_stk = (CPU_STK *)malloc(stk_size);
    if (p_stk != (CPU_STK *)0) {
        Create the task and pass it "p_stk" as the base address of the stack;
    }
    :
    :
}
```

See section 5-2 "Determining the Size of a Stack" on page 92.

F5-2(5)   A task can also have access to global variables. However, because µC/OS-III is a preemptive kernel care must be taken with code when accessing such variables as they may be shared between multiple tasks. Fortunately, µC/OS-III provides mechanisms to help with the management of such shared resources (semaphores, mutexes and more).

F5-2(6)   A task may also have access to one or more Input/Output (I/O) devices (also known as *peripherals*). In fact, it is common practice to assign tasks to manage I/O devices.

5

5-1 ASSIGNING TASK PRIORITIES

Sometimes task priorities are both obvious and intuitive. For example, if the most important aspect of the embedded system is to perform some type of control and it is known that the control algorithm must be responsive then it is best to assign the control task(s) a high priority while display and operator interface tasks are assigned low priority. However, most of the time, assigning task priorities is not so cut and dry because of the complex nature of real-time systems. In most systems, not all tasks are considered critical, and non-critical tasks should obviously be given low priorities.

An interesting technique called rate monotonic scheduling (RMS) assigns task priorities based on how often tasks execute. Simply put, tasks with the highest rate of execution are given the highest priority. However, RMS makes a number of assumptions, including:

- All tasks are periodic (they occur at regular intervals).

- Tasks do not synchronize with one another, share resources, or exchange data.

- The CPU must always execute the highest priority task that is ready to run. In other words, preemptive scheduling must be used.

Given a set of n tasks that are assigned RMS priorities, the basic RMS theorem states that all task hard real-time deadlines are always met if the following inequality holds true:

$$\sum_i \frac{E_i}{T_i} \leq n \left(2^{1/n} - 1 \right)$$

Where E_i corresponds to the maximum execution time of task i, and T_i corresponds to the execution period of task i. In other words, E_i/T_i corresponds to the fraction of CPU time required to execute task i.

Table 5-1 shows the value for size $n(2^{1/n} - 1)$ based on the number of tasks. The upper bound for an infinite number of tasks is given by $\ln(2)$, or 0.693, which means that meeting all hard real-time deadlines based on RMS, CPU use of all time-critical tasks should be less than 70 percent!

Note that one can still have (and generally does) non time-critical tasks in a system and thus use close to 100 percent of the CPU's time. However, using 100 percent of your CPU's time is not a desirable goal as it does not allow for code changes and added features. As a rule of thumb, always design a system to use less than 60 to 70 percent of the CPU.

RMS says that the highest rate task has the highest priority. In some cases, the highest rate task might not be the most important task. The application dictates how to assign priorities. However, RMS is an interesting starting point.

Number of Tasks	$n(2^{1/n}-1)$
1	1.00
2	0.828
3	0.779
4	0.756
5	0.743
:	:
:	:
:	:
Infinite	0.693

Table 5-1 **Allowable CPU usage based on number of tasks**

5

5-2 DETERMINING THE SIZE OF A STACK

The size of the stack required by the task is application specific. When sizing the stack, however, one must account for the nesting of all the functions called by the task, the number of local variables to be allocated by all functions called by the task, and the stack requirements for all nested interrupt service routines. In addition, the stack must be able to store all CPU registers and possibly Floating-Point Unit (FPU) registers if the processor has a FPU. As a general rule in embedded systems, avoid writing recursive code.

It is possible to manually figure out the stack space needed by adding all the memory required by all function call nesting (1 pointer each function call for the return address), plus all the memory required by all the arguments passed in those function calls, plus storage for a full CPU context (depends on the CPU), plus another full CPU context for each nested ISRs (if the CPU doesn't have a separate stack to handle ISRs), plus whatever stack space is needed by those ISRs. Adding all this up is a tedious chore and the resulting number is a minimum requirement. Most likely one would not make the stack size that precise in order to account for "surprises." The number arrived at should probably be multiplied by some safety factor, possibly 1.5 to 2.0. This calculation assumes that the exact path of the code is known at all times, which is not always possible. Specifically, when calling a function such as `printf()` or some other library function, it might be difficult or nearly impossible to even guess just how much stack space `printf()` will require. In this case, start with a fairly large stack space and monitor the stack usage at run-time to see just how much stack space is actually used after the application runs for a while.

There are really cool and clever compilers/linkers that provide this information in a link map. For each function, the link map indicates the worst-case stack usage. This feature clearly enables one to better evaluate stack usage for each task. It is still necessary to add the stack space for a **full CPU** context plus, another **full CPU** context for each nested ISR (if the CPU does not have a separate stack to handle ISRs), plus whatever stack space is needed by those ISRs. Again, allow for a safety net and multiply this value by some factor.

Always monitor stack usage at run-time while developing and testing the product as stack overflows occur often and can lead to some curious behaviors. In fact, whenever someone mentions that his or her application behaves "strangely," insufficient stack size is the first thing that comes to mind.

5-3 DETECTING TASK STACK OVERFLOWS

1) Using an MMU or MPU

Stack overflows are easily detected if the processor has a Memory Management Unit (MMU) or a Memory Protection Unit (MPU). Basically, MMUs and MPUs are special hardware devices integrated alongside the CPU that can be configured to detect when a task attempts to access invalid memory locations, whether code, data, or stack. Setting up an MMU or MPU is well beyond the scope of this book.

2) Using a CPU with stack overflow detection

Some processors, however, do have simple stack pointer overflow detection registers. When the CPU's stack pointer goes below (or above depending on stack growth) the value set in this register, an exception is generated and the exception handler ensures that the offending code does not do further damage (possibly issue a warning about the faulty code). The `.StkLimitPtr` field in the `OS_TCB` (see Task Control Blocks) is provided for this purpose as shown in Figure 5-3. Note that the position of the stack limit is typically set at a valid location in the task's stack with sufficient room left on the stack to handle the exception itself (assuming the CPU does not have a separate exception stack). In most cases, the position can be fairly close to `&MyTaskStk[0]`.

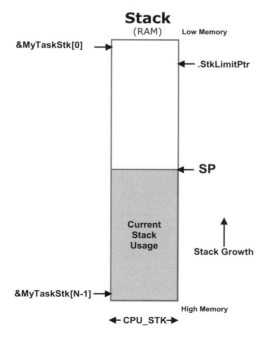

Figure 5-3 **Hardware detection of stack overflows**

As a reminder, the location of the `.StkLimitPtr` is determined by the "`stk_limit`" argument passed to `OSTaskCreate()`, when the task is created as shown below:

```
OS_TCB   MtTaskTCB;
CPU_STK MyTaskStk[1000];


OSTaskCreate(&MyTaskTCB,
             "MyTaskName",
             MyTask,
             &MyTaskArg,
             MyPrio,
             &MyTaskStk[0],   /* Stack base address                                   */
              100,            /* Set .StkLimitPtr to trigger exception at stack usage > 90% */
             1000,            /* Total stack size (in CPU_STK elements)                */
             MyTaskQSize,
             MyTaskTimeQuanta,
             (void *)0,
             MY_TASK_OPT,
             &err);
```

Of course, the value of `.StkLimitPtr` used by the CPU's stack overflow detection hardware needs to be changed whenever µC/OS-III performs a context switch. This can be tricky because the value of this register may need to be changed so that it first points to **NULL**, then change the CPU's stack pointer, and finally set the value of the stack checking register to the value saved in the TCB's `.StkLimitPtr`. Why? Because if the sequence is not followed, the exception could be generated as soon as the stack pointer or the stack overflow detection register is changed. One can avoid this problem by first changing the stack overflow detection register to point to a location that ensures the stack pointer is never invalid (thus the **NULL** as described above). Note that I assumed here that the stack grows from high memory to low memory but the concept works in a similar fashion if the stack grows in the opposite direction.

3) Software-based stack overflow detection

Whenever µC/OS-III switches from one task to another, it calls a "hook" function (`OSTaskSwHook()`), which allows the µC/OS-III port programmer to extend the capabilities of the context switch function. So, if the processor doesn't have hardware stack pointer overflow detection, it's still possible to "simulate" this feature by adding code in the context switch hook function and, perform the overflow detection in software. Specifically, before a task is *switched* in, the code should ensure that the stack pointer to load into the CPU does not exceed the "limit" placed in `.StkLimitPtr`. Because the software implementation cannot detect the stack overflow "as soon" as the stack pointer exceeds the value of .StkLimitPtr, it is important to position the value of .StkLimitPtr in the stack fairly far from &MyTaskStk[0], as shown in Figure 5-4. A software implementation such as this is not as reliable as a hardware-based detection mechanism but still prevents a possible stack overflow. Of course, the .StkLimitPtr field would be set using OSTaskCreate() as shown above but this time, with a location further away from &MyTaskStk[0].

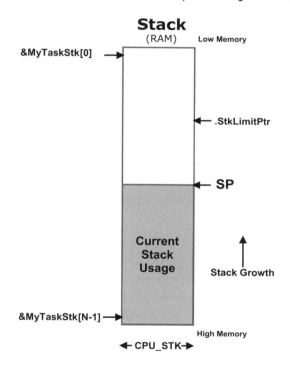

Figure 5-4 **Software detection of stack overflows, monitoring .StkLimitPtr**

4) Counting the amount of free stack space

Another way to check for stack overflows is to allocate more stack space than is anticipated to be used for the stack, then, monitor and possibly display actual maximum stack usage at run-time. This is fairly easy to do. First, the task stack needs to be cleared (i.e., filled with zeros) when the task is created. Next, a low priority task *walks the stack* of each task created, from the bottom (&MyTaskStk[0]) towards the top, counting the number of zero entries. When the task finds a non-zero value, the process is stopped and the usage of the stack can be computed (in number of bytes used or as a percentage). Then, adjust the size of the stacks (by recompiling the code) to allocate a more *reasonable* value (either increase or decrease the amount of stack space for each task). For this to be effective, however, run the application long enough for the stack to grow to its highest value. This is illustrated in Figure 5-5. µC/OS-III provides a function that performs this calculation at run-time, `OSTaskStkChk()` and in fact, this function is called by `OS_StatTask()` to compute stack usage for every task created in the application (to be described later).

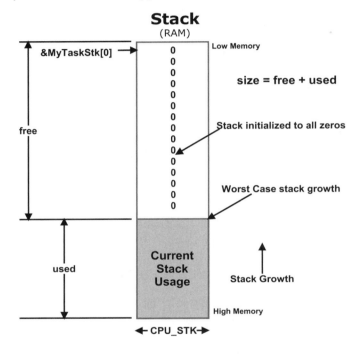

Figure 5-5 **Software detection of stack overflows, walking the stack**

5-4 TASK MANAGEMENT SERVICES

µC/OS-III provides a number of task-related services to call from the application. These services are found in **OS_TASK.C** and they all start with **OSTask???()**. The type of service they perform groups task-related services:

Group	Functions
General	OSTaskCreate() OSTaskDel() OSTaskChangePrio() OSTaskRegSet() OSTaskRegGet() OSTaskSuspend() OSTaskResume() OSTaskTimeQuantaSet()
Signaling a Task (See also Chapter 14, "Synchronization" on page 257)	OSTaskSemPend() OSTaskSemPost() OSTaskSemPendAbort()
Sending Messages to a Task (See also Chapter 15, "Message Passing" on page 295)	OSTaskQPend() OSTaskQPost() OSTaskQPendAbort() OSTaskQFlush()

Table 5-2 **Task Management Services**

A complete description of all µC/OS-III task related services is provided in Appendix A, "µC/OS-III API Reference Manual" on page 381.

5

5-5 TASK MANAGEMENT INTERNALS

5-5-1 TASK STATES

From a µC/OS-III user point of view, a task can be in any one of five states as shown in Figure 5-6. Internally, µC/OS-III does not need to keep track of the dormant state and the other states are tracked slightly differently. This will be discussed after a discussion on task states from the user's point of view. Figure 5-6 also shows which µC/OS-III functions are used to move from one state to another. The diagram is actually simplified as state transitions are a bit more complicated than this.

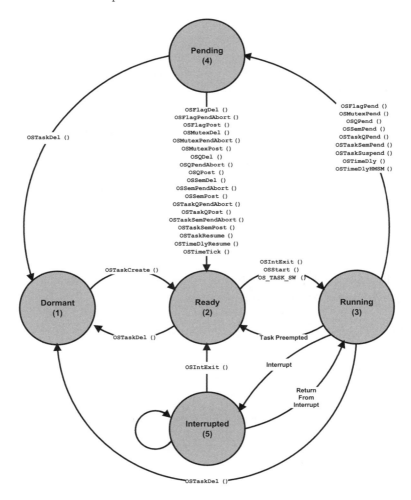

Figure 5-6 **Five basic states of a task**

F5-6(1) The *Dormant* state corresponds to a task that resides in memory but has not been made available to µC/OS-III.

A task is made available to µC/OS-III by calling a function to create the task, **OSTaskCreate()**. The task code actually resides in code space but µC/OS-III needs to be informed about it.

When it is no longer necessary for µC/OS-III to manage a task, call the task delete function, **OSTaskDel()**. **OSTaskDel()** does not actually delete the code of the task, it is simply not eligible to access the CPU.

F5-6(2) The *Ready* state corresponds to a ready-to-run task, but is not the most important task ready. There can be any number of tasks ready and µC/OS-III keeps track of all ready tasks in a **ready list** (discussed later). This list is sorted by priority.

F5-6(3) The most important ready-to-run task is placed in the *Running* state. On a single CPU, only one task can be running at any given time.

The task selected to run on the CPU is *switched in* by µC/OS-III from the ready state when the application code calls **OSStart()**, or when µC/OS-III calls either **OSIntExit()** or **OS_TASK_SW()**.

As previously discussed, tasks must wait for an event to occur. A task waits for an event by calling one of the functions that brings the task to the pending state if the event has not occurred.

F5-6(4) Tasks in the *Pending* state are placed in a special list called a *pend-list* (or wait list) associated with the event the task is waiting for. When waiting for the event to occur, the task does not consume CPU time. When the event occurs, the task is placed back into the ready list and µC/OS-III decides whether the newly readied task is the most important ready-to-run task. If this is the case, the currently running task will be preempted (placed back in the ready list) and the newly readied task is given control of the CPU. In other words, the newly readied task will run immediately if it is the most important task.

5

Note that the **OSTaskSuspend()** function unconditionally blocks a task and this task will not actually wait for an event to occur but in fact, waits until another task calls **OSTaskResume()** to make the task ready to run.

F5-6(5)   Assuming that CPU interrupts are enabled, an interrupting device will suspend execution of a task and execute an Interrupt Service Routine (ISR). ISRs are typically events that tasks wait for. Generally speaking, an ISR should simply notify a task that an event occurred and let the task process the event. ISRs should be as short as possible and most of the work of handling the interrupting devices should be done at the task level where it can be managed by μC/OS-III. ISRs are only allowed to make "Post" calls (i.e., **OSFlagPost()**, **OSQPost()**, **OSSemPost()**, **OSTaskQPost()** and **OSTaskSemPost()**). The only post call not allowed to be made from an ISR is OSMutexPost() since mutexes, as will be addressed later, are assumed to be services that are only accessible at the task level.

As the state diagram indicates, an interrupt can interrupt another interrupt. This is called **interrupt nesting** and most processors allow this. However, interrupt nesting easily leads to stack overflow if not managed properly.

Internally, μC/OS-III keeps track of task states using the state machine shown in Figure 5-7. The task state is actually maintained in a variable that is part of a data structure associated with each task, the task's TCB. The task state diagram was referenced throughout the design of μC/OS-III when implementing most of μC/OS-III's services. The number in parentheses is the state number of the task and thus, a task can be in any one of eight (8) states (see **OS.H, OS_TASK_STATE_???**).

Note that the diagram does not keep track of a dormant task, as a dormant task is not known to μC/OS-III. Also, interrupts and interrupt nesting is tracked differently as will be explained further in the text.

This state diagram should be quite useful to understand how to use several functions and their impact on the state of tasks. In fact, I'd highly recommend that the reader bookmark the page of the diagram.

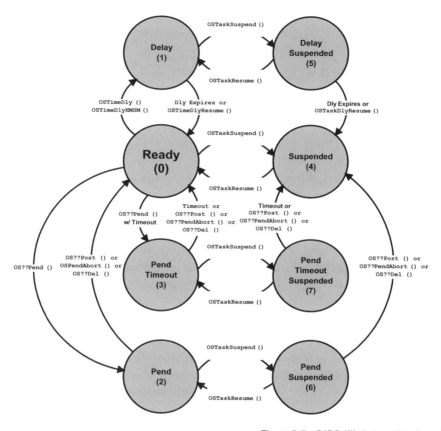

Figure 5-7 **µC/OS-III's internal task state machine**

F5-7(1)   State 0 occurs when a task is ready to run. Every task "wants" to be ready to run as that is the only way it gets to perform their duties.

F5-7(2)   A task can decide to wait for time to expire by calling either `OSTimeDly()` or `OSTimeDlyHMSM()`. When the time expires or the delay is cancelled (by calling `OSTimeDlyResume()`), the task returns to the ready state.

F5-7(3)   A task can wait for an event to occur by calling one of the pend (i.e., wait) functions (`OSFlagPend()`, `OSMutexPend()`, `OSQPend()`, `OSSemPend()`, `OSTaskQPend()`, or `OSTaskSemPend()`), and specify to wait forever for the event to occur. The pend terminates when the event occurs (i.e., a task or an ISR performs a "post"), the awaited object is deleted or, another task decides to abort the pend.

5

F5-7(4)   A task can wait for an event to occur as indicated, but specify that it is willing to wait a certain amount of time for the event to occur. If the event is not posted within that time, the task is readied, then the task is notified that a timeout occurred. Again, the pend terminates when the event occurs (i.e., a task or an ISR performs a "post"), the object awaited is deleted or, another task decides to abort the pend.

F5-7(5)   A task can suspend itself or another task by calling **OSTaskSuspend()**. The only way the task is allowed to resume execution is by calling **OSTaskResume()**. Suspending a task means that a task will not be able to run on the CPU until it is resumed by another task.

F5-7(6)   A delayed task can also be suspended by another task. In this case, the effect is additive. In other words, the delay must complete (or be resumed by **OSTimeDlyResume()**) and the suspension must be removed (by another task which would call **OSTaskResume()**) in order for the task to be able to run.

F5-7(7)   A task waiting on an event to occur may be suspended by another task. Again, the effect is additive. The event must occur and the suspension removed (by another task) in order for the task to be able to run. Of course, if the object that the task is pending on is deleted or, the pend is aborted by another task, then one of the above two condition is removed. The suspension , however, must be explicitly removed.

F5-7(8)   A task can wait for an event, but only for a certain amount of time, and the task could also be suspended by another task. As one might expect, the suspension must be removed by another task (or the same task that suspended it in the first place), and the event needs to either occur or timeout while waiting for the event.

5-5-2 TASK CONTROL BLOCKS (TCBs)

A task control block (TCB) is a data structure used by kernels to maintain information about a task. Each task requires its own TCB and, for µC/OS-III, the user assigns the TCB in user memory space (RAM). The address of the task's TCB is provided to µC/OS-III when calling task-related services (i.e., **OSTask???()** functions). The task control block data structure is declared in **OS.H** as shown in Listing 5-3. Note that the fields are actually commented in **OS.H**, and some of the fields are conditionally compiled based on whether or not certain features are desired. Both are not shown here for clarity.

Also, it is important to note that even when the user understands what the different fields of the **OS_TCB** do, the application code must never directly access these (especially change them). In other words, **OS_TCB** fields must only be accessed by µC/OS-III and not the code.

```
struct os_tcb {
    CPU_STK         *StkPtr;
    void            *ExtPtr;
    CPU_STK         *StkLimitPtr;
    OS_TCB          *NextPtr;
    OS_TCB          *PrevPtr;
    OS_TCB          *TickNextPtr;
    OS_TCB          *TickPrevPtr;
    OS_TICK_SPOKE   *TickSpokePtr;
    OS_CHAR         *NamePtr;
    CPU_STK         *StkBasePtr;
    OS_TASK_PTR      TaskEntryAddr;
    void            *TaskEntryArg;
    OS_PEND_DATA    *PendDataTblPtr;
    OS_OBJ_QTY       PendDataEntries;
    CPU_TS           TS;
    void            *MsgPtr;
    OS_MSG_SIZE      MsgSize;
    OS_MSG_Q         MsgQ;
    CPU_TS           MsgQPendTime;
    CPU_TS           MsgQPendTimeMax;
    OS_FLAGS         FlagsPend;
    OS_OPT           FlagsOpt;
    OS_FLAGS         FlagsRdy;
```

5

```
        OS_REG                RegTbl[OS_TASK_REG_TBL_SIZE];
        OS_SEM_CTR            SemCtr;
        CPU_TS                SemPendTime;
        CPU_TS                SemPendTimeMax;
        OS_NESTING_CTR        SuspendCtr;
        CPU_STK_SIZE          StkSize;
        CPU_STK_SIZE          StkUsed;
        CPU_STK_SIZE          StkFree;
        OS_OPT                Opt;
        OS_TICK               TickCtrPrev;
        OS_TICK               TickCtrMatch;
        OS_TICK               TickRemain;
        OS_TICK               TimeQuanta;
        OS_TICK               TimeQuantaCtr;
        OS_CPU_USAGE          CPUUsage;
        OS_CTX_SW_CTR         CtxSwCtr;
        CPU_TS                CyclesDelta;
        CPU_TS                CyclesStart;
        OS_CYCLES             CyclesTotal;
        CPU_TS                IntDisTimeMax;
        CPU                   SchedLockTimeMax;
        OS_STATE              PendOn;
        OS_STATUS             PendStatus;
        OS_STATE              TaskState;
        OS_PRIO               Prio;
        OS_TCB                DbgNextPtr;
        OS_TCB                DbgPrevPtr;
        CPU_CHAR              DbgNamePtr;
    };
```

Listing 5-3 **OS_TCB Data Structure**

.StkPtr

This field contains a pointer to the current top-of-stack for the task. µC/OS-III allows each task to have its own stack and each stack can be any size. **.StkPtr** should be the only field in the **OS_TCB** data structure accessed from assembly language code (for the context-switching code). This field is therefore placed as the first entry in the structure making access easier from assembly language code (it will be at offset zero in the data structure).

.ExtPtr

This field contains a pointer to a user-definable pointer to extend the TCB as needed. This pointer is easily accessible from assembly language.

.StkLimitPtr

The field contains a pointer to a location in the task's stack to set a *watermark* limit for stack growth and is determined from the value of the "**stk_limit**" argument passed to **OSTaskCreate()**. Some processors have special registers that automatically check the value of the stack pointer at run-time to ensure that the stack does not overflow. **.StkLimitPtr** may be used to set this register during a context switch. Alternatively, if the processor does not have such a register, this can be "simulated" in software. However, it is not as reliable as a hardware solution. If this feature is not used then the value of "**stk_limit**" can be set to **0** when calling **OSTaskCreate()**. See also section 5-3 "Detecting Task Stack Overflows" on page 93).

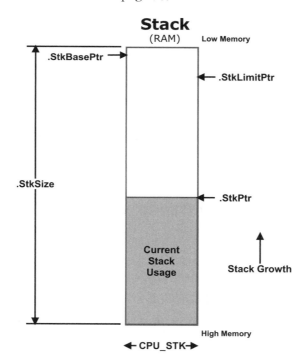

.NextPtr and .PrevPtr

These pointers are used to doubly link **OS_TCBs** in the ready list. A doubly linked list allows **OS_TCBs** to be quickly inserted and removed from the list.

.TickNextPtr and .TickPrevPtr

These pointers are used to doubly link **OS_TCBs** in the list of tasks waiting for time to expire or to timeout from pend calls. Again, a doubly linked list allows **OS_TCBs** to be quickly inserted and removed from the list.

.TickSpokePtr

This pointer is used to know which spoke in the "tick wheel" the task is linked to. The tick wheel will be described in "Chapter 9, "Interrupt Management" on page 163."

.NamePtr

This pointer allows a name (an ASCII string) to be assigned to each task. Having a name is useful when debugging, since it is user friendly compared to displaying the address of the OS_TCB. Storage for the ASCII string is assumed to be in user space in code memory (ASCII string declared as a const) or in RAM.

.StkBasePtr

This field points to the base address of the task's stack. The stack base is typically the lowest address in memory where the stack for the task resides. A task stack is declared as follows:

```
CPU_STK MyTaskStk[???];
```

CPU_STK is the data type you must use to declare task stacks and ??? is the size of the stack associated with the task. The base address is always &MyTaskStk[0].

.TaskEntryAddr

This field contains the entry address of the task. As previously mentioned, a task is declared as shown below and this field contains the address of MyTask.

```
void  MyTask (void *p_arg);
```

.TaskEntryArg

This field contains the value of the argument that is passed to the task when the task starts. As previously mentioned, a task is declared as shown below and this field contains the value of p_arg.

```
void  MyTask (void *p_arg);
```

.PendDataTblPtr

µC/OS-III allows the task to pend on any number of semaphores or message queues simultaneously. This pointer points to a table containing information about the pended objects.

.PendDataEntries

This field works with the `.PendDataTblPtr`, indicating the number of objects a task is pending on at the same time.

.TS

This field is used to store a "time stamp" of when an event that the task was waiting on occurred. When the task resumes execution, this time stamp is returned to the caller.

.MsgPtr

When a message is sent to a task, this field contains the message received. This field only exists in a TCB if message queue services (`OS_CFG_Q_EN` is set to 1 in `OS_CFG.H`), or task message queue services, are enabled (`OS_CFG_TASK_Q_EN` is set to 1 in `OS_CFG.H`) at compile time.

.MsgSize

When a message is sent to a task, this field contains the size (in number of bytes) of the message received. This field only exists in a TCB if message queue services (`OS_CFG_Q_EN` is set to 1 in `OS_CFG.H`), or task message queue services, (`OS_CFG_TASK_Q_EN` is set to 1 in `OS_CFG.H`) are enabled at compile time.

.MsgQ

µC/OS-III allows tasks or ISRs to send messages directly to tasks. Because of this, a message queue is actually built into each TCB. This field only exists in a TCB if task message queue services are enabled at compile time (`OS_CFG_TASK_Q_EN` is set to 1 in `OS_CFG.H`). `.MsgQ` is used by the `OSTaskQ???()` services.

.MsgQPendTime

This field contains the amount of time for a message to arrive. When `OSTaskQPost()` is called, the current time stamp is read and stored in the message. When `OSTaskQPend()` returns, the current time stamp is read again and the difference between the two times is stored in this variable. A debugger or µC/Probe can be used to indicate the time taken for a message to arrive by displaying this field.

This field is only available if setting `OS_CFG_TASK_PROFILE_EN` to 1 in `OS_CFG.H`.

.MsgQPendTimeMax

This field contains the maximum amount of time it takes for a message to arrive. It is a peak detector of the value of **.MsgQPendTime**. The peak can be reset by calling **OSStatReset()**.

This field is only available if setting **OS_CFG_TASK_PROFILE_EN** to 1 in **OS_CFG.H**.

.FlagsPend

When a task pends on event flags, this field contains the event flags (i.e., bits) that the task is pending on. This field only exists in a TCB if event flags services are enabled at compile time (**OS_CFG_FLAG_EN** is set to 1 in **OS_CFG.H**).

.FlagsOpt

When a task pends on event flags, this field contains the type of pend (pend on any event flag bit specified in **.FlagsPend** or all event flag bits specified in **.FlagsPend**). This field only exists in a TCB if event flags services are enabled at compile time (**OS_CFG_FLAG_EN** is set to 1 in **OS_CFG.H**).

.FlagsRdy

This field contains the event flags that were posted and that the task was waiting on. In other words, it allows a task to know which event flags made the task ready to run. This field only exists in a TCB if event flags services are enabled at compile time (**OS_CFG_FLAG_EN** is set to 1 in **OS_CFG.H**).

.RegTbl[]

This field contains a table of "registers" that are task-specific. These registers are different than CPU registers. Task registers allow for the storage of such task-specific information as task ID, "**errno**" common in some software components, and more. Task registers may also store task-related data that needs to be associated with the task at run time. Note that the data type for elements of this array is **OS_REG**, which can be declared at compile time to be nearly anything. However, all registers must be of this data type. This field only exists in a TCB if task registers are enabled at compile time (**OS_CFG_TASK_REG_TBL_SIZE** is greater than 0 in **OS_CFG.H**).

.SemCtr

This field contains a semaphore counter associated with the task. Each task has its own semaphore built-in. An ISR or another task can signal a task using this semaphore. **.SemCtr** is therefore used to keep track of how many times the task is signaled. **.SemCtr** is used by **OSTaskSem???()** services.

.SemPendTime

This field contains the amount of time taken for the semaphore to be signaled. When OSTaskSemPost() is called, the current time stamp is read and stored in the OS_TCB (see .TS). When OSTaskSemPend() returns, the current time stamp is read again and the difference between the two times is stored in this variable. This field can be displayed by a debugger or µC/Probe to indicate how much time it took for the task to be signaled.

This field is only available when setting OS_CFG_TASK_PROFILE_EN to 1 in OS_CFG.H.

.SemPendTimeMax

This field contains the maximum amount of time it took for the task to be signaled. It is a peak detector of the value of .SemPendTime. The peak can be reset by calling OSStatReset().

This field is only available if setting OS_CFG_TASK_PROFILE_EN to 1 in OS_CFG.H.

.SuspendCtr

This field is used by OSTaskSuspend() and OSTaskResume() to keep track of how many times a task is suspended. Task suspension can be nested. When .SuspendCtr is 0, all suspensions are removed. This field only exists in a TCB if task suspension is enabled at compile time (OS_CFG_TASK_SUSPEND_EN is set to 1 in OS_CFG.H).

.StkSize

This field contains the size (in number of CPU_STK elements) of the stack associated with the task. Recall that a task stack is declared as follows:

```
CPU_STK MyTaskStk[???];
```

.StkSize is the value of ??? in the above array.

.StkUsed and .StkFree

µC/OS-III is able to compute (at run time) the amount of stack space a task actually uses and how much stack space remains. This is accomplished by a function called OSTaskStkChk(). Stack usage computation assumes that the task's stack is "cleared" when the task is created. In other words, when calling OSTaskCreate(), it is expected that the following options be specified: OS_TASK_OPT_STK_CLR and OS_TASK_OPT_STK_CHK. OSTaskCreate() will then clear all the RAM used for the task's stack.

μC/OS-III provides an internal task called OS_StatTask() that checks the stack of each of the tasks at run-time. OS_StatTask() typically runs at a low priority so that it does not interfere with the application code. OS_StatTask() saves the value computed for each task in the TCB of each task in these fields, which represents the maximum number of stack bytes used and the amount of stack space still unused by the task. These fields only exist in a TCB if the statistic task is enabled at compile time (OS_CFG_STAT_TASK_STK_CHK_EN is set to 1 in OS_CFG.H).

.Opt

This field saves the "options" passed to OSTaskCreate() when the task is created (see OS_TASK_OPT_??? in OS.H). Note that task options are additive.

.TickCtrPrev

This field stores the previous value of OSTickCtr when OSTimeDly() is called with the OS_OPT_TIME_PERIODIC option.

.TickCtrMatch

When a task is waiting for time to expire, or pending on an object with a timeout, the task is placed in a special list of tasks waiting for time to expire. When in this list, the task waits for .TickCtrMatch to match the value of the "tick counter" (OSTickCtr). When a match occurs, the task is removed from that list.

.TickRemain

This field is computed at run time by OS_TickTask() to compute the amount of time (expressed in "ticks") left before a delay or timeout expires. This field is useful for debuggers or run-time monitors for display purposes.

.TimeQuanta and .TimeQuantaCtr

These fields are used for time slicing. When multiple tasks are ready to run at the same priority, .TimeQuanta determines how much time (in ticks) the task will execute until it is preempted by μC/OS-III so that the next task at the same priority gets a chance to execute. .TimeQuantaCtr keeps track of the remaining number of ticks for this to happen and is loaded with .TimeQuanta at the beginning of the task's time slice.

.CPUUsage

This field is computed by OS_StatTask() if OS_CFG_TASK_PROFILE_EN is set to 1 in OS_CFG.H. .CPUUsage contains the CPU usage of a task in percent (0 to 100%).

.CtxSwCtr

This field keeps track of how often the task has executed (not how long it has executed). This field is generally used by debuggers or run-time monitors to see if a task is executing (the value of this field would be non-zero and would be incrementing). The field is enabled at compile time when OS_CFG_TASK_PROFILE_EN is set to 1.

.CyclesDelta

.CyclesDelta is computed during a context switch and contains the value of the current time stamp (obtained by calling OS_TS_GET()) minus the value of .CyclesStart. This field is generally used by debuggers or a run-time monitor to see how long a task takes to execute. The field is enabled at compile time when OS_CFG_TASK_PROFILE_EN is set to 1.

.CyclesStart

This field is used to measure the execution time of a task. .CyclesStart is updated when µC/OS-III performs a context switch. .CyclesStart contains the value of the current time stamp (it calls OS_TS_GET()) when a task switch occurs. This field is generally used by debuggers or a run-time monitor to see how long a task takes to execute. The field is enabled at compile time when OS_CFG_TASK_PROFILE_EN is set to 1.

.CyclesTotal

This field accumulates the value of .CyclesDelta, so it contains the total execution time of a task. This is typically a 64-bit value because of the accumulation of cycles over time. Using a 64-bit value ensures that we can accumulate CPU cycles for almost 600 years even if the CPU is running at 1 GHz! Of course, it's assumed that the compiler supports 64-bit data types.

.IntDisTimeMax

This field keeps track of the maximum interrupt disable time of the task. The field is updated only if µC/CPU supports interrupt disable time measurements. This field is available only if setting OS_CFG_TASK_PROFILE_EN to 1 in OS_CFG.H and µC/CPU's CPU_CFG_TIME_MEAS_INT_DIS_EN is defined in DCPU_CFG.H.

.SchedLockTimeMax

The field keeps track of the maximum scheduler lock time of the task.

This field is available only if you set OS_CFG_TASK_PROFILE_EN to 1 and OS_CFG_SCHED_LOCK_TIME_MEAS_EN is set to 1 in OS_CFG.H.

5

.PendOn

This field indicates upon what the task is pending and contains OS_TASK_PEND_ON_??? (see OS.H).

.PendStatus

This field indicates the outcome of a pend and contains OS_STATUS_PEND_??? (see OS.H).

.TaskState

This field indicates the current state of a task and contains one of the eight (8) task states that a task can be in, see OS_TASK_STATE_??? (see OS.H).

.Prio

This field contains the current priority of a task. .Prio is a value between 0 and OS_CFG_PRIO_MAX-1. In fact, the idle task is the only task at priority OS_CFG_PRIO_MAX-1.

.DbgNextPtr

This field contains a pointer to the next OS_TCB in a doubly linked list of OS_TCBs. OS_TCBs are placed in this list by OSTaskCreate(). This field is only present if OS_CFG_DBG_EN is set to 1 in OS_CFG.H. the current priority of a task.

.DbgPrevPtr

This field contains a pointer to the previous OS_TCB in a doubly linked list of OS_TCBs. OS_TCBs are placed in this list by OSTaskCreate(). This field is only present if OS_CFG_DBG_EN is set to 1 in OS_CFG.H.

.DbgNamePtr

This field contains a pointer to the name of the object that the task is pending on when the task is pending on an event flag group, a semaphore, a mutual exclusion semaphore or a message queue. This information is quite useful during debugging and thus, this field is only present if OS_CFG_DBG_EN is set to 1 in OS_CFG.H.

5-6 INTERNAL TASKS

During initialization, µC/OS-III creates a minimum of two (2) internal tasks (OS_IdleTask() and OS_TickTask()) and, three (3) optional tasks (OS_StatTask(), OS_TmrTask() and OS_IntQTask()). The optional tasks are created based on the value of compile-time #defines found in OS_CFG.H.

5

5-6-1 THE IDLE TASK (OS_IdleTask())

OS_IdleTask() is the very first task created by μC/OS-III and always exists in a μC/OS-III-based application. The priority of the idle task is always set to OS_CFG_PRIO_MAX-1. In fact, OS_IdleTask() is the only task that is ever allowed to be at this priority and, as a safeguard, when other tasks are created, OSTaskCreate() ensures that there are no other tasks created at the same priority as the idle task. The idle task runs whenever there are no other tasks that are ready to run. The important portions of the code for the idle task are shown below (refer to OS_CORE.C for the complete code).

```
void  OS_IdleTask (void *p_arg)
{
    while (DEF_ON) {                     (1)
        OS_CRITICAL_ENTER();
        OSIdleTaskCtr++;                 (2)
        OSTaskStatCtr++;
        OS_CRITICAL_EXIT();
        OSIdleTaskHook();                (3)
    }
}
```

Listing 5-4 **Idle Task**

L5-4(1)   The idle task is a "true" infinite loop that never calls functions to "wait for an event". This is because, on most processors, when there is "nothing to do," the processor still executes instructions. When μC/OS-III determines that there is no other higher-priority task to run, μC/OS-III "parks" the CPU in the idle task. Instead of having an empty "for loop" doing nothing, this "idle" time is used to do something useful.

L5-4(2)   Two counters are incremented whenever the idle task runs.

OSIdleTaskCtr is typically defined as a 32-bit unsigned integer (see OS.H). OSIdleTaskCtr is reset once when μC/OS-III is initialized. OSIdleTaskCtr is used to indicate "activity" in the idle task. In other words, if one monitors and displays OSIdleTaskCtr, one should expect to see a value between 0x00000000 and 0xFFFFFFFF. The rate at which OSIdleTaskCtr increments depend on how busy the CPU is at running the application code. The faster the increment, the less work the CPU has to do in application tasks.

`OSStatTaskCtr` is also typically defined as a 32-bit unsigned integer (see `OS.H`) and is used by the statistic task (described later) to get a sense of CPU utilization at run time.

L5-4(3)   Every time through the loop, `OS_IdleTask()` calls `OSIdleTaskHook()`, which is a function that is declared in the µC/OS-III port for the processor used. `OSIdleTaskHook()` allows the implementer of the µC/OS-III port to perform additional processing during idle time. It is very important for this code to not make calls that would cause the idle task to "wait for an event". This is generally not a problem as most programmers developing µC/OS-III ports know to follow this simple rule.

`OSIdleTaskHook()` may be used to place the CPU in low-power mode for battery-powered applications or to simply not waste energy as shown in the pseudo-code below. However, doing this means that `OSStatTaskCtr` cannot be used to measure CPU utilization (described later).

```
void  OSIdleTaskHook (void)
{
    /* Place the CPU in low power mode */
}
```

Typically, most processors exit low-power mode when an interrupt occurs. Depending on the processor, however, the Interrupt Service Routine (ISR) may have to write to "special" registers to return the CPU to its full or desired speed. If the ISR wakes up a high-priority task (every task is higher in priority than the idle task) then the ISR will not immediately return to the interrupted idle task, but instead switch to the higher-priority task. When the higher-priority task completes its work and waits for its event to occur, µC/OS-III causes a context switch to return to `OSIdleTaskHook()` just "after" the instruction that caused the CPU to enter low-power mode. In turn, `OSIdleTaskHook()` returns to `OS_IdleTask()` and causes another iteration through the "for loop."

5-6-2 THE TICK TASK (OS_TickTask())

Nearly every RTOS requires a periodic time source called a *Clock Tick* or *System Tick* to keep track of time delays and timeouts. µC/OS-III's clock tick handling is encapsulated in the file OS_TICK.C.

OS_TickTask() is a task created by µC/OS-III and its priority is configurable by the user through µC/OS-III's configuration file OS_CFG_APP.H (see OS_CFG_TICK_TASK_PRIO). Typically OS_TickTask() is set to a relatively high priority. In fact, the priority of this task is set slightly lower than the most important tasks.

OS_TickTask() is used by µC/OS-III to keep track of tasks waiting for time to expire or, for tasks that are pending on kernel objects with a timeout. OS_TickTask() is a periodic task and it waits for signals from the tick ISR (described in Chapter 9, "Interrupt Management" on page 163) as shown in Figure 5-8.

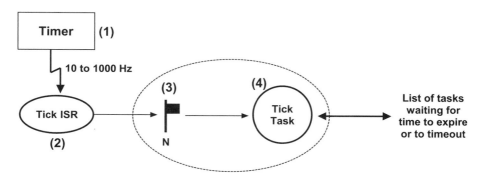

Figure 5-8 **Tick ISR and Tick Task relationship**

F5-8(1)   A hardware timer is generally used and configured to generate an interrupt at a rate between 10 and 1000 Hz (see OS_CFG_TICK_RATE in OS_CFG_APP.H). This timer is generally called the *Tick Timer*. The actual rate to use depends on such factors as: processor speed, desired time resolution, and amount of allowable overhead to handle the tick timer, etc.

The tick interrupt does not have to be generated by a timer and, in fact, it can come from other regular time sources such as the power-line frequency (50 or 60 Hz), which are known to be fairly accurate over long periods of time.

F5-8(2)   Assuming CPU interrupts are enabled, the CPU accepts the tick interrupt, preempts the current task, and vectors to the tick ISR. The tick ISR must call `OSTimeTick()` (see `OS_TIME.C`), which accomplishes most of the work needed by µC/OS-III. The tick ISR then clears the timer interrupt (and possibly reloads the timer for the next interrupt). However, some timers may need to be taken care of prior to calling `OSTimeTick()` instead of after as shown below.

```
void  TickISR (void)
{
    OSTimeTick();
    /* Clear tick interrupt source              */
    /* Reload the timer for the next interrupt */
}
```

or,

```
void  TickISR (void)
{
    /* Clear tick interrupt source              */
    /* Reload the timer for the next interrupt */
    OSTimeTick();
}
```

`OSTimeTick()` calls `OSTimeTickHook()` at the very beginning of `OSTimeTick()` to give the opportunity to the µC/OS-III port developer to react as soon as possible upon servicing the tick interrupt.

F5-8(3)   `OSTimeTick()` calls a service provided by µC/OS-III to signal the tick task and make that task ready to run. The tick task executes as soon as it becomes the most important task. The reason the tick task might not run immediately is that the tick interrupt could have interrupted a task higher in priority than the tick task and, upon completion of the tick ISR, µC/OS-III will resume the interrupted task.

F5-8(4)   When the tick task executes, it goes through a list of all tasks that are waiting for time to expire or are waiting on a kernel object with a timeout. From this point forward, this will be called the tick list. The tick task will make ready to run all of the tasks in the tick list for which time or timeout has expired. The process is explained below.

µC/OS-III may need to place literally hundreds of tasks (if an application has that many tasks) in the tick list. The tick list is implemented in such a way that it does not take much CPU time to determine if time has expired for those tasks placed in the tick list and, possibly makes those tasks ready to run. The tick list is implemented as shown in Figure 5-9.

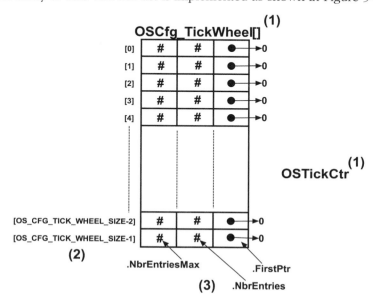

Figure 5-9 **Empty Tick List**

F5-9(1)   The tick list consists of a table (OSCfg_TickWheel[]) and a counter (OSTickCtr).

F5-9(2)   The table contains up to OS_CFG_TICK_WHEEL_SIZE entries, which is a compile time configuration value (see OS_CFG_APP.H). The number of entries depends on the amount of memory (RAM) available to the processor and the maximum number of tasks in the application. A good starting point for OS_CFG_TICK_WHEEL_SIZE may be: #Tasks / 4. It is recommended not to make OS_CFG_TICK_WHEEL_SIZE an even multiple of the tick rate. If the tick rate is 1000 Hz and one has 50 tasks in the application, avoid setting OS_CFG_TICK_WHEEL_SIZE to 10 or 20 (use 11 or 23 instead). Actually, prime numbers are good choices. Although it is not really possible to plan at compile time what will happen at run time, ideally, the number of tasks waiting in each entry of the table will be distributed uniformly.

5

F5-9(3)   Each entry in the table contains three fields: **.NbrEntriesMax**, **.NbrEntries** and **.FirstPtr**.

.NbrEntries indicates the number of tasks linked to this table entry.

.NbrEntriesMax keeps track of the highest number of entries in the table. This value is reset when the application code calls **OSStatReset()**.

.FirstPtr contains a pointer to a doubly linked list of tasks (through the tasks **OS_TCB**) belonging to the list, at that table position.

The counter is incremented by **OS_TickTask()** each time the task is signaled by the tick ISR.

Tasks are automatically inserted in the tick list when the application programmer calls a **OSTimeDly???()** function, or when an **OS???Pend()** call is made with a non-zero timeout value.

Example 5-1

Using an example to illustrate the process of inserting a task in the tick list, let's assume that the tick list is completely empty, **OS_CFG_TICK_WHEEL_SIZE** is configured to 12, and the current value of **OSTickCtr** is 10 as shown in Figure 5-10. A task is placed in the tick list when **OSTimeDly()** is called and assume **OSTimeDly()** is called as follows:

```
    :
OSTimeDly(1, OS_OPT_TIME_DLY, &err);
    :
```

Referring to the µC/OS-III reference manual in Appendix A, notice that this action indicates to µC/OS-III to delay the current task for 1 tick. Since **OSTickCtr** has a value of 10, the task will be put to sleep until **OSTickCtr** reaches 11 or at the very next clock tick interrupt. Tasks are inserted in the **OSCfg_TickWheel[]** table using the following equation:

```
MatchValue                    = OSTickCtr + dly
Index into OSCfg_TickWheel[] = MatchValue % OS_CFG_TICK_WHEEL_SIZE
```

Where "**dly**" is the value passed in the first argument of **OSTimeDly()** or, 1 in this example. We therefore obtain the following:

```
MatchValue                     =  10 + 1
Index into OSCfg_TickWheel[] = (10 + 1) % 12
```

or,

```
MatchValue                     = 11
Index into OSCfg_TickWheel[] = 11
```

Because of the "circular" nature of the table (a modulo operation using the size of the table), the table is referred to as a *tick wheel* and each entry is a *spoke* in the wheel.

The OS_TCB of the task being delayed is entered at index 11 in OSCfg_TickWheel[] (i.e., spoke 11 using the wheel analogy). The OS_TCB of the task is inserted in the first entry of the list (i.e., pointed to by OSCfg_TickWheel[11].FirstPtr), and the number of entries at spoke 11 is incremented (i.e., OSCfg_TickWheel[11].NbrEntries will be 1). Notice that the OS_TCB also links back to &OSCfg_TickWheel[11] and the "MatchValue" are placed in the OS_TCB field .TickCtrMatch. Since this is the first task inserted in the tick list at spoke 11, the .TickNextPtr and .TickPrevPtr both point to NULL.

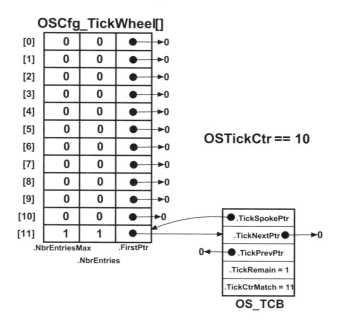

Figure 5-10 **Inserting a task in the tick list**

OSTimeDly() takes care of a few other details. Specifically, the task is removed from μC/OS-III's ready list (described in Chapter 6, "The Ready List" on page 129) since the task is no longer eligible to run (because it is waiting for time to expire). Also, the scheduler is called because μC/OS-III will need to run the next most important ready-to-run task.

If the next task to run also happens to call OSTimeDly() "before" the next tick arrives and calls OSTimeDly() as follows:

```
    :
    OSTimeDly(13, OS_OPT_TIME_DLY, &err);
    :
```

μC/OS-III will calculate the match value and spoke as follows:

```
MatchValue                    =  10 + 13
OSCfg_TickWheel[] spoke number = (10 + 13) % 12
```

or,

```
MatchValue                    =  23
OSCfg_TickWheel[] spoke number =  11
```

The "second task" will be inserted at the same table entry as shown in Figure 5-11. Tasks sharing the same spoke are sorted in ascending order such that the task with the least amount of time remaining is placed at the head of the list.

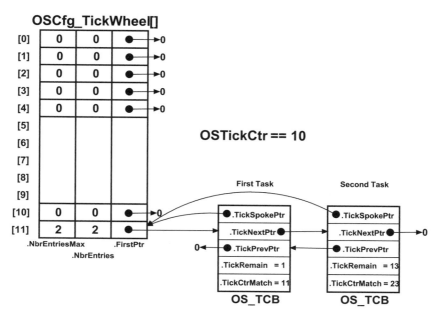

Figure 5-11 **Inserting a second task in the tick list**

When the tick task executes (see OS_TickTask() and also OS_TickListUpdate() in OS_TICK.C), it starts incrementing OSTickCtr and determines which table entry (i.e., which spoke) needs to be processed. Then, if there are tasks in the list at this entry (i.e., .FirstPtr is not NULL), each OS_TCB is examined to determine whether the .TickCtrMatch value "matches" OSTickCtr and, if so, we remove the OS_TCB from the list. If the task is only waiting for time to expire, it will be placed in the ready list (described later). If the task is pending on an object, not only will the task be removed from the tick list, but it will also be removed from the list of tasks waiting on that object. The search through the list terminates as soon as OSTickCtr does not match the task's .TickCtrMatch value; since there is no point in looking any further in the list.

Note that OS_TickTask() does most of its work in a critical section when the tick list is updated. However, because the list is sorted, the critical section has a chance to be fairly short.

5

5-6-3 THE STATISTIC TASK (OS_StatTask())

µC/OS-III contains an internal task that provides such run-time statistics as overall CPU utilization (0 to 100%), per-task CPU utilization (0-100%), and per-task stack usage.

The statistic task is optional in a µC/OS-III application and its presence is controlled by a compile-time configuration constant OS_CFG_STAT_TASK_EN defined in OS_CFG.H. Specifically, the code is included in the build when OS_CFG_STAT_TASK_EN is set to 1.

Also, the priority of this task and the location and size of the statistic task's stack is configurable via OS_CFG_APP.H (OS_CFG_STAT_TASK_PRIO).

If the application uses the statistic task, it should call OSStatTaskCPUUsageInit() from the first, and only the application task created in the main() function as shown in Listing 5-5. The startup code should create only one task before calling OSStart(). The single task created is, of course, allowed to create other tasks, but only after calling OSStatTaskCPUUsageInit().

```
void main (void)                           (1)
{
    OS_ERR  err;
    :
    OSInit(&err);                          (2)
    if (err != OS_ERR_NONE) {
        /* Something wasn't configured properly, µC/OS-III not properly initialized  */
    }
    /* (3) Create ONE task (we'll call it AppTaskStart() for sake of discussion)    */
    :
    OSStart(&err);                         (4)
}


void AppTaskStart (void *p_arg)
{
    OS_ERR  err;
    :
    /* (5) Initialize the tick interrupt                                        */
#if OS_CFG_STAT_TASK_EN > 0
    OSStatTaskCPUUsageInit(&err);          (6)
#endif
    :
    /* (7) Create other tasks                                                   */
    while (DEF_ON) {
        /* AppTaskStart() body                                                  */
    }
}
```

Listing 5-5 **Proper startup for computing CPU utilization**

L5-5(1)   The C compiler should start up the CPU and bring it to **main()** as is typical in most C applications.

L5-5(2)   **main()** calls **OSInit()** to initialize µC/OS-III. It is assumed that the statistics task is enabled by setting **OS_CFG_STAT_TASK_EN** to 1 in **OS_CFG_APP.H**. Always examine µC/OS-III's returned error code to make sure the call was done properly. Refer to **OS.H** for a list of possible errors, **OS_ERR_???**.

L5-5(3)   As the comment indicates, creates a single task called **AppTaskStart()** in the example (its name is left to the creator's discretion). When creating this task, give it a fairly high priority (do not use priority 0 since it's reserved for µC/OS-III).

5

Normally, µC/OS-III allows the user to create as many tasks as are necessary prior to calling **OSStart()**. However, when the statistic task is used to compute overall CPU utilization, it is necessary to create only one task.

L5-5(4)   Call **OSStart()** to let µC/OS-III start the highest-priority task which, should be **AppTaskStart()**. At this point, there should be either four or five tasks created (the timer task is optional): µC/OS-III creates up to four tasks (**OS_IdleTask()**, **OS_TickTask()**, **OS_StatTask()** and **OS_TaskTmr()**), and now **AppTaskStart()**.

L5-5(5)   The start task should then configure and enable tick interrupts. This most likely requires that the user initialize the hardware timer used for the clock tick and have it interrupt at the rate specified by **OS_CFG_STAT_TASK_RATE** (see **OS_CFG_APP.H**). Additionally, Micriµm provides sample projects that include a basic board-support package (BSP). The BSP initializes many aspects of the CPU as well as the periodic time source required by µC/OS-III. If available, the user may utilize BSP services by calling **BSP_Init()** from the startup task. After this point, no further time source initialization is required by the user.

L5-5(6)   Call **OSStatTaskCPUUsageInit()**. This function determines the maximum value that **OSStatTaskCtr** (see **OS_IdleTask()**) can count up to for 1/**OS_CFG_STAT_TASK_RATE** second when there are no other tasks running in the system (apart for the other µC/OS-III tasks). For example, if the system does not contain an application task and **OSStatTaskCtr** counts from 0 to 10,000,000 for 1/**OS_CFG_STAT_TASK_RATE** second, when adding tasks, and the test is redone every 1/**OS_CFG_STAT_TASK_RATE** second, the **OSStatTaskCtr** will not reach 10,000,000 and actual CPU utilization is determined as follows:

$$CPU\_Utilization_{\%} = \left(100 - \frac{100 \times OSTaskStatCtr}{OSTaskStatCtr_{Max}}\right)$$

For example, if when redoing the test, **OSStatTaskCtr** reaches 7,500,000 the CPU is busy 25% of its time running application tasks:

$$25\% = \left(100 - \frac{100 \times 7,500,000}{10,000,000}\right)$$

L5-5(7)   `AppTaskStart()` can then create other application tasks as needed.

As previously described, µC/OS-III stores run-time statistics for a task in each task's `OS_TCB`.

`OS_StatTask()` also computes stack usage of all created tasks by calling `OSTaskStkChk()` and stores the return values of this function (free and used stack space) in the `.StkFree` and `.StkUsed` field of the task's `OS_TCB`, respectively.

5-6-4 THE TIMER TASK (`OS_TmrTask()`)

µC/OS-III provides timer services to the application programmer. Code to handle timers is found in `OS_TMR.C`.

The timer task is optional in a µC/OS-III application and its presence is controlled by the compile-time configuration constant `OS_CFG_TMR_EN` defined in `OS_CFG.H`. Specifically, the code is included in the build when `OS_CFG_TMR_EN` is set to 1.

Timers are countdown counters that perform an action when the counter reaches zero. The action is provided by the user through a callback function. A callback function is a function that the user declares and that will be called when the timer expires. The callback can thus be used to turn on or off a light, a motor, or perform whatever action needed. It is important to note that the callback function is called from the context of the timer task. The application programmer may create an unlimited number of timers (limited only by the amount of available RAM). Timer management is fully described in Chapter 12, "Timer Management" on page 199 and the timer services available to the application programmer are described in Appendix A, "µC/OS-III API Reference Manual" on page 381.

`OS_TmrTask()` is a task created by µC/OS-III (this assumes setting `OS_CFG_TMR_EN` to 1 in `OS_CFG.H`) and its priority is configurable by the user through µC/OS-III's configuration file `OS_CFG_APP.H` (see `OS_CFG_TMR_TASK_PRIO`). `OS_TmrTask()` is typically set to a medium priority.

OS_TmrTask() is a periodic task using the same interrupt source that was used to generate clock ticks. However, timers are generally updated at a slower rate (i.e., typically 10 Hz) and the timer tick rate is divided down in software. In other words, if the tick rate is 1000 Hz and the desired timer rate is 10 Hz, the timer task will be signaled every 100th tick interrupt as shown in Figure 5-12.

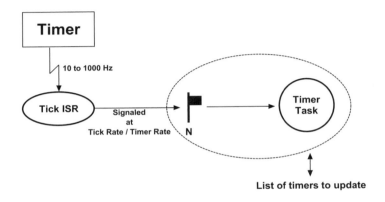

Figure 5-12 **Tick ISR and Timer Task relationship**

5-6-5 THE ISR HANDLER TASK (OS_IntQTask())

When setting the compile-time configuration constant OS_CFG_ISR_POST_DEFERRED_EN in OS_CFG.H to 1, μC/OS-III creates a task (called OS_IntQTask()) responsible for "deferring" the action of OS service post calls from ISRs.

As described in Chapter 4, "Critical Sections" on page 75, μC/OS-III manages critical sections either by disabling/enabling interrupts, or by locking/unlocking the scheduler. If selecting the latter method (i.e., setting OS_CFG_ISR_POST_DEFERRED_EN to 1), μC/OS-III "post" functions called from interrupts are not allowed to manipulate such internal data structures as the ready list, pend lists, and others.

When an ISR calls one of the "post" functions provided by μC/OS-III, a copy of the data posted and the desired destination is placed in a special "holding" queue. When all nested ISRs complete, μC/OS-III context switches to the ISR handler task (OS_IntQTask()), which "re-posts" the information placed in the holding queue to the appropriate task(s). This extra step is performed to reduce the amount of interrupt disable time that would otherwise be necessary to remove tasks from wait lists, insert them in the ready list, and perform other time-consuming operations.

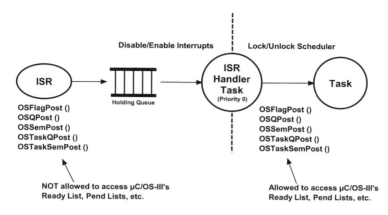

Figure 5-13 **ISR Handler Task**

`OS_IntQTask()` is created by µC/OS-III and always runs at priority 0 (i.e., the highest priority). If `OS_CFG_ISR_POST_DEFERRED_EN` is set to 1, no other task will be allowed to use priority 0.

5-7 SUMMARY

A task is a simple program that thinks it has the CPU all to itself. On a single CPU, only one task executes at any given time. µC/OS-III supports multitasking and allows the application to have any number of tasks. The maximum number of tasks is actually only limited by the amount of memory (both code and data space) available to the processor.

A task can be implemented as a run-to-completion task in which the task deletes itself when it is finished or more typically as an infinite loop, waiting for events to occur and processing those events.

A task needs to be created. When creating a task, it is necessary to specify the address of an `OS_TCB` to be used by the task, the priority of the task, and an area in RAM for the task's stack. A task can also perform computations (CPU bound task), or manage one or more I/O (Input/Output) devices.

µC/OS-III creates up to five internal tasks: the idle task, tick task, ISR handler task, statistics task, and timer task. The idle and tick tasks are always created while statistics and timer tasks are optional.

5

6

The Ready List

Tasks that are ready to execute are placed in the Ready List. The ready list consists of two parts: a bitmap containing the priority levels that are ready and a table containing pointers to all the tasks ready.

6-1 PRIORITY LEVELS

Figures 5-1 to 5-3 show the bitmap of priorities that are ready. The "width" of the table depends on the data type **CPU_DATA** (see **CPU.H**), which can either be 8-, 16- or 32-bits. The width depends on the processor used.

µC/OS-III allows up to **OS_CFG_PRIO_MAX** different priority levels (see **OS_CFG.H**). In µC/OS-III, a low-priority number corresponds to a high-priority level. Priority level zero (0) is thus the highest priority level. Priority **OS_CFG_PRIO_MAX-1** is the lowest priority level. µC/OS-III uniquely assigns the lowest priority to the idle task. No other tasks are allowed at this priority level. If there are tasks that are ready-to-run at a given a priority level, then its corresponding bit is set (i.e., 1) in the bitmap table. Notice in Figures 5-1 to 5-3 that "priority levels" are numbered from left to right and, the priority level increases (moves toward lower priority) with an increase in table index. The order was chosen to be able to use a special instruction called Count Leading Zeros (CLZ), which is found on many modern processors. This instruction greatly accelerates the process of determining the highest priority level.

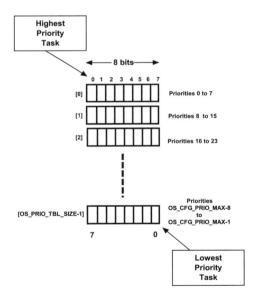

Figure 6-1 **CPU_DATA declared as a CPU_INT08U**

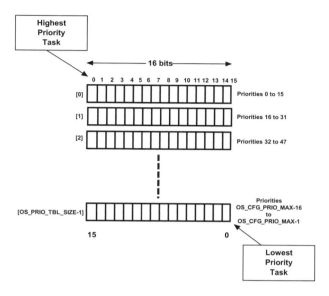

Figure 6-2 **CPU_DATA declared as a CPU_INT16U**

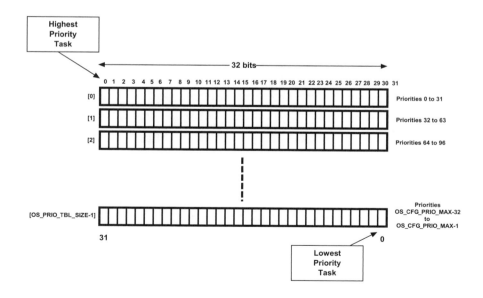

Figure 6-3 **CPU_DATA declared as a CPU_INT32U**

OS_PRIO.C contains the code to set, clear, and search the bitmap table. These functions are internal to µC/OS-III and are placed in OS_PRIO.C to allow them to be optimized in assembly language by replacing OS_PRIO.C with an assembly language equivalent OS_PRIO.ASM, when necessary.

Function	Description
OS_PrioGetHighest()	Find the highest priority level
OS_PrioInsert()	Set bit corresponding to priority level in the bitmap table
OS_PrioRemove()	Clear bit corresponding to priority level in the bitmap table

Table 6-1 **Priority Level access functions**

To determine the highest priority level that contains ready-to-run tasks, the bitmap table is scanned until the first bit set in the lowest bit position is found using OS_PrioGetHighest(). The code for this function is shown in Listing 6-1.

```
OS_PRIO  OS_PrioGetHighest (void)
{
    CPU_DATA   *p_tbl;
    OS_PRIO     prio;


    prio  = (OS_PRIO)0;
    p_tbl = &OSPrioTbl[0];
    while (*p_tbl == (CPU_DATA)0) {            (1)
        prio += sizeof(CPU_DATA) * 8u;        (2)
        p_tbl++;
    }
    prio += (OS_PRIO)CPU_CntLeadZeros(*p_tbl); (3)
    return (prio);
}
```

Listing 6-1 **Finding the highest priority level**

L6-1(1)   OS_PrioGetHighest() scans the table from OSPrioTbl[] until a non-zero entry is found. The loop will always terminate because there will always be a non-zero entry in the table because of the idle task.

L6-1(2)   Each time a zero entry is found, we move to the next table entry and increment "**prio**" by the width (in number of bits) of each entry. If each entry is 32-bits wide, "**prio**" is incremented by 32.

L6-1(3)   Once the first non-zero entry is found, the number of "**leading zeros**" of that entry is simply added and return the priority level back to the caller. Counting the number of zeros is a CPU-specific function so that if a particular CPU has a built-in CLZ instruction, it is up to the implementer of the CPU port to take advantage of this feature. If the CPU used does not provide that instruction, the functionality must be implemented in C.

The function **CPU_CntLeadZeros()** simply counts how many zeros there are in a **CPU_DATA** entry starting from the left (i.e., most significant bit). For example, assuming 32 bits, **0xF0001234** results in 0 leading zeros and **0x00F01234** results in 8 leading zeros.

At first view, the linear path through the table might seem inefficient. However, if the number of priority levels is kept low, the search is quite fast. In fact, there are several optimizations to streamline the search. For example, if using a 32-bit processor and you are satisfied with limiting the number of different priority levels to 64, the above code can be optimized as shown in Listing 6-2. In fact, some processors have built-in "Count Leading Zeros" instructions and thus, the code can be written with just a few lines of assembly language. Remember that with µC/OS-III, 64 priority levels does not mean that the user is limited to 64 tasks since with µC/OS-III, any number of tasks are possible at a given priority level.

```
OS_PRIO  OS_PrioGetHighest (void)
{
    OS_PRIO  prio;


    if (OSPrioTbl[0] != (OS_PRIO_BITMAP)0) {
        prio = OS_CntLeadingZeros(OSPrioTbl[0]);
    } else {
        prio = OS_CntLeadingZeros(OSPrioTbl[1]) + 32;
    }
    return (prio);
}
```

Listing 6-2 **Finding the highest priority level within 64 levels**

6-2 THE READY LIST

Tasks that are ready to run are placed in the Ready List. As shown in Figure 6-1, the ready list is an array (`OSRdyList[]`) containing `OS_CFG_PRIO_MAX` entries, with each entry defined by the data type `OS_RDY_LIST` (see `OS.H`). An `OS_RDY_LIST` entry consists of three fields: `.Entries`, `.TailPtr` and `.HeadPtr`.

`.Entries` contains the number of ready-to-run tasks at the priority level corresponding to the entry in the ready list. `.Entries` is set to zero (0) if there are no tasks ready to run at a given priority level.

`.TailPtr` and `.HeadPtr` are used to create a doubly linked list of all the tasks that are ready at a specific priority. `.HeadPtr` points to the head of the list and `.TailPtr` points to its tail.

The "index" into the array is the priority level associated with a task. For example, if a task is created at priority level 5 then it will be inserted in the table at `OSRdyList[5]` if that task is ready to run.

Table 6-2 shows the functions that µC/OS-III uses to manipulate entries in the ready list. These functions are internal to µC/OS-III and the application code must never call them.

Function	Description
OS_RdyListInit()	Initialize the ready list to "empty" (see Figure 6-4)
OS_RdyListInsert()	Insert a TCB into the ready list
OS_RdyListInsertHead()	Insert a TCB at the head of the list
OS_RdyListInsertTail()	Insert a TCB at the tail of the list
OS_RdyListMoveHeadToTail()	Move a TCB from the head to the tail of the list
OS_RdyListRemove()	Remove a TCB from the ready list

Table 6-2 **Ready List access functions**

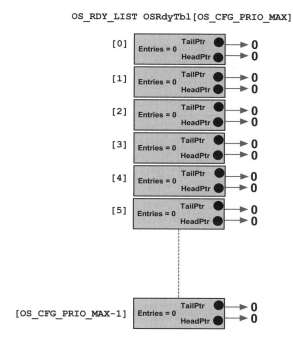

OS_RDY_LIST OSRdyTbl[OS_CFG_PRIO_MAX]

Figure 6-4 **Empty Ready List**

Assuming all internal µC/OS-III's tasks are enabled, Figure 6-5 shows the state of the ready list after calling **OSInit()** (i.e., µC/OS-III's initialization). It is assumed that each µC/OS-III task had a unique priority. With µC/OS-III, this does not have to be the case.

F6-4(1)   There is only one entry in **OSRdyList[OS_CFG_PRIO_MAX-1]**, the idle task.

F6-4(2)   The list points to OS_TCBs. Only relevant fields of the TCB are shown. The **.PrevPtr** and **.NextPtr** are used to form a doubly linked list of **OS_TCBs** associated to tasks at the same priority. For the idle task, these fields always point to **NULL**.

F6-4(3)   **Priority** 0 is reserved to the ISR handler task when **OS_CFG_ISR_DEFERRED_EN** is set to 1 in **OS_CFG.H**. In this case, this is the only task that can run at priority 0.

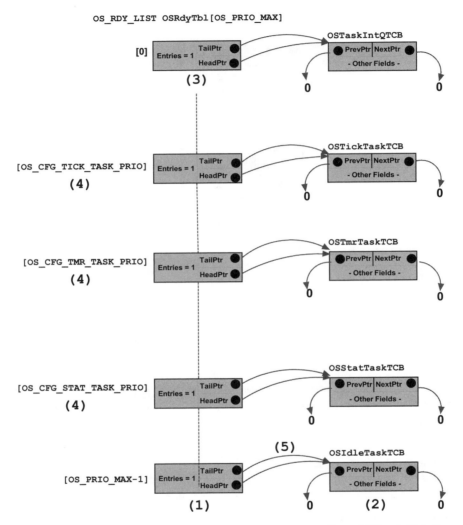

Figure 6-5 **Ready List after calling OSInit()**

F6-5(1) The tick task and the other two optional tasks have their own priority level, as shown. µC/OS-III enables the user to have multiple tasks at the same priority and thus, the tasks could be set up as shown. Typically, one would set the priority of the tick task higher than the timer task and, the timer task higher in priority than the statistic task.

F6-5(2) Both the tail and head pointers point to the same TCB when there is only one TCB at a given priority level.

6-3 ADDING TASKS TO THE READY LIST

Tasks are added to the ready list by a number of µC/OS-III services. The most obvious service is OSTaskCreate(), which always creates a task in the ready-to-run state and adds the task to the ready list. As shown in Figure 6-6, when creating a task, and specifying a priority level where tasks already exist (two in this example) in the ready list at that priority level, OSTaskCreate() will insert the new task at the end of the list of tasks at that priority level.

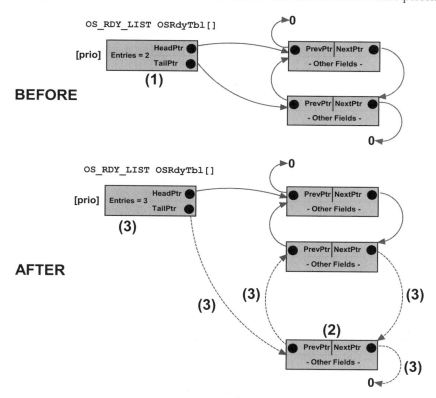

Figure 6-6 **Inserting a newly created task in the ready list**

F6-6(1)   Before calling OSTaskCreate() (in this example), two tasks were in the ready list at priority "prio".

F6-6(2)   A new TCB is passed to OSTaskCreate() and, µC/OS-III initialized the contents of that TCB.

F6-6(3)   **OSTaskCreate()** calls **OS_RdyListInsertTail()**, which links the new TCB to the ready list by setting up four pointers and also incrementing the .Entries field of **OSRdyList[prio]**. Not shown in Figure 6-6 is that **OSTaskCreate()** also calls **OS_PrioInsert()** to set the bit in the bitmap table. Of course, this operation is not necessary as there are already entries in the list at this priority. However, **OS_PrioInsert()** is a very fast call and thus it should not affect performance.

The reason the new TCB is added to the end of the list is that the current head of the list could be the task creator and, at the same priority, there is no reason to make the new task the next task to run. In fact, a task being made ready will be inserted at the tail of the list if the current task is at the same priority. However, if a task is being made ready at a different priority than the current task, it will be inserted at the head of the list.

6-4 SUMMARY

µC/OS-III supports any number of different priority levels. However, 256 different priority levels should be sufficient for the most complex applications and most systems will not require more than 64 levels.

The ready list consist of two data structures: a bitmap table that keeps track of which priority level is ready, and a table containing a list of all the tasks ready at each priority level.

Processors having "count leading zeros" instructions can accelerate the table lookup process used in determining the highest priority task.

Chapter

7

Scheduling

The scheduler, also called the dispatcher, is a part of µC/OS-III responsible for determining which task runs next. µC/OS-III is a *preemptive, priority-based kernel*. Each task is assigned a priority based on its importance. The priority for each task depends on the application, and µC/OS-III supports multiple tasks at the same priority level.

The word preemptive means that when an event occurs, and that event makes a more important task ready to run, then µC/OS-III will immediately give control of the CPU to that task. Thus, when a task signals or sends a message to a higher-priority task, the current task is suspended and the higher-priority task is given control of the CPU. Similarly, if an Interrupt Service Routine (ISR) signals or sends a message to a higher priority task, when the message is completed, the interrupted task remains suspended, and the new higher priority task resumes.

7-1 PREEMPTIVE SCHEDULING

µC/OS-III handles event posting from interrupts using two different methods: Direct and Deferred Post. These will be discussed in greater detail in Chapter 9, "Interrupt Management" on page 163. From a scheduling point of view, the end result of the two methods is the same; the highest priority and ready task will receive the CPU as shown in Figures 6-1 and 6-2.

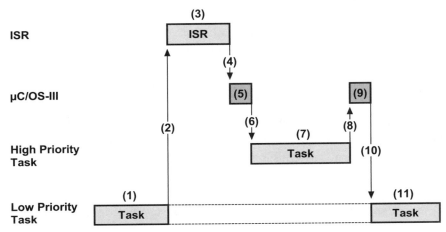

Figure 7-1 **Preemptive scheduling – Direct Method**

F7-1(1)   A low priority task is executing, and an interrupt occurs.

F7-1(2)   If interrupts are enabled, the CPU vectors (i.e., jumps) to the ISR that is responsible for servicing the interrupting device.

F7-1(3)   The ISR services the device and signals or sends a message to a higher-priority task waiting to service this device. This task is thus ready to run.

F7-1(4)   When the ISR completes its work it makes a service call to µC/OS-III.

F7-1(5)
F7-1(6)   Since there is a more important ready-to-run task, µC/OS-III decides to not return to the interrupted task but switches to the more important task. See Chapter 8, "Context Switching" on page 153 for details on how this works.

F7-1(7)

F7-1(8)   The higher priority task services the interrupting device and, when finished, calls µC/OS-III asking it to wait for another interrupt from the device.

F7-1(9)

F7-1(10)   µC/OS-III blocks the high-priority task until the next device interrupts. Since the device has not interrupted a second time, µC/OS-III switches back to the original task (the one that was interrupted).

F7-1(11)   The interrupted task resumes execution, exactly at the point where it was interrupted.

Figure 7-2 shows that µC/OS-III performs a few extra steps when it is configured for the Deferred Post method. Notice that the end results is the same; the high-priority task preempts the low-priority one.

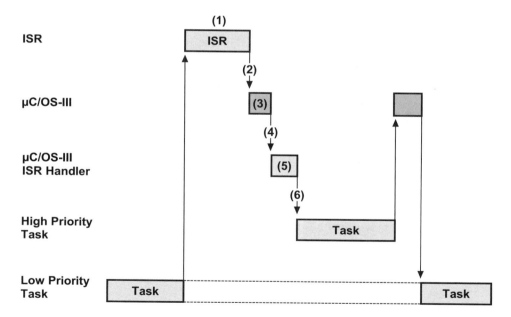

Figure 7-2 **Preemptive scheduling – Deferred Post Method**

F7-2(1)   The ISR services the device and, instead of signaling or sending the message to the task, µC/OS-III (through the POST call) places the post call into a special queue and makes a very high-priority task (actually the highest-possible priority) ready to run. This task is called the *ISR Handler Task*.

F7-2(2)   When the ISR completes its work, it makes a service call to µC/OS-III.

F7-2(3)

F7-2(4)   Since the ISR made the ISR Handler Task ready to run, µC/OS-III switches to that task.

F7-2(5)

F7-2(6)   The ISR Handler Task then removes the post call from the message queue and reissues the post. This time, however, it does it at the task level instead of the ISR level. The reason this extra step is performed is to keep interrupt disable time as small as possible. See Chapter 9, "Interrupt Management" on page 163 to find out more on the subject. When the queue is emptied, µC/OS-III removes the ISR Handler Task from the ready list and switches to the task that was signaled or sent a message.

7-2 SCHEDULING POINTS

Scheduling occurs at scheduling points and nothing special must be done in the application code since scheduling occurs automatically based on the conditions described below.

A task signals or sends a message to another task:
This occurs when the task signaling or sending the message calls one of the post services, OS???Post(). Scheduling occurs towards the end of the OS???Post() call. Note that scheduling does not occur if one specifies (as part of the post call) to not invoke the scheduler (i.e., set the option argument to OS_OPT_POST_NO_SCHED).

A task calls OSTimeDly() or OSTimeDlyHMSM():
If the delay is non-zero, scheduling always occurs since the calling task is placed in a list waiting for time to expire. Scheduling occurs as soon as the task is inserted in the wait list.

A task waits for an event to occur and the event has not yet occurred:
This occurs when one of the OS???Pend() functions are called. The task is placed in the wait list for the event and, if a non-zero timeout is specified, then the task is also inserted in the list of tasks waiting to timeout. The scheduler is then called to select the next most important task to run.

If a task aborts a pend:
A task is able to abort the wait (i.e., pend) of another task by calling OS???PendAbort(). Scheduling occurs when the task is removed from the wait list for the specified kernel object.

If a task is created:
The newly created task may have a higher priority than the task's creator. In this case, the scheduler is called.

If a task is deleted:
When terminating a task, the scheduler is called if the current task is deleted.

If a kernel object is deleted:
If you delete an event flag group, a semaphore, a message queue, or a mutual exclusion semaphore, if tasks are waiting on the kernel object, those tasks will be made ready to run and the scheduler will be called to determine if any of the tasks have a higher priority than the task that deleted the kernel object.

A task changes the priority of itself or another task:
The scheduler is called when a task changes the priority of another task (or itself) and the new priority of that task is higher than the task that changed the priority.

A task suspends itself by calling OSTaskSuspend():
The scheduler is called since the task that called OSTaskSuspend() is no longer able to execute, and must be resumed by another task.

A task resumes another task that was suspended by OSTaskSuspend():
The scheduler is called if the resumed task has a higher priority than the task that calls OSTaskResume().

At the end of all nested ISRs:
The scheduler is called at the end of all nested ISRs to determine whether a more important task is made ready to run by one of the ISRs. The scheduling is actually performed by OSIntExit() instead of OSSched().

The scheduler is unlocked by calling OSSchedUnlock():
The scheduler is unlocked after being locked. Lock the scheduler by calling OSSchedLock(). Note that locking the scheduler can be nested and the scheduler must be unlocked a number of times equal to the number of locks.

A task gives up its time quanta by calling OSSchedRoundRobinYield():
This assumes that the task is running alongside with other tasks at the same priority and the currently running task decides that it can give up its time quanta and let another task run.

The user calls OSSched():
The application code can call OSSched() to run the scheduler. This only makes sense if calling OS???Post() functions and specifying OS_OPT_POST_NO_SCHED so that multiple posts can be accomplished without running the scheduler on every post. Of course, in the above situation, the last post can be a post without the OS_OPT_POST_NO_SCHED option.

7-3 ROUND-ROBIN SCHEDULING

When two or more tasks have the same priority, µC/OS-III allows one task to run for a predetermined amount of time (called a *Time Quanta*) before selecting another task. This process is called *Round-Robin Scheduling* or *Time Slicing*. If a task does not need to use its full time quanta it can voluntarily give up the CPU so that the next task can execute. This is called *Yielding*. µC/OS-III allows the user to enable or disable round robin scheduling at run time.

Figure 7-3 shows a timing diagram with tasks running at the same priority. There are three tasks that are ready to run at priority "X". For sake of illustration, the time quanta occurs every 4th clock tick. This is shown as a darker tick mark.

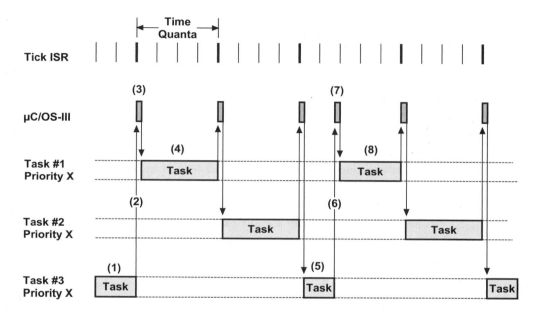

Figure 7-3 **Round Robin Scheduling**

F7-3(1)   Task #3 is executing. During that time, tick interrupts occur but the time quanta have not expired yet for Task #3.

F7-3(2)   On the 4th tick interrupt, the time quanta for Task #3 expire.

F7-3(3)   µC/OS-III resumes Task #1 since it was the next task in the list of tasks at priority "X" that was ready to run.

F7-3(4)   Task #1 executes until its time quanta expires (i.e., after four ticks).

F7-3(5)

F7-3(6)

F7-3(7)   Here Task #3 executes but decides to give up its time quanta by calling the µC/OS-III function **OSSchedRoundRobinYield( )**, which causes the next task in the list of tasks ready at priority "X" to execute. An interesting thing occurred when µC/OS-III scheduled Task #1. It reset the time quanta for that task to four ticks so that the next time quanta will expire four ticks from this point.

F7-3(8)   Task #1 executes for its full time quanta.

µC/OS-III allows the user to change the time quanta at run time through the **OSSchedRoundRobinCfg( )** function (see Appendix A, "µC/OS-III API Reference Manual" on page 381). This function also allows round robin scheduling to be enabled/disabled, and the ability to change the default time quanta.

µC/OS-III also enables the user to specify the time quanta on a per-task basis. One task could have a time quanta of 1 tick, another 12, another 3, and yet another 7, etc. The time quanta of a task is specified when the task is created. The time quanta of a task may also be changed at run time through the function **OSTaskTimeQuantaSet( )**.

7-4 SCHEDULING INTERNALS

Scheduling is performed by two functions: **OSSched()** and **OSIntExit()**. **OSSched()** is called by task level code while **OSIntExit()** is called by ISRs. Both functions are found in **OS_CORE.C**.

Figure 7-1 illustrates the two sets of data structures that the scheduler uses; the priority ready bitmap and the ready list as described in Chapter 6, "The Ready List" on page 129.

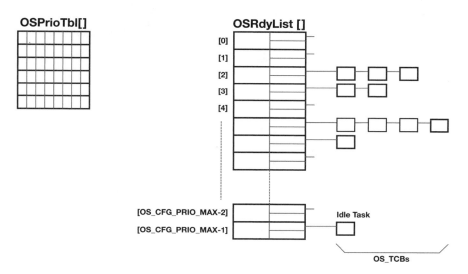

Figure 7-4 **Priority ready bitmap and Ready list**

7-4-1 OSSched()

The pseudo code for the task level scheduler, OSSched() is shown in Listing 7-1.

```
void  OSSched (void)
{
    Disable interrupts;
    if (OSIntNestingCtr > 0) {                              (1)
        return;
    }
    if (OSSchedLockNestingCtr > 0) {                        (2)
        return;
    }
    Get highest priority ready;                             (3)
    Get pointer to OS_TCB of next highest priority task;   (4)
    if (OSTCBNHighRdyPtr != OSTCBCurPtr) {                  (5)
        Perform task level context switch;
    }
    Enable interrupts;
}
```

Listing 7-1 **OSSched() pseudocode**

L7-1(1)   OSSched() starts by making sure it is not called from an ISR as OSSched() is the task level scheduler. Instead, an ISR must call OSIntExit(). If OSSched() is called by an ISR, OSSched() simply returns.

L7-1(2)   The next step is to make sure the scheduler is not locked. If the code calls OSSchedLock() the user does not want to run the scheduler and the function just returns.

L7-1(3)   OSSched() determines the priority of the highest priority task ready by scanning the bitmap OSPrioTbl[] as described in Chapter 6, "The Ready List" on page 129.

L7-1(4)   Once it is known which priority is ready, index into the OSRdyList[] and extract the OS_TCB at the head of the list (i.e., OSRdyList[highest priority].HeadPtr). At this point, it is known which OS_TCB to switch to and which OS_TCB to save to as this was the task that called OSSched(). Specifically, OSTCBCurPtr points to the current task's OS_TCB and OSTCBHighRdyPtr points to the new OS_TCB to switch to.

7

L7-1(5)   If the user is not attempting to switch to the same task that is currently running, **OSSched()** calls the code that will perform the context switch (see Chapter 8, "Context Switching" on page 153). As the code indicates, however, the task level scheduler calls a task-level function to perform the context switch.

Notice that the scheduler and the context switch runs with interrupts disabled. This is necessary because this process needs to be atomic.

7-4-2 OSIntExit()

The pseudo code for the ISR level scheduler, **OSIntExit()** is shown in Listing 7-2. Note that interrupts are assumed to be disabled when **OSIntExit()** is called.

```
void  OSIntExit (void)
{
    if (OSIntNestingCtr == 0) {                          (1)
        return;
    }
    OSIntNestingCtr--;
    if (OSIntNestingCtr > 0) {                           (2)
        return;
    }
    if (OSSchedLockNestingCtr > 0) {                     (3)
        return;
    }
    Get highest priority ready;                          (4)
    Get pointer to OS_TCB of next highest priority task; (5)
    if (OSTCBHighRdyPtr != OSTCBCurPtr) {                (6)
        Perform ISR level context switch;
    }
}
```

Listing 7-2 **OSIntExit() pseudocode**

L7-2(1)   **OSIntExit()** starts by making sure that the call to **OSIntExit()** will not cause **OSIntNestingCtr** to wrap around. This would be extremely and unlikely occurrence, but not worth taking a chance that it might.

L7-2(2)   **OSIntExit()** decrements the nesting counter as **OSIntExit()** is called at the end of an ISR. If all ISRs have not nested, the code simply returns. There is no need to run the scheduler since there are still interrupts to return to.

7

L7-2(3)   `OSIntExit()` checks to see that the scheduler is not locked. If it is, `OSIntExit()` does not run the scheduler and simply returns to the interrupted task that locked the scheduler.

L7-2(4)   Finally, this is the last nested ISR (we are returning to task-level code) and the scheduler is not locked. Therefore, we need to find the highest priority task that needs to run.

L7-2(5)   Again, we extract the highest priority `OS_TCB` from `OSRdyList[ ]`.

L7-2(6)   If the highest-priority task is not the current task µC/OS-III performs an ISR level context switch. The ISR level context switch is different as it is assumed that the interrupted task's context was saved at the beginning of the ISR and it is only left to restore the context of the new task to run. This is described in Chapter 8, "Context Switching" on page 153.

7-4-3 OS_SchedRoundRobin()

When the time quanta for a task expires and there are multiple tasks at the same priority, µC/OS-III will select and run the next task that is ready to run at the current priority. `OS_SchedRoundRobin()` is the code used to perform this operation. `OS_SchedRoundRobin()` is either called by `OSTimeTick()` or `OS_IntQTask()`. `OS_SchedRoundRobin()` is found in `OS_CORE.C`.

`OS_SchedRoundRobin()` is called by `OSTimeTick()` when you selected the Direct Method of posting (see Chapter 9, "Interrupt Management" on page 163). `OS_SchedRoundRobin()` is called by `OS_IntQTask()` when selecting the Deferred Post Method of posting, described in Chapter 8.

The pseudo code for the round-robin scheduler is shown in Listing 7-3.

```
void  OS_SchedRoundRobin (void)
{
    if (OSSchedRoundRobinEn != TRUE) {                      (1)
        return;
    }
    if (Time quanta counter > 0) {                          (2)
        Decrement time quanta counter;
    }
    if (Time quanta counter > 0) {
        return;
    }
    if (Number of OS_TCB at current priority level < 2) {   (3)
        return;
    }
    if (OSSchedLockNestingCtr > 0) {                         (4)
        return;
    }
    Move OS_TCB from head of list to tail of list;          (5)
    Reload time quanta for current task;                    (6)
}
```

Listing 7-3 **OS_SchedRoundRobin() pseudocode**

L7-3(1)   OS_SchedRoundRobin() starts by making sure that round robin scheduling is enabled. Recall that to enable round robin scheduling, one must call OSSchedRoundRobinCfg().

L7-3(2)   The time quanta counter, which resides inside the **OS_TCB** of the running task, is decremented. If the value is still non-zero then OS_SchedRoundRobin() returns.

L7-3(3)   Once the time quanta counter reaches zero, check to see that there are other ready-to-run tasks at the current priority. If there are none, return. Round robin scheduling only applies when there are multiple tasks at the same priority and the task doesn't completes its work within its time quanta.

L7-3(4)   OS_SchedRoundRobin() also returns if the scheduler is locked.

L7-3(5)   Next, OS_SchedRoundRobin() move the **OS_TCB** of the current task from the head of the ready list to the end.

L7-3(6) The time quanta for the task at the head of the list are loaded. Each task may specify its own time quanta when the task is created or through `OSTaskTimeQuantaSet()`. If specifying 0, µC/OS-III assumes the default time quanta, which corresponds to the value in the variable `OSSchedRoundRobinDfltTimeQuanta`.

7-5 SUMMARY

µC/OS-III is a preemptive scheduler so it will always execute the highest priority task that is ready to run.

µC/OS-III allows for multiple tasks at the same priority. If there are multiple ready-to-run tasks, µC/OS-III will round robin between these tasks.

Scheduling occurs at specific scheduling points, when the application calls µC/OS-III functions.

µC/OS-III has two schedulers: `OSSched()`, which is called by task-level code, and `OSIntExit()` called at the end of each ISR.

8

Context Switching

When µC/OS-III decides to run a different task (see Chapter 7, "Scheduling" on page 139), it saves the current task's context, which typically consists of the CPU registers, onto the current task's stack and restores the context of the new task and resumes execution of that task. This process is called a *Context Switch*.

Context switching adds overhead. The more registers a CPU has, the higher the overhead. The time required to perform a context switch is generally determined by how many registers must be saved and restored by the CPU.

The context switch code is generally part of a processor's *port* of µC/OS-III. A port is the code needed to adapt µC/OS-III to the desired processor. This code is placed in special C and assembly language files: **OS_CPU.H**, **OS_CPU_C.C** and **OS_CPU_A.ASM**. Chapter 18, "Porting µC/OS-III" on page 341, Porting µC/OS-III provides more details on the steps needed to port µC/OS-III to different CPU architectures.

In this chapter, we will discuss the context switching process in generic terms using a fictitious CPU as shown in Figure 8-1. Our fictitious CPU contains 16 integer registers (R0 to R15), a separate ISR stack pointer, and a separate status register (SR). Every register is 32 bits wide and each of the 16 integer registers can hold either data or an address. The program counter (or instruction pointer) is R15 and there are two separate stack pointers labeled R14 and R14". R14 represents a task stack pointer (TSP), and R14" represents an ISR stack pointer (ISP). The CPU automatically switches to the ISR stack when servicing an exception or interrupt. The task stack is accessible from an ISR (i.e., we can push and pop elements onto the task stack when in an ISR), and the interrupt stack is also accessible from a task.

8

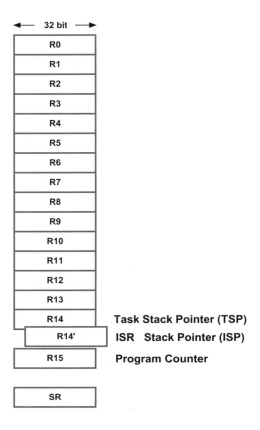

Figure 8-1 **Fictitious CPU**

In µC/OS-III, the stack frame for a ready task is always setup to look as if an interrupt has just occurred and all processor registers were saved onto it. Tasks enter the ready state upon creation and thus their stack frames are pre-initialized by software in a similar manner. Using our fictitious CPU, we'll assume that a stack frame for a task that is ready to be restored is shown in Figure 8-2.

The task stack pointer points to the last register saved onto the task's stack. The program counter and status registers are the first registers saved onto the stack. In fact, these are saved automatically by the CPU when an exception or interrupt occurs (assuming interrupts are enabled) while the other registers are pushed onto the stack by software in the exception handler. The stack pointer (R14) is not actually saved on the stack but instead is saved in the task's OS_TCB.

The interrupt stack pointer points to the current top-of-stack for the interrupt stack, which is a different memory area. When an ISR executes, the processor uses R14" as the stack pointer for function calls and local arguments.

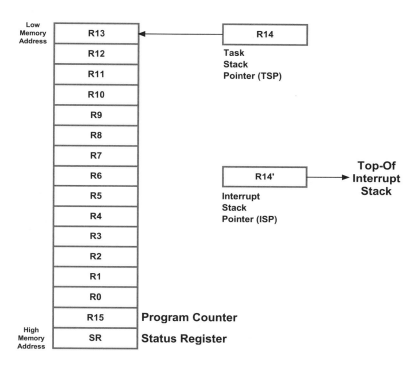

Figure 8-2 **CPU register stacking order of ready task**

There are two types of context switches: one performed from a task and another from an ISR. The task level context switch is implemented by the code in OSCtxSw( ), which is actually invoked by the macro OS_TASK_SW( ). A macro is used as there are many ways to invoke OSCtxSw( ) such as software interrupts, trap instructions, or simply calling the function.

The ISR context switch is implemented by OSIntCtxSw( ). The code for both functions is typically written in assembly language and is found in a file called OS_CPU_A.ASM.

8-1   OSCtxSw()

OSCtxSw() is called when the task level scheduler (OSSched()) determines that a new high priority task needs to execute. Figure 8-3 shows the state of several µC/OS-III variables and data structures just prior to calling OSCtxSw().

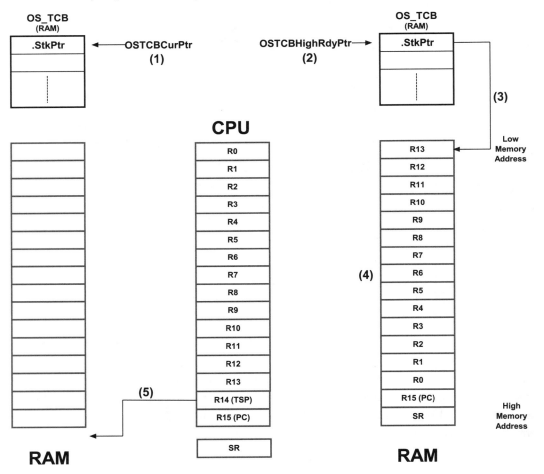

Figure 8-3 **Variables and data structures prior to calling OSCtxSw()**

F8-3(1)   OSTCBCurPtr points to the OS_TCB of the task that is currently running and that called OSSched().

F8-3(2)   OSSched() finds the new task to run by having OSTCBHighRdyPtr point to its OS_TCB.

F8-3(3)   **OSTCBHighRdyPtr->StkPtr** points to the top of stack of the new task to run.

F8-3(4)   When µC/OS-III creates or suspends a task, it always leaves the stack frame to look as if an interrupt just occurred and all the registers saved onto it. This represents the expected state of the task so it can be resumed.

F8-3(5)   The CPU's stack pointer points within the stack area (i.e., RAM) of the task that called **OSSched()**. Depending on how **OSCtxSw()** is invoked, the stack pointer may be pointing at the return address of **OSCtxSw()**.

Figure 8-4 shows the steps involved in performing the context switch as implemented by **OSCtxSw()**.

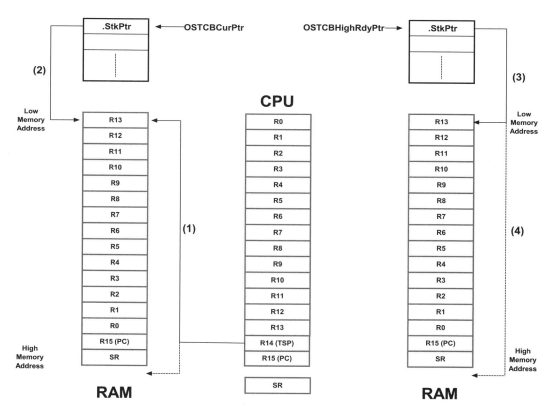

Figure 8-4 **Operations performed by OSCtxSw()**

F8-4(1)   **OSCtxSw( )** begins by saving the status register and program counter of the current task onto the current task's stack. The saving order of register depends on how the CPU expects the registers on the stack frame when an interrupt occurs. In this case, it is assumed that the SR is stacked first. The remaining registers are then saved onto the stack.

F8-4(2)   **OSCtxSw( )** saves the contents of the CPU's stack pointer into the **OS_TCB** of the task being suspended. In other words, **OSTCBCurPtr->StkPtr = R14**.

F8-4(3)   **OSCtxSw( )** then loads the CPU stack pointer with the saved top-of-stack from the new task's **OS_TCB**. In other words, **R14 = OSTCBHighRdyPtr->StkPtr**.

F8-4(4)   Finally, **OSCtxSw( )** retrieves the CPU register contents from the new stack. The program counter and status registers are generally retrieved at the same time by executing a return from interrupt instruction.

8-2   OSIntCtxSw()

OSIntCtxSw() is called when the ISR level scheduler (OSIntExit()) determines that a new high priority task is ready to execute. Figure 8-5 shows the state of several μC/OS-III variables and data structures just prior to calling OSIntCtxSw().

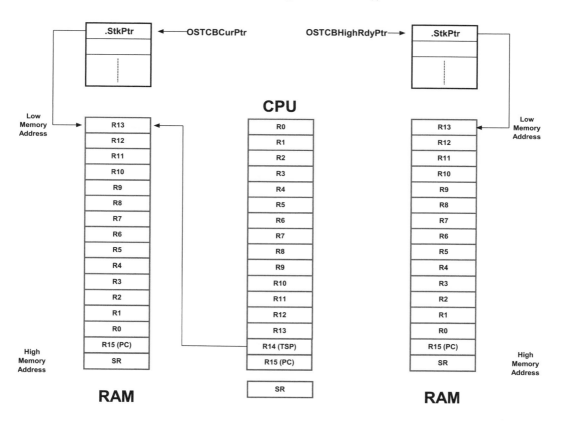

Figure 8-5 **Variables and data structures prior to calling OSIntCtxSw()**

μC/OS-III assumes that CPU registers are saved onto the task's stack at the beginning of an ISR (see Chapter 9, "Interrupt Management" on page 163). Because of this, notice that OSTCBCurPtr->StkPtr contains a pointer to the top-of-stack pointer of the task being suspended (the one on the left). OSIntCtxSw() does not have to worry about saving the CPU registers of the suspended task since that is already finished.

Figure 8-6 shows the operations performed by OSIntCtxSw( ) to complete the second half of the context switch. This is exactly the same process as the second half of OSCtxSw( ).

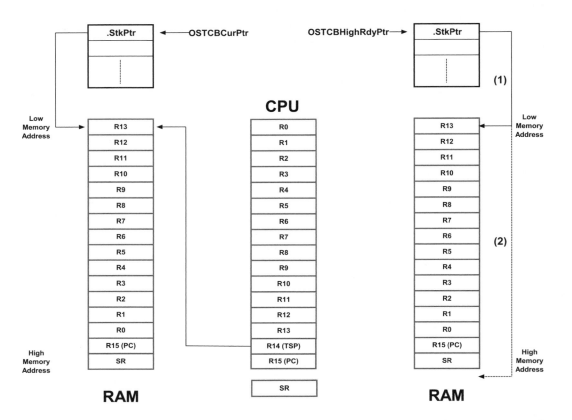

Figure 8-6 **Operations performed by OSIntCtxSw()**

F8-6(1)   OSIntCtxSw( ) loads the CPU stack pointer with the saved top-of-stack from the new task's OS_TCB. R14 = OSTCBHighRdyPtr->StkPtr.

F8-6(2)   OSIntCtxSw( ) then retrieves the CPU register contents from the new stack. The program counter and status registers are generally retrieved at the same time by executing a return from interrupt instruction.

8-3 SUMMARY

A context switch consists of saving the context (i.e., CPU registers) associated with one task and restoring the context of a new, higher-priority task.

The new task to be switched to is determined by **OSSched()** when a context switch is initiated by task level code, and **OSIntExit()** when initiated by an ISR.

OSCtxSw() performs the context switch for **OSSched()** and **OSIntCtxSw()** performs the context switch for **OSIntExit()**. However, **OSIntCtxSw()** only needs to perform the second half of the context switch because it is assumed that the ISR saved CPU registers upon entry to the ISR.

8

8

Chapter

9

Interrupt Management

An *interrupt* is a hardware mechanism used to inform the CPU that an asynchronous event occurred. When an interrupt is recognized, the CPU saves part (or all) of its context (i.e., registers) and jumps to a special subroutine called an *Interrupt Service Routine* (ISR). The ISR processes the event, and – upon completion of the ISR – the program either returns to the interrupted task, or the highest priority task, if the ISR made a higher priority task ready to run.

Interrupts allow a microprocessor to process events when they occur (i.e., asynchronously), which prevents the microprocessor from continuously *polling* (looking at) an event to see if it occurred. Task level response to events is typically better using interrupt mode as opposed to polling mode, however at the possible cost of increased interrupt latency. Microprocessors allow interrupts to be ignored or recognized through the use of two special instructions: disable interrupts and enable interrupts, respectively.

In a real-time environment, interrupts should be disabled as little as possible. Disabling interrupts affects interrupt latency possibly causing interrupts to be missed.

Processors generally allow interrupts to be nested, which means that while servicing an interrupt, the processor recognizes and services other (more important) interrupts.

One of the most important specifications of a real-time kernel is the maximum amount of time that interrupts are disabled. This is called *interrupt disable time*. All real-time systems disable interrupts to manipulate critical sections of code and re-enable interrupts when critical sections are completed. The longer interrupts are disabled, the higher the interrupt latency.

Interrupt response is defined as the time between the reception of the interrupt and the start of the user code that handles the interrupt. Interrupt response time accounts for the entire overhead involved in handling an interrupt. Typically, the processor's context (CPU registers) is saved on the stack before the user code is executed.

Interrupt recovery is defined as the time required for the processor to return to the interrupted code or to a higher priority task if the ISR made such a task ready to run.

Task latency is defined as the time it takes from the time the interrupt occurs to the time task level code resumes.

9-1 HANDLING CPU INTERRUPTS

There are many popular CPU architectures on the market today, and most processors typically handle interrupts from a multitude of sources. For example, a UART receives a character, an Ethernet controller receives a packet, a DMA controller completes a data transfer, an Analog-to-Digital Converter (ADC) completes an analog conversion, a timer expires, *etc.*

In most cases, an *interrupt controller* captures all of the different interrupts presented to the processor as shown in Figure 9-1 (note that the "CPU Interrupt Enable/Disable" is typically part of the CPU, but is shown here separately for sake of the illustration).

Interrupting devices signal the interrupt controller, which then prioritizes the interrupts and presents the highest-priority interrupt to the CPU.

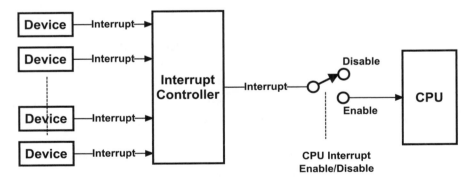

Figure 9-1 **Interrupt controllers**

Modern interrupt controllers have built-in intelligence that enable the user to prioritize interrupts, remember which interrupts are still pending and, in many cases, have the interrupt controller provide the address of the ISR (also called the vector address) directly to the CPU.

If "global" interrupts (i.e., the switch in Figure 9-1) are disabled, the CPU will ignore requests from the interrupt controller, but they will be held pending by the interrupt controller until the CPU re-enables interrupts.

CPUs deal with interrupts using one of two models:

1   All interrupts *vector* to a single interrupt handler.

2   Each interrupt *vectors* directly to an interrupt handler.

Before discussing these two methods, it is important to understand how µC/OS-III handles CPU interrupts.

9-2 TYPICAL µC/OS-III INTERRUPT SERVICE ROUTINE (ISR)

µC/OS-III requires that an interrupt service routine be written in assembly language. However, if a C compiler supports in-line assembly language, the ISR code can be placed directly into a C source file. The pseudo-code for a typical ISR when using µC/OS-III is shown in Listing 9-1.

```
MyISR:                                                           (1)
    Disable all interrupts;                                      (2)
    Save the CPU registers;                                      (3)
    OSIntNestingCtr++;                                           (4)
    if (OSIntNestingCtr == 1) {                                  (5)
        OSTCBCurPtr->StkPtr = Current task's CPU stack pointer register value;
    }
    Clear interrupting device;                                   (6)
    Re-enable interrupts (optional);                             (7)
    Call user ISR;                                               (8)
    OSIntExit();                                                 (9)
    Restore the CPU registers;                                   (10)
    Return from interrupt;                                       (11)
```

Listing 9-1 **ISRs under µC/OS-III (assembly language)**

9

L9-1(1)   As mentioned above, an ISR is typically written in assembly language. **MyISR** corresponds to the name of the handler that will handle the interrupting device.

L9-1(2)   It is important that all interrupts are disabled before going any further. Some processors have interrupts disabled whenever an interrupt handler starts. Others require the user to explicitly disable interrupts as shown here. This step may be tricky if a processor supports different interrupt priority levels. However, there is always a way to solve the problem.

L9-1(3)   The first thing the interrupt handler must do is save the context of the CPU onto the interrupted task's stack. On some processors, this occurs automatically. However, on most processors it is important to know how to save the CPU registers onto the task's stack. Save the full "context" of the CPU, which may also include Floating-Point Unit (FPU) registers if the CPU used is equipped with an FPU.

Certain CPUs also automatically switch to a special stack just to process interrupts (i.e., an interrupt stack). This is generally beneficial as it avoids using up valuable task stack space. However, for µC/OS-III, the context of the interrupted task needs to be saved onto that task's stack.

If the processor does not have a dedicated stack pointer to handle ISRs then it is possible to implement one in software. Specifically, upon entering the ISR, simply save the current task stack, switch to a dedicated ISR stack, and when done with the ISR switch back to the task stack. Of course, this means that there is additional code to write, however the benefits are enormous since it is not necessary to allocate extra space on the task stacks to accommodate for worst case interrupt stack usage including interrupt nesting.

L9-1(4)   Next, either call **OSIntEnter()**, or simply increment the variable **OSIntNestingCtr** in assembly language. This is generally quite easy to do and is more efficient than calling **OSIntEnter()**. As its name implies, **OSIntNestingCtr** keeps track of the interrupt nesting level.

L9-1(5)   If this is the first nested interrupt, save the current value of the stack pointer of the interrupted task into its **OS_TCB**. The global pointer **OSTCBCurPtr** conveniently points to the interrupted task's OS_TCB. The very first field in

OS_TCB is where the stack pointer needs to be saved. In other words, OSTCBCurPtr->StkPtr happens to be at offset 0 in the OS_TCB (this greatly simplifies assembly language).

L9-1(6)   At this point, clear the interrupting device so that it does not generate another interrupt until it is ready to do so. The user does not want the device to generate the same interrupt if re-enabling interrupts (refer to the next step). However, most people defer the clearing of the source and prefer to perform the action within the user ISR handler in "C."

L9-1(7)   At this point, it is safe to re-enable interrupts if the developer wants to support nested interrupts. This step is optional.

L9-1(8)   At this point, further processing can be deferred to a C function called from assembly language. This is especially useful if there is a large amount of processing to do in the ISR handler. However, as a general rule, keep the ISRs as short as possible. In fact, it is best to simply signal or send a message to a task and let the task handle the details of servicing the interrupting device.

The ISR must call one of the following functions: OSSemPost(), OSTaskSemPost(), OSFlagPost(), OSQPost() or OSTaskQPost(). This is necessary since the ISR will notify a task, which will service the interrupting device. These are the only functions able to be called from an ISR and they are used to signal or send a message to a task. However, if the ISR does not need to call one of these functions, consider writing the ISR as a "Short Interrupt Service Routine," as described in the next section.

L9-1(9)   When completing the ISR, the user must call OSIntExit() to tell μC/OS-III that the ISR has completed. OSIntExit() simply decrements OSIntNestingCtr and, if OSIntNestingCtr goes to 0, this indicates that the ISR will return to task-level code (instead of a previously interrupted ISR). μC/OS-III will need to determine whether there is a higher priority task that needs to run because of one of the nested ISRs. In other words, the ISR might have signaled or sent a message to a higher- priority task waiting for this signal or message. In this case, μC/OS-III will context switch to this higher priority task instead of returning to the interrupted task. In this latter case, OSIntExit() does not actually return, but takes a different path.

L9-1(10)   If the ISR signaled or sent a message to a lower-priority task than the interrupted task, **OSIntExit()** returns. This means that the interrupted task is still the highest-priority task to run and it is important to restore the previously saved registers.

L9-1(11)   The ISR performs a return from interrupts and so resumes the interrupted task.

NOTE: From this point on, (1) to (6) will be referred to as the *ISR Prologue* and (9) to (11) as the ISR Epilogue.

9-3 SHORT INTERRUPT SERVICE ROUTINE (ISR)

The above sequence assumes that the ISR signals or sends a message to a task. However, in many cases, the ISR may not need to notify a task and can simply perform all of its work within the ISR (assuming it can be done quickly). In this case, the ISR will appear as shown in Listing 9-2.

```
MyShortISR:                                          (1)
    Save enough registers as needed by the ISR;      (2)
    Clear interrupting device;                       (3)
    DO NOT re-enable interrupts;                     (4)
    Call user ISR;                                    (5)
    Restore the saved CPU registers;                 (6)
    Return from interrupt;                            (7)
```

Listing 9-2 **Short ISRs with µC/OS-III**

L9-2(1)   As mentioned above, an ISR is typically written in assembly language. **MyShortISR** corresponds to the name of the handler that will handle the interrupting device.

L9-2(2)   Here, save sufficient registers as required to handle the ISR.

L9-2(3)   The user may want to clear the interrupting device to prevent it from generating the same interrupt once the ISR returns.

L9-2(4)   *Do not* re-enable interrupts at this point since another interrupt could make μC/OS-III calls, forcing a context switch to a higher-priority task. This means that the above ISR would complete, but at a much later time.

L9-2(5)   Now take care of the interrupting device in assembly language or call a C function, if necessary.

L9-2(6)   Once finished, simply restore the saved CPU registers.

L9-2(7)   Perform a return from interrupt to resume the interrupted task.

Short ISRs, as described above, should be the exception and not the rule since μC/OS-III has no way of knowing when these ISRs occur.

9-4 ALL INTERRUPTS VECTOR TO A COMMON LOCATION

Even though an interrupt controller is present in most designs, some CPUs still vector to a common interrupt handler, and an ISR queries the interrupt controller to determine the source of the interrupt. At first glance, this might seem silly since most interrupt controllers are able to force the CPU to jump directly to the proper interrupt handler. It turns out, however, that for μC/OS-III, it is easier to have the interrupt controller vector to a single ISR handler than to vector to a unique ISR handler for each source. Listing 9-3 describes the sequence of events to be performed when the interrupt controller forces the CPU to vector to a single location.

```
An interrupt occurs;                                    (1)
The CPU vectors to a common location;                   (2)
The ISR code performs the "ISR prologue"                (3)
The C handler performs the following:                   (4)
    while (there are still interrupts to process) {     (5)
        Get vector address from interrupt controller;
        Call interrupt handler;
    }
The "ISR epilogue" is executed;                         (6)
```

Listing 9-3 **Single interrupt vector for all interrupts**

L9-3(1)   An interrupt occurs from any device. The interrupt controller activates the interrupt pin on the CPU. If there are other interrupts that occur after the first one, the interrupt controller will latch them and properly prioritize the interrupts.

L9-3(2)   The CPU vectors to a single interrupt handler address. In other words, all interrupts are to be handled by this one interrupt handler.

L9-3(3)   Execute the "ISR prologue" code needed by µC/OS-III. as previously described. This ensures that all ISRs will be able to make µC/OS-III "post" calls.

L9-3(4)   Call a µC/OS-III C handler, which will continue processing the ISR. This makes the code easier to write (and read). Notice that interrupts are not re-enabled.

L9-3(5)   The µC/OS-III C handler then interrogates the interrupt controller and asks it: "Who caused the interrupt?" The interrupt controller will either respond with a number (1 to N) or with the address of the interrupt handler for the interrupting device. Of course, the µC/OS-III C handler will know how to handle the specific interrupt controller since the C handler is written specifically for that controller.

If the interrupt controller provides a number between 1 and N, the C handler simply uses this number as an index into a table (in ROM or RAM) containing the address of the interrupt service routine servicing the interrupting device. A RAM table is handy to change interrupt handlers at run-time. For many embedded systems, however, the table may also reside in ROM.

If the interrupt controller responds with the address of the interrupt service routine, the C handler only needs to call this function.

In both of the above cases, all interrupt handlers need to be declared as follows:

```
void MyISRHandler (void);
```

There is one such handler for each possible interrupt source (obviously, each having a unique name).

The "**while**" loop terminates when there are no other interrupting devices to service.

L9-3(6)   The µC/OS-III "ISR epilogue" is executed to see if it is necessary to return to the interrupted task, or switch to a more important one.

A couple of interesting points to notice:

■   If another device caused an interrupt before the C handler had a chance to query the interrupt controller, most likely the interrupt controller will capture that interrupt. In fact, if that second device happens to be a higher-priority interrupting device, it will most likely be serviced first, as the interrupt controller will prioritize the interrupts.

■   The loop will not terminate until all pending interrupts are serviced. This is similar to allowing nested interrupts, but better, since it is not necessary to redo the ISR prologue and epilogue.

The disadvantage of this method is that a high priority interrupt that occurs after the servicing of another interrupt that has already started must wait for that interrupt to complete before it will be serviced. So, the latency of any interrupt, regardless of priority, can be as long as it takes to process the longest interrrupt.

9-5 EVERY INTERRUPT VECTORS TO A UNIQUE LOCATION

If the interrupt controller vectors directly to the appropriate interrupt handler, each of the ISRs must be written in assembly language as described in section 9-2 "Typical µC/OS-III Interrupt Service Routine (ISR)" on page 165. This, of course, slightly complicates the design. However, copy and paste the majority of the code from one handler to the other and just change what is specific to the actual device.

If the interrupt controller allows the user to query it for the source of the interrupt, it may be possible to simulate the mode in which all interrupts vector to the same location by simply setting all vectors to point to the same location. Most interrupt controllers that vector to a unique location, however, do not allow users to query it for the source of the interrupt since, by definition, having a unique vector for all interrupting devices should not be necessary.

9-6 DIRECT AND DEFERRED POST METHODS

µC/OS-III handles event posting from interrupts using two different methods: Direct and Deferred Post. The method used in the application is selected by changing the value of OS_CFG_ISR_POST_DEFERRED_EN in OS_CFG.H (this assumes you have access to µC/OS-III's source code). When set to 0, µC/OS-III uses the Direct Post Method and when set to 1, µC/OS-III uses the Deferred Post Method.

As far as application code and ISRs are concerned, these two methods are completely transparent. It is not necessary to change anything except the configuration value OS_CFG_ISR_POST_DEFERRED_EN to switch between the two methods. Of course, changing the configuration constant will require recompiling the product and µC/OS-III.

Before explaining why to use one versus the other, let us review their differences.

9-6-1 DIRECT POST METHOD

The Direct Post Method is used by µC/OS-II and is replicated in µC/OS-III. Figure 9-2 shows a task diagram of what takes place in a Direct Post.

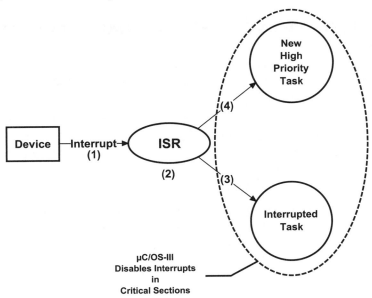

Figure 9-2 **Direct Post Method**

F9-2(1)   A device generates an interrupt.

F9-2(2)   The Interrupt Service Routine (ISR) responsible to handle the device executes (assuming interrupts are enabled). The device interrupt is generally the event a task is waiting for. The task waiting for this interrupt to occur either has a higher priority than the interrupted task, or lower (or equal) in priority.

F9-2(3)   If the ISR made a lower (or equal) priority task ready to run then upon completion of the ISR, μC/OS-III returns to the interrupted task exactly at the point the interrupt occurred.

F9-2(4)   If the ISR made a higher priority task ready to run, μC/OS-III will context switch to the new higher-priority task since the more important task was waiting for this device interrupt.

F9-2(5)   In the Direct Post Method, μC/OS-III must protect critical sections by disabling interrupts as some of these critical sections can be accessed by ISRs.

The above discussion assumed that interrupts were enabled and that the ISR could respond quickly to the interrupting device. However, if the application code makes μC/OS-III service calls (and it will at some point), it is possible that interrupts would be disabled. When `OS_CFG_ISR_POST_DEFERRED_EN` is set to 0, μC/OS-III disables interrupts while accessing critical sections. Thus, interrupts will not be responded to until μC/OS-III re-enables interrupts. Of course, attempts were made to keep interrupt disable times as short as possible, but there are complex features of μC/OS-III that disable interrupts for a longer period than the user would like.

The key factor in determining whether to use the Direct Post Method is generally the μC/OS-III interrupt disable time. This is fairly easy to determine since the μC/CPU files provided with the μC/OS-III port for the processor used includes code to measure maximum interrupt disable time. This code can be enabled (assumes you have the source code) for testing purposes and removed when ready to deploy the product. The user would typically not want to leave measurement code in production code to avoid introducing measurement artifacts. Once instrumented, let the application run for sufficiently long and read the variable `CPU_IntDisMeasMaxRaw_cnts`. The resolution (in time) of this variable depends on the timer used during the measurement.

Determine the interrupt latency, interrupt response, interrupt recovery, and task latency by adding the execution times of the code involved for each, as shown below.

Interrupt Latency   =   Maximum interrupt disable time;

Interrupt Response   =   Interrupt latency
                          + Vectoring to the interrupt handler
                          + ISR prologue;

Interrupt Recovery   =   Handling of the interrupting device
                          + Posting a signal or a message to a task
                          + OSIntExit()
                          + OSIntCtxSw();

Task Latency   =   Interrupt response
                          + Interrupt recovery
                          + Time scheduler is locked;

The execution times of the µC/OS-III ISR prologue, ISR epilogue, OSIntExit(), and OSIntCtxSw(), can be measured independently and should be fairly constant.

It should also be easy to measure the execution time of a post call by using OS_TS_GET().

In the Direct Post Method, the scheduler is locked only when handling timers and therefore, task latency should be fast if there are not too many timers with short callbacks expiring at the same time. See Chapter 12, "Timer Management" on page 199. µC/OS-III is also able to measure the amount of time the scheduler is locked, providing task latency.

9-6-2 DEFERRED POST METHOD

In the Deferred Post Method (OS_CFG_ISR_POST_DEFERRED_EN is set to 1), instead of disabling interrupts to access critical sections, μC/OS-III locks the scheduler. This avoids having other tasks access critical sections while allowing interrupts to be recognized and serviced. In the Deferred Post Method, interrupts' are almost never disabled. The Deferred Post Method is, however, a bit more complex as shown in Figure 9-3.

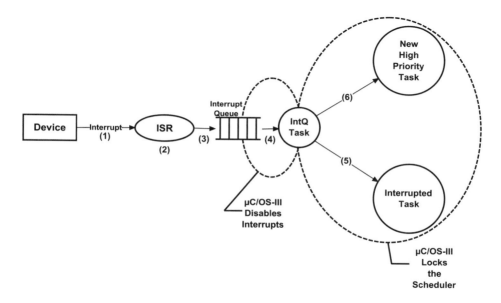

Figure 9-3 **Deferred Post Method block diagram**

F9-3(1)   A device generates an interrupt.

F9-3(2)   The ISR responsible for handling the device executes (assuming interrupts are enabled). The device interrupt is the event that a task was waiting for. The task waiting for this interrupt to occur is either higher in priority than the interrupted task, lower, or equal in priority.

F9-3(3)   The ISR calls one of the post services to signal or send a message to a task. However, instead of performing the post operation, the ISR queues the actual post call along with arguments in a special queue called the *Interrupt Queue*. The ISR then makes the *Interrupt Queue Handler Task* ready to run. This task is internal to μC/OS-III and is always the highest priority task (i.e., Priority 0).

F9-3(4)   At the end of the ISR, µC/OS-III always context switches to the interrupt queue handler task, which then extracts the post command from the queue. We disable interrupts to prevent another interrupt from accessing the interrupt queue while the queue is being emptied. The task then re-enables interrupts, locks the scheduler, and performs the post call as if the post was performed at the task level all along. This effectively manipulates critical sections at the task level.

F9-3(5)   When the interrupt queue handler task empties the interrupt queue, it makes itself not ready to run and then calls the scheduler to determine which task must run next. If the original interrupted task is still the highest priority task, µC/OS-III will resume that task.

F9-3(6)   If, however, a more important task was made ready to run because of the post, µC/OS-III will context switch to that task.

All the extra processing is performed to avoid disabling interrupts during critical sections of code. The extra processing time only consist of copying the post call and arguments into the queue, extracting it back out of the queue, and performing an extra context switch.

Similar to the Direct Post Method, it is easy to determine interrupt latency, interrupt response, interrupt recovery, and task latency, by adding execution times of the pieces of code involved for each as shown below.

Interrupt Latency   =   Maximum interrupt disable time;

Interrupt Response   =   Interrupt latency
                          + Vectoring to the interrupt handler
                          + ISR prologue;

Interrupt Recovery   =   Handling of the interrupting device
                          + Posting a signal or a message to the Interrupt Queue
                          + `OSIntExit()`
                          + `OSIntCtxSw()` to Interrupt Queue Handler Task;

Task Latency	=	Interrupt response
		+ Interrupt recovery
		+ Re-issue the post to the object or task
		+ Context switch to task
		+ Time scheduler is locked;

The execution times of the µC/OS-III ISR prologue, ISR epilogue, **OSIntExit()**, and **OSIntCtxSw()**, can be measured independently and should be constant.

It should also be easy to measure the execution time of a post call by using **OS_TS_GET()**. In fact, the post calls should be short in the Deferred Post Method because it only involves copying the post call and its arguments into the interrupt queue.

The difference is that in the Deferred Post Method, interrupts are disabled for a very short amount of time and thus, the first three metrics should be fast. However, task latency is higher as µC/OS-III locks the scheduler to access critical sections.

9

9

9-7 DIRECT VS. DEFERRED POST METHOD

In the Direct Post Method, μC/OS-III disables interrupts to access critical sections. In comparison, while in the Deferred Post Method, μC/OS-III locks the scheduler to access the same critical sections.

In the Deferred Post Method, μC/OS-III must still disable interrupts to access the interrupt queue. However, the interrupt disable time is very short and fairly constant.

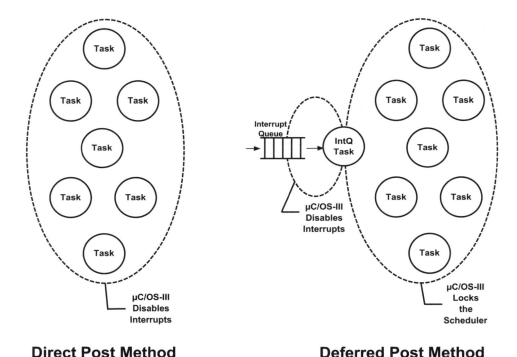

Direct Post Method   **Deferred Post Method**

Figure 9-4 **Direct vs. Deferred Post Methods**

If interrupt disable time is critical in the application because there are very fast interrupt sources and the interrupt disable time of μC/OS-III is not acceptable using the Direct Post Method, use the Deferred Post Method.

However, if you are planning on using the features listed in Table 9-1, consider using the Deferred Post Method, described in the next section.

Feature	Reason
Multiple tasks at the same priority	Although this is an important feature of µC/OS-III, multiple tasks at the same priority create longer critical sections. However, if there are only a few tasks at the same priority, interrupt latency will be relatively small. If the user does not create multiple tasks at the same priority, the Direct Post Method is recommended.
Event Flags Chapter 14, "Synchronization" on page 257	If multiple tasks are waiting on different events, going through all of the tasks waiting for events requires a fair amount of processing time, which means longer critical sections. If only a few tasks (approximately one to five) are waiting on an event flag group, the critical section will be short enough to use the Direct Post Method.
Pend on multiple objects Chapter 16, "Pending On Multiple Objects" on page 319	Pending on multiple objects is probably the most complex feature provided by µC/OS-III and requires interrupts to be disabled for fairly long periods of time when using the Direct Post Method. If pending on multiple objects, the Deferred Post Method is highly recommended. If the application does not use this feature, the user may select the Direct Post Method.
Broadcast on Post calls See OSSemPost() and OSQPost() descriptions.	µC/OS-III disables interrupts while processing a post to multiple tasks in a broadcast. If not using the broadcast option, use the Direct Post Method. Note that broadcasts only apply to semaphores and message queues.

Table 9-1 **µC/OS-III features to avoid when using the Direct Post Method**

9-8 THE CLOCK TICK (OR SYSTEM TICK)

µC/OS-III-based systems generally require the presence of a periodic time source called the *clock tick* or *system tick*.

A hardware timer configured to generate an interrupt at a rate between 10 and 1000 Hz provides the clock tick. A tick source may also be obtained by generating an interrupt from an AC power line (typically 50 or 60 Hz). In fact, one can easily derive 100 or 120 Hz by detecting zero crossings of the power line.

The clock tick interrupt can be viewed as the system's heartbeat. The rate is application specific and depends on the desired resolution of this time source. However, the faster the tick rate, the higher the overhead imposed on the system.

The clock tick interrupt allows μC/OS-III to delay tasks for an integral number of clock ticks and provide timeouts when tasks are waiting for events to occur.

The clock tick interrupt must call **OSTimeTick()**. The pseudocode for **OSTimeTick()** is shown in Listing 9-4.

```
void  OSTimeTick (void)
{
    OSTimeTickHook();                                       (1)
#if OS_CFG_ISR_POST_DEFERRED_EN > 0u
    Get timestamp;                                          (2)
    Post "time tick" to the Interrupt Queue;
#else
    Signal the Tick Task;                                   (3)
    Run the round-robin scheduling algorithm;              (4)
    Signal the timer task;                                  (5)
#endif
}
```

Listing 9-4 **OSTimeTick() pseudocode**

L9-4(1)   The time tick ISR starts by calling a hook function, **OSTimeTickHook()**. The hook function allows the implementer of the μC/OS-III port to perform additional processing when a tick interrupt occurs. In turn, the tick hook can call a user-defined tick hook if its corresponding pointer, **OS_AppTimeTickHookPtr**, is non-**NULL**. The reason the hook is called first is to give the application immediate access to this periodic time source. This can be useful to read sensors at a regular interval (not as subject to jitter), update Pulse Width Modulation (PWM) registers, and more.

L9-4(2)   If μC/OS-III is configured for the Deferred Post Method, μC/OS-III reads the current timestamp and defers the call to signal the tick task by placing an appropriate entry in the interrupt queue. The tick task will thus be signaled by the Interrupt Queue Handler Task.

L9-4(3)   If µC/OS-III is configured for the Direct Post Method, µC/OS-III signals the tick task so that it can process the time delays and timeouts.

L9-4(4)   µC/OS-III runs the round-robin scheduling algorithm to determine whether the time slot for the current task has expired.

L9-4(5)   The tick task is also used as the time base for the timers (see Chapter 13, "Resource Management" on page 215).

A common misconception is that a system tick is always needed with µC/OS-III. In fact, many low-power applications may not implement the system tick because of the power required to maintain the tick list. In other words, it is not reasonable to continuously power down and power up the product just to maintain the system tick. Since µC/OS-III is a preemptive kernel, an event other than a tick interrupt can wake up a system placed in low power mode by either a keystroke from a keypad or other means. Not having a system tick means that the user is not allowed to use time delays and timeouts on system calls. This is a decision required to be made by the designer of the low-power product.

9-9 SUMMARY

µC/OS-III provides services to manage interrupts. An ISR should be short in length, and signal or send a message to a task, which is responsible for servicing the interrupting device.

ISRs that are short and do not need to signal or send a message to a task, are not required to do so.

µC/OS-III supports processors that vector to a single ISR for all interrupting devices, or to a unique ISR for each device.

µC/OS-III supports two methods: Direct and Deferred Post. The Direct Post Method assumes that µC/OS-III critical sections are protected by disabling interrupts. The Deferred Post Method locks the scheduler when µC/OS-III accesses critical sections of code.

µC/OS-III assumes the presence of a periodic time source for applications requiring time delays and timeouts on certain services.

9

10

Pend Lists (or Wait Lists)

A task is placed in a *Pend List* (also called a *Wait List*) when it is waiting on a semaphore to be signaled, a mutual exclusion semaphore to be released, an event flag group to be posted, or a message queue to be posted.

See ...	For ...	Kernel Object
Chapter 13, "Resource Management" on page 215	Semaphores Mutual Exclusion Semaphores	OS_SEM OS_MUTEX
Chapter 14, "Synchronization" on page 257	Semaphores Event Flags	OS_SEM OS_FLAG_GRP
Chapter 15, "Message Passing" on page 295	Message Queues	OS_Q

Table 10-1 **Kernel objects that have Pend Lists**

A pend list is similar to the *Ready List*, except that instead of keeping track of tasks that are ready-to-run, the pend list keeps track of tasks waiting for an object to be posted. In addition, the pend list is sorted by priority; the highest priority task waiting on the object is placed at the head of the list, and the lowest priority task waiting on the object is placed at the end of the list.

A pend list is a data structure of type **OS_PEND_LIST**, which consists of three fields as shown in Figure 10-1.

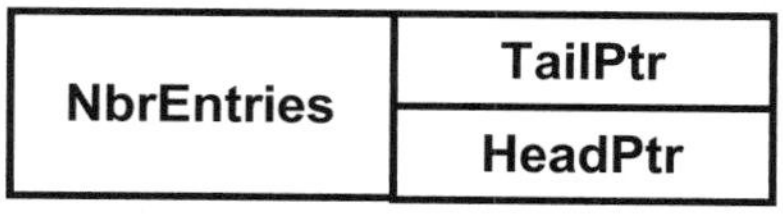

NbrEntries	TailPtr
	HeadPtr

Figure 10-1 **Pend List**

.NbrEntries	Contains the current number of entries in the pend list. Each entry in the pend list points to a task that is waiting for the kernel object to be posted.
.TailPtr	Is a pointer to the last task in the list (i.e., the lowest priority task).
.HeadPtr	Is a pointer to the first task in the list (i.e., the highest priority task).

Figure 10-2 indicates that each kernel object using a pend list contains the same three fields at the beginning of the kernel object that we called an **OS_PEND_OBJ**. Notice that the first field is always a "Type" which allows µC/OS-III to know if the kernel object is a semaphore, a mutual exclusion semaphore, an event flag group, or a message queue object.

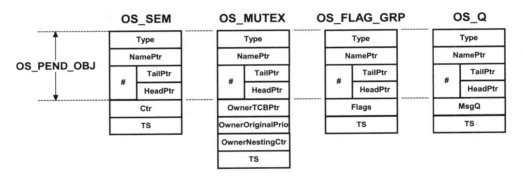

Figure 10-2 **OS_PEND_OBJ at the beginning of certain kernel objects**

Table 10-2 shows that the "Type" field of each of the above objects is initialized to contain four ASCII characters when the respective object is created. This allows the user to identify these objects when performing a memory dump using a debugger.

Kernel Object	Type
Semaphore	'S" "E" "M" "A"
Mutual Exclusion Semaphore	'M" "U" "T" "X"
Event Flag Group	'F" "L" "A" "G"
Message Queue	'Q" "U" "E" "U"

Table 10-2 **Kernel objects with initialized "Type" field**

A pend list does not actually point to a task's **OS_TCB**, but instead points to **OS_PEND_DATA** objects as shown in Figure 10-3. Also, an **OS_PEND_DATA** structure is allocated dynamically on the current task's stack when a task is placed on a pend list. This implies that a task stack needs to be able to allocate storage for this data structure.

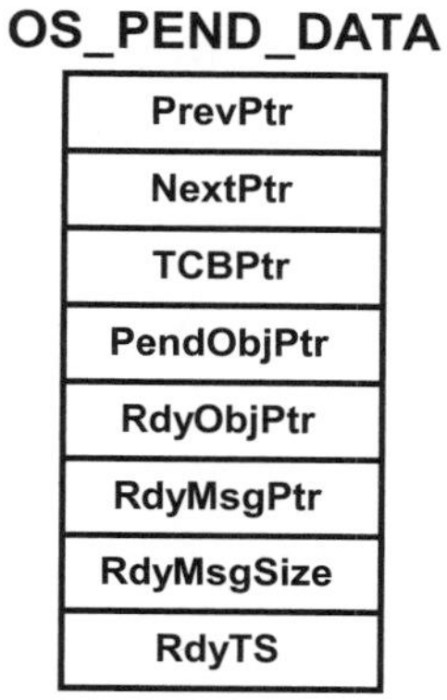

OS_PEND_DATA

PrevPtr
NextPtr
TCBPtr
PendObjPtr
RdyObjPtr
RdyMsgPtr
RdyMsgSize
RdyTS

Figure 10-3 **Pend Data**

.PrevPtr   Is a pointer to an **OS_PEND_DATA** entry in the pend list. This pointer points to a higher or equal priority task waiting on the kernel object.

.NextPtr   Is a pointer to an **OS_PEND_DATA** entry in the pend list. This pointer points to a lower or equal priority task waiting on the kernel object.

.TCBPtr   Is a pointer to the **OS_TCB** of the task waiting on the pend list.

.PendObjPtr   Is a pointer to the kernel object that the task is pending on. In other words, this pointer can point to an **OS_SEM**, **OS_MUTEX**, **OS_FLAG_GRP** or **OS_Q** by using an **OS_PEND_OBJ** as the common data structure.

.RdyObjPtr   Is a pointer to the kernel object that is ready if the task actually waits for multiple kernel objects. See Chapter 16, "Pending On Multiple Objects" on page 319 for more on this.

`.RdyMsgPtr`	Is a pointer to the message posted through `OSQPost()` if the task is pending on multiple kernel objects. Again, see Chapter 16, "Pending On Multiple Objects" on page 319.
`.RdyTS`	Is a timestamp of when the kernel object was posted. This is used when a task pends on multiple kernel objects as described in Chapter 16, "Pending On Multiple Objects" on page 319.

Figure 10-4 exhibits how all data structures connect to each other when tasks are inserted in a pend list. This drawing assumes that there are two tasks waiting on a semaphore.

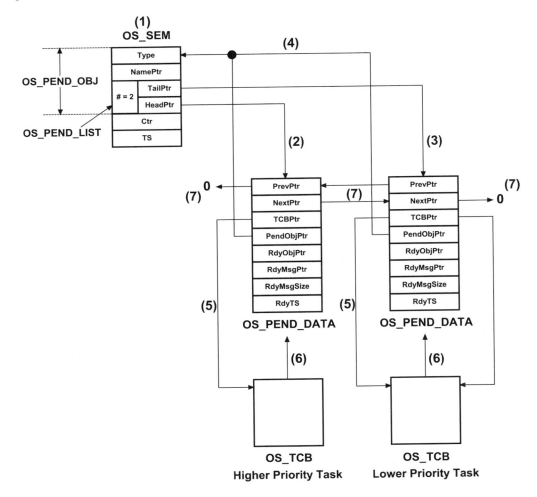

Figure 10-4 **Pend Data**

F9-4(1)   The **OS_SEM** data type contains an **OS_PEND_OBJ**, which in turn contains an **OS_PEND_LIST**. The **.NbrEntries** field in the pend list indicates that there are two tasks waiting on the semaphore.

F9-4(2)   The **.HeadPtr** field of the pend list points to the **OS_PEND_DATA** structure associated with the highest priority task waiting on the semaphore.

F9-4(3)   The **.TailPtr** field of the pend list points to the **OS_PEND_DATA** structure associated with the lowest priority task waiting on the semaphore.

F9-4(4)   Both **OS_PEND_DATA** structures in turn point back to the **OS_SEM** data structure. The pointers think they are pointing to an **OS_PEND_OBJ**. We know that the **OS_PEND_OBJ** is a semaphore by examining the **.Type** field of the **OS_PEND_OBJ**.

F9-4(5)   Each **OS_PEND_DATA** structure points to its respective **OS_TCB**. In other words, we know which task is pending on the semaphore.

F9-4(6)   Each task points back to the **OS_PEND_DATA** structure.

F9-4(7)   Finally, the **OS_PEND_DATA** structure forms a doubly linked list so that the µC/OS-III can easily add or remove entries in this list.

Although this may seem complex, the reasoning will become apparent in Chapter 16, "Pending On Multiple Objects" on page 319. For now, assume all of the links are necessary.

Table 10-3 shows the functions that µC/OS-III uses to manipulate entries in a pend list. These functions are internal to µC/OS-III and the application code must never call them. The code is found in **OS_CORE.C**.

10

Function	Description
OS_PendListChangePrio()	Change the priority of a task in a pend list
OS_PendListInit()	Initialize a pend list
OS_PendListInsertHead()	Insert an OS_PEND_DATA at the head of the pend list
OS_PendListInsertPrio()	Insert an OS_PEND_DATA in priority order in the pend list
OS_PendListRemove()	Remove multiple OS_PEND_DATA from the pend list
OS_PendListRemove1()	Remove single OS_PEND_DATA from the pend list

Table 10-3 **Pend List access functions**

10-1 SUMMARY

μC/OS-III keeps track of tasks waiting for semaphores, mutual exclusion semaphores, event flag groups and message queues using pend lists.

A pend list consists of a data structure of type **OS_PEND_LIST**. The pend list is further encapsulated into another data type called an **OS_PEND_OBJ**.

Tasks are not directly linked to the pend list but instead are linked through an intermediate data structure called an **OS_PEND_DATA** which is allocated on the stack of the task waiting on the kernel object.

Application code must not access pend lists, since these are internal to μC/OS-III.

Chapter

11

Time Management

µC/OS-III provides time-related services to the application programmer.

In Chapter 9, "Interrupt Management" on page 163, it was established that µC/OS-III generally requires (as do most kernels) that the user provide a periodic interrupt to keep track of time delays and timeouts. This periodic time source is called a clock tick and should occur between 10 and 1000 times per second, or Hertz (see **OS_CFG_TICK_RATE_HZ** in **OS_CFG_APP.H**). The actual frequency of the clock tick depends on the desired tick resolution of the application. However, the higher the frequency of the ticker, the higher the overhead.

µC/OS-III provides a number of services to manage time as summarized in Table 11-1, and the code is found in **OS_TIME.C**.

Function Name	Operation
OSTimeDly()	Delay execution of a task for "n" ticks
OSTimeDlyHMSM()	Delay a task for a user specified time in HH:MM:SS.mmm
OSTimeDlyResume()	Resume a delayed task
OSTimeGet()	Obtain the current value of the tick counter
OSTimeSet()	Set the tick counter to a new value
OSTimeTick()	Signal the occurrence of a clock tick

Table 11-1 **Time Services API summary**

The application programmer should refer to Appendix A, "µC/OS-III API Reference Manual" on page 381 for a detailed description of these services.

11-1 OSTimeDly()

A task calls this function to suspend execution until some time expires. The calling function will not execute until the specified time expires. This function allows three modes: relative, periodic and absolute.

Listing 11-1 shows how to use OSTimeDly() in relative mode.

```
void  MyTask (void *p_arg)
{
    OS_ERR   err;
    :
    :
    while (DEF_ON) {
        :
        :
        OSTimeDly(2,                             (1)
                    OS_OPT_TIME_DLY,             (2)
                    &err);                       (3)
        /* Check "err" */                        (4)
        :
        :
    }
}
```

Listing 11-1 **OSTimeDly() - Relative**

L11-1(1)   The first argument specifies the amount of time delay (in number of ticks) from when the function is called. For example if the tick rate (OS_CFG_TICK_RATE_HZ in OS_CFG_APP.H) is set to 1000 Hz, the user is asking to suspend the current task for approximately 2 milliseconds. However, the value is not accurate since the count starts from the next tick which could occur almost immediately. This will be explained shortly.

L11-1(2)   Specifying OS_OPT_TIME_DLY indicates that the user wants to use "relative" mode.

L11-1(3)   As with most µC/OS-III services an error return value will be returned. The example should return OS_ERR_NONE as the arguments are all valid. Refer to Chapter 11, "Time Management" on page 189 for a list of possible error codes.

L11-1(4)   Always check the error code returned by μC/OS-III. If "**err**" does not contain
             OS_ERR_NONE, **OSTimeDly()** did not perform the intended work. For example,
             another task could remove the time delay suspension by calling
             OSTimeDlyResume() and when **MyTask()** returns, it would not have returned
             because the time had expired.

             As mentioned above, the delay is not accurate. Refer to Figure 11-1 and its
             description below to understand why.

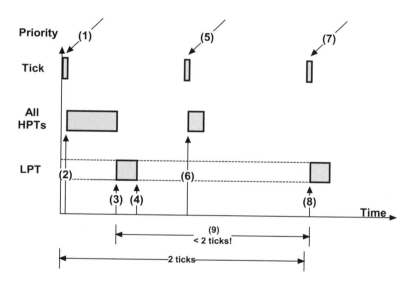

Figure 11-1 **OSTimeDly() - Relative**

F11-1(1)   We get a tick interrupt and μC/OS-III services the ISR.

F11-1(2)   At the end of the ISR, all Higher Priority Tasks (HPTs) execute. The execution
             time of HPTs is unknown and can vary.

F11-1(3)   Once all HPTs have executed, μC/OS-III runs the task that has called
             OSTimeDly() as shown above. For the sake of discussion, it is assumed that
             this task is a lower priority task (LPT).

F11-1(4)   The task calls `OSTimeDly()` and specifies to delay for two ticks in "relative" mode. At this point, μC/OS-III places the current task in the tick list where it will wait for two ticks to expire. The delayed task consumes zero CPU time while waiting for the time to expire.

F11-1(5)   The next tick occurs. If there are HPTs waiting for this particular tick, μC/OS-III will schedule them to run at the end of the ISR.

F11-1(6)   The HPTs execute.

F11-1(7)   The next tick interrupt occurs. This is the tick that the LPT was waiting for and will now be made ready to run by μC/OS-III.

F11-1(8)   Since there are no HPTs to execute on this tick, μC/OS-III switches to the LPT.

F11-1(9)   Given the execution time of the HPTs, the time delay is not exactly two ticks, as requested. In fact, it is virtually impossible to obtain a delay of exactly the desired number of ticks. One might ask for a delay of two ticks, but the very next tick could occur almost immediately after calling `OSTimeDly()`! Just imagine what might happen if all HPTs took longer to execute and pushed (3) and (4) further to the right. In this case, the delay would actually appear as one tick instead of two.

`OSTimeDly()` can also be called with the `OS_OPT_TIME_PERIODIC` option as shown in Listing 11-2. This option allows delaying the task until the tick counter reaches a certain periodic match value and thus ensures that the spacing in time is always the same as it is not subject to CPU load variations.

μC/OS-III determines the "match value" of `OSTickCtr` to determine when the task will need to wake up based on the desired period. This is shown in Figure 11-2. μC/OS-III checks to ensure that if the match is computed such that it represents a value that has already gone by then, the delay will be zero.

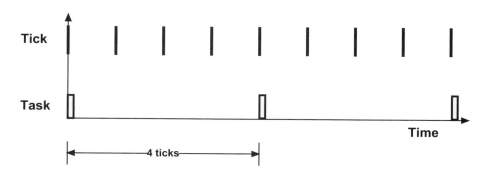

Figure 11-2 **OSTimeDly() - Periodic**

```
void  MyTask (void *p_arg)
{
    OS_ERR    err;
    :
    :
    while (DEF_ON) {
        OSTimeDly(4,                           (1)
                    OS_OPT_TIME_PERIODIC,      (2)
                    &err);
        /* Check "err" */                      (3)
        :
        :
    }
}
```

Listing 11-2 **OSTimeDly() - Periodic**

L11-2(1)   The first argument specifies the period for the task to execute, specifically every four ticks. Of course, if the task is a low-priority task, µC/OS-III only schedules and runs the task based on its priority relative to what else needs to be executed.

L11-2(2)   Specifying **OS_OPT_TIME_PERIODIC** indicates that the task is to be ready to run when the tick counter reaches the desired period from the previous call.

L11-2(3)   You should always check the error code returned by µC/OS-III.

Relative and Periodic modes might not look different, but they are. In Relative mode, it is possible to miss one of the ticks when the system is heavily loaded, missing a tick or more on occasion. In Periodic mode, the task may still execute later, but it will always be synchronized to the desired number of ticks. In fact, Periodic mode is the preferred mode to use to implement a time-of-day clock.

Finally, you can use the absolute mode to perform a specific action at a fixed time after power up. For example, turn off a light 10 seconds after the product powers up. In this case, you would specify **OS_OPT_TIME_MATCH** while "**dly**" actually corresponds to the desired value of **OSTickCtr** you want to reach.

To summarize, the task will wake up when **OSTickCtr** reaches the following value:

Value of "opt"	Task wakes up when
OS_OPT_TIME_DLY	OSTickCtr + dly
OS_OPT_TIME_PERIODIC	OSTCBCurPtr->TickCtrPrev + dly
OS_OPT_TIME_MATCH	dly

11-2 `OSTimeDlyHMSM()`

A task may call this function to suspend execution until some time expires by specifying the length of time in a more user-friendly way. Specifically, specify the delay in hours, minutes, seconds, and milliseconds (thus the **HMSM**). This function only works in "Relative" mode.

Listing 11-3 indicates how to use `OSTimeDlyHMSM()`.

```
void  MyTask (void *p_arg)
{
    OS_ERR  err;
    :
    :
    while (DEF_ON) {
        :
        :
        OSTimeDlyHMSM(0,                              (1)
                      0,
                      1,
                      0,
                      OS_OPT_TIME_HMSM_STRICT,        (2)
                      &err);                          (3)
        /* Check "err" */
        :
        :
    }
}
```

Listing 11-3 **OSTimeDlyHMSM()**

L11-3(1)   The first four arguments specify the amount of time delay (in hours, minutes, seconds, and milliseconds) from this point in time. In the above example, the task should delay by 1 second. The resolution greatly depends on the tick rate. For example, if the tick rate (**OS_CFG_TICK_RATE_HZ** in **OS_CFG_APP.H**) is set to 1000 Hz there is technically a resolution of 1 millisecond. If the tick rate is 100 Hz then the delay of the current task is in increments of 10 milliseconds. Again, given the relative nature of this call, the actual delay may not be accurate.

L11-3(2)   Specifying **OS_OPT_TIME_HMSM_STRICT** verifies that the user strictly passes valid values for hours, minutes, seconds and milliseconds. Valid hours are 0 to 99, valid minutes are 0 to 59, valid seconds are 0 to 59, and valid milliseconds are 0 to 999.

If specifying **OS_OPT_TIME_HMSM_NON_STRICT**, the function will accept nearly any value for hours (between 0 to 999), minutes (from 0 to 9999), seconds (any value, up to **65,535**), and milliseconds (any value, up to **4,294,967,295**). **OSTimeDlyHMSM(203, 101, 69, 10000)** may be accepted. Whether or not this makes sense is a different story.

The reason hours is limited to 999 is that time delays typically use 32-bit values to keep track of ticks. If the tick rate is set at 1000 Hz then, it is possible to only track 4,294,967 seconds, which corresponds to 1,193 hours, and therefore 999 is a reasonable limit.

L11-3(3)   As with most µC/OS-III services the user will receive an error return value. The example should return **OS_ERR_NONE** since the arguments are all valid. Refer to Appendix A, "µC/OS-III API Reference Manual" on page 381 for a list of possible error codes.

Even though µC/OS-III allows for very long delays for tasks, it is actually not recommended to delay tasks for a long time. There is no indication that the task is actually "alive" unless it is possible to monitor the amount of time remaining for the delay. It is better to have the task wake up approximately every minute or so, and have it "tell you" that it is still ok.

OSTimeDly() and **OSTimeDlyHMSM()** are often used to create periodic tasks (tasks that execute periodically). For example, it is possible to have a task that scans a keyboard every 50 milliseconds and another task that reads analog inputs every 10 milliseconds, etc.

11-3 `OSTimeDlyResume()`

A task can resume another task that called `OSTimeDly()` or `OSTimeDlyHMSM()` by calling `OSTimeDlyResume()`. Listing 11-4 shows how to use `OSTimeDlyResume()`. The task that delayed itself will not know that it was resumed, but will think that the delay expired. Because of this, use this function with great care.

```c
OS_TCB  MyTaskTCB;


void  MyTask (void *p_arg)
{
    OS_ERR  err;
    :
    :
    while (1) {
        :
        :
        OSTimeDly(10,
                  OS_OPT_TIME_DLY,
                  &err);
        /* Check "err" */
        :
        :
    }
}


void  MyOtherTask (void *p_arg)
{
    OS_ERR  err;
    :
    :
    while (1) {
        :
        :
        OSTimeDlyResume(&MyTaskTCB,
                        &err);
        /* Check "err" */
        :
        :
    }
}
```

Listing 11-4 **OSTimeDlyResume()**

11-4 `OSTimeSet()` **AND** `OSTimeGet()`

µC/OS-III increments a tick counter every time a tick interrupt occurs. This counter allows the application to make coarse time measurements and have some notion of time (after power up).

`OSTimeGet()` allows the user to take a snapshot of the tick counter. As shown in a previous section, use this value to delay a task for a specific number of ticks and repeat this periodically without losing track of time.

`OSTimeSet()` allows the user to change the current value of the tick counter. Although µC/OS-III allows for this, it is recommended to use this function with great care.

11–5 OSTimeTick()

The tick Interrupt Service Routine (ISR) must call this function every time a tick interrupt occurs. µC/OS-III uses this function to update time delays and timeouts on other system calls. OSTimeTick() is considered an internal function to µC/OS-III.

11-6 SUMMARY

µC/OS-III provides services to applications so that tasks can suspend their execution for user-defined time delays. Delays are either specified by a number of clock ticks or hours, minutes, seconds, and milliseconds.

Application code can resume a delayed task by calling `OSTimeDlyResume()`. However, its use is not recommended because resumed task will not know that they were resumed as opposed to the time delay expired.

µC/OS-III keeps track of the number of ticks occurring since power up or since the number of ticks counter was last changed by `OSTimeSet()`. The counter may be read by the application code using `OSTimeGet()`.

12

Timer Management

μC/OS-III provides timer services to the application programmer and code to handle timers is found in **OS_TMR.C**. Timer services are enabled when setting **OS_CFG_TMR_EN** to 1 in **OS_CFG.H**.

Timers are down counters that perform an *action* when the counter reaches zero. The user provides the action through a *callback* function (or simply *callback*). A callback is a user-declared function that will be called when the timer expires. The callback can be used to turn a light on or off, start a motor, or perform other actions. However, it is important to never make blocking calls within a callback function (i.e., call **OSTimeDly()**, **OSTimeDlyHMSM()**, **OS???Pend()**, or anything that causes the timer task to block or be deleted).

Timers are useful in protocol stacks (retransmission timers, for example), and can also be used to poll I/O devices at predefined intervals.

An application can have any number of timers (limited only by the amount of RAM available). Timer services in μC/OS-III start with the **OSTmr???()** prefix, and the services available to the application programmer are described in Appendix A, "μC/OS-III API Reference Manual" on page 381.

The resolution of all the timers managed by μC/OS-III is determined by the configuration constant: **OS_CFG_TMR_TASK_RATE_HZ**, which is expressed in Hertz (Hz). So, if the timer task (described later) rate is set to 10, all timers have a resolution of 1/10th of a second (ticks in the diagrams to follow). In fact, this is the typical recommended value for the timer task. Timers are to be used with "coarse" granularity.

µC/OS-III provides a number of services to manage timers as summarized in Table 12-1.

Function Name	Operation
OSTmrCreate()	Create and specify the operating mode of the timer.
OSTmrDel()	Delete a timer.
OSTmrRemainGet()	Obtain the remaining time left before the timer expires.
OSTmrStart()	Start (or restart) a timer.
OSTmrStateGet()	Obtain the current state of a timer.
OSTmrStop()	Stop the countdown process of a timer.

Table 12-1 **Timer API summary**

A timer needs to be created before it can be used. Create a timer by calling **OSTmrCreate()** and specify a number of arguments to this function based on how the timer is to operate. Once the timer operation is specified, its operating mode cannot be changed unless the timer is deleted and recreated. The function prototype for **OSTmrCreate()** is shown below as a quick reference:

```
void   OSTmrCreate (OS_TMR                *p_tmr,             /* Pointer to timer      */
                    CPU_CHAR              *p_name,            /* Name of timer, ASCII */
                    OS_TICK               dly,               /* Initial delay         */
                    OS_TICK               period,            /* Repeat period         */
                    OS_OPT                opt,               /* Options               */
                    OS_TMR_CALLBACK_PTR   p_callback,        /* Fnct to call at 0     */
                    void                  *p_callback_arg,    /* Arg. to callback      */
                    OS_ERR                *p_err)
```

Once created, a timer can be started (or restarted) and stopped as often as is necessary. Timers can be created to operate in one of three modes: One-shot, Periodic (no initial delay), and Periodic (with initial delay).

12-1 ONE-SHOT TIMERS

As its name implies, a one-shot timer will countdown from its initial value, call the callback function when it reaches zero, and stop. Figure 12-1 shows a timing diagram of this operation. The countdown is initiated by calling OSTmrStart(). At the completion of the time delay, the callback function is called, assuming a callback function was provided when the timer was created. Once completed, the timer does not do anything unless restarted by calling OSTmrStart(), at which point the process starts over.

Terminate the countdown process of a timer (before it reaches zero) by calling OSTmrStop(). In this case, specify that the callback function be called or not.

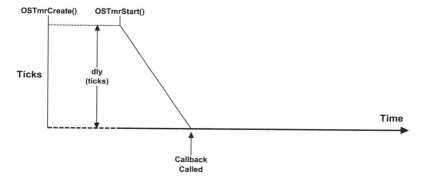

Figure 12-1 **One Shot Timers (dly > 0, period == 0)**

As shown in Figure 12-2, a one-shot timer is retriggered by calling OSTmrStart() before the timer reaches zero. This feature can be used to implement watchdogs and similar safeguards.

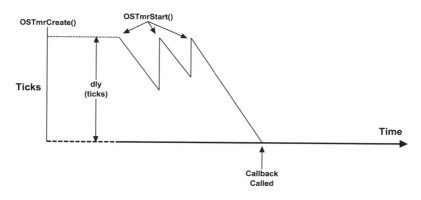

Figure 12-2 **Retriggering a One Shot Timer**

201

12-2 PERIODIC (NO INITIAL DELAY)

As indicated in Figure 12-3, timers can be configured for periodic mode. When the countdown expires, the callback function is called, the timer is automatically reloaded, and the process is repeated. If specifying a delay of zero (i.e., **dly == 0**) when the timer is created, when started, the timer immediately uses the "**period**" as the reload value. Calling **OSTmrStart()** at any point in the countdown restarts the process.

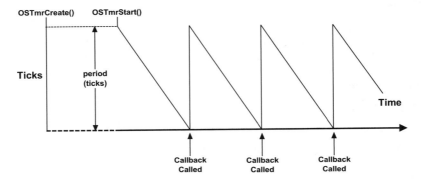

Figure 12-3 **Periodic Timers (dly == 0, period > 0)**

12-3 PERIODIC (WITH INITIAL DELAY)

As shown in Figure 12-4, timers can be configured for periodic mode with an initial delay that is different than its period. The first countdown count comes from the "**dly**" argument passed in the **OSTmrCreate()** call, and the reload value is the "**period**". Calling **OSTmrStart()** restarts the process including the initial delay.

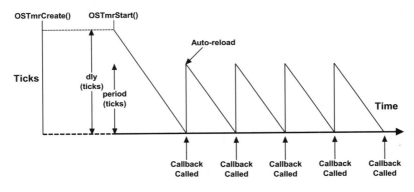

Figure 12-4 **Periodic Timers (dly > 0, period > 0)**

12-4 TIMER MANAGEMENT INTERNALS

12-4-1 TIMER MANAGEMENT INTERNALS - TIMERS STATES

Figure 12-5 shows the state diagram of a timer.

Tasks can call **OSTmrStateGet()** to find out the state of a timer. Also, at any time during the countdown process, the application code can call **OSTmrRemainGet()** to find out how much time remains before the timer reaches zero (0). The value returned is expressed in "timer ticks." If timers are decremented at a rate of 10 Hz then a count of 50 corresponds to 5 seconds. If the timer is in the stop state, the time remaining will correspond to either the initial delay (one shot or periodic with initial delay), or the period if the timer is configured for periodic without initial delay.

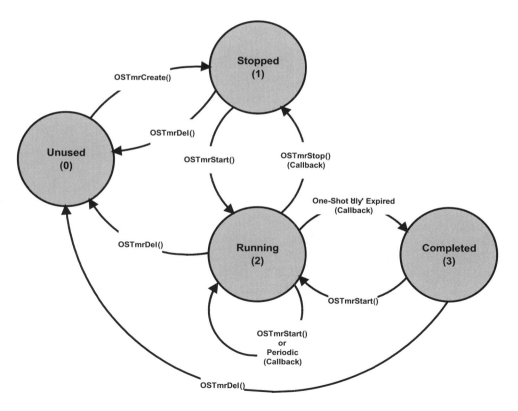

Figure 12-5 **Timer State Diagram**

F12-5(1)   The "Unused" state is a timer that has not been created or has been "deleted." In other words, µC/OS-III does not know about this timer.

F12-5(2)   When creating a timer or calling **OSTmrStop()**, the timer is placed in the "stopped" state.

F12-5(3)   A timer is placed in running state when calling **OSTmrStart()**. The timer stays in that state unless it's stopped, deleted, or completes its one shot.

F12-5(4)   The "Completed" state is the state a one-shot timer is in when its delay expires.

12-4-2 TIMER MANAGEMENT INTERNALS - OS_TMR

A timer is a kernel object as defined by the **OS_TMR** data type (see **OS.H**) as shown in Listing 12-1.

The services provided by µC/OS-III to manage timers are implemented in the file **OS_TMR.C**. A µC/OS-III licensee has access to the source code. In this case, timer services are enabled at compile time by setting the configuration constant **OS_CFG_TMR_EN** to 1 in **OS_CFG.H**.

```
    typedef  struct  os_tmr  OS_TMR;                (1)


struct  os_tmr {
    OS_OBJ_TYPE          Type;                      (2)
    CPU_CHAR             *NamePtr;                   (3)
    OS_TMR_CALLBACK_PTR  CallbackPtr;               (4)
    void                 *CallbackPtrArg;            (5)
    OS_TMR               *NextPtr;                   (6)
    OS_TMR               *PrevPtr;
    OS_TICK              Match;                      (7)
    OS_TICK              Remain;                     (8)
    OS_TICK              Dly;                        (9)
    OS_TICK              Period;                    (10)
    OS_OPT               Opt;                       (11)
    OS_STATE             State;                     (12)
};
```

Listing 12-1 **OS_TMR data type**

L12-1(1)   In µC/OS-III, all structures are given a data type. In fact, all data types start with "**OS_**" and are all uppercase. When a timer is declared, simply use **OS_TMR** as the data type of the variable used to declare the timer.

L12-1(2)   The structure starts with a "**Type**" field, which allows it to be recognized by µC/OS-III as a timer. Other kernel objects will also have a "**Type**" as the first member of the structure. If a function is passed a kernel object, µC/OS-III is able to confirm that it is passed the proper data type. For example, if passing a message queue (**OS_Q**) to a timer service (for example **OSTmrStart()**) then µC/OS-III will be able to recognize that an invalid object was passed, and return an error code accordingly.

L12-1(3)   Each kernel object can be given a name for easier recognition by debuggers or µC/Probe. This member is simply a pointer to an ASCII string which is assumed to be NUL terminated.

L12-1(4)   The **.CallbackPtr** member is a pointer to a function that is called when the timer expires. If a timer is created and passed a **NULL** pointer, a callback would not be called when the timer expires.

L12-1(5)   If there is a non-**NULL** **.CallbackPtr** then the application code could have also specified that the callback be called with an argument when the timer expires. This is the argument that would be passed in this call.

L12-1(6)   **.NextPtr** and **.PrevPtr** are pointers used to link a timer in a doubly linked list. These are described later.

L12-1(7)   A timer expires when the timer manager variable **OSTmrTickCtr** reaches the value stored in a timer's **.Match** field. This is also described later.

L12-1(8)   The **.Remain** contains the amount of time remaining for the timer to expire. This value is updated once per **OS_CFG_TMR_WHEEL_SIZE** (see **OS_CFG_APP.H**) that the timer task executes (described later). The value is expressed in multiples of **1/OS_CFG_TMR_TASK_RATE_HZ** of a second (see **OS_CFG_APP.H**).

12

L12-1(9)   The **.Dly** field contains the one-shot time when the timer is configured (i.e., created) as a one-shot timer and the initial delay when the timer is created as a periodic timer. The value is expressed in multiples of 1/**OS_CFG_TMR_TASK_RATE_HZ** of a second (see **OS_CFG_APP.H**).

L12-1(10)   The **.Period** is the timer period when the timer is created to operate in periodic mode. The value is expressed in multiples of 1/**OS_CFG_TMR_TASK_RATE_HZ** of a second (see **OS_CFG_APP.H**).

L12-1(11)   The **.Opt** field contains options as passed to **OSTmrCreate()**.

L12-1(12)   The **.State** field represents the current state of the timer (see Figure 12-5).

Even if the internals of the **OS_TMR** data type are understood, the application code should never access any of the fields in this data structure directly. Instead, always use the Application Programming Interfaces (APIs) provided with µC/OS-III.

12-4-3 TIMER MANAGEMENT INTERNALS - TIMER TASK

OS_TmrTask() is a task created by µC/OS-III (assumes setting **OS_CFG_TMR_EN** to 1 in **OS_CFG.H**) and its priority is configurable by the user through µC/OS-III's configuration file **OS_CFG_APP.H** (see **OS_CFG_TMR_TASK_PRIO**). **OS_TmrTask()** is typically set to a medium priority.

OS_TmrTask() is a periodic task and uses the same interrupt source used to generate clock ticks. However, timers are generally updated at a slower rate (i.e., typically 10 Hz or so) and thus, the timer tick rate is divided down in software. If the tick rate is 1000 Hz and the desired timer rate is 10 Hz then the timer task will be signaled every 100th tick interrupt as shown in Figure 12-6.

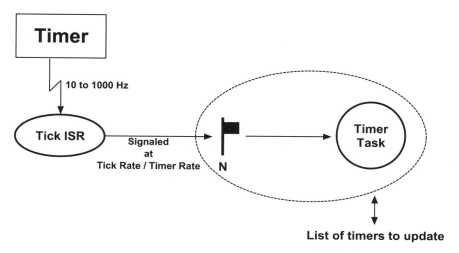

Figure 12-6 **Tick ISR and Timer Task relationship**

Figure 12-7 shows timing diagram associated with the timer management task.

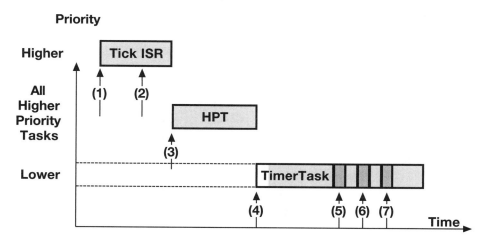

Figure 12-7 **Timing Diagram**

F12-7(1)   The tick ISR occurs and assumes interrupts are enabled and executes.

F12-7(2)   The tick ISR signals the tick task that it is time for it to update timers.

F12-7(3)   The tick ISR terminates, however there are higher priority tasks that need to execute (assuming the timer task has a lower priority). Therefore, µC/OS-III runs the higher priority task(s).

F12-7(4)   When all higher priority tasks have executed, µC/OS-III switches to the timer task and determines that there are three timers that expired.

F12-7(5)   The callback for the first timer is executed.

F12-7(6)   The callback for the second expired timer is executed.

F12-7(7)   The callback for the third expired timer is executed.

There are a few interesting things to notice:

■ Execution of the callback functions is performed within the context of the timer task. This means that the application code will need to make sure there is sufficient stack space for the timer task to handle these callbacks.

■ The callback functions are executed one after the other based on the order they are found in the timer list.

■ The execution time of the timer task greatly depends on how many timers expire and how long each of the callback functions takes to execute. Since the callbacks are provided by the application code they have a large influence on the execution time of the timer task.

■ The timer callback functions must never wait on events that would delay the timer task for excessive amounts of time, if not forever.

■ Callbacks are called with the scheduler locked, so you should ensure that callbacks execute as quickly as possible.

12-4-4 TIMER MANAGEMENT INTERNALS - TIMER LIST

µC/OS-III might need to literally maintain hundreds of timers (if an application requires that many). The timer list management needs to be implemented such that it does not take too much CPU time to update the timers. The timer list works similarly to a tick list as shown in Figure 12-8.

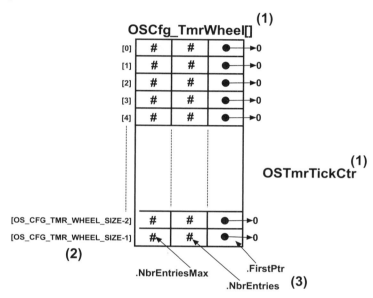

Figure 12-8 **Empty Timer List**

F12-8(1)   The timer list consists of a table (OSCfg_TmrWheel[]) and a counter (OSTmrTickCtr).

F12-8(2)   The table contains up to OS_CFG_TMR_WHEEL_SIZE entries, which is a compile time configuration value (see OS_CFG_APP.H). The number of entries depends on the amount of RAM available to the processor and the maximum number of timers in the application. A good starting point for OS_CFG_TMR_WHEEL_SIZE might be: #Timers/4. It is not recommended to make OS_CFG_TMR_WHEEL_SIZE an even multiple of the timer task rate. In other words, if the timer task is 10 Hz, avoid setting OS_CFG_TMR_WHEEL_SIZE to 10 or 100 (use 11 or 101 instead). Also, use prime numbers for the timer wheel size. Although it is not really possible to plan at compile time what will happen at run time, ideally the number of timers waiting in each entry of the table is distributed uniformly.

F12-8(3)   Each entry in the table contains three fields: **.NbrEntriesMax**, **.NbrEntries** and **.FirstPtr**. **.NbrEntries** indicates how many timers are linked to this table entry. **.NbrEntriesMax** keeps track of the highest number of entries in the table. Finally, **.FirstPtr** contains a pointer to a doubly linked list of timers (through the tasks **OS_TMR**) belonging into the list at that table position.

The counter is incremented by **OS_TmrTask()** every time the tick ISR signals the task.

Timers are inserted in the timer list by calling **OSTmrStart()**. However, a timer must be created before it can be used.

An example to illustrate the process of inserting a timer in the timer list is as follows. Let's assume that the timer list is completely empty, **OS_CFG_TMR_WHEEL_SIZE** is configured to 9, and the current value of **OSTmrTickCtr** is 12 as shown in Figure 12-9. A timer is placed in the timer list when calling **OSTmrStart()**, and assumes that the timer was created with a delay of 1 and that this timer will be a one-shot timer as follows:

```
OS_TMR  MyTmr1;
OS_TMR  MyTmr2;


void MyTask (void *p_arg)
{
    OS_ERR  err;


    while (DEF_ON) {
        :
        OSTmrCreate((OS_TMR              *)&MyTmr1,
                    (OS_CHAR             *)"My Timer #1",
                    (OS_TICK             )1,
                    (OS_TICK             )0,
                    (OS_OPT              )OS_OPT_TMR_ONE_SHOT,
                    (OS_TMR_CALLBACK_PTR )0;
                    (OS_ERR              *)&err;
        /* Check 'err" */
        OSTmrStart ((OS_TMR *)&MyTmr1,
                    (OS_ERR *)&err);
        /* Check "err" */
        // Continues in the next code listing!
```

Listing 12-2 **Creating and Starting a timer**

Since **OSTmrTickCtr** has a value of 12, the timer will expire when **OSTmrTickCtr** reaches 13, or during the next time the timer task is signaled. Timers are inserted in the **OSCfg_TmrWheel[]** table using the following equation:

```
MatchValue                    = OSTmrTickCtr + dly
Index into OSCfg_TmrWheel[]   = MatchValue % OS_CFG_TMR_WHEEL_SIZE
```

Where "**dly**" (in this example) is the value passed in the third argument of **OSTmrCreate()** (i.e., 1 in this example). Again, using the example, we arrive at the following:

```
MatchValue                    = 12 + 1
Index into OSCfg_TickWheel[]  = 13 % 9
```

or,

```
MatchValue                    = 13
Index into OSCfg_TickWheel[]  = 4
```

Because of the "circular" nature of the table (a modulo operation using the size of the table), the table is referred to as a timer wheel, and each entry is a spoke in the wheel.

The timer is entered at index 4 in the timer wheel, **OSCfg_TmrWheel[]**. In this case, the **OS_TMR** is placed at the head of the list (i.e., pointed to by **OSCfg_TmrWheel[4].FirstPtr**), and the number of entries at index 4 is incremented (i.e., **OSCfg_TmrWheel[4].NbrEntries** will be 1). "**MatchValue**" is placed in the **OS_TMR** field **.Match**. Since this is the first timer inserted in the timer list at index 4, the **.NextPtr** and **.PrevPtr** both point to **NULL**.

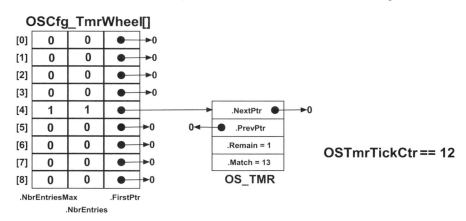

Figure 12-9 **Inserting a timer in the timer list**

211

The code below shows creating and starting another timer. This is performed "before" the timer task is signaled.

```
// Continuation of code from previous code listing.
:
:
OSTmrCreate((OS_TMR                *)&MyTmr2,
            (OS_CHAR               *)"My Timer #2",
            (OS_TICK               )10,
            (OS_TICK               )0,
            (OS_OPT                )OS_OPT_TMR_ONE_SHOT,
            (OS_TMR_CALLBACK_PTR)0;
            (OS_ERR                *)&err;
    /* Check 'err" */
OSTmrStart ((OS_TMR *)&MyTmr,
            (OS_ERR *)&err);
    /* Check 'err" */
    }
}
```

Listing 12-3 **Creating and Starting a timer - continued**

µC/OS-III will calculate the match value and index as follows:

```
MatchValue                  = 12 + 10
Index into OSCfg_TmrWheel[] = 22 % 9
```

or,

```
MatchValue                  = 22
Index into OSCfg_TickWheel[] =  4
```

The "second timer" will be inserted at the same table entry as shown in Figure 12-10, but sorted so that the timer with the least amount of time remaining before expiration is placed at the head of the list, and the timer with the longest to wait at the end.

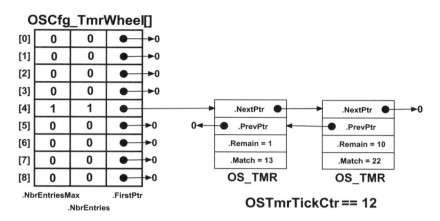

Figure 12-10 **Inserting a second timer in the tick list**

When the timer task executes (see `OS_TmrTask()` in `OS_TMR.C`), it starts by incrementing `OSTmrTickCtr` and determines which table entry (i.e., spoke) it needs to update. Then, if there are timers in the list at this entry (i.e., `.FirstPtr` is not `NULL`), each `OS_TMR` is examined to determine whether the `.Match` value "matches" `OSTmrTickCtr` and, if so, the `OS_TMR` is removed from the list and `OS_TmrTask()` calls the timer callback function, assuming one was defined when the timer was created. The search through the list terminates as soon as `OSTmrTickCtr` does not match the timer's `.Match` value. There is no point in looking any further in the list since the list is already sorted.

Note that `OS_TmrTask()` does most of its work with the scheduler locked. However, because the list is sorted, and the search through the list terminates as soon as there no longer is a match, the critical section should be fairly short.

12-5 SUMMARY

Timers are down counters that perform an action when the counter reaches zero. The action is provided by the user through a callback function.

µC/OS-III allows application code to create any number of timers (limited only by the amount of RAM available).

The callback functions are executed in the context of the timer task with the scheduler locked. Keep callback functions as short and as fast as possible and do not have the callbacks make blocking calls.

13

Resource Management

This chapter will discuss services provided by µC/OS-III to manage shared resources. A shared resource is typically a variable (static or global), a data structure, table (in RAM), or registers in an I/O device.

When protecting a shared resource it is preferred to use mutual exclusion semaphores, as will be described in this chapter. Other methods are also presented.

Tasks can easily share data when all tasks exist in a single address space and can reference global variables, pointers, buffers, linked lists, ring buffers, etc. Although sharing data simplifies the exchange of information between tasks, it is important to ensure that each task has exclusive access to the data to avoid contention and data corruption.

For example, when implementing a module that performs a simple time-of-day algorithm in software, the module obviously keeps track of hours, minutes and seconds. The **TimeOfDay()** task may appear as that shown in Listing 13-1.

Imagine if this task was preempted by another task because an interrupt occurred, and, the other task was more important than the **TimeOfDay()** task) after setting the Minutes to 0. Now imagine what will happen if this higher priority task wants to know the current time from the time-of-day module. Since the Hours were not incremented prior to the interrupt, the higher-priority task will read the time incorrectly and, in this case, it will be incorrect by a whole hour.

The code that updates variables for the **TimeOfDay()** task must treat all of the variables indivisibly (or atomically) whenever there is possible preemption. Time-of-day variables are considered shared resources and any code that accesses those variables must have exclusive access through what is called a critical section. µC/OS-III provides services to protect shared resources and enables the easy creation of critical sections.

```
CPU_INT08U  Hours;
CPU_INT08U  Minutes;
CPU_INT08U  Seconds;


void  TimeOfDay (void *p_arg)
{
    OS_ERR  err;


    (void)&p_arg;
    while (DEF_ON) {
        OSTimeDlyHMSM(0,
                      0,
                      1,
                      0,
                      OS_OPT_TIME_HMSM_STRICT,
                      &err);
        /* Examine "err" to make sure the call was successful */
        Seconds++;
        if (Seconds > 59) {
            Seconds = 0;
            Minutes++;
            if (Minutes > 59) {
                Minutes = 0;
                Hours++;
                if (Hours > 23) {
                    Hours = 0;
                }
            }
        }
    }
}
```

Listing 13-1 **Faulty Time-Of-Day clock task**

The most common methods of obtaining exclusive access to shared resources and to create *critical sections* are:

■ disabling interrupts

■ disabling the scheduler

■ using semaphores

■ using mutual exclusion semaphores (a.k.a. a mutex)

The mutual exclusion mechanism used depends on how fast the code will access a shared resource, as shown in Table 13-1.

Resource Sharing Method	When should you use?
Disable/Enable Interrupts	When access to shared resource is very quick (reading from or writing to few variables) and access is faster than µC/OS-III's interrupt disable time. It is highly recommended to not use this method as it impacts interrupt latency.
Locking/Unlocking the Scheduler	When access time to the shared resource is longer than µC/OS-III's interrupt disable time, but shorter than µC/OS-III's scheduler lock time. Locking the scheduler has the same effect as making the task that locks the scheduler the highest-priority task. It is recommended not to use this method since it defeats the purpose of using µC/OS-III. However, it is a better method than disabling interrupts, as it does not impact interrupt latency.
Semaphores	When all tasks that need to access a shared resource do not have deadlines. This is because semaphores may cause unbounded priority inversions (described later). However, semaphore services are slightly faster (in execution time) than mutual-exclusion semaphores.
Mutual Exclusion Semaphores	This is the preferred method for accessing shared resources, especially if the tasks that need to access a shared resource have deadlines. Remember that µC/OS-III's mutual exclusion semaphores have a built-in priority inheritance mechanism, which avoids unbounded priority inversions. However, mutual exclusion semaphore services are slightly slower (in execution time) than semaphores since the priority of the owner may need to be changed, which requires CPU processing.

13

Table 13-1 **Resource sharing**

13-1 DISABLE/ENABLE INTERRUPTS

The easiest and fastest way to gain exclusive access to a shared resource is by disabling and enabling interrupts, as shown in the pseudo-code in Listing 13-2.

```
Disable Interrupts;
Access the resource;
Enable  Interrupts;
```

Listing 13-2 **Disabling and Enabling Interrupts**

µC/OS-III uses this technique (as do most, if not all, kernels) to access certain internal variables and data structures, ensuring that these variables and data structures are manipulated atomically. However, disabling and enabling interrupts are actually CPU-related functions rather than OS-related functions and functions in CPU-specific files are provided to accomplish this (see the CPU.H file of the processor being used). The services provided in the CPU module are called µC/CPU. Each different target CPU architecture has its own set of µC/CPU-related files.

```
void OS_Function (void)
{
    CPU_SR_ALLOC();             (1)


    CPU_CRITICAL_ENTER();       (2)
    Access the resource;        (3)
    CPU_CRITICAL_EXIT();        (4)
}
```

Listing 13-3 **Using CPU macros to disable and enable interrupts**

L13-3(1)   The **CPU_SR_ALLOC()** macro is required when the other two macros that disable/enable interrupts are used. This macro simply allocates storage for a local variable to hold the value of the current interrupt disable status of the CPU. If interrupts are already disabled we do not want to enable them upon exiting the critical section.

L13-3(2)   **CPU_CRITICAL_ENTER()** saves the current state of the CPU interrupt disable
flag(s) in the local variable allocated by **CPU_SR_ALLOC()** and disables all
maskable interrupts.

L13-3(3)   The critical section of code is then accessed without fear of being changed by
either an ISR or another task because interrupts are disabled. In other words,
this operation is now atomic.

L13-3(4)   **CPU_CRITICAL_EXIT()** restores the previously saved interrupt disable status of
the CPU from the local variable.

CPU_CRITICAL_ENTER() and **CPU_CRITICAL_EXIT()** are always used in pairs. Interrupts
should be disabled for as short a time as possible as disabling interrupts impacts the
response of the system to interrupts. This is known as interrupt latency. Disabling and
enabling is used only when changing or copying a few variables.

Note, this is the only way that a task can share variables or data structures with an ISR.
µC/CPU provides a way to actually measure interrupt latency.

When using µC/OS-III, interrupts may be disabled for as much time as µC/OS-III does,
without affecting *interrupt latency*. Obviously, it is important to know how long µC/OS-III
disables interrupts, which depends on the CPU used.

Although this method works, avoid disabling interrupts as it affects the responsiveness of
the system to real-time events.

13

13-2 LOCK/UNLOCK

If the task does not share variables or data structures with an ISR, disable and enable μC/OS-III's scheduler while accessing the resource, as shown in Listing 13-4.

```
void OS_Function (void)
{
    CPU_SR_ALLOC();                 (1)
    CPU_CRITICAL_ENTER();           (2)
    Access the resource;            (3)
    CPU_CRITICAL_EXIT();            (4)
}
```

Listing 13-4 **Accessing a resource with the scheduler locked**

Using this method, two or more tasks share data without the possibility of contention. Note that while the scheduler is locked, interrupts are enabled and if an interrupt occurs while in the critical section, the ISR is executed immediately. At the end of the ISR, the kernel always returns to the interrupted task even if a higher priority task is made ready to run by the ISR. Since the ISR returns to the interrupted task, the behavior of the kernel is similar to that of a non-preemptive kernel (while the scheduler is locked).

OSSchedLock() and OSSchedUnlock() can be nested up to 250 levels deep. The scheduler is invoked only when OSSchedUnlock() is called the same number of times the application called OSSchedLock().

After the scheduler is unlocked, μC/OS-III performs a context switch if a higher priority task is ready to run.

μC/OS-III will not allow the user to make blocking calls when the scheduler is locked. If the application were able to make blocking calls, the application would most likely fail.

Although this method works well, avoid disabling the scheduler as it defeats the purpose of having a preemptive kernel. Locking the scheduler makes the current task the highest priority task.

13-3 SEMAPHORES

A semaphore originally was a mechanical signaling mechanism. The railroad industry used the device to provide a form of mutual exclusion for railroads tracks shared by more than one train. In this form, the semaphore signaled trains by closing a set of mechanical arms to block a train from a section of track that was currently in use. When the track became available, the arm would swing up and the waiting train would then proceed.

The notion of using a semaphore in software as a means of synchronization was invented by the Dutch computer scientist Edgser Dijkstra in 1959. In computer software, a semaphore is a protocol mechanism offered by most multitasking kernels. Semaphores, originally used to control access to shared resources, now are used for synchronization as described in Chapter 14, "Synchronization" on page 257. However, it is useful to describe how semaphores can be used to share resources. The pitfalls of semaphores will be discussed in a later section.

A semaphore was originally a "lock mechanism" and code acquired the key to this lock to continue execution. Acquiring the key means that the executing task has permission to enter the section of otherwise locked code. Entering a section of locked code causes the task to wait until the key becomes available.

Typically, two types of semaphores exist: binary semaphores and counting semaphores. As its name implies, a binary semaphore can only take two values: 0 or 1. A counting semaphore allows for values between 0 and 255, 65,535, or 4,294,967,295, depending on whether the semaphore mechanism is implemented using 8, 16, or 32 bits, respectively. For μC/OS-III, the maximum value of a semaphore is determined by the data type **OS_SEM_CTR** (see **OS_TYPE.H**), which can be changed as needed (assuming μC/OS-III's source code is available). Along with the semaphore's value, μC/OS-III also keeps track of tasks waiting for the semaphore's availability.

Only tasks are allowed to use semaphores when semaphores are used for sharing resources; ISRs are not allowed.

A semaphore is a kernel object defined by the **OS_SEM** data type, which is defined by the structure os_sem (see **OS.H**). The application can have any number of semaphores (limited only by the amount of RAM available).

13

There are a number of operations the application is able to perform on semaphores, summarized in Table 13-2. In this chapter, only three functions used most often are discussed: **OSSemCreate()**, **OSSemPend()**, and **OSSemPost()**. Other functions are described in Appendix A, "µC/OS-III API Reference Manual" on page 381. When semaphores are used for sharing resources, every semaphore function must be called from a task and never from an ISR. The same limitation does not apply when using semaphores for signaling, as described later in Chapter 13.

Function Name	Operation
OSSemCreate()	Create a semaphore.
OSSemDel()	Delete a semaphore.
OSSemPend()	Wait on a semaphore.
OSSemPendAbort()	Abort the wait on a semaphore.
OSSemPost()	Release or signal a semaphore.
OSSemSet()	Force the semaphore count to a desired value.

Table 13-2 **Semaphore API summary**

13-3-1 BINARY SEMAPHORES

A task that wants to acquire a resource must perform a Wait (or Pend) operation. If the semaphore is available (the semaphore value is greater than 0), the semaphore value is decremented, and the task continues execution (owning the resource). If the semaphore's value is 0, the task performing a Wait on the semaphore is placed in a waiting list. µC/OS-III allows a timeout to be specified. If the semaphore is not available within a certain amount of time, the requesting task is made ready to run, and an error code (indicating that a timeout has occurred) is returned to the caller.

A task releases a semaphore by performing a Signal (or Post) operation. If no task is waiting for the semaphore, the semaphore value is simply incremented. If there is at least one task waiting for the semaphore, the highest-priority task waiting on the semaphore is made ready to run, and the semaphore value is not incremented. If the readied task has a higher priority than the current task (the task releasing the semaphore), a context switch occurs and the higher-priority task resumes execution. The current task is suspended until it again becomes the highest-priority task that is ready to run.

The operations described above are summarized using the pseudo-code shown in Listing 13-5.

```
OS_SEM  MySem;                             (1)


void  main (void)
{
    OS_ERR  err;
    :
    :
    OSInit(&err);
    :
    OSSemCreate(&MySem,                    (2)
                "My Semaphore",            (3)
                1,                         (4)
                &err);                     (5)
    /* Check "err" */
    :
    /* Create task(s) */
    :
    OSStart(&err);
    (void)err;
}
```

Listing 13-5 **Using a semaphore to access a shared resource**

L13-5(1)   The application must declare a semaphore as a variable of type **OS_SEM**. This variable will be referenced by other semaphore services.

L13-5(2)   Create a semaphore by calling **OSSemCreate()** and pass the address to the semaphore allocated in (1). The semaphore must be created before it can be used by other tasks. Here, the semaphore is initialized in startup code (i.e., **main ()**), however it could also be initialized by a task (but it must be initialized before it is used).

L13-5(3)   Assign an ASCII name to the semaphore, which can be used by debuggers or µC/Probe to easily identify the semaphore. Storage for the ASCII characters is typically in ROM, which is typically more plentiful than RAM. If it is necessary to change the name of the semaphore at runtime, store the characters in an array in RAM and simply pass the address of the array to **OSSemCreate()**. Of course, the array must be NUL terminated.

L13-5(4)   Specify the initial value of the semaphore. Initialize the semaphore to 1 when the semaphore is used to access a single shared resource (as in this example).

L13-5(5)   **OSSemCreate()** returns an error code based on the outcome of the call. If all the arguments are valid, err will contain **OS_ERR_NONE**. Refer to the description of **OSSemCreate()** in Appendix A, "µC/OS-III API Reference Manual" on page 381 for a list of other error codes and their meaning.

```
void Task1 (void *p_arg)
{
    OS_ERR   err;
    CPU_TS   ts;


    while (DEF_ON) {
        :
        OSSemPend(&MySem,                      (6)
                  0,                           (7)
                  OS_OPT_PEND_BLOCKING,        (8)
                  &ts,                         (9)
                  &err);                       (10)
        switch (err) {
            case OS_ERR_NONE:
                Access Shared Resource;        (11)
                OSSemPost(&MySem,              (12)
                          OS_OPT_POST_1,       (13)
                          &err);               (14)
                /* Check "err" */
                break;

            case OS_ERR_PEND_ABORT:
                /* The pend was aborted by another task    */
                break;

            case OS_ERR_OBJ_DEL:
                /* The semaphore was deleted               */
                break;

            default:
                /* Other errors                            */
        }
        :
    }
}
```

Listing 13-6 **Using a semaphore to access a shared resource**

L13-6(6)   The task pends (or waits) on the semaphore by calling **OSSemPend()**. The application must specify the desired semaphore to wait upon, and the semaphore must have been previously created.

L13-6(7)   The next argument is a timeout specified in number of clock ticks. The actual timeout depends on the tick rate. If the tick rate (see **OS_CFG_APP.H**) is set to 1000, a timeout of 10 ticks represents 10 milliseconds. Specifying a timeout of zero (0) means waiting forever for the semaphore.

L13-6(8)   The third argument specifies how to wait. There are two options: **OS_OPT_PEND_BLOCKING** and **OS_OPT_PEND_NON_BLOCKING**. The blocking option means that if the semaphore is not available, the task calling **OSSemPend()** will wait until the semaphore is posted or until the timeout expires. The non-blocking option indicates that if the semaphore is not available, **OSSemPend()** will return immediately and not wait. This last option is rarely used when using a semaphore to protect a shared resource.

L13-6(9)   When the semaphore is posted, μC/OS-III reads a "timestamp" and returns this timestamp when **OSSemPend()** returns. This feature allows the application to know "when" the post happened and the semaphore was released. At this point, **OS_TS_GET()** is read to get the current timestamp and compute the difference, indicating the length of the wait.

L13-6(10)   **OSSemPend()** returns an error code based on the outcome of the call. If the call is successful, err will contain **OS_ERR_NONE**. If not, the error code will indicate the reason for the error. See Appendix A, "μC/OS-III API Reference Manual" on page 381 for a list of possible error code for **OSSemPend()**. Checking for error return values is important since other tasks might delete or otherwise abort the pend. However, it is not a recommended practice to delete kernel objects at run time as the action may cause serious problems.

L13-6(11)   The resource can be accessed when **OSSemPend()** returns, if there are no errors.

L13-6(12)   When finished accessing the resource, simply call **OSSemPost()** and specify the semaphore to be released.

L13-6(13)   **OS_OPT_POST_1** indicates that the semaphore is signaling a single task, if there are many tasks waiting on the semaphore. In fact, always specify this option when a semaphore is used to access a shared resource.

L13-6(14)   As with most μC/OS-III functions, specify the address of a variable that will receive an error message from the call.

```
void  Task2 (void *p_arg)
{
    OS_ERR   err;
    CPU_TS   ts;


    while (DEF_ON) {
        :
        OSSemPend(&MySem,                          (15)
                  0,
                  OS_OPT_PEND_BLOCKING,
                  &ts,
                  &err);
        switch (err) {
            case OS_ERR_NONE:
                Access Shared Resource;
                OSSemPost(&MySem,
                          OS_OPT_POST_1,
                          &err);
                /* Check "err" */
                break;

            case OS_ERR_PEND_ABORT:
                /* The pend was aborted by another task    */
                break;

            case OS_ERR_OBJ_DEL:
                /* The semaphore was deleted                */
                break;

            default:
                /* Other errors                            */
        }
        :
    }
}
```

Listing 13-7 **Using a semaphore to access a shared resource**

L13-7(15)   Another task wanting to access the shared resource needs to use the same procedure to access the shared resource.

Semaphores are especially useful when tasks share I/O devices. Imagine what would happen if two tasks were allowed to send characters to a printer at the same time. The printer would contain interleaved data from each task. For instance, the printout from Task 1 printing "I am Task 1," and Task 2 printing "I am Task 2," could result in "I Ia amm T Tasask k1 2". In this case, use a semaphore and initialize it to 1 (i.e., a binary semaphore). The rule is simple: to access the printer each task must first obtain the resource's semaphore. Figure 13-1 shows tasks competing for a semaphore to gain exclusive access to the printer. Note that a key, indicating that each task must obtain this key to use the printer, represents the semaphore symbolically.

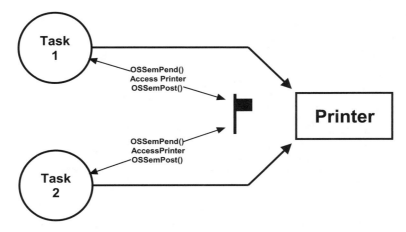

Figure 13-1 **Using a semaphore to access a printer**

The above example implies that each task knows about the existence of the semaphore to access the resource. It is almost always better to encapsulate the critical section and its protection mechanism. Each task would therefore not know that it is acquiring a semaphore when accessing the resource. For example, an RS-232C port is used by multiple tasks to send commands and receive responses from a device connected at the other end as shown in Figure 13-2.

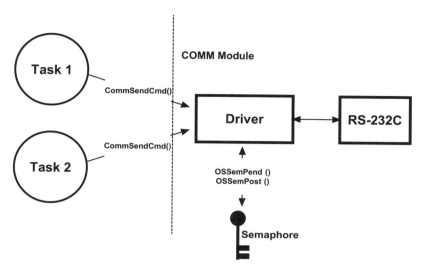

Figure 13-2 **Hiding a semaphore from a task**

The function **CommSendCmd()** is called with three arguments: the ASCII string containing the command, a pointer to the response string from the device, and finally, a timeout in case the device does not respond within a certain amount of time. The pseudo-code for this function is shown in Listing 13-8.

```
APP_ERR  CommSendCmd (CPU_CHAR  *cmd,
                      CPU_CHAR  *response,
                      OS_TICK    timeout)
{
    Acquire serial port's semaphore;
    Send "cmd" to device;
    Wait for response with "timeout";
    if (timed out) {
        Release serial port's semaphore;
        return (error code);
    } else {
        Release serial port's semaphore;
        return (no error);
    }
}
```

Listing 13-8 **Encapsulating the use of a semaphore**

Each task that needs to send a command to the device must call this function. The semaphore is assumed to be initialized to 1 (i.e., available) by the communication driver initialization routine. The first task that calls CommSendCmd() acquires the semaphore, proceeds to send the command, and waits for a response. If another task attempts to send a command while the port is busy, this second task is suspended until the semaphore is released. The second task appears simply to have made a call to a normal function that will not return until the function performs its duty. When the semaphore is released by the first task, the second task acquires the semaphore and is allowed to use the RS-232C port.

13-3-2 COUNTING SEMAPHORES

A counting semaphore is used when elements of a resource can be used by more than one task at the same time. For example, a counting semaphore is used in the management of a buffer pool, as shown in Figure 13-3. Assume that the buffer pool initially contains 10 buffers. A task obtains a buffer from the buffer manager by calling BufReq(). When the buffer is no longer needed, the task returns the buffer to the buffer manager by calling BufRel(). The pseudo-code for these functions is shown in Listing 13-9.

The buffer manager satisfies the first 10 buffer requests because the semaphore is initialized to 10. When all buffers are used, a task requesting a buffer is suspended until a buffer becomes available. Use µC/OS-III's OSMemGet() and OSMemPut() (see Chapter 17, "Memory Management" on page 329) to obtain a buffer from the buffer pool. When a task is finished with the buffer it acquired, the task calls BufRel() to return the buffer to the buffer manager and the buffer is inserted into the linked list before the semaphore is signaled. By encapsulating the interface to the buffer manager in BufReq() and BufRel(), the caller does not need to be concerned with actual implementation details.

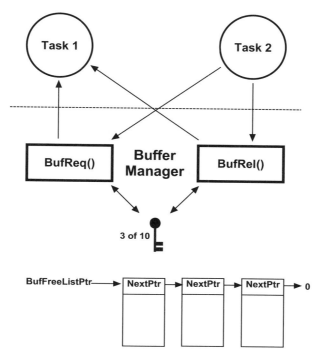

Figure 13-3 **Using a counting semaphore**

```
BUF  *BufReq (void)
{
    BUF  *ptr;



    Wait on semaphore;
    ptr = OSMemGet(...) ;               /* Get a buffer      */
    return (ptr);
}



void  BufRel (BUF *ptr)
{
    OSMemPut(..., (void *)ptr, ...);    /* Return the buffer */
    Signal semaphore;
}
```

Listing 13-9 **Buffer management using a semaphore.**

13

Note that the details of creating the memory partition are removed since this is discussed in Chapter 17, "Memory Management" on page 329. The semaphore is used here to extend the memory management capabilities of µC/OS-III, and to provide it with a blocking mechanism. However, only tasks can make `BufReq()` and `BufRel()` calls.

13-3-3 NOTES ON SEMAPHORES

Using a semaphore to access a shared resource does not increase interrupt latency. If an ISR or the current task makes a higher priority task ready to run while accessing shared data, the higher priority task executes immediately.

An application may have as many semaphores as required to protect a variety of different resources. For example, one semaphore may be used to access a shared display, another to access a shared printer, another for shared data structures, and another to protect a pool of buffers, etc. However, it is preferable to use semaphores to protect access to I/O devices rather than memory locations.

Semaphores are often overused. The use of a semaphore to access a simple shared variable is overkill in most situations. The overhead involved in acquiring and releasing the semaphore consumes valuable CPU time. Perform the job more efficiently by disabling and enabling interrupts, however there is an indirect cost to disabling interrupts: even higher priority tasks that do not share the specific resource are blocked from using the CPU. Suppose, for instance, that two tasks share a 32-bit integer variable. The first task increments the variable, while the second task clears it. When considering how long a processor takes to perform either operation, it is easy to see that a semaphore is not required to gain exclusive access to the variable. Each task simply needs to disable interrupts before performing its operation on the variable and enable interrupts when the operation is complete. A semaphore should be used if the variable is a floating-point variable and the microprocessor does not support hardware floating-point operations. In this case, the time involved in processing the floating-point variable may affect interrupt latency if interrupts are disabled.

Semaphores are subject to a serious problem in real-time systems called priority inversion, which is described in section 13-3-5 "Priority Inversions" on page 238.

13-3-4 SEMAPHORE INTERNALS (FOR RESOURCE SHARING)

As previously mentioned, a semaphore is a kernel object as defined by the **OS_SEM** data type, which is derived from the structure **os_sem** (see **OS.H**) as shown in Listing 13-10.

The services provided by µC/OS-III to manage semaphores are implemented in the file **OS_SEM.C**. µC/OS-III licensees have access to the source code. In this case, semaphore services are enabled at compile time by setting the configuration constant **OS_CFG_SEM_EN** to 1 in **OS_CFG.H**.

```
typedef  struct  os_sem  OS_SEM;                    (1)


struct  os_sem {
    OS_OBJ_TYPE            Type;                     (2)
    CPU_CHAR              *NamePtr;                  (3)
    OS_PEND_LIST          PendList;                  (4)
    OS_SEM_CTR            Ctr;                       (5)
    CPU_TS                TS;                        (6)
};
```

Listing 13-10 **OS_SEM data type**

L13-10(1)   In µC/OS-III, all structures are given a data type. All data types start with "**OS_**" and are uppercase. When a semaphore is declared, simply use **OS_SEM** as the data type of the variable used to declare the semaphore.

L13-10(2)   The structure starts with a "Type" field, which allows it to be recognized by µC/OS-III as a semaphore. Other kernel objects will also have a ".**Type**" as the first member of the structure. If a function is passed a kernel object, µC/OS-III will confirm that it is being passed the proper data type. For example, if passing a message queue (**OS_Q**) to a semaphore service (for example **OSSemPend()**), µC/OS-III will recognize that an invalid object was passed, and return an error code accordingly.

L13-10(3)   Each kernel object can be given a name for easier recognition by debuggers or µC/Probe. This member is simply a pointer to an ASCII string, which is assumed to be NUL terminated.

L13-10(4)   Since it is possible for multiple tasks to wait (or pend) on a semaphore, the semaphore object contains a pend list as described in Chapter 10, "Pend Lists (or Wait Lists)" on page 183.

L13-10(5)   A semaphore contains a counter. As explained above, the counter can be implemented as either an 8-, 16- or 32-bit value, depending on how the data type **OS_SEM_CTR** is declared in **OS_TYPE.H**.

µC/OS-III does not make a distinction between binary and counting semaphores. The distinction is made when the semaphore is created. If creating a semaphore with an initial value of 1, it is a binary semaphore. When creating a semaphore with a value > 1, it is a counting semaphore. In the next chapter, we discover that a semaphore is more often used as a signaling mechanism and therefore, the semaphore counter is initialized to zero.

L13-10(6)   A semaphore contains a timestamp used to indicate the last time the semaphore was posted. µC/OS-III assumes the presence of a free-running counter that allows the application to make time measurements. When the semaphore is posted, the free-running counter is read and the value is placed in this field, which is returned when **OSSemPend()** is called. The value of this field is more useful when a semaphore is used as a signaling mechanism (see Chapter 14, "Synchronization" on page 257), as opposed to a resource-sharing mechanism.

Even if the user understands the internals of the **OS_SEM** data type, the application code should never access any of the fields in this data structure directly. Instead, always use the APIs provided with µC/OS-III.

As previously mentioned, semaphores must be created before they can be used by an application.

A task waits on a semaphore before accessing a shared resource by calling **OSSemPend()** as shown in Listing 13-11 (see Appendix A, "µC/OS-III API Reference Manual" on page 381 for details regarding the arguments).

```
OS_SEM  MySem;


void MyTask (void *p_arg)
{
    OS_ERR   err;
    CPU_TS   ts;

    :
    while (DEF_ON) {
        :
        OSSemPend(&MySem,                 /* (1) Pointer to semaphore                     */
                 10,                      /*     Wait up until this time for the semaphore */
                 OS_OPT_PEND_BLOCKING, /*     Option(s)                                */
                 &ts,                     /*     Returned timestamp of when sem. was released */
                 &err);                   /*     Pointer to Error returned                */
        :
        /* Check "err" */                 /* (2)                                          */
        :
        OSSemPost(&MySem,                 /* (3) Pointer to semaphore                     */
                 OS_OPT_POST_1,           /*     Option(s) … always OS_OPT_POST_1         */
                 &err);                   /*     Pointer to Error returned                */
        /* Check "err" */
        :
        :

    }
}
```

Listing 13-11 **Pending on and Posting to a Semaphore**

L13-11(1)   When called, **OSSemPend()** starts by checking the arguments passed to this
function to make sure they have valid values.

If the semaphore counter (**.Ctr** of **OS_SEM**) is greater than zero, the counter is
decremented and **OSSemPend()** returns. If **OSSemPend()** returns without error,
then the task now owns the shared resource.

When the semaphore counter is zero, this indicates that another task owns the
semaphore, and the calling task may need to wait for the semaphore to be
released. If specifying **OS_OPT_PEND_NON_BLOCKING** as the option (the
application does not want the task to block), **OSSemPend()** returns immediately
to the caller and the returned error code indicates that the semaphore is
unavailable. Use this option if the task does not want to wait for the resource to
be available, and would prefer to do something else and check back later.

If specifying the OS_OPT_PEND_BLOCKING option, the calling task will be inserted in the list of tasks waiting for the semaphore to become available. The task is inserted in the list by priority order and therefore, the highest priority task waiting on the semaphore is at the beginning of the list.

If specifying a non-zero timeout, the task will also be inserted in the tick list. A zero value for a timeout indicates that the user is willing to wait forever for the semaphore to be released. Most of the time, specify an infinite timeout when using the semaphore in resource sharing. Adding a timeout may temporarily break a deadlock, however, there are better ways of preventing deadlock at the application level (e.g., never hold more than one semaphore at the same time; resource ordering; etc.).

The scheduler is called since the current task is no longer able to run (it is waiting for the semaphore to be released). The scheduler will then run the next highest-priority task that is ready to run.

When the semaphore is released and the task that called OSSemPend() is again the highest-priority task, µC/OS-III examines the task status to determine the reason why OSSemPend() is returning to its caller. The possibilities are:

1) The semaphore was given to the waiting task

2) The pend was aborted by another task

3) The semaphore was not posted within the specified timeout

4) The semaphore was deleted

When OSSemPend() returns, the caller is notified of the above outcome through an appropriate error code.

L13-11(2)   If **OSSemPend()** returns with err set to **OS_ERR_NONE**, assume that you now have access to the resource.

If err contains anything else, **OSSemPend()** either timed out (if the timeout argument was non-zero), the pend was aborted by another task, or the semaphore was deleted by another task. It is always important to examine the returned error code and not assume that everything went well.

L13-11(3)   When the task is finished accessing the resource, it needs to call **OSSemPost()** and specify the same semaphore. Again, **OSSemPost()** starts by checking the arguments passed to this function to make sure there are valid values.

OSSemPost() then calls **OS_TS_GET()** to obtain the current timestamp so it can place that information in the semaphore to be used by **OSSemPend()**.

OSSemPost() checks to see if any tasks are waiting for the semaphore. If not, **OSSemPost()** simply increments **p_sem->Ctr**, saves the timestamp in the semaphore, and returns.

If there are tasks waiting for the semaphore to be released, **OSSemPost()** extracts the highest-priority task waiting for the semaphore. This is a fast operation as the pend list is sorted by priority order.

When calling **OSSemPost()**, it is possible to specify as an option to not call the scheduler. This means that the post is performed, but the scheduler is not called even if a higher priority task waits for the semaphore to be released. This allows the calling task to perform other post functions (if needed) and make all posts take effect simultaneously without the possibility of context switching in between each post.

13

13-3-5 PRIORITY INVERSIONS

Priority inversion is a problem in real-time systems, and occurs only when using a priority-based preemptive kernel. Figure 13-4 illustrates a priority-inversion scenario. Task H (high priority) has a higher priority than Task M (medium priority), which in turn has a higher priority than Task L (low priority).

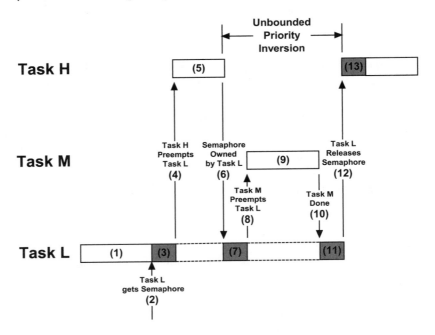

Figure 13-4 **Unbounded priority Inversion**

F13-4(1)   Task H and Task M are both waiting for an event to occur and Task L is executing.

F13-4(2)   At some point, Task L acquires a semaphore, which it needs before it can access a shared resource.

F13-4(3)   Task L performs operations on the acquired resource.

F13-4(4)   The event that Task H was waiting for occurs, and the kernel suspends Task L and start executing Task H since Task H has a higher priority.

F13-4(5)   Task H performs computations based on the event it just received.

F13-4(6)   Task H now wants to access the resource that Task L currently owns (i.e., it attempts to get the semaphore that Task L owns). Because Task L owns the resource, Task H is placed in a list of tasks waiting for the semaphore to be free.

F13-4(7)   Task L is resumed and continues to access the shared resource.

F13-4(8)   Task L is preempted by Task M since the event that Task M was waiting for occurred.

F13-4(9)   Task M handles the event.

F13-4(10)   When Task M completes, the kernel relinquishes the CPU back to Task L.

F13-4(11)   Task L continues accessing the resource.

F13-4(12)   Task L finally finishes working with the resource and releases the semaphore. At this point, the kernel knows that a higher-priority task is waiting for the semaphore, and a context switch takes place to resume Task H.

F13-4(13)   Task H has the semaphore and can access the shared resource.

So, what happened here is that the priority of Task H has been reduced to that of Task L since it waited for the resource that Task L owned. The trouble begins when Task M preempted Task L, further delaying the execution of Task H. This is called an *unbounded priority inversion*. It is unbounded because any medium priority can extend the time Task H has to wait for the resource. Technically, if all medium-priority tasks have known worst-case periodic behavior and bounded execution times, the priority inversion time is computable. This process, however, may be tedious and would need to be revised every time the medium priority tasks change.

This situation can be corrected by raising the priority of Task L, only during the time it takes to access the resource, and restore the original priority level when the task is finished. The priority of Task L should be raised up to the priority of Task H. μC/OS-III contains a special type of semaphore that does just that called a mutual-exclusion semaphore.

13

13-4 MUTUAL EXCLUSION SEMAPHORES (MUTEX)

µC/OS-III supports a special type of binary semaphore called a mutual exclusion semaphore (also known as a mutex) that eliminates unbounded priority inversions. Figure 13-5 shows how priority inversions are bounded using a Mutex.

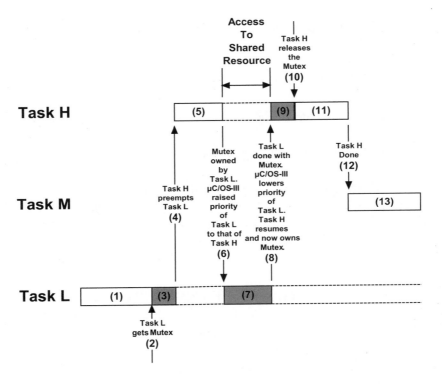

Figure 13-5 **Using a mutex to share a resource**

F13-5(1)   Task H and Task M are both waiting for an event to occur and Task L is executing.

F13-5(2)   At some point, Task L acquires a mutex, which it needs before it is able to access a shared resource.

F13-5(3)   Task L performs operations on the acquired resource.

F13-5(4)   The event that Task H waited for occurs and the kernel suspends Task L and begins executing Task H since Task H has a higher priority.

F13-5(5)   Task H performs computations based on the event it just received.

F13-5(6)   Task H now wants to access the resource that Task L currently owns (i.e., it attempts to get the mutex from Task L). Given that Task L owns the resource, μC/OS-III raises the priority of Task L to the same priority as Task H to allow Task L to finish with the resource and prevent Task L from being preempted by medium-priority tasks.

F13-5(7)   Task L continues accessing the resource, however it now does so while it is running at the same priority as Task H. Note that Task H is not actually running since it is waiting for Task L to release the mutex. In other words, Task H is in the mutex wait list.

F13-5(8)   Task L finishes working with the resource and releases the mutex. μC/OS-III notices that Task L was raised in priority and thus lowers Task L to its original priority. After doing so, μC/OS-III gives the mutex to Task H, which was waiting for the mutex to be released.

F13-5(9)   Task H now has the mutex and can access the shared resource.

F13-5(10)   Task H is finished accessing the shared resource, and frees up the mutex.

F13-5(11)   There are no higher-priority tasks to execute, therefore Task H continues execution.

F13-5(12)   Task H completes and decides to wait for an event to occur. At this point, μC/OS-III resumes Task M, which was made ready to run while Task H or Task L were executing.

F13-5(13)   Task M executes.

Note that there is no priority inversion, only resource sharing. Of course, the faster Task L accesses the shared resource and frees up the mutex, the better.

μC/OS-III implements full-priority inheritance and therefore if a higher priority requests the resource, the priority of the owner task will be raised to the priority of the new requestor.

A mutex is a kernel object defined by the **OS_MUTEX** data type, which is derived from the structure **os_mutex** (see **OS.H**). An application may have an unlimited number of mutexes (limited only by the RAM available).

Only tasks are allowed to use mutual exclusion semaphores (ISRs are not allowed).

µC/OS-III enables the user to nest ownership of mutexes. If a task owns a mutex, it can own the same mutex up to 250 times. The owner must release the mutex an equivalent number of times. In several cases, an application may not be immediately aware that it called **OSMutexPend()** multiple times, especially if the mutex is acquired again by calling a function as shown in Listing 13-12.

```
OS_MUTEX           MyMutex;
SOME_STRUCT        MySharedResource;


void  MyTask (void *p_arg)
{
    OS_ERR   err;
    CPU_TS   ts;


    :
    while (DEF_ON) {
        OSMutexPend((OS_MUTEX *)&MyMutex,                       (1)
                    (OS_TICK  )0,
                    (OS_OPT   )OS_OPT_PEND_BLOCKING,
                    (CPU_TS  *)&ts,
                    (OS_ERR  *)&err);
        /* Check 'err"                             */     (2)
        /* Acquire shared resource if no error     */
        MyLibFunction();                                  (3)
        OSMutexPost((OS_MUTEX *)&MyMutex,                 (7)
                    (OS_OPT   )OS_OPT_POST_NONE,
                    (OS_ERR  *)&err);
        /* Check "err"                             */
    }
}
```

```
void  MyLibFunction (void)
{
    OS_ERR  err;
    CPU_TS  ts;


    OSMutexPend((OS_MUTEX *)&MyMutex,                          (4)
                (OS_TICK  )0,
                (OS_OPT   )OS_OPT_PEND_BLOCKING,
                (CPU_TS  *)&ts,
                (OS_ERR  *)&err);
    /* Check "err"                      */
    /* Access shared resource if no error  */               (5)
    OSMutexPost((OS_MUTEX *)&MyMutex,                          (6)
                (OS_OPT   )OS_OPT_POST_NONE,
                (OS_ERR  *)&err);
    /* Check "err"                      */
}
```

Listing 13-12 **Nesting calls to OSMutexPend()**

L13-12(1) A task starts by pending on a mutex to access shared resources. **OSMutexPend()** sets a nesting counter to 1.

L13-12(2) Check the error return value. If no errors exist, **MyTask()** owns **MySharedResource**.

L13-12(3) A function is called that will perform additional work.

L13-12(4) The designer of **MyLibFunction()** knows that, to access **MySharedResource**, it must acquire the mutex. Since the calling task already owns the mutex, this operation should not be necessary. However, **MyLibFunction()** could have been called by yet another function that might not need access to **MySharedResource**. µC/OS-III allows nested mutex pends, so this is not a problem. The mutex nesting counter is thus incremented to 2.

L13-12(5) **MyLibFunction()** can access the shared resource.

L13-12(6)   The mutex is released and the nesting counter is decremented back to 1. Since this indicates that the mutex is still owned by the same task, nothing further needs to be done, and **OSMutexPost()** simply returns. **MyLibFunction()** returns to its caller.

L13-12(7)   The mutex is released again and, this time, the nesting counter is decremented back to 0 indicating that other tasks can now acquire the mutex.

Always check the return value of **OSMutexPend()** (and any kernel call) to ensure that the function returned because you properly obtained the mutex, and not because the return from **OSMutexPend()** was caused by the mutex being deleted, or because another task called **OSMutexPendAbort()** on this mutex.

As a general rule, do not make function calls in critical sections. All mutual exclusion semaphore calls should be in the leaf nodes of the source code (e.g., in the low level drivers that actually touches real hardware or in other reentrant function libraries).

There are a number of operations that can be performed on a mutex, as summarized in Table 13-3. However, in this chapter, we will only discuss the three functions that most often used: **OSMutexCreate()**, **OSMutexPend()**, and **OSMutexPost()**. Other functions are described in Appendix A, "µC/OS-III API Reference Manual" on page 381.

Function Name	Operation
OSMutexCreate()	Create a mutex.
OSMutexDel()	Delete a mutex.
OSMutexPend()	Wait on a mutex.
OSMutexPendAbort()	Abort the wait on a mutex.
OSMutexPost()	Release a mutex.

Table 13-3 **Mutex API summary**

13-4-1 MUTUAL EXCLUSION SEMAPHORE INTERNALS

A mutex is a kernel object defined by the **OS_MUTEX** data type, which is derived from the structure **os_mutex** (see **OS.H**) as shown in Listing 13-13:

```
typedef  struct  os_mutex  OS_MUTEX;          (1)


struct  os_mutex {
    OS_OBJ_TYPE          Type;               (2)
    CPU_CHAR             *NamePtr;            (3)
    OS_PEND_LIST         PendList;            (4)
    OS_TCB               *OwnerTCBPtr;        (5)
    OS_PRIO              OwnerOriginalPrio;   (6)
    OS_NESTING_CTR       OwnerNestingCtr;     (7)
    CPU_TS               TS;                  (8)
};
```

13

Listing 13-13 **OS_MUTEX data type**

L13-13(1)   In μC/OS-III, all structures are given a data type. All data types begin with "**OS_**" and are uppercase. When a mutex is declared, simply use **OS_MUTEX** as the data type of the variable used to declare the mutex.

L13-13(2)   The structure starts with a "Type" field, which allows it to be recognized by μC/OS-III as a mutex. Other kernel objects may also have a "**.Type**" as the first member of the structure. If a function is passed a kernel object, μC/OS-III will be able to confirm that it is being passed the proper data type. For example, if passing a message queue (**OS_Q**) to a mutex service (for example **OSMutexPend()**), μC/OS-III will recognize that the application passed an invalid object and return an error code accordingly.

L13-13(3)   Each kernel object can be given a name to make them easier to recognize by debuggers or μC/Probe. This member is simply a pointer to an ASCII string, which is assumed to be **NUL** terminated.

L13-13(4)   Because it is possible for multiple tasks to wait (or pend on a mutex), the mutex object contains a pend list as described in Chapter 10, "Pend Lists (or Wait Lists)" on page 183.

L13-13(5)   If the mutex is owned by a task, it will point to the **OS_TCB** of that task.

L13-13(6)   If the mutex is owned by a task, this field contains the "original" priority of the task that owns the mutex. This field is required in case the priority of the task must be raised to a higher priority to prevent unbounded priority inversions.

L13-13(7)   µC/OS-III allows a task to "acquire" the same mutex multiple times. In order for the mutex to be released, the owner must release the mutex the same number of times that it was acquired. Nesting can be performed up to 250-levels deep.

L13-13(8)   A mutex contains a timestamp, used to indicate the last time it was released. µC/OS-III assumes the presence of a free-running counter that allows applications to make time measurements. When the mutex is released, the free-running counter is read and the value is placed in this field, which is returned when **OSMutexPend()** returns.

Application code should never access any of the fields in this data structure directly. Instead, always use the APIs provided with µC/OS-III.

A mutual exclusion semaphore (mutex) must be created before it can be used by an application. Listing 13-14 shows how to create a mutex.

```
OS_MUTEX  MyMutex;                        (1)


void  MyTask (void *p_arg)
{
    OS_ERR  err;
    :
    :
    OSMutexCreate(&MyMutex,               (2)
                  "My Mutex",             (3)
                  &err);                  (4)
    /* Check "err" */
    :
    :
}
```

Listing 13-14 **Creating a mutex**

L13-14(1) The application must declare a variable of type **OS_MUTEX**. This variable will be referenced by other mutex services.

L13-14(2) Create a mutex by calling **OSMutexCreate()** and pass the address to the mutex allocated in (1).

L13-14(3) Assign an ASCII name to the mutex, which can be used by debuggers or µC/Probe to easily identify this mutex. There are no practical limits to the length of the name since µC/OS-III stores a pointer to the ASCII string, and not to the actual characters that makes up the string.

L13-14(4) **OSMutexCreate()** returns an error code based on the outcome of the call. If all the arguments are valid, err will contain **OS_ERR_NONE**.

Note that since a mutex is always a binary semaphore, there is no need to initialize a mutex counter.

A task waits on a mutual exclusion semaphore before accessing a shared resource by calling **OSMutexPend()** as shown in Listing 13-15 (see Appendix A, "µC/OS-III API Reference Manual" on page 381 for details regarding the arguments).

13

```
OS_MUTEX  MyMutex;


void MyTask (void *p_arg)
{
    OS_ERR  err;
    CPU_TS  ts;
    :
    while (DEF_ON) {
        :
        OSMutexPend(&MyMutex,             /* (1) Pointer to mutex                      */
                    10,                   /*     Wait up until this time for the mutex */
                    OS_OPT_PEND_BLOCKING, /*     Option(s)                             */
                    &ts,                  /*     Timestamp of when mutex was released  */
                    &err);                /*     Pointer to Error returned             */
        :
        /* Check "err"                        (2)                                      */
        :
        OSMutexPost(&MyMutex,             /* (3) Pointer to mutex                      */
                    OS_OPT_POST_NONE,
                    &err);                /*     Pointer to Error returned             */
        /* Check "err"                                                                 */
        :
        :
    }
}
```

Listing 13-15 **Pending (or waiting) on a Mutual Exclusion Semaphore**

L13-15(1)   When called, **OSMutexPend()** starts by checking the arguments passed to this function to make sure they have valid values.

If the mutex is available, **OSMutexPend()** assumes the calling task is now the owner of the mutex and stores a pointer to the task's **OS_TCB** in **p_mutex->OwnerTCPPtr**, saves the priority of the task in **p_mutex->OwnerOriginalPrio**, and sets a mutex nesting counter to 1. **OSMutexPend()** then returns to its caller with an error code of **OS_ERR_NONE**.

If the task that calls **OSMutexPend()** already owns the mutex, **OSMutexPend()** simply increments a nesting counter. Applications can nest calls to **OSMutexPend()** up to 250-levels deep. In this case, the error returned will indicate **OS_ERR_MUTEX_OWNER**.

If the mutex is already owned by another task and OS_OPT_PEND_NON_BLOCKING is specified, OSMutexPend() returns since the task is not willing to wait for the mutex to be released by its owner.

If the mutex is owned by a lower-priority task, μC/OS-III will raise the priority of the owner to match the priority of the current task.

If specifying OS_OPT_PEND_BLOCKING as the option, the calling task will be inserted in the list of tasks waiting for the mutex to be available. The task is inserted in the list by priority order and the highest priority task waiting on the mutex is at the beginning of the list.

If further specifying a non-zero timeout, the task will also be inserted in the tick list. A zero value for a timeout indicates a willingness to wait forever for the mutex to be released.

The scheduler is then called since the current task is no longer able to run (it is waiting for the mutex to be released). The scheduler will then run the next highest-priority task that is ready to run.

When the mutex is finally released and the task that called OSMutexPend() is again the highest-priority task, a task status is examined to determine the reason why OSMutexPend() is returning to its caller. The possibilities are:

1) The mutex was given to the waiting task

2) The pend was aborted by another task

3) The mutex was not posted within the specified timeout

4) The mutex was deleted

When OSMutexPend() returns, the caller is notified of the outcome through an appropriate error code.

13

L13-15(2)   If OSMutexPend() returns with err set to OS_ERR_NONE, assume that the calling task now owns the resource and can proceed with accessing it. If err contains anything else, then OSMutexPend() either timed out (if the timeout argument was non-zero), the pend was aborted by another task, or the mutex was deleted by another task. It is always important to examine returned error codes and not assume everything went as planned.

If "err" is OS_ERR_NESTING_OWNER, then the caller attempted to pend on the same mutex.

L13-15(3)   When your task is finished accessing the resource, it must call OSMutexPost() and specify the same mutex. Again, OSMutexPost() starts by checking the arguments passed to this function to make sure they contain valid values.

OSMutexPost() now calls OS_TS_GET() to obtain the current timestamp and place that information in the mutex, which will be used by OSMutexPend().

OSMutexPost() decrements the nesting counter and, if still non-zero, OSMutexPost() returns to the caller. In this case, the current owner has not fully released the mutex. The error code will indicate OS_ERR_MUTEX_NESTING.

If there are no tasks waiting for the mutex, OSMutexPost() sets p_mutex->OwnerTCBPtr to a NULL pointer and clears the mutex nesting counter.

If µC/OS-III had to raise the priority of the mutex owner, it is returned to its original priority at this time.

The highest-priority task waiting on the mutex is then extracted from the pend list and given the mutex. This is a fast operation since the pend list is sorted by priority.

The scheduler is called to see if the new mutex owner has a higher priority than the current task. If so, µC/OS-III will switch context to the new mutex owner.

You should note that you should only acquire one mutex at a time. In fact, it's highly recommended that when you acquire a mutex, you don't acquire any other kernel objects.

13-5 SHOULD YOU USE A SEMAPHORE INSTEAD OF A MUTEX?

A semaphore can be used instead of a mutex if none of the tasks competing for the shared resource have deadlines to be satisfied.

However, if there are deadlines to meet, you should use a mutex prior to accessing shared resources. Semaphores are subject to unbounded priority inversions, while mutex are not.

13-6 DEADLOCKS (OR DEADLY EMBRACE)

A *deadlock*, also called a **deadly embrace**, is a situation in which two tasks are each unknowingly waiting for resources held by the other.

Assume Task T1 has exclusive access to Resource R1 and Task T2 has exclusive access to Resource R2 as shown in the pseudo-code of Listing 13-16.

```
void T1 (void *p_arg)
{
    while (DEF_ON) {
        Wait for event to occur;        (1)
        Acquire M1;                     (2)
        Access  R1;                     (3)
        :
        :
        \--------  Interrupt!           (4)
        :
        :                               (8)
        Acquire M2;                     (9)
        Access  R2;
    }
}
```

```
void  T2 (void *p_arg)
{
    while (DEF_ON) {
        Wait for event to occur;         (5)
        Acquire M2;                      (6)
        Access  R2;
        :
        :
        Acquire M1;                      (7)
        Access  R1;
    }
}
```

Listing 13-16 **Deadlock problem**

L13-16(1)   Assume that the event that task T1 is waiting for occurs and T1 is now the highest priority task that must execute.

L13-16(2)   Task T1 executes and acquires M1.

L13-16(3)   Resource R1 is accessed.

L13-16(4)   An interrupt occurs causing the CPU to switch to task T2 as T2 is now the highest-priority task. Actually, this could be a blocking call when the task is suspended and the CPU is given to another task.

L13-16(5)   The ISR is the event that task T2 was waiting for and therefore T2 resumes execution.

L13-16(6)   Task T2 acquires mutex M2 and is able to access resource R2.

L13-16(7)   Task T2 tries to acquire mutex M1, but μC/OS-III knows that mutex M1 is owned by another task.

L13-16(8)   μC/OS-III switches back to task T1 because Task T2 can no longer continue. It needs mutex M1 to access resource R1.

L13-16(9)   Task T1 now tries to access mutex M2 but, unfortunately, mutex M2 is owned by task T2. At this point, the two tasks are deadlocked.

Techniques used to avoid deadlocks are for tasks to:

- Never acquire more than one mutex at a time

- Never acquire a mutex directly (i.e., let them be hidden inside drivers and reentrant library calls)

- Acquire all resources before proceeding

- Always acquire resources in the same order

µC/OS-III allows the calling task to specify a timeout when acquiring a semaphore or a mutex. This feature allows a deadlock to be broken, but the same deadlock may then recur later, or many times later. If the semaphore or mutex is not available within a certain period of time, the task requesting the resource resumes execution. µC/OS-III returns an error code indicating that a timeout occurred. A return error code prevents the task from thinking it has properly obtained the resource.

13

The pseudo-code avoids deadlocks by first acquiring all resources as shown in Listing 13-17.

```
void T1 (void *p_arg)
{
    while (DEF_ON) {
        Wait for event to occur;
        Acquire M1;
        Acquire M2;
        Access  R1;
        Access  R2;
    }
}


void  T2 (void *p_arg)
{
    while (DEF_ON) {
        Wait for event to occur;
        Acquire M1;
        Acquire M2;
        Access  R1;
        Access  R2;
    }
}
```

Listing 13-17 **Deadlock avoidance – acquire all first and in the same order**

The pseudo-code to acquire all of the mutexes in the same order is shown in Listing 13-18. This is similar to the previous example, except that it is not necessary to acquire all the mutexes first, only to make sure that the mutexes are acquired in the same order for both tasks.

```
void T1 (void *p_arg){
    while (DEF_ON) {
        Wait for event to occur;
        Acquire M1;
        Access  R1;
        Acquire M2;
        Access  R2;
    }
}


void  T2 (void *p_arg)
{
    while (DEF_ON) {
        Wait for event to occur;
        Acquire M1;
        Access  R1;
        Acquire M2;
        Access  R2;
    }
}
```

13

Listing 13-18 **Deadlock avoidance – acquire in the same order**

13-7 SUMMARY

The mutual exclusion mechanism used depends on how fast code will access the shared resource, as shown in Table 13-4.

Resource Sharing Method	When should you use?
Disable/Enable Interrupts	When access to shared resource is very quick (reading from or writing to just a few variables) and the access is actually faster than µC/OS-III's interrupt disable time. It is highly recommended to not use this method as it impacts interrupt latency.
Locking/Unlocking the Scheduler	When access time to the shared resource is longer than µC/OS-III's interrupt disable time, but shorter than µC/OS-III's scheduler lock time. Locking the scheduler has the same effect as making the task that locks the scheduler the highest priority task. It is recommended to not use this method since it defeats the purpose of using µC/OS-III. However, it's a better method than disabling interrupts as it does not impact interrupt latency.
Semaphores	When all tasks that need to access a shared resource do not have deadlines. This is because semaphores can cause unbounded priority inversions. However, semaphore services are slightly faster (in execution time) than mutual exclusion semaphores.
Mutual Exclusion Semaphores	This is the preferred method for accessing shared resources, especially if the tasks that need to access a shared resource have deadlines. Remember that mutual exclusion semaphores have a built-in priority inheritance mechanism, which avoids unbounded priority inversions. However, mutual exclusion semaphore services are slightly slower (in execution time) than semaphores, because the priority of the owner may need to be changed, which requires CPU processing.

Table 13-4 **Resource sharing summary**

14

Synchronization

This chapter focuses on how tasks can synchronize their activities with Interrupt Service Routines (ISRs), or other tasks.

When an ISR executes, it can signal a task telling the task that an event of interest has occurred. After signaling the task, the ISR exits and, depending on the signaled task priority, the scheduler is run. The signaled task may then service the interrupting device, or otherwise react to the event. Serving interrupting devices from task level is preferred whenever possible, since it reduces the amount of time that interrupts are disabled and the code is easier to debug.

There are two basic mechanisms for synchronizations in µC/OS-III: semaphores and event flags.

14-1 SEMAPHORES

As defined in Chapter 13, "Resource Management" on page 215, a semaphore is a protocol mechanism offered by most multitasking kernels. Semaphores were originally used to control access to shared resources. However, better mechanisms exist to protect access to shared resources, as described in Chapter 12. Semaphores are best used to synchronize an ISR to a task, or synchronize a task with another task as shown in Figure 14-1.

Note that the semaphore is drawn as a flag to indicate that it is used to signal the occurrence of an event. The initial value for the semaphore is typically zero (0), indicating the event has not yet occurred.

The value "N" next to the flag indicates that the semaphore can accumulate events or credits. It is possible to initialize the semaphore with a value other than zero, indicating that the semaphore initially contains that number of events. An ISR (or a task) can post (or signal) multiple times to a semaphore and the semaphore will remember how many times it was posted.

Also, the small hourglass close to the receiving task indicates that the task has an option to specify a timeout. This timeout indicates that the task is willing to wait for the semaphore to be signaled (or posted to) within a certain amount of time. If the semaphore is not signaled within that time, µC/OS-III resumes the task and returns an error code indicating that the task was made ready to run because of a timeout and not the semaphore was signaled.

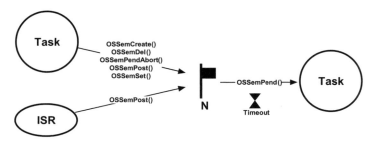

Figure 14-1 µC/OS-III Semaphore Services

There are a number of operations to perform on semaphores as summarized in Table 14-1 and Figure 14-1. However, in this chapter, we will only discuss the three functions used most often: OSSemCreate(), OSSemPend(), and OSSemPost(). The other functions are described in Appendix A, "µC/OS-III API Reference Manual" on page 381. Also note that every semaphore function is callable from a task, but only OSSemPost() can be called by an ISR

Function Name	Operation
OSSemCreate()	Create a semaphore.
OSSemDel()	Delete a semaphore.
OSSemPend()	Wait on a semaphore.
OSSemPendAbort()	Abort the wait on a semaphore.
OSSemPost()	Signal a semaphore.
OSSemSet()	Force the semaphore count to a desired value.

Table 14-1 **Semaphore API summary**

When used for synchronization, a semaphore keeps track of how many times it was signaled using a counter. The counter can take values between 0 and 255, 65,535, or 4,294,967,295, depending on whether the semaphore mechanism is implemented using 8, 16, or 32 bits, respectively. For µC/OS-III, the maximum value of a semaphore is determined by the data type **OS_SEM_CTR** (see **OS_TYPE.H**), which is changeable, as needed (assuming access to µC/OS-III's source code). Along with the semaphore's value, µC/OS-III keeps track of tasks waiting for the semaphore to be signaled.

14

14-1-1 UNILATERAL RENDEZVOUS

Figure 14-2 shows that a task can be synchronized with an ISR (or another task) by using a semaphore. In this case, no data is exchanged, however there is an indication that the ISR or the task (on the left) has occurred. Using a semaphore for this type of synchronization is called a unilateral rendezvous.

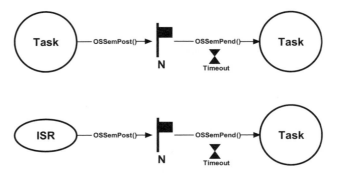

Figure 14-2 **Unilateral Rendezvous**

A unilateral rendezvous is used when a task initiates an I/O operation and waits (i.e., call OSSemPend()) for the semaphore to be signaled (posted). When the I/O operation is complete, an ISR (or another task) signals the semaphore (i.e., calls **OSSemPost( )**), and the task is resumed. This process is also shown on the timeline of Figure 14-3 and described below. The code for the ISR and task is shown in Listing 14-1.

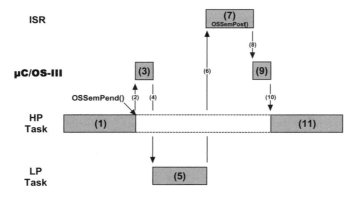

Figure 14-3 **Unilateral Rendezvous, Timing Diagram**

F14-3(1)   A high priority task is executing. The task needs to synchronize with an ISR (i.e., wait for the ISR to occur) and call OSSemPend().

F14-3(2)
F14-3(3)
F14-3(4)   Since the ISR has not occurred, the task will be placed in the waiting list for the semaphore until the event occurs The scheduler in µC/OS-III will then select the next most important task and context switch to that task.

F14-3(5)   The low-priority task executes.

F14-3(6)   The event that the original task was waiting for occurs. The lower-priority task is immediately preempted (assuming interrupts are enabled), and the CPU vectors to the interrupt handler for the event.

F14-3(7)
F14-3(8)   The ISR handles the interrupting device and then calls OSSemPost() to signal the semaphore. When the ISR completes, µC/OS-III is called.

F14-3(9)
F14-3(10)   µC/OS-III notices that a higher-priority task is waiting for this event to occur and context switches back to the original task.

F14-3(11)   The original task resumes execution immediately after the call to OSSemPend().

14

```
OS_SEM  MySem;


void MyISR (void)
{
    OS_ERR  err;


    /* Clear the interrupting device */
    OSSemPost(&MySem,                      (7)
             OS_OPT_POST_1,
             &err);
    /* Check "err" */
}


void MyTask (void *p_arg)
{
    OS_ERR  err;
    CPU_TS  ts;
    :
    :
    while (DEF_ON) {
        OSSemPend(&MySem,                  (1)
                 10,
                 OS_OPT_PEND_BLOCKING,
                 &ts,
                 &err);
        /* Check "err" */                  (11)
        :
        :
    }
}
```

Listing 14-1 **Pending (or waiting) on a Semaphore**

A few interesting things are worth noting about this process. First, the task does not need to know about the details of what happens behind the scenes. As far as the task is concerned, it called a function (**OSSemPend( )**) that will return when the event it is waiting for occurs. Second, µC/OS-III maximizes the use of the CPU by selecting the next most important task, which executes until the ISR occurs. In fact, the ISR may not occur for many milliseconds and, during that time, the CPU will work on other tasks. As far as the task that is waiting for the semaphore is concerned, it does not consume CPU time while it is waiting. Finally, the task waiting for the semaphore will execute immediately after the event occurs (assuming it is the most important task that needs to run).

14-1-2 CREDIT TRACKING

As previously mentioned, a semaphore "remembers" how many times it was signaled (or posted to). In other words, if the ISR occurs multiple times before the task waiting for the event becomes the highest-priority task, the semaphore will keep count of the number of times it was signaled. When the task becomes the highest priority ready-to-run task, it will execute without blocking as many times as there were ISRs signaled. This is called Credit Tracking and is illustrated in Figure 14-4 and described below.

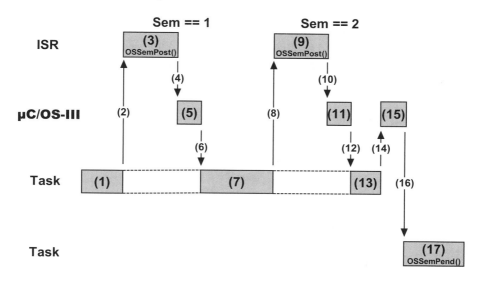

Figure 14-4 **Semaphore Credit Tracking**

F14-4(1)   A high-priority task is executing.

F14-4(2)

F14-4(3)   An event meant for a lower-priority task occurs which preempts the task (assuming interrupts are enabled). The ISR executes and posts the semaphore. At this point the semaphore count is 1.

F14-4(4)

F14-4(5)

F14-4(6)   μC/OS-III is called at the end of the ISR to see if the ISR caused a higher-priority task to be ready to run. Since the ISR was an event that a lower-priority task was waiting on, μC/OS-III will resume execution of the higher-priority task at the exact point where it was interrupted.

F14-4(7)   The high-priority task is resumed and continues execution.

F14-4(8)

F14-4(9)   The interrupt occurs a second time. The ISR executes and posts the semaphore. At this point the semaphore count is 2.

F14-4(10)

F14-4(11)

F14-4(12)   µC/OS-III is called at the end of the ISR to see if the ISR caused a higher-priority task to be ready to run. Since the ISR was an event that a lower-priority task was waiting on, µC/OS-III resumes execution of the higher-priority task at the exact point where it was interrupted.

F14-4(13)

F14-4(14)   The high-priority task resumes execution and actually terminates the work it was doing. This task will then call one of the µC/OS-III services to wait for "its" event to occur.

F14-4(15)

F14-4(16)   µC/OS-III will then select the next most important task, which happens to be the task waiting for the event and will context switch to that task.

F14-4(17)   The new task executes and will know that the ISR occurred twice since the semaphore count is two. The task will handle this accordingly.

14-1-3 MULTIPLE TASKS WAITING ON A SEMAPHORE

It is possible for more than one task to wait on the same semaphore, each with its own timeout as illustrated in Figure 14-5.

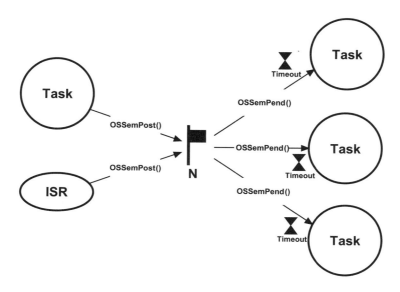

Figure 14-5 **Multiple Tasks waiting on a Semaphore**

When the semaphore is signaled (whether by an ISR or task), µC/OS-III makes the highest-priority task waiting on the semaphore ready to run. However, it is also possible to specify that all tasks waiting on the semaphore be made ready to run. This is called broadcasting and is accomplished by specifying **OS_OPT_POST_ALL** as an option when calling **OSSemPost()**. If any of the waiting tasks has a higher priority than the previously running task, µC/OS-III will execute the highest-priority task made ready by **OSSemPost()**.

Broadcasting is a common technique used to synchronize multiple tasks and have them start executing at the same time. However, some of the tasks that we want to synchronize might not be waiting for the semaphore. It is fairly easy to resolve this problem by combining semaphores and event flags. This will be described after examining event flags.

14-1-4 SEMAPHORE INTERNALS (FOR SYNCHRONIZATION)

Note that some of the material presented in this section is also contained in Chapter 13, "Resource Management" on page 215, as semaphores were also discussed in that chapter. However, the material presented here will be applicable to semaphores used for synchronization and thus will differ somewhat.

A counting semaphore allows values between 0 and 255, 65,535, or 4,294,967,295, depending on whether the semaphore mechanism is implemented using 8, 16, or 32 bits, respectively. For µC/OS-III, the maximum value of a semaphore is determined by the data type **OS_SEM_CTR** (see **OS_TYPE.H**), which can be changed as needed (assuming access to µC/OS-III's source code). Along with the semaphore's value, µC/OS-III keeps track of tasks waiting for the semaphore's availability.

The application programmer can create an unlimited number of semaphores (limited only by available RAM). Semaphore services in µC/OS-III start with the **OSSem???()** prefix, and services available to the application programmer are described in Appendix A, "µC/OS-III API Reference Manual" on page 381. Semaphore services are enabled at compile time by setting the configuration constant **OS_CFG_SEM_EN** to **1** in **OS_CFG.H**.

Semaphores must be created before they can be used by the application. Listing 14-3 shows how to create a semaphore.

As previously mentioned, a semaphore is a kernel object as defined by the **OS_SEM** data type, which is derived from the structure os_sem (see **OS.H**) as shown in Listing 14-2.

The services provided by µC/OS-III to manage semaphores are implemented in the file **OS_SEM.C**. µC/OS-III licensees, have access to the source code.

```
typedef  struct  os_sem  OS_SEM;                (1)


struct  os_sem {
    OS_OBJ_TYPE          Type;                  (2)
    CPU_CHAR             *NamePtr;              (3)
    OS_PEND_LIST          PendList;             (4)
    OS_SEM_CTR            Ctr;                  (5)
    CPU_TS                TS;                   (6)
};
```

Listing 14-2 **OS_SEM data type**

L14-2(1)   In μC/OS-III, all structures are given a data type. In fact, all data types start with "**OS_**" and are all uppercase. When a semaphore is declared, simply use **OS_SEM** as the data type of the variable used to declare the semaphore.

L14-2(2)   The structure starts with a "**Type**" field, which allows it to be recognized by μC/OS-III as a semaphore. In other words, other kernel objects will also have a "**Type**" as the first member of the structure. If a function is passed a kernel object, μC/OS-III will confirm that it is being passed the proper data type. For example, if passing a message queue (**OS_Q**) to a semaphore service (for example **OSSemPend()**), μC/OS-III will recognize that an invalid object was passed, and return an error code accordingly.

L14-2(3)   Each kernel object can be given a name to make them easier to be recognized by debuggers or μC/Probe. This member is simply a pointer to an ASCII string, which is assumed to be **NUL** terminated.

L14-2(4)   Since it is possible for multiple tasks to be waiting (or pending) on a semaphore, the semaphore object contains a pend list as described in Chapter 10, "Pend Lists (or Wait Lists)" on page 183.

L14-2(5)   A semaphore contains a counter. As explained above, the counter can be implemented as either an 8-, 16- or 32-bit value, depending on how the data type **OS_SEM_CTR** is declared in **OS_TYPE.H**.

μC/OS-III keeps track of how many times the semaphore is signaled with this counter and this field is typically initialized to zero by **OSSemCreate()**.

14

267

L14-2(6)   A semaphore contains a time stamp, which is used to indicate the last time the semaphore was signaled (or posted to). µC/OS-III assumes the presence of a free-running counter that allows the application to make time measurements. When the semaphore is signaled, the free-running counter is read and the value is placed in this field, which is returned when **OSSemPend()** is called. This value allows the application to determine either when the signal was performed, or how long it took for the task to get control of the CPU from the signal. In the latter case, call **OS_TS_GET()** to determine the current timestamp and compute the difference.

Even for users who understand the internals of the **OS_SEM** data type, the application code should never access any of the fields in this data structure directly. Instead, always use the APIs provided with µC/OS-III.

Semaphores must be created before they can be used by an application. Listing 14-3 shows how to create a semaphore.

```
OS_SEM  MySem;                      (1)


void  MyCode (void)
{
    OS_ERR  err;
    :
    OSSemCreate(&MySem,             (2)
                "My Semaphore",     (3)
                (OS_SEM_CTR)0,      (4)
                &err);              (5)
    /* Check "err" */
    :
}
```

Listing 14-3 **Creating a Semaphore**

L14-3(1)   The application must declare a variable of type **OS_SEM**. This variable will be referenced by other semaphore services.

L14-3(2)   Create a semaphore by calling **OSSemCreate()** and pass the address to the semaphore allocated in (1).

L14-3(3)   Assign an ASCII name to the semaphore, which can be used by debuggers or µC/Probe to easily identify this semaphore.

L14-3(4)   Initialize the semaphore to zero (0) when using a semaphore as a signaling mechanism.

L14-3(5)   OSSemCreate() returns an error code based on the outcome of the call. If all arguments are valid, err will contain OS_ERR_NONE.

OSSemCreate() performs a check on the arguments passed to this function and only initializes the contents of the variable of type OS_SEM used for signaling.

A task waits for a signal from an ISR or another task by calling OSSemPend() as shown in Listing 14-4 (see Appendix A, "µC/OS-III API Reference Manual" on page 381 for details regarding the arguments).

```
OS_SEM  MySem;                      (1)


void  MyCode (void)
{
    OS_ERR  err;
    :
    OSSemCreate(&MySem,             (2)
                "My Semaphore",     (3)
                (OS_SEM_CTR)0,      (4)
                &err);              (5)
    /* Check "err" */
    :
}
```

14

Listing 14-4 **Pending (or waiting) on a Semaphore**

L14-4(1)   When called, OSSemPend() starts by checking the arguments passed to this function to make sure they have valid values.

If the semaphore counter (.Ctr of OS_SEM) is greater than zero, the counter is decremented and OSSemPend() returns, which indicates that the signal occurred. This is the outcome that the caller expects.

If the semaphore counter is zero, this indicates that the signal has not occurred and the calling task might need to wait for the semaphore to be released. If specifying OS_OPT_PEND_NON_BLOCKING as the option (the task is not to block), OSSemPend() returns immediately to the caller and the returned error code will indicate that the signal did not occur.

If specifying OS_OPT_PEND_BLOCKING as the option, the calling task will be inserted in the list of tasks waiting for the semaphore to be signaled. The task is inserted in the list by priority order with the highest priority task waiting on the semaphore at the beginning of the list as shown in Figure 14-6.

If further specifying a non-zero timeout, the task will also be inserted in the tick list. A zero value for a timeout indicates that the calling task is willing to wait forever for the semaphore to be signaled.

The scheduler is then called as the current task is not able to run (it is waiting for the semaphore to be signaled). The scheduler will then run the next highest-priority task that is ready to run.

When the semaphore is signaled and the task that called OSSemPend() is again the highest-priority task, a task status is examined to determine the reason why OSSemPend() is returning to its caller. The possibilities are:

1) The semaphore was signaled

2) The pend was aborted by another task

3) The semaphore was not signaled within the specified timeout

4) The semaphore was deleted

When OSSemPend() returns, the caller is notified of the above outcome through an appropriate error code.

L14-4(2)   If OSSemPend() returns with err set to OS_ERR_NONE, assume that the semaphore was signaled and the task can proceed with servicing the ISR or task that caused the signal. If err contains anything else, OSSemPend() either timed out (if the timeout argument was non-zero), the pend was aborted by another task, or the semaphore was deleted by another task. It is always important to examine returned error code and not assume everything went as expected.

To signal a task (either from an ISR or a task), simply call **OSSemPost()** as shown in Listing 14-5.

```
OS_SEM  MySem;


void MyISR (void)
{
    OS_ERR  err;
    :
    OSSemPost(&MySem,                 (1)
              OS_OPT_POST_1,          (2)
              &err);                  (3)
    /* Check "err" */
    :
    :
}
```

Listing 14-5 **Posting (or signaling) a Semaphore**

L14-5(1)   Your task signals (or posts to) the semaphore by calling **OSSemPost()**. Specify the semaphore to post by passing its address. The semaphore must have been previously created.

L14-5(2)   The next argument specifies how the task wants to post. There are a number of options to choose from.

Specify **OS_OPT_POST_1**, which indicates posting to only one task in case there are multiple tasks waiting on the semaphore. The task that will be made ready to run will be the highest-priority task waiting on the semaphore. If there are multiple tasks at the same priority, only one of them will be made ready-to-run. As shown in Figure 14-6, tasks waiting are in priority order (HPT means High Priority Task and LPT means Low Priority Task). It is a fast operation to extract the HPT from the list.

If specifying **OS_OPT_POST_ALL**, all tasks waiting on the semaphore will be posted and made ready to run.

The calling task can "add" the option **OS_OPT_POST_NO_SCHED** to either of the two previous options to indicate that the scheduler is not to be called at the end of **OSSemPost()**, possibly because additional postings will be performed, and rescheduling should take place when finished. This means that the signal is performed, but the scheduler is not called even if a higher-priority task was waiting for the semaphore to be signaled. This allows the calling task to perform other post functions (if needed) and make all the posts take effect simultaneously. Note that **OS_OPT_POST_NO_SCHED** is "additive," meaning that it can be used with either of the previous options. You can specify:

```
OS_OPT_POST_1
OS_OPT_POST_ALL
OS_OPT_POST_1   + OS_OPT_POST_NO_SCHED
OS_OPT_POST_ALL + OS_OPT_POST_NO_SCHED
```

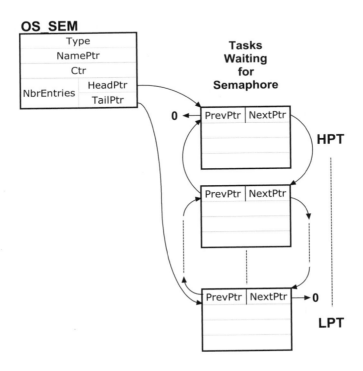

Figure 14-6 **Tasks waiting for semaphore**

L14-5(3)   OSSemPost() returns an error code based on the outcome of the call. If the call was successful, err will contain OS_ERR_NONE. If not, the error code will indicate the reason for the error (see Appendix A, "µC/OS-III API Reference Manual" on page 381 for a list of possible error codes for OSSemPost().

14-2 TASK SEMAPHORE

Signaling a task using a semaphore is a very popular method of synchronization and, in µC/OS-III, each task has its own built-in semaphore. This feature not only simplifies code, but is also more efficient than using a separate semaphore object. The semaphore, which is built into each task, is shown in Figure 14-7.

Task semaphore services in µC/OS-III start with the OSTaskSem???() prefix, and the services available to the application programmer are described in Appendix A, "µC/OS-III API Reference Manual" on page 381. Task semaphores are built into µC/OS-III and cannot be disabled at compile time as can other services. The code for task semaphores is found in OS_TASK.C.

Use this feature if the code knows which task to signal when the event occurs. For example, if receiving an interrupt from an Ethernet controller, signal the task responsible for processing the received packet as it is preferable to perform this processing using a task instead of the ISR.

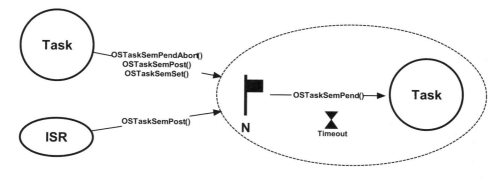

Figure 14-7 **Semaphore built-into a Task**

There are a number of operations to perform on task semaphores, summarized in Table 14-2.

Function Name	Operation
OSTaskSemPend()	Wait on a task semaphore.
OSTaskSemPendAbort()	Abort the wait on a task semaphore.
OSTaskSemPost()	Signal a task.
OSTaskSemSet()	Force the semaphore count to a desired value.

Table 14-2 **Task Semaphore API summary**

14-2-1 PENDING (i.e., WAITING) ON A TASK SEMAPHORE

When a task is created, it automatically creates an internal semaphore with an initial value of zero (0). Waiting on a task semaphore is quite simple, as shown in Listing 14-6.

```
void MyTask (void *p_arg)
{
    OS_ERR  err;
    CPU_TS  ts;
    :
    while (DEF_ON) {
        OSTaskSemPend(10,                       (1)
                      OS_OPT_PEND_BLOCKING,     (2)
                      &ts,                       (3)
                      &err);                     (4)
        /* Check "err" */
        :
        :
    }
}
```

Listing 14-6 **Pending (or waiting) on Task's internal semaphore**

L14-6(1)   A task pends (or waits) on the task semaphore by calling **OSTaskSemPend()**. There is no need to specify which task, as the current task is assumed. The first argument is a timeout specified in number of clock ticks. The actual timeout obviously depends on the tick rate. If the tick rate (see **OS_CFG_APP.H**) is set to 1000, a timeout of 10 ticks represents 10 milliseconds. Specifying a timeout of zero (0) means that the task will wait forever for the task semaphore.

L14-6(2)   The second argument specifies how to pend. There are two options: **OS_OPT_PEND_BLOCKING** and **OS_OPT_PEND_NON_BLOCKING**. The blocking option means that, if the task semaphore has not been signaled (or posted to), the task will wait until the semaphore is signaled, the pend is aborted by another task or, until the timeout expires.

L14-6(3)   When the semaphore is signaled, μC/OS-III reads a "timestamp" and places it in the receiving task's **OS_TCB**. When **OSTaskSemPend()** returns, the value of the timestamp is placed in the local variable "**ts**". This feature captures "when" the signal actually happened. **Call OS_TS_GET()** to read the current timestamp and compute the difference. This establishes how long it took for the task to receive the signal from the posting task or ISR.

L14-6(4)   **OSTaskSemPend()** returns an error code based on the outcome of the call. If the call was successful, err will contain **OS_ERR_NONE**. If not, the error code will indicate the reason of the error (see Appendix A, "μC/OS-III API Reference Manual" on page 381 for a list of possible error code for **OSTaskSemPend()**.

14-2-2 POSTING (i.e., SIGNALING) A TASK SEMAPHORE

An ISR or a task signals a task by calling **OSTaskSemPost()**, as shown in Listing 14-7.

```
OS_TCB  MyTaskTCB;


void MyISR (void *p_arg)
{
    OS_ERR  err;
    :
    OSTaskSemPost(&MyTaskTCB,              (1)
                  OS_OPT_POST_NONE,        (2)
                  &err);                   (3)
    /* Check "err" */
    :
    :
}
```

Listing 14-7 **Posting (or signaling) a Semaphore**

L14-7(1) A task posts (or signals) the task by calling **OSTaskSemPost()**. It is necessary to pass the address of the desired task's **OS_TCB**. Of course, the task must exist.

L14-7(2) The next argument specifies how the user wants to post. There are only two choices.

Specify **OS_OPT_POST_NONE**, which indicates the use of the default option of calling the scheduler after posting the semaphore.

Or, specify **OS_OPT_POST_NO_SCHED** to indicate that the scheduler is not to be called at the end of **OSTaskSemPost()**, possibly because there will be additional postings, and rescheduling would take place when finished (the last post would not specify this option).

L14-7(3) **OSTaskSemPost()** returns an error code based on the outcome of the call. If the call was successful, err will contain **OS_ERR_NONE**. If not, the error code will indicate the reason of the error (see Appendix A, "µC/OS-III API Reference Manual" on page 381 for a list of possible error codes for **OSTaskSemPost()**.

14

14-2-3 BILATERAL RENDEZVOUS

Two tasks can synchronize their activities by using two task semaphores, as shown in Figure 14-8, and is called a *bilateral rendezvous*. A bilateral rendezvous is similar to a unilateral rendezvous, except that both tasks must synchronize with one another before proceeding. A bilateral rendezvous cannot be performed between a task and an ISR because an ISR cannot wait on a semaphore.

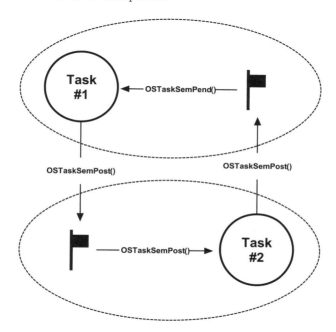

Figure 14-8 **Bilateral Rendezvous**

The code for a bilateral rendezvous is shown in Listing 14-8. Of course, a bilateral rendezvous can use two separate semaphores, but the built-in task semaphore makes setting up this type of synchronization quite straightforward.

```
OS_TCB   MyTask1_TCB;
OS_TCB   MyTask2_TCB;


void Task1 (void *p_arg)
{
    OS_ERR   err;
    CPU_TS   ts;

    while (DEF_ON) {
        :
        OSTaskSemPost(&MyTask2_TCB,              (1)
                      OS_OPT_POST_NONE,
                      &err);
        /* Check 'err" */
        OSTaskSemPend(0,                         (2)
                      OS_OPT_PEND_BLOCKING,
                      &ts,
                      &err);
        /* Check 'err" */
        :
    }
}


void Task2 (void *p_arg)
{
    OS_ERR   err;
    CPU_TS   ts;

    while (DEF_ON) {
        :
        OSTaskSemPost(&MyTask1_TCB,              (3)
                      OS_OPT_POST_NONE,
                      &err);
        /* Check 'err" */
        OSTaskSemPend(0,                         (4)
                      OS_OPT_PEND_BLOCKING,
                      &ts,
                      &err);
        /* Check 'err" */
        :
    }
}
```

Listing 14-8 **Tasks synchronizing their activities**

L14-8(1)   Task #1 is executing and signals Task #2's semaphore.

L14-8(2)   Task #1 pends on its internal semaphore to synchronize with Task #2. Because Task #2 has not executed yet, Task #1 is blocked waiting on its semaphore to be signaled. μC/OS-III context switches to Task #2.

L14-8(3)   Task #2 executes, and signals Task #1's semaphore.

L14-8(4)   Since it has already been signaled, Task #2 is now synchronized to Task #1. If Task #1 is higher in priority than Task #2, μC/OS-III will switch back to Task #1. If not, Task #2 continues execution.

14-3 EVENT FLAGS

Event flags are used when a task needs to synchronize with the occurrence of multiple events. The task can be synchronized when any of the events have occurred, which is called disjunctive synchronization (logical OR). A task can also be synchronized when all events have occurred, which is called conjunctive synchronization (logical AND). Disjunctive and conjunctive synchronization are shown in Figure 14-9.

The application programmer can create an unlimited number of event flag groups (limited only by available RAM). Event flag services in μC/OS-III start with the `OSFlag???()` prefix. The services available to the application programmer are described in Appendix A, "μC/OS-III API Reference Manual" on page 381.

The code for event flag services is found in the file `OS_FLAG.C`, and is enabled at compile time by setting the configuration constant `OS_CFG_FLAG_EN` to 1 in `OS_CFG.H`.

14

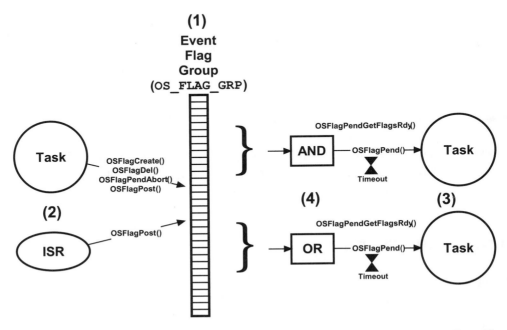

Figure 14-9 **Event Flags**

F14-9(1)   A µC/OS-III "event flag group" is a kernel object of type **OS_FLAG_GRP** (see **OS.H**), and consists of a series of bits (8-, 16- or 32-bits, based on the data type **OS_FLAGS** defined in **OS_TYPE.H**). The event flag group also contains a list of tasks waiting for some (or all) of the bits to be set (1) or clear (0). An event flag group must be created before it can be used by tasks and ISRs. Create event flags prior to starting µC/OS-III, or by a startup task in the application code.

F14-9(2)   Tasks or ISRs can post to event flags. In addition, only tasks can create, delete, and stop other task from pending on event flag groups.

F14-9(3)   A task can wait (i.e., pend) on any number of bits in an event flag group (i.e., a subset of all the bits). As with all µC/OS-III pend calls, the calling task can specify a timeout value such that if the desired bits are not posted within a specified amount of time (in ticks), the pending task is resumed and informed about the timeout.

F14-9(4)   The task can specify whether it wants to wait for "any" subset of bits (OR) to be set (or clear), or wait for "all" bits in a subset of bit (AND) to be set (or clear).

There are a number of operations to perform on event flags, as summarized in Table 14-3.

Table 14-3 **Event Flags API summary**

Function Name	Operation
OSFlagCreate()	Create an event flag group
OSFlagDel()	Delete an event flag group
OSFlagPend()	Pend (i.e., wait) on an event flag group
OSFlagPendAbort()	Abort waiting on an event flag group
OSFlagPendGetFlagsRdy()	Get flags that caused task to become ready
OSFlagPost()	Post flag(s) to an event flag group

14-3-1 USING EVENT FLAGS

When a task or an ISR posts to an event flag group, all tasks that have their wait conditions satisfied will be resumed.

It's up to the application to determine what each bit in an event flag group means and it is possible to use as many event flag groups as needed. In an event flag group you can, for example, define that bit #0 indicates that a temperature sensor is too low, bit #1 may indicate a low battery voltage, bit #2 could indicate that a switch was pressed, etc. The code (tasks or ISRs) that detects these conditions would set the appropriate event flag by calling **OSFlagPost()** and the task(s) that would respond to those conditions would call **OSFlagPend()**.

Listing 14-9 shows how to use event flags.

14

```
#define     TEMP_LOW    (OS_FLAGS)0x0001                        (1)
#define     BATT_LOW    (OS_FLAGS)0x0002
#define     SW_PRESSED  (OS_FLAGS)0x0004

OS_FLAG_GRP  MyEventFlagGrp;                                    (2)

void main (void)
{
   OS_ERR  err;

   OSInit(&err);
   :
   OSFlagCreate(&MyEventFlagGrp,                                (3)
               "My Event Flag Group",
               (OS_FLAGS)0,
               &err);
   /* Check 'err" */
   :
   OSStart(&err);
}


void  MyTask (void *p_arg)                                      (4)
{
   OS_ERR  err;
   CPU_TS  ts;

   while (DEF_ON) {
       OSFlagPend(&MyEventFlagGrp,                              (5)
               TEMP_LOW + BATT_LOW,
               (OS_TICK )0,
               (OS_OPT)OS_OPT_PEND_FLAG_SET_ANY,
               &ts,
               &err);
       /* Check 'err" */
       :
   }
}
```

```
void  MyISR (void)                                      (6)
{
    OS_ERR  err;
    :
    OSFlagPost(&MyEventFlagGrp,                          (7)
               BAT_LOW,
               (OS_OPT)OS_OPT_POST_FLAG_SET,
               &err);
    /* Check 'err" */
    :
}
```

Listing 14-9 **Using Event Flags**

L14-9(1)   Define some bits in the event flag group.

L14-9(2)   Declare an object of type **OS_FLAG_GRP**. This object will be referenced in all subsequent µC/OS-III calls that apply to this event flag group. For the sake of discussions, assume that event flags are declared to be 16-bits in **OS_TYPE.H** (i.e., of type **CPU_INT16U**).

L14-9(3)   Event flag groups must be "created" before they can be used. The best place to do this is in your startup code as it ensures that no tasks, or ISR, will be able to use the event flag group until µC/OS-III is started. In other words, the best place is to create the event flag group is in **main()**. In the example, the event flag was given a name and all bits start in their cleared state (i.e., all zeros).

L14-9(4)   Assume that the application created "**MyTask()**" which will be pending on the event flag group.

L14-9(5)   To pend on an event flag group, call **OSFlagPend()** and pass it the address of the desired event flag group.

The second argument specifies which bits the task will be waiting to be set (assuming the task is triggered by set bits instead of cleared bits).

Specify how long to wait for these bits to be set. A timeout value of zero (0) indicates that the task will wait forever. A non-zero value indicates the number of ticks the task will wait until it is resumed if the desired bits are not set.

Specifying **OS_OPT_FLAG_SET_ANY** indicates that the task will wake up if either of the two bits specified is set.

A timestamp is read and saved when the event flag group is posted to. This timestamp can be used to determine the response time to the event.

OSFlagPend() performs a number of checks on the arguments passed (i.e., did you pass **NULL** pointers, invalid options, etc.), and returns an error code based on the outcome of the call. If the call was successful "err" will be set to **OS_ERR_NONE**.

L14-9(6)   An ISR (it can also be a task) is setup to detect when the battery voltage of the product goes low (assuming the product is battery operated). The ISR signals the task, letting the task perform whatever corrective action is needed.

L14-9(7)   The desired event flag group is specified in the post call as well as which flag the ISR is setting. The third option specifies that the error condition will be "flagged" as a set bit. Again, the function sets "err" based on the outcome of the call.

Event flags are generally used for two purposes: status and transient events. Typically use different event flag groups to handle each of these as shown in Listing 14-10.

Tasks or ISRs can report status information such as a temperature that has exceeded a certain value, that RPM is zero on an engine or motor, or there is fuel in the tank, and more. This status information cannot be "consumed" by the tasks waiting for these events, because the status is managed by other tasks or ISRs. Event flags associated with status information are monitored by other task by using non-blocking wait calls.

Tasks will report transient events such as a switch was pressed, an object was detected by a motion sensor, an explosion occurred, etc. The task that responds to these events will typically block waiting for any of those events to occur and "consume" the event.

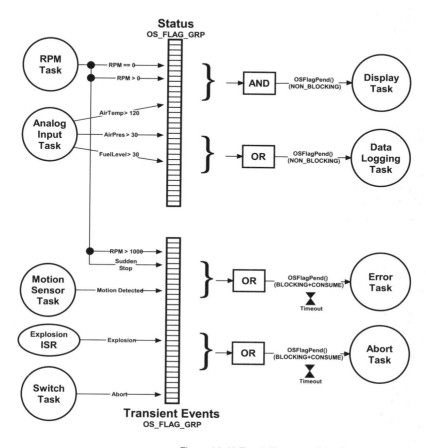

Figure 14-10 **Event Flags used for Status and Transient Events**

14-3-2 EVENT FLAGS INTERNALS

The application programmer can create an unlimited number of event flag groups (limited only by available RAM). Event flag services in µC/OS-III start with OSFlag and the services available to the application programmer are described in Appendix A, "µC/OS-III API Reference Manual" on page 381. Event flag services are enabled at compile time by setting the configuration constant OS_CFG_FLAG_EN to 1 in OS_CFG.H.

An event flag group is a kernel object as defined by the OS_FLAG_GRP data type, which is derived from the structure os_flag_grp (see OS.H) as shown in Listing 14-10.

The services provided by μC/OS-III to manage event flags are implemented in the file **OS_FLAG.C**. μC/OS-III licensees have access to the source code.

```
typedef  struct  os_flag_grp  OS_FLAG_GRP;    (1)


struct  os_flag_grp {
    OS_OBJ_TYPE         Type;               (2)
    CPU_CHAR            *NamePtr;           (3)
    OS_PEND_LIST        PendList;           (4)
    OS_FLAGS            Flags;              (5)
    CPU_TS              TS;                 (6)
};
```

Listing 14-10 **OS_FLAG_GRP data type**

L14-10(1)   In μC/OS-III, all structures are given a data type. In fact, all data types start with "**OS_**" and are uppercase. When an event flag group is declared, simply use **OS_FLAG_GRP** as the data type of the variable used to declare the event flag group.

L14-10(2)   The structure starts with a "**Type**" field, which allows it to be recognized by μC/OS-III as an event flag group. In other words, other kernel objects will also have a "**Type**" as the first member of the structure. If a function is passed a kernel object, μC/OS-III will be able to confirm that it is being passed the proper data type. For example, if passing a message queue (**OS_Q**) to an event flag service (for example **OSFlagPend( )**), μC/OS-III will be able to recognize that an invalid object was passed, and return an error code accordingly.

L14-10(3)   Each kernel object can be given a name to make them easier to be recognized by debuggers or μC/Probe. This member is simply a pointer to an ASCII string, which is assumed to be **NUL** terminated.

L14-10(4)   Because it is possible for multiple tasks to be waiting (or pending) on an event flag group, the event flag group object contains a pend list as described in Chapter 10, "Pend Lists (or Wait Lists)" on page 183.

L14-10(5)   An event flag group contains a series of flags (i.e., bits), and this member contains the current state of these flags. The flags can be implemented using either an 8-, 16- or 32-bit value depending on how the data type **OS_FLAGS** is declared in **OS_TYPE.H**.

L14-10(6)   An event flag group contains a timestamp used to indicate the last time the event flag group was posted to. µC/OS-III assumes the presence of a free-running counter that allows users to make time measurements. When the event flag group is posted to, the free-running counter is read and the value is placed in this field, which is returned when **OSFlagPend()** is called. This value allows an application to determine either when the post was performed, or how long it took for your the to obtain control of the CPU from the post. In the latter case, call **OS_TS_GET()** to determine the current timestamp and compute the difference.

Even if the user understands the internals of the **OS_FLAG_GRP** data type, application code should never access any of the fields in this data structure directly. Instead, always use the APIs provided with µC/OS-III.

Event flag groups must be created before they can be used by an application as shown in Listing 14-11.

```
OS_FLAG_GRP  MyEventFlagGrp;               (1)


void  MyCode (void)
{
    OS_ERR  err;
    :
    OSFlagCreate(&MyEventFlagGrp,          (2)
               "My Event Flag Group",      (3)
               (OS_FLAGS)0,                (4)
               &err);                      (5)
    /* Check 'err" */
    :
}
```

Listing 14-11 **Creating a Event Flag Group**

14

L14-11(1)   The application must declare a variable of type **OS_FLAG_GRP**. This variable will be referenced by other event flag services.

L14-11(2)   Create an event flag group by calling **OSFlagCreate()** and pass the address to the event flag group allocated in (1).

L14-11(3)   Assign an ASCII name to the event flag group, which can be used by debuggers or μC/Probe to easily identify this event flag group. μC/OS-III stores a pointer to the name so there is no practical limit to its size, except that the ASCII string needs to be **NUL** terminated.

L14-11(4)   Initialize the flags inside the event flag group to zero (0) unless the task and ISRs signal events with bits cleared instead of bits set. If using cleared bits, initialize all the bits to ones (1).

L14-11(5)   **OSFlagCreate()** returns an error code based on the outcome of the call. If all the arguments are valid, err will contain **OS_ERR_NONE**.

A task waits for one or more event flag bits either from an ISR or another task by calling **OSFlagPend()** as shown in Listing 14-12 (see Appendix A, "μC/OS-III API Reference Manual" on page 381 for details regarding the arguments).

```
OS_FLAG_GRP  MyEventFlagGrp;


void MyTask (void *p_arg)
{
    OS_ERR  err;
    CPU_TS  ts;
    :
    while (DEF_ON) {
        :
        OSFlagPend(&MyEventFlagGrp,          /* (1) Pointer to event flag group      */
                   (OS_FLAGS)0x0F,           /*      Which bits to wait on            */
                   10,                       /*      Maximum time to wait             */
                   OS_OPT_PEND_BLOCKING +
                   OS_OPT_PEND_FLAG_SET_ANY, /*      Option(s)                        */
                   &ts,                      /*      Timestamp of when posted to      */
                   &err);                    /*      Pointer to Error returned        */
        /* Check "err"                          (2)                                   */
        :
        :
    }
}
```

Listing 14-12 **Pending (or waiting) on an Event Flag Group**

14

L14-12(1)   When called, **OSFlagPend()** starts by checking the arguments passed to this function to ensure they have valid values. If the bits the task is waiting for are set (or cleared depending on the option), **OSFlagPend()** returns and indicate which flags satisfied the condition. This is the outcome that the caller expects.

If the event flag group does not contain the flags that the caller is looking for, the calling task might need to wait for the desired flags to be set (or cleared). If specifying **OS_OPT_PEND_NON_BLOCKING** as the option (the task is not to block), **OSFlagPend()** returns immediately to the caller and the returned error code indicates that the bits have not been set (or cleared).

If specifying **OS_OPT_PEND_BLOCKING** as the option, the calling task will be inserted in the list of tasks waiting for the desired event flag bits. The task is not inserted in priority order but simply inserted at the beginning of the list. This is done because whenever bits are set (or cleared), it is necessary to examine all tasks in this list to see if their desired bits have been satisfied.

If further specifying a non-zero timeout, the task will also be inserted in the tick list. A zero value for a timeout indicates that the calling task is willing to wait forever for the desired bits.

The scheduler is then called since the current task is no longer able to run (it is waiting for the desired bits). The scheduler will run the next highest-priority task that is ready to run.

When the event flag group is posted to and the task that called **OSFlagPend()** has its desired bits set or cleared, a task status is examined to determine the reason why **OSFlagPend()** is returning to its caller. The possibilities are:

1) The desired bits were set (or cleared)

2) The pend was aborted by another task

3) The bits were not set (or cleared) within the specified timeout

4) The event flag group was deleted

When **OSFlagPend()** returns, the caller is notified of the above outcome through an appropriate error code.

L14-12(2)   If **OSFlagPend()** returns with err set to **OS_ERR_NONE**, assume that the desired bits were set (or cleared) and the task can proceed with servicing the ISR or task that created those events. If err contains anything else, **OSFlagPend()** either timed out (if the timeout argument was non-zero), the pend was aborted by another task or, the event flag group was deleted by another task. It is always important to examine the returned error code and not assume everything went as planned.

To set (or clear) event flags (either from an ISR or a task), simply call **OSFlagPost()**, as shown in Listing 14-13.

```
OS_FLAG_GRP  MyEventFlagGrp;

void MyISR (void)
{
    OS_ERR  err;
    :
    OSFlagPost(&MyEventFlagGrp,        (1)
               (OS_FLAGS)0x0C,          (2)
               OS_OPT_POST_FLAG_SET,    (3)
               &err);                   (4)
    /* Check 'err" */
    :
    :
}
```

Listing 14-13 **Posting flags to an Event Flag Group**

L14-13(1)   A task posts to the event flag group by calling **OSFlagPost()**. Specify the desired event flag group to post by passing its address. Of course, the event flag group must have been previously created.

L14-13(2)   The next argument specifies which bit(s) the ISR (or task) will be setting or clearing in the event flag group.

L14-13(3)   Specify **OS_OPT_POST_FLAG_SET** or **OS_OPT_POST_FLAG_CLR**.

If specifying **OS_OPT_POST_FLAG_SET**, the bits specified in the second arguments will set the corresponding bits in the event flag group. For example, if **MyEventFlagGrp.Flags** contains 0x03, the code in Listing 14-13 will change **MyEventFlagGrp.Flags** to 0x0F.

If specifying **OS_OPT_POST_FLAG_CLR**, the bits specified in the second arguments will clear the corresponding bits in the event flag group. For example, if **MyEventFlagGrp.Flags** contains 0x0F, the code in Listing 14-13 will change **MyEventFlagGrp.Flags** to 0x03.

When calling **OSFlagPost()** specify as an option (i.e., **OS_OPT_POST_NO_SCHED**) to not call the scheduler. This means that the post is performed, but the scheduler is not called even if a higher-priority task was waiting for the event flag group. This allows the calling task to perform other post functions (if needed) and make all the posts take effect simultaneously.

L14-13(4)   **OSFlagPost()** returns an error code based on the outcome of the call. If the call was successful, err will contain **OS_ERR_NONE**. If not, the error code will indicate the reason of the error (see Appendix A, "μC/OS-III API Reference Manual" on page 381 for a list of possible error codes for **OSFlagPost()**.

14-4 SYNCHRONIZING MULTIPLE TASKS

Synchronizing the execution of multiple tasks by broadcasting to a semaphore is a commonly used technique. It may be important to have multiple tasks start executing at the same time. Obviously, on a single processor, only one task will actually execute at one time. However, the start of their execution will be synchronized to the same time. This is called a multiple task rendezvous. However, some of the tasks synchronized might not be waiting for the semaphore when the broadcast is performed. It is fairly easy to resolve this problem by combining semaphores and event flags, as shown in Figure 14-11. For this to work properly, the task on the left needs to have a lower priority than the tasks waiting on the semaphore.

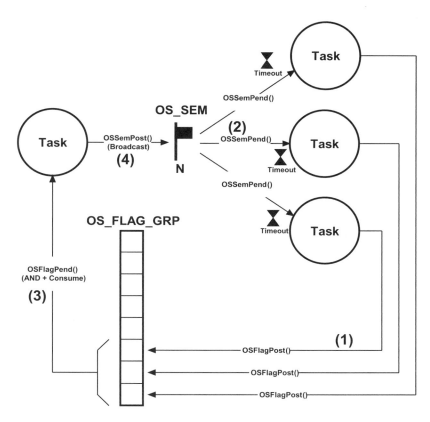

Figure 14-11 **Multiple Task Rendezvous**

F14-11(1) Each task that needs to synchronize at the rendezvous needs to set an event flag bit (and specify OS_OPT_POST_NO_SCHED).

F14-11(2) The task needs to wait for the semaphore to be signaled.

F14-11(3) The task that will be broadcasting must wait for "all" of the event flags corresponding to each task to be set.

F14-11(4) When all waiting tasks are ready, the task that will synchronize the waiting task issues a broadcast to the semaphore.

14-5 SUMMARY

Three methods are presented to allow an ISR or a task to signal one or more tasks: semaphores, task semaphores, and event flags.

Both semaphores and task semaphores contain a counter allowing them to perform credit tracking and accumulate the occurrence of events. If an ISR or task needs to signal a single task (as opposed to multiple tasks when the event occurs), it makes sense to use a task semaphore since it prevents the user from having to declare an external semaphore object. Also, task semaphore services are slightly faster (in execution time) than semaphores.

Event flags are used when a task needs to synchronize with the occurrence of one or more events. However, event flags cannot perform credit tracking since a single bit (as opposed to a counter) represents each event.

14

15

Message Passing

It is sometimes necessary for a task or an ISR to communicate information to another task. This information transfer is called *inter-task* communication. Information can be communicated between tasks in two ways: through global data, or by sending messages.

As seen in Chapter 13, "Resource Management" on page 215, when using global variables, each task or ISR must ensure that it has exclusive access to variables. If an ISR is involved, the only way to ensure exclusive access to common variables is to disable interrupts. If two tasks share data, each can gain exclusive access to variables either by disabling interrupts, locking the scheduler, using a semaphore, or preferably, using a mutual-exclusion semaphore. Note that a task can only communicate information to an ISR by using global variables. A task is not aware when a global variable is changed by an ISR, unless the ISR signals the task, or the task polls the contents of a variable periodically.

Messages can either be sent to an intermediate object called a *message queue*, or directly to a task since in µC/OS-III, each task has its own built-in message queue. Use an external message queue if multiple tasks are to wait for messages. Send a message directly to a task if only one task will process the data received.

When a task waits for a message to arrive, it does not consume CPU time.

15-1 MESSAGES

A message consists of a pointer to data, a variable containing the size of the data being pointed to, and a timestamp indicating when the message was sent. The pointer can point to a data area or even a function. Obviously, the sender and the receiver must agree as to the contents and the meaning of the message. In other words, the receiver of the message will know the meaning of the message received to be able to process it. For example, an Ethernet controller receives a packet and sends a pointer to this packet to a task that knows how to handle the packet.

The message contents must always remain in scope since the data is actually sent by reference instead of by value. In other words, data sent is not copied. Consider using dynamically allocated memory as described in Chapter 17, "Memory Management" on page 329. Alternatively, pass pointers to a global variable, a global data structure, a global array, or a function, etc.

15-2 MESSAGE QUEUES

A message queue is a kernel object allocated by the application. In fact, you can allocate any number of message queues. The only limit is the amount of RAM available.

There are a number of operations that the user can perform on message queues, summarized in Figure 15-1. However, an ISR can only call OSQPost(). A message queue must be created before sending messages through it.

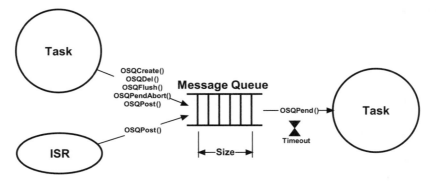

Figure 15-1 **Operations on message queue**

Message queues are drawn as a first-in, first-out pipe (FIFO). However, with µC/OS-III, it is possible to post messages in last-in, first-out order (LIFO). The LIFO mechanism is useful when a task or an ISR must send an "urgent" message to a task. In this case, the message bypasses all other messages already in the message queue. The size of the message queue is configurable at run time.

The small hourglass close to the receiving task indicates that the task has an option to specify a timeout. This timeout indicates that the task is willing to wait for a message to be sent to the message queue within a certain amount of time. If the message is not sent within that time, µC/OS-III resumes the task and returns an error code indicating that the task was made ready to run because of a timeout, and not because the message was received. It is possible to specify an infinite timeout and indicate that the task is willing to wait forever for the message to arrive.

The message queue also contains a list of tasks waiting for messages to be sent to the message queue. Multiple tasks can wait on a message queue as shown in Figure 15-2. When a message is sent to the message queue, the highest priority task waiting on the message queue receives the message. Optionally, the sender can *broadcast* a message to all tasks waiting on the message queue. In this case, if any of the tasks receiving the message from the broadcast has a higher priority than the task sending the message (or interrupted task, if the message is sent by an ISR), µC/OS-III will run the highest-priority task that is waiting. Notice that not all tasks must specify a timeout; some tasks may want to wait forever.

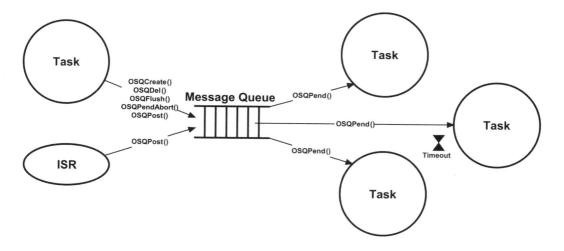

Figure 15-2 **Multiple tasks waiting on a message queue**

15-3 TASK MESSAGE QUEUE

It is fairly rare to find applications where multiple tasks wait on a single message queue. Because of this, a message queue is built into each task and the user can send messages directly to a task without going through an external message queue object. This feature not only simplifies the code but, is also more efficient than using a separate message queue object. The message queue that is built into each task is shown in Figure 15-3.

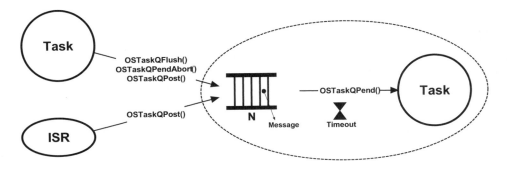

Figure 15-3 **Task message queue**

Task message queue services in μC/OS-III start with the `OSTaskQ???()` prefix, and services available to the application programmer are described in Appendix A, "μC/OS-III API Reference Manual" on page 381. Setting `OS_CFG_TASK_EN` in `OS_CFG.H` enables task message queue services. The code for task message queue management is found in `OS_TASK.C`.

Use this feature if the code knows which task to send the message(s) to. For example, if receiving an interrupt from an Ethernet controller, send the address of the received packet to the task that will be responsible for processing the received packet.

15

15-4 BILATERAL RENDEZVOUS

Two tasks can synchronize their activities by using two message queues, as shown in Figure 15-4. This is called a *bilateral rendezvous* and works the same as with semaphores except that both tasks may send messages to each other. A bilateral rendezvous cannot be performed between a task and an ISR since an ISR cannot wait on a message queue.

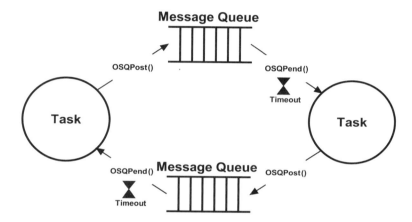

Figure 15-4 **Bilateral Rendezvous**

15

In a bilateral rendezvous, each message queue holds a maximum of one message. Both message queues are initially created empty. When the task on the left reaches the rendezvous point, it sends a message to the top message queue and waits for a message to arrive on the bottom message queue. Similarly, when the task on the right reaches its rendezvous point, it sends a message to the message queue on the bottom and waits for a message to arrive on the top message queue.

Figure 15-5 shows how to use task-message queues to perform a bilateral rendezvous.

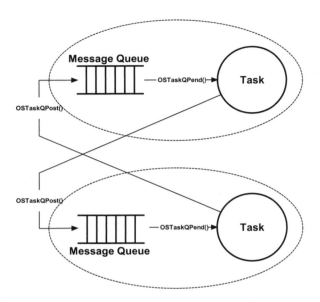

Figure 15-5 **Figure Bilateral Rendezvous with task message queues**

15-5 FLOW CONTROL

Task-to-task communication often involves data transfer from one task to another. One task produces data while the other *consumes* it. However, data processing takes time and consumers might not consume data as fast as it is produced. In other words, it is possible for the producer to overflow the message queue if a higher-priority task preempts the consumer. One way to solve this problem is to add flow control in the process as shown in Figure 15-6.

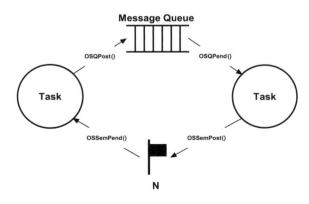

Figure 15-6 **Producer and consumer tasks with flow control**

Here, a counting semaphore is used, initialized with the number of allowable messages that can be sent by the consumer. If the consumer cannot queue more than 10 messages, the counting semaphore contains a count of 10.

As shown in the pseudo code of Listing 15-1, the producer must wait on the semaphore before it is allowed to send a message. The consumer waits for messages and, when processed, signals the semaphore.

```
Producer Task:
Pend on Semaphore;
Send message to message queue;

Consumer Task:
Wait for message from message queue;
Signal the semaphore;
```

Listing 15-1 **Producer and consumer flow control**

Combining the task message queue and task semaphores (see Chapter 14, "Synchronization" on page 257), it is easy to implement flow control as shown in Figure 15-7. In this case, however, `OSTaskSemSet()` must be called immediately after creating the task to set the value of the task semaphore to the same value as the maximum number of allowable messages in the task message queue.

15

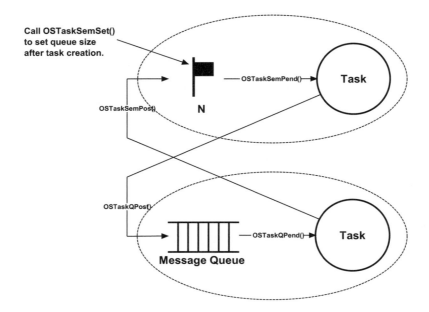

Call OSTaskSemSet()
to set queue size
after task creation.

OSTaskSemPend()

Task

OSTaskSemPost()

N

OSTaskQPost()

OSTaskQPend()

Task

Message Queue

Figure 15-7 **Flow control with task semaphore and task message queue**

15-6 KEEPING THE DATA IN SCOPE

The messages sent typically point to data structures, variables, arrays, tables, etc. However, it is important to realize that the data must remain static until the receiver of the data completes its processing of the data. Once sent, the sender must not touch the sent data. This seems obvious, however it is easy to forget.

One possibility is to use the fixed-size memory partition manager provided with µC/OS-III (see Chapter 17, "Memory Management" on page 329) to dynamically allocate and free memory blocks used to pass the data. Figure 15-8 shows an example. For sake of illustration, assume that a device is sending data bytes to the UART in packets using a protocol. In this case, the first byte of a packet is unique and the end-of-packet byte is also unique.

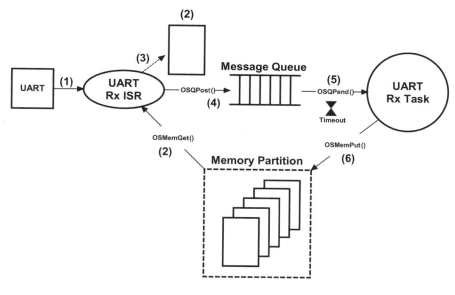

Figure 15-8 **Using memory partitions for message contents**

F15-8(1)   Here, a UART generates an interrupt when characters are received.

F15-8(2)   The pseudo-code in Listing 15-2 shows what the UART ISR code might look like. There are a lot of details omitted for sake of simplicity. The ISR reads the byte received from the UART and sees if it corresponds to a start of packet. If it is, a buffer is obtained from the memory partition.

F15-8(3)   The received byte is then placed in the buffer.

F15-8(4)   If the data received is an end-of-packet byte, simply post the address of the buffer to the message queue so that the task can process the received packet.

F15-8(5)   If the message sent makes the UART task the highest priority task, μC/OS-III will switch to that task at the end of the ISR instead of returning to the interrupted task. The task retrieves the packet from the message queue. Note that the OSQPend() call also returns the number of bytes in the packet and a time stamp indicating when the message was sent.

F15-8(6)   When the task is finished processing the packet, the buffer is returned to the memory partition it came from by calling OSMemPut().

15

```
void  UART_ISR (void)
{
    OS_ERR  err;


    RxData = Read byte from UART;
    if (RxData == Start of Packet) {            /* See if we need a new buffer    */
        RxDataPtr = OSMemGet(&UART_MemPool,     /* Yes                            */
                        &err);
        RxDataCtr = 0;
    } else {
        RxDataCtr++;                            /* Update number of bytes received */
    }
    if (RxData == End of Packet byte) {         /* See if we got a full packet    */
        OSQPost((OS_Q       *)&UART_Q,          /* Yes, post to task for processing */
                (void       *)RxDataPtr,
                (OS_MSG_SIZE)RxDataCtr,
                (OS_OPT     )OS_OPT_POST_FIFO,
                (OS_ERR     *)&err);
        RxDataPtr = NULL;                       /* Don't point to sent buffer     */
        RxDataCtr = 0;
    } else; {
        *RxDataPtr++ = RxData;                  /* Save the byte received         */
    }
}
```

Listing 15-2 **UART ISR Pseudo-code**

15-7 USING MESSAGE QUEUES

Table 15-1 shows a summary of message-queue services available from µC/OS-III. Refer to Appendix A, "µC/OS-III API Reference Manual" on page 381 for a full description on their use.

Function Name	Operation
OSQCreate()	Create a message queue.
OSQDel()	Delete a message queue.
OSQFlush()	Empty the message queue.
OSQPend()	Wait for a message.
OSQPendAbort()	Abort waiting for a message.
OSQPost()	Send a message through a message queue.

Table 15-1 **Message queue API summary**

Table 15-2 is a summary of task message queue services available from µC/OS-III. Refer to Appendix A, "µC/OS-III API Reference Manual" on page 381, for a full description on how to their use.

Function Name	Operation
OSTaskQPend()	Wait for a message.
OSTaskQPendAbort()	Abort the wait for a message.
OSTaskQPost()	Send a message to a task.
OSTaskQFlush()	Empty the message queue.

Table 15-2 **Task message queue API summary**

15

Figure 15-9 shows an example of using a message queue when determining the speed of a rotating wheel.

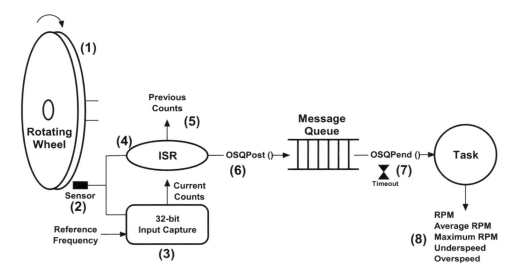

Figure 15-9 **Measuring RPM**

F15-9(1)   The goal is to measure the RPM of a rotating wheel.

F15-9(2)   A sensor is used to detect the passage of a hole in the wheel. In fact, to receive additional resolution, the wheel could contain multiple holes that are equally spaced.

F15-9(3)   A 32-bit input capture register is used to capture the value of a free-running counter when the hole is detected.

F15-9(4)   An interrupt is generated when the hole is detected. The ISR reads the current count of the input capture register and subtracts the value of the previous capture to receive the time it took for one rotation (assuming only a single hole).

```
Delta Counts    = Current Counts - Previous Counts;
Previous Counts = Current Counts;
```

F15-9(5)   The delta counts are sent to a message queue. Since a message is actually a pointer, if the pointer is 32-bits wide on the processor in use, simply cast the 32-bit delta counts to a pointer and send this through the message queue. A safer and more portable approach is to dynamically allocate storage to hold the delta counts using a memory block from µC/OS-III's memory management services (see Chapter 17, "Memory Management" on page 329) and send the address of the allocated memory block.

F15-9(6)   When the message is sent, the RPM measurement task wakes up and computes the RPM as follows:

```
RPM = 60 * Reference Frequency / Delta Counts;
```

The user may specify a timeout on the pend call and the task will wake up if a message is not sent within the timeout period. This allows the user to easily detect that the wheel is not rotating and therefore, the RPM is 0.

F15-9(7)   Along with computing RPM, the task can also compute average RPM, maximum RPM, and whether the speed is above or below thresholds, etc.

15

A few interesting things are worth noting about the above example. First, the ISR is very short; read the input capture and post the delta counts to the task to accomplish the time-consuming math. Second, with the timeout on the pend, it is easy to detect that the wheel is stopped. Finally, the task can perform additional calculations and can further detect such errors as the wheel spinning too fast or too slow. In fact, the task can notify other tasks about these errors, if needed.

Listing 15-3 shows how to implement the RPM measurement example using µC/OS-III's message queue services. Some of the code is pseudo-code, while the calls to µC/OS-III services are actual calls with their appropriate arguments.

```
OS_Q        RPM_Q;                                              (1)
CPU_INT32U  DeltaCounts;
CPU_INT32U  CurrentCounts;
CPU_INT32U  PreviousCounts;


void main (void)
{
    OS_ERR  err ;
    :
    OSInit(&err) ;                                             (2)
    :
    OSQCreate((OS_Q     *)&RPM_Q,
            (CPU_CHAR *)"My Queue",
            (OS_MSG_QTY)10,
            (OS_ERR    *)&err);
    :
    OSStart(&err);
}


void RPM_ISR (void)                                           (3)
{
    OS_ERR  err;


    Clear the interrupt from the sensor;
    CurrentCounts  = Read the input capture;
    DeltaCounts    = CurrentCounts - PreviousCounts;
    PreviousCounts = CurrentCounts;
    OSQPost((OS_Q     *)&RPM_Q,                               (4)
        (void      *)DeltaCounts,
        (OS_MSG_SIZE)sizeof(void *),
        (OS_OPT     )OS_OPT_POST_FIFO,
        (OS_ERR    *)&err);
}
```

15

```
void RPM_Task (void *p_arg)
{
    CPU_INT32U   delta;
    OS_ERR       err;
    OS_MSG_SIZE  size;
    CPU_TS       ts;


    DeltaCounts    = 0;
    PreviousCounts = 0;
    CurrentCounts  = 0;
    while (DEF_ON) {
        delta = (CPU_INT32U)OSQPend((OS_Q        *)&RPM_Q,            (5)
                                    (OS_TICK      )OS_CFG_TICK_RATE * 10,
                                    (OS_OPT       )OS_OPT_PEND_BLOCKING,
                                    (OS_MSG_SIZE *)&size,
                                    (CPU_TS      *)&ts,
                                    (OS_ERR      *)&err);
        if (err == OS_ERR_TIMEOUT) {                                 (6)
            RPM = 0;
        } else {
            if (delta > 0u) {
                RPM = 60 * Reference Frequency / delta;              (7)
            }
        }
        Compute average RPM;                                         (8)
        Detect maximum RPM;
        Check for overspeed;
        Check for underspeed;
        :
        :
    }
}
```

Listing 15-3 **Pseudo-code of RPM measurement**

L15-3(1)   Variables are declared. Notice that it is necessary to allocate storage for the message queue itself.

L15-3(2)   Call **OSInit()** and create the message queue before it is used. The best place to do this is in startup code.

L15-3(3)   The RPM ISR clears the sensor interrupt and reads the value of the 32-bit input capture. Note that it is possible to read RPM if there is only a 16-bit input capture. The problem with a 16-bit input capture is that it is easy for it to overflow, especially at low RPMs.

The RPM ISR also computes delta counts directly in the ISR. It is just as easy to post the current counts and let the task compute the delta. However, the subtraction is a fast operation and does not significantly increase ISR processing time.

L15-3(4)   Send the delta counts to the RPM task, responsible for computing the RPM and perform additional computations. Note that the message gets lost if the queue is full when the user attempts to post. This happens if data is generated faster than it is processed. Unfortunately, it is not possible to implement flow control in the example because it is dealing with an ISR.

L15-3(5)   The RPM task starts by waiting for a message from the RPM ISR by pending on the message queue. The third argument specifies the timeout. In this case, ten seconds worth of timeout is specified. However, the value chosen depends on the requirements of an application.

Also notice that the ts variable contains the timestamp of when the post was completed. Determine the time it took for the task to respond to the message received by calling **OS_TS_GET( )**, and subtract the value of **ts**:

```
response_time = OS_TS_GET() - ts;
```

L15-3(6)   If a timeout occurs, assume the wheel is no longer spinning.

L15-3(7)   The RPM is computed from the delta counts received, and from the reference frequency of the free-running counter.

L15-3(8)   Additional computations are performed as needed. In fact, messages can be sent to different tasks in case error conditions are detected. The messages would be processed by the other tasks. For example, if the wheel spins too fast, another task can initiate a shutdown on the device that is controlling the wheel speed.

In Listing 15-4, OSQPost() and OSQPend() are replaced with OSTaskQPost() and OSTaskQPend() for the RPM measurement example. Notice that the code is slightly simpler to use and does not require creating a separate message queue object. However, when creating the RPM task, it is important to specify the size of the message queue used by the task and compile the application code with **OS_CFG_TASK_Q_EN** set to 1. The differences between using message queues and the task's message queue will be explained.

```
OS_TCB      RPM_TCB;                                        (1)
OS_STK      RPM_Stk[1000];
CPU_INT32U  DeltaCounts ;
CPU_INT32U  CurrentCounts ;
CPU_INT32U  PreviousCounts ;


void main (void)
{
    OS_ERR  err ;
    :
    OSInit(&err) ;
    :
    void  OSTaskCreate ((OS_TCB      *)&RPM_TCB,             (2)
                        (CPU_CHAR    *)"RPM Task",
                        (OS_TASK_PTR )RPM_Task,
                        (void        *)0,
                        (OS_PRIO     )10,
                        (CPU_STK     *)&RPM_Stk[0],
                        (CPU_STK_SIZE )100,
                        (CPU_STK_SIZE )1000,
                        (OS_MSG_QTY  )10,
                        (OS_TICK     )0,
                        (void        *)0,
                        (OS_OPT      )(OS_OPT_TASK_STK_CHK + OS_OPT_TASK_STK_CLR),
                        (OS_ERR      *)&err);
    :
    OSStart(&err);
}
```

```
void RPM_ISR (void)
{
    OS_ERR  err;

    Clear the interrupting from the sensor;
    CurrentCounts  = Read the input capture;
    DeltaCounts    = CurrentCounts — PreviousCounts;
    PreviousCounts = CurrentCounts;
    OSTaskQPost((OS_TCB     *)&RPM_TCB,                       (3)
                (void        *)DeltaCounts,
                (OS_MSG_SIZE)sizeof(DeltaCounts),
                (OS_OPT      )OS_OPT_POST_FIFO,
                (OS_ERR     *)&err);
}


void RPM_Task (void *p_arg)
{
    CPU_INT32U   delta;
    OS_ERR       err;
    OS_MSG_SIZE  size;
    CPU_TS       ts;


    DeltaCounts    = 0;
    PreviousCounts = 0;
    CurrentCounts  = 0;
    while (DEF_ON) {
        delta = (CPU_INT32U)OSTaskQPend((OS_TICK       )OS_CFG_TICK_RATE * 10,   (4)
                                        (OS_OPT        )OS_OPT_PEND_BLOCKING,
                                        (OS_MSG_SIZE *)&size,
                                        (CPU_TS       *)&ts,
                                        (OS_ERR       *)&err);
        if (err == OS_ERR_TIMEOUT) {
            RPM = 0;
        } else {
            if (delta > 0u) {
                RPM = 60 * ReferenceFrequency / delta;
            }
        }
        Compute average RPM;
        Detect maximum RPM;
        Check for overspeed;
        Check for underspeed;
        :
        :
    }
}
```

Listing 15-4 **Pseudo-code of RPM measurement**

L15-4(1)   Instead of declaring a message queue, it is important to know the OS_TCB of the task that will be receiving messages.

L15-4(2)   The RPM task is created and a queue size of 10 entries is specified. Of course, hard-coded values should not be specified in a real application, but instead, use #defines. Fixed numbers are used here for sake of illustration.

L15-4(3)   Instead of posting to a message queue, the ISR posts the message directly to the task, specifying the address of the OS_TCB of the task. This is known since the OS_TCB is allocated when creating the task.

L15-4(4)   The RPM task starts by waiting for a message from the RPM ISR by calling OSTaskQPend(). This is an inherent call so it is not necessary to specify the address of the OS_TCB to pend on as the current task is assumed. The second argument specifies the timeout. Here, ten seconds worth of timeout is specified, which corresponds to 6 RPM.

15-8 CLIENTS AND SERVERS

Another interesting use of message queues is shown in Figure 15-10. Here, a task (the server) is used to monitor error conditions that are sent to it by other tasks or ISRs (clients). For example, a client detects whether the RPM of the rotating wheel has been exceeded, another client detects whether an over-temperature exists, and yet another client detects that a user pressed a shutdown button. When the clients detect error conditions, they send a message through the message queue. The message sent indicates the error detected, which threshold was exceeded, the error code that is associated with error conditions, or even suggests the address of a function that will handle the error, and more.

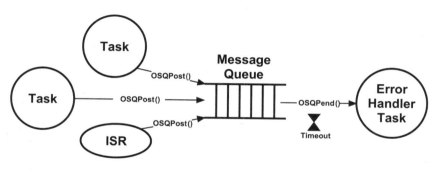

Figure 15-10 **Clients and Servers**

313

15-9 MESSAGE QUEUES INTERNALS

As previously described, a message consists of a pointer to actual data, a variable indicating the size of the data being pointed to and a timestamp indicating when the message was actually sent. When sent, a message is placed in a data structure of type OS_MSG, shown in Figure 15-11.

The sender and receiver are unaware of this data structure since everything is hidden through the APIs provided by µC/OS-III.

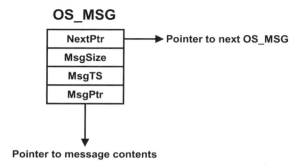

Figure 15-11 **OS_MSG structure**

µC/OS-III maintains a pool of free OS_MSGs. The total number of available messages in the pool is determined by the value of OS_CFG_MSG_POOL_SIZE found in OS_CFG_APP.H. When µC/OS-III is initialized, OS_MSGs are linked in a single linked list as shown in Figure 15-12. Notice that the free list is maintained by a data structure of type OS_MSG_POOL, which contains three fields: .NextPtr, which points to the free list; .NbrFree, which contains the number of free OS_MSGs in the pool; and finally .NbrUsed, which contains the number of OS_MSGs allocated to application.

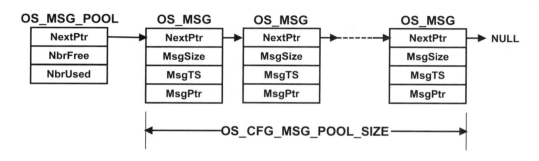

Figure 15-12 **Pool of free OS_MSGs**

Messages are queued using a data structure of type OS_MSG_Q, as shown in Figure 15-13.

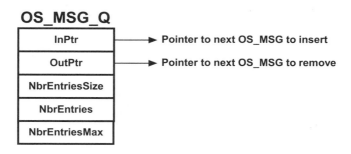

Figure 15-13 **OS_MSG_Q structure**

.InPtr   This field contains a pointer to where the next OS_MSG will be inserted in the queue. In fact, the OS_MSG will be inserted "after" the OS_MSG pointed to.

.OutPtr   This field contains a pointer to where the next OS_MSG will be extracted.

.NbrEntriesSize   This field contains the maximum number of OS_MSGs that the queue will hold. If an application attempts to send a message and the .NbrEntries matches this value, the queue is considered to be full and the OS_MSG will not be inserted.

.NbrEntries   This field contains the current number of OS_MSGs in the queue.

.NbrEntriesMax   This field contains the highest number of OS_MSGs existing in the queue at any given time.

A number of internal functions are used by µC/OS-III to manipulate the free list and messages. Specifically, OS_MsgQPut() inserts an OS_MSG in an OS_MSG_Q, OS_MsgQGet() extracts an OS_MSG from an OS_MSG_Q, and OS_MsgQFreeAll() returns all OS_MSGs in an OS_MSG_Q to the pool of free OS_MSGs. There are other OS_MsgQ??() functions in OS_MSG.C that are used during initialization.

Figure 15-14 shows an example of an **OS_MSG_Q** when four **OS_MSGs** are inserted.

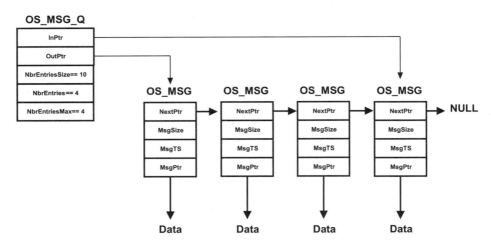

Figure 15-14 **OS_MSG_Q with four OS_MSGs**

OS_MSG_Qs are used inside two additional data structures: **OS_Q** and **OS_TCB**. Recall that an **OS_Q** is declared when creating a message queue object. An **OS_TCB** is a task control block and, as previously mentioned, each **OS_TCB** can have its own message queue when the configuration constant **OS_CFG_TASK_Q_EN** is set to 1 in **OS_CFG.H**. Figure 15-15 shows the contents of an **OS_Q** and partial contents of an **OS_TCB** containing an **OS_MSG_Q**. The **OS_MSG_Q** data structure is shown as an "exploded view" to emphasize the structure within the structure.

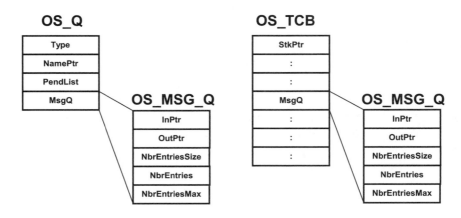

Figure 15-15 **OS_Q and OS_TCB each contain an OS_MSG_Q**

15-10 SUMMARY

Message queues are useful when a task or an ISR is to send data to another task. The data sent must remain in scope as it is actually sent by reference instead of by value. In other words, the data sent is not copied.

The task waiting for the data will not consume CPU time while waiting for a message to be sent to it.

If it is known which task is responsible for servicing messages sent by producers, use task message queue (i.e., **OSTaskQ???()**) services since they are simple and fast. Task message queue services are enabled when **OS_CFG_TASK_Q_EN** is set to 1 in **OS_CFG.H**.

If multiple tasks must wait for messages from the same message queue, allocate an **OS_Q** and have the tasks wait for messages to be sent to the queue. Alternatively, broadcast special messages to all tasks waiting on a message queue. Regular message queue services are enabled when **OS_CFG_Q_EN** is set to 1 in **OS_CFG.H**.

Messages are sent using an **OS_MSG** data structure obtained by µC/OS-III from a pool. Set the maximum number of messages that can be sent to a message queue, or as many messages as are available in the pool.

15

15

16

Pending On Multiple Objects

In Chapter 10, "Pend Lists (or Wait Lists)" on page 183 we saw how multiple tasks can pend (or wait) on a single kernel object such as a semaphore, mutual exclusion semaphore, event flag group, or message queue. In this chapter, we will see how tasks can pend on multiple objects. However, µC/OS-III only allows for pend on multiple semaphores and/or message queues. In other words, it is not possible to pend on multiple event flag groups or mutual exclusion semaphores.

As shown in Figure 16-1, a task can pend on any number of semaphores or message queues at the same time. The first semaphore or message queue posted will make the task ready to run and compete for CPU time with other tasks in the ready list. As shown, a task pends on multiple objects by calling `OSPendMulti()` and specifies an optional timeout value. The timeout applies to all of the objects. If none of the objects are posted within the specified timeout, the task resumes with an error code indicating that the pend timed out.

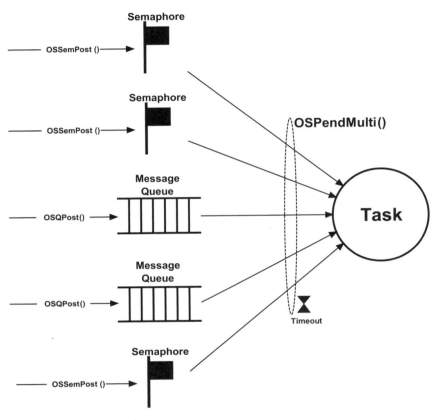

Figure 16-1 **Task pending on multiple objects**

Listing 16-1 shows the function prototype of `OSPendMulti()` and Figure 16-2 exhibits an array of **OS_PEND_DATA** elements.

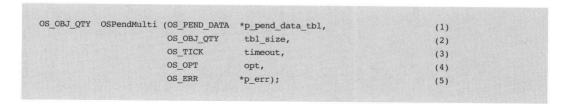

```
OS_OBJ_QTY  OSPendMulti (OS_PEND_DATA  *p_pend_data_tbl,      (1)
                         OS_OBJ_QTY     tbl_size,             (2)
                         OS_TICK        timeout,              (3)
                         OS_OPT         opt,                  (4)
                         OS_ERR        *p_err);               (5)
```

Listing 16-1 **OSPendMulti() prototype**

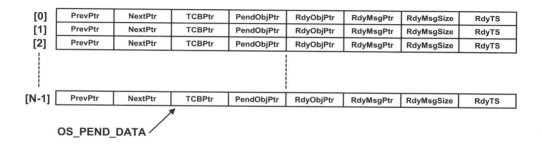

OS_PEND_DATA

Figure 16-2 **Array of OS_PEND_DATA**

16

L16-1(1)   `OSPendMulti()` is passed an array of **OS_PEND_DATA** elements. The caller must instantiate an array of **OS_PEND_DATA**. The size of the array depends on the total number of kernel objects that the task wants to pend on. For example, if the task wants to pend on three semaphores and two message queues then the array contains five **OS_PEND_DATA** elements as shown below:

```
OS_PEND_DATA   my_pend_multi_tbl[5];
```

The calling task needs to initialize the `.PendObjPtr` of each element of the array to point to each of the objects to be pended on. For example:

```
OS_SEM  MySem1;
OS_SEM  MySem2;
OS_SEM  MySem3;
OS_Q    MyQ1;
OS_Q    MyQ2;


void  MyTask (void)
{
    OS_ERR          err;
    OS_PEND_DATA  my_pend_multi_tbl[5];
    :
    while (DEF_ON) {
        :
        my_pend_multi_tbl[0].PendObjPtr = (OS_PEND_OBJ)&MySem1;        (6)
        my_pend_multi_tbl[1].PendObjPtr = (OS_PEND_OBJ)&MySem2;
        my_pend_multi_tbl[2].PendObjPtr = (OS_PEND_OBJ)&MySem3;
        my_pend_multi_tbl[3].PendObjPtr = (OS_PEND_OBJ)&MyQ1;
        my_pend_multi_tbl[4].PendObjPtr = (OS_PEND_OBJ)&MyQ2;
        OSPendMulti((OS_PEND_DATA *)&my_pend_multi_tbl[0],
                    (OS_OBJ_QTY    )5,
                    (OS_TICK       )0,
                    (OS_OPT        )OS_OPT_PEND_BLOCKING,
                    (OS_ERR      *)&err);
        /* Check 'err" */
        :
    }
}
```

L16-1(2)   This argument specifies the size of the **OS_PEND_DATA** table. In the above example, this is 5.

L16-1(3)   Specify whether or not to timeout in case none of the objects are posted within a certain amount of time. A non-zero value indicates the number of ticks to timeout. Specifying zero indicates the task will wait forever for any of the objects to be posted.

L16-1(4)   The "opt" argument specifies whether to wait for objects to be posted (set opt to **OS_OPT_PEND_BLOCKING**) or, not block if none of the objects have already been posted (set opt to **OS_OPT_PEND_NON_BLOCKING**).

F16-2(1) As with most µC/OS-III function calls, specify the address of a variable that will receive an error code based on the outcome of the function call. See Appendix A, "µC/OS-III API Reference Manual" on page 381 for a list of possible error codes. As always, it is highly recommended to examine the error return code.

F16-2(2) Note that all objects are cast to **OS_PEND_OBJ** data types.

When called, **OSPendMulti()** first starts by validating that all of the objects specified in the **OS_PEND_DATA** table are either an **OS_SEM** or an **OS_Q**. If not, an error code is returned.

Next, **OSPendMulti()** goes through the **OS_PEND_DATA** table to see if any of the objects have already posted. If so, **OSPendMulti()** fills the following fields in the table: **.RdyObjPtr**, **.RdyMsgPtr**, **.RdyMsgSize** and **.RdyTS**.

.RdyObjPtr is a pointer to the object if the object has been posted. For example, if the first object in the table is a semaphore and the semaphore has been posted to, **my_pend_multi_tbl[0].RdyObjPtr** is set to **my_pend_multi_tbl[0].PendObjPtr**.

.RdyMsgPtr is a pointer to a message if the object in the table at this entry is a message queue and a message was received from the message queue.

.RdyMsgSize is the size of the message received if the object in the table at this entry is a message queue and a message was received from the message queue.

.RdyTS is the timestamp of when the object posted. This allows the user to know when a semaphore or message queue posts.

If there are no objects posted, then **OSPendMulti()** places the current task in the wait list of all the objects that it is pending on. This is a complex and tedious process for **OSPendMulti()** since there can be other tasks in the pend list of some of these objects we are pending on.

To indicate how tricky things get, Figure 16-3 is an example of a task pending on two semaphores.

16

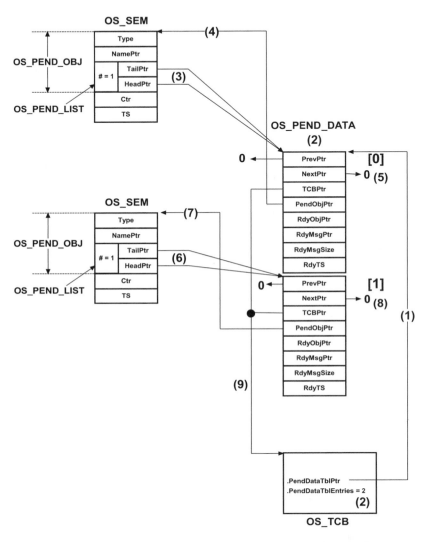

Figure 16-3 **Task pending on two semaphores**

F16-3(1)   A pointer to the base address of the **OS_PEND_DATA** table is placed in the **OS_TCB** of the task placed in the pend list of the two semaphores.

F16-3(2)   The numbers of entries in the **OS_PEND_DATA** table are also placed in the **OS_TCB**. Again, this task is waiting on two semaphores and therefore there are two entries in the table.

F16-3(3)   Entry [0] of the **OS_PEND_DATA** table is linked to the semaphore object specified by that entry's **.PendObjPtr**.

F16-3(4)   This pointer was specified by the caller of **OSPendMulti()**.

F16-3(5)   Since there is only one task in the pend list of the semaphore, the **.PrevPtr** and **.NextPtr** are pointing to **NULL**.

F16-3(6)   The second semaphore points to the second entry in the **OS_PEND_DATA** table.

F16-3(7)   This pointer was specified by the caller of **OSPendMulti()**.

F16-3(8)   The second semaphore only has one entry in its pend list. Therefore the **.PrevPtr** and **.NextPtr** both point to **NULL**.

F16-3(9)   **OSPendMulti()** links back each **OS_PEND_DATA** entry to the task that is waiting on the two semaphores.

Figure 16-4 is a more complex example where one task is pending on two semaphores while another task also pends on one of the two semaphores. The examples presented so far only show semaphores, but they could be combinations of semaphores and message queues.

16

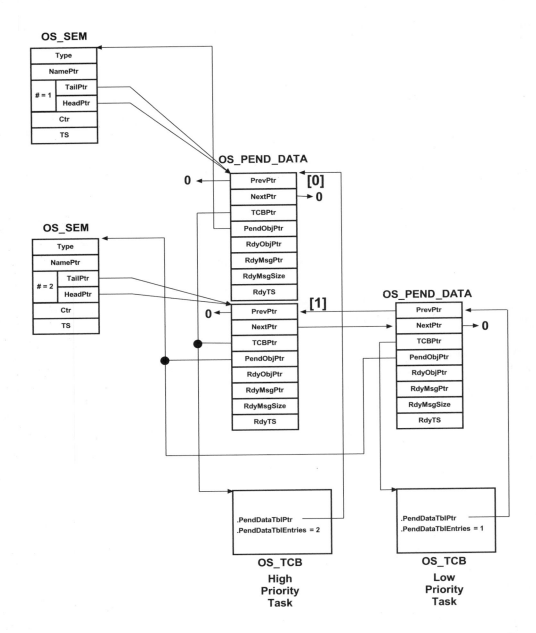

Figure 16-4 **Tasks pending on semaphores**

When either an ISR or a task signals or sends a message to one of the objects that the task is pending on, OSPendMulti() returns, indicating in the OS_PEND_DATA table which object was posted. This is done by only filling in "one" of the .RdyObjPtr entries, the one that corresponds to the object posted as shown in Figure 16-2.

Only one of the entries in the OS_PEND_DATA table will have a .RdyObjPtr with a non-NULL value while all the other entries have the .RdyObjPtr set to NULL. Going back to the case where a task waits on five semaphores and two message queues, if the first message queue is posted while the task is pending on all those objects, the OS_PEND_DATA table will be as shown in Figure 16-5.

	.PrevPtr	.NextPtr	.TCBPtr	.PendObjPtr	.RdyObjPtr	.RdyMsgPtr	.RdyMsgSize	.RdyTS
[0]	0	0	TCBPtr	PendObjPtr	0	0	0	0
[1]	0	0	TCBPtr	PendObjPtr	0	0	0	0
[2]	0	0	TCBPtr	PendObjPtr	0	0	0	0
[3]	0	0	TCBPtr	&MyQ1	&MyQ1	Msg Ptr	Msg Size	Timestamp
[4]	0	0	TCBPtr	PendObjPtr	0	0	0	0

Figure 16-5 **Message queue #1 posted before timeout expired**

16-1 SUMMARY

µC/OS-III allows tasks to pend on multiple kernel objects.

OSPendMulti() can only pend on multiple semaphores and message queues, not event flags and mutual-exclusion semaphores.

If the objects are already posted when OSPendMulti() is called, µC/OS-III will specify which of the objects in the list of objects have already been posted.

If none of the objects are posted, OSPendMulti() will place the calling task in the pend list of all the desired objects. OSPendMulti() will return as soon as one of the objects is posted. In this case, OSPendMulti() will indicate which object was posted.

OSPendMulti() is a complex function that has potentially long critical sections.

16

327

16

Chapter

17

Memory Management

An application can allocate and free dynamic memory using any ANSI C compiler's **malloc()** and **free()** functions, respectively. However, using **malloc()** and **free()** in an embedded real-time system may be dangerous. Eventually, it might not be possible to obtain a single contiguous memory area due to fragmentation. Fragmentation is the development of a large number of separate free areas (i.e., the total free memory is fragmented into small, non-contiguous pieces). Execution time of **malloc()** and **free()** is generally nondeterministic given the algorithms used to locate a contiguous block of free memory.

µC/OS-III provides an alternative to **malloc()** and **free()** by allowing an application to obtain fixed-sized memory blocks from a partition made from a contiguous memory area, as illustrated in Figure 17-1. All memory blocks are the same size, and the partition contains an integral number of blocks. Allocation and deallocation of these memory blocks is performed in constant time and is deterministic. The partition itself is typically allocated statically (as an array), but can also be allocated by using **malloc()** as long as it is never freed.

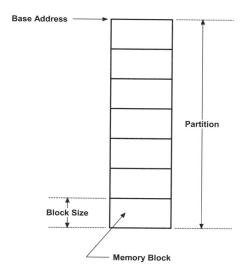

Figure 17-1 **Memory Partition**

As indicated in Figure 17-2, more than one memory partition may exist in an application and each one may have a different number of memory blocks and be a different size. An application can obtain memory blocks of different sizes based upon requirements. However, a specific memory block must always be returned to the partition that it came from. This type of memory management is not subject to fragmentation except that it is possible to run out of memory blocks. It is up to the application to decide how many partitions to have and how large each memory block should be within each partition.

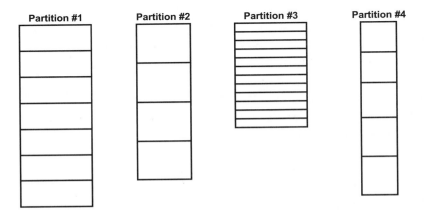

Figure 17-2 **Multiple Memory Partitions**

17-1 CREATING A MEMORY PARTITION

Before using a memory partition, it must be created. This allows µC/OS-III to know something about the memory partition so that it can manage their allocation and deallocation. Once created, a memory partition is as shown in Figure 17-3. Calling OSMemCreate() creates a memory partition.

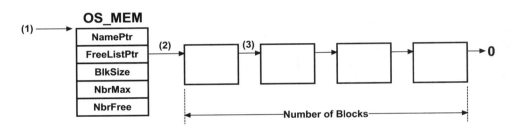

Figure 17-3 **Created Memory Partition**

F17-3(1)   When creating a partition, the application code supplies the address of a
            memory partition control block (**OS_MEM**). Typically, this memory control block
            is allocated from static memory, however it can also be obtained from the heap
            by calling **malloc()**. The application code should however never deallocate it.

F17-3(2)   **OSMemCreate()** organizes the continuous memory provided into a singly
            linked list and stores the pointer to the beginning of the list in the **OS_MEM**
            structure.

F17-3(3)   Each memory block must be large enough to hold a pointer. Given the nature
            of the linked list, a block needs to be able to point to the next block.

Listing 17-1 indicates how to create a memory partition with μC/OS-III.

```
OS_MEM        MyPartition;                                      (1)
CPU_INT08U    MyPartitionStorage[12][100];                      (2)


void  main (void)                                               (3)
{
    OS_ERR   err;
    :
    :
    OSInit(&err);
    :
    OSMemCreate((OS_MEM     *)&MyPartition,                     (4)
                (CPU_CHAR   *)"My Partition",                   (5)
                (void       *)&MyPartitionStorage[0][0],        (6)
                (OS_MEM_QTY ) 12,                               (7)
                (OS_MEM_SIZE)100,                               (8)
                (OS_ERR     *)&err);                            (9)
    /* Check 'err" */
    :
    :
    OSStart(&err);
}
```

Listing 17-1 **Creating a memory partition**

L17-1(1)   An application needs to allocate storage for a memory partition control block.
            This can be a static allocation as shown here or **malloc()** can be used in the code.
            However, the application code must not deallocate the memory control block.

L17-1(2)   The application also needs to allocate storage for the memory that will be split into memory blocks. This can also be a static allocation or **malloc()** can be used. The same reasoning applies. Do not deallocate this storage since other tasks may rely on the existence of this storage.

L17-1(3)   Memory partition must be created before allocating and deallocating blocks from the partition. One of the best places to create memory partitions is in **main()** prior to starting the multitasking process. Of course, an application can call a function from **main()** to do this instead of actually placing the code directly in **main()**.

L17-1(4)   Pass the address of the memory partition control block to **OSMemCreate()**. Never reference any of the internal members of the **OS_MEM** data structure. Instead, use µC/OS-III's API.

L17-1(5)   Assign a name to the memory partition. There is no limit to the length of the ASCII string as µC/OS-III saves a pointer to the ASCII string in the partition control block and not the actual characters.

L17-1(6)   Pass the base address of the storage area reserved for the memory blocks.

L17-1(7)   Specify how many memory blocks are available from this memory partition. Hard coded numbers are used for the sake of the illustration but one should instead use **#define** constants.

L17-1(8)   Specify the size of each memory block in the partition. Again, a hard coded value is used for illustration, which is not recommended in real code.

L17-1(9)   As with most µC/OS-III services, **OSMemCreate()** returns an error code indicating the outcome of the service. The call is successful if "**err**" contains **OS_ERR_NONE**.

Listing 17-2 shows how to create a memory partition with µC/OS-III, this time using **malloc()** to allocate storage. Do not deallocate the memory control block or the storage for the partition.

```
OS_MEM      *MyPartitionPtr;                                    (1)


void  main (void)
{
    OS_ERR    err;
    void    *p_storage;
    :
    OSInit(&err);
    :
    MyPartitionPtr = (OS_MEM *)malloc(sizeof(OS_MEM));          (2)
    if (MyPartitionPtr != (OS_MEM *)0) {
        p_storage = malloc(12 * 100);                          (3)
        if (p_storage != (void *)0) {
            OSMemCreate((OS_MEM     *)MyPartitionPtr,           (4)
                        (CPU_CHAR   *)"My Partition",
                        (void       *)p_storage,               (5)
                        (OS_MEM_QTY ) 12,                      (6)
                        (OS_MEM_SIZE)100,                      (6)
                        (OS_ERR     *)&err);
            /* Check 'err" */
        }
    }
    :
    OSStart(&err);
}
```

Listing 17-2 **Creating a memory partition**

17

L17-2(1)   Instead of allocating static storage for the memory partition control block, assign a pointer that receives the OS_MEM allocated using `malloc()`.

L17-2(2)   The application allocates storage for the memory control block.

L17-2(3)   Allocate storage for the memory partition.

L17-2(4)   Pass a pointer to the allocated memory control block to `OSMemCreate()`.

L17-2(5)   Pass the base address of the storage used for the partition.

L17-2(6)   Finally, pass the number of blocks and the size of each block so that µC/OS-III creates the linked list of 12 blocks of 100 bytes each. Again, hard coded numbers are used, but these would typically be replaced by `#defines`.

17-2 GETTING A MEMORY BLOCK FROM A PARTITION

Application code can request a memory block from a partition by calling **OSMemGet()** as shown in Listing 17-3. The code assumes that the partition was already created.

```
OS_MEM       MyPartition;                                              (1)
CPU_INT08U  *MyDataBlkPtr;


void  MyTask (void *p_arg)
{
    OS_ERR  err;


    :
    while (DEF_ON) {
        :
        MyDataBlkPtr = (CPU_INT08U *)OSMemGet((OS_MEM    *)&MyPartition,  (2)
                                              (OS_ERR    *)&err);
        if (err == OS_ERR_NONE) {                                        (3)
            /* You have a memory block from the partition */
        }
        :
        :
    }
}
```

Listing 17-3 **Obtaining a memory block from a partition**

L17-3(1)   The memory partition control block must be accessible by all tasks or ISRs that will be using the partition.

L17-3(2)   Simply call **OSMemGet()** to obtain a memory block from the desired partition. A pointer to the allocated memory block is returned. This is similar to **malloc()**, except that the memory block comes from a pool that is guaranteed to not fragment.

L17-3(3)   It is important to examine the returned error code to ensure that there are free memory blocks and that the application can start putting content in the memory blocks.

17-3 RETURNING A MEMORY BLOCK TO A PARTITION

The application code must return an allocated memory block back to the proper partition when finished. Do this by calling **OSMemPut()** as shown in Listing 17-4. The code assumes that the partition was already created.

```
OS_MEM       MyPartition;                                    (1)
CPU_INT08U  *MyDataBlkPtr;


void  MyTask (void *p_arg)
{
    OS_ERR  err;


    :
    while (DEF_ON) {
        :
        OSMemPut((OS_MEM  *)&MyPartition,                    (2)
                 (void     *)MyDataBlkPtr,                    (3)
                 (OS_ERR   *)&err);
        if (err == OS_ERR_NONE) {                            (4)
            /* You properly returned the memory block to the partition */
        }
        :
        :
    }
}
```

Listing 17-4 **Returning a memory block to a partition**

L17-4(1)   The memory partition control block must be accessible by all tasks or ISRs that will be using the partition.

L17-4(2)   Simply call **OSMemPut()** to return the memory block back to the memory partition. Note that there is no check to see whether the proper memory block is being returned to the proper partition (assuming you have multiple different partitions). It is therefore important to be careful (as is necessary when designing embedded systems).

L17-4(3)   Pass the pointer to the data area that is allocated so that it can be returned to the pool. Note that a "**void ***" is assumed.

L17-4(4)   Examine the returned error code to ensure that the call was successful.

335

17-4 USING MEMORY PARTITIONS

Memory management services are enabled at compile time by setting the configuration constant OS_CFG_MEM_EN to 1 in OS_CFG.H.

There are a number of operations to perform on memory partitions as summarized in Table 13-1.

Function Name	Operation
OSMemCreate()	Create a memory partition.
OSMemGet()	Obtain a memory block from a memory partition.
OSMemPut()	Return a memory block to a memory partition.

Table 17-1 **Memory Partition API summary**

OSMemCreate() can only be called from task-level code, but OSMemGet() and OSMemPut() can be called by Interrupt Service Routines (ISRs).

Listing 17-4 shows an example of how to use the dynamic memory allocation feature of µC/OS-III, as well as message-passing capabilities (see Chapter 15, "Message Passing" on page 295). In this example, the task on the left reads and checks the value of analog inputs (pressures, temperatures, and voltage) and sends a message to the second task if any of the analog inputs exceed a threshold. The message sent contains information about which channel had the error, an error code, an indication of the severity of the error, and other information.

Error handling in this example is centralized. Other tasks, or even ISRs, can post error messages to the error-handling task. The error-handling task could be responsible for displaying error messages on a monitor (a display), logging errors to a disk, or dispatching other tasks to take corrective action based on the error.

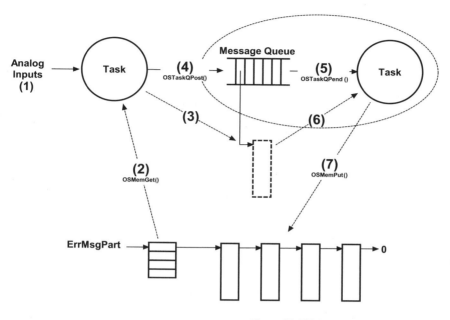

Figure 17-4 **Using a Memory Partition – non blocking**

F17-4(1)   The analog inputs are read by the task. The task determines that one of the inputs is outside a valid range and an error message needs to be sent to the error handler.

F17-4(2)   The task then obtains a memory block from a memory partition so that it can place information regarding the detected error.

F17-4(3)   The task writes this information to the memory block. As mentioned above, the task places the analog channel that is at fault, an error code, an indication of the severity, possible solutions, and more. There is no need to store a timestamp in the message, as time stamping is a built-in feature of µC/OS-III so the receiving task will know when the message was posted.

F17-4(4)   Once the message is complete, it is posted to the task that will handle such error messages. Of course the receiving task needs to know how the information is placed in the message. Once the message is sent, the analog input task is no longer allowed (by convention) to access the memory block since it sent it out to be processed.

F17-4(5)   The error handler task (on the right) normally pends on the message queue. This task will not execute until a message is sent to it.

F17-4(6)   When a message is received, the error handler task reads the contents of the message and performs necessary action(s). As indicated, once sent, the sender will not do anything else with the message.

F17-4(7)   Once the error handler task is finished processing the message, it simply returns the memory block to the memory partition. The sender and receiver therefore need to know about the memory partition or, the sender can pass the address of the memory partition as part of the message and the error handler task will know where to return the memory block.

Sometimes it is useful to have a task wait for a memory block in case a partition runs out of blocks. µC/OS-III does not support pending on partitions, but it is possible to support this requirement by adding a counting semaphore (see Chapter 13, "Resource Management" on page 215) to guard the memory partition. This is illustrated in Figure 17-5.

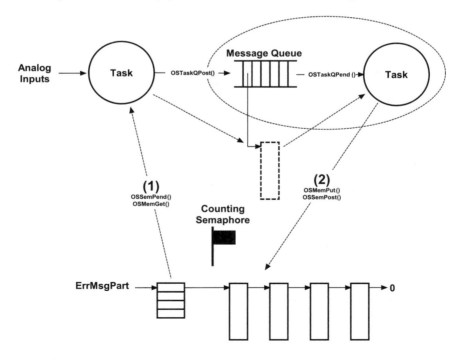

Figure 17-5 **Using a Memory Partition - blocking**

F17-5(1)   To obtain a memory block, simply obtain the semaphore by calling OSSemPend() and call OSMemGet() to receive the memory block.

F17-5(2)   To release a block, simply return the memory block by calling OSMemPut() and signal the semaphore by calling OSSemPost().

The above operations must be performed in order.

Note that the user may call OSMemGet() and OSMemPut() from an ISR since these functions do not block and in fact, execute very quickly. However, you cannot use blocking calls from ISRs.

17-5 SUMMARY

Do not use malloc() and free() in embedded systems since they lead to fragmentation.

It is possible to use malloc() to allocate memory from the heap, but do not deallocate the memory.

The application programmer can create an unlimited number of memory partitions (limited only by the amount of available RAM).

Memory partition services in µC/OS-III start with the OSMem???() prefix, and the services available to the application programmer are described in Appendix A, "µC/OS-III API Reference Manual" on page 381.

Memory management services are enabled at compile time by setting the configuration constant OS_CFG_MEM_EN to 1 in OS_CFG.H.

OSMemGet() and OSMemPut() can be called from ISRs.

17

17

18

Porting μC/OS-III

This chapter describes in general terms how to adapt μC/OS-III to different processors. Adapting μC/OS-III to a microprocessor or a microcontroller is called porting. Most of μC/OS-III is written in C for portability. However, it is still necessary to write processor-specific code in C and assembly language. μC/OS-III manipulates processor registers, which can only be done using assembly language. Porting μC/OS-III to different processors is relatively easy as μC/OS-III was designed to be portable and, since μC/OS-III is similar to μC/OS-II, the user can start from a μC/OS-II port. If there is already a port for the processor to be used, it is not necessary to read this chapter unless, of course, there is an interest in knowing how μC/OS-III processor-specific code works.

μC/OS-III can run on a processor if it satisfies the following general requirements:

■ The processor has an ANSI C compiler that generates reentrant code.

■ The processor supports interrupts and can provide an interrupt that occurs at regular intervals (typically between 10 and 1000 Hz).

■ Interrupts can be disabled and enabled.

■ The processor supports a hardware stack that accommodates a fair amount of data (possibly many kilobytes).

■ The processor has instructions to save and restore the stack pointer and other CPU registers, either on the stack or in memory.

■ The processor has access to sufficient RAM for μC/OS-III's variables and data structures as well as internal task stacks.

■ The compiler should support 64-bit data types (typically "long long").

Figure 18-1 shows the µC/OS-III architecture and its relationship with other software components and hardware. When using µC/OS-III in an application, the user is responsible for providing application software and µC/OS-III configuration sections.

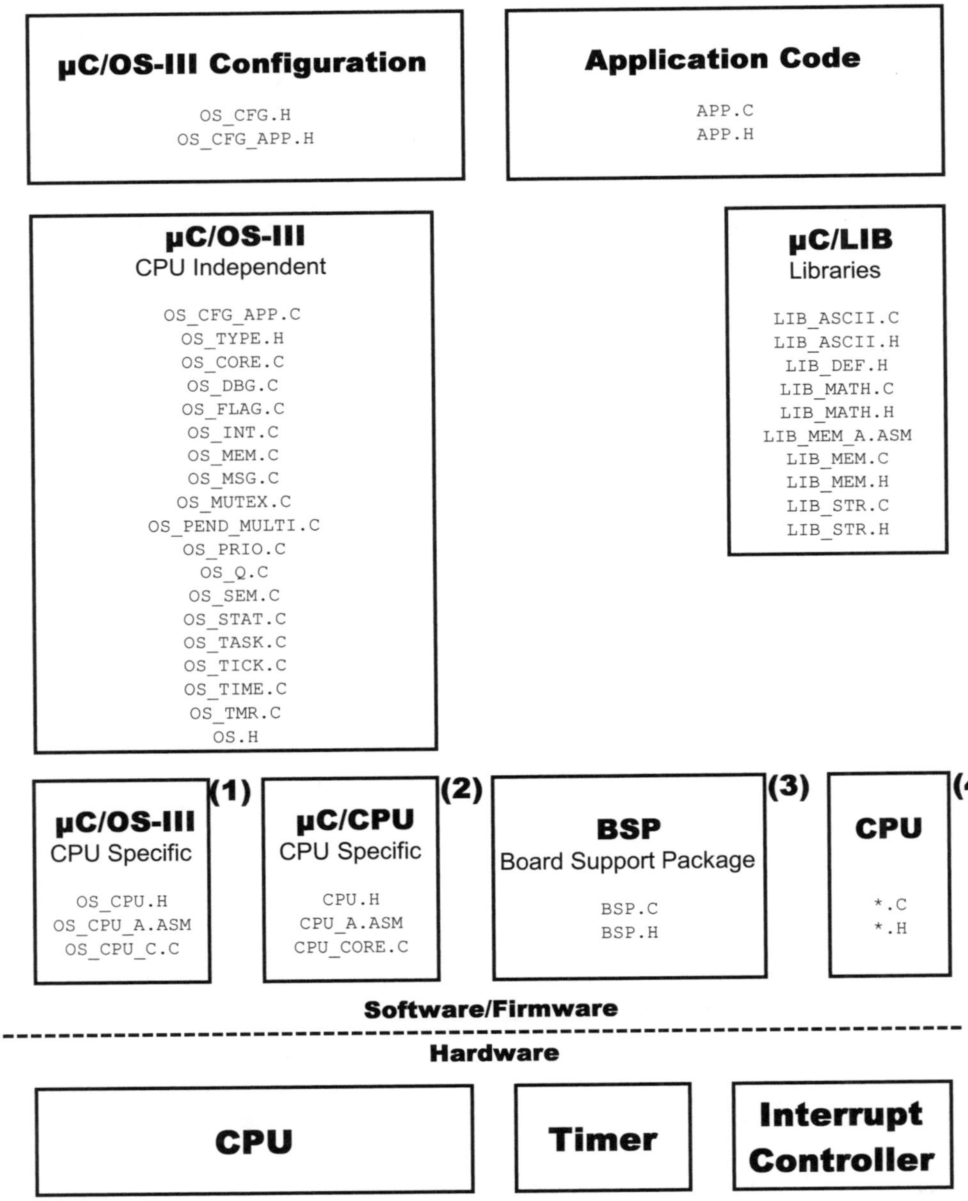

µC/OS-III Configuration

OS_CFG.H
OS_CFG_APP.H

Application Code

APP.C
APP.H

µC/OS-III
CPU Independent

OS_CFG_APP.C
OS_TYPE.H
OS_CORE.C
OS_DBG.C
OS_FLAG.C
OS_INT.C
OS_MEM.C
OS_MSG.C
OS_MUTEX.C
OS_PEND_MULTI.C
OS_PRIO.C
OS_Q.C
OS_SEM.C
OS_STAT.C
OS_TASK.C
OS_TICK.C
OS_TIME.C
OS_TMR.C
OS.H

µC/LIB
Libraries

LIB_ASCII.C
LIB_ASCII.H
LIB_DEF.H
LIB_MATH.C
LIB_MATH.H
LIB_MEM_A.ASM
LIB_MEM.C
LIB_MEM.H
LIB_STR.C
LIB_STR.H

(1)
µC/OS-III
CPU Specific

OS_CPU.H
OS_CPU_A.ASM
OS_CPU_C.C

(2)
µC/CPU
CPU Specific

CPU.H
CPU_A.ASM
CPU_CORE.C

(3)
BSP
Board Support Package

BSP.C
BSP.H

(4)
CPU

*.C
*.H

Software/Firmware
- -
Hardware

CPU

Timer

Interrupt Controller

Figure 18-1 µC/OS-III architecture

F18-1(1)   A µC/OS-III port consists of writing or changing the contents of three kernel-specific files: **OS_CPU.H**, **OS_CPU_A.ASM** and **OS_CPU_C.C**.

F18-1(2)   A port also involves writing or changing the contents of three CPU specific files: **CPU.H**, **CPU_A.ASM** and **CPU_CORE.C**.

F18-1(3)   A Board Support Package (BSP) is generally necessary to interface µC/OS-III to a timer (which is used for the clock tick) and an interrupt controller.

F18-1(4)   Some semiconductor manufacturers provide source and header files to access on-chip peripherals. These are contained in CPU/MCU specific files.

Porting µC/OS-III is quite straightforward once the subtleties of the target processor and the C compiler/assembler are understood. Depending on the processor, a port consists of writing or changing between 100 and 400 lines of code, which takes a few hours to a few days to accomplish. The easiest thing to do, however, is to modify an existing port from a processor that is similar to the one intended for use.

A µC/OS-III port looks very much like a µC/OS-II port. Since µC/OS-II was ported to well over 45 different CPU architectures it is easy to start from a µC/OS-II port. Converting a µC/OS-II port to µC/OS-III takes approximately an hour. The process is described in Appendix C, "Migrating from µC/OS-II to µC/OS-III" on page 605.

A port involves three aspects: CPU, OS and board-specific code. The board-specific code is often called a *Board Support Package* (BSP) and from µC/OS-III's point of view, requires very little.

18

18-1 µC/CPU

CPU-specific code is related to the CPU and the compiler in use, and less so with µC/OS-III. For example, disabling and enabling interrupts and the word width of the stack, whether the stack grows from high-to-low memory or from low-to-high memory and more are all CPU specific and not OS specific. Micrium encapsulates CPU functions and data types into a module called µC/CPU.

Table 18-1 shows the name of µC/CPU files and where they should be placed on the computer used to develop a µC/OS-III-based application.

File	Directory
CPU_DEF.H	\Micrium\Software\uC-CPU\
CPU.H	\Micrium\Software\uC-CPU\<processor>\<compiler>
CPU_C.C	\Micrium\Software\uC-CPU\<processor>\<compiler>
CPU_CFG.H	\Micrium\Software\uC-CPU\CFG\TEMPLATE
CPU_CORE.C	\Micrium\Software\uC-CPU\
CPU_CORE.H	\Micrium\Software\uC-CPU\
CPU_A.ASM	\Micrium\Software\uC-CPU\<processor>\<compiler>

Table 18-1 **µC/CPU files and directories**

Here, <processor> is the name of the processor that the **CPU*.*** files apply to, and <compiler> is the name of the compiler that these files assume because of different assembly language directives that different tool chains use.

The above source files for the CPU that came with this book are found when downloading the code from the Micrium website.

CPU_DEF.H

This file should not require any changes. **CPU_DEF.H** declares **#define** constants that are used by Micrium software components.

CPU.H

Many CPUs have different word lengths and **CPU.H** declares a series of type definitions that ensure portability. Specifically, at Micriµm, C data types **int**, **short**, **long**, **char**, *etc.*, are not used. Instead, clearer data types are defined. Consult compiler documentation to determine whether the standard declarations described below must be changed for the CPU/compiler used. When using a 32-bit CPU, the declarations below should work without change.

```
typedef                 void        CPU_VOID;
typedef   unsigned  char        CPU_CHAR;
typedef   unsigned  char        CPU_BOOLEAN;
typedef   unsigned  char        CPU_INT08U;
typedef     signed  char        CPU_INT08S;
typedef   unsigned  short       CPU_INT16U;
typedef     signed  short       CPU_INT16S;
typedef   unsigned  int         CPU_INT32U;
typedef     signed  int         CPU_INT32S;
typedef   unsigned  long  long  CPU_INT64U;
typedef     signed  long  long  CPU_INT64S;
typedef             float       CPU_FP32;
typedef             double      CPU_FP64;
typedef   volatile  CPU_INT08U  CPU_REG08;
typedef   volatile  CPU_INT16U  CPU_REG16;
typedef   volatile  CPU_INT32U  CPU_REG32;
typedef   volatile  CPU_INT64U  CPU_REG64;
typedef             void        (*CPU_FNCT_VOID)(void);
typedef             void        (*CPU_FNCT_PTR )(void *);
typedef   CPU_INT32U            CPU_ADDR;
typedef   CPU_INT32U            CPU_DATA;
typedef   CPU_DATA              CPU_ALIGN;
typedef   CPU_ADDR              CPU_SIZE_T;
typedef   CPU_INT32U            CPU_STK;          (1)
typedef   CPU_ADDR              CPU_STK_SIZE;
typedef   CPU_INT16U            CPU_ERR;
typedef   CPU_INT32U            CPU_SR;           (2)
typedef   CPU_INT32U            CPU_TS;           (3)
```

18

(1)   Especially important for µC/OS-III is the definition of the **CPU_STK** data type, which sets the width of a stack entry. Specifically, is the width of data pushed to and popped from the stack 8 bits, 16 bits, 32 bits or 64 bits?

(2)   **CPU_SR** defines the data type for the processor's status register (SR) that generally holds the interrupt disable status.

(3)   The **CPU_TS** is a time stamp used to determine when an operation occurred, or to measure the execution time of code.

CPU.H also declares macros to disable and enable interrupts: **CPU_CRITICAL_ENTER( )** and **CPU_CRITICAL_EXIT( )**, respectively. Finally, **CPU.H** declares function prototypes for a number of functions found in either **CPU_C.C** or **CPU_CORE.C**.

CPU_C.C

This is an optional file containing CPU-specific functions to set the interrupt controller, timer prescalers, and more. Most implementations will not contain this file.

CPU_CFG.H

This is a configuration file to be copied into the product directory and changed based on the options to exercise in µC/CPU. The file contains **#define** constants that may need to be changed based on the desired use of µC/CPU. For example, to assign a "name" to the CPU, the name can be queried and displayed. Also, to name the CPU, one must specify the length of the ASCII string.

CPU_CORE.C

This file is generic and does not need to be changed. However it must be included in all builds. **CPU_CORE.C** defines such functions as **CPU_Init( )**, **CPU_CntLeadZeros( )**, and code to measure maximum CPU interrupt disable time.

CPU_Init( ) must be called before calling OSInit( ).

CPU_CntLeadZeros( ) is used by the µC/OS-III scheduler to find the highest priority ready task (see Chapter 7, "Scheduling" on page 139). **CPU_CORE.C** implements a count leading zeros in C. However, if the processor used provides a built-in instruction to count leading zeros, define

CPU_CFG_LEAD_ZEROS_ASM_PRESENT, and replace this function by an assembly language equivalent (in **CPU_A.ASM**). It is important to properly declare **CPU_CFG_DATA_SIZE** in **CPU.H** for this function to work.

CPU_CORE.C also includes code that allows you to read timestamps. µC/CPU timestamps (CPU_TS) are 32-bit values. However, µC/CPU can return a 64-bit timestamp since µC/CPU keeps track of overflows of the low part of the 64-bit timestamp. Also use timestamps to determine when events occur, or to measure the execution time of code. Timestamp support requires a 16- or 32-bit free-running counter/timer that can be read. The code to read this timer will be placed in the BSP (Board Support Package) of the evaluation board or target board used.

CPU_CORE.H

This header file is required by **CPU_CORE.C** to define function prototypes.

CPU_A.ASM

This file contains assembly language code to implement such functions as disabling and enabling interrupts, a more efficient count leading zeros function, and more. At a minimum, this file should implement **CPU_SR_Save()** and **CPU_SR_Restore()**.

CPU_SR_Save() reads the current value of the CPU status register where the current interrupt disable flag resides and returns this value to the caller. However, before returning, **CPU_SR_Save()** must disable all interrupts. **CPU_SR_Save()** is actually called by the macro **CPU_CRITICAL_ENTER()**.

CPU_SR_Restore() restores the CPU's status register to a previously saved value. **CPU_SR_Restore()** is called from the macro **CPU_CRITICAL_EXIT()**.

18-2 µC/OS-III PORT

Table 18-2 shows the name of µC/OS-III files and where they are typically found.

File	Directory
OS_CPU.H	\Micrium\Software\uCOS-III\Ports\<processor>\<compiler>\
OS_CPU_A.ASM	\Micrium\Software\uCOS-III\Ports\<processor>\<compiler>\
OS_CPU_C.C	\Micrium\Software\uCOS-III\Ports\<processor>\<compiler>\

Table 18-2 **µC/OS-III files and directories**

Here, <processor> is the name of the processor that the **OS_CPU*.*** files apply to, and <compiler> is the name of the compiler that these files assume because of the different assembly language directives that different tool chains use.

OS_CPU.H

This file must define the macro **OS_TASK_SW()**, which is called by **OSSched()** to perform a task-level context switch. The macro can translate directly to a call to **OSCtxSw()**, trigger a software interrupt, or a **TRAP.** The choice depends on the CPU architecture.

18

OS_CPU.H must also define the macro OS_TS_GET() which obtains the current time stamp. It is expected that the time stamp is type CPU_TS, which is typically declared as at least a 32-bit value.

OS_CPU.H also defines function prototypes for OSCtxSw(), OSIntCtxSw(), OSStartHighRdy() and possibly other functions required by the port.

OS_CPU_A.ASM

This file contains the implementation of the following assembly language functions:

```
OSStartHighRdy()
OSCtxSw()
OSIntCtxSw()
```

and optionally,

```
OSTickISR()
```

OSTickISR() may optionally be placed in OS_CPU_A.ASM if it does not change from one product to another. The functions in this file are implemented in assembly language since they manipulate CPU registers, which is typically not possible from C. The functions are described in Appendix A, "µC/OS-III API Reference Manual" on page 381.

OS_CPU_C.C

This file contains the implementation of the following C functions:

```
OSIdleTaskHook()
OSInitHook()
OSStatTaskHook()
OSTaskCreateHook()
OSTaskDelHook()
OSTaskReturnHook()
OSTaskStkInit()
OSTaskSwHook()
OSTimeTickHook()
```

The functions are described in Appendix A, "µC/OS-III API Reference Manual" on page 381. OS_CPU_C.C can declare other functions as needed by the port, however the above functions are mandatory.

18-3 BOARD SUPPORT PACKAGE (BSP)

A board support package refers to code associated with the actual evaluation board or the target board used. For example, the BSP defines functions to turn LEDs on or off, reads push-button switches, initializes peripheral clocks, etc., providing nearly any functionality to multiple products/projects.

Names of typical BSP files include:

```
BSP.C
BSP.H
BSP_INT.C
BSP_INT.H
```

All files are generally placed in a directory as follows:

```
\Micrium\Software\EvalBoards\<manufacturer>\
<board_name>\<compiler>\BSP\
```

Here, **<manufacturer>** is the name of the evaluation board or target board manufacturer, **<board_name>** is the name of the evaluation or target board and <compiler> is the name of the compiler that these files assume, although most should be portable to different compilers since the BSP is typically written in C.

BSP.C and BSP.H

These files normally contain functions and their definitions such as **BSP_Init()**, **BSP_LED_On()**, **BSP_LED_Off()**, **BSP_LED_Toggle()**, **BSP_PB_Rd()**, and others. It is up to the user to decide if the functions in this file start with the prefix **BSP_**. In other words, use **LED_On()** and **PB_Rd()** if this is clearer. However, it is a good practice to encapsulate this type of functionality in a BSP type file.

In BSP.C, add **CPU_TS_TmrInit()** to initialize the µC/CPU timestamp feature. This function must return the number 16 if using a 16-bit timer and 0 for a 32-bit timer.

CPU_TS_TmrGet() is responsible for reading the value of a 16- or 32-bit free-running timer. If the timer is 16 bits, this function will need to return the value of the timer, but shifted to the left 16 places so that it looks like a 32-bit timer. If the timer is 32 bits, simply return the current value of the timer. Note that the timer is assumed to be an up counter. If the timer counts down, the BSP code will need to return the ones-complement of the timer value (prior to the shift).

BSP_INT.C and BSP_INT.H

These files are typically used to declare interrupt controller related functions. For example, code that enables or disables specific interrupts from the interrupt controller, acknowledges the interrupt controller, and code to handle all interrupts if the CPU vectors to a single location when an interrupt occurs (see Chapter 9, "Interrupt Management" on page 163). The pseudo code below shows an example of the latter.

```
void  BSP_IntHandler (void)                                      (1)
{
    CPU_FNCT_VOID   p_isr;

    while (interrupts being asserted) {                          (2)
        p_isr = Read the highest priority interrupt from the controller; (3)
        if (p_isr != (CPU_FNCT_VOID)0) {                        (4)
            (*p_isr)();                                          (5)
        }
        Acknowledge interrupt controller;                       (6)
    }
}
```

(1)   Here assume that the handler for the interrupt controller is called from the assembly language code that saves the CPU registers upon entering an ISR (see Chapter 9, "Interrupt Management" on page 163).

(2)   The handler queries the interrupt controller to ask it for the address of the ISR that needs to be executed in response to the interrupt. Some interrupt controllers return an integer value that corresponds to the source. In this case, simply use this integer value as an index into a table (RAM or ROM) where those vectors are placed.

(3)   The interrupt controller is asked to provide the highest priority interrupt pending. It is assumed here that the CPU may receive multiple simultaneous interrupts (or closely spaced interrupts), and that the interrupt will prioritize the interrupts received. The CPU will then service each interrupt in priority order instead of on a first-come basis. However, the scheme used greatly depends on the interrupt controller itself.

(4)   Check to ensure that the interrupt controller did not return a **NULL** pointer.

(5)   Simply call the ISR associated with the interrupt device.

(6)   The interrupt controller generally needs to be acknowledged so that it knows that the interrupt presented is taken care of.

18-4 SUMMARY

A port involves three aspects: CPU, OS and board specific (BSP) code.

µC/OS-III port consists of writing or changing the contents of three kernel specific files: **OS_CPU.H**, **OS_CPU_A.ASM** and **OS_CPU_C.C**.

It is necessary to write or change the content of three CPU specific files: **CPU.H**, **CPU_A.ASM** and **CPU_C.C**.

Finally create or change a Board Support Package (BSP) for the evaluation board or target board being used.

A µC/OS-III port is similar to a µC/OS-II port, therefore start from one of the many µC/OS-II ports already available (see Appendix C, "Migrating from µC/OS-II to µC/OS-III" on page 605).

18

18

Chapter

19

Run-Time Statistics

µC/OS-III performs substantial run-time statistics that can be displayed by kernel-aware debuggers and/or µC/Probe. Specifically, it is possible to ascertain the total number of context switches, maximum interrupt disable time, maximum scheduler lock time, CPU usage, stack space used on a per-task basis, the RAM used by µC/OS-III, and much more.

No other real-time kernel provides as much run-time information as µC/OS-III. This information is quite useful during debugging as it provides a sense of how well an application is running and the resources being used.

µC/OS-III also provides information about the configuration of the system. Specifically, the amount of RAM used by µC/OS-III, including all internal variables and task stacks.

The µC/OS-III variables described in this chapter should be displayed and never changed.

19-1 GENERAL STATISTICS – RUN-TIME

The following is a list of µC/OS-III variables that are not associated to any specific task:

OSCfg_TickWheel[i].NbrEntries
The tick wheel contains up to **OS_CFG_TICK_WHEEL_SIZE** "spokes" (see **OS_CFG_APP.H**), and each spoke contains the **.NbrEntries** field, which holds the current number of entries in that spoke.

OSCfg_TickWheel[i].NbrEntriesMax
The **.NbrEntriesMax** field holds the maximum (i.e., peak) number of entries in a spoke.

OSCfg_TmrWheel[i].NbrEntries
The tick wheel contains up to **OS_CFG_TMR_WHEEL_SIZE** "spokes" (see **OS_CFG_APP.H**), and each spoke contains the **.NbrEntries** field, which holds the current number of entries in that spoke.

OSCfg_TmrWheel[i].NbrEntriesMax
The **.NbrEntriesMax** field holds the maximum (i.e., peak) number of entries in a spoke.

OSIdleTaskCtr
This variable contains a counter that is incremented every time the idle task infinite loop runs.

OSIntNestingCtr
This variable contains the interrupt nesting level. 1 means servicing the first level of interrupt nesting, 2 means the interrupt was interrupted by another interrupt, etc.

OSIntDisTimeMax
This variable contains the maximum interrupt disable time (in **CPU_TS** units).

OSRunning
This variable indicates that multitasking has started.

OSIntQNbrEntries
This variable indicates the current number of entries in the interrupt handler queue.

OSIntQOvfCtr

This variable shows the number of attempts to post a message from an interrupt to the interrupt handler queue, and there was not enough room to place the post call. In other words, how many times an interrupt was not being able to be serviced by its corresponding task. This value should always be 0 if the interrupt handler queue is sized large enough. If the value is non-zero, increase the size of the interrupt handler queue. A non-zero value may also indicate that the processor is not fast enough.

OSIntQTaskTimeMax

This variable contains the maximum execution time of the Interrupt Queue Handler Task (in CPU_TS units).

OSFlagQty

This variable indicates the number of event flag groups created. This variable is only declared if OS_CFG_FLAG_EN is set to 1 in OS_CFG.H.

OSMemQty

This variable indicates the number of fixed-sized memory partitions created by the application. This variable is only declared if OS_CFG_MEM_EN is set to 1 in OS_CFG.H.

OSMsgPool.NbrFree

The variable indicates the number of free OS_MSGs in the message pool. This number should never be zero since that indicate that the application is no longer able to send messages. This variable is only declared if OS_CFG_Q_EN is set to 1, or OS_CFG_TASK_Q_EN is set to 1 in OS_CFG.H.

OSMsgPool.NbrUsed

This variable indicates the number of OS_MSGs currently used by the application. This variable is only declared if OS_CFG_Q_EN is set to 1, or OS_CFG_TASK_Q_EN is set to 1 in OS_CFG.H.

OSMutexQty

This variable indicates the number of mutual exclusion semaphores created by the application. This variable is only declared if OS_CFG_MUTEX_EN is set to 1 in OS_CFG.H.

OSRdyList[i].NbrEntries

It is useful to examine how many entries there are in the ready list at each priority.

19

OSSchedLockTimeMax

This variable indicates the maximum amount of time the scheduler was locked irrespective of which task did the locking. It represents the global scheduler lock time. This value is expressed in **CPU_TS** units. The variable is only declared if **OS_CFG_SCHED_LOCK_TIME_MEAS_EN** is set to 1 in **OS_CFG.H**.

OSSchedLockTimeMaxCur

This variable indicates the maximum amount of time the scheduler was locked. This value is expressed in **CPU_TS** units and is reset by the context switch code so that it can track the scheduler lock time on a per-task basis. This variable is only declared if **OS_CFG_SCHED_LOCK_TIME_MEAS_EN** is set to 1 in **OS_CFG.H**.

OSSchedLockNestingCtr

This variable keeps track of the nesting level of the scheduler lock.

OSSchedRoundRobinEn

This variable indicates whether or not round robin scheduling is enabled.

OSSemQty

This variable indicates the number of semaphores created by your application. This variable is only declared if **OS_CFG_SEM_EN** is set to 1 in **OS_CFG.H**.

OSStatTaskCPUUsage

This variable indicates the CPU usage of the application expressed as a percentage. A value of 10 indicates that 10% of the CPU is used, while 90% of the time the CPU is idling. This variable is only declared if **OS_CFG_STAT_TASK_EN** is set to 1 in **OS_CFG.H**.

OSStatTaskCtr

This variable contains a counter that is incremented every time the idle task infinite loop runs. This variable is only declared if **OS_CFG_STAT_TASK_EN** is set to 1 in **OS_CFG.H**.

OSStatTaskCtrMax

This variable contains the maximum number of times the idle task loop runs in 0.1 second. This value is used to measure the CPU usage of the application. This variable is only declared if **OS_CFG_STAT_TASK_EN** is set to 1 in **OS_CFG.H**.

OSStatTaskTimeMax

This variable contains the maximum execution time of the statistic task (in **CPU_TS** units). It is only declared if **OS_CFG_STAT_TASK_EN** is set to 1 in **OS_CFG.H**.

OSTaskCtxSwCtr

This variable accumulates the number of context switches performed by μC/OS-III.

OSTaskQty

The variable contains the total number of tasks created in the application.

OSTickCtr

This variable is incremented every time the tick task executes.

OSTickTaskTimeMax

This variable contains the maximum execution time of the tick task (in **CPU_TS** units).

OSTmrQty

This variable indicates the number of timers created by the application. It is only declared if **OS_CFG_TMR_EN** is set to 1 in **OS_CFG.H**.

OSTmrCtr

This variable is incremented every time the timer task executes.

OSTmrTaskTimeMax

This variable contains the maximum execution time of the timer task (in **CPU_TS** units). It is only declared if **OS_CFG_TMR_EN** is set to 1 in **OS_CFG.H**.

19

19-2 PER-TASK STATISTICS – RUN-TIME

μC/OS-III maintains statistics for each task at run-time. This information is saved in the task's **OS_TCB**.

.CPUUsage

This variable keeps track of CPU usage of the task as a percentage of the total CPU usage. For example if the task's **.CPUUsage** is 20%, and the total CPU usages from **OSTaskStatCPUUsage** is 10%, this variable represents 2% of total CPU usage.

The variable is only declared when **OS_CFG_TASK_PROFILE_EN** is set to 1 in **OS_CFG.H**.

.CtxSwCtr

This variable keeps track of the number of times a task is context switched to. This variable should increment. If it does not increment, the task is not running. At a minimum, the counter should at least have a value of one since a task is always created ready to run.

This variable is only declared when **OS_CFG_TASK_PROFILE_EN** is set to 1 in **OS_CFG.H**.

.IntDisTimeMax

This variable keeps track of the maximum interrupt disable time of a task (in **CPU_TS** units). This variable shows how each task affects interrupt latency.

The variable is only declared when **OS_CFG_TASK_PROFILE_EN** is set to 1 in **OS_CFG.H** and defines **CPU_CFG_INT_DIS_MEAS_EN** in **CPU_CFG.H**.

.MsgQ.NbrEntries

This variable indicates the number of entries currently waiting in the message queue of a task. This variable is only declared when **OS_CFG_TASK_Q_EN** is set to 1 in **OS_CFG.H**.

.MsgQ.NbrEntriesMax

This variable indicates the maximum number of entries placed in the message queue of a task. This variable is only declared when **OS_CFG_TASK_Q_EN** is set to 1 in **OS_CFG.H**.

.MsgQ.NbrEntriesSize

This variable indicates the maximum number of entries that a task message queue is able to accept before it is full.

This variable is only declared when **OS_CFG_TASK_Q_EN** is set to 1 in **OS_CFG.H**.

.MsgQ.PendTime

This variable indicates the amount of time it took for a task or an ISR to send a message to the task (in CPU_TS units).

The variable is only declared when OS_CFG_TASK_PROFILE_EN is set to 1 in OS_CFG.H.

.MsgQ.PendTimeMax

This variable indicates the maximum amount of time it took for a task or an ISR to send a message to the task (in CPU_TS units).

This variable is only declared when OS_CFG_TASK_PROFILE_EN is set to 1 in OS_CFG.H.

.PendOn

This variable indicates what a task is pending on if the task is in a pend state. Possible values are:

0	Nothing
1	Pending on an event flag group
2	Pending on the task's message queue
3	Pending on multiple objects
4	Pending on a mutual exclusion semaphore
5	Pending on a message queue
6	Pending on a semaphore
7	Pending on a task's semaphore

.Prio

This corresponds to the priority of the task. This might change at run time depending on whether or not the task owns a mutual exclusion semaphore, or the user changes the priority of the task by calling OSTaskChangePrio().

.SchedLockTimeMax

This variable keeps track of the maximum time a task locks the scheduler (in CPU_TS units). This variable allows the application to see how each task affects task latency. The variable is declared only when OS_CFG_TASK_PROFILE_EN and OS_CFG_SCHED_LOCK_TIME_MEAS_EN are set to 1 in OS_CFG.H.

19

.SemPendTime

This variable indicates the amount of time it took for a task or ISR to signal the task (in CPU_TS units).

This variable is only declared when OS_CFG_TASK_PROFILE_EN is set to 1 in OS_CFG.H.

.SemPendTimeMax

This variable indicates the maximum amount of time it took for a task or an ISR to signal the task (in CPU_TS units).

This variable is only declared when OS_CFG_TASK_PROFILE_EN is set to 1 in OS_CFG.H.

.State

This variable indicates the current state of a task. The possible values are:

0	Ready
1	Delayed
2	Pending
3	Pending with Timeout
4	Suspended
5	Delayed and Suspended
6	Pending and Suspended
7	Pending, Delayed and Suspended

.StkFree

This variable indicates the amount of stack space (in bytes) unused by a task. This value is determined by the statistic task if OS_CFG_TASK_STAT_STK_CHK_EN is set to 1 in OS_CFG.H.

.StkUsed

This variable indicates the maximum stack usage (in bytes) of a task. This value is determined by the statistic task if OS_CFG_TASK_STAT_STK_CHK_EN is set to 1 in OS_CFG.H.

.TickRemain

This variable indicates the amount of time left (in clock ticks) until a task time delay expires, or the task times out waiting on a kernel object such as a semaphore, message queue, or other.

19

19-3 KERNEL OBJECT – RUN-TIME

It is possible to examine the run-time values of certain kernel objects as described below.

SEMAPHORES

.NamePtr

This is a pointer to an ASCII string used to provide a name to the semaphore. The ASCII string can have any length as long as it is NUL terminated.

.PendList.NbrEntries

Each semaphore contains a wait list of tasks waiting for the semaphore to be signaled. The variable represents the number of entries in the wait list.

.Ctr

This variable represents the current count of the semaphore.

.TS

This variable contains the timestamp of when the semaphore was last signaled.

MUTUAL EXCLUSION SEMAPHORES

.NamePtr

This is a pointer to an ASCII string used to provide a name to the mutual exclusion semaphore. The ASCII string can have any length as long as it is NUL terminated.

.PendList.NbrEntries

Each mutual exclusion semaphore contains a list of tasks waiting for the semaphore to be released. The variable represents the number of entries in the wait list.

.OwnerOriginalPrio

This variable holds the original priority of the task that owns the mutual exclusion semaphore.

.OwnerTCBPtr->Prio

Dereferencing the pointer to the OS_TCB of the mutual exclusion semaphore owner allows the application to determine whether a task priority was changed.

.OwnerNestingCtr

This variable indicates how many times the owner of the mutual exclusion semaphore requested the semaphore.

.TS

This variable contains the timestamp of when the mutual exclusion semaphore was last released.

MESSAGE QUEUES

.NamePtr

This is a pointer to an ASCII string used to provide a name to the message queue. The ASCII string can have any length, as long as it is **NUL** terminated.

.PendList.NbrEntries

Each message queue contains a wait list of tasks waiting for messages to be sent to the queue. The variable represents the number of entries in the wait list.

.MsgQ.NbrEntries

This variable represents the number of messages currently in the message queue.

.MsgQ.NbrEntriesMax

This variable represents the maximum number of messages ever placed in the message queue.

.MsgQ.NbrEntriesSize

This variable represents the maximum number of messages that can be placed in the message queue.

EVENT FLAGS

.NamePtr

This is a pointer to an ASCII string used to provide a name to the event flag group. The ASCII string can have any length, as long as it is **NUL** terminated.

.PendList.NbrEntries

Each event flag group contains a wait list of tasks waiting for event flags to be set or cleared. This variable represents the number of entries in the wait list.

.Flags

This variable contains the current value of the event flags in an event flag group.

.TS

This variable contains the timestamp of when the event flag group was last posted.

MEMORY PARTITIONS

.NamePtr

This is a pointer to an ASCII string that is used to provide a name to the memory partition. The ASCII string can have any length as long as it is **NUL** terminated.

.BlkSize

This variable contains the block size (in bytes) for the memory partition.

.NbrMax

This variable contains the maximum number of memory blocks belonging to the memory partition.

.NbrFree

This variable contains the number of memory blocks that are available from memory partition. The number of memory blocks in use is given by:

```
.NbrMax - .NbrFree
```

19

19-4 OS_DBG.C – **STATIC**

OS_DBG.C is provided in µC/OS-III as some debuggers are not able to read the values of #define constants. Specifically, OS_DBG.C contains ROM variables initialized to #define constants so that users can read them with any debugger.

Below is a list of ROM variables provided in OS_DBG.C, along with their descriptions. These variables use approximately 100 bytes of code space.

The application code can examine these variables and you do not need to access them in a critical region as they reside in code space and are therefore not changeable.

ROM Variable	Data Type	Value
OSDbg_DbgEn	CPU_INT08U	OS_CFG_DBG_EN

When 1, this variable indicates that ROM variables in OS_DBG.C will be compiled. This value is set in OS_CFG.H.

ROM Variable	Data Type	Value
OSDbg_ArgChkEn	CPU_INT08U	OS_CFG_ARG_CHK_EN

When 1, this variable indicates that run-time argument checking is enabled. This means that µC/OS-III will check the validity of the values of arguments passed to functions. The feature is enabled in OS_CFG.H.

ROM Variable	Data Type	Value
OSDbg_AppHooksEn	CPU_INT08U	OS_CFG_DBG_EN

When 1, the variable indicates whether application hooks will be available to the application programmer, and the pointers listed below are declared. This value is set in **OS_CFG.H**.

OS_AppTaskCreateHookPtr;
OS_AppTaskDelHookPtr;
OS_AppTaskReturnHookPtr;
OS_AppIdleTaskHookPtr;
OS_AppStatTaskHookPtr;
OS_AppTaskSwHookPtr;
OS_AppTimeTickHookPtr;

ROM Variable	Data Type	Value
OSDbg_EndiannessTest	CPU_INT32U	0x12345678

This variable allows the kernel awareness debugger or µC/Probe to determine the endianness of the CPU. This is easily done by looking at the lowest address in memory where this variable is saved. If the value is 0x78 then the CPU is a little endian machine. If it's 0x12, it is a big endian machine.

ROM Variable	Data Type	Value
OSDbg_CalledFromISRChkEn	CPU_INT08U	OS_CFG_CALLED_FROM_ISR_CHK_EN

When 1, this variable indicates that µC/OS-III will perform run-time checking to see if a function that is not supposed to be called from an ISR, is called from an ISR. This value is set in **OS_CFG.H**.

19

ROM Variable	Data Type	Value
OSDbg_FlagEn	CPU_INT08U	OS_CFG_FLAG_EN

When 1, this variable indicates that µC/OS-III's event flag services are available to the application programmer. This value is set in **OS_CFG.H**.

ROM Variable	Data Type	Value
OSDbg_FlagDelEn	CPU_INT08U	OS_CFG_FLAG_DEL_EN

When 1, this variable indicates that the **OSFlagDel()** function is available to the application programmer. This value is set in **OS_CFG.H**.

ROM Variable	Data Type	Value
OSDbg_FlagModeClrEn	CPU_INT08U	OS_CFG_FLAG_MODE_CLR_EN

When 1, this variable indicates that cleared flags can be used instead of set flags when posting and pending on event flags. This value is set in **OS_CFG.H**.

ROM Variable	Data Type	Value
OSDbg_FlagPendAbortEn	CPU_INT08U	OS_CFG_FLAG_PEND_ABORT_EN

When 1, this variable indicates that the **OSFlagPendAbort()** function is available to the application programmer. This value is set in **OS_CFG.H**.

ROM Variable	Data Type	Value
OSDbg_FlagGrpSize	CPU_INT16U	sizeof(OS_FLAG_GRP)

This variable indicates the memory footprint (in RAM) of an event flag group (in bytes). This data type is declared in **OS.H**.

ROM Variable	Data Type	Value
OSDbg_FlagWidth	CPU_INT16U	sizeof(OS_FLAGS)

This variable indicates the word width (in bytes) of event flags. If event flags are declared as **CPU_INT08U**, this variable will be 1, if declared as a **CPU_INT16U**, this variable will be 2, etc. This data type is declared in **OS_TYPE.H**.

ROM Variable	Data Type	Value
OSDbg_IntQSize	CPU_INT16U	sizeof(OS_INT_Q)

This variable indicates the size of the **OS_INT_Q** data type, which is used to queue up deferred posts. The value of this variable is zero if **OS_CFG_ISR_POST_DEFERRED_EN** is 0 in **OS_CFG.H**.

ROM Variable	Data Type	Value
OSDbg_ISRPostDeferredEn	CPU_INT08U	OS_CFG_ISR_POST_DEFERRED_EN

When 1, this variable indicates that an ISR will defer posts to task-level code. This value is set in **OS_CFG.H**.

ROM Variable	Data Type	Value
OSDbg_MemEn	CPU_INT08U	OS_CFG_MEM_EN

When 1, this variable indicates that µC/OS-III's memory management services are available to the application. This value is set in **OS_CFG.H**.

ROM Variable	Data Type	Value
OSDbg_MemSize	CPU_INT16U	sizeof(OS_MEM)

This variable indicates the RAM footprint (in bytes) of a memory partition control block.

19

ROM Variable	Data Type	Value
OSDbg_MsgEn	CPU_INT08U	OS_CFG_MSG_EN

When 1, this variable indicates that the application either enabled message queues, or task message queues, or both. This value is set in **OS_CFG.H** by **ORing** the value of **OS_CFG_Q_EN** and **OS_CFG_TASK_Q_EN**.

ROM Variable	Data Type	Value
OSDbg_MsgSize	CPU_INT16U	sizeof(OS_MSG)

This variable indicates the RAM footprint (in bytes) of an OS_MSG data structure.

ROM Variable	Data Type	Value
OSDbg_MsgPoolSize	CPU_INT16U	sizeof(OS_MSG_POOL)

This variable indicates the RAM footprint (in bytes) of an **OS_MSG_POOL** data structure.

ROM Variable	Data Type	Value
OSDbg_MsgQSize	CPU_INT16U	sizeof(OS_MSG_Q)

This variable indicates the RAM footprint (in number of bytes) of an **OS_MSG_Q** data type.

ROM Variable	Data Type	Value
OSDbg_MutexEn	CPU_INT08U	OS_CFG_MUTEX_EN

When 1, this variable indicates that μC/OS-III's mutual exclusion semaphore management services are available to the application. This value is set in **OS_CFG.H**.

ROM Variable	Data Type	Value
OSDbg_MutexDelEn	CPU_INT08U	OS_CFG_MUTEX_DEL_EN

When 1, this variable indicates that the function OSMutexDel() is available to the application. This value is set in OS_CFG.H.

ROM Variable	Data Type	Value
OSDbg_MutexPendAbortEn	CPU_INT08U	OS_CFG_MUTEX_PEND_ABORT_EN

When 1, the variable indicates that the function OSMutexPendAbort() is available to the application. This value is set in OS_CFG.H.

ROM Variable	Data Type	Value
OSDbg_MutexSize	CPU_INT16U	sizeof(OS_MUTEX)

This variable indicates the RAM footprint (in number of bytes) of an OS_MUTEX data type.

ROM Variable	Data Type	Value
OSDbg_ObjTypeChkEn	CPU_INT08U	OS_CFG_OBJ_TYPE_CHK_EN

When 1, this variable indicates that μC/OS-III will check for valid object types at run time. μC/OS-III will make sure the application is accessing a semaphore if calling OSSem???() functions, accessing a message queue when calling OSQ???() functions, etc. This value is set in OS_CFG.H.

ROM Variable	Data Type	Value
OSDbg_PendMultiEn	CPU_INT08U	OS_CFG_PEND_MULTI_EN

When 1, this variable indicates that μC/OS-III's service to pend on multiple objects (semaphores or message queues) is available to the application. This value is set in OS_CFG.H.

19

ROM Variable	Data Type	Value
OSDbg_PendDataSize	CPU_INT16U	sizeof(OS_PEND_DATA)

This variable indicates the RAM footprint (in bytes) of an **OS_PEND_DATA** data type.

ROM Variable	Data Type	Value
OSDbg_PendListSize	CPU_INT16U	sizeof(OS_PEND_LIST)

This variable indicates the RAM footprint (in bytes) of an OS_PEND_LIST data type.

ROM Variable	Data Type	Value
OSDbg_PendObjSize	CPU_INT16U	sizeof(OS_PEND_OBJ)

This variable indicates the RAM footprint (in bytes) of an **OS_PEND_OBJ** data type.

ROM Variable	Data Type	Value
OSDbg_PrioMax	CPU_INT16U	OS_CFG_PRIO_MAX

This variable indicates the maximum number of priorities that the application will support.

ROM Variable	Data Type	Value
OSDbg_PtrSize	CPU_INT16U	sizeof(void *)

This variable indicates the size (in bytes) of a pointer.

ROM Variable	Data Type	Value
OSDbg_QEn	CPU_INT08U	OS_CFG_Q_EN

When 1, this variable indicates that µC/OS-III's message queue services are available to the application. This value is set in **OS_CFG.H**.

ROM Variable	Data Type	Value
OSDbg_QDelEn	CPU_INT08U	OS_CFG_Q_DEL_EN

When 1, this variable indicates that the function OSQDel() is available to the application. This value is set in OS_CFG.H.

ROM Variable	Data Type	Value
OSDbg_QFlushEn	CPU_INT08U	OS_CFG_Q_FLUSH_EN

When 1, this variable indicates that the function OSQFlush() is available to the application. This value is set in OS_CFG.H.

ROM Variable	Data Type	Value
OSDbg_QPendAbortEn	CPU_INT08U	OS_CFG_Q_PEND_ABORT_EN

When 1, this variable indicates that the function OSQPendAbort() is available to the application. This value is set in OS_CFG.H.

ROM Variable	Data Type	Value
OSDbg_QSize	CPU_INT16U	

This variable indicates the RAM footprint (in number of bytes) of an OS_Q data type.

19

ROM Variable	Data Type	Value
OSDbg_SchedRoundRobinEn	CPU_INT08U	OS_CFG_ROUND_ROBIN_EN

When 1, this variable indicates that the µC/OS-III round robin scheduling feature is available to the application. This value is set in OS_CFG.H.

ROM Variable	Data Type	Value
OSDbg_SemEn	CPU_INT08U	OS_CFG_SEM_EN

When 1, this variable indicates that µC/OS-III's semaphore management services are available to the application. This value is set in **OS_CFG.H**.

ROM Variable	Data Type	Value
OSDbg_SemDelEn	CPU_INT08U	OS_CFG_SEM_DEL_EN

When 1, this variable indicates that the function **OSSemDel()** is available to the application. This value is set in **OS_CFG.H**.

ROM Variable	Data Type	Value
OSDbg_SemPendAbortEn	CPU_INT08U	OS_CFG_SEM_PEND_ABORT_EN

When 1, this variable indicates that the function **OSSemPendAbort()** is available to the application. This value is set in **OS_CFG.H**.

ROM Variable	Data Type	Value
OSDbg_SemSetEn	CPU_INT08U	OS_CFG_SEM_SET_EN

When 1, this variable indicates that the function **OSSemSet()** is available to the application. This value is set in **OS_CFG.H**.

ROM Variable	Data Type	Value
OSDbg_RdyList	CPU_INT16U	sizeof(OS_RDY_LIST)

This variable indicates the RAM footprint (in bytes) of an **OS_RDY_LIST** data type.

ROM Variable	Data Type	Value
OSDbg_RdyListSize	CPU_INT32U	sizeof(OSRdyList)

This variable indicates the RAM footprint (in bytes) of the ready list.

ROM Variable	Data Type	Value
OSDbg_StkWidth	CPU_INT08U	sizeof(CPU_STK)

This variable indicates the word size of a stack entry (in bytes). If a stack entry is declared as **CPU_INT08U**, this value will be 1, if a stack entry is declared as **CPU_INT16U**, the value will be 2, etc.

ROM Variable	Data Type	Value
OSDbg_StatTaskEn	CPU_INT08U	OS_CFG_STAT_TASK_EN

When 1, this variable indicates that μC/OS-III's statistic task is enabled. This value is set in **OS_CFG.H**.

ROM Variable	Data Type	Value
OSDbg_StatTaskStkChkEn	CPU_INT08U	OS_CFG_STAT_TASK_STK_CHK_EN

When 1, this variable indicates that μC/OS-III will perform run-time stack checking by walking the stack of each task to determine the usage of each. This value is set in **OS_CFG.H**.

ROM Variable	Data Type	Value
OSDbg_TaskChangePrioEn	CPU_INT08U	OS_CFG_TASK_CHANGE_PRIO_EN

When 1, this variable indicates that the function **OSTaskChangePrio()** is available to the application. This value is set in **OS_CFG.H**.

19

ROM Variable	Data Type	Value
OSDbg_TaskDelEn	CPU_INT08U	OS_CFG_TASK_DEL_EN

When 1, this variable indicates that the function OSTaskDel() is available to the application. This value is set in OS_CFG.H.

ROM Variable	Data Type	Value
OSDbg_TaskQEn	CPU_INT08U	OS_CFG_TASK_Q_EN

When 1, this variable indicates that OSTaskQ???() services are available to the application. This value is set in OS_CFG.H.

ROM Variable	Data Type	Value
OSDbg_TaskQPendAbortEn	CPU_INT08U	OS_CFG_TASK_Q_PEND_ABORT_EN

When 1, this variable indicates that the function OSTaskQPendAbort() is available to the application. This value is set in OS_CFG.H.

ROM Variable	Data Type	Value
OSDbg_TaskProfileEn	CPU_INT08U	OS_CFG_TASK_PROFILE_EN

When 1, this variable indicates that task profiling is enabled, and that µC/OS-III will perform run-time performance measurements on a per-task basis. Specifically, when 1, µC/OS-III will keep track of how many context switches each task makes, how long a task disables interrupts, how long a task locks the scheduler, and more. This value is set in OS_CFG.H.

ROM Variable	Data Type	Value
OSDbg_TaskRegTblSize	CPU_INT16U	OS_CFG_TASK_REG_TBL_SIZE

This variable indicates how many entries each task register table can accept.

19

ROM Variable	Data Type	Value
OSDbg_TaskSemPendAbortEn	CPU_INT08U	OS_CFG_TASK_SEM_PEND_ABORT_EN

When 1, this variable indicates that the function **OSTaskSemPendAbort()** is available to the application. This value is set in **OS_CFG.H**.

ROM Variable	Data Type	Value
OSDbg_TaskSuspendEn	CPU_INT08U	OS_CFG_TASK_SUSPEND_EN

When 1, this variable indicates that the function **OSTaskSuspend()** is available to the application. This value is set in **OS_CFG.H**.

ROM Variable	Data Type	Value
OSDbg_TCBSize	CPU_INT16U	sizeof(OS_TCB)

This variable indicates the RAM footprint (in bytes) of an **OS_TCB** data structure.

ROM Variable	Data Type	Value
OSDbg_TickSpokeSize	CPU_INT16U	sizeof(OS_TICK_SPOKE)

This variable indicates the RAM footprint (in bytes) of an **OS_TICK_SPOKE** data structure.

19

ROM Variable	Data Type	Value
OSDbg_TimeDlyHMSMEn	CPU_INT08U	OS_CFG_TIME_DLY_HMSM_EN

When 1, this variable indicates that the function **OSTimeDlyHMSM()** is available to the application. This value is set in **OS_CFG.H**.

ROM Variable	Data Type	Value
OSDbg_TimeDlyResumeEn	CPU_INT08U	OS_CFG_TIME_DLY_RESUME_EN

When 1, this variable indicates that the function **OSTimeDlyResume()** is available to the application. This value is set in **OS_CFG.H**.

ROM Variable	Data Type	Value
OSDbg_TmrEn	CPU_INT08U	OS_CFG_TMR_EN

When 1, this variable indicates that **OSTmr???()** services are available to the application. This value is set in **OS_CFG.H**.

ROM Variable	Data Type	Value
OSDbg_TmrDelEn	CPU_INT08U	OS_CFG_TMR_DEL_EN

When 1, this variable indicates that the function **OSTmrDel()** is available to the application. This value is set in **OS_CFG.H**.

ROM Variable	Data Type	Value
OSDbg_TmrSize	CPU_INT16U	sizeof(OS_TMR)

This variable indicates the RAM footprint (in bytes) of an **OS_TMR** data structure.

ROM Variable	Data Type	Value
OSDbg_TmrSpokeSize	CPU_INT16U	sizeof(OS_TMR_SPOKE)

This variable indicates the RAM footprint (in bytes) of an **OS_TMR_SPOKE** data structure.

ROM Variable	Data Type	Value
OSDbg_VersionNbr	CPU_INT16U	OS_VERSION

This variable indicates the current version of µC/OS-III multiplied by 1000. For example version 3.00.4 will show as 3004.ZZ

ROM Variable	Data Type	Value
OSDbg_DataSize	CPU_INT32U	Size of all RAM variables

This variable indicates the RAM footprint (in bytes) of the internal µC/OS-III variables for the current configuration.

19-5 OS_CFG_APP.C – **STATIC**

As with **OS_DBG.C**, **OS_CFG_APP.C** defines a number of ROM variables. These variables, however, reflect the run-time configuration of an application. Specifically, the user will be able to know the RAM footprint (in bytes) of µC/OS-III task stacks, the message pool, and more.

Below is a list of ROM variables provided in **OS_APP_CFG.C**, along with their descriptions. These variables represent approximately 100 bytes of code space.

Application code can examine these variables and the application does not need to access them in a critical region since they reside in code space and are therefore not changeable.

19

ROM Variable	Data Type	Value
OSCfg_IdleTaskStkSizeRAM	CPU_INT32U	sizeof(OSCfg_IdleTaskStk)

This variable indicates the RAM footprint (in bytes) of the µC/OS-III idle task stack.

ROM Variable	Data Type	Value
OSCfg_IntQSizeRAM	CPU_INT32U	sizeof(OSCfg_IntQ)

This variable indicates the RAM footprint (in bytes) of the μC/OS-III interrupt handler task queue.

ROM Variable	Data Type	Value
OSCfg_IntQTaskStkSizeRAM	CPU_INT32U	sizeof(OSCfg_IntQTaskStk)

This variable indicates the RAM footprint (in bytes) of the μC/OS-III interrupt queue handler task stack.

ROM Variable	Data Type	Value
OSCfg_ISRStkSizeRAM	CPU_INT32U	sizeof(OSCfg_ISRStk)

This variable indicates the RAM footprint (in bytes) of the dedicated Interrupt Service Routine (ISR) stack.

ROM Variable	Data Type	Value
OSCfg_MsgPoolSizeRAM	CPU_INT32U	sizeof(OSCfg_MsgPool)

This variable indicates the RAM footprint (in bytes) of the message pool.

ROM Variable	Data Type	Value
OSCfg_StatTaskStkSizeRAM	CPU_INT32U	sizeof(OSCfg_StatTaskStk)

This variable indicates the RAM footprint (in bytes) of the μC/OS-III statistic task stack.

ROM Variable	Data Type	Value
OSCfg_TickTaskStkSizeRAM	CPU_INT32U	sizeof(OSCfg_TickTaskStk)

This variable indicates the RAM footprint (in bytes) of the μC/OS-III tick task stack.

ROM Variable	Data Type	Value
OSCfg_TickWheelSizeRAM	CPU_INT32U	sizeof(OSCfg_TickWheel)

This variable indicates the RAM footprint (in bytes) of the tick wheel.

ROM Variable	Data Type	Value
OSCfg_TmrWheelSizeRAM	CPU_INT32U	sizeof(OSCfg_TmrWheel)

This variable indicates the RAM footprint (in bytes) of the timer wheel.

ROM Variable	Data Type	Value
OSCfg_DataSizeRAM	CPU_INT32U	Total of all configuration RAM

This variable indicates the RAM footprint (in bytes) of all of the configuration variables declared in OS_CFG_APP.C.

19-6 SUMMARY

This chapter presented a number of variables that can be read by a debugger and/or µC/Probe.

These variables provide run-time and compile-time (static) information regarding µC/OS-III-based applications. The µC/OS-III variables allow users to monitor RAM footprint, task stack usage, context switches, CPU usage, the execution time of many operations, and more.

The application must never change (i.e., write to) any of these variables.

19

µC/OS-III API Reference Manual

This chapter provides a reference to µC/OS-III services. Each of the user-accessible kernel services is presented in alphabetical order. The following information is provided for each entry:

- A brief description of the service

- The function prototype

- The filename of the source code

- The **#define** constant required to enable code for the service

- A description of the arguments passed to the function

- A description of returned value(s)

- Specific notes and warnings regarding use of the service

- One or two examples of how to use the function

Many functions return error codes. These error codes should be checked by the application to ensure that the µC/OS-III function performed its operation as expected.

The next few pages summarizes most of the services provided by µC/OS-III. The function calls in bold are commonly used.

A-1 TASK MANAGEMENT

```
void
OSTaskChangePrio    (OS_TCB      *p_tcb,
                     OS_PRIO      prio,
                     OS_ERR      *p_err);
```

```
void
OSTaskCreate        (OS_TCB      *p_tcb,
                     CPU_CHAR    *p_name,
                     OS_TASK_PTR *p_task,
                     void        *p_arg,
                     OS_PRIO      prio,
                     CPU_STK     *p_stk_base,
                     CPU_STK_SIZE stk_limit,
                     CPU_STK_SIZE stk_size,
                     OS_MSG_QTY   q_size,
                     OS_TICK      time_quanta,
                     void        *p_ext,
                     OS_OPT       opt,
                     OS_ERR      *p_err);
```

```
Values for "opt":
    OS_OPT_TASK_NONE
    OS_OPT_TASK_STK_CHK
    OS_OPT_TASK_STK_CLR
    OS_OPT_TASK_SAVE_FP
```

```
void
OSTaskDel           (OS_TCB      *p_tcb,
                     OS_ERR      *p_err);
```

```
OS_REG
OSTaskRegGet        (OS_TCB      *p_tcb,
                     OS_REG_ID    id,
                     OS_ERR      *p_err);
```

```
void
OSTaskRegSet        (OS_TCB      *p_tcb,
                     OS_REG_ID    id,
                     OS_REG       value,
                     OS_ERR      *p_err);
```

```
void
OSTaskResume        (OS_TCB      *p_tcb,
                     OS_ERR      *p_err);
```

```
void
OSTaskSuspend       (OS_TCB      *p_tcb,
                     OS_ERR      *p_err);
```

```
void
OSTaskStkChk        (OS_TCB      *p_tcb,
                     CPU_STK_SIZE *p_free,
                     CPU_STK_SIZE *p_used,
                     OS_ERR      *p_err);
```

```
void
OSTaskTimeQuantaSet (OS_TCB      *p_tcb,
                     OS_TICK      time_quanta,
                     OS_ERR      *p_err);
```

A-2 TIME MANAGEMENT

```
void
OSTimeDly       (OS_TICK    dly,
                 OS_OPT     opt,
                 OS_ERR     *p_err);
```

Values for "opt":
  OS_OPT_TIME_HMSM_STRICT
  OS_OPT_TIME_HMSM_NON_STRICT

```
void
OSTimeDlyHMSM   (CPU_INT16U hours,
                 CPU_INT16U minutes,
                 CPU_INT16U seconds
                 CPU_INT32U milli,
                 OS_OPT     opt,
                 OS_ERR     *p_err);
```

```
void
OSTimeDlyResume (OS_TCB     *p_tcb,
                 OS_ERR     *p_err);
```

```
OS_TICK
OSTimeGet       (OS_ERR     *p_err);
```

```
void
OSTimeSet       (OS_TICK    ticks,
                 OS_ERR     *p_err);
```

A-3 MUTUAL EXCLUSION SEMAPHORES – RESOURCE MANAGEMENT

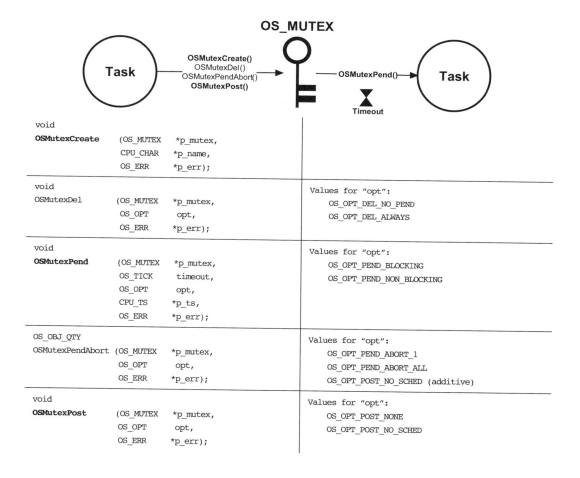

```
void
OSMutexCreate    (OS_MUTEX    *p_mutex,
                 CPU_CHAR     *p_name,
                 OS_ERR       *p_err);
```

```
void
OSMutexDel       (OS_MUTEX    *p_mutex,
                 OS_OPT       opt,
                 OS_ERR       *p_err);
```

Values for "opt":
  OS_OPT_DEL_NO_PEND
  OS_OPT_DEL_ALWAYS

```
void
OSMutexPend      (OS_MUTEX    *p_mutex,
                 OS_TICK      timeout,
                 OS_OPT       opt,
                 CPU_TS       *p_ts,
                 OS_ERR       *p_err);
```

Values for "opt":
  OS_OPT_PEND_BLOCKING
  OS_OPT_PEND_NON_BLOCKING

```
OS_OBJ_QTY
OSMutexPendAbort (OS_MUTEX    *p_mutex,
                 OS_OPT       opt,
                 OS_ERR       *p_err);
```

Values for "opt":
  OS_OPT_PEND_ABORT_1
  OS_OPT_PEND_ABORT_ALL
  OS_OPT_POST_NO_SCHED (additive)

```
void
OSMutexPost      (OS_MUTEX    *p_mutex,
                 OS_OPT       opt,
                 OS_ERR       *p_err);
```

Values for "opt":
  OS_OPT_POST_NONE
  OS_OPT_POST_NO_SCHED

A-4 EVENT FLAGS – SYNCHRONIZATION

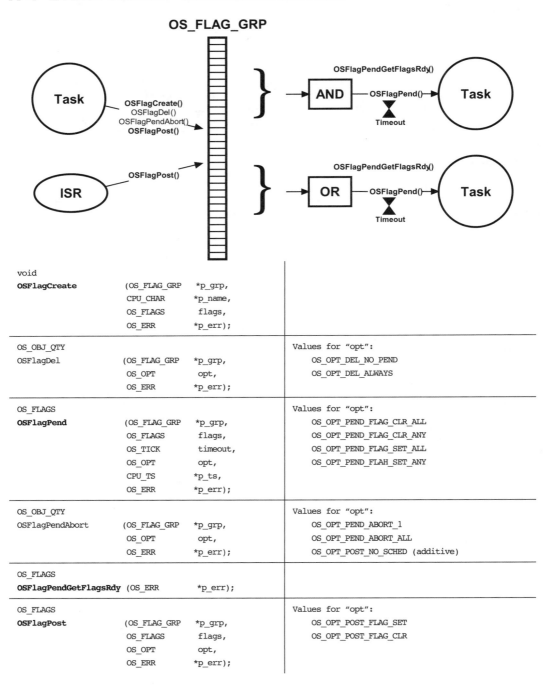

`void`	
OSFlagCreate `(OS_FLAG_GRP  *p_grp,`	
`CPU_CHAR     *p_name,`	
`OS_FLAGS      flags,`	
`OS_ERR       *p_err);`	

`OS_OBJ_QTY`	Values for "opt":
`OSFlagDel   (OS_FLAG_GRP  *p_grp,`	`OS_OPT_DEL_NO_PEND`
`OS_OPT        opt,`	`OS_OPT_DEL_ALWAYS`
`OS_ERR       *p_err);`	

`OS_FLAGS`	Values for "opt":
OSFlagPend `(OS_FLAG_GRP  *p_grp,`	`OS_OPT_PEND_FLAG_CLR_ALL`
`OS_FLAGS      flags,`	`OS_OPT_PEND_FLAG_CLR_ANY`
`OS_TICK       timeout,`	`OS_OPT_PEND_FLAG_SET_ALL`
`OS_OPT        opt,`	`OS_OPT_PEND_FLAH_SET_ANY`
`CPU_TS       *p_ts,`	
`OS_ERR       *p_err);`	

`OS_OBJ_QTY`	Values for "opt":
`OSFlagPendAbort  (OS_FLAG_GRP  *p_grp,`	`OS_OPT_PEND_ABORT_1`
`OS_OPT        opt,`	`OS_OPT_PEND_ABORT_ALL`
`OS_ERR       *p_err);`	`OS_OPT_POST_NO_SCHED (additive)`

`OS_FLAGS`	
OSFlagPendGetFlagsRdy `(OS_ERR        *p_err);`	

`OS_FLAGS`	Values for "opt":
OSFlagPost `(OS_FLAG_GRP  *p_grp,`	`OS_OPT_POST_FLAG_SET`
`OS_FLAGS      flags,`	`OS_OPT_POST_FLAG_CLR`
`OS_OPT        opt,`	
`OS_ERR       *p_err);`	

A-5 SEMAPHORES – SYNCHRONIZATION

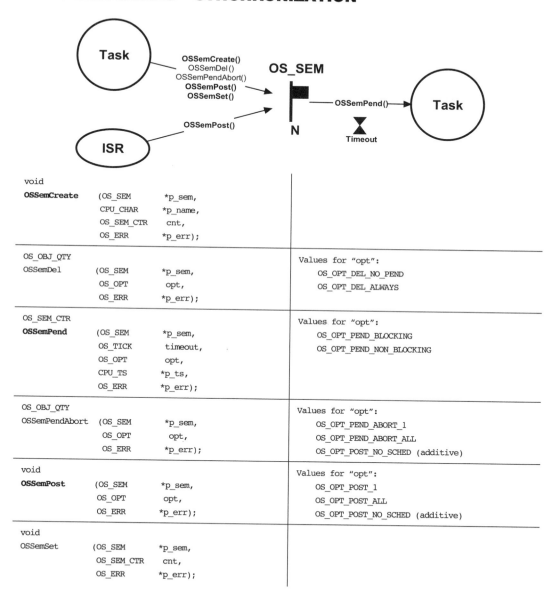

```
void
OSSemCreate      (OS_SEM       *p_sem,
                  CPU_CHAR     *p_name,
                  OS_SEM_CTR   cnt,
                  OS_ERR       *p_err);
```

```
OS_OBJ_QTY
OSSemDel         (OS_SEM       *p_sem,
                  OS_OPT       opt,
                  OS_ERR       *p_err);
```

Values for "opt":
    OS_OPT_DEL_NO_PEND
    OS_OPT_DEL_ALWAYS

```
OS_SEM_CTR
OSSemPend        (OS_SEM       *p_sem,
                  OS_TICK      timeout,
                  OS_OPT       opt,
                  CPU_TS       *p_ts,
                  OS_ERR       *p_err);
```

Values for "opt":
    OS_OPT_PEND_BLOCKING
    OS_OPT_PEND_NON_BLOCKING

```
OS_OBJ_QTY
OSSemPendAbort   (OS_SEM       *p_sem,
                  OS_OPT       opt,
                  OS_ERR       *p_err);
```

Values for "opt":
    OS_OPT_PEND_ABORT_1
    OS_OPT_PEND_ABORT_ALL
    OS_OPT_POST_NO_SCHED (additive)

```
void
OSSemPost        (OS_SEM       *p_sem,
                  OS_OPT       opt,
                  OS_ERR       *p_err);
```

Values for "opt":
    OS_OPT_POST_1
    OS_OPT_POST_ALL
    OS_OPT_POST_NO_SCHED (additive)

```
void
OSSemSet         (OS_SEM       *p_sem,
                  OS_SEM_CTR   cnt,
                  OS_ERR       *p_err);
```

A-6 TASK SEMAPHORES – SYNCHRONIZATION

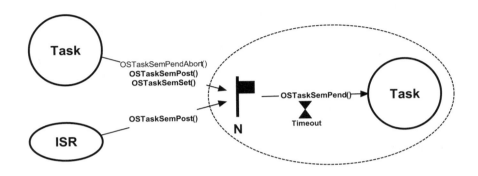

OS_SEM_CTR			Values for "opt":
OSTaskSemPend	(OS_TICK	timeout,	OS_OPT_PEND_BLOCKING
	OS_OPT	opt,	OS_OPT_PEND_NON_BLOCKING
	CPU_TS	*p_ts,	
	OS_ERR	*p_err);	

CPU_BOOLEAN			Values for "opt":
OSTaskSemPendAbort	(OS_TCB	*p_tcb,	OS_OPT_POST_NONE
	OS_OPT	opt,	OS_OPT_POST_NO_SCHED
	OS_ERR	*p_err);	

OS_SEM_CTR			Values for "opt":
OSTaskSemPost	(OS_TCB	*p_tcb,	OS_OPT_POST_NONE
	OS_OPT	opt,	OS_OPT_POST_NO_SCHED
	OS_ERR	*p_err);	

OS_SEM_CTR			
OSTaskSemSet	(OS_TCB	*p_tcb,	
	OS_SEM_CTR	cnt,	
	OS_ERR	*p_err);	

A-7 MESSAGE QUEUES – MESSAGE PASSING

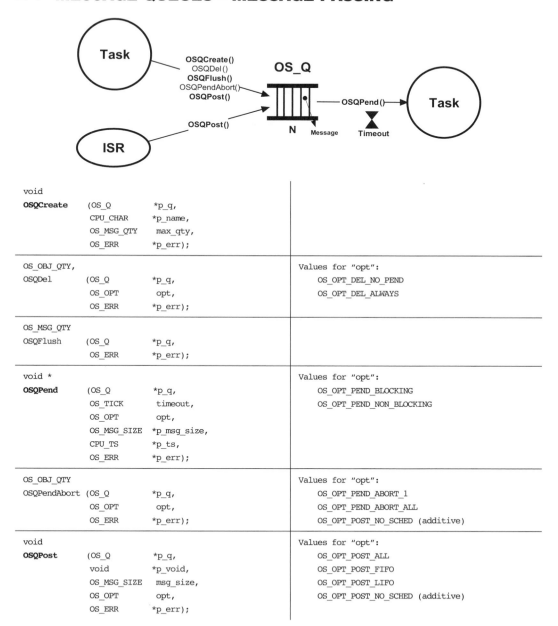

```
void
OSQCreate      (OS_Q        *p_q,
                CPU_CHAR     *p_name,
                OS_MSG_QTY   max_qty,
                OS_ERR       *p_err);
```

```
OS_OBJ_QTY,
OSQDel         (OS_Q        *p_q,
                OS_OPT       opt,
                OS_ERR       *p_err);
```
Values for "opt":
   OS_OPT_DEL_NO_PEND
   OS_OPT_DEL_ALWAYS

```
OS_MSG_QTY
OSQFlush       (OS_Q        *p_q,
                OS_ERR       *p_err);
```

```
void *
OSQPend        (OS_Q        *p_q,
                OS_TICK      timeout,
                OS_OPT       opt,
                OS_MSG_SIZE  *p_msg_size,
                CPU_TS       *p_ts,
                OS_ERR       *p_err);
```
Values for "opt":
   OS_OPT_PEND_BLOCKING
   OS_OPT_PEND_NON_BLOCKING

```
OS_OBJ_QTY
OSQPendAbort  (OS_Q         *p_q,
                OS_OPT       opt,
                OS_ERR       *p_err);
```
Values for "opt":
   OS_OPT_PEND_ABORT_1
   OS_OPT_PEND_ABORT_ALL
   OS_OPT_POST_NO_SCHED (additive)

```
void
OSQPost        (OS_Q        *p_q,
                void         *p_void,
                OS_MSG_SIZE  msg_size,
                OS_OPT       opt,
                OS_ERR       *p_err);
```
Values for "opt":
   OS_OPT_POST_ALL
   OS_OPT_POST_FIFO
   OS_OPT_POST_LIFO
   OS_OPT_POST_NO_SCHED (additive)

A-8 TASK MESSAGE QUEUES – MESSAGE PASSING

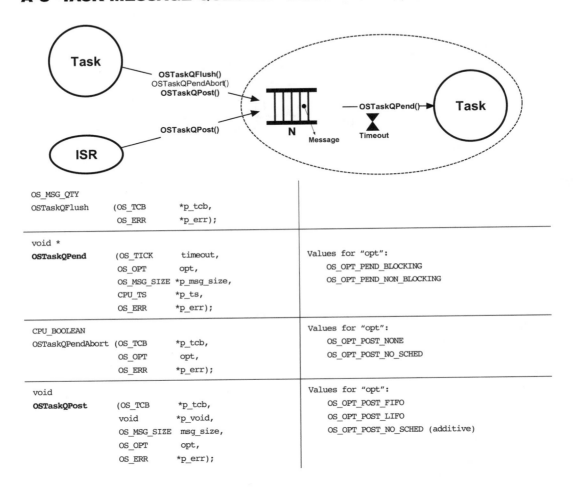

```
OS_MSG_QTY
OSTaskQFlush      (OS_TCB        *p_tcb,
                   OS_ERR        *p_err);
```

```
void *
OSTaskQPend       (OS_TICK       timeout,
                   OS_OPT        opt,
                   OS_MSG_SIZE   *p_msg_size,
                   CPU_TS        *p_ts,
                   OS_ERR        *p_err);
```

Values for "opt":
   OS_OPT_PEND_BLOCKING
   OS_OPT_PEND_NON_BLOCKING

```
CPU_BOOLEAN
OSTaskQPendAbort  (OS_TCB        *p_tcb,
                   OS_OPT        opt,
                   OS_ERR        *p_err);
```

Values for "opt":
   OS_OPT_POST_NONE
   OS_OPT_POST_NO_SCHED

```
void
OSTaskQPost       (OS_TCB        *p_tcb,
                   void          *p_void,
                   OS_MSG_SIZE   msg_size,
                   OS_OPT        opt,
                   OS_ERR        *p_err);
```

Values for "opt":
   OS_OPT_POST_FIFO
   OS_OPT_POST_LIFO
   OS_OPT_POST_NO_SCHED (additive)

A-9 PENDING ON MULTIPLE OBJECTS

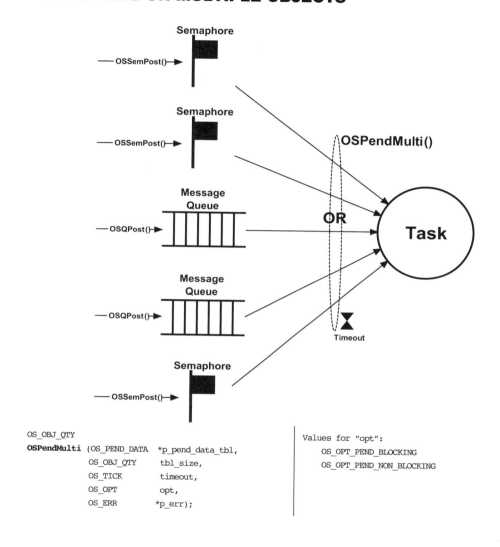

```
OS_OBJ_QTY
OSPendMulti (OS_PEND_DATA  *p_pend_data_tbl,
            OS_OBJ_QTY     tbl_size,
            OS_TICK        timeout,
            OS_OPT         opt,
            OS_ERR         *p_err);
```

```
Values for "opt":
    OS_OPT_PEND_BLOCKING
    OS_OPT_PEND_NON_BLOCKING
```

A-10 TIMERS

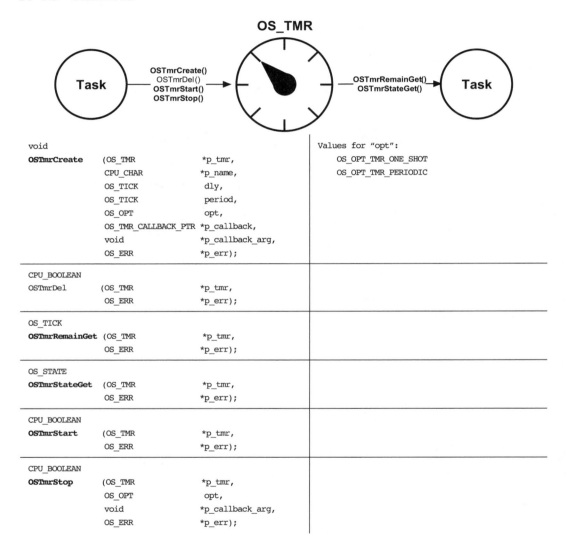

void			Values for "opt":
OSTmrCreate	(OS_TMR	*p_tmr,	OS_OPT_TMR_ONE_SHOT
	CPU_CHAR	*p_name,	OS_OPT_TMR_PERIODIC
	OS_TICK	dly,	
	OS_TICK	period,	
	OS_OPT	opt,	
	OS_TMR_CALLBACK_PTR *p_callback,		
	void	*p_callback_arg,	
	OS_ERR	*p_err);	

CPU_BOOLEAN		
OSTmrDel	(OS_TMR	*p_tmr,
	OS_ERR	*p_err);

OS_TICK		
OSTmrRemainGet	(OS_TMR	*p_tmr,
	OS_ERR	*p_err);

OS_STATE		
OSTmrStateGet	(OS_TMR	*p_tmr,
	OS_ERR	*p_err);

CPU_BOOLEAN		
OSTmrStart	(OS_TMR	*p_tmr,
	OS_ERR	*p_err);

CPU_BOOLEAN		
OSTmrStop	(OS_TMR	*p_tmr,
	OS_OPT	opt,
	void	*p_callback_arg,
	OS_ERR	*p_err);

A-11 FIXED-SIZE MEMORY PARTITIONS – MEMORY MANAGEMENT

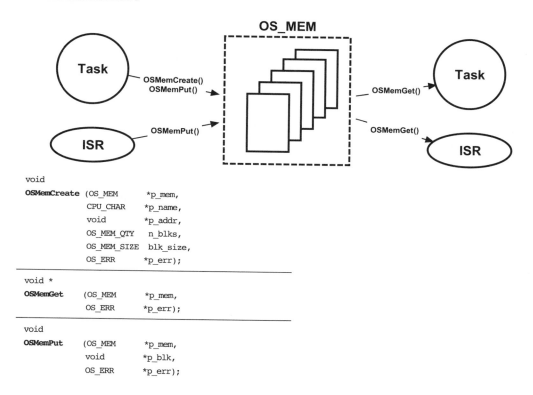

```
void
OSMemCreate (OS_MEM      *p_mem,
             CPU_CHAR    *p_name,
             void        *p_addr,
             OS_MEM_QTY  n_blks,
             OS_MEM_SIZE blk_size,
             OS_ERR      *p_err);
```

```
void *
OSMemGet   (OS_MEM      *p_mem,
            OS_ERR      *p_err);
```

```
void
OSMemPut   (OS_MEM      *p_mem,
            void        *p_blk,
            OS_ERR      *p_err);
```

OSCtxSw()

void OSCtxSw (void)

File	Called from	Code enabled by
OS_CPU_A.ASM	OSSched()	N/A

OSCtxSw() is called from the macro OS_TASK_SW(), which in turn is called from OSSched() to perform a task-level context switch. Interrupts are disabled when OSCtxSw() is called.

Prior to calling OSCtxSw(), OSSched() sets OSTCBCurPtr to point at the OS_TCB of the task that is being switched out, and OSTCBHighRdyPtr to point at the OS_TCB of the task being switched in.

Arguments

None

Returned Values

None

Notes/Warnings

None

Example

The pseudocode for OSCtxSw() follows:

```
void  OSCtxSw (void)
{
    Save all CPU registers;                        (1)
    OSTCBCurPtr->StkPtr = SP;                       (2)
    OSTaskSwHook();                                 (3)
    OSPrioCur          = OSPrioHighRdy;             (4)
    OSTCBCurPtr        = OSTCBHighRdyPtr;           (5)
    SP                 = OSTCBHighRdyPtr->StkPtr;   (6)
    Restore all CPU registers;                      (7)
    Return from interrupt;                          (8)
}
```

(1)   OSCtxSw() must save all of the CPU registers onto the current task's stack. OSCtxSw() is called from the context of the task being switched out. Therefore, the CPU stack pointer is pointing to the proper stack. The user must save all of the registers in the same order as if an ISR started and all the CPU registers were saved on the stack. The stacking order should therefore match that of OSTaskStkInit().

(2)   Save the current task's stack pointer into the current task's OS_TCB.

(3)   Next, OSCtxSw() must call OSTaskSwHook().

(4)   Copy OSPrioHighRdy to OSPrioCur.

(5)   Copy OSTCBHighRdyPtr to OSTCBCurPtr since the current task is now the task being switched in.

(6)   Restore the stack pointer of the new task, which is found in the OS_TCB of the new task.

(7)   Restore all the CPU registers from the new task's stack.

(8)   Finally, OSCtxSw() must execute a return from interrupt instruction.

OSFlagCreate()

```
void  OSFlagCreate (OS_FLAG_GRP  *p_grp,
                    CPU_CHAR      *p_name,
                    OS_FLAGS      flags,
                    OS_ERR        *p_err)
```

File	Called from	Code enabled by
OS_FLAG.C	Task or startup code	OS_CFG_FLAG_EN

OSFlagCreate() is used to create and initialize an event flag group. µC/OS-III allows the user to create an unlimited number of event flag groups (limited only by the amount of RAM in the system).

Arguments

p_grp is a pointer to an event flag group that must be allocated in the application. The user will need to declare a "global" variable as shown, and pass a pointer to this variable to **OSFlagCreate()**:

    `OS_FLAG_GRP  MyEventFlag;`

p_name is a pointer to an ASCII string used for the name of the event flag group. The name can be displayed by debuggers or by µC/Probe.

flags contains the initial value of the flags to store in the event flag group.

p_err is a pointer to a variable that is used to hold an error code. The error code can be one of the following:

OS_ERR_NONE	if the call is successful and the event flag group has been created.
OS_ERR_CREATE_ISR	if attempting to create an event flag group from an ISR, w is not allowed.
OS_ERR_NAME	if **p_name** is a **NULL** pointer.
OS_ERR_OBJ_CREATED	if the object passed has already been created.
OS_ERR_OBJ_PTR_NULL	if **p_grp** is a **NULL** pointer.

Returned Values

None

Notes/Warnings

1. Event flag groups must be created by this function before they can be used by the other event flag group services.

Example

```
OS_FLAG_GRP  EngineStatus;


void main (void)
{
    OS_ERR  err;

    OSInit(&err);                       /* Initialize μC/OS-III               */
    :
    :
    OSFlagCreate(&EngineStatus,
                 "Engine Status",
                 (OS_FLAGS)0,
                 &err);                 /* Create a flag grp containing the engine's status */
    /* Check "err" */
    :
    :
    OSStart();                          /* Start Multitasking                 */
}
```

OSFlagDel()

```
void OSFlagDel (OS_FLAG_GRP *p_grp,
                OS_OPT       opt,
                OS_ERR      *p_err);
```

File	Called from	Code enabled by
OS_FLAG.C	Task	OS_CFG_FLAG_EN and OS_CFG_FLAG_DEL_EN

OSFlagDel() is used to delete an event flag group. This function should be used with care since multiple tasks may be relying on the presence of the event flag group. Generally, before deleting an event flag group, first delete all of the tasks that access the event flag group. Also, it is recommended that the user not delete kernel objects at run time.

Arguments

p_grp   is a pointer to the event flag group to delete.

opt   specifies whether the user wants to delete the event flag group only if there are no pending tasks (OS_OPT_DEL_NO_PEND), or whether the event flag group should always be deleted regardless of whether or not tasks are pending (OS_OPT_DEL_ALWAYS). In this case, all pending task are readied.

p_err   is a pointer to a variable used to hold an error code. The error code can be one of the following:

OS_ERR_NONE	if the call is successful and the event flag group has been deleted.
OS_ERR_DEL_ISR	if the user attempts to delete an event flag group from an ISR.
OS_ERR_OBJ_PTR_NULL	if p_grp is a NULL pointer.
OS_ERR_OBJ_TYPE	if p_grp is not pointing to an event flag group.
OS_ERR_OPT_INVALID	if the user does not specify one of the options mentioned in the opt argument.
OS_ERR_TASK_WAITING	if one or more tasks are waiting on the event flag group and OS_OPT_DEL_NO_PEND is specified.

Returned Values

0 if no task was waiting on the event flag group, or an error occurs.

> 0 if one or more tasks waiting on the event flag group are now readied and informed

Notes/Warnings

1. Use this call with care as other tasks might expect the presence of the event flag group.

Example

```c
OS_FLAG_GRP  EngineStatusFlags;


void Task (void *p_arg)
{
    OS_ERR      err;
    OS_OBJ_QTY  qty;

    (void)&p_arg;
    while (DEF_ON) {
        :
        :
        qty = OSFlagDel(&EngineStatusFlags,
                        OS_OPT_DEL_ALWAYS,
                        &err);
        /* Check "err" */
        :
        :
    }
}
```

OSFlagPend()

```
OS_FLAGS  OSFlagPend (OS_FLAG_GRP *p_grp,
                      OS_FLAGS     flags,
                      OS_TICK      timeout,
                      OS_OPT       opt,
                      CPU_TS      *p_ts,
                      OS_ERR      *p_err)
```

File	Called from	Code enabled by
OS_FLAG.C	Task	OS_CFG_FLAG_EN

OSFlagPend() allows the task to wait for a combination of conditions (i.e., events or bits) to be set (or cleared) in an event flag group. The application can wait for any condition to be set or cleared, or for all conditions to be set or cleared. If the events that the calling task desires are not available, the calling task is blocked (optional) until the desired conditions are satisfied, the specified timeout expires, the event flag is deleted, or the pend is aborted by another task.

Arguments

p_grp   is a pointer to the event flag group.

flags   is a bit pattern indicating which bit(s) (i.e., flags) to check. The bits wanted are specified by setting the corresponding bits in flags. If the application wants to wait for bits 0 and 1 to be set, specify 0x03.

timeout   allows the task to resume execution if the desired flag(s) is(are) not received from the event flag group within the specified number of clock ticks. A timeout value of 0 indicates that the task wants to wait forever for the flag(s). The timeout value is not synchronized with the clock tick. The timeout count begins decrementing on the next clock tick, which could potentially occur immediately.

opt   specifies whether all bits are to be set/cleared or any of the bits are to be set/cleared. Specify the following arguments:

OS_OPT_PEND_FLAG_CLR_ALL   Check all bits in flags to be clear (0)
OS_OPT_PEND_FLAG_CLR_ANY   Check any bit in flags to be clear (0)

OS_OPT_PEND_FLAG_SET_ALL   Check all bits in flags to be set (1)

OS_OPT_PEND_FLAG_SET_ANY   Check any bit in flags to be set (1)

The user may also specify whether the flags are consumed by "adding" OS_OPT_PEND_FLAG_CONSUME to the opt argument. For example, to wait for any flag in a group and then clear the flags that satisfy the condition, set opt to:

OS_OPT_PEND_FLAG_SET_ANY + OS_OPT_PEND_FLAG_CONSUME

Finally, you can specify whether the user wants to block if the flag(s) are available or not. The user must "add" the following options:

OS_OPT_PEND_BLOCKING

OS_OPT_PEND_NON_BLOCKING

Note that the timeout argument should be set to 0 when specifying OS_OPT_PEND_NON_BLOCKING, since the timeout value is irrelevant using this option.

p_ts   is a pointer to a timestamp indicating when the flags were posted, the pend was aborted, or the event flag group was deleted. If passing a **NULL** pointer (i.e., (**CPU_TS** *)0), the user will not obtain the timestamp. Passing a **NULL** pointer is valid, and indicates that the user does not need the timestamp.

A timestamp is useful when the task desires to know when the event flag group was posted or how long it took for the task to resume after the event flag group was posted. In the latter case, the user must call **OS_TS_GET()** and compute the difference between the current value of the timestamp and ***p_ts**, as shown:

delta = OS_TS_GET() - *p_ts;

p_err   is a pointer to an error code and can be:

OS_ERR_NONE	No error.
OS_ERR_OBJ_PTR_NULL	if **p_grp** is a **NULL** pointer.
OS_ERR_OBJ_TYPE	**p_grp** is not pointing to an event flag group.
OS_ERR_OPT_INVALID	the user specified an invalid option.
OS_ERR_PEND_ABORT	the wait on the flags was aborted by another task that called **OSFlagPendAbort()**.

`OS_ERR_PEND_ISR`	An attempt was made to call OSFlagPend from an ISR, which is not allowed.
`OS_ERR_SCHED_LOCKED`	When calling this function while the scheduler was locked.
`OS_ERR_PEND_WOULD_BLOCK`	`if` specifying non-blocking but the flags were not available and the call would block if the user had specified `OS_OPT_PEND_BLOCKING`.
`OS_ERR_TIMEOUT`	the flags are not available within the specified amount of time.

Returned Values

The flag(s) that cause the task to be ready, 0 if either none of the flags are ready, or indicate an error occurred.

Notes/Warnings

1. The event flag group must be created before it is used.

Example

```
#define   ENGINE_OIL_PRES_OK   0x01
#define   ENGINE_OIL_TEMP_OK   0x02
#define   ENGINE_START         0x04


OS_FLAG_GRP  EngineStatus;

void Task (void *p_arg)
{
    OS_ERR   err;
    OS_FLAGS value;
    CPU_TS   ts;


    (void)&p_arg;
    while (DEF_ON) {
        value = OSFlagPend(&EngineStatus,
                           ENGINE_OIL_PRES_OK   + ENGINE_OIL_TEMP_OK,
                           OS_FLAG_WAIT_SET_ALL + OS_FLAG_CONSUME,
                           10,
                           OS_OPT_PEND_BLOCKING,
                           &ts,
                           &err);
        /* Check "err" */
        :
        :
    }
}
```

OSFlagPendAbort()

```
OS_OBJ_QTY  OSFlagPendAbort (OS_SEM  *p_grp,
                             OS_OPT    opt,
                             OS_ERR   *p_err)
```

File	Called from	Code enabled by
OS_FLAG.C	Task	OS_CFG_FLAG_EN and OS_CFG_FLAG_PEND_ABORT_EN

OSFlagPendAbort() aborts and readies any tasks currently waiting on an event flag group. This function should be used by another task to fault abort the wait on the event flag group, rather than to normally signal the event flag group via OSFlagPost().

Arguments

p_grp   is a pointer to the event flag group for which pend(s) must be aborted.

opt   determines the type of abort performed.

OS_OPT_PEND_ABORT_1	Aborts the pend of only the highest priority task waiting on the event flag group.
OS_OPT_PEND_ABORT_ALL	Aborts the pend of all the tasks waiting on the event flag group.
OS_OPT_POST_NO_SCHED	Specifies that the scheduler should not be called even if the pend of a higher priority task is aborted. Scheduling will need to occur from another function.
	Use this option if the task calling OSFlagPendAbort() will perform additional pend aborts, rescheduling will take place at completion, and when multiple pend aborts are to take effect simultaneously.

p_err is a pointer to a variable that holds an error code. **OSFlagPendAbort()** sets ***p_err** to one of the following:

OS_ERR_NONE	at least one task waiting on the event flag group was readied and informed of the aborted wait. Check the return value for the number of tasks where a wait on the event flag group was aborted.
OS_ERR_OBJ_PTR_NULL	if **p_grp** is a **NULL** pointer.
OS_ERR_OBJ_TYPE	if **p_grp** is not pointing to an event flag group.
OS_ERR_OPT_INVALID	if specifying an invalid option.
OS_ERR_PEND_ABORT_ISR	This function cannot be called from an ISR.
OS_ERR_PEND_ABORT_NONE	No task was aborted since no task was waiting.

Returned Value

OSFlagPendAbort() returns the number of tasks made ready to run by this function. Zero indicates that no tasks were pending on the event flag group and thus this function had no effect.

Notes/Warnings

1. Event flag groups must be created before they are used.

Example

```
OS_FLAG_GRP  EngineStatus;


void Task (void *p_arg)
{
    OS_ERR      err;
    OS_OBJ_QTY  nbr_tasks;


    (void)&p_arg;
    while (DEF_ON) {
        :
        :
        nbr_tasks = OSFlagPendAbort(&EngineStatus,
                                    OS_OPT_PEND_ABORT_ALL,
                                    &err);
        /* Check "err" */
        :
        :
    }
}
```

OSFlagPendGetFlagsRdy()

`OS_FLAGS  OSFlagPendGetFlagsRdy (OS_ERR  *p_err)`

File	Called from	Code enabled by
OS_FLAG.C	Task	OS_CFG_FLAG_EN

`OSFlagPendGetFlagsRdy()` is used to obtain the flags that caused the current task to be ready to run. This function allows the user to know "Who done it!"

Arguments

p_err   is a pointer to an error code and can be:

> OS_ERR_NONE   No error.
>
> OS_ERR_PEND_ISR   When attempting to call this function from an ISR.

Returned Value

The value of the flags that caused the current task to become ready to run.

Notes/Warnings

1. The event flag group must be created before it is used.

Example

```
#define  ENGINE_OIL_PRES_OK   0x01
#define  ENGINE_OIL_TEMP_OK   0x02
#define  ENGINE_START         0x04


OS_FLAG_GRP  EngineStatus;


void Task (void *p_arg)
{
    OS_ERR    err;
    OS_FLAGS  value;
    OS_FLAGS  flags_rdy;


    (void)&p_arg;
    while (DEF_ON) {
        value     = OSFlagPend(&EngineStatus,
                               ENGINE_OIL_PRES_OK   + ENGINE_OIL_TEMP_OK,
                               OS_FLAG_WAIT_SET_ALL + OS_FLAG_CONSUME,
                               10,
                               &err);
        /* Check "err" */
        flags_rdy = OSFlagPendGetFlagsRdy(&err);
        /* Check "err" */
        :
        :
    }
}
```

OSFlagPost()

```
OS_FLAGS  OSFlagPost (OS_FLAG_GRP  *p_grp,
                      OS_FLAGS      flags,
                      OS_OPT        opt,
                      OS_ERR        *p_err)
```

File	Called from	Code enabled by
OS_FLAG.C	Task or ISR	OS_CFG_FLAG_EN

Set or clear event flag bits by calling **OSFlagPost()**. The bits set or cleared are specified in a bit mask (i.e., the flags argument). **OSFlagPost()** readies each task that has its desired bits satisfied by this call. The user can set or clear bits that are already set or cleared.

Arguments

p_grp   is a pointer to the event flag group.

flags   specifies which bits to be set or cleared. If opt is **OS_OPT_POST_FLAG_SET**, each bit that is set in flags will set the corresponding bit in the event flag group. For example to set bits 0, 4, and 5, set flags to 0x31 (note that bit 0 is the least significant bit). If opt is **OS_OPT_POST_FLAG_CLR**, each bit that is set in flags will clear the corresponding bit in the event flag group. For example to clear bits 0, 4, and 5, specify flags as 0x31 (again, bit 0 is the least significant bit).

opt   indicates whether the flags are set (**OS_OPT_POST_FLAG_SET**) or cleared (**OS_OPT_POST_FLAG_CLR**).

The user may also "add" **OS_OPT_POST_NO_SCHED** so that µC/OS-III will not call the scheduler after the post.

p_err   is a pointer to an error code and can be:

OS_ERR_NONE	the call is successful.
OS_ERR_FLAG_INVALID_OPT	specify an invalid option.
OS_ERR_OBJ_PTR_NULL	the user passed a **NULL** pointer.
OS_ERR_OBJ_TYPE	the user is not pointing to an event flag group.

Returned Value

The new value of the event flags.

Notes/Warnings

1 Event flag groups must be created before they are used.

2 The execution time of this function depends on the number of tasks waiting on the event flag group. However, the execution time is still deterministic.

3 Although the example below shows that we are posting from a task, **OSFlagPost()** can also be called from an ISR.

Example

```
#define  ENGINE_OIL_PRES_OK   0x01
#define  ENGINE_OIL_TEMP_OK   0x02
#define  ENGINE_START         0x04


OS_FLAG_GRP  EngineStatusFlags;


void  TaskX (void *p_arg)
{
    OS_ERR    err;
    OS_FLAGS  flags;


    (void)&p_arg;
    while (DEF_ON) {
        :
        :
        flags = OSFlagPost(&EngineStatusFlags,
                    ENGINE_START,
                    OS_OPT_POST_FLAG_SET,
                    &err);
        /* Check 'err" */
        :
        :
    }
}
```

OSIdleTaskHook()

```
void  OSIdleTaskHook (void);
```

File	Called from	Code enabled by
OS_CPU_C.C	OS_IdleTask() ONLY	N/A

This function is called by OS_IdleTask().

OSIdleTaskHook() is part of the CPU port code and this function *must not* be called by the application code. OSIdleTaskHook() is used by the μC/OS-III port developer.

OSIdleTaskHook() runs in the context of the idle task so that it is important to make sure there is sufficient stack space in the idle task. OSIdleTaskHook() *must not* make any OS???Pend() calls, call OSTaskSuspend() or OSTimeDly???(). In other words, this function must never be allowed to make a blocking call.

Arguments

None

Returned Value

None

Notes/Warnings

1. Never make blocking calls from OSIdleTaskHook().

2. *Do not* call this function from you application.

Example

The code below calls an application-specific hook that the application programmer can define. The user can simply set the value of OS_AppIdleTaskHookPtr to point to the desired hook function which in this case assumes s defined in OS_APP_HOOKS.C. The idle task calls OSIdleTaskHook() which in turns calls App_OS_IdleTaskHook() through OS_AppIdleTaskHookPtr.

This feature is very useful when there is a processor that can enter low-power mode. When µC/OS-III has no other task to run, the processor can be put to sleep waiting for an interrupt to wake it up.

```
void  App_OS_IdleTaskHook (void)                          /* See OS_APP_HOOKS.C   */
{
    /* Your code goes here! */
    /* Put the CPU in low power mode (optional) */
}


void App_OS_SetAllHooks (void)                            /* OS_APP_HOOKS.C       */
{
    CPU_SR_ALLOC();

    CPU_CRITICAL_ENTER();
    :
    OS_AppIdleTaskHookPtr = App_OS_IdleTaskHook;
    :
    CPU_CRITICAL_EXIT();
}


void  OSIdleTaskHook (void)                               /* See OS_CPU_C.C       */
{
#if OS_CFG_APP_HOOKS_EN > 0u
    if (OS_AppIdleTaskHookPtr != (OS_APP_HOOK_VOID)0) {   /* Call application hook */
        (*OS_AppIdleTaskHookPtr)();
    }
#endif
}
```

OSInit()

```
void OSInit (OS_ERR *p_err);
```

File	Called from	Code enabled by
OS_CORE.C	Startup code only	N/A

OSInit() initializes µC/OS-III and it must be called prior to calling any other µC/OS-III function. Including OSStart()which will start multitasking.

Arguments

p_err   is a pointer to an error code and can be:

OS_ERR_NONE   initialization was successful.

OS_ERR_????   some other OS_ERR_???? value returned by a sub-function of OSInit().

Returned Values

None

Notes/Warnings

1. OSInit() must be called before OSStart().

2. OSInit() returns as soon as it detects an error in any of the sub-functions it calls. For example, if OSInit() encounters a problem initializing the task manager, an appropriate error code will be returned and OSInit() will not go any further. It is therefore important that the user checks the error code before starting multitasking.

Example

```
void main (void)
{
    OS_ERR  err;


        :
    OSInit(&err);                    /* Initialize µC/OS-III            */
    /* Check "err" */
        :
        :
    OSStart(&err);                   /* Start Multitasking             */
    /* Check "err" */               /* Code not supposed to end up here! */
}
```

OSInitHook()

```
void OSInitHook (void);
```

File	Called from	Code enabled by
OS_CPU_C.C	OSInit()	Always enabled

OSInitHook() is a function that is called by µC/OS-III's initialization code, OSInit(). OSInitHook() is typically implemented by the port implementer for the processor used. This hook allows the port to be extended to do such tasks as setup exception stacks, floating-point registers, and more. OSInitHook() is called at the beginning of OSInit(), before any µC/OS-III task and data structure have been initialized.

Arguments

None

Returned Values

None

Notes/Warnings

None

Example

```c
void OSInitHook (void)                          /* See OS_CPU_C.C       */
{
    /* Perform any initialization code necessary by the port */
}
```

OSIntCtxSw()

```
void  OSIntCtxSw (void)
```

File	Called from	Code enabled by
OS_CPU_A.ASM	OSIntExit()	N/A

OSIntCtxSw() is called from **OSIntExit()** to perform a context switch when all nested interrupts have returned.

Interrupts are disabled when **OSIntCtxSw()** is called.

OSIntExit() sets **OSTCBCurPtr** to point at the **OS_TCB** of the task that is switched out and OSTCBHighRdyPtr to point at the **OS_TCB** of the task that is switched in.

Arguments

None

Returned Values

None

Notes/Warnings

None

Example

The pseudocode for OSIntCtxSw() is shown below. Notice that the code does only half of what OSCtxSw() did. The reason is that OSIntCtxSw() is called from an ISR and it is assumed that all of the CPU registers of the interrupted task were saved at the beginning of the ISR. OSIntCtxSw() therefore only must restore the context of the new, high-priority task.

```
void  OSIntCtxSw (void)
{
    OSTaskSwHook();                                    (1)
    OSPrioCur        = OSPrioHighRdy;                  (2)
    OSTCBCurPtr      = OSTCBHighRdyPtr;                 (3)
    SP               = OSTCBHighRdyPtr->StkPtr;        (4)
    Restore all CPU registers;                         (5)
    Return from interrupt;                             (6)
}
```

(1)   OSIntCtxSw() must call OSTaskSwHook().

(2)   Copy OSPrioHighRdy to OSPrioCur.

(3)   Copy OSTCBHighRdyPtr to OSTCBCurPtr because the current task will now be the new task.

(4)   Restore the stack pointer of the new task, which is found in the OS_TCB of the new task.

(5)   Restore all the CPU registers from the new task's stack.

(6)   Execute a return from interrupt instruction.

OSIntEnter()

void OSIntEnter (void);

File	Called from	Code enabled by
OS_CORE.C	ISR only	N/A

OSIntEnter() notifies µC/OS-III that an ISR is being processed, which allows µC/OS-III to keep track of interrupt nesting. OSIntEnter() is used in conjunction with OSIntExit(). This function is generally called at the beginning of ISRs. Note that on some CPU architectures, it must be written in assembly language (shown below in pseudo code):

```
MyISR:
    Save CPU registers;
    OSIntEnter();                /* Or, OSIntNestingCtr++ */
    :
    Process ISR;
    :
    OSIntExit();
    Restore CPU registers;
    Return from interrupt;
```

Arguments

None

Returned Values

None

Notes/Warnings

1. This function must not be called by task-level code.

2. Iincrement the interrupt-nesting counter (OSIntNestingCtr) directly in the ISR to avoid the overhead of the function call/return. It is safe to increment OSIntNestingCtr in the ISR since interrupts are assumed to be disabled when OSIntNestingCtr is incremented. However, that is not true for all CPU architectures. Make sure interrupts are disabled in the ISR before directly incrementing OSIntNestingCtr.

3. It is possible to nest interrupts up to 250 levels deep.

OSIntExit()

```
void OSIntExit (void);
```

File	Called from	Code enabled by
OS_CORE.C	ISR only	N/A

OSIntExit() notifies µC/OS-III that an ISR is complete, which allows µC/OS-III to keep track of interrupt nesting. OSIntExit() is used in conjunction with OSIntEnter(). When the last nested interrupt completes, OSIntExit() determines if a higher priority task is ready to run. If so, the interrupt returns to the higher priority task instead of the interrupted task.

This function is typically called at the end of ISRs as follows, and on some CPU architectures, it must be written in assembly language (shown below in pseudo code):

```
MyISR:
    Save CPU registers;
    OSIntEnter();
        :
    Process ISR;
        :
    OSIntExit();
    Restore CPU registers;
    Return from interrupt;
```

Arguments

None

Returned Value

None

Notes/Warnings

1. This function must not be called by task-level code. Also, if directly incrementing OSIntNestingCtr, instead of calling OSIntEnter(), the user must still call OSIntExit().

OSMemCreate()

```
void  OSMemCreate (OS_MEM      *p_mem,
                   CPU_CHAR    *p_name,
                   void        *p_addr,
                   OS_MEM_QTY   n_blks,
                   OS_MEM_SIZE  blk_size,
                   OS_ERR      *p_err)
```

File	Called from	Code enabled by
OS_MEM.C	Task or startup code	OS_CFG_MEM_EN

OSMemCreate() creates and initializes a memory partition. A memory partition contains a user-specified number of fixed-size memory blocks. An application may obtain one of these memory blocks and, when completed, release the block back to the same partition where the block originated.

Arguments

p_mem   is a pointer to a memory partition control block that must be allocated in the application. It is assumed that storage will be allocated for the memory control blocks in the application. In other words, the user will declare a "global" variable as follows, and pass a pointer to this variable to OSMemCreate():

```
OS_MEM  MyMemPartition;
```

p_name   is a pointer to an ASCII string to provide a name to the memory partition. The name can be displayed by debuggers or µC/Probe.

p_addr   is the address of the start of a memory area used to create fixed-size memory blocks. Memory partitions may be created either using static arrays or malloc() during startup. Note that the partition *must* align on a pointer boundary. Thus, if a pointer is 16-bits wide. the partition must start on a memory location with an address that ends with 0, 2, 4, 6, 8, etc. If a pointer is 32-bits wide, the partition must start on a memory location with an address that ends in 0, 4, 8 of C. The easiest way to ensure this is to create a static array as follows:

```
void *MyMemArray[N][M * sizeof(void *)]
```

Never deallocate memory blocks that were allocated from the heap to prevent fragmentation of your heap. It is quite acceptable to allocate memory blocks from the heap as long as the user does not deallocate them.

n_blks   contains the number of memory blocks available from the specified partition. Specify at least two memory blocks per partition.

blk_size   specifies the size (in bytes) of each memory block within a partition. A memory block must be large enough to hold at least a pointer. Also, the size of a memory block must be a multiple of the size of a pointer. If a pointer is 32-bits wide then the block size must be 4, 8, 12, 16, 20, etc. bytes (i.e., a multiple of 4 bytes).

p_err   is a pointer to a variable that holds an error code:

OS_ERR_NONE	if the memory partition is created successfully
OS_ERR_MEM_INVALID_BLKS	if the user does not specify at least two memory blocks per partition
OS_ERR_MEM_INVALID_P_ADDR	if specifying an invalid address (i.e., **p_addr** is a **NULL** pointer) or the partition is not properly aligned.
OS_ERR_MEM_INVALID_SIZE	if the user does not specify a block size that can contain at least a pointer variable, and if it is not a multiple of a pointer-size variable.

Returned Value

None

Notes/Warnings

1. Memory partitions must be created before they are used.

Example

```
OS_MEM       CommMem;
CPU_INT32U   *CommBuf[16][32];          /* 16 buffers of 32 words of 32 bits */


void  main (void)
{
    OS_ERR  err;


    OSInit(&err);                       /* Initialize µC/OS-III              */
    :
    :
    OSMemCreate(&CommMem,
                "Comm Buffers",
                &CommBuf[0][0],
                16,
                32 * sizeof(CPU_INT32U),
                &err);
    /* Check "err" */
    :
    :
    OSStart(&err);                      /* Start Multitasking                */
}
```

OSMemGet()

```
void  *OSMemGet (OS_MEM  *p_mem,
                 OS_ERR   *p_err)
```

File	Called from	Code enabled by
OS_MEM.C	Task or ISR	OS_CFG_MEM_EN

OSMemGet() obtains a memory block from a memory partition. It is assumed that the application knows the size of each memory block obtained. Also, the application must return the memory block [using OSMemPut()] to the same memory partition when it no longer requires it. OSMemGet() may be called more than once until all memory blocks are allocated.

Arguments

p_mem   is a pointer to the desired memory partition control block.

p_err   is a pointer to a variable that holds an error code:

OS_ERR_NONE	if a memory block is available and returned to the application.
OS_ERR_MEM_INVALID_P_MEM	if p_mem is a NULL pointer.
OS_ERR_MEM_NO_FREE_BLKS	if the memory partition does not contain additional memory blocks to allocate.

Returned Value

OSMemGet() returns a pointer to the allocated memory block if one is available. If a memory block is not available from the memory partition, OSMemGet() returns a NULL pointer. It is up to the application to "cast" the pointer to the proper data type since OSMemGet() returns a void *.

Notes/Warnings

1. Memory partitions must be created before they are used.

2. This is a non-blocking call and this function can be called from an ISR.

Example

```
OS_MEM   CommMem;


void Task (void *p_arg)
{
    OS_ERR       err;
    CPU_INT08U  *p_msg;


    (void)&p_arg;
    while (DEF_ON) {
        p_msg = (CPU_INT08U *)OSMemGet(&CommMem,
                                       &err);
        /* Check "err" */
        :
        :
    }
}
```

OSMemPut()

```
void   OSMemPut (OS_MEM   *p_mem,
                 void      *p_blk,
                 OS_ERR    *p_err)
```

File	Called from	Code enabled by
OS_MEM.C	Task or ISR	OS_CFG_MEM_EN

OSMemPut() returns a memory block back to a memory partition. It is assumed that the user will return the memory block to the same memory partition from which it was allocated.

Arguments

p_mem   is a pointer to the memory partition control block.

p_blk   is a pointer to the memory block to be returned to the memory partition.

p_err   is a pointer to a variable that holds an error code:

OS_ERR_NONE	if a memory block is available and returned to the application.
OS_ERR_MEM_INVALID_P_BLK	if the user passed a **NULL** pointer for the memory block being returned to the memory partition.
OS_ERR_MEM_INVALID_P_MEM	if **p_mem** is a **NULL** pointer.
OS_ERR_MEM_MEM_FULL	if returning a memory block to an already full memory partition. This would indicate that the user freed more blocks that were allocated and potentially did not return some of the memory blocks to the proper memory partition.

Returned Value

None

Notes/Warnings

1. Memory partitions must be created before they are used.

2. Return a memory block to the proper memory partition.

3. Call this function from an ISR or a task.

Example

```
OS_MEM       CommMem;
CPU_INT08U  *CommMsg;


void Task (void *p_arg)
{
    OS_ERR err;


    (void)&p_arg;
    while (DEF_ON) {
        OSMemPut(&CommMem,
                 (void *)CommMsg,
                 &err);
        /* Check "err" */
        :
        :
    }
}
```

OSMutexCreate()

```
void  OSMutexCreate (OS_MUTEX   *p_mutex,
                     CPU_CHAR   *p_name,
                     OS_ERR     *p_err)
```

File	Called from	Code enabled by
OS_MUTEX.C	Task or startup code	OS_CFG_MUTEX_EN

OSMutexCreate() is used to create and initialize a mutex. A mutex is used to gain exclusive access to a resource.

Arguments

p_mutex   is a pointer to a mutex control block that must be allocated in the application. The user will need to declare a "global" variable as follows, and pass a pointer to this variable to OSMutexCreate():

OS_MUTEX MyMutex;

p_name   is a pointer to an ASCII string used to assign a name to the mutual exclusion semaphore. The name may be displayed by debuggers or μC/Probe.

p_err   is a pointer to a variable that is used to hold an error code:

OS_ERR_NONE	if the call is successful and the mutex has been created.
OS_ERR_CREATE_ISR	if attempting to create a mutex from an ISR.
OS_ERR_OBJ_CREATED	if p_mutex already points to a mutex. This indicates that the mutex is already created.
OS_ERR_OBJ_PTR_NULL	if p_mutex is a NULL pointer.
OS_ERR_OBJ_TYPE	if p_mutex points to a different type of object (semaphore, message queue or timer).

Returned Value

None

Notes/Warnings

1. Mutexes must be created before they are used.

Example

```
OS_MUTEX  DispMutex;


void main (void)
{
    OS_ERR  err;


    :
    OSInit(&err);                           /* Initialize µC/OS-III        */
    :
    :
    OSMutexCreate(&DispMutex,               /* Create Display Mutex        */
                  "Display Mutex",
                  &err);
    /* Check "err" */

    :
    :
    OSStart(&err);                          /* Start Multitasking          */
}
```

OSMutexDel()

```
void  OSMutexDel (OS_MUTEX  *p_mutex,
                  OS_OPT     opt,
                  OS_ERR    *p_err)
```

File	Called from	Code enabled by
OS_MUTEX.C	Task	OS_CFG_MUTEX_EN and OS_CFG_MUTEX_DEL_EN

OSMutexDel() is used to delete a mutex. This function should be used with care because multiple tasks may rely on the presence of the mutex. Generally speaking, before deleting a mutex, first delete all the tasks that access the mutex. However, as a general rule, do not delete kernel objects at run-time.

Arguments

p_mutex   is a pointer to the mutex to delete.

opt   specifies whether to delete the mutex only if there are no pending tasks (OS_OPT_DEL_NO_PEND), or whether to always delete the mutex regardless of whether tasks are pending or not (OS_OPT_DEL_ALWAYS). In this case, all pending task are readied.

p_err   is a pointer to a variable that is used to hold an error code:

OS_ERR_NONE	if the call is successful and the mutex has been deleted.
OS_ERR_DEL_ISR	if attempting to delete a mutex from an ISR.
OS_ERR_OBJ_PTR_NULL	if p_mutex is a NULL pointer.
OS_ERR_OBJ_TYPE	if p_mutex is not pointing to a mutex.
OS_ERR_OPT_INVALID	if the user does not specify one of the two options mentioned in the opt argument.
OS_ERR_TASK_WAITING	if one or more task are waiting on the mutex and OS_OPT_DEL_NO_PEND is specified.

Returned Value

The number of tasks that were waiting for the mutex and 0 if an error occurred.

Notes/Warnings

1. Use this call with care as other tasks may expect the presence of the mutex.

Example

```
OS_MUTEX  DispMutex;


void Task (void *p_arg)
{
    OS_ERR  err;


    (void)&p_arg;
    while (DEF_ON) {
        :
        :
        OSMutexDel(&DispMutex,
                   OS_OPT_DEL_ALWAYS,
                   &err);
        /* Check "err" */
        :
        :
    }
}
```

OSMutexPend()

```
void   OSMutexPend (OS_MUTEX    *p_mutex,
                    OS_TICK      timeout,
                    OS_OPT       opt,
                    CPU_TS      *p_ts,
                    OS_ERR      *p_err)
```

File	Called from	Code enabled by
OS_MUTEX.C	Task only	OS_CFG_MUTEX_EN

OSMutexPend() is used when a task requires exclusive access to a resource. If a task calls OSMutexPend() and the mutex is available, OSMutexPend() gives the mutex to the caller and returns to its caller. Note that nothing is actually given to the caller except that if p_err is set to OS_ERR_NONE, the caller can assume that it owns the mutex.

However, if the mutex is already owned by another task, OSMutexPend() places the calling task in the wait list for the mutex. The task waits until the task that owns the mutex releases the mutex and therefore the resource, or until the specified timeout expires. If the mutex is signaled before the timeout expires, µC/OS-III resumes the highest-priority task that is waiting for the mutex.

Note that if the mutex is owned by a lower-priority task, OSMutexPend() raises the priority of the task that owns the mutex to the same priority as the task requesting the mutex. The priority of the owner will be returned to its original priority when the owner releases the mutex (see OSMutexPost()).

OSMutexPend() allows nesting. The same task can call OSMutexPend() multiple times. However, the same task must then call OSMutexPost() an equivalent number of times to release the mutex.

Arguments

p_mutex   is a pointer to the mutex.

timeout   specifies a timeout value (in clock ticks) and is used to allow the task to resume execution if the mutex is not signaled (i.e., posted to) within the specified timeout. A timeout value of 0 indicates that the task wants to wait forever for the mutex. The timeout value is not synchronized with the clock tick. The timeout count is decremented on the next clock tick, which could potentially occur immediately.

opt   determines whether the user wants to block if the mutex is not available or not. This argument must be set to either:

            OS_OPT_PEND_BLOCKING, or

            OS_OPT_PEND_NON_BLOCKING

            Note that the timeout argument should be set to 0 when specifying OS_OPT_PEND_NON_BLOCKING since the timeout value is irrelevant using this option.

p_ts   is a pointer to a timestamp indicating when the mutex was posted, the pend was aborted, or the mutex was deleted. If passing a **NULL** pointer (i.e., (**CPU_TS** *)0), the user will not receive the timestamp. In other words, passing a **NULL** pointer is valid and indicates that the timestamp is not required.

            A timestamp is useful when it is important for a task to know when the mutex was posted, or how long it took for the task to resume after the mutex was posted. In the latter case, the user must call **OS_TS_GET()** and compute the difference between the current value of the timestamp and ***p_ts**. In other words:

            delta = OS_TS_GET() - *p_ts;

p_err   is a pointer to a variable that is used to hold an error code:

OS_ERR_NONE	if the call is successful and the mutex is available.
OS_ERR_MUTEX_NESTING	if the calling task already owns the mutex and it has not posted all nested values.
OS_ERR_MUTEX_OWNER	if the calling task already owns the mutex.
OS_ERR_OBJ_PTR_NULL	if **p_mutex** is a **NULL** pointer.

OS_ERR_OBJ_TYPE	if the user did not pass a pointer to a mutex.
OS_ERR_OPT_INVALID	if a valid option is not specified.
OS_ERR_PEND_ISR	if attempting to acquire the mutex from an ISR.
OS_ERR_SCHED_LOCKED	if calling this function when the scheduler is locked
OS_ERR_TIMEOUT	if the mutex is not available within the specified timeout.

Returned Value

None

Notes/Warnings

1. Mutexes must be created before they are used.

2. Do not suspend the task that owns the mutex. Also, do not have the mutex owner wait on any other µC/OS-III objects (i.e., semaphore, event flag, or queue), and delay the task that owns the mutex. The code should release the resource as quickly as possible.

Example

```
OS_MUTEX  DispMutex;


void  DispTask (void *p_arg)
{
    OS_ERR  err;
    CPU_TS  ts;


    (void)&p_arg;
    while (DEF_ON) {
        :
        OSMutexPend(&DispMutex,
                    0,
                    OS_OPT_PEND_BLOCKING,
                    &ts,
                    &err);
        /* Check "err" */
    }
}
```

OSMutexPendAbort()

```
void OSMutexPendAbort (OS_MUTEX   *p_mutex,
                       OS_OPT      opt,
                       OS_ERR     *p_err)
```

File	Called from	Code enabled by
OS_MUTEX.C	Task	OS_CFG_MUTEX_EN and OS_CFG_MUTEX_PEND_ABORT_EN

OSMutexPendAbort() aborts and readies any tasks currently waiting on a mutex. This function should be used to fault-abort the wait on the mutex rather than to normally signal the mutex via OSMutexPost().

Arguments

p_mutex   is a pointer to the mutex.

opt   specifies whether to abort only the highest-priority task waiting on the mutex or all tasks waiting on the mutex:

OS_OPT_PEND_ABORT_1	to abort only the highest-priority task waiting on the mutex.
OS_OPT_PEND_ABORT_ALL	to abort all tasks waiting on the mutex.
OS_OPT_POST_NO_SCHED	specifies that the scheduler should not be called even if the pend of a higher-priority task has been aborted. Scheduling will need to occur from another function. The user would select this option if the task calling OSMutexPendAbort() will be doing additional pend aborts, rescheduling should not take place until all tasks are completed, and multiple pend aborts should take place simultaneously.

p_err   is a pointer to a variable that is used to hold an error code:

OS_ERR_NONE	if at least one task was aborted. Check the return value for the number of tasks aborted.
OS_ERR_OBJ_PTR_NULL	if **p_mutex** is a **NULL** pointer.
OS_ERR_OBJ_TYPE	if the user does not pass a pointer to a mutex.
OS_ERR_OPT_INVALID	if the user specified an invalid option.
OS_ERR_PEND_ABORT_ISR	if attempting to call this function from an ISR
OS_ERR_PEND_ABORT_NONE	if no tasks were aborted.

Returned Value

OSMutexPendAbort() returns the number of tasks made ready to run by this function. Zero indicates that no tasks were pending on the mutex and therefore this function had no effect.

Notes/Warnings

1. Mutexes must be created before they are used.

Example

```
OS_MUTEX  DispMutex;


void  DispTask (void *p_arg)
{
    OS_ERR      err;
    OS_OBJ_QTY  qty;


    (void)&p_arg;
    while (DEF_ON) {
        :
        :
        qty = OSMutexPendAbort(&DispMutex,
                               OS_OPT_PEND_ABORT_ALL,
                               &err);
        /* Check "err" */
    }
}
```

OSMutexPost()

```
void OSMutexPost (OS_MUTEX  *p_mutex,
                  OS_OPT     opt,
                  OS_ERR    *p_err);
```

File	Called from	Code enabled by
OS_MUTEX.C	Task	OS_CFG_MUTEX_EN

A mutex is signaled (i.e., released) by calling **OSMutexPost()**. Call this function only if acquiring the mutex by first calling **OSMutexPend()**. If the priority of the task that owns the mutex has been raised when a higher priority task attempted to acquire the mutex, at that point, the original task priority of the task is restored. If one or more tasks are waiting for the mutex, the mutex is given to the highest-priority task waiting on the mutex. The scheduler is then called to determine if the awakened task is now the highest-priority task ready to run, and if so, a context switch is done to run the readied task. If no task is waiting for the mutex, the mutex value is simply set to available (**DEF_TRUE**).

Arguments

p_mutex   is a pointer to the mutex.

opt   determines the type of POST performed.

OS_OPT_POST_NONE	No special option selected.
OS_OPT_POST_NO_SCHED	Do not call the scheduler after the post, therefore the caller is resumed even if the mutex was posted and tasks of higher priority are waiting for the mutex.
	Use this option if the task calling **OSMutexPost()** will be doing additional posts, if the user does not want to reschedule until all is complete, and multiple posts should take effect simultaneously.

p_err   is a pointer to a variable that is used to hold an error code:

OS_ERR_NONE	if the call is successful and the mutex is available.
OS_ERR_MUTEX_NESTING	if the owner of the mutex has the mutex nested and it has not fully un-nested the mutex yet.
OS_ERR_MUTEX_NOT_OWNER	if the caller is not the owner of the mutex and therefore is not allowed to release it.
OS_ERR_OBJ_PTR_NULL	if **p_mutex** is a **NULL** pointer.
OS_ERR_OBJ_TYPE	if not passing a pointer to a mutex.
OS_ERR_POST_ISR	if attempting to post the mutex from an ISR.

Returned Value

None

Notes/Warnings

1. Mutexes must be created before they are used.

2. Do not call this function from an ISR.

Example

```
OS_MUTEX  DispMutex;


void  TaskX (void *p_arg)
{
    OS_ERR  err;



    (void)&p_arg;
    while (DEF_ON) {
        :
        OSMutexPost(&DispMutex,
                    OS_OPT_POST_NONE,
                    &err);
        /* Check "err" */
        :
    }
}
```

OSPendMulti()

```
OS_OBJ_QTY   OSPendMulti(OS_PEND_DATA  *p_pend_data_tbl,
                         OS_OBJ_QTY     tbl_size,
                         OS_TICK        timeout,
                         OS_OPT         opt,
                         OS_ERR         *p_err);
```

File	Called from	Code enabled by
OS_PEND_MULTI.C	Task	OS_CFG_PEND_MULTI_EN && (OS_CFG_Q_EN || OS_CFG_SEM_EN)

OSPendMulti() is used when a task expects to wait on multiple kernel objects, specifically semaphores or message queues. If more than one such object is ready when OSPendMulti() is called, then all available objects and messages, if any, are returned as ready to the caller. If no objects are ready, OSPendMulti() suspends the current task until either:

■ an object becomes ready,

■ a timeout occurs,

■ one or more of the tasks are deleted or pend aborted or,

■ one or more of the objects are deleted.

If an object becomes ready, and multiple tasks are waiting for the object, μC/OS-III resumes the highest-priority task waiting on that object.

A pended task suspended with OSTaskSuspend() can still receive a message from a multi-pended message queue, or obtain a signal from a multi-pended semaphore. However, the task remains suspended until it is resumed by calling OSTaskResume().

Arguments

p_pend_data_tbl   is a pointer to an OS_PEND_DATA table. This table will be used by the caller to understand the outcome of this call. Also, the caller *must* initialize the .PendObjPtr field of the OS_PEND_DATA field for each object that the caller wants to pend on (see example below).

`tbl_size`   is the number of entries in the **OS_PEND_DATA** table pointed to by **p_pend_data_tbl**. This value indicates how many objects the task will be pending on.

`timeout`   specifies the amount of time (in clock ticks) that the calling task is willing to wait for objects to be posted. A timeout value of 0 indicates that the task wants to wait forever for any of the multi-pended objects. The timeout value is not synchronized with the clock tick. The timeout count begins decrementing on the next clock tick, which could potentially occur immediately.

`p_err`   is a pointer to a variable that holds an error code:

OS_ERR_NONE	if any of the multi-pended objects are ready.
OS_ERR_OBJ_TYPE	if any of the **.PendObjPtr** in the **p_pend_data_tbl** is a **NULL** pointer, not a semaphore, or not a message queue.
OS_ERR_OPT_INVALID	if specifying an invalid option.
OS_ERR_PEND_ABORT	indicates that a multi-pended object was aborted; check the **.RdyObjPtr** of the **p_pend_data_tbl** to know which object was aborted. The first non-**NULL** **.RdyObjPtr** is the object that was aborted.
OS_ERR_PEND_DEL	indicates that a multi-pended object was deleted; check the **.RdyObjPtr** of the **p_pend_data_tbl** to know which object was deleted. The first non-**NULL** **.RdyObjPtr** is the object that was deleted.
OS_ERR_PEND_ISR	if calling this function from an ISR.
OS_ERR_PEND_LOCKED	if calling this function when the scheduler is locked.
OS_ERR_PEND_WOULD_BLOCK	if the caller does not want to block and no object is ready.
OS_ERR_PTR_INVALID	if **p_pend_data_tbl** is a **NULL** pointer.
OS_ERR_TIMEOUT	if no multi-pended object is ready within the specified timeout.

Returned Value

OSPendMulti() returns the number of multi-pended objects that are ready. If an object is pend aborted or deleted, the return value will be 1. Examine the value of *p_err to know the exact outcome of this call. If no multi-pended object is ready within the specified timeout period, or because of any error, the .RdyObjPtr in the p_pend_data_tbl array will all be NULL.

When objects are posted, the OS_PEND_DATA fields of p_pend_data_tbl contains additional information about the posted objects:

.RdyObjPtr	Contains a pointer to the object ready or posted to, or NULL pointer if the object was not ready or posted to.
.RdyMsgPtr	If the object pended on was a message queue and the queue was posted to, this field contains the message.
.RdyMsgSize	If the object pended on was a message queue and the queue was posted to, this field contains the size of the message (in number of bytes).
.RdyTS	If the object pended on was posted to, this field contains the timestamp as to when the object was posted. Note that if the object is deleted or pend-aborted, this field contains the timestamp of when the condition occurred.

Notes/Warnings

1. Message queue or semaphore objects must be created before they are used.

2. Do call OSPendMulti() from an ISR.

3. The user cannot multi-pend on event flags and mutexes.

Example

```
OS_SEM  Sem1;
OS_SEM  Sem2;
OS_Q    Q1;
OS_Q    Q2;


void Task(void *p_arg)
{
    OS_PEND_DATA  pend_data_tbl[4];
    OS_ERR        err;
    OS_OBJ_QTY    nbr_rdy;


    (void)&p_arg;
    while (DEF_ON) {
        :
        pend_data_tbl[0].PendObjPtr = (OS_PEND_OBJ *)Sem1;
        pend_data_tbl[1].PendObjPtr = (OS_PEND_OBJ *)Sem2;
        pend_data_tbl[2].PendObjPtr = (OS_PEND_OBJ *)Q1;
        pend_data_tbl[3].PendObjPtr = (OS_PEND_OBJ *)Q2;
        nbr_rdy = OSPendMulti(&pend_data_tbl[0],
                              4,
                              0,
                              OS_OPT_PEND_BLOCKING,
                              &err);
        /* Check "err" */
        :
        :
    }
}
```

OSQCreate()

```
void  OSQCreate (OS_Q        *p_q,
                 CPU_CHAR    *p_name,
                 OS_MSG_QTY   max_qty,
                 OS_ERR      *p_err)
```

File	Called from	Code enabled by
OS_Q.C	Task or startup code	OS_CFG_Q_EN and OS_CFG_MSG_EN

OSQCreate() creates a message queue. A message queue allows tasks or ISRs to send pointer-sized variables (messages) to one or more tasks. The meaning of the messages sent are application specific.

Arguments

p_q   is a pointer to the message queue control block. It is assumed that storage for the message queue will be allocated in the application. The user will need to declare a "global" variable as follows, and pass a pointer to this variable to OSQCreate():

OS_Q MyMsgQ;

p_name   is a pointer to an ASCII string used to name the message queue. The name can be displayed by debuggers or µC/Probe.

msg_size   indicates the maximum size of the message queue (must be non-zero). If the user intends to not limit the size of the queue, simply pass a very large number. Of course, if there are not enough OS_MSGs in the pool of OS_MSGs, the post call (i.e., OSQPost()) will simply fail and an error code will indicate that there are no more OS_MSGs to use.

p_err   is a pointer to a variable that is used to hold an error code:

OS_ERR_NONE	if the call is successful and the mutex has been created.
OS_ERR_CREATE_ISR	if attempting to create the message queue from an ISR.
OS_ERR_NAME	if **p_name** is a **NULL** pointer.
OS_ERR_OBJ_CREATED	if **p_q** is already pointing to a message queue. In other words, the user is trying to create a message queue that has already been created.
OS_ERR_OBJ_PTR_NULL	if **p_q** is a **NULL** pointer.
OS_ERR_Q_SIZE	if the size specified is 0.

Returned Value

None

Notes/Warnings

1. Queues must be created before they are used.

Example

```
OS_Q    CommQ;


void main (void)
{
    OS_ERR    err;


    OSInit(&err);                    /* Initialize µC/OS-III  */
    :
    :
    OSQCreate(&CommQ,
             "Comm Queue",
             10,
             &err);                  /* Create COMM Q         */
    /* Check "err" */
    :
    :
    OSStart();                       /* Start Multitasking    */
}
```

OSQDel()

```
OS_OBJ_QTY  OSQDel (OS_Q    *p_q,
                    OS_OPT   opt,
                    OS_ERR   *p_err)
```

File	Called from	Code enabled by
OS_Q.C	Task	OS_CFG_Q_EN and OS_CFG_Q_DEL_EN

OSQDel() is used to delete a message queue. This function should be used with care since multiple tasks may rely on the presence of the message queue. Generally speaking, before deleting a message queue, first delete all the tasks that can access the message queue. However, it is highly recommended that you do not delete kernel objects at run time.

Arguments

p_q   is a pointer to the message queue to delete.

opt   specifies whether to delete the queue only if there are no pending tasks (**OS_OPT_DEL_NO_PEND**), or always delete the queue regardless of whether tasks are pending or not (**OS_OPT_DEL_ALWAYS**). In this case, all pending task are readied.

p_err   is a pointer to a variable that is used to hold an error code. The error code can be one of the following:

OS_ERR_NONE	if the call is successful and the message queue has been deleted.
OS_ERR_DEL_ISR	if the user attempts to delete the message queue from an ISR.
OS_ERR_OBJ_PTR_NULL	if passing a **NULL** pointer for **p_q**.
OS_ERR_OBJ_TYPE	if **p_q** is not pointing to a queue.
OS_ERR_OPT_INVALID	if not specifying one of the two options mentioned in the opt argument.
OS_ERR_TASK_WAITING	if one or more tasks are waiting for messages at the message queue and it is specified to only delete if no task is pending.

Returned Value

The number of tasks that were waiting on the message queue and 0 if an error is detected.

Notes/Warnings

1. Message queues must be created before they can be used.

2. This function must be used with care. Tasks that would normally expect the presence of the queue *must* check the return code of OSQPend().

Example

```
OS_Q  DispQ;


void Task (void *p_arg)
{
    OS_ERR  err;


    (void)&p_arg;
    while (DEF_ON) {
        :
        :
        OSQDel(&DispQ,
               OS_OPT_DEL_ALWAYS,
               &err);
        /* Check "err" */
        :
        :
    }
}
```

OSQFlush()

```
OS_MSG_QTY  OSQFlush (OS_Q    *p_q,
                      OS_ERR  *p_err)
```

File	Called from	Code enabled by
OS_Q.C	Task	OS_CFG_Q_EN and OS_CFG_Q_FLUSH_EN

OSQFlush() empties the contents of the message queue and eliminates all messages sent to the queue. This function takes the same amount of time to execute regardless of whether tasks are waiting on the queue (and thus no messages are present), or the queue contains one or more messages. OS_MSGs from the queue are simply returned to the free pool of OS_MSGs.

Arguments

p_q   is a pointer to the message queue.

p_err   is a pointer to a variable that will contain an error code returned by this function.

OS_ERR_NONE	if the message queue is flushed.
OS_ERR_FLUSH_ISR	if calling this function from an ISR
OS_ERR_OBJ_PTR_NULL	if p_q is a NULL pointer.
OS_ERR_OBJ_TYPE	if you attempt to flush an object other than a message queue.

Returned Value

The number of OS_MSG entries freed from the message queue. Note that the OS_MSG entries are returned to the free pool of OS_MSGs.

Notes/Warnings

1. Queues must be created before they are used.

2. Use this function with great care. When flushing a queue, you lose the references to what the queue entries are pointing to, potentially causing 'memory leaks'. The data that the user is pointing to that is referenced by the queue entries should, most likely, be de-allocated (i.e., freed). To flush a queue that contains entries, instead use OSQPend() with the OS_OPT_PEND_NON_BLOCKING option.

Example

```
OS_Q   CommQ;


void Task (void *p_arg)
{
    OS_ERR   err;


    (void)&p_arg;
    while (DEF_ON) {
        :
        :
        entries = OSQFlush(&CommQ,
                           &err);
        /* Check "err" */
        :
        :
    }
}
```

OSQPend()

```
void  *OSQPend (OS_Q         *p_q,
                OS_TICK       timeout,
                OS_OPT        opt,
                OS_MSG_SIZE  *p_msg_size,
                CPU_TS       *p_ts,
                OS_ERR       *p_err)
```

File	Called from	Code enabled by
OS_Q.C	Task	OS_CFG_Q_EN and OS_CFG_MSG_EN

OSQPend() is used when a task wants to receive messages from a message queue. The messages are sent to the task via the message queue either by an ISR, or by another task using the OSQPost() call. The messages received are pointer-sized variables, and their use is application specific. If at least one message is already present in the message queue when OSQPend() is called, the message is retrieved and returned to the caller.

If no message is present in the message queue and OS_OPT_PEND_BLOCKING is specified for the opt argument, OSQPend() suspends the current task (assuming the scheduler is not locked) until either a message is received, or a user-specified timeout expires. If a message is sent to the message queue and multiple tasks are waiting for such a message, μC/OS-III resumes the highest priority task that is waiting.

A pended task suspended with OSTaskSuspend() can receive a message. However, the task remains suspended until it is resumed by calling OSTaskResume().

If no message is present in the queue and OS_OPT_PEND_NON_BLOCKING is specifed for the opt argument, OSQPend() returns to the caller with an appropriate error code, and returns a NULL pointer.

Arguments

p_q is a pointer to the queue from which the messages are received.

timeout allows the task to resume execution if a message is not received from the message queue within the specified number of clock ticks. A timeout value of 0 indicates that the task is willing to wait forever for a message. The timeout value is not synchronized with the clock tick. The timeout count starts decrementing on the next clock tick, which could potentially occur immediately.

opt determines whether or not to block if a message is not available in the queue. This argument must be set to either:

OS_OPT_PEND_BLOCKING, or

OS_OPT_PEND_NON_BLOCKING

Note that the timeout argument should be set to 0 when specifying OS_OPT_PEND_NON_BLOCKING, since the timeout value is irrelevant using this option.

p_msg_size is a pointer to a variable that will receive the size of the message (in number of bytes).

p_ts is a pointer to a variable that will receive the timestamp of when the message was received. If passing a **NULL** pointer (i.e., (**CPU_TS** *)0), the timestamp will not be returned. Passing a **NULL** pointer is valid, and indicates that the user does not need the timestamp.

A timestamp is useful when the user wants the task to know when the message queue was posted, or how long it took for the task to resume after the message queue was posted. In the latter case, call **OS_TS_GET()** and compute the difference between the current value of the timestamp and *p_ts. In other words:

delta = OS_TS_GET() - *p_ts;

p_err   is a pointer to a variable used to hold an error code.

OS_ERR_NONE	if a message is received.
OS_ERR_OBJ_PTR_NULL	if p_q is a NULL pointer.
OS_ERR_OBJ_TYPE	if p_q is not pointing to a message queue.
OS_ERR_PEND_ABORT	if the pend was aborted because another task called OSQPendAbort().
OS_ERR_PEND_ISR	if the function is called from an ISR.
OS_ERR_PEND_WOULD_BLOCK	if this function is called with the opt argument set to OS_OPT_PEND_NON_BLOCKING, and no message is in the queue.
OS_ERR_SCHED_LOCKED	if calling this function when the scheduler is locked.
OS_ERR_TIMEOUT	if a message is not received within the specified timeout.

Returned Value

The message (i.e., a pointer) or a NULL pointer if no messages has been received. Note that it is possible for the actual message to be NULL pointers, so check the returned error code instead of relying on the returned value.

Notes/Warnings

1. Queues must be created before they are used.

2. The user cannot call OSQPend() from an ISR.

Example

```
OS_Q   CommQ;


void CommTask (void *p_arg)
{
    OS_ERR      err;
    void        *p_msg;
    OS_MSG_SIZE msg_size;
    CPU_TS      ts;


    (void)&p_arg;
    while (DEF_ON) {
        :
        :
        p_msg = OSQPend(CommQ,
                        100,
                        OS_OPT_PEND_BLOCKING,
                        &msg_size,
                        &ts,
                        &err);
        /* Check "err" */
        :
        :
    }
}
```

OSQPendAbort()

```
OS_OBJ_QTY  OSQPendAbort (OS_Q    *p_q,
                          OS_OPT   opt,
                          OS_ERR  *p_err)
```

File	Called from	Code enabled by
OS_Q.C	Task only	OS_CFG_Q_EN and
		OS_CFG_Q_PEND_ABORT_EN

OSQPendAbort() aborts and readies any tasks currently waiting on a message queue. This function should be used to fault-abort the wait on the message queue, rather than to signal the message queue via OSQPost().

Arguments

p_q   is a pointer to the queue for which pend(s) need to be aborted.

opt   determines the type of abort to be performed.

OS_OPT_PEND_ABORT_1	Aborts the pend of only the highest-priority task waiting on the message queue.
OS_OPT_PEND_ABORT_ALL	Aborts the pend of all tasks waiting on the message queue.
OS_OPT_POST_NO_SCHED	specifies that the scheduler should not be called, even if the pend of a higher-priority task has been aborted. Scheduling will need to occur from another function.
	Use this option if the task calling OSQPendAbort() is doing additional pend aborts, rescheduling is not performed until completion, and multiple pend aborts are to take effect simultaneously.

p_err   is a pointer to a variable that holds an error code:

OS_ERR_NONE	at least one task waiting on the message queue was readied and informed of the aborted wait. Check the return value for the number of tasks whose wait on the message queue was aborted.
OS_ERR_PEND_ABORT_ISR	if called from an ISR
OS_ERR_PEND_ABORT_NONE	if no task was pending on the message queue
OS_ERR_OBJ_PTR_NULL	if p_q is a NULL pointer.
OS_ERR_OBJ_TYPE	if p_q is not pointing to a message queue.
OS_ERR_OPT_INVALID	if an invalid option is specified.

Returned Value

OSQPendAbort() returns the number of tasks made ready to run by this function. Zero indicates that no tasks were pending on the message queue, therefore this function had no effect.

Notes/Warnings

1. Queues must be created before they are used.

Example

```
OS_Q   CommQ;


void CommTask(void *p_arg)
{
    OS_ERR      err;
    OS_OBJ_QTY  nbr_tasks;


    (void)&p_arg;
    while (DEF_ON) {
        :
        :
        nbr_tasks = OSQPendAbort(&CommQ,
                                 OS_OPT_PEND_ABORT_ALL,
                                 &err);
        /* Check "err" */
        :
        :
    }
}
```

OSQPost()

```
void   OSQPost (OS_Q         *p_q,
               void          *p_void,
               OS_MSG_SIZE   msg_size,
               OS_OPT        opt,
               OS_ERR        *p_err)
```

File	Called from	Code enabled by
OS_Q.C	Task or ISR	OS_CFG_Q_EN

OSQPost() sends a message to a task through a message queue. A message is a pointer-sized variable, and its use is application specific. If the message queue is full, an error code is returned to the caller. In this case, OSQPost() immediately returns to its caller, and the message is not placed in the message queue.

If any task is waiting for a message to be posted to the message queue, the highest-priority task receives the message. If the task waiting for the message has a higher priority than the task sending the message, the higher-priority task resumes, and the task sending the message is suspended; that is, a context switch occurs. Message queues can be first-in first-out (OS_OPT_POST_FIFO), or last-in-first-out (OS_OPT_POST_LIFO) depending of the value specified in the opt argument.

If any task is waiting for a message at the message queue, OSQPost() allows the user to either post the message to the highest-priority task waiting at the queue (opt set to OS_OPT_POST_FIFO or OS_OPT_POST_LIFO), or to all tasks waiting at the message queue (opt is set to OS_OPT_POST_ALL). In either case, scheduling occurs unless opt is also set to OS_OPT_POST_NO_SCHED.

Arguments

p_q   is a pointer to the message queue being posted to.

p_void   is the actual message posted. p_void is a pointer-sized variable. Its meaning is application specific.

msg_size   specifies the size of the message (in number of bytes).

| opt | determines the type of POST performed. The last two options may be added to either `OS_OPT_POST_FIFO` or `OS_OPT_POST_LIFO` to create different combinations: |

`OS_OPT_POST_FIFO`	POST message to the end of the queue (FIFO), or send message to a single waiting task.
`OS_OPT_POST_LIFO`	POST message to the front of the queue (LIFO), or send message to a single waiting task
`OS_OPT_POST_ALL`	POST message to ALL tasks that are waiting on the queue. This option can be added to either `OS_OPT_POST_FIFO` or `OS_OPT_POST_LIFO`.
`OS_OPT_POST_NO_SCHED`	Do not call the scheduler after the post and therefore the caller is resumed, even if the message was posted to a message queue with tasks having a higher priority than the caller. Use this option if the task (or ISR) calling `OSQPost()` will do additional posts, the user does not want to reschedule until finished, and, multiple posts are to take effect simultaneously.

| p_err | is a pointer to a variable that will contain an error code returned by this function. |

`OS_ERR_NONE`	if no tasks were waiting on the queue. In this case, the return value is also 0.
`OS_ERR_MSG_POOL_EMPTY`	if there are no more `OS_MSG` structures to use to store the message.
`OS_ERR_OBJ_PTR_NULL`	if `p_q` is a `NULL` pointer.
`OS_ERR_OBJ_TYPE`	if `p_q` is not pointing to a message queue.
`OS_ERR_Q_MAX`	if the queue is full and therefore cannot accept more messages.

Returned Value

None

Notes/Warnings

1. Queues must be created before they are used.

2. Possible combinations of options are:

```
OS_OPT_POST_FIFO
OS_OPT_POST_LIFO
OS_OPT_POST_FIFO + OS_OPT_POST_ALL
OS_OPT_POST_LIFO + OS_OPT_POST_ALL
OS_OPT_POST_FIFO + OS_OPT_POST_NO_SCHED
OS_OPT_POST_LIFO + OS_OPT_POST_NO_SCHED
OS_OPT_POST_FIFO + OS_OPT_POST_ALL + OS_OPT_POST_NO_SCHED
OS_OPT_POST_LIFO + OS_OPT_POST_ALL + OS_OPT_POST_NO_SCHED
```

3. Although the example below shows calling OSQPost() from a task, it can also be called from an ISR.

Example

```c
OS_Q          CommQ;
CPU_INT08U    CommRxBuf[100];


void CommTaskRx (void *p_arg)
{
    OS_ERR   err;


    (void)&p_arg;
    while (DEF_ON) {
        :
        :
        OSQPost(&CommQ,
                &CommRxBuf[0],
                sizeof(CommRxBuf),
                OS_OPT_POST_OPT_FIFO + OS_OPT_POST_ALL + OS_OPT_POST_NO_SCHED,
                &err);
        /* Check "err" */
        :
        :
    }
}
```

OSSafetyCriticalStart()

void OSSafetyCriticalStart (void)

File	Called from	Code enabled by
OS_CORE.C	Task	OS_SAFETY_CRITICAL_IEC61508

OSSafetyCriticalStart() allows your code to notify µC/OS-III that you are done initializing and creating all kernel objects. After calling OSSafetyCriticalStart(), your application code will no longer be allowed to create kernel objects.

Arguments

None

Returned Value

None

Notes/Warnings

None

Example

```
void AppStartTask (void *p_arg)
{
    (void)&p_arg;
    /* Create tasks and other kernel objects           */
    OSSafetyCriticalStart();
    /* Your code is no longer allowed to create kernel objects */
    while (DEF_ON) {
        :
        :
    }
}
```

OSSched()

`void OSSched (void)`

File	Called from	Code enabled by
OS_CORE.C	Task	N/A

OSSched() allows a task to call the scheduler. Use this function if creating a series of "posts" and specifing OS_OPT_POST_NO_SCHED as a post option.

OSSched() can only be called by task-level code. Also, if the scheduler is locked (i.e., OSSchedLock() was previously called), then OSSched() will have no effect.

If a higher-priority task than the calling task is ready to run, OSSched() will context switch to that task.

Arguments

None

Returned Value

None

Notes/Warnings

None

Example

```
void TaskX (void *p_arg)
{
    (void)&p_arg;
    while (DEF_ON) {
        :
        OS??Post(…);          /* Posts with OS_OPT_POST_NO_SCHED option     */
        /* Check "err" */
        OS??Post(…);
        /* Check "err" */
        OS??Post(…);
        /* Check "err" */
        :
        OSSched();            /* Run the scheduler                          */
        :
    }
}
```

OSSchedLock()

`void OSSchedLock (OS_ERR *p_err)`

File	Called from	Code enabled by
OS_CORE.C	Task or ISR	N/A

OSSchedLock() prevents task rescheduling until its counterpart, OSSchedUnlock(), is called. The task that calls OSSchedLock() retains control of the CPU, even though other higher-priority tasks are ready to run. However, interrupts are still recognized and serviced (assuming interrupts are enabled). OSSchedLock() and OSSchedUnlock() must be used in pairs.

μC/OS-III allows OSSchedLock() to be nested up to 250 levels deep. Scheduling is enabled when an equal number of OSSchedUnlock() calls have been made.

Arguments

p_err   is a pointer to a variable that will contain an error code returned by this function.

OS_ERR_NONE   the scheduler is locked.

OS_ERR_LOCK_NESTING_OVF   if the user called this function too many times.

OS_ERR_OS_NOT_RUNNING   if the function is called before calling OSStart().

Returned Value

None

Notes/Warnings

1. After calling OSSchedLock(), the application must not make system calls that suspend execution of the current task; that is, the application cannot call OSTimeDly(), OSTimeDlyHMSM(), OSFlagPend(), OSSemPend(), OSMutexPend(), or OSQPend(). Since the scheduler is locked out, no other task is allowed to run, and the system will lock up.

Example

```
void TaskX (void *p_arg)
{
    OS_ERR  err;


    (void)&p_arg;
    while (DEF_ON) {
        :
        OSSchedLock(&err);      /* Prevent other tasks to run          */
        /* Check "err" */
        :                       /* Code protected from context switch */
        OSSchedUnlock(&err);    /* Enable other tasks to run           */
        /* Check "err" */
        :
    }
}
```

OSSchedRoundRobinCfg()

```
void  OSSchedRoundRobinCfg (CPU_BOOLEAN  en,
                            OS_TICK       dflt_time_quanta,
                            OS_ERR        *p_err)
```

File	Called from	Code enabled by
OS_CORE.C	Task or startup code	OS_CFG_SCHED_ROUND_ROBIN_EN

OSSchedRoundRobinCfg() is used to enable or disable round-robin scheduling.

Arguments

en

when set to **DEF_ENABLED** enables round-robin scheduling, and when set to **DEF_DISABLED** disables it.

dflt_time_quanta

is the default time quanta given to a task. This value is used when a task was created and specified a value of 0 for the time quanta. In other words, if the user did not specify a non-zero for the task's time quanta, this is the value that will be used. If passing 0 for this argument, μC/OS-III will assume a time quanta of 1/10 the tick rate. For example, if the tick rate is 1000 Hz and 0 for dflt_time_quanta is specified, μC/OS-III will set the time quanta to 10 milliseconds.

p_err

is a pointer to a variable that is used to hold an error code:

OS_ERR_NONE   if the call is successful.

Returned Value

None

Notes/Warnings

None

Example

```
void main (void)
{
    OS_ERR  err;


    :
    OSInit(&err);                   /* Initialize µC/OS-III        */
    :
    :
    OSSchedRoundRobinCfg(DEF_ENABLED,
                         10,
                         &err);
    /* Check "err" */
    :
    :
    OSStart(&err);                  /* Start Multitasking          */
}
```

OSSchedRoundRobinYield()

void OSSchedRoundRobinYield (OS_ERR *p_err);

File	Called from	Code enabled by
OS_CORE.C	Task	OS_CFG_SCHED_ROUND_ROBIN_EN

OSSchedRoundRobinYield() is used to voluntarily give up a task's time slot, assuming that there are other tasks running at the same priority.

Arguments

p_err   is a pointer to a variable used to hold an error code:

OS_ERR_NONE	if the call was successful.
OS_ERR_ROUND_ROBIN_1	if there is only one task at the current priority level that is ready to run.
OS_ERR_ROUND_ROBIN_DISABLED	if round-robin scheduling has not been enabled. See OSSchedRoundRobinCfg() to enable or disable.
OS_ERR_SCHED_LOCKED	if the scheduler is locked and µC/OS-III cannot switch tasks.
OS_ERR_YIELD_ISR	if calling this function from an ISR.

Returned Value

None

Notes/Warnings

None

Example

```
void Task (void *p_arg)
{
    OS_ERR  err;


    (void)&p_arg;
    while (DEF_ON) {
        :
        :
        OSSchedRoundRobinYield(&err); /* Give up the CPU to the next task at same priority */
        /* Check "err" */
        :
        :
    }
}
```

OSSchedUnlock()

```
void OSSchedUnlock(OS_ERR  *p_err);
```

File	Called from	Code enabled by
OS_CORE.C	Task or ISR	N/A

OSSchedUnlock() re-enables task scheduling whenever it is paired with OSSchedLock().

Arguments

p_err   is a pointer to a variable that will contain an error code returned by this function.

OS_ERR_NONE	the call is successful and the scheduler is no longer locked.
OS_ERR_OS_NOT_RUNNING	if calling this function before calling OSStart().
OS_ERR_SCHED_LOCKED	if the scheduler is still locked. This would indicate that scheduler lock has not fully unnested
OS_ERR_SCHED_NOT_LOCKED	if the user did not call OSSchedLock().

Returned Value

None

Notes/Warnings

None

Example

```
void TaskX (void *p_arg)
{
    OS_ERR  err;


    (void)&p_arg;
    while (DEF_ON) {
        :
        OSSchedLock(&err);      /* Prevent other tasks to run          */
        /* Check "err" */
        :                       /* Code protected from context switch */
        OSSchedUnlock(&err);    /* Enable other tasks to run           */
        /* Check "err" */
        :
    }
}
```

OSSemCreate()

```
void   OSSemCreate (OS_SEM      *p_sem,
                    CPU_CHAR    *p_name,
                    OS_SEM_CTR  cnt,
                    OS_ERR      *p_err)
```

File	Called from	Code enabled by
OS_SEM.C	Task or startup code	OS_CFG_SEM_EN

OSSemCreate() initializes a semaphore. Semaphores are used when a task wants exclusive access to a resource, needs to synchronize its activities with an ISR or a task, or is waiting until an event occurs. Use a semaphore to signal the occurrence of an event to one or multiple tasks, and use mutexes to guard share resources. However, technically, semaphores allow for both.

Arguments

p_sem   is a pointer to the semaphore control block. It is assumed that storage for the semaphore will be allocated in the application. In other words, declare a "global" variable as follows, and pass a pointer to this variable to OSSemCreate():

OS_SEM MySem;

p_name   is a pointer to an ASCII string used to assign a name to the semaphore. The name can be displayed by debuggers or µC/Probe.

cnt   specifies the initial value of the semaphore.

If the semaphore is used for resource sharing, set the initial value of the semaphore to the number of identical resources guarded by the semaphore. If there is only one resource, the value should be set to 1 (this is called a binary semaphore). For multiple resources, set the value to the number of resources (this is called a counting semaphore).

If using a semaphore as a signaling mechanism, set the initial value to 0.

p_err   is a pointer to a variable used to hold an error code:

OS_ERR_NONE	if the call is successful and the semaphore has been created.
OS_ERR_CREATE_ISR	if calling this function from an ISR.
OS_ERR_NAME	if **p_name** is a **NULL** pointer.
OS_ERR_OBJ_CREATED	if the semaphore is already created.
OS_ERR_OBJ_PTR_NULL	if **p_q** is a **NULL** pointer.
OS_ERR_OBJ_TYPE	if **p_sem** has been initialized to a different object type.

Returned Value

None

Notes/Warnings

Semaphores must be created before they are used.

Example

```
OS_SEM  SwSem;


void main (void)
{
    OS_ERR  err;


    :
    OSInit(&err);                   /* Initialize µC/OS-III            */
    :
    :
    OSSemCreate(&SwSem,             /* Create Switch Semaphore         */
                "Switch Semaphore",
                0,
                &err);
    /* Check "err" */
    :
    :
    OSStart(&err);                  /* Start Multitasking              */
}
```

OSSemDel()

```
void  OSSemDel (OS_SEM  *p_sem,
               OS_OPT   opt,
               OS_ERR   *p_err)
```

File	Called from	Code enabled by
OS_SEM.C	Task	OS_CFG_SEM_EN and OS_CFG_SEM_DEL_EN

OSSemDel() is used to delete a semaphore. This function should be used with care as multiple tasks may rely on the presence of the semaphore. Generally speaking, before deleting a semaphore, first delete all the tasks that access the semaphore. As a rule, it is highly recommended to not delete kernel objects at run time.

Deleting the semaphore will not de-allocate the object. In other words, storage for the variable will still remain at the same location unless the semaphore is allocated dynamically from the heap. The dynamic allocation of objects has its own set of problems. Specifically, it is not recommended for embedded systems to allocate (and de-allocate) objects from the heap given the high likelihood of fragmentation.

Arguments

p_sem   is a pointer to the semaphore.

opt   specifies one of two options: OS_OPT_DEL_NO_PEND or OS_OPT_DEL_ALWAYS.

OS_OPT_DEL_NO_PEND specifies to delete the semaphore only if no task is waiting on the semaphore. Because no task is "currently" waiting on the semaphore does not mean that a task will not attempt to wait for the semaphore later. How would such a task handle the situation waiting for a semaphore that was deleted? The application code will have to deal with this eventuality.

OS_OPT_DEL_ALWAYS specifies deleting the semaphore, regardless of whether tasks are waiting on the semaphore or not. If there are tasks waiting on the semaphore, these tasks will be made ready to run and informed (through an appropriate error code) that the reason the task is readied is that the semaphore it was waiting on was deleted. The same reasoning applies with the other option, how will the tasks handle the fact that the semaphore they want to wait for is no longer available?

p_err   is a pointer to a variable used to hold an error code. The error code may be one of the following:

OS_ERR_NONE	if the call is successful and the semaphore has been deleted.
OS_ERR_DEL_ISR	if attempting to delete the semaphore from an ISR.
OS_ERR_OBJ_PTR_NULL	if **p_sem** is a **NULL** pointer.
OS_ERR_OBJ_TYPE	if **p_sem** is not pointing to a semaphore.
OS_ERR_OPT_INVALID	if one of the two options mentioned in the opt argument is not specified.
OS_ERR_TASK_WAITING	if one or more tasks are waiting on the semaphore.

Returned Value

None

Notes/Warnings

Use this call with care because other tasks might expect the presence of the semaphore.

Example

```
OS_SEM  SwSem;


void Task (void *p_arg)
{
    OS_ERR  err;


    (void)&p_arg;
    while (DEF_ON) {
        :
        :
        OSSemDel(&SwSem,
                 OS_OPT_DEL_ALWAYS,
                 &err);
        /* Check "err" */
        :
        :
    }
}
```

OSSemPend()

```
OS_SEM_CTR   OSSemPend (OS_SEM    *p_sem,
                        OS_TICK    timeout,
                        OS_OPT     opt,
                        CPU_TS    *p_ts,
                        OS_ERR    *p_err)
```

File	Called from	Code enabled by
OS_SEM.C	Task only	OS_CFG_SEM_EN

OSSemPend() is used when a task wants exclusive access to a resource, needs to synchronize its activities with an ISR or task, or is waiting until an event occurs.

When the semaphore is used for resource sharing, if a task calls OSSemPend() and the value of the semaphore is greater than 0, OSSemPend() decrements the semaphore and returns to its caller. However, if the value of the semaphore is 0, OSSemPend() places the calling task in the waiting list for the semaphore. The task waits until the owner of the semaphore (which is always a task in this case) releases the semaphore by calling OSSemPost(), or the specified timeout expires. If the semaphore is signaled before the timeout expires, µC/OS-III resumes the highest-priority task waiting for the semaphore.

When the semaphore is used as a signaling mechanism, the calling task waits until a task or an ISR signals the semaphore by calling OSSemPost(), or the specified timeout expires. If the semaphore is signaled before the timeout expires, µC/OS-III resumes the highest-priority task waiting for the semaphore.

A pended task that has been suspended with OSTaskSuspend() can obtain the semaphore. However, the task remains suspended until it is resumed by calling OSTaskResume().

OSSemPend() also returns if the pend is aborted or, the semaphore is deleted.

Arguments

p_sem   is a pointer to the semaphore.

timeout   allows the task to resume execution if a semaphore is not posted within the specified number of clock ticks. A timeout value of 0 indicates that the task waits forever for the semaphore. The timeout value is not synchronized with the clock tick. The timeout count begins decrementing on the next clock tick, which could potentially occur immediately.

opt   specifies whether the call is to block if the semaphore is not available, or not block.

> **OS_OPT_PEND_BLOCKING**   to block the caller until the semaphore is available or a timeout occurs.
>
> **OS_OPT_PEND_NON_BLOCKING**   if the semaphore is not available, **OSSemPend()** will not block but return to the caller with an appropriate error code.

p_ts   is a pointer to a variable that will receive a timestamp of when the semaphore was posted, pend aborted, or deleted. Passing a **NULL** pointer is valid and indicates that a timestamp is not required.

A timestamp is useful when the task must know when the semaphore was posted or, how long it took for the task to resume after the semaphore was posted. In the latter case, call **CPU_BOOLEAN()** and compute the difference between the current value of the timestamp and ***p_ts**. In other words:

```
delta = OS_TS_GET() - *p_ts;
```

p_err   is a pointer to a variable used to hold an error code:

OS_ERR_NONE	if the semaphore is available.
OS_ERR_OBJ_DEL	if the semaphore was deleted.
OS_ERR_OBJ_PTR_NULL	if **p_sem** is a **NULL** pointer.
OS_ERR_OBJ_TYPE	if **p_sem** is not pointing to a semaphore.
OS_ERR_PEND_ABORT	if the pend was aborted
OS_ERR_PEND_ISR	if this function is called from an ISR.
OS_ERR_PEND_WOULD_BLOCK	if this function is called as specified OS_OPT_PEND_NON_BLOCKING, and the semaphore was not available.
OS_ERR_SCHED_LOCKED	if calling this function when the scheduler is locked.

OS_ERR_TIMEOUT   if the semaphore is not signaled within the specified timeout.

Returned Value

The new value of the semaphore count.

Notes/Warnings

1. Semaphores must be created before they are used.

Example

```
OS_SEM   SwSem;


void DispTask (void *p_arg)
{
    OS_ERR   err;
    CPU_TS   ts;


    (void)&p_arg;
    while (DEF_ON) {
        :
        :
        OSSemPend(&SwSem,
                  0,
                  OS_OPT_PEND_BLOCKING,
                  &ts,
                  &err);
        /* Check "err" */
    }
}
```

OSSemPendAbort()

```
OS_OBJ_QTY  OSSemPendAbort (OS_SEM  *p_sem,
                            OS_OPT   opt,
                            OS_ERR  *p_err)
```

File	Called from	Code enabled by
OS_SEM.C	Task only	OS_CFG_SEM_EN and OS_CFG_SEM_PEND_ABORT_EN

OSSemPendAbort() aborts and readies any task currently waiting on a semaphore. This function should be used to fault-abort the wait on the semaphore, rather than to normally signal the semaphore via OSSemPost().

Arguments

p_sem   is a pointer to the semaphore for which pend(s) need to be aborted.

opt   determines the type of abort performed.

<table>
<tr><td>OS_OPT_PEND_ABORT_1</td><td>Aborts the pend of only the highest-priority task waiting on the semaphore.</td></tr>
<tr><td>OS_OPT_PEND_ABORT_ALL</td><td>Aborts the pend of all the tasks waiting on the semaphore.</td></tr>
<tr><td>OS_OPT_POST_NO_SCHED</td><td>Specifies that the scheduler should not be called, even if the pend of a higher-priority task has been aborted. Scheduling will need to occur from another function.

Use this option if the task calling OSSemPendAbort() will be doing additional pend aborts, reschedule takes place when finished, and multiple pend aborts are to take effect simultaneously.</td></tr>
<tr><td>p_err</td><td>Is a pointer to a variable that holds an error code. OSSemPendAbort() sets *p_err to one of the following:</td></tr>
</table>

OS_ERR_NONE	At least one task waiting on the semaphore was readied and informed of the aborted wait. Check the return value for the number of tasks whose wait on the semaphore was aborted.
OS_ERR_OBJ_PTR_NULL	if **p_sem** is a **NULL** pointer.
OS_ERR_OBJ_TYPE	if **p_sem** is not pointing to a semaphore.
OS_ERR_OPT_INVALID	if an invalid option is specified.
OS_ERR_PEND_ABORT_ISR	This function is called from an ISR.
OS_ERR_PEND_ABORT_NONE	No task was aborted because no task was waiting.

Returned Value

OSSemPendAbort() returns the number of tasks made ready to run by this function. Zero indicates that no tasks were pending on the semaphore and therefore, the function had no effect.

Notes/Warnings

Semaphores must be created before they are used.

Example

```
OS_SEM   SwSem;


void CommTask(void *p_arg)
{
    OS_ERR      err;
    OS_OBJ_QTY  nbr_tasks;


    (void)&p_arg;
    while (DEF_ON) {
        :
        :
        nbr_tasks = OSSemPendAbort(&SwSem,
                           OS_OPT_PEND_ABORT_ALL,
                           &err);
        /* Check "err" */
        :
        :
    }
}
```

OSSemPost()

```
OS_SEM_CTR   OSSemPost (OS_SEM   *p_sem,
                        OS_OPT    opt,
                        OS_ERR    *p_err)
```

File	Called from	Code enabled by
OS_SEM.C	Task or ISR	OS_CFG_SEM_EN

A semaphore is signaled by calling **OSSemPost()**. If the semaphore value is 0 or more, it is incremented, and **OSSemPost()** returns to its caller. If tasks are waiting for the semaphore to be signaled, **OSSemPost()** removes the highest-priority task pending for the semaphore from the waiting list and makes this task ready to run. The scheduler is then called to determine if the awakened task is now the highest-priority task that is ready to run.

Arguments

p_sem   is a pointer to the semaphore.

opt   determines the type of post performed.

OS_OPT_POST_1	Post and ready only the highest-priority task waiting on the semaphore.
OS_OPT_POST_ALL	Post to all tasks waiting on the semaphore. ONLY use this option if the semaphore is used as a signaling mechanism and NEVER when the semaphore is used to guard a shared resource. It does not make sense to tell all tasks that are sharing a resource that they can all access the resource.
OS_OPT_POST_NO_SCHED	This option indicates that the caller does not want the scheduler to be called after the post. This option can be used in combination with ONE of the two previous options.

Use this option if the task (or ISR) calling **OSSemPost()** will be doing additional, the user does not want to reschedule until all done, and multiple posts are to take effect simultaneously.

p_err   is a pointer to a variable that holds an error code:

OS_ERR_NONE	if no tasks are waiting on the semaphore. In this case, the return value is also 0.
OS_ERR_OBJ_PTR_NULL	if **p_sem** is a **NULL** pointer.
OS_ERR_OBJ_TYPE	if **p_sem** is not pointing to a semaphore.
OS_ERR_SEM_OVF	if the post would have caused the semaphore counter to overflow.

Returned Value

The current value of the semaphore count

Notes/Warnings

1. Semaphores must be created before they are used.

2. You can also post to a semaphore from an ISR but the semaphore must be used as a signaling mechanism and not to protect a shared resource.

Example

```
OS_SEM  SwSem;


void TaskX (void *p_arg)
{
    OS_ERR      err;
    OS_SEM_CTR  ctr;


    (void)&p_arg;
    while (DEF_ON) {
        :
        :
        ctr = OSSemPost(&SwSem,
                        OS_OPT_POST_1 + OS_OPT_POST_NO_SCHED,
                        &err);
        /* Check "err" */
        :
        :
    }
}
```

OSSemSet()

```
void  OSSemSet (OS_SEM     *p_sem,
               OS_SEM_CTR  cnt,
               OS_ERR     *p_err)
```

File	Called from	Code enabled by
OS_SEM.C	Task	OS_CFG_SEM_EN and OS_CFG_SEM_SET_EN

OSSemSet() is used to change the current value of the semaphore count. This function is normally selected when a semaphore is used as a signaling mechanism. OSSemSet() can then be used to reset the count to any value. If the semaphore count is already 0, the count is only changed if there are no tasks waiting on the semaphore.

Arguments

p_sem   is a pointer to the semaphore that is used as a signaling mechanism.

cnt   is the desired count that the semaphore should be set to.

p_err   is a pointer to a variable used to hold an error code:

OS_ERR_NONE	if the count was changed or, not changed, because one or more tasks was waiting on the semaphore.
OS_ERR_OBJ_PTR_NULL	if **p_sem** is a **NULL** pointer.
OS_ERR_OBJ_TYPE	if **p_sem** is not pointing to a semaphore.
OS_ERR_SET_ISR	if this function was called from an ISR.
OS_ERR_TASK_WAITING	if tasks are waiting on the semaphore.

Returned Value

None

Notes/Warnings

Do not use this function if the semaphore is used to protect a shared resource.

Example

```
OS_SEM  SwSem;


void Task (void *p_arg)
{
    OS_ERR  err;


    (void)&p_arg;
    while (DEF_ON) {
        OSSemSet(&SwSem,        /* Reset the semaphore count */
                 0,
                 &err);
        /* Check "err" */
        :
        :
    }
}
```

OSStart()

```
void  OSStart (OS_ERR  *p_err)
```

File	Called from	Code enabled by
OS_CORE.C	Startup code only	N/A

OSStart() starts multitasking under µC/OS-III. This function is typically called from startup code after calling OSInit(). OSStart() will not return to the caller. Once µC/OS-III is running, calling OSStart() again will have no effect.

Arguments

p_err   is a pointer to a variable used to hold an error code:

OS_ERR_FATAL_RETURN	if we ever return to this function.
OS_ERR_OS_RUNNING	if the kernel is already running. In other words, if this function has already been called.

Returned Value

None

Notes/Warnings

OSInit() must be called prior to calling OSStart(). OSStart() should only be called once by the application code. However, if calling OSStart() more than once, nothing happens on the second and subsequent calls.

Example

```
void main (void)
{
    OS_ERR   err;

                                    /* User Code          */
    :
    OSInit(&err);                   /* Initialize µC/OS-III */
    /* Check "err" */
    :                               /* User Code          */
    :
    OSStart(&err);                  /* Start Multitasking  */
    /* Any code here should NEVER be executed! */
}
```

OSStartHighRdy()

void OSStartHighRdy (void)

File	Called from	Code enabled by
OS_CPU_A.ASM	OSStart()	N/A

OSStartHighRdy() is responsible for starting the highest-priority task that was created prior to calling OSStart().

Arguments

None

Returned Values

None

Notes/Warnings

None

Example

The pseudocode for OSStartHighRdy() is shown below.

```
void  OSStartHighRdy (void)
{
    OSTaskSwHook();                          (1)
    SP = OSTCBHighRdyPtr->StkPtr;            (2)
    Pop CPU registers off the task's stack;  (3)
    Return from interrupt;                   (4)
}
```

(1)   OSStartHighRdy() must call OSTaskSwHook().

When called, OSTCBCurPtr and OSTCBHighRdyPtr both point to the OS_TCB of the highest-priority task created.

OSTaskSwHook() should check that OSTCBCurPtr is not equal to OSTCBHighRdyPtr as this is the first time OSTaskSwHook() is called and there is not a task that is switched out.

(2)   Load the CPU stack pointer register with the top-of-stack (TOS) of the task being started. The TOS is found in the `.StkPtr` field of the `OS_TCB`. For convenience, the `.StkPtr` field is the very first field of the `OS_TCB` data structure. This makes it easily accessible from assembly language.

(3)   Pop the registers from the task's stack frame. Recall that the registers should have been placed on the stack frame in the same order as if they were pushed at the beginning of an interrupt service routine.

(4)   Perform a return from interrupt, which starts the task as if it was resumed when returning from a real interrupt.

OSStatReset()

void OSStatReset (OS_ERR *p_err)

File	Called from	Code enabled by
OS_STAT.C	Task Level Only	OS_CFG_STAT_TASK_EN

OSStatReset() is used to reset statistical variables maintained by µC/OS-III. Specifically, the per-task maximum interrupt disable time, maximum scheduler lock time, maximum amount of time a message takes to reach a task queue, the maximum amount of time it takes a signal to reach a task and more.

Arguments

p_err   is a pointer to a variable used to hold an error code:

      OS_ERR_NONE   the call was successful.

      OS_ERR_STAT_RESET_ISR   if the call was attempted from an ISR.

Returned Value

None

Notes/Warnings

None

Example

```
void TaskX (void *p_arg)
{
    OS_ERR   err;

    (void)&p_arg;
    while (DEF_ON) {
        :
        :
        OSStatReset(&err);
        /* Check "err" */
        :
        :
    }
}
```

OSStatTaskCPUUsageInit()

void   OSStatTaskCPUUsageInit (void)

File	Called from	Code enabled by
OS_STAT.C	Startup code only	OS_CFG_TASK_STAT_EN

OSStatTaskCPUUsageInit() determines the maximum value that a 32-bit counter can reach when no other task is executing. This function must be called when only one task is created in the application and when multitasking has started. This function must be called from the first and only task created by the application.

Arguments

p_err   is a pointer to a variable used to hold an error code:

> OS_ERR_NONE   Always returns this value.

Returned Value

None

Notes/Warnings

None

Example

```
void FirstAndOnlyTask (void *p_arg)
{
    :
    :
#if OS_CFG_TASK_STAT_EN > 0
    OSStatTaskCPUUsageInit(); /* Compute CPU capacity with no task running */
#endif
    :
    OSTaskCreate(_);            /* Create the other tasks                  */
    OSTaskCreate(_);
    :
    while (DEF_ON) {
        :
        :
    }
}
```

OSStatTaskHook()

```
void OSStatTaskHook (void);
```

File	Called from	Code enabled by
OS_CPU_C.C	OSStatTask()	Always enabled

OSStatTaskHook() is a function called by µC/OS-III's statistic task, OSStatTask(). OSStatTaskHook() is generally implemented by the port implementer for the processor used. This hook allows the port to perform additional statistics for the processor used.

Arguments

None

Returned Values

None

Notes/Warnings

None

Example

The code below calls an application-specific hook that an application programmer can define. For this, the user can simply set the value of OS_AppStatTaskHookPtr to point to the desired hook function (see App_OS_SetAllHooks() in OS_APP_HOOKS.C).

In the example below, OSStatTaskHook() calls App_OS_StatTaskHook() if the pointer OS_AppStatTaskHookPtr is set to that function.

```
void  App_OS_StatTaskHook (void)                        /* OS_APP_HOOKS.C      */
{
    /* Your code goes here! */
}



void App_OS_SetAllHooks (void)                          /* OS_APP_HOOKS.C      */
{
    CPU_SR_ALLOC();

    CPU_CRITICAL_ENTER();
    :
    OS_AppStatTaskHookPtr = App_OS_StatTaskHook;
    :
    CPU_CRITICAL_EXIT();
}



void  OSStatTaskHook (void)                             /* OS_CPU_C.C          */
{
#if OS_CFG_APP_HOOKS_EN > 0u
    if (OS_AppStatTaskHookPtr != (OS_APP_HOOK_VOID)0) {  /* Call application hook */
        (*OS_AppStatTaskHookPtr)();
    }
#endif
}
```

OSTaskChangePrio()

```
void  OSTaskChangePrio (OS_TCB    *p_tcb,
                        OS_PRIO   prio_new,
                        OS_ERR    *p_err)
```

File	Called from	Code enabled by
OS_TASK.C	Task	OS_CFG_TASK_CHANGE_PRIO_EN

When you creating a task (see **OSTaskCreate()**), you also specify the priority of the task being created. In most cases, it is not necessary to change the priority of the task at run time. However, it is sometimes useful to do so, and **OSTaskChangePrio()** allows this to take place.

If the task is ready to run, **OSTaskChangePrio()** simply changes the position of the task in µC/OS-III's ready list. If the task is waiting on an event, **OSTaskChangePrio()** will change the position of the task in the pend list of the corresponding object, so that the pend list remains sorted by priority.

Because µC/OS-III supports multiple tasks at the same priority, there are no restrictions on the priority that a task can have, except that task priority zero (0) is reserved by µC/OS-III, and priority **OS_PRIO_MAX-1** is used by the idle task.

Note that a task priority cannot be changed from an ISR.

Arguments

p_tcb   is a pointer to the **OS_TCB** of the task for which the priority is being changed. If passing a **NULL** pointer, the priority of the current task is changed.

prio_new   is the new task's priority. This value must never be set to **OS_CFG_PRIO_MAX-1**, or higher and you must not use priority 0 since they are reserved for µC/OS-III.

p_err   is a pointer to a variable that will receive an error code:

OS_ERR_NONE   if the task's priority is changed.
OS_ERR_TASK_CHANGE_PRIO_ISR   if attempting to change the task's priority from an ISR.

491

OS_ERR_PRIO_INVALID	if the priority of the task specified is invalid. By specifying a priority greater than or equal to OS_PRIO_MAX-1, or 0.

Returned Value

None

Notes/Warnings

None

Example

```
OS_TCB  MyTaskTCB;


void TaskX (void *p_arg)
{
    OS_ERR  err;


    while (DEF_ON) {
        :
        :
        OSTaskChangePrio(&MyTaskTCB,     /* Change the priority of "MyTask" to 10 */
                         10,
                         &err);
        /* Check "err" */
        :
    }
}
```

OSTaskCreate()

```
void   OSTaskCreate (OS_TCB         *p_tcb,
                     CPU_CHAR       *p_name,
                     OS_TASK_PTR     p_task,
                     void           *p_arg,
                     OS_PRIO         prio,
                     CPU_STK        *p_stk_base,
                     CPU_STK_SIZE    stk_limit,
                     CPU_STK_SIZE    stk_size,
                     OS_MSG_QTY      q_size,
                     OS_TICK         time_quanta,
                     void           *p_ext,
                     OS_OPT          opt,
                     OS_ERR         *p_err)
```

File	Called from	Code enabled by
OS_TASK.C	Task or startup code	N/A

Tasks must be created in order for µC/OS-III to recognize them as tasks. Create a task by calling **OSTaskCreate()** and provide arguments specifying to µC/OS-III how the task will be managed. Tasks are always created in the ready-to-run state.

Tasks can be created either prior to the start of multitasking (i.e., before calling **OSStart()**), or by a running task. A task cannot be created by an ISR. A task must either be written as an infinite loop, or delete itself once completed. If the task code returns by mistake, µC/OS-III will terminate the task by calling **OSTaskDel((OS_TCB *)0, &err))**. At Micrium, we like the "**while (DEF_ON)**" to implement infinite loops because, by convention, we use a **while** loop when we don't know how many iterations a loop will do. This is the case of an infinite loop. We use **for** loops when we know how many iterations a loop will do.

Task as an infinite loop:

```
void MyTask (void *p_arg)
{
    /* Local variables                                          */


    /* Do something with 'p_arg'                                */
    /* Task initialization                                      */
    while (DEF_ON) {       /* Task body, as an infinite loop.   */
        :
        :
        /* Must call one of the following services:             */
        /*    OSFlagPend()                                      */
        /*    OSMutexPend()                                     */
        /*    OSQPend()                                         */
        /*    OSSemPend()                                       */
        /*    OSTimeDly()                                       */
        /*    OSTimeDlyHMSM()                                   */
        /*    OSTaskQPend()                                     */
        /*    OSTaskSemPend()                                   */
        /*    OSTaskSuspend()     (Suspend self)                */
        /*    OSTaskDel()         (Delete  self)                */
        :
        :
    }
}
```

Run to completion task:

```
void MyTask (void *p_arg)
{
    OS_ERR  err;
    /* Local variables                                          */


    /* Do something with 'p_arg'                                */
    /* Task initialization                                      */
    /* Task body (do some work)                                 */
    OSTaskDel((OS_TCB *)0, &err);
    /* Check 'err"                                              */
}
```

Arguments

p_tcb   is a pointer to the task's **OS_TCB** to use. It is assumed that storage for the TCB of the task will be allocated by the user code. Declare a "global" variable as follows, and pass a pointer to this variable to **OSTaskCreate( )**:

```
OS_TCB MyTaskTCB;
```

p_name   is a pointer to an ASCII string (NUL terminated) to assign a name to the task. The name can be displayed by debuggers or by µC/Probe.

p_task   is a pointer to the task (i.e., the name of the function).

p_arg   is a pointer to an optional data area, which is used to pass parameters to the task when it is created. When µC/OS-III runs the task for the first time, the task will think that it was invoked, and passed the argument **p_arg**. For example, create a generic task that handles an asynchronous serial port. **p_arg** can be used to pass task information about the serial port it will manage: the port address, baud rate, number of bits, parity, and more. **p_arg** is the argument received by the task shown below.

```
void MyTask (void *p_arg)
{
    while (DEF_ON) {
        Task code;
    }
}
```

prio   is the task priority. The lower the number, the higher the priority (i.e., the importance) of the task. If **OS_CFG_ISR_POST_DEFERRED_EN** is set to 1, the user may not use priority 0.

Task priority must also have a lower number than **OS_CFG_PRIO_MAX-1**. Priorities 0, 1, **OS_CFG_PRIO_MAX-2** and **OS_CFG_PRIO_MAX-1** are reserved. In other words, a task should have a priority between 2 and **OOS_CFG_PRIO_MAX-3**, inclusively.

p_stk_base is a pointer to the task's stack base address. The task's stack is used to store local variables, function parameters, return addresses, and possibly CPU registers during an interrupt.

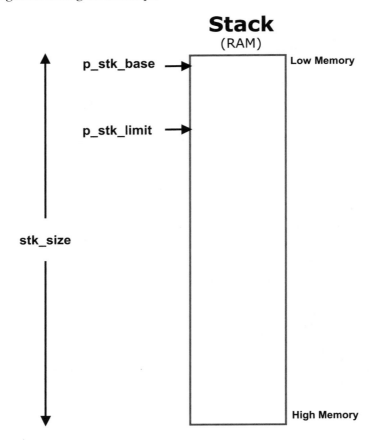

The task stack must be declared as follows:

```
CPU_STK MyTaskStk[xxx];
```

The user would then pass **p_stk_base** the address of the first element of this array or, &MyTaskStk[0]. "xxx" represents the size of the stack.

The size of this stack is determined by the task's requirements and the anticipated interrupt nesting (unless the processor has a separate stack just for interrupts). Determining the size of the stack involves knowing how many bytes are required for storage of local variables for the task itself and all nested functions, as well as requirements for interrupts (accounting for nesting).

Note that you can allocate stack space for a task from the heap but, in this case, never delete the task and free the stack space as this can cause the heap to fragment, which is not desirable in embedded systems.

`stk_limit` is used to locate, within the task's stack, a watermark limit that can be used to monitor and ensure that the stack does not overflow.

If the processor does not have hardware stack overflow detection, or this feature is not implemented in software by the port developer, this value may be used for other purposes. For example, some processors have two stacks, a hardware and a software stack. The hardware stack typically keeps track of function call nesting and the software stack is used to pass function arguments. `stk_limit` may be used to set the size of the hardware stack as shown below.

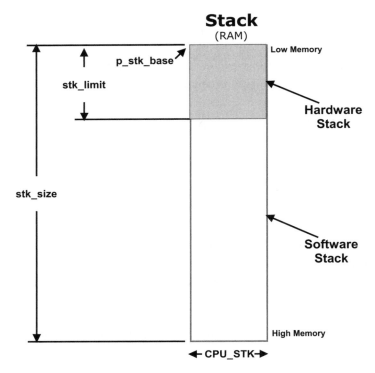

stk_size   specifies the size of the task's stack in number of elements. If **CPU_STK** is set to
             CPU_INT08U (see **OS_TYPE.H**), **stk_size** corresponds to the number of bytes
             available on the stack. If **CPU_STK** is set to **CPU_INT16U**, then **stk_size**
             contains the number of 16-bit entries available on the stack. Finally, if **CPU_STK**
             is set to **CPU_INT32U**, **stk_size** contains the number of 32-bit entries available
             on the stack.

q_size   A μC/OS-III task contains an optional internal message queue
             (if **OS_TASK_Q_EN** > 0). This argument specifies the maximum number of
             messages that the task can receive through this message queue. The user may
             specify that the task is unable to receive messages by setting the argument to 0.

time_quanta the amount of time (in clock ticks) for the time quanta when
             round robin is enabled. If you specify 0, then the default time
             quanta will be used which is the tick rate divided by 10.

p_ext   is a pointer to a user-supplied memory location (typically a data structure) used as a TCB extension. For example, the user memory can hold the contents of floating-point registers during a context switch.

opt   contains task-specific options. Each option consists of one bit. The option is selected when the bit is set. The current version of µC/OS-III supports the following options:

OS_OPT_TASK_NONE	specifies that there are no options.
OS_OPT_TASK_STK_CHK	specifies whether stack checking is allowed for the task.
OS_OPT_TASK_STK_CLR	specifies whether the stack needs to be cleared.
OS_OPT_TASK_SAVE_FP	specifies whether floating-point registers are saved. This option is only valid if the processor has floating-point hardware and the processor-specific code saves the floating-point registers.

p_err   is a pointer to a variable that will receive an error code:

OS_ERR_NONE	if the function is successful.
OS_ERR_NAME	if **p_name** is a **NULL** pointer.
OS_ERR_PRIO_INVALID	if prio is higher than the maximum value allowed (i.e., > **OS_PRIO_MAX-1**). Also, if the user set **OS_CFG_ISR_POST_DEFERRED_EN** to 1 and tried to use priority 0.
OS_ERR_STK_INVALID	if specifying a **NULL** pointer for **p_stk_base**.
OS_ERR_STK_SIZE_INVALID	if specifying a stack size smaller than what is currently specified by **OS_CFG_STK_SIZE_MIN** (see the **OS_CFG.H**).
OS_ERR_TASK_CREATE_ISR	if attempting to create the task from an ISR.
OS_ERR_TASK_INVALID	if specifying a **NULL** pointer for **p_task**
OS_ERR_TCB_INVALID	if specifying a **NULL** pointer for **p_tcb**.

Returned Value

None

Notes/Warnings

1. The stack must be declared with the CPU_STK type.

2. A task must always invoke one of the services provided by μC/OS-III to wait for time to expire, suspend the task, or wait on an object (wait on a message queue, event flag, mutex, semaphore, a signal or a message to be sent directly to the task). This allows other tasks to gain control of the CPU.

3. Do not use task priorities 0, 1, OS_PRIO_MAX-2 and OS_PRIO_MAX-1 because they are reserved for use by μC/OS-III.

Example

OSTaskCreate() can be called from main() (in C), or a previously created task.

```
OS_TCB  MyTaskTCB;                      /*  (1) Storage for task's TCB            */
CPU_STK MyTaskStk[200];


void  MyTask (void *p_arg)              /*  (3) The address of the task is its name  */
{
    while (DEF_ON) {
        /* Wait for an event */
        /* My task body      */
    }
}


void SomeCode (void)
{
    OS_ERR  err;
    :
    :
    OSTaskCreate (&MyTaskTCB,           /*  (1) Address of TCB assigned to the task  */
                  "My Task",            /*  (2) Name you want to give the task       */
                  MyTask,               /*  (3) Address of the task itself           */
                  (void *)0,            /*  (4) "p_arg" is not used                  */
                  12,                   /*  (5) Priority you want to assign to the task */
                  &MyTaskStk[0],        /*  (6) Base address of task's stack         */
                  10,                   /*  (7) Watermark limit for stack growth     */
                  200,                  /*  (8) Stack size in number of CPU_STK elements */
                  5,                    /*  (9) Size of task message queue           */
                  10,                   /*  (10) Time quanta (in number of ticks)    */
                  (void *)0,            /*  (11) Extension pointer is not used       */
                  OS_OPT_TASK_STK_CHK + OS_OPT_TASK_STK_CLR, /* (12) Options        */
                  &err);                             /*  (13) Error code            */
    /* Check "err"                                      (14)                         */
    :
    :
}
```

(1)   In order to create a task, allocate storage for a TCB and pass a pointer to this TCB to **OSTaskCreate()**.

(2)   Assign an ASCII name to the task by passing a pointer to an ASCII string. The ASCII string may be allocated in code space (i.e., ROM), or data space (i.e., RAM). In either case, it is assumed that the code can access that memory.

(3)   Pass the address of the task to **OSTaskCreate()**. In C, the address of a function is simply the name of the function.

(4)   To provide additional data to **MyTask()**, simply pass a pointer to such data. In this case, **MyTask()** did not need such data and therefore, a **NULL** pointer is passed.

(5)   The user must assign a priority to the task. The priority specifies the importance of this task with respect to other tasks. A low-priority value indicates a high priority. Priority 0 is the highest priority (reserved for an internal task) and a priority up to **OS_PRIO_MAX-2** can be specified (see **OS_CFG.H**). Note that **OS_PRIO_MAX-1** is also reserved for an internal task, the idle task.

(6)   The next argument specifies the "base address" of the task's stack. In this case, it is simply the base address of the array **MyTaskStk[]**. Note that it is possible to simply specify the name of the array. I prefer to make it clear by writing **&MyTaskStk[0]**.

(7)   Set the watermark limit for stack growth. If the processor port does not use this field then either set this value to **0**.

(8)   µC/OS-III also needs to know the size of the stack for the task. This allows µC/OS-III to perform stack checking at run time.

(9)   µC/OS-III allows tasks or ISRs to send messages directly to a task. This argument specifies how many such messages can be received by this task.

(10)   This argument specifies how much time (in number of ticks) this task will run on the CPU before µC/OS-III will force the CPU away from this task and run the next task at the same priority (if there are more than one task at the same priority that is ready to run).

(11)   µC/OS-III allows the user to "extend" the capabilities of the TCB by allowing passing a pointer to some memory location that could contain additional information about the task. For example, there may be a CPU that supports floating-point math and the user would likely need to save the floating-point registers during a context switch. This pointer could point to the storage area for these registers.

(12)   When creating a task, options must be specified. Specifically, such options as, whether the stack of the task will be cleared (i.e., filled with 0x00) when the task is created (**OS_OPT_TASK_STK_CLR**), whether μC/OS-III will be allowed to check for stack usage (**OS_OPT_TASK_STK_CHK**), whether the CPU supports floating-point math, and whether the task will make use of the floating-point registers and therefore need to save and restore them during a context switch (**OS_OPT_TASK_SAVE_FP**). The options are additive.

(13)   Most of μC/OS-III's services return an error code indicating the outcome of the call. The error code is always returned as a pointer to a variable of type **OS_ERR**. The user must allocate storage for this variable prior to calling **OSTaskCreate()**. By the way, a pointer to an error variable is always the last argument, which makes it easy to remember.

(14)   It is highly recommended that the user examine the error code whenever calling a μC/OS-III function. If the call is successful, the error code will always be **OS_ERR_NONE**. If the call is not successful, the returned code will indicate the reason for the failure (see **OS_ERR_???** in **OS.H**).

OSTaskCreateHook()

void OSTaskCreateHook (OS_TCB *p_tcb)

File	Called from	Code enabled by
OS_CPU_C.C	OSTaskCreate() ONLY	N/A

This function is called by **OSTaskCreate()** just before adding the task to the ready list. When **OSTaskCreateHook()** is called, all of the **OS_TCB** fields are assumed to be initialized. **OSTaskCreateHook()** is called after initializing the **OS_TCB** fields and setting up the stack frame for the task, before the task is placed in the ready list.

OSTaskCreateHook() is part of the CPU port code and this function *must not* be called by the application code. **OSTaskCreateHook()** is actually used by the µC/OS-III port developer.

Use this hook to initialize and store the contents of floating-point registers, MMU registers, or anything else that can be associated with a task. Typically, store this additional information in memory allocated by the application.

Arguments
p_tcb   is a pointer to the TCB of the task being created. Note that the **OS_TCB** has been validated by **OSTaskCreate()** and is guaranteed to not be a **NULL** pointer when **OSTaskCreateHook()** is called.

Returned Value
None

Notes/Warnings
Do not call this function from the application.

Example
The code below calls an application-specific hook that the application programmer can define. The user can simply set the value of **OS_AppTaskCreateHookPtr** to point to the desired hook function as shown in the example. **OSTaskCreate()** calls

OSTaskCreateHook() which in turns calls **App_OS_TaskCreateHook()** through OS_AppTaskCreateHookPtr. As can be seen, when called, the application hook is passed the address of the **OS_TCB** of the newly created task.

```
void  App_OS_TaskCreateHook (OS_TCB *p_tcb)              /* OS_APP_HOOKS.C      */
{
    /* Your code goes here! */
}


void App_OS_SetAllHooks (void)                           /* OS_APP_HOOKS.C      */
{
    CPU_SR_ALLOC();

    CPU_CRITICAL_ENTER();
    :
    OS_AppTaskCreateHookPtr = App_OS_TaskCreateHook;
    :
    CPU_CRITICAL_EXIT();
}


void  OSTaskCreateHook (OS_TCB *p_tcb)                    /* OS_CPU_C.C          */
{
#if OS_CFG_APP_HOOKS_EN > 0u
    if (OS_AppTaskCreateHookPtr != (OS_APP_HOOK_TCB)0) {  /* Call application hook */
        (*OS_AppTaskCreateHookPtr)(p_tcb);
    }
#endif
}
```

OSTaskDel()

```
void   OSTaskDel (OS_TCB   *p_tcb,
                  OS_ERR   *p_err)
```

File	Called from	Code enabled by
OS_TASK.C	Task	OS_CFG_TASK_DEL_EN

When a task is no longer needed, it can be deleted. Deleting a task does not mean that the code is removed, but that the task code is no longer managed by μC/OS-III. OSTaskDel() can be used when creating a task that will only run once. In this case, the task must not return but instead call OSTaskDel((OS_TCB *)0, &err), specifying to μC/OS-III to delete the currently running task.

A task may also delete another task by specifying to OSTaskDel() the address of the OS_TCB of the task to delete.

Once a task is deleted, its OS_TCB and stack may be reused to create another task. This assumes that the task's stack requirement of the new task is satisfied by the stack size of the deleted task.

Even though μC/OS-III allows the user to delete tasks at run time, it is recommend that such actions be avoided. Why? Because a task can "own" resources that are shared with other tasks. Deleting the task that owns resource(s) without first relinquishing the resources could lead to strange behaviors and possible deadlocks.

Arguments

p_tcb   is a pointer to the TCB of the task to delete or, a **NULL** pointer for the calling task to delete itself. If deleting the calling task, the scheduler will be invoked so that the next highest-priority task is executed.

p_err   is a pointer to a variable that will receive an error code:

OS_ERR_NONE   if the desired task was deleted (unless the task deleted itself in which case there are no errors to return).

OS_ERR_TASK_DEL_IDLE   if attempting to delete the ilde task.

OS_ERR_TASK_DEL_ISR	if calling OSTaskDel() from an ISR.
OS_ERR_TASK_DEL_INVALID	if attempting to delete the ISR Handler task while OS_CFG_ISR_POST_DEFERRED_EN is set to 1.

Returned Value

None

Notes/Warnings

1. OSTaskDel() verifies that the user is not attempting to delete the µC/OS-III idle task and the ISR handler task.

2. Be careful when deleting a task that owns resources.

Example

```
OS_TCB  MyTaskTCB;


void TaskX (void *p_arg)
{
    OS_ERR  err;


    while (DEF_ON) {
        :
        :
        OSTaskDel(&MyTaskTCB,
                  &err);
        /* Check "err" */
        :
        :
    }
}
```

OSTaskDelHook()

```
void  OSTaskDelHook (OS_TCB  *p_tcb);
```

File	Called from	Code enabled by
OS_CPU_C.C	OSTaskDel() ONLY	N/A

This function is called by **OSTaskDel()** after the task is removed from the ready list or any pend list.

Use this hook to deallocate storage assigned to the task.

OSTaskDelHook() is part of the CPU port code and this function *must not* be called by the application code. **OSTaskDelHook()** is actually used by the µC/OS-III port developer.

Arguments

p_tcb   is a pointer to the TCB of the task being created. Note that the **OS_TCB** has been validated by **OSTaskDel()** and is guaranteed to not be a **NULL** pointer when **OSTaskDelHook()** is called.

Returned Value

None

Notes/Warnings

Do not call this function from the application.

Example

The code below calls an application-specific hook that the application programmer can define. The user can simply set the value of **OS_AppTaskDelHookPtr** to point to the desired hook function. **OSTaskDel()** calls **OSTaskDelHook()** which in turns calls **App_OS_TaskDelHook()** through **OS_AppTaskDelHookPtr**. As can be seen, when called, the application hook is passed the address of the **OS_TCB** of the task being deleted.

```
void  App_OS_TaskDelHook (OS_TCB *p_tcb)                /* OS_APP_HOOKS.C      */
{
    /* Your code goes here! */
}


void App_OS_SetAllHooks (void)                          /* OS_APP_HOOKS.C      */
{
    CPU_SR_ALLOC();

    CPU_CRITICAL_ENTER();
    :
    OS_AppTaskDelHookPtr = App_OS_TaskDelHook;
    :
    CPU_CRITICAL_EXIT();
}



void  OSTaskDelHook (OS_TCB *p_tcb)                      /* OS_CPU_C.C          */
{
#if OS_CFG_APP_HOOKS_EN > 0u
    if (OS_AppTaskDelHookPtr != (OS_APP_HOOK_TCB)0) {    /* Call application hook */
        (*OS_AppTaskDelHookPtr)(p_tcb);
    }
#endif
}
```

OSTaskQPend()

```
void   *OSTaskQPend (OS_TICK        timeout,
                     OS_OPT         opt,
                     OS_MSG_SIZE    *p_msg_size,
                     CPU_TS         *p_ts,
                     OS_ERR         *p_err)
```

File	Called from	Code enabled by
OS_TASK.C	Task	OS_CFG_TASK_Q_EN and OS_CFG_MSG_EN

OSTaskQPend() allows a task to receive messages directly from an ISR or another task, without going through an intermediate message queue. In fact, each task has a built-in message queue if the configuration constant OS_TASK_Q_EN is set to 1. The messages received are pointer-sized variables, and their use is application specific. If at least one message is already present in the message queue when OSTaskQPend() is called, the message is retrieved and returned to the caller.

If no message is present in the task's message queue and OS_OPT_PEND_BLOCKING is specified for the opt argument, OSTaskQPend() suspends the current task (assuming the scheduler is not locked) until either a message is received, or a user-specified timeout expires. A pended task that is suspended with OSTaskSuspend() can receive messages. However, the task remains suspended until it is resumed by calling OSTaskResume().

If no message is present in the task's message queue and OS_OPT_PEND_NON_BLOCKING is specified for the opt argument, OSTaskQPend() returns to the caller with an appropriate error code and returns a NULL pointer.

Arguments

timeout   allows the task to resume execution if a message is not received from a task or an ISR within the specified number of clock ticks. A timeout value of 0 indicates that the task wants to wait forever for a message. The timeout value is not synchronized with the clock tick. The timeout count starts decrementing on the next clock tick, which could potentially occur immediately.

opt   determines whether or not the user wants to block if a message is not available in the task's queue. This argument must be set to either:

OS_OPT_PEND_BLOCKING, or

OS_OPT_PEND_NON_BLOCKING

Note that the timeout argument should be set to 0 when OS_OPT_PEND_NON_BLOCKING is specified, since the timeout value is irrelevant using this option.

p_msg_size   is a pointer to a variable that will receive the size of the message.

p_ts   is a pointer to a timestamp indicating when the task's queue was posted, or the pend aborted. If passing a **NULL** pointer (i.e., (**CPU_TS** *)0), the timestamp will not returned. In other words, passing a **NULL** pointer is valid and indicates that the timestamp is not necessary.

A timestamp is useful when the task must know when the task message queue was posted, or how long it took for the task to resume after the task message queue was posted. In the latter case, call **OS_TS_GET()** and compute the difference between the current value of the timestamp and *p_ts. In other words:

delta = OS_TS_GET() - *p_ts;

p_err   is a pointer to a variable used to hold an error code.

OS_ERR_NONE	if a message is received.
OS_ERR_PEND_ABORT	if the pend was aborted because another task called OSTaskQPendAbort().
OS_ERR_PEND_ISR	if calling this function from an ISR.
OS_ERR_PEND_WOULD_BLOCK	if calling this function with the opt argument set to OS_OPT_PEND_NON_BLOCKING and no message is in the task's message queue.
OS_ERR_SCHED_LOCKED	if calling this function when the scheduler is locked and the user wanted to block.

| OS_ERR_TIMEOUT | if a message is not received within the specified timeout. |

Returned Value

The message if no error or a **NULL** pointer upon error. Examine the error code since it is possible to send **NULL** pointer messages. In other words, a **NULL** pointer does not mean an error occurred. *p_err must be examined to determine the reason for the error.

Notes/Warnings

Do not call **OSTaskQPend()** from an ISR.

Example

```
void CommTask (void *p_arg)
{
    OS_ERR       err;
    void        *p_msg;
    OS_MSG_SIZE  msg_size;
    CPU_TS       ts;


    (void)&p_arg;
    while (DEF_ON) {
        :
        :
        p_msg = OSTaskQPend(100,
                            OS_OPT_PEND_BLOCKING,
                            &msg_size,
                            &ts,
                            &err);
        /* Check "err" */
        :
        :
    }
}
```

OSTaskQPendAbort()

```
CPU_BOOLEAN   OSTaskQPendAbort (OS_TCB   *p_tcb,
                                OS_OPT    opt,
                                OS_ERR   *p_err)
```

File	Called from	Code enabled by
OS_Q.C	Task	OS_CFG_TASK_Q_EN and OS_CFG_TASK_Q_PEND_ABORT_EN

OSTaskQPendAbort() aborts and readies a task currently waiting on its built-in message queue. This function should be used to fault-abort the wait on the task's message queue, rather than to normally signal the message queue via OSTaskQPost().

Arguments

p_tcb   is a pointer to the task for which the pend needs to be aborted. Note that it doesn't make sense to pass a **NULL** pointer or the address of the calling task's TCB since, by definition, the calling task cannot be pending.

opt   provides options for this function.

OS_OPT_POST_NONE	No option specified.
OS_OPT_POST_NO_SCHED	specifies that the scheduler should not be called even if the pend of a higher priority task has been aborted. Scheduling will need to occur from another function.
	Use this option if the task calling **OSTaskQPendAbort()** will do additional pend aborts, rescheduling will take place when completed, and multiple pend aborts should take effect simultaneously.

p_err   is a pointer to a variable that holds an error code:

OS_ERR_NONE	the task was readied by another task and it was informed of the aborted wait.
OS_ERR_PEND_ABORT_ISR	if called from an ISR

OS_ERR_PEND_ABORT_NONE	if the task was not pending on the task's message queue.
OS_ERR_PEND_ABORT_SELF	if p_tcb is a NULL pointer. The user is attempting to pend abort the calling task which makes no sense as the caller, by definition, is not pending.

Returned Value

OSTaskQPendAbort() returns DEF_TRUE if the task was made ready to run by this function. DEF_FALSE indicates that the task was not pending, or an error occurred.

Notes/Warnings

None

Example

```
OS_TCB   CommRxTaskTCB;


void CommTask (void *p_arg)
{
    OS_ERR      err;
    CPU_BOOLEAN aborted;


    (void)&p_arg;
    while (DEF_ON) {
        :
        :
        aborted = OSTaskQPendAbort(&CommRxTaskTCB,
                                   OS_OPT_POST_NONE,
                                   &err);
        /* Check "err" */
        :
        :
    }
}
```

OSTaskQPost()

```
void  OSTaskQPost (OS_TCB       *p_tcb,
                   void         *p_void,
                   OS_MSG_SIZE  msg_size,
                   OS_OPT       opt,
                   OS_ERR       *p_err)
```

File	Called from	Code enabled by
OS_Q.C	Task or ISR	OS_CFG_TASK_Q_EN and OS_CFG_MSG_EN

OSTaskQPost() sends a message to a task through its local message queue. A message is a pointer-sized variable, and its use is application specific. If the task's message queue is full, an error code is returned to the caller. In this case, OSTaskQPost() immediately returns to its caller, and the message is not placed in the message queue.

If the task receiving the message is waiting for a message to arrive, it will be made ready to run. If the receiving task has a higher priority than the task sending the message, the higher-priority task resumes, and the task sending the message is suspended; that is, a context switch occurs. A message can be posted as first-in first-out (FIFO), or last-in-first-out (LIFO), depending on the value specified in the **opt** argument. In either case, scheduling occurs unless **opt** is set to OS_OPT_POST_NO_SCHED.

Arguments

p_tcb   is a pointer to the TCB of the task. Note that it is possible to post a message to the calling task (i.e., self) by specifying a **NULL** pointer, or the address of its TCB.

p_void   is the actual message sent to the task. p_void is a pointer-sized variable and its meaning is application specific.

msg_size   specifies the size of the message posted (in number of bytes).

opt   determines the type of POST performed. Of course, it does not make sense to post LIFO and FIFO simultaneously, so these options are exclusive:

OS_OPT_POST_FIFO	POST message to task, or place at the end of the queue if the task is not waiting for messages.
OS_OPT_POST_LIFO	POST message to task, or place at the front of the queue if the task is not waiting for messages.
OS_OPT_POST_NO_SCHED	Do not call the scheduler after the post and therefore the caller is resumed.
	Use this option if the task (or ISR) calling **OSTaskQPost()** will be doing additional posts, the user does not want to reschedule until all done, and multiple posts are to take effect simultaneously. **p_err** is a pointer to a variable that will contain an error code returned by this function.
OS_ERR_NONE	if the call was successful and the message was posted to the task's message queue.
OS_ERR_MSG_POOL_EMPTY	if running out of **OS_MSG** to hold the message being posted.
OS_ERR_Q_MAX	if the task's message queue is full and cannot accept more messages.

Returned Value

None

Notes/Warnings

None

Example

```
OS_TCB      CommRxTaskTCB;
CPU_INT08U  CommRxBuf[100];


void CommTaskRx (void *p_arg)
{
    OS_ERR   err;


    (void)&p_arg;
    while (DEF_ON) {
        :
        OSTaskQPost(&CommRxTaskTCB,
                   (void *)&CommRxBuf[0],
                   sizeof(CommRxBuf),
                   OS_OPT_POST_FIFO,
                   &err);
        /* Check "err" */
        :
    }
}
```

OSTaskRegGet()

```
OS_REG   OSTaskRegGet (OS_TCB      *p_tcb,
                       OS_REG_ID   id,
                       OS_ERR      *p_err)
```

File	Called from	Code enabled by
OS_TASK.C	Task	OS_CFG_TASK_REG_TBL_SIZE > 0

µC/OS-III allows the user to store task-specific values in task registers. Task registers are different than CPU registers and are used to save such information as "errno," which are common in software components. Task registers can also store task-related data to be associated with the task at run time such as I/O register settings, configuration values, etc. A task may have as many as **OS_CFG_TASK_REG_TBL_SIZE** registers, and all registers have a data type of **OS_REG**. However, **OS_REG** can be declared at compile time (see **OS_TYPE.H**) to be nearly anything (8-, 16-, 32-, 64-bit signed or unsigned integer, or floating-point).

As shown below, a task is register is changed by calling **OSTaskRegSet()** and read by calling **OSTaskRegGet()**. The desired task register is specified as an argument to these functions and can take a value between 0 and **OS_CFG_TASK_REG_TBL_SIZE-1**.

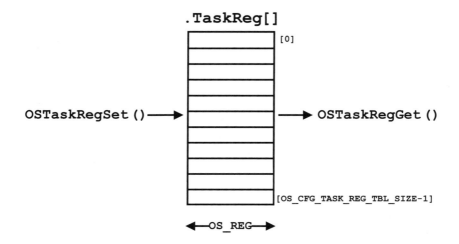

Arguments

p_tcb   is a pointer to the TCB of the task the user is receiving a task-register value from. A **NULL** pointer indicates that the user wants the value of a task register of the calling task.

id   is the identifier of the task register and valid values are from 0 to OS_CFG_TASK_REG_TBL_SIZE-1.

p_err   is a pointer to a variable that will contain an error code returned by this function.

         OS_ERR_NONE   if the call was successful and the function returned the value of the desired task register.

         OS_ERR_REG_ID_INVALID   if a valid task register identifier is not specified.

Returned Value

The current value of the task register.

Notes/Warnings

None

Example

```
OS_TCB  MyTaskTCB;


void TaskX (void *p_arg)
{
    OS_ERR  err;
    OS_REG  reg;


    while (DEF_ON) {
        :
        reg = OSTaskRegGet(&MyTaskTCB,
                           5,
                           &err);
        /* Check "err" */
        :
    }
}
```

OSTaskRegSet()

```
void  OSTaskRegSet (OS_TCB      *p_tcb,
                    OS_REG_ID   id,
                    OS_REG      value,
                    OS_ERR      *p_err)
```

File	Called from	Code enabled by
OS_TASK.C	Task	OS_CFG_TASK_REG_TBL_SIZE > 0

µC/OS-III allows the user to store task-specific values in task registers. Task registers are different than CPU registers and are used to save such information as "errno," which are common in software components. Task registers can also store task-related data to be associated with the task at run time such as I/O register settings, configuration values, etc. A task may have as many as **OS_CFG_TASK_REG_TBL_SIZE** registers, and all registers have a data type of **OS_REG**. However, **OS_REG** can be declared at compile time to be nearly anything (8-, 16-, 32-, 64-bit signed or unsigned integer, or floating-point).

As shown below, a task is register is changed by calling **OSTaskRegSet()**, and read by calling **OSTaskRegGet()**. The desired task register is specified as an argument to these functions and can take a value between 0 and **OS_CFG_TASK_REG_TBL_SIZE**-1.

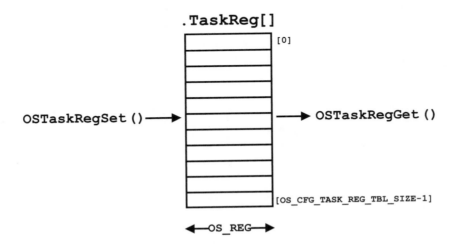

Arguments

p_tcb   is a pointer to the TCB of the task you are setting. A **NULL** pointer indicates that the user wants to set the value of a task register of the calling task.

id   is the identifier of the task register and valid values are from 0 to OS_CFG_TASK_REG_TBL_SIZE-1.

value   is the new value of the task register specified by **id**.

p_err   is a pointer to a variable that will contain an error code returned by this function.

         OS_ERR_NONE   if the call was successful, and the function set the value of the desired task register.

         OS_ERR_REG_ID_INVALID   if a valid task register identifier is not specified.

Returned Value

None

Notes/Warnings

None

Example

```
OS_TCB  MyTaskTCB;


void TaskX (void *p_arg)
{
    OS_ERR  err;


    while (DEF_ON) {
        :
        reg = OSTaskRegSet(&MyTaskTCB,
                           5,
                           23,
                           &err);
        /* Check "err" */
        :
    }
}
```

OSTaskReturnHook()

```
void   OSTaskReturnHook (void);
```

File	Called from	Code enabled by
OS_CPU_C.C	OS_TaskReturn() ONLY	N/A

This function is called by OS_TaskReturn(). OS_TaskReturn() is called if the user accidentally returns from the task code. In other words, the task should either be implemented as an infinite loop and never return, or the task must call OSTaskDel((OS_TCB *)0, &err) to delete itself to prevent it from exiting.

OSTaskReturnHook() is part of the CPU port code and this function *must not* be called by the application code. OSTaskReturnHook() is actually used by the µC/OS-III port developer.

Note that after calling OSTaskReturnHook(), OS_TaskReturn() will actually delete the task by calling:

```
OSTaskDel((OS_TCB *)0,
          &err)
```

Arguments

p_tcb   is a pointer to the TCB of the task that is not behaving as expected. Note that the OS_TCB is validated by OS_TaskReturn(), and is guaranteed to not be a NULL pointer when OSTaskReturnHook() is called.

Returned Value

None

Notes/Warnings

Do not call this function from the application.

Example

The code below calls an application-specific hook that the application programmer can define. For this, the user can simply set the value of OS_AppTaskReturnHookPtr to point to the desired hook function as shown in the example. If a task returns and forgets to call

OSTaskDel((OS_TCB *)0, &err) then μC/OS-III will call OSTaskReturnHook() which in turns calls App_OS_TaskReturnHook() through OS_AppTaskReturnHookPtr. When called, the application hook is passed the address of the OS_TCB of the task returning.

```c
void  App_OS_TaskReturnHook (OS_TCB  *p_tcb)            /* OS_APP_HOOKS.C       */
{
    /* Your code goes here! */
}


void App_OS_SetAllHooks (void)                          /* OS_APP_HOOKS.C       */
{
    CPU_SR_ALLOC();

    CPU_CRITICAL_ENTER();
    :
    OS_AppTaskReturnHookPtr = App_OS_TaskReturnHook;
    :
    CPU_CRITICAL_EXIT();
}


void  OSTaskReturnHook (OS_TCB *p_tcb)                  /* OS_CPU_C.C           */
{
#if OS_CFG_APP_HOOKS_EN > 0u
    if (OS_AppTaskReturnHookPtr != (OS_APP_HOOK_TCB)0) {   /* Call application hook */
        (*OS_AppTaskReturnHookPtr)(p_tcb);
    }
#endif
}
```

OSTaskResume()

```
void  OSTaskResume (OS_TCB  *p_tcb,
                    OS_ERR  *p_err)
```

File	Called from	Code enabled by
OS_TASK.C	Task	OS_CFG_TASK_SUSPEND_EN

OSTaskResume() resumes a task suspended through the OSTaskSuspend() function. In fact, OSTaskResume() is the only function that can unsuspend a suspended task. Obviously, the suspended task can only be resumed by another task. If the suspended task is also waiting on another kernel object such as an event flag, semaphore, mutex, message queue etc., the suspension will simply be lifted (i.e., removed), but the task will continue waiting for the object.

The user can "nest" suspension of a task by calling OSTaskSuspend() and therefore must call OSTaskResume() an equivalent number of times to resume such a task. In other words, if suspending a task five times, it is necessary to unsuspend the same task five times to remove the suspension of the task.

Arguments

p_tcb   is a pointer to the TCB of the task that is resuming. A NULL pointer is not a valid value as one cannot resume the calling task because, by definition, the calling task is running and is not suspended.

p_err   is a pointer to a variable that will contain an error code returned by this function.

OS_ERR_NONE	if the call was successful and the desired task is resumed.
OS_ERR_TASK_RESUME_ISR	if calling this function from an ISR.
OS_ERR_TASK_RESUME_SELF	if passing a NULL pointer for p_tcb. It is not possible to resume the calling task since, if suspended, it cannot be executing.
OS_ERR_TASK_NOT_SUSPENDED	if the task attempting to be resumed is not suspended.

Returned Value

None

Notes/Warnings

None

Example

```
OS_TCB   TaskY;


void TaskX (void *p_arg)
{
    OS_ERR err;


    while (DEF_ON) {
        :
        :
        OSTaskResume(&TaskY,
                     &err);      /* Resume suspended task    */
        /* Check "err" */
        :
        :
    }
}
```

OSTaskSemPend()

```
OS_SEM_CTR  OSTaskSemPend (OS_TICK   timeout,
                           OS_OPT    opt,
                           CPU_TS   *p_ts,
                           OS_ERR   *p_err)
```

File	Called from	Code enabled by
OS_TASK.C	Task	Always enabled

OSTaskSemPend() allows a task to wait for a signal to be sent by another task or ISR without going through an intermediate object such as a semaphore. If the task was previously signaled when OSTaskSemPend() is called then, the caller resumes.

If no signal was received by the task and OS_OPT_PEND_BLOCKING is specified for the opt argument, OSTaskSemPend() suspends the current task (assuming the scheduler is not locked) until either a signal is received, or a user-specified timeout expires. A pended task suspended with OSTaskSuspend() can receive signals. However, the task remains suspended until it is resumed by calling OSTaskResume().

If no signals were sent to the task and OS_OPT_PEND_NON_BLOCKING was specified for the opt argument, OSTaskSemPend() returns to the caller with an appropriate error code and returns a signal count of 0.

Arguments

timeout   allows the task to resume execution if a signal is not received from a task or an ISR within the specified number of clock ticks. A timeout value of 0 indicates that the task wants to wait forever for a signal. The timeout value is not synchronized with the clock tick. The timeout count starts decrementing on the next clock tick, which could potentially occur immediately.

opt   determines whether the user wants to block or not, if a signal was not sent to the task. Set this argument to either:

     OS_OPT_PEND_BLOCKING, or

     OS_OPT_PEND_NON_BLOCKING

Note that the timeout argument should be set to 0 when specifying OS_OPT_PEND_NON_BLOCKING, since the timeout value is irrelevant using this option.

p_ts   is a pointer to a timestamp indicating when the task's semaphore was posted, or the pend was aborted. If passing a NULL pointer (i.e., (CPU_TS *)0) the timestamp will not be returned. In other words, passing a NULL pointer is valid and indicates that the timestamp is not necessary.

A timestamp is useful when the task is to know when the semaphore was posted, or how long it took for the task to resume after the semaphore was posted. In the latter case, call OS_TS_GET() and compute the difference between the current value of the timestamp and *p_ts. In other words:

delta = OS_TS_GET() - *p_ts;

p_err   is a pointer to a variable used to hold an error code.

OS_ERR_NONE	if a signal is received.
OS_ERR_PEND_ABORT	if the pend was aborted because another task called OSTaskSemPendAbort().
OS_ERR_PEND_ISR	if calling this function from an ISR.
OS_ERR_PEND_WOULD_BLOCK	if calling this function with the opt argument set to OS_OPT_PEND_NON_BLOCKING, and no signal was received.
OS_ERR_SCHED_LOCKED	if calling this function when the scheduler is locked and the user wanted the task to block.
OS_ERR_TIMEOUT	if a signal is not received within the specified timeout.

Returned Value

The current value of the signal counter after it has been decremented. In other words, the number of signals still remaining in the signal counter.

Notes/Warnings

Do not call OSTaskSemPend() from an ISR.

Example

```
void CommTask(void *p_arg)
{
    OS_ERR      err;
    OS_SEM_CTR  ctr;
    CPU_TS      ts;


    (void)&p_arg;
    while (DEF_ON) {
        :
        ctr = OSTaskSemPend(100,
                            OS_OPT_PEND_BLOCKING,
                            &ts,
                            &err);
        /* Check "err" */
        :
    }
}
```

OSTaskSemPendAbort()

```
CPU_BOOLEAN  OSTaskSemPendAbort (OS_TCB  *p_tcb,
                                 OS_OPT   opt,
                                 OS_ERR  *p_err)
```

File	Called from	Code enabled by
OS_TASK.C	Task	OS_CFG_TASK_SEM_PEND_ABORT_EN

OSTaskSemPendAbort() aborts and readies a task currently waiting on its built-in semaphore. This function should be used to fault-abort the wait on the task's semaphore, rather than to normally signal the task via OSTaskSemPost().

Arguments

p_tcb   is a pointer to the task for which the pend must be aborted. Note that it does not make sense to pass a **NULL** pointer or the address of the calling task's TCB since, by definition, the calling task cannot be pending.

opt   provides options for this function.

OS_OPT_POST_NONE	no option specified, call the scheduler by default.
OS_OPT_POST_NO_SCHED	specifies that the scheduler should not be called even if the pend of a higher-priority task has been aborted. Scheduling will need to occur from another function. Use this option if the task calling OSTaskSemPendAbort() will be doing additional pend aborts, rescheduling will not take place until finished, and multiple pend aborts are to take effect simultaneously.

p_err   is a pointer to a variable that holds an error code:

OS_ERR_NONE	the pend was aborted for the specified task.
OS_ERR_PEND_ABORT_ISR	if called from an ISR
OS_ERR_PEND_ABORT_NONE	if the task was not waiting for a signal.
OS_ERR_PEND_ABORT_SELF	if p_tcb is a **NULL** pointer or the TCB of the calling task is specified. The user is attempting to pend abort the calling task, which makes no sense since, by definition, the calling task is not pending.

Returned Value

OSTaskSemPendAbort() returns DEF_TRUE if the task was made ready to run by this function. DEF_FALSE indicates that the task was not pending, or an error occurred.

Notes/Warnings

None

Example

```
OS_TCB   CommRxTaskTCB;


void CommTask (void *p_arg)
{
    OS_ERR      err;
    CPU_BOOLEAN aborted;


    (void)&p_arg;
    while (DEF_ON) {
        :
        :
        aborted = OSTaskSemPendAbort(&CommRxTaskTCB,
                                     OS_OPT_POST_NONE,
                                     &err);
        /* Check "err" */
        :
        :
    }
}
```

OSTaskSemPost()

```
OS_SEM_CTR   OSTaskSemPost (OS_TCB    *p_tcb,
                            OS_OPT     opt,
                            OS_ERR    *p_err)
```

File	Called from	Code enabled by
OS_TASK.C	Task or ISR	Always enabled

OSTaskSemPost() sends a signal to a task through it's local semaphore.

If the task receiving the signal is actually waiting for a signal to be received, it will be made ready to run and, if the receiving task has a higher priority than the task sending the signal, the higher-priority task resumes, and the task sending the signal is suspended; that is, a context switch occurs. Note that scheduling only occurs if opt is set to **OS_OPT_POST_NONE**, because the **OS_OPT_POST_NO_SCHED** option does not cause the scheduler to be called.

Arguments

p_tcb   is a pointer to the TCB of the task being signaled. A **NULL** pointer indicates that the user is sending a signal to itself.

opt   provides options to the call.

OS_OPT_POST_NONE	No option, by default the scheduler will be called.
OS_OPT_POST_NO_SCHED	Do not call the scheduler after the post, therefore the caller is resumed. Use this option if the task (or ISR) calling OSTaskSemPost() will be doing additional posts, reschedule waits until all is done, and multiple posts are to take effect simultaneously.

p_err   is a pointer to a variable that will contain an error code returned by this function.

OS_ERR_NONE	if the call was successful and the signal was sent.

OS_ERR_SEM_OVF   the post would have caused the semaphore
                          counter to overflow.

Returned Value

The current value of the task's signal counter, or 0 if called from an ISR and
OS_CFG_ISR_POST_DEFERRED_EN is set to 1.

Notes/Warnings

None

Example

```
OS_TCB          CommRxTaskTCB;


void CommTaskRx (void *p_arg)
{
    OS_ERR      err;
    OS_SEM_CTR  ctr;


    (void)&p_arg;
    while (DEF_ON) {
        :
        ctr = OSTaskSemPost(&CommRxTaskTCB,
                            OS_OPT_POST_NONE,
                            &err);
        /* Check "err" */
        :
    }
}
```

OSTaskSemSet()

```
OS_SEM_CTR  OSTaskSemSet (OS_TCB     *p_tcb,
                          OS_SEM_CTR  cnt;
                          OS_ERR     *p_err)
```

File	Called from	Code enabled by
OS_TASK.C	Task or ISR	Always Enabled

OSTaskSemSet() allows the user to set the value of the task's signal counter. Set the signal counter of the calling task by passing a **NULL** pointer for p_tcb.

Arguments

p_tcb   is a pointer to the task's **OS_TCB** to clear the signal counter. A **NULL** pointer indicates that the user wants to clear the caller's signal counter.

cnt   the desired value for the task semaphore counter.

p_err   is a pointer to a variable that will contain an error code·returned by this function.

OS_ERR_NONE	if the call was successful and the signal counter was cleared.
OS_ERR_SET_ISR	if calling this function from an ISR

Returned Value

The value of the signal counter prior to setting it.

Notes/Warnings

None

Example

```
OS_TCB   TaskY;


void TaskX (void *p_arg)
{
    OS_ERR err;


    while (DEF_ON) {
        :
        :
        OSTaskSemSet(&TaskY,
                     0,
                     &err);
        /* Check "err" */
        :
        :
    }
}
```

OSTaskStatHook()

void OSTaskStatHook (void);

File	Called from	Code enabled by
OS_CPU_C.C	OS_TaskStat() ONLY	OS_CFG_TASK_STAT_EN

This function is called by **OS_TaskStat()**.

OSTaskStatHook() is part of the CPU port code and *must not* be called by the application code. **OSTaskStatHook()** is actually used by the µC/OS-III port developer.

Arguments

None

Returned Value

None

Notes/Warnings

Do not call this function from the application.

Example

The code below calls an application-specific hook that the application programmer can define. The user can simply set the value of **OS_AppStatTaskHookPtr** to point to the desired hook function as shown in the example. The statistic task calls **OSStatTaskHook()** which in turns calls **App_OS_StatTaskHook()** through **OS_AppStatTaskHookPtr**.

```
void  App_OS_StatTaskHook (void)                         /* OS_APP_HOOKS.C        */
{
    /* Your code goes here! */
}


void App_OS_SetAllHooks (void)                           /* OS_APP_HOOKS.C        */
{
    CPU_SR_ALLOC();

    CPU_CRITICAL_ENTER();
    :
    OS_AppStatTaskHookPtr = App_OS_StatTaskHook;
    :
    CPU_CRITICAL_EXIT();
}


void  OSStatTaskHook (void)                              /* OS_CPU_C.C            */
{
#if OS_CFG_APP_HOOKS_EN > 0u
    if (OS_AppStatTaskHookPtr != (OS_APP_HOOK_VOID)0) {   /* Call application hook */
        (*OS_AppStatTaskHookPtr)();
    }
#endif
}
```

OSTaskStkChk()

```
void  OSTaskStkChk (OS_TCB        *p_tcb,
                    CPU_STK_SIZE  *p_free,
                    CPU_STK_SIZE  *p_used,
                    OS_ERR        *p_err)
```

File	Called from	Code enabled by
OS_TASK.C	Task	OS_CFG_TASK_STAT_CHK_EN

OSTaskStkChk() determines a task's stack statistics. Specifically, it computes the amount of free stack space, as well as the amount of stack space used by the specified task. This function requires that the task be created with the OS_TASK_OPT_STK_CHK and OS_TASK_OPT_STK_CLR options.

Stack sizing is accomplished by walking from the bottom of the stack and counting the number of 0 entries on the stack until a non-zero value is found. It is possible to not set the OS_TASK_OPT_STK_CLR when creating the task if the startup code clears all RAM, and tasks are not deleted (this reduces the execution time of OSTaskCreate()).

µC/OS-III's statistic task calls OSTaskStkChk() for each task created and stores the results in each task's OS_TCB so your application doesn't need to call this function if the statistic task is enabled.

Arguments

p_tcb   is a pointer to the TCB of the task where the stack is being checked. A NULL pointer indicates that the user is checking the calling task's stack.

p_free   is a pointer to a variable of type CPU_STK_SIZE and will contain the number of free "bytes" on the stack of the task being inquired about.

p_used   is a pointer to a variable of type CPU_STK_SIZE and will contain the number of used "bytes" on the stack of the task being inquired about.

p_err   is a pointer to a variable that will contain an error code returned by this function.

OS_ERR_NONE	if the call was successful.
OS_ERR_PTR_INVALID	if either p_free or p_used are **NULL** pointers.
OS_ERR_TASK_NOT_EXIST	if the stack pointer of the task is a **NULL** pointer.
OS_ERR_TASK_OPT	if **OS_OPT_TASK_STK_CHK** is not specififed whencreating the task being checked.
OS_ERR_TASK_STK_CHK_ISR	if calling this function from an ISR.

Returned Value

None

Notes/Warnings

1. Execution time of this task depends on the size of the task's stack.

2. The application can determine the total task stack space (in number of bytes) by adding the value of *p_free and *p_used.

3. The **#define CPU_CFG_STK_GROWTH** must be declared (typically from **OS_CPU.H**). When this **#define** is set to **CPU_STK_GROWTH_LO_TO_HI**, the stack grows from low memory to high memory. When this **#define** is set to **CPU_STK_GROWTH_HI_TO_LO**, the stack grows from high memory to low memory.

Example

```
OS_TCB  MyTaskTCB;


void Task (void *p_arg)
{
    OS_ERR      err;
    CPU_STK_SIZE  n_free;
    CPU_STK_SIZE  n_used;


    (void)&p_arg;
    while (DEF_ON) {
        :
        :
        OSTaskStkChk(&MyTaskTCB,
                    &n_free,
                    &n_used,
                    &err);
        /* Check "err" */
        :
        :
    }
}
```

OSTaskStkInit()

```
void OSTaskStkInit (OS_TASK_PTR    p_task,
                    void           *p_arg,
                    CPU_STK        *p_stk_base,
                    CPU_STK        *p_stk_limit,
                    CPU_STK_SIZE   stk_size,
                    OS_OPT         opt);
```

File	Called from	Code enabled by
OS_CPU_C.C	OSTaskCreate() ONLY	N/A

This function is called by **OSTaskCreate()** to setup the stack frame of the task being created. Typically, the stack frame will look as if an interrupt just occurred, and all CPU registers were pushed onto the task's stack. The stacking order of CPU registers is very CPU specific.

OSTaskStkInit() is part of the CPU port code and this function *must not* be called by the application code. **OSTaskStkInit()** is actually defined by the µC/OS-III port developer.

Arguments

p_task   is the address of the task being created (see MyTask below). Tasks must be declared as follows:

```
void   MyTask (void *p_arg)
{
    /* Do something with "p_arg" (optional) */
    while (DEF_ON) {
        /* Wait for an event to occur */
        /* Do some work            */
    }
}
```

Or,

```
void    MyTask (void  *p_arg)
{
    OS_ERR  err;


    /* Do something with "p_arg" (optional) */
    /* Do some work                         */
    OSTaskDel((OS_TCB *)0,
             &err);
}
```

p_arg   is the argument that the task will receive when the task first start (see code above).

p_stk_base   is the base address of the task's stack. This is typically the lowest address of the area of storage reserved for the task stack. In other words, if declaring the task's stack as follows:

```
CPU_STK  MyTaskStk[100];
```

OSTaskCreate() would pass &OSMyTaskStk[0] to p_stk_base.

p_stk_limit   is the address of the task's stack limit watermark. This pointer is the same pointer passed to OSTaskCreate().

stk_size   is the size of the task's stack in number of CPU_STK elements. In the example above, the stack size is 100.

opt   is the options pass to OSTaskCreate() for the task being created.

Returned Value

The new top of stack after the task's stack is initialized. OSTaskStkInit() will place values on the task's stack and will return the new pointer of the stack pointer for the task. The value returned is very processor specific. For some processors, the returned value will point to the last value placed on the stack while, with other processors, the returned value will point at the next free stack entry.

Notes/Warnings

Do not call this function from the application.

Example

The pseudo code below shows the typical steps performed by this function. Consult an existing µC/OS-III port for examples. Here it is assumed that the stack grows from high memory to low memory.

```
CPU_STK  *OSTaskStkInit (OS_TASK_PTR   p_task,
                         void          *p_arg,
                         CPU_STK       *p_stk_base,
                         CPU_STK       *p_stk_limit,
                         CPU_STK_SIZE  stk_size,
                         OS_OPT        opt)
{
    CPU_STK  *p_stk;


    p_stk    = &p_stk_base[stk_size – 1u];                    (1)
    *p_stk-- = Initialize the stack as if an interrupt just occurred; (2)
    return (p_stk);                                           (3)
}
```

(1)   'p_stk" is set to the top-of-stack. It is assumed that the stack grows from high memory locations to lower ones. If the stack of the CPU grew from low memory locations to higher ones, the user would simply set "p_stk" to point at the base. However, this also means that it would be necessary to initialize the stack frame in the opposite direction.

(2)   Store the CPU registers onto the stack using the same stacking order as used when an interrupt service routine (ISR) saves the registers at the beginning of the ISR. The value of the register contents on the stack is typically not important. However, there are some values that are critical. Specifically, place the address of the task in the proper location on the stack frame and it may be important to load the value of the CPU register and possibly pass the value of "p_arg" in one of the CPU registers. Finally, if the task is to return by mistake, it is a good idea to place the address of "OS_TaskReturn()" in the proper location on the stack frame. This ensures that a faulty returning task is intercepted by µC/OS-III.

(3)   Finally, return the value of the stack pointer at the new top-of-stack frame. Some processors point to the last stored location, while others point to the next empty location. Consult the processor documentation so that the return value points at the proper location.

Below is a complete example showing **OSTaskCreate()** which calls **OSTaskStkInit()** with the proper arguments.

```
CPU_STK  MyTaskStk[100];
OS_TCB   MyTaskTCB;


void  MyTask (void *p_arg)
{
    /* Do something with "parg" (optional) */
}


void  main (void)
{
    OS_ERR  err;
    :
    :
    OSInit(&err);
    /* Check "err" */
    :
    OSTaskCreate ((OS_TCB        *)&MyTaskTCB,
                  (CPU_CHAR      *)"My Task",
                  (OS_TASK_PTR   )MyTask,            /* "p_task"     of OSTaskStkInit() */
                  (void          *)0,                /* "p_arg"      of OSTaskStkInit() */
                  (OS_PRIO       )prio,
                  (CPU_STK       *)&MyTaskStk[0],    /* "p_stk_base" of OSTaskStkInit() */
                  (CPU_STK_SIZE  )10,                /* "p_stk_limit" of OSTaskStkInit() */
                  (CPU_STK_SIZE  )100,               /* "stk_size"   of OSTaskStkInit() */
                  (OS_MSG_QTY    )0,
                  (OS_TICK       )0,
                  (void          *)0,
                  (OS_OPT        )(OS_OPT_TASK_STK_CLR + OS_OPT_TASK_STK_CHK),  /* "opt" */
                  (OS_ERR        *)&err);
    /* Check "err" */
    :
    :
    OSStart(&err);
    /* Check "err" */
}
```

OSTaskSuspend()

```
void    OSTaskSuspend (OS_TCB  *p_tcb,
                       OS_ERR  *p_err)
```

File	Called from	Code enabled by
OS_TASK.C	Task	OS_CFG_TASK_SUSPEND_EN

OSTaskSuspend() suspends (or blocks) execution of a task unconditionally. The calling task may be suspended by specifying a **NULL** pointer for p_tcb, or simply by passing the address of its **OS_TCB**. In this case, another task needs to resume the suspended task. If the current task is suspended, rescheduling occurs, and µC/OS-III runs the next highest priority task ready to run. The only way to resume a suspended task is to call **OSTaskResume()**.

Task suspension is additive, which means that if the task being suspended is delayed until n ticks expire, the task is resumed only when both the time expires and the suspension is removed. Also, if the suspended task is waiting for a semaphore and the semaphore is signaled, the task is removed from the semaphore wait list (if it is the highest-priority task waiting for the semaphore), but execution is not resumed until the suspension is removed.

The user can "nest" suspension of a task by calling **OSTaskSuspend()** and therefore it is important to call **OSTaskResume()** an equivalent number of times to resume the task. If suspending a task five times, it is necessary to unsuspend the same task five times to remove the suspension of the task.

Arguments

p_tcb   is a pointer to the TCB of the task the user is suspending. A **NULL** pointer indicates suspension of the calling task.

p_err   is a pointer to a variable that will contain an error code returned by this function.

OS_ERR_NONE	if the call was successful and the desired task was suspended.
OS_ERR_TASK_SUSPEND_ISR	if the function is called from an ISR.

OS_ERR_TASK_SUSPEND_IDLE   if attempting to suspend the idle task. This is not allowed since the idle task must always exist.

OS_ERR_TASK_SUSPEND_INT_HANDLER if attempting to suspend the ISR handler task. This is not allowed since the ISR handler task is a µC/OS-III internal task.

Returned Value

None

Notes/Warnings

1. OSTaskSuspend() and OSTaskResume() must be used in pairs.

2. A suspended task can only be resumed by OSTaskResume().

Example

```
void TaskX (void *p_arg)
{
    OS_ERR   err;

    (void)&p_arg;
    while (DEF_ON) {
        :
        :
        OSTaskSuspend((OS_TCB *)0,
                       &err);        /* Suspend current task          */
        /* Check "err" */
        :
    }
}
```

OSTaskSwHook()

```
void  OSTaskSwHook (void)
```

File	Called from	Code enabled by
OS_CPU_C.C	OSCtxSw() or OSIntCtxSw()	N/A

OSTaskSwHook() is always called by either OSCtxSw() or OSIntCtxSw() (see OS_CPU_A.ASM), just after saving the CPU registers onto the task being switched out. This hook function allows the port developer to perform additional operations (if needed) when µC/OS-III performs a context switch.

Before calling OSTaskSwHook(), OSTCBCurPtr is set to point at the OS_TCB of the task being switched out, and OSTCBHighRdyPtr points at the OS_TCB of the new task being switched in.

The code shown in the example below should be included in all implementations of OSTaskSwHook(), and is used for performance measurements. This code is written in C for portability.

Arguments

None

Returned Values

None

Notes/Warnings

None

Example

The code below calls an application specific hook that the application programmer can define. The user can simply set the value of OS_AppTaskSwHookPtr to point to the desired hook function. When µC/OS-III performs a context switch, it calls OSTaskSwitchHook() which in turn calls App_OS_TaskSwHook() through OS_AppTaskSwHookPtr.

```
void  App_OS_TaskSwHook (void)                      /* OS_APP_HOOKS.C      */
{
    /* Your code goes here! */
}


void App_OS_SetAllHooks (void)                      /* OS_APP_HOOKS.C      */
{
    CPU_SR_ALLOC();

    CPU_CRITICAL_ENTER();
    :
    OS_AppTaskSwHookPtr = App_OS_TaskSwHook;
    :
    CPU_CRITICAL_EXIT();
}
```

```
void  OSTaskSwHook (void)                              /* OS_CPU_C.C            */
{
#if OS_CFG_TASK_PROFILE_EN > 0u
    CPU_TS     ts;
#endif
#ifdef  CPU_CFG_TIME_MEAS_INT_DIS_EN
    CPU_TS     int_dis_time;
#endif


#if OS_CFG_APP_HOOKS_EN > 0u
    if (OS_AppTaskSwHookPtr != (OS_APP_HOOK_VOID)0) {
        (*OS_AppTaskSwHookPtr)();
    }
#endif
#if OS_CFG_TASK_PROFILE_EN > 0u
    ts = OS_TS_GET();
    if (OSTCBCurPtr != OSTCBHighRdyPtr) {
        OSTCBCurPtr->CyclesDelta = ts - OSTCBCurPtr->CyclesStart;
        OSTCBCurPtr->CyclesTotal = OSTCBCurPtr->CyclesTotal + OSTCBCurPtr->CyclesDelta;
    }
    OSTCBHighRdyPtr->CyclesStart = ts;
#ifdef  CPU_CFG_INT_DIS_MEAS_EN
    int_dis_time = CPU_IntDisMeasMaxCurReset();
    if (int_dis_time > OSTCBCurPtr->IntDisTimeMax) {
        OSTCBCurPtr->IntDisTimeMax = int_dis_time;
    }
#endif
#if OS_CFG_SCHED_LOCK_TIME_MEAS_EN > 0u
    if (OSSchedLockTimeMaxCur > OSTCBCurPtr->SchedLockTimeMax) {
        OSTCBCurPtr->SchedLockTimeMax = OSSchedLockTimeMaxCur;
        OSSchedLockTimeMaxCur         = (CPU_TS)0;
    }
#endif
#endif
}
```

OSTaskTimeQuantaSet()

```
void    OSTaskTimeQuantaSet (OS_TCB   *p_tcb,
                             OS_TICK  time_quanta,
                             OS_ERR   *p_err)
```

File	Called from	Code enabled by
OS_TASK.C	Task only	OS_CFG_SCHED_ROUND_ROBIN_EN

OSTaskTimeQuantaSet() is used to change the amount of time a task is given when time slicing multiple tasks running at the same priority.

Arguments

p_tcb   is a pointer to the TCB of the task for which the time quanta is being set. A **NULL** pointer indicates that the user is changing the time quanta for the calling task.

time_quanta   specifies the amount of time (in ticks) that the task will run when µC/OS-III is time slicing between tasks at the same priority. Specifying 0 indicates that the default time as specified will be used when calling the function OSSchedRoundRobinCfg(), or OS_CFG_TICK_RATE_HZ / 10 if you never called OSSchedRoundRobinCfg().

Do not specify a "large" value for this argument as this means that the task will execute for that amount of time when multiple tasks are ready to run at the same priority. The concept of time slicing is to allow other equal-priority tasks a chance to run. Typical time quanta periods should be approximately 10 mS. A too small value results in more overhead because of the additional context switches.

p_err   is a pointer to a variable that will contain an error code returned
                       by this function.

     OS_ERR_NONE   if the call was successful and the time quanta
                                    for the task was changed.
     OS_ERR_SET_ISR   if calling this function from an ISR.

Returned Value

None

Notes/Warnings

Do not specify a large value for time_quanta.

Example

```
void TaskX (void *p_arg)
{
    OS_ERR  err;


    while (DEF_ON) {
        :
        :
        OSTaskTimeQuantaSet((OS_TCB *)0,
                            OS_CFG_TICK_RATE_HZ / 4;
                            &err);
        /* Check "err" */
        :
    }
}
```

OSTickISR()

void OSTickISR (void)

File	Called from	Code enabled by
OS_CPU_A.ASM	Tick interrupt	N/A

OSTickISR() is invoked by the tick interrupt, and the function is generally written in assembly language. However, this depends on how interrupts are handled by the processor. (see Chapter 9, "Interrupt Management" on page 163).

Arguments

None

Returned Values

None

Notes/Warnings

None

Example

The code below indicates how to write OSTickISR() if all interrupts vector to a common location, and the interrupt handler simply calls OSTickISR(). As indicated, this code can be written completely in C and can be placed either in OS_CPU_C.C of the μC/OS-III port, or in the board support package (BSP.C) and be reused by applications using the same BSP.

```
void  OSTickISR (void)
{
    Clear the tick interrupt;
    OSTimeTick();
}
```

The pseudo code below shows how to write OSTickISR() if each interrupt directly vectors to its own interrupt handler. The code, in this case, would be written in assembly language and placed either in OS_CPU_A.ASM of the μC/OS-III port, or in the board support package (BSP.C).

```
void OSTickISR (void)
{
    Save all the CPU registers onto the current task's stack;
    if (OSIntNestingCtr == 0) {
        OSTCBCurPtr->StkPtr = SP;
    }
    OSIntNestingCtr++;
    Clear the tick interrupt;
    OSTimeTick();
    OSIntExit();
    Restore the CPU registers from the stack;
    Return from interrupt;
}
```

OSTimeDly()

```
void OSTimeDly (OS_TICK   dly,
                OS_OPT    opt,
                OS_ERR    *p_err)
```

File	Called from	Code enabled by
OS_TIME.C	Task only	N/A

OSTimeDly() allows a task to delay itself for an integral number of clock ticks. The delay can either be relative (delay from current time), periodic (delay occurs at fixed intervals) or absolute (delay until we reach some time).

In relative mode, rescheduling always occurs when the number of clock ticks is greater than zero. A delay of 0 means that the task is not delayed, and OSTimeDly() returns immediately to the caller.

In periodic mode, you must specify a non-zero period otherwise the function returns immediately with an appropriate error code. The period is specified in "ticks".

In absolute mode, rescheduling always occurs since all delay values are valid.

The actual delay time depends on the tick rate (see OS_CFG_TICK_RATE_HZ).

Arguments

dly   is the desired delay expressed in number of clock ticks. Depending on the value of the **opt** field, delays can be relative or absolute.

A relative delay means that the delay is started from the "**current time + dly**".

A periodic delay means the period (in number of ticks).

An absolute delay means that the task will wake up when OSTaskTickCtr reaches the value specified by **dly**.

opt   is used to indicate whether the delay is absolute or relative:

OS_OPT_TIME_DLY	Specifies a relative delay.
OS_OPT_TIME_PERIODIC	Specifies periodic mode.
OS_OPT_TIME_MATCH	Specifies that the task will wake up when **OSTaskTickCtr** reaches the value specified by **dly**

p_err   is a pointer to a variable that will contain an error code returned by this function.

OS_ERR_NONE	if the call was successful, and the task has returned from the desired delay.
OS_ERR_OPT_INVALID	if a valid option is not specified.
OS_ERR_TIME_DLY_ISR	if calling this function from an ISR.
OS_ERR_TIME_ZERO_DLY	if specifying a delay of 0 when the option was set to **OS_OPT_TIME_DLY**. Note that a value of 0 is valid when setting the option to **OS_OPT_TIME_MATCH**.

Returned Value

None

Notes/Warnings

None

Example

```
void TaskX (void *p_arg)
{
  OS_ERR  err;


  while (DEF_ON) {
    :
    :
    OSTimeDly(10,
              OS_OPT_TIME_PERIODIC,
              &err);
    /* Check "err" */
    :
    :
  }
}
```

OSTimeDlyHMSM()

```
void   OSTimeDlyHMSM (CPU_INT16U  hours,
                      CPU_INT16U  minutes,
                      CPU_INT16U  seconds,
                      CPU_INT32U  milli,
                      OS_OPT      opt,
                      OS_ERR      *p_err)
```

File	Called from	Code enabled by
OS_TIME.C	Task only	OS_CFG_TIME_DLY_HMSM_EN

OSTimeDlyHMSM() allows a task to delay itself for a user-specified period that is specified in hours, minutes, seconds, and milliseconds. This format is more convenient and natural than simply specifying ticks as is true in the case of OSTimeDly(). Rescheduling always occurs when at least one of the parameters is non-zero. The delay is relative from the time this function is called.

µC/OS-III allows the user to specify nearly any value when indicating that this function is not to be strict about the values being passed (opt == OS_OPT_TIME_HMSM_NON_STRICT). This is a useful feature, for example, to delay a task for thousands of milliseconds.

Arguments

hours   is the number of hours the task is delayed. Depending on the **opt** value, the valid range is 0..99 (OS_OPT_TIME_HMSM_STRICT), or 0..999 (OS_OPT_TIME_HMSM_NON_STRICT). Please note that it *not* recommended to delay a task for many hours because feedback from the task will not be available for such a long period of time.

minutes   is the number of minutes the task is delayed. The valid range of values is 0 to 59 (OS_OPT_TIME_HMSM_STRICT), or 0..9,999 (OS_OPT_TIME_HMSM_NON_STRICT). Please note that it *not* recommended to delay a task for tens to hundreds of minutes because feedback from the task will not be available for such a long period of time.

seconds   is the number of seconds the task is delayed. The valid range of values is 0 to 59 (OS_OPT_TIME_HMSM_STRICT), or 0..65,535 (OS_OPT_TIME_HMSM_NON_STRICT).

milli is the number of milliseconds the task is delayed. The valid range of values is 0 to 999 (`OS_OPT_TIME_HMSM_STRICT`), or 0..4,294,967,295 (`OS_OPT_TIME_HMSM_NON_STRICT`). Note that the resolution of this argument is in multiples of the tick rate. For instance, if the tick rate is set to 100Hz, a delay of 4 ms results in no delay. Also, the delay is rounded to the nearest tick. Thus, a delay of 15 ms actually results in a delay of 20 ms.

opt is the desired mode and can be either:

    `OS_OPT_TIME_HMSM_STRICT` (see above)
    `OS_OPT_TIME_HMSM_NON_STRICT`(see above)

p_err is a pointer to a variable that contains an error code returned by this function.

`OS_ERR_NONE`	if the call was successful and the task has returned from the desired delay.
`OS_ERR_TIME_DLY_ISR`	if calling this function from an ISR.
`OS_ERR_TIME_INVALID_HOURS`	if not specifying a valid value for hours.
`OS_ERR_TIME_INVALID_MINUTES`	if not specifying a valid value for minutes.
`OS_ERR_TIME_INVALID_SECONDS`	if not specifying a valid value for seconds.
`OS_ERR_TIME_INVALID_MILLISECONDS`	if not specifying a valid value for milliseconds.
`OS_ERR_TIME_ZERO_DLY`	if specifying a delay of 0 because all the time arguments are 0.

Returned Value

None

Notes/Warnings

1. Note that `OSTimeDlyHMSM(0,0,0,0,OS_OPT_TIME_HMSM_???,&err)` (i.e., hours, minutes, seconds, milliseconds are 0) results in no delay, and the function returns to the caller.

2. The total delay (in ticks) must not exceed the maximum acceptable value that an `OS_TICK` variable can hold. Typically `OS_TICK` is a 32-bit value.

Example

```
void TaskX (void *p_arg)
{
    OS_ERR  err;


    while (DEF_ON) {
        :
        :
        OSTimeDlyHMSM(0,
                      0,
                      1,
                      0,
                      OS_OPT_TIME_HMSM_STRICT,
                      &err);                  /* Delay task for 1 second */
        /* Check "err" */
        :
        :
    }
}
```

OSTimeDlyResume()

```
void  OSTimeDlyResume (OS_TCB  *p_tcb,
                       OS_ERR  *p_err)
```

File	Called from	Code enabled by
OS_TIME.C	Task only	OS_CFG_TIME_DLY_RESUME_EN

OSTimeDlyResume() resumes a task that has been delayed through a call to either OSTimeDly(), or OSTimeDlyHMSM().

Arguments

p_tcb   is a pointer to the TCB of the task that is resuming. A **NULL** pointer is not valid since it would indicate that the user is attempting to resume the current task and that is not possible as the caller cannot possibly be delayed.

p_err   is a pointer to a variable that contains an error code returned by this function.

OS_ERR_NONE	if the call was successful and the task was resumed.
OS_ERR_STATE_INVALID	if the task is in an invalid state.
OS_ERR_TIME_DLY_RESUME_ISR	if calling this function from an ISR.
OS_ERR_TIME_NOT_DLY	if the task was not delayed.
OS_ERR_TASK_SUSPENDED	if the task to resume is suspended and will remain suspended.

Returned Value

None

Notes/Warnings

Do not call this function to resume a task that is waiting for an event with timeout.

Example

```
OS_TCB   AnotherTaskTCB;


void TaskX (void *p_arg)
{
    OS_ERR   err;


    while (DEF_ON) {
        :
        OSTimeDlyResume(&AnotherTaskTCB,
                        &err);
        /* Check "err" */
        :
    }
}
```

OSTimeGet()

```
OS_TICK  OSTimeGet (OS_ERR  *p_err)
```

File	Called from	Code enabled by
OS_TIME.C	Task + ISR	N/A

OSTimeGet() obtains the current value of the system clock. Specifically, it returns a snapshot of the variable OSTaskTickCtr. The system clock is a counter of type OS_TICK that counts the number of clock ticks since power was applied, or since OSTaskTickCtr was last set by OSTimeSet().

Arguments

p_err   is a pointer to a variable that contains an error code returned by this function.

OS_ERR_NONE   if the call was successful.

Returned Value

The current value of OSTaskTickCtr (in number of ticks).

Notes/Warnings

None

Example

```
void TaskX (void *p_arg)
{
    OS_TICK  clk;
    OS_ERR   err;


    while (DEF_ON) {
        :
        :
        clk = OSTimeGet(&err);  /* Get current value of system clock */
        /* Check "err" */
        :
        :
    }
}
```

OSTimeSet()

```
void  OSTimeSet (OS_TICK  ticks,
                OS_ERR   *p_err)
```

File	Called from	Code enabled by
OS_TIME.C	Task + ISR	N/A

OSTimeSet() sets the system clock. The system clock is a counter, which has a data type of OS_TICK, and it counts the number of clock ticks since power was applied. or since the system clock was last set.

Arguments

ticks   is the desired value for the system clock, in ticks.

p_err   is a pointer to a variable that will contain an error code returned by this function.

       OS_ERR_NONE   if the call was successful.

Returned Value

None

Notes/Warnings

You should be careful when using this function because other tasks may depend on the current value of the tick counter (OSTickCtr). Specifically, a task may delay itself (see OSTimeDly() and specify to wake up when OSTickCtr reaches a specific value.

Example

```
void TaskX (void *p_arg)
{
    OS_ERR   err;


    while (DEF_ON) {
        :
        :
        OSTimeSet(0,
                  &err);          /* Reset the system clock  */
        /* Check "err" */
        :
        :
    }
}
```

OSTimeTick()

void   OSTimeTick (void)

File	Called from	Code enabled by
OS_TIME.C	ISR	N/A

OSTimeTick() "announces" that a tick has just occurred, and that time delays and timeouts need to be updated. This function must be called from the tick ISR.

Arguments

None

Returned Value

None

Notes/Warnings

None

Example

```
void MyTickISR (void)
{
    /* Clear interrupt source */
    OSTimeTick();
    :
    :
}
```

OSTimeTickHook()

```
void  OSTimeTickHook (void);
```

File	Called from	Code enabled by
OS_CPU_C.C	OSTimeTick() ONLY	N/A

This function is called by **OSTimeTick()**, which is assumed to be called from an ISR. **OSTimeTickHook()** is called at the very beginning of **OSTimeTick()** to give priority to user or port-specific code when the tick interrupt occurs.

If the **#define OS_APP_HOOKS_EN** is set to 1 in **OS_CFG.H**, **OSTimeTickHook()** will call **AppTimeTickHook()**.

OSTimeTickHook() is part of the CPU port code and the function *must not* be called by the application code. **OSTimeTickHook()** is actually used by the µC/OS-III port developer.

Arguments

None

Returned Value

None

Notes/Warnings

Do not call this function from the application.

Example

The code below calls an application-specific hook that the application programmer can define. The user can simply set the value of OS_AppTimeTickHookPtr to point to the desired hook function OSTimeTickHook() is called by OSTimeTick() which in turn calls App_OS_TimeTickHook() through the pointer OS_AppTimeTickHookPtr.

```
void  App_OS_TimeTickHook (void)                    /* OS_APP_HOOKS.C        */
{
    /* Your code goes here! */
}


void App_OS_SetAllHooks (void)                      /* OS_APP_HOOKS.C        */
{
    CPU_SR_ALLOC();

    CPU_CRITICAL_ENTER();
    :
    OS_AppTimeTickHookPtr = App_OS_TimeTickHook;
    :
    CPU_CRITICAL_EXIT();
}


void  OSTimeTickHook (void)                         /* OS_CPU_C.C            */
{
#if OS_CFG_APP_HOOKS_EN > 0u
    if (OS_AppTimeTickHookPtr != (OS_APP_HOOK_VOID)0) {   /* Call application hook */
        (*OS_AppTimeTickHookPtr)();
    }
#endif
}
```

OSTmrCreate()

```
void   OSTmrCreate (OS_TMR              *p_tmr,
                    CPU_CHAR            *p_name,
                    OS_TICK              dly,
                    OS_TICK              period,
                    OS_OPT               opt,
                    OS_TMR_CALLBACK_PTR  p_callback,
                    void                *p_callback_arg,
                    OS_ERR              *p_err)
```

File	Called from	Code enabled by
OS_TMR.C	Task Only	OS_CFG_TMR_EN

OSTmrCreate() allows the user to create a software timer. The timer can be configured to run continuously (opt set to **OS_TMR_OPT_PERIODIC**), or only once (opt set to **OS_TMR_OPT_ONE_SHOT**). When the timer counts down to 0 (from the value specified in period), an optional "callback" function can be executed. The callback can be used to signal a task that the timer expired, or perform any other function. However, it is recommended to keep the callback function as short as possible.

The timer is created in the "stop" mode and therefore the user *must* call **OSTmrStart()** to actually start the timer. If configuring the timer for ONE-SHOT mode, and the timer expires, call **OSTmrStart()** to retrigger the timer, or **OSTmrDel()** to delete the timer if it is not necessary to retrigger it, or not use the timer anymore. Note: use the callback function to delete the timer if using the ONE-SHOT mode.

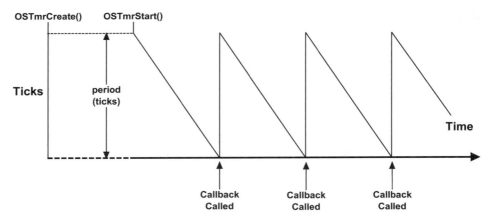

PERIODIC MODE (see "**opt**") – **dly** > 0, **period** > 0

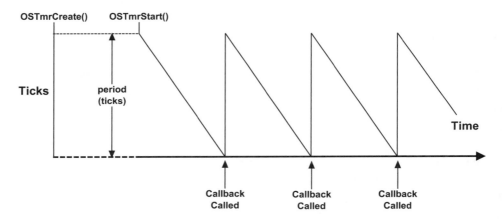

PERIODIC MODE (see "**opt**") – " == 0

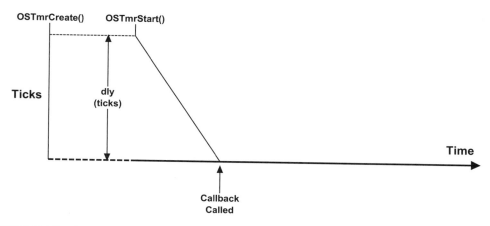

ONE-SHOT MODE (see "opt") – dly > 0, period == 0

Arguments

p_tmr   is a pointer to the timer-control block of the desired timer. It is assumed that storage for the timer will be allocated in the application. In other words, declare a "global" variable as follows, and pass a pointer to this variable to OSTmrCreate():

```
OS_TMR MyTmr;
```

p_name   is a pointer to an ASCII string (NUL terminated) used to assign a name to the timer. The name can be displayed by debuggers or µC/Probe.

dly   specifies the initial delay (specified in timer tick units) used by the timer (see drawing above). If the timer is configured for ONE-SHOT mode, this is the timeout used. If the timer is configured for PERIODIC mode, this is the timeout to wait before the timer enters periodic mode. The units of this time depends on how often the user will call OSTmrSignal() (see OSTimeTick()). If OSTmrSignal() is called every 1/10 of a second (i.e., OS_CFG_TMR_TASK_RATE_HZ set to 10), dly specifies the number of 1/10 of a second before the delay expires. Note that the timer is *not* started when it is created.

period   specifies the period repeated by the timer if configured for PERIODIC mode. Set the "period" to 0 when using ONE-SHOT mode. The units of time depend on how often `OSTmrSignal()` is called. If `OSTmrSignal()` is called every 1/10 of a second (i.e., `OS_CFG_TMR_TASK_RATE_HZ` set to 10), the period specifies the number of 1/10 of a second before the timer times out.

opt   is used to specify whether the timer is to be ONE-SHOT or PERIODIC:

        `OS_OPT_TMR_ONE_SHOT` `ONE-SHOT` mode
        `OS_OPT_TMR_PERIODIC` `PERIODIC` mode

p_callback is a pointer to a function that will execute when the timer expires (ONE-SHOT mode), or every time the period expires (PERIODIC mode). A **NULL** pointer indicates that no action is to be performed upon timer expiration. The callback function must be declared as follows:

        `void MyCallback (OS_TMR *p_tmr, void *p_arg);`

When called, the callback will be passed the pointer to the timer as well as an argument (**p_callback_arg**), which can be used to indicate to the callback what to do. Note that the user is allowed to call all of the timer related functions (i.e., `OSTmrCreate()`, `OSTmrDel()`, `OSTmrStateGet()`, `OSTmrRemainGet()`, `OSTmrStart()`, and `OSTmrStop()`) from the callback function.

Do not make blocking calls within callback functions.

p_callback_arg   is an argument passed to the callback function when the timer expires (ONE-SHOT mode), or every time the period expires (PERIODIC mode). The pointer is declared as a "**void ***" so it can point to any data.

p_err   is a pointer to a variable that contains an error code returned by this function.

`OS_ERR_NONE`	if the call was successful.
`OS_ERR_OBJ_CREATED`	if the timer was already created
`OS_ERR_OBJ_PTR_NULL`	if `p_tmr` is a **NULL** pointer
`OS_ERR_TMR_INVALID_DLY`	if specifying an invalid delay in ONE-SHOT mode. In other words, it is not allowed to delay for 0 in ONE-SHOT mode.

OS_ERR_TMR_INVALID_PERIOD	if specifying an invalid period in PERIODIC mode. It is not allowed to have a 0 period in PERIODIC.
OS_ERR_TMR_INVALID_OPT	if not specifying a valid options.
OS_ERR_TMR_ISR	if calling this function from an ISR.

Returned Values

None.

Notes/Warnings

1. *Do not* call this function from an ISR.

2. The timer is *not* started when it is created. To start the timer, call `OSTmrStart()`.

3. *Do not* make blocking calls within callback functions.

4. Keep callback functions as short as possible.

Example

```
OS_TMR  CloseDoorTmr;


void Task (void *p_arg)
{
    OS_ERR   err;


    (void)&p_arg;
    while (DEF_ON) {
        OSTmrCreate(&CloseDoorTmr,          /* p_tmr            */
                    "Door close",           /* p_name           */
                     10,                    /* dly              */
                     100,                   /* period           */
                     OS_OPT_TMR_PERIODIC,   /* opt              */
                     DoorCloseFnct,         /* p_callback       */
                     0,                     /* p_callback_arg   */
                     &err);                 /* p_err            */
        /* Check "err" */
    }
}


void  DoorCloseFnct (void *p_arg)
{
    /* Close the door! */
}
```

OSTmrDel()

```
CPU_BOOLEAN   OSTmrDel(OS_TMR   *p_tmr,
                       OS_ERR    *p_err)
```

File	Called from	Code enabled by
OS_TMR.C	Task only	OS_CFG_TMR_EN and OS_CFG_TMR_DEL_EN

OSTmrDel() allows the user to delete a timer. If a timer was running it will be stopped, then deleted. If the timer has already timed out and is therefore stopped, it will simply be deleted.

It is up to the user to delete unused timers. If deleting a timer, *Do not* reference it again.

Arguments

p_tmr   is a pointer to the timer to be deleted.

p_err   a pointer to an error code and can be any of the following:

OS_ERR_NONE	if the timer was deleted.
OS_ERR_OBJ_TYPE	if the user did not pass a pointer to a timer.
OS_ERR_TMR_INVALID	if p_tmr is a NULL pointer.
OS_ERR_TMR_ISR	This function is called from an ISR, which is *not* allowed.
OS_ERR_TMR_INACTIVE	p_tmr is pointing to an inactive timer. In other words, this error appears when pointing to a timer that has been deleted or was not created.
OS_ERR_TMR_INVALID_STATE	the timer is in an invalid state.

Returned Values

DEF_TRUE if the timer was deleted, DEF_FALSE if not.

Notes/Warnings

1. Examine the return value to make sure what is received from this function is valid.

2. *Do not* call this function from an ISR.

3. When deleting a timer, *do not* reference it again.

Example

```
OS_TMR  CloseDoorTmr;


void Task (void *p_arg)
{
    OS_ERR      err;
    CPU_BOOLEAN  deleted;


    (void)&p_arg;
    while (DEF_ON) {
        deleted = OSTmrDel(&CloseDoorTmr,
                           &err);
        /* Check "err" */
    }
}
```

OSTmrRemainGet()

```
OS_TICK   OSTmrRemainGet(OS_TMR *p_tmr,
                         OS_ERR *p_err);
```

File	Called from	Code enabled by
OS_TMR.C	Task only	OS_CFG_TMR_EN

OSTmrRemainGet() allows the user to obtain the time remaining (before timeout) of the specified timer. The value returned depends on the rate (in Hz) at which the timer task is signaled (see OS_CFG_TMR_TASK_RATE_HZ). If OS_CFG_TMR_TASK_RATE_HZ is set to 10, the value returned is the number of 1/10 of a second before the timer times out. If the timer has timed out, the value returned is 0.

Arguments

p_tmr   is a pointer to the timer the user is inquiring about.

p_err   a pointer to an error code and can be any of the following:

OS_ERR_NONE	if the function returned the time remaining for the timer.
OS_ERR_OBJ_TYPE	'p_tmr" is not pointing to a timer.
OS_ERR_TMR_INVALID	if p_tmr is a NULL pointer.
OS_ERR_TMR_ISR	This function is called from an ISR, which is *not* allowed.
OS_ERR_TMR_INACTIVE	p_tmr is pointing to an inactive timer. In other words, this error will appear when pointing to a timer that has been deleted or was not created.
OS_ERR_TMR_INVALID_STATE	the timer is in an invalid state.

Returned Values

The time remaining for the timer. The value returned depends on the rate (in Hz) at which the timer task is signaled (see OS_CFG_TMR_TASK_RATE_HZ). If OS_CFG_TMR_TASK_RATE_HZ is set to 10 the value returned is the number of 1/10 of a second before the timer times out. If specifying an invalid timer, the returned value will be 0. If the timer expired, the returned value will be 0.

Notes/Warnings

1. Examine the returned error code to ensure the results from this function are valid.

2. *Do not* call this function from an ISR.

Example

```
OS_TICK    TimeRemainToCloseDoor;
OS_TMR     CloseDoorTmr;


void Task (void *p_arg)
{
    OS_ERR     err;


    (void)&p_arg;
    while (DEF_ON) {
        TimeRemainToCloseDoor = OSTmrRemainGet(&CloseDoorTmr,
                                               &err);

        /* Check "err" */
    }
}
```

OSTmrStart()

```
CPU_BOOLEAN  OSTmrStart (OS_TMR   *p_tmr,
                         OS_ERR   *p_err);
```

File	Called from	Code enabled by
OS_TMR.C	Task	OS_CFG_TMR_EN

OSTmrStart() allows the user to start (or restart) the countdown process of a timer. The timer *must* have previously been created.

Arguments

p_tmr   is a pointer to the timer to start (or restart).

p_err   a pointer to an error code and can be any of the following:

> OS_ERR_NONE   if the timer was started.
>
> OS_ERR_OBJ_TYPE   'p_tmr" is not pointing to a timer.
>
> OS_ERR_TMR_INVALID   if p_tmr is a NULL pointer.
>
> OS_ERR_TMR_INACTIVE   p_tmr is pointing to an inactive timer. In other words, this error occurs if pointing to a timer that has been deleted or was not created.
>
> OS_ERR_TMR_INVALID_STATE   the timer is in an invalid state.
>
> OS_ERR_TMR_ISR   This function was called from an ISR, which is *not* allowed.

Returned Values

DEF_TRUE   if the timer was started

DEF_FALSE   if an error occurred.

Notes/Warnings

1. *Do not* call this function from an ISR.

2. The timer *must* have previously been created.

Example

```
OS_TMR       CloseDoorTmr;


void Task (void *p_arg)
{
    OS_ERR      err;
    CPU_BOOLEAN status;


    (void)&p_arg;
    while (DEF_ON) {
        status = OSTmrStart(&CloseDoorTmr,
                            &err);
        /* Check "err" */
    }
}
```

OSTmrStateGet()

```
OS_STATE   OSTmrStateGet(OS_TMR   *p_tmr,
                         OS_ERR   *p_err);
```

File	Called from	Code enabled by
OS_TMR.C	Task only	OS_CFG_TMR_EN

OSTmrStateGet() allows the user to obtain the current state of a timer. A timer can be in one of four states:

OS_TMR_STATE_UNUSED	the timer has not been created
OS_TMR_STATE_STOPPED	the timer is created but has not yet started, or has been stopped.
OS_TMR_STATE_COMPLETED	the timer is in *one-shot* mode, and has completed its delay.
OS_TMR_STATE_RUNNING	the timer is currently running

Arguments

p_tmr   is a pointer to the timer that the user is inquiring about. This pointer is returned when the timer is created (see OSTmrCreate()).

p_err   a pointer to an error code and can be any of the following:

OS_ERR_NONE	if the function returned the state of the timer.
OS_ERR_OBJ_TYPE	p_tmr is not pointing to a timer.
OS_ERR_TMR_INVALID	if p_tmr is a NULL pointer.
OS_ERR_TMR_INVALID_STATE	the timer is in an invalid state.
OS_ERR_TMR_ISR	This function was called from an ISR, which is *not* allowed.

Returned Values

The state of the timer (see description).

Notes/Warnings

1. Examine the return value to ensure the results from this function are valid.

2. *Do not* call this function from an ISR.

Example

```
OS_STATE   CloseDoorTmrState;
OS_TMR     CloseDoorTmr;


void Task (void *p_arg)
{
    OS_ERR  err;


    (void)&p_arg;
    while (DEF_ON) {
        CloseDoorTmrState = OSTmrStateGet(&CloseDoorTmr,
                                          &err);
        /* Check "err" */
    }
}
```

OSTmrStop()

```
CPU_BOOLEAN   OSTmrStop (OS_TMR    *p_tmr,
                        OS_OPT     opt,
                        void       *p_callback_arg,
                        OS_ERR     *p_err)
```

File	Called from	Code enabled by
OS_TMR.C	Task	OS_CFG_TMR_EN

OSTmrStop() allows the user to stop a timer. The user may execute the callback function of the timer when it is stopped, and pass this callback function a different argument than was specified when the timer was started. This allows the callback function to know that the timer was stopped since the callback argument can be set to indicate this (this is application specific). If the timer is already stopped, the callback function is not called.

Arguments

p_tmr   is a pointer to the timer control block of the desired timer.

opt   is used to specify options:

OS_OPT_TMR_NONE	No option
OS_OPT_TMR_CALLBACK	Run the callback function with the argument specified when the timer was created.
OS_OPT_TMR_CALLBACK_ARG	Run the callback function, but use the argument passed in OSTmrStop() instead of the one specified when the task was created.

p_callback_arg   is a new argument to pass the callback functions (see options above).

p_err   is a pointer to a variable that contains an error code returned by this function.

OS_ERR_NONE	if the call was successful.
OS_ERR_OBJ_TYPE	if p_tmr is not pointing to a timer object.
OS_ERR_TMR_INACTIVE	the timer cannot be stopped since it is inactive.

OS_ERR_TMR_INVALID	When passing a **NULL** pointer for the **p_tmr** argument.
OS_ERR_TMR_INVALID_OPT	if the user did not specify a valid option.
OS_ERR_TMR_INVALID_STATE	the timer is in an invalid state.
OS_ERR_TMR_ISR	if calling this function from an ISR.
OS_ERR_TMR_NO_CALLBACK	if the timer lacks a callback function. This should be specified when the timer is created.
OS_ERR_TMR_STOPPED	if the timer is currently stopped.

Returned Values

DEF_TRUE   if the timer was stopped (even if it was already stopped).

DEF_FALSE   if an error occurred.

Notes/Warnings

1. Examine the returned error code to make ensure the results from this function are valid.

2. *Do not* call this function from an ISR.

3. The callback function is *not* called if the timer is already stopped.

Example

```
OS_TMR  CloseDoorTmr;


void Task (void *p_arg)
{
    OS_ERR     err;


    (void)&p_arg;
    while (DEF_ON) {
        OSTmrStop(&CloseDoorTmr,
                OS_TMR_OPT_CALLBACK,
                (void *)0,
                &err);
        /* Check "err" */
    }
}
```

OSVersion()

```
CPU_INT16U OSVersion (OS_ERR  *p_err);
```

File	Called from	Code enabled by
OS_CORE.C	Task or ISR	N/A

OSVersion() obtains the current version of µC/OS-III.

Arguments

p_err   is a pointer to a variable that contains an error code returned by this function. Currently, OSVersion() always return:

      OS_ERR_NONE

Returned Value

The version is returned as x.yy multiplied by 1000. For example, v3.00.0 is returned as 3000.

Notes/Warnings

None

Example

```
void TaskX (void *p_arg)
{
    CPU_INT16U  os_version;
    OS_ERR      err;


    while (DEF_ON) {
        :
        :
        os_version = OSVersion(&err);  /* Obtain µC/OS-III's version      */
        /* Check "err" */
        :
        :
    }
}
```

B

µC/OS-III Configuration Manual

Three (3) files are used to configure µC/OS-III as highlighted in Figure B-1: OS_CFG.H, OS_TYPE.H, and OS_CFG_APP.H.

Table B-1 shows where these files are typically located on your on a computer.

File	Directory
OS_CFG.H	\Micrium\Software\uCOS-III\Cfg\Template
OS_CFG_APP.H	\Micrium\Software\uCOS-III\Cfg\Template
OS_TYPE.H	\Micrium\Software\uCOS-III\Source

Table B-1 **Configuration files and directories**

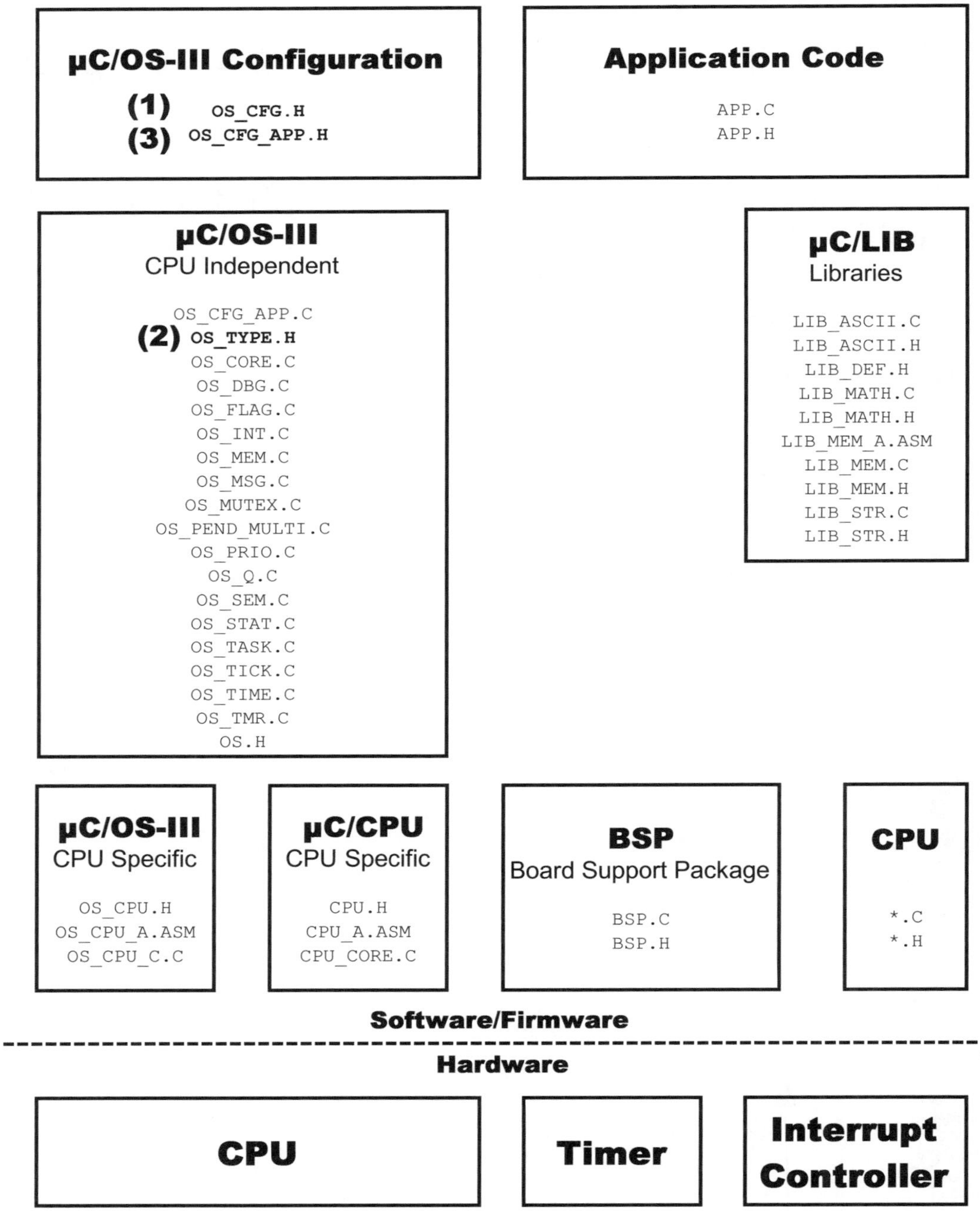

Figure B-1 **Task pending on multiple objects**

FB-1(1)   **µC/OS-III Features (OS_CFG.H):**

OS_CFG.H is used to determine which features are needed from µC/OS-III for an application (i.e., product). Specifically, this file allows a user to determine whether to include semaphores, mutexes, event flags, run-time argument checking, etc. If µC/OS-III is provided in linkable object form, the available features are determined in advanced.

If using a pre-compiled µC/OS-III library, make sure to use the same OS_CFG.H file used to build this library so that all the data types properly match up.

FB-1(2)   **µC/OS-III Data Types (OS_TYPE.H):**

OS_TYPE.H establishes µC/OS-III-specific data types used when building an application. It specifies the size of variables used to represent task priorities, the size of a semaphore count, and more. This file contains recommended data types for µC/OS-III, however these can be altered to make better use of the CPU's natural word size. For example, on some 32-bit CPUs, it is better to declare boolean variables as 32-bit values for performance considerations, even though an 8-bit quantity is more space efficient (assuming performance is more important than footprint).

The port developer typically makes those decisions, since altering the contents of the file requires a deep understanding of the CPU and, most important, how data sizes affect µC/OS-III.

If using a pre-compiled µC/OS-III library, make sure to use the same OS_TYPE.H file used to build this library so that all the data types properly match up.

FB-1(3)   **µC/OS-III Stacks, Pools and other data sizes (OS_CFG_APP.H):**

µC/OS-III can be configured at the application level through **#define** constants in OS_CFG_APP.H even if µC/OS-III is provided in linkable object form. The **#defines** allows a user to specify stack sizes for all µC/OS-III internal tasks: the idle task, statistic task, tick task, timer task, and the ISR handler task. OS_CFG_APP.H also allows users to specify task priorities (except for the idle task since it is always the lowest priority), the tick rate, tick wheel size, the timer wheel size, and more.

You can simply copy OS_CFG_APP.H into the project directory and alter the contents of this file for the application. Once altered, simply re-compile OS_CFG_APP.C, and link the object file produced by the compiler with the rest of the μC/OS-III application. OS_CFG_APP.C "maps" the #define constants defined in OS_CFG_APP.H to variables (placed in code space, i.e., ROM) that μC/OS-III uses at initialization. This process is necessary to allow using μC/OS-III in linkable object form. μC/OS-III licensees will have full source code for μC/OS-III.

The contents of the three configuration files will be described in the following sections.

B-1 μC/OS-III FEATURES (OS_CFG.H)

Compile-time configuration allows users to determine which features to enable and those features that are not needed. This assumes that the user has the μC/OS-III source code. With compile-time configuration, the code and data sizes of μC/OS-III (i.e., its footprint) can be reduced by enabling only the desired functionality.

Compile-time configuration is accomplished by setting a number of #define constants in a file called OS_CFG.H that the application is expected to provide. With the full source code for μC/OS-III, simply copy OS_CFG.H into the application directory and change the copied file to satisfy the application's requirements. This way, OS_CFG.H is not recreated from scratch.

The compile-time configuration #defines are listed below in alphabetic order and are not necessarily found in this order in OS_CFG.H.

OS_CFG_APP_HOOKS_EN

When set to 1, this #define specifies that application-defined hooks can be called from μC/OS-III's hooks. This allows the application code to extend the functionality of μC/OS-III. Specifically:

The μC/OS-III hook ...	Calls the Application-define hook through...
OSIdleTaskHook()	OS_AppIdleTaskHookPtr
OSInitHook()	None
OSStatTaskHook()	OS_AppStatTaskHookPtr
OSTaskCreateHook()	OS_AppTaskCreateHookPtr

The µC/OS-III hook ...	Calls the Application-define hook through...
OSTaskDelHook()	OS_AppTaskDelHookPtr
OSTaskReturnHook()	OS_AppTaskReturnHookPtr
OSTaskSwHook()	OS_AppTaskSwHookPtr
OSTimeTickHook()	OS_AppTimeTickHookPtr

Application hook functions could be declared as shown in the code below.

```
void  App_OS_TaskCreateHook (OS_TCB *p_tcb)
{
    /* Your code here */
}

void  App_OS_TaskDelHook (OS_TCB *p_tcb)
{
    /* Your code here */
}

void  App_OS_TaskReturnHook (OS_TCB *p_tcb)
{
    /* Your code here */
}

void  App_OS_IdleTaskHook (void)
{
    /* Your code here */
}

void  App_OS_StatTaskHook (void)
{
    /* Your code here */
}

void  App_OS_TaskSwHook (void)
{
    /* Your code here */
}

void  App_OS_TimeTickHook (void)
{
    /* Your code here */
}
```

It's also up to a user to set the value of the pointers so that they point to the appropriate functions as shown below. The pointers do not have to be set in **main()** but, set them after calling **OSInit()**.

```
void  main (void)
{
    OS_ERR  err;


    OSInit(&err);
    :
    :
    OS_AppTaskCreateHookPtr = (OS_APP_HOOK_TCB )App_OS_TaskCreateHook;
    OS_AppTaskDelHookPtr    = (OS_APP_HOOK_TCB )App_OS_TaskDelHook;
    OS_AppTaskReturnHookPtr = (OS_APP_HOOK_TCB )App_OS_TaskReturnHook;
    OS_AppIdleTaskHookPtr   = (OS_APP_HOOK_VOID)App_OS_IdleTaskHook;
    OS_AppStatTaskHookPtr   = (OS_APP_HOOK_VOID)App_OS_StatTaskHook;
    OS_AppTaskSwHookPtr     = (OS_APP_HOOK_VOID)App_OS_TaskSwHook;
    OS_AppTimeTickHookPtr   = (OS_APP_HOOK_VOID)App_OS_TimeTickHook;
    :
    :
    OSStart(&err);
}
```

Note that not every hook function need to be defined, only the ones the user wants to place in the application code.

Also, if you don't intend to extend µC/OS-III's hook through these application hooks, set **OS_CFG_APP_HOOKS_EN** to 0 to save RAM (i.e., the pointers).

OS_CFG_ARG_CHK_EN

OS_CFG_ARG_CHK_EN determines whether the user wants most of µC/OS-III functions to perform argument checking. When set to 1, µC/OS-III ensures that pointers passed to functions are non-**NULL**, that arguments passed are within allowable range, that options are valid, and more. When set to 0, **OS_CFG_ARG_CHK_EN** reduces the amount of code space and processing time required by µC/OS-III. Set **OS_CFG_ARG_CHK_EN** to 0 if you are certain that the arguments are correct.

µC/OS-III performs argument checking in over 40 functions. Therefore, you can save a few hundred bytes of code space by disabling this check. However, always enable argument checking until you are certain the code can be trusted.

OS_CFG_CALLED_FROM_ISR_CHK_EN

OS_CFG_CALLED_FROM_ISR_CHK_EN determines whether most of µC/OS-III functions are to confirm that the function is not called from an ISR. In other words, most of the functions from µC/OS-III should be called by task-level code except "post" type functions (which can also be called from ISRs). By setting this **#define** to 1 µC/OS-III is told to make sure that functions that are only supposed to be called by tasks are not called by ISRs. It's highly recommended to set this **#define** to 1 until absolutely certain that the code is behaving correctly and that task-level functions are always called from tasks. Set this **#define** to 0 to save code space and, of course, processing time.

µC/OS-III performs this check in approximately 50 functions. Therefore, you can save a few hundred bytes of code space by disabling this check.

OS_CFG_DBG_EN

When set to 1, this **#define** adds ROM constants located in **OS_DBG.C** to help support kernel aware debuggers. Specifically, a number of named ROM variables can be queried by a debugger to find out about compiled-in options. For example, a debugger can find out the size of an **OS_TCB**, µC/OS-III's version number, the size of an event flag group (**OS_FLAG_GRP**), and much more.

OS_CFG_FLAG_EN

OS_CFG_FLAG_EN enables (when set to 1) or disables (when set to 0) code generation of event flag services and data structures. This reduces the amount of code and data space needed when an application does not require event flags. When **OS_CFG_FLAG_EN** is set to 0, it is not necessary to enable or disable any of the other **OS_CFG_FLAG_xxx** **#define** constants in this section.

OS_CFG_FLAG_DEL_EN

OS_CFG_FLAG_DEL_EN enables (when set to 1) or disables (when set to 0) code generation of the function **OSFlagDel()**.

OS_CFG_FLAG_MODE_CLR_EN

OS_CFG_FLAG_MODE_CLR_EN enables (when set to 1) or disables (when set to 0) code generation used to wait for event flags to be 0 instead of 1. Generally, wait for event flags to be set. However, the user may also want to wait for event flags to be clear and in this case, enable this option.

B

OS_CFG_FLAG_PEND_ABORT_EN

OS_CFG_FLAG_PEND_ABORT_EN enables (when set to 1) or disables (when set to 0) code generation of the function OSFlagPendAbort().

OS_CFG_ISR_POST_DEFERRED_EN

When set to 1, OS_CFG_ISR_POST_DEFERRED_EN reduces interrupt latency since interrupts are not disabled during most critical sections of code within µC/OS-III. Instead, the scheduler is locked during the processing of these critical sections. The advantage of setting OS_CFG_ISR_POST_DEFERRED_EN to 1 is that interrupt latency is lower, however, ISR to task response is slightly higher. It is recommended to set

OS_CFG_ISR_POST_DEFERRED_EN to 1 when enabling the following services, as setting this #define to 0 would potentially make interrupt latency unacceptably high:

µC/OS-III Services	Enabled by ...
Event Flags	OS_CFG_FLAG_EN
Multiple Pend	OS_CFG_PEND_MULTI_EN
OS???Post() with broadcast	
OS???Del() with OS_OPT_DEL_ALWAYS	
OS???PendAbort()	

The compromise to make is:

> OS_CFG_ISR_POST_DEFERRED_EN set to 1
> Short interrupt latency, longer ISR-to-task response.

> OS_CFG_ISR_POST_DEFERRED_EN set to 0
> Long interrupt latency (see table above), shorter ISR-to-task response.

OS_CFG_MEM_EN

OS_CFG_MEM_EN enables (when set to 1) or disables (when set to 0) code generation of the µC/OS-III partition memory manager and its associated data structures. This feature allows users to reduce the amount of code and data space needed when an application does not require the use of memory partitions.

OS_CFG_MUTEX_EN

OS_CFG_MUTEX_EN enables (when set to 1) or disables (when set to 0) the code generation of all mutual exclusion semaphore services and data structures. This feature allows users to reduce the amount of code and data space needed when an application does not require the use of mutexes. When OS_CFG_MUTEX_EN is set to 0, there is no need to enable or disable any of the other OS_CFG_MUTEX_XXX #define constants in this section.

OS_CFG_MUTEX_DEL_EN

OS_CFG_MUTEX_DEL_EN enables (when set to 1) or disables (when set to 0) code generation of the function OSMutexDel().

OS_CFG_MUTEX_PEND_ABORT_EN

OS_CFG_MUTEX_PEND_ABORT_EN enables (when set to 1) or disables (when set to 0) code generation of the function OSMutexPendAbort().

OS_CFG_OBJ_TYPE_CHK_EN

OS_CFG_OBJ_TYPE_CHK_EN determines whether most of µC/OS-III functions should check to see if the function is manipulating the proper object. In other words, if attempting to post to a semaphore, is the user in fact passing a semaphore object or another object by mistake? It is recommended to set this #define to 1 until absolutely certain that the code is behaving correctly and the user code is always pointing to the proper objects. Set this #define to 0 to save code space as well as data space. µC/OS-III object type checking is done nearly 30 times, and it is possible to save a few hundred bytes of code space and processing time by disabling this check.

OS_CFG_PEND_MULTI_EN

This constant determines whether the code to support pending on multiple events (i.e., semaphores or message queues) will be enabled (1) or not (0).

OS_CFG_PRIO_MAX

OS_CFG_PRIO_MAX specifies the maximum number of priorities available in the application. Specifying OS_CFG_PRIO_MAX to just the number of priorities the user intends to use, reduces the amount of RAM needed by µC/OS-III.

In µC/OS-III, task priorities can range from 0 (highest priority) to a maximum of 255 (lowest possible priority) when the data type OS_PRIO is defined as a CPU_INT08U. However, in μC/OS-III, there is no practical limit to the number of available priorities. Specifically, if defining **OS_PRIO** as a CPU_INT16U, there can be up to 65536 priority levels. It is recommended to leave **OS_PRIO** defined as a CPU_INT08U and use only 256 different priority levels (i.e., 0..255), which is generally sufficient for every application. Always set the value of **OS_CFG_PRIO_MAX** to even multiples of 8 (8, 16, 32, 64, 128, 256, etc.). The higher the number of different priorities, the more RAM μC/OS-III will consume.

An application cannot create tasks with a priority number higher than or equal to

OS_CFG_PRIO_MAX. In fact, μC/OS-III reserves priority **OS_CFG_PRIO_MAX-1** for itself; **OS_CFG_PRIO_MAX-1** is reserved for the idle task **OS_IdleTask()**. Additionally, do not use priority 0 for an application since it is reserved by μC/OS-III's ISR handler task. The priorities of the application tasks can therefore take a value between 1 and **OS_CFG_PRIO_MAX-2** (inclusive).

To summarize, there are two priority levels to avoid in an application:

Priority	Reserved by μC/OS-III for ...
0	The ISR Handler Task (OS_IntQTask())
1	Reserved
2	Reserved
OS_CFG_PRIO_MAX-2	Reserved
OS_CFG_PRIO_MAX-1	The idle task (OS_IdleTask())

OS_CFG_Q_EN

OS_CFG_Q_EN enables (when set to 1) or disables (when set to 0) code generation of message queue services and data structures. This reduces the amount of code space needed when an application does not require the use of message queues. When OS_CFG_Q_EN is set to 0, do not enable or disable any of the other **OS_CFG_Q_XXX** #define constants in this section.

OS_CFG_Q_DEL_EN

OS_CFG_Q_DEL_EN enables (when set to 1) or disables (when set to 0) code generation of the function OSQDel().

OS_CFG_Q_FLUSH_EN

OS_CFG_Q_FLUSH_EN enables (when set to 1) or disables (when set to 0) code generation of the function OSQFlush().

OS_CFG_Q_PEND_ABORT_EN

OS_CFG_Q_PEND_ABORT_EN enables (when set to 1) or disables (when set to 0) code generation of the function OSQPendAbort().

OS_CFG_SCHED_LOCK_TIME_MEAS_EN

This constant enables (when set to 1) or disables (when set to 0) code generation to measure the amount of time the scheduler is locked. This is useful when determining task latency.

OS_CFG_SCHED_ROUND_ROBIN_EN

This constant enables (when set to 1) or disables (when set to 0) code generation for the round-robin feature of µC/OS-III.

OS_CFG_SEM_EN

OS_CFG_SEM_EN enables (when set to 1) or disables (when set to 0) code generation of the semaphore manager and associated data structures. This reduces the amount of code and data space needed when an application does not require the use of semaphores. When OS_CFG_SEM_EN is set to 0, it is not necessary to enable or disable any of the other OS_CFG_SEM_XXX #define constants in this section.

OS_CFG_SEM_DEL_EN

OS_CFG_SEM_DEL_EN enables (when set to 1) or disables (when set to 0) code generation of the function OSSemDel().

OS_CFG_SEM_PEND_ABORT_EN

OS_CFG_SEM_PEND_ABORT_EN enables (when set to 1) or disables (when set to 0) code generation of the function OSSemPendAbort().

OS_CFG_SEM_SET_EN

OS_CFG_SEM_SET_EN enables (when set to 1) or disables (when set to 0) code generation of the function OSSemSet().

OS_CFG_STAT_TASK_EN

OS_CFG_STAT_TASK_EN specifies whether or not to enable µC/OS-III's statistic task, as well as its initialization function. When set to 1, the statistic task OS_StatTask() and statistic task initialization function are enabled. OS_StatTask() computes the CPU usage of an application, stack usage of each task, the CPU usage of each task at run time and more.

When enabled, OS_StatTask() executes at a rate of OS_CFG_STAT_TASK_RATE_HZ (see OS_CFG_APP.H), and computes the value of OSStatTaskCPUUsage, which is a variable that contains the percentage of CPU used by the application. OS_StatTask() calls OSStatTaskHook() every time it executes so that the user can add their own statistics as needed. See OS_STAT.C for details on the statistic task. The priority of OS_StatTask() is configurable by the application code (see OS_CFG_APP.H).

OS_StatTask() also computes stack usage of each task created when the #define

OS_CFG_STAT_TASK_STK_CHK_EN is set to 1. In this case, OS_StatTask() calls OSTaskStkChk() for each task and the result is placed in the task's TCB. The .StkFree and .StkUsed field of the task's TCB represents the amount of free space (in bytes) and amount of used space, respectively.

When OS_CFG_STAT_TASK_EN is set to 0, all variables used by the statistic task are not declared (see OS.H). This, of course, reduces the amount of RAM needed by µC/OS-III when not enabling the statistic task. When setting OS_CFG_STAT_TASK_EN to 1, statistics will be determined at a rate of OS_CFG_STAT_TASK_RATE_HZ (see OS_CFG_APP.H).

OS_CFG_STAT_TASK_STK_CHK_EN

This constant allows the statistic task to call OSTaskStkChk() for each task created. For this to happen, OS_CFG_STAT_TASK_EN needs to be set to 1 (i.e., the statistic task needs to be enabled). However, call OSStatStkChk() from one of the tasks to obtain this information about the task(s).

OS_CFG_STK_SIZE_MIN

This #define specifies the minimum stack size (in CPU_STK elements) for each task. This is used by µC/OS-III to verify that sufficient stack space is provided for when each task is created. Suppose the full context of a processor consists of 16 registers of 32 bits. Also, suppose CPU_STK is declared as being of type CPU_INT32U, at a bare minimum, set OS_CFG_STK_SIZE_MIN to 16. However, it would be quite unwise to not accommodate for storage of local variables, function call returns, and possibly nested ISRs. Refer to the "port" of the processor used to see how to set this minimum. Again, this is a safeguard to make sure task stacks have sufficient stack space.

OS_CFG_TASK_CHANGE_PRIO_EN

OS_CFG_TASK_CHANGE_PRIO_EN enables (when set to 1) or disables (when set to 0) code generation of the function OSTaskChangePrio().

OS_CFG_TASK_DEL_EN

OS_CFG_TASK_DEL_EN enables (when set to 1) or disables (when set to 0) code generation of the function OSTaskDel().

OS_CFG_TASK_Q_EN

OS_CFG_TASK_Q_EN enables (when set to 1) or disables (when set to 0) code generation of the OSTaskQXXX() functions used to send and receive messages directly to/from tasks and ISRs. Sending messages directly to a task is more efficient than sending messages using a message queue because there is no pend list associated with messages sent to a task.

OS_CFG_TASK_Q_PEND_ABORT_EN

OS_CFG_TASK_Q_PEND_ABORT_EN enables (when set to 1) or disables (when set to 0) code generation of code for the function OSTaskQPendAbort().

OS_CFG_TASK_PROFILE_EN

This constant allows variables to be allocated in each task's OS_TCB to hold performance data about each task. If OS_CFG_TASK_PROFILE_EN is set to 1, each task will have a variable to keep track of the number of times a task is switched to, the task execution time, the percent CPU usage of the task relative to the other tasks and more. The information made available with this feature is highly useful when debugging, but requires extra RAM.

OS_CFG_TASK_REG_TBL_SIZE

This constant allows each task to have task context variables. Use task variables to store such elements as "errno", task identifiers and other task-specific values. The number of variables that a task contains is set by this constant. Each variable is identified by a unique identifier from 0 to OS_CFG_TASK_REG_TBL_SIZE-1. Also, each variable is declared as having an OS_REG data type (see OS_TYPE.H). If OS_REG is a CPU_INT08U, all variables in this table are of this type.

OS_CFG_TASK_SEM_PEND_ABORT_EN

OS_CFG_TASK_SEM_PEND_ABORT_EN enables (when set to 1) or disables (when set to 0) code generation of code for the function OSTaskSemPendAbort().

OS_CFG_TASK_SUSPEND_EN

OS_CFG_TASK_SUSPEND_EN enables (when set to 1) or disables (when set to 0) code generation of the functions OSTaskSuspend() and OSTaskResume(), which allows the application to explicitly suspend and resume tasks, respectively. Suspending and resuming a task is useful when debugging, especially if calling these functions via a terminal interface at run time.

OS_CFG_TIME_DLY_HMSM_EN

OS_CFG_TIME_DLY_HMSM_EN enables (when set to 1) or disables (when set to 0) the code generation of the function OSTimeDlyHMSM(), which is used to delay a task for a specified number of hours, minutes, seconds, and milliseconds.

OS_CFG_TIME_DLY_RESUME_EN

OS_CFG_TIME_DLY_RESUME_EN enables (when set to 1) or disables (when set to 0) the code generation of the function OSTimeDlyResume().

OS_CFG_TMR_EN

Enables (when set to 1) or disables (when set to 0) the code generation of timer management services.

OS_CFG_TMR_DEL_EN

OS_CFG_TMR_DEL_EN enables (when set to 1) or disables (when set to 0) the code generation of the function OSTmrDel().

B-2 DATA TYPES (OS_TYPE.H)

OS_TYPE.H contains the data types used by µC/OS-III, which should only be altered by the implementer of the µC/OS-III port. If the user only has access to a compiled µC/OS-III library or object code, make sure to use the same OS_TYPE.H used to compile the library in order to use µC/OS-III. Of course, if there is access to the source code of both the port and µC/OS-III, you can alter the contents of OS_TYPE.H. However, it is important to understand how each of the data types that are being changed will affect the operation of µC/OS-III-based applications.

The reason to change **OS_TYPE.H** is that processors may work better with specific word sizes. For example, a 16-bit processor will likely be more efficient at manipulating 16-bit values and a 32-bit processor more comfortable with 32-bit values, even at the cost of extra RAM. In other words, the user may need to choose between processor performance and RAM footprint.

If changing "any" of the data types, copy **OS_TYPE.H** in the project directory and change that file (not the original **OS_TYPE.H** that comes with the µC/OS-III release). Of course, to change the data types, the user must have the full source code for µC/OS-III and recompile all of the code using the new data types.

Recommended data type sizes are specified in comments in **OS_TYPE.H**.

B-3 µC/OS-III STACKS, POOLS AND OTHER (OS_CFG_APP.H)

µC/OS-III allows the user to configure the sizes of the idle task stack, statistic task stack, message pool, tick wheel, timer wheel, debug tables, and more. This is done through OS_CFG_APP.H.

OS_CFG_TASK_STK_LIMIT_PCT_EMPTY

This **#define** sets the position (as a percentage to empty) of the stack limit for the idle, statistic, tick, interrupt queue handler, and timer tasks stacks. In other words, the amount of space to leave before the stack is empty. For example if the stack contains 1000 **CPU_STK** entries and the user declares **OS_CFG_TASK_STK_LIMIT_PCT_EMPTY** to 10, the stack limit will be set when the stack reaches 90% full, or 10% empty.

If the stack of the processor grows from high memory to low memory, the limit would be set towards the "base address" of the stack, i.e., closer to element 0 of the stack.

If the processor used does not offer automatic stack limit checking, set this **#define** to 0.

OS_CFG_IDLE_TASK_STK_SIZE

This **#define** sets the size of the idle task's stack as follows:

```
CPU_STK OSCfg_IdleTaskStk[OS_CFG_IDLE_TASK_STK_SIZE];
```

Note that the stack size needs to be at least greater than **OS_CFG_STK_SIZE_MIN**.

OS_CFG_INT_Q_SIZE

If OS_CFG_ISR_POST_DEFERRED_EN is set to 1 (see OS_CFG.H), this #define specifies the number of entries that can be placed in the interrupt queue. The size of this queue depends on how many interrupts could occur in the time it takes to process interrupts by the ISR Handler Task. The size also depends on whether or not to allow interrupt nesting. A good start point is approximately 10 entries.

OS_CFG_INT_Q_TASK_STK_SIZE

If OS_CFG_ISR_POST_DEFERRED_EN is set to 1 (see OS_CFG.H) then this #define sets the size of the ISR handler task's stack as follows:

```
CPU_STK OSCfg_IntQTaskStk[OS_CFG_INT_Q_TASK_STK_SIZE];
```

Note that the stack size needs to be at least greater than OS_CFG_STK_SIZE_MIN.

OS_CFG_ISR_STK_SIZE

This specifies the size of µC/OS-III's interrupt stack (in CPU_STK elements, see OS_TYPE.H). Note that the stack size needs to accommodate for worst case interrupt nesting, assuming the processor supports interrupt nesting.

OS_CFG_MSG_POOL_SIZE

This entry specifies the number of OS_MSGs available in the pool of OS_MSGs. The size is specified in number of OS_MSG elements. The message pool is declared in OS_CFG_APP.C as follows:

```
OS_MSG   OSCfg_MsgPool[OS_CFG_MSG_POOL_SIZE];
```

OS_CFG_STAT_TASK_PRIO

This #define allows a user to specify the priority assigned to the µC/OS-III statistic task. It is recommended to make this task a very low priority and possibly even one priority level just above the idle task, or, OS_CFG_PRIO_MAX-2.

OS_CFG_STAT_TASK_RATE_HZ

This #define defines the execution rate (in Hz) of the statistic task. It is recommended to make this rate an even multiple of the tick rate (see OS_CFG_TICK_RATE_HZ).

OS_CFG_STAT_TASK_STK_SIZE

This #define sets the size of the statistic task's stack as follows:

CPU_STK OSCfg_StatTaskStk[OS_CFG_STAT_TASK_STK_SIZE];

Note that the stack size needs to be at least greater than OS_CFG_STK_SIZE_MIN.

OS_CFG_TICK_RATE_HZ

This #define specifies the rate in Hertz of µC/OS-III's tick interrupt. The tick rate should be set between 10 and 1000 Hz. The higher the rate, the more overhead it will impose on the processor. The desired rate depends on the granularity required for time delays and timeouts.

OS_CFG_TICK_TASK_PRIO

This #define specifies the priority to assign to the µC/OS-III tick task. It is recommended to make this task a fairly high priority, but it does not need to be the highest. The priority assigned to this task must be greater than 0 and less than OS_CFG_PRIO_MAX-1.

OS_CFG_TICK_TASK_STK_SIZE

This entry specifies the size of µC/OS-III's tick task stack (in CPU_STK elements). Note that the stack size must be at least greater than OS_CFG_STK_SIZE_MIN.

OS_CFG_TICK_WHEEL_SIZE

This #define determines the number of entries in the OSTickWheel[] table. This "wheel" reduces the number of tasks to be updated by the tick task. The size of the wheel should be a fraction of the number of tasks expected in the application.

This value should be a number between 4 and 1024. Task management overhead is somewhat determined by the size of the wheel. A large number of entries might reduce the overhead for tick management but would require more RAM. Each entry requires a pointer and a counter of the number of entries in each "spoke" of the wheel. This counter is typically a 16-bit value. It is recommended that OS_CFG_TICK_WHEEL_SIZE not be a multiple of the tick rate. If the application has many tasks, a large wheel size is recommended. As a starting value, use a prime number (3, 5, 7, 11, 13, 17, 19, 23, etc.).

OS_CFG_TMR_TASK_PRIO

This #define allows a user to specify the priority to assign to the µC/OS-III timer task. It is recommended to make this task a medium-to-low priority, depending on how fast the timer task will execute (see OS_CFG_TMR_TASK_RATE_HZ), how many timers running in the application, and the size of the timer wheel, etc. The priority assigned to this task must be greater than 0 and less than OS_CFG_PRIO_MAX-1.

Start with these simple rules:

■ The faster the timer rate, the higher the priority to assign to this task.

■ The higher the timer wheel size, the higher the priority to assign this task.

■ The higher the number of timers in the system, the lower the priority.

In other words:

High Timer Rate	Higher Priority
High Timer Wheel Size	Higher Priority
High Number of Timers	Lower Priority

OS_CFG_TMR_TASK_RATE_HZ

This #define specifies the rate in Hertz of µC/OS-III's timer task. The timer task rate should typically be set to 10 Hz. However, timers can run at a faster rate at the price of higher processor overhead. Note that OS_CFG_TMR_TASK_RATE_HZ MUST be an integer multiple of OS_CFG_TICK_TASK_RATE_HZ. In other words, if setting OS_CFG_TICK_TASK_RATE_HZ to 1000, do not set OS_CFG_TMR_TASK_RATE_HZ to 11 since 90.91 ticks would be required for every timer update, and 90.91 is not an integer multiple. Use approximately 10 Hz in this example.

OS_CFG_TMR_TASK_STK_SIZE

This #define sets the size of the timer task's stack as follows:

```
CPU_STK OSCfg_TmrTaskStk[OS_CFG_TMR_TASK_STK_SIZE];
```

Note that the stack size needs to be at least greater than OS_CFG_STK_SIZE_MIN.

OS_CFG_TMR_WHEEL_SIZE

Timers are updated using a rotating wheel mechanism. This "wheel" reduces the number of timers to be updated by the timer manager task. The size of the wheel should be a fraction of the number of timers in the application.

This value should be a number between 4 and 1024. Timer management overhead is somewhat determined by the size of the wheel. A large number of entries might reduce the overhead for timer management but would require more RAM. Each entry requires a pointer and a counter of the number of entries in each "spoke" of the wheel. This counter is typically a 16-bit value. It is recommended that this value *not* be a multiple of the tick rate. If an application has many timers a large wheel size is recommended. As a starting value, use a prime number (3, 5, 7, 11, 13, 17, 19, 23, etc.).

Appendix

C

Migrating from µC/OS-II to µC/OS-III

µC/OS-III is a completely new real-time kernel with roots in µC/OS-II. Portions of the µC/OS-II Application Programming Interface (API) function names are the same, but the arguments passed to the functions have, in some places, drastically changed.

Appendix C explains several differences between the two real-time kernels. However, access to µC/OS-II and µC/OS-III source files best highlights the differences.

Table C-1 is a feature-comparison chart for µC/OS-II and µC/OS-III.

Feature	µC/OS-II	µC/OS-III
Year of introduction	1998/2002	2009
Book	Yes	Yes
Source code available (Licensees only)	Yes	Yes
Preemptive Multitasking	Yes	Yes
Maximum number of tasks	255	Unlimited
Number of tasks at each priority level	1	Unlimited
Round Robin Scheduling	No	Yes
Semaphores	Yes	Yes
Mutual Exclusion Semaphores (Nestable)	Yes	Yes
Event Flags	Yes	Yes
Message Mailboxes (not needed)	Yes	No
Message Queues	Yes	Yes
Fixed Sized Memory Management	Yes	Yes
Signal a task without requiring a semaphore	No	Yes
Send messages to a task without requiring a message queue	No	Yes
Software Timers	Yes	Yes
Task suspend/resume (Nestable)	Yes	Yes
Deadlock prevention	Yes	Yes
Scalable	Yes	Yes
Code Footprint	6K to 26K	6K to 20K
Data Footprint	1K+	1K+
ROMable	Yes	Yes
Run-time configurable	No	Yes
Feature	µC/OS-II	µC/OS-III
Compile-time configurable	Yes	Yes

Feature	µC/OS-II	µC/OS-III
ASCII names for each kernel object	Yes	Yes
Interrupt Latency	1200~	< 1000~
Pend on multiple objects	Yes	Yes
Task registers	Yes	Yes
Built-in performance measurements	Limited	Extensive
User definable hook functions	Yes	Yes
Time stamps on posts	No	Yes
Built-in Kernel Awareness support	Yes	Yes
Optimizable Scheduler in assembly language	No	Yes
Tick handling at task level	No	Yes
Source code available	Yes	Yes
Number of services	~90	~70
MISRA-C:1998 (except 5 rules)	Yes	N/A
MISRA-C:2004 (except 5 rules)	No	Yes
DO178B Level A and EUROCAE ED-12B	Yes	In progress
Medical FDA pre-market notification (510(k)) and pre-market approval (PMA)	Yes	In progress
SIL3/SIL4 IEC for transportation and nuclear systems	Yes	In progress
IEC-61508	Yes	In progress

Table C-1 **µC/OS-II and µC/OS-III features comparison chart**

C-1 DIFFERENCES IN SOURCE FILE NAMES AND CONTENTS

Table C-2 shows the source files used in both kernels. Note that a few of the files have the same or similar name. Even though µC/OS-III has more source files, the final compiled footprint is actually smaller for a full configuration.

µC/OS-II	µC/OS-III	Note
	OS_APP_HOOKS.C	(1)
	OS_CFG_APP.C	(2)
	OS_CFG_APP.H	(3)
OS_CFG_R.H	OS_CFG.H	(4)
OS_CORE.C	OS_CORE.C	
OS_CPU.H	OS_CPU.H	(5)
OS_CPU_A.ASM	OS_CPU_A.ASM	(5)
OS_CPU_C.C	OS_CPU_C.C	(5)
OS_DBG_R.C	OS_DBG.C	(6)
OS_FLAG.C	OS_FLAG.C	
	OS_INT.C	(7)
	OS_PEND_MULTI.C	(8)
	OS_PRIO.C	(9)
OS_MBOX.C		(10)
OS_MEM.C	OS_MEM.C	
	OS_MSG.C	(11)
OS_MUTEX.C	OS_MUTEX.C	
OS_Q.C	OS_Q.C	
OS_SEM.C	OS_SEM.C	
	OS_STAT.C	(12)
OS_TASK.C	OS_TASK.C	
OS_TIME.C	OS_TIME.C	
OS_TMR.C	OS_TMR.C	
	OS_VAR.C	(13)
	OS_TYPE.H	(14)
UCOS_II.H	OS.H	(15)

Table C-2 µC/OS-II and µC/OS-III files

TC-2(1)   µC/OS-II does not have this file, which is now provided for convenience so the user can add application hooks. Copy this file to the application directory and edit the contents of the file.

TC-2(2)   **OS_CFG_APP.C** did not exist in µC/OS-II. This file needs to be added to a project build for µC/OS-III.

TC-2(3)   In µC/OS-II, all configuration constants were placed in **OS_CFG.H**. In µC/OS-III, some of the configuration constants are placed in this file, while others are in **OS_CFG.H**. **OS_CFG_APP.H** contains application-specific configurations such as the size of the idle task stack, tick rate, and others.

TC-2(4)   In µC/OS-III, **OS_CFG.H** is reserved for configuring certain features of the kernel. For example, are any of the semaphore services required, and will the application have fixed-sized memory partition management?

TC-2(5)   These are the port files and a few variables and functions will need to be changed when using a µC/OS-II port as a starting point for the µC/OS-III port.

µC/OS-II variable changes to ...	... in µC/OS-III
OSIntNesting	OSIntNestingCtr
OSTCBCur	OSTCBCurPtr
OSTCBHighRdy	OSTCBHighRdyPtr
µC/OS-II function changes to ...	**... in µC/OS-III**
OSInitHookBegin()	OSInitHook()
OSInitHookEnd()	N/A
OSTaskStatHook()	OSStatTaskHook()
OSTaskIdleHook()	OSIdleTaskHook()
OSTCBInitHook()	N/A
OSTaskStkInit()	OSTaskStkInit()

The name of **OSTaskStkInit()** is the same but it is listed here since the code for it needs to be changed slightly as several arguments passed to this function are different. Specifically, instead of passing the top-of-stack as in µC/OS-II, **OSTaskStkInit()** is passed the base address and the size of the task stack.

TC-2(6)   In µC/OS-III, **OS_DBG.C** should always be part of the build. In µC/OS-II, the equivalent file (**OS_DBG_R.C**) was optional.

TC-2(7)   **OS_INT.C** contains the code for the Interrupt Queue handler, which is a new feature in µC/OS-III, allowing post calls from ISRs to be deferred to a task-level handler. This is done to reduce interrupt latency (see Chapter 9, "Interrupt Management" on page 163).

TC-2(8)   Both kernels allow tasks to pend on multiple kernel objects. In µC/OS-II, this code is found in **OS_CORE.C**, while in µC/OS-III, the code is placed in a separate file.

TC-2(9)   The code to determine the highest priority ready-to-run task is isolated in µC/OS-III and placed in **OS_PRIO.C**. This allows the port developer to replace this file by an assembly language equivalent file, especially if the CPU used supports certain bit manipulation instructions and a count leading zeros (CLZ) instruction.

TC-2(10)   µC/OS-II provides message mailbox services. A message mailbox is identical to a message queue of size one. µC/OS-III does not have these services since they can be easily emulated by message queues.

TC-2(11)   Management of messages for message queues is encapsulated in **OS_MSG.C** in µC/OS-III.

TC-2(12)   The statistics task and its support functions have been extracted out of **OS_CORE.C** and placed in **OS_STAT.C** for µC/OS-III.

TC-2(13)   All the µC/OS-III variables are instantiated in a file called **OS_VAR.C**.

TC-2(14)   In µC/OS-III, the size of most data types is better adapted to the CPU architecture used. In µC/OS-II, the size of a number of these data types was assumed.

TC-2(15)   In µC/OS-II, the main header file is called **UCOS_II.H**. In µC/OS-III, it is renamed to **OS.H**.

C-2 CONVENTION CHANGES

There are a number of convention changes from µC/OS-II to µC/OS-III. The most notable is the use of CPU-specific data types. Table C-3 shows the differences between the data types used in both kernels.

µC/OS-II (`OS_CPU.H`)	µC/CPU (`CPU.H`)	Note
BOOLEAN	CPU_BOOLEAN	
INT8S	CPU_INT8S	
INT8U	CPU_INT8U	
INT16S	CPU_INT16S	
INT16U	CPU_INT16U	
INT32S	CPU_INT32S	
INT32U	CPU_INT32U	
OS_STK	CPU_OS_STK	(1)
OS_CPU_SR	CPU_SR	(2)
µC/OS-II (`OS_CFG.H`)	**µC/CPU (`CPU.H`)**	
OS_STK_GROWTH	CPU_CFG_STK_GROWTH	(3)

Table C-3 µC/OS-II vs. µC/OS-III basic data types

TC-3(1)   A task stack in µC/OS-II is declared as an **OS_STK**, which is now replaced by a CPU specific data type **CPU_STK**. These two data types are equivalent, except that defining the width of the CPU stack in µC/CPU makes more sense.

TC-3(2)   It also makes sense to declare the CPU's status register in µC/CPU.

TC-3(3)   Stack growth (high-to-low or low-to-high memory) is declared in µC/CPU since stack growth is a CPU feature and not an OS one.

Another convention change is the use of the acronym "**cfg**" which stands for configuration. Now, all **#define** configuration constants and variables have the "**CFG**" or "**Cfg**" acronym in them as shown in Table C-4. Table C-4 shows the configuration constants that have been moved from **OS_CFG.H** to **OS_CFG_APP.H**. This is done because µC/OS-III is configurable at the application level instead of just at compile time as with µC/OS-II.

µC/OS-II (OS_CFG.H)	µC/OS-III (OS_CFG_APP.H)	Note
	OS_CFG_MSG_POOL_SIZE	
	OS_CFG_ISR_STK_SIZE	
	OS_CFG_TASK_STK_LIMIT_PCT_EMPTY	
OS_TASK_IDLE_STK_SIZE	OS_CFG_IDLE_TASK_STK_SIZE	
	OS_CFG_INT_Q_SIZE	
	OS_CFG_INT_Q_TASK_STK_SIZE	
	OS_CFG_STAT_TASK_PRIO	
	OS_CFG_STAT_TASK_RATE_HZ	
OS_TASK_STAT_SIZE	OS_CFG_STAT_TASK_STK_SIZE	
OS_TICKS_PER_SEC	OS_CFG_TICK_RATE_HZ	(1)
	OS_CFG_TICK_TASK_PRIO	
	OS_CFG_TICK_TASK_STK_SIZE	
	OS_CFG_TICK_WHEEL_SIZE	
	OS_CFG_TMR_TASK_PRIO	
OS_TMR_CFG_TICKS_PER_SEC	OS_CFG_TMR_TASK_RATE_HZ	
OS_TASK_TMR_STK_SIZE	OS_CFG_TMR_TASK_STK_SIZE	
OS_TMR_CFG_WHEEL_SIZE	OS_CFG_TMR_WHEEL_SIZE	

Table C-4 µC/OS-III uses "CFG" in configuration

TC-4(1)   The very useful **OS_TICKS_PER_SEC** in µC/OS-II was renamed to **OS_CFG_TICK_RATE_HZ** in µC/OS-III. The "**HZ**" indicates that this **#define** represents Hertz (i.e., ticks per second).

Table C-5 shows additional configuration constants added to **OS_CFG.H**, while several µC/OS-II constants were either removed or renamed.

µC/OS-II (OS_CFG.H)	µC/OS-III (OS_CFG.H)	Note
OS_APP_HOOKS_EN	OS_CFG_APP_HOOKS_EN	
OS_ARG_CHK_EN	OS_CFG_ARG_CHK_EN	
	OS_CFG_CALLED_FROM_ISR_CHK_EN	
OS_DEBUG_EN	OS_CFG_DBG_EN	(1)
OS_EVENT_MULTI_EN	OS_CFG_PEND_MULTI_EN	
OS_EVENT_NAME_EN		(2)
	OS_CFG_ISR_POST_DEFERRED_EN	
OS_MAX_EVENTS		(3)
OS_MAX_FLAGS		(3)
OS_MAX_MEM_PART		(3)
OS_MAX_QS		(3)
OS_MAX_TASKS		(3)
	OS_CFG_OBJ_TYPE_CHK_EN	
OS_LOWEST_PRIO	OS_CFG_PRIO_MAX	
	OS_CFG_SCHED_LOCK_TIME_MEAS_EN	
	OS_CFG_SCHED_ROUND_ROBIN_EN	
	OS_CFG_STK_SIZE_MIN	
OS_FLAG_EN	OS_CFG_FLAG_EN	
OS_FLAG_ACCEPT_EN		(6)
OS_FLAG_DEL_EN	OS_CFG_FLAG_DEL_EN	
OS_FLAG_WAIT_CLR_EN	OS_CFG_FLAG_MODE_CLR_EN	
OS_FLAG_NAME_EN		(2)
OS_FLAG_NBITS		(4)
OS_FLAG_QUERY_EN		(5)
	OS_CFG_PEND_ABORT_EN	
OS_MBOX_EN		
OS_MBOX_ACCEPT_EN		(6)

µC/OS-II (OS_CFG.H)	µC/OS-III (OS_CFG.H)	Note
OS_MBOX_DEL_EN		
OS_MBOX_PEND_ABORT_EN		
OS_MBOX_POST_EN		
OS_MBOX_POST_OPT_EN		
OS_MBOX_QUERY_EN		(5)
OS_MEM_EN	OS_CFG_MEM_EN	
OS_MEM_NAME_EN		(2)
OS_MEM_QUERY_EN		(5)
OS_MUTEX_EN	OS_CFG_MUTEX_EN	
OS_MUTEX_ACCEPT_EN		(6)
OS_MUTEX_DEL_EN	OS_CFG_MUTEX_DEL_EN	
	OS_CFG_MUTEX_PEND_ABORT_EN	
OS_MUTEX_QUERY_EN		(5)
OS_Q_EN	OS_CFG_Q_EN	
OS_Q_ACCEPT_EN		(6)
OS_Q_DEL_EN	OS_CFG_Q_DEL_EN	
OS_Q_FLUSH_EN	OS_CFG_Q_FLUSH_EN	
	OS_CFG_Q_PEND_ABORT_EN	
OS_Q_POST_EN		(7)
OS_Q_POST_FRONT_EN		(7)
OS_Q_POST_OPT_EN		(7)
OS_Q_QUERY_EN		(5)
OS_SCHED_LOCK_EN		
OS_SEM_EN	OS_CFG_SEM_EN	
OS_SEM_ACCEPT_EN		(6)
OS_SEM_DEL_EN	OS_CFG_SEM_DEL_EN	
OS_SEM_PEND_ABORT_EN	OS_CFG_SEM_PEND_ABORT_EN	

µC/OS-II (OS_CFG.H)	µC/OS-III (OS_CFG.H)	Note
OS_SEM_QUERY_EN		(5)
OS_SEM_SET_EN	OS_CFG_SEM_SET_EN	
OS_TASK_STAT_EN	OS_CFG_STAT_TASK_EN	
OS_TASK_STK_CHK_EN	OS_CFG_STAT_TASK_STK_CHK_EN	
OS_TASK_CHANGE_PRIO_EN	OS_CFG_TASK_CHANGE_PRIO_EN	
OS_TASK_CREATE_EN		
OS_TASK_CREATE_EXT_EN		
OS_TASK_DEL_EN	OS_CFG_TASK_DEL_EN	
OS_TASK_NAME_EN		(2)
	OS_CFG_TASK_Q_EN	
	OS_CFG_TASK_Q_PEND_ABORT_EN	
OS_TASK_QUERY_EN		(5)
OS_TASK_PROFILE_EN	OS_CFG_TASK_PROFILE_EN	
	OS_CFG_TASK_REG_TBL_SIZE	
	OS_CFG_TASK_SEM_PEND_ABORT_EN	
OS_TASK_SUSPEND_EN	OS_CFG_TASK_SUSPEND_EN	
OS_TASK_SW_HOOK_EN		
OS_TICK_STEP_EN		(8)
OS_TIME_DLY_HMSM_EN	OS_CFG_TIME_DLY_HMSM_EN	
OS_TIME_DLY_RESUME_EN	OS_CFG_TIME_DLY_RESUME_EN	
OS_TIME_GET_SET_EN		
OS_TIME_TICK_HOOK_EN		
OS_TMR_EN	OS_CFG_TMR_EN	
OS_TMR_CFG_NAME_EN		(2)
OS_TMR_DEL_EN	OS_CFG_TMR_DEL_EN	

Table C-5 **µC/OS-III uses "CFG" in configuration**

615

TC-5(1)   **DEBUG** is replaced with **DBG**.

TC-5(2)   In μC/OS-II, all kernel objects have ASCII names after creation. In μC/OS-III, ASCII names are assigned when the object is created.

TC-5(3)   In μC/OS-II, it is necessary to declare the maximum number of kernel objects (number of tasks, number of event flag groups, message queues, etc.) at compile time. In μC/OS-III, all kernel objects are allocated at run time so it is no longer necessary to specify the maximum number of these objects. This feature saves valuable RAM as it is no longer necessary to over allocate objects.

TC-5(4)   In μC/OS-II, event-flag width must be declared at compile time through **OS_FLAG_NBITS**. In μC/OS-III, this is accomplished by defining the width (i.e., number of bits) in **OS_TYPE.H** through the data type **OS_FLAG**. The default is typically 32 bits.

TC-5(5)   μC/OS-III does not provide query services to the application.

TC-5(6)   μC/OS-III does not directly provide "**accept**" function calls as with μC/OS-II. Instead, **OS???Pend()** functions provide an option that emulates the "**accept**" functionality.

TC-5(7)   In μC/OS-II, there are a number of "**post**" functions. The features offered are now combined in the **OS???Post()** functions in μC/OS-III.

TC-5(8)   The μC/OS-View feature **OS_TICK_STEP_EN** is not present in μC/OS-III since μC/OS-View is an obsolete product.

C-3 VARIABLE NAME CHANGES

Some of the variable names in µC/OS-II are changed for µC/OS-III to be more consistent with coding conventions. Significant variables are shown in Table C-6.

µC/OS-II (uCOS_II.H)	µC/OS-III (OS.H)	Note
OSCtxSwCtr	OSTaskCtxSwCtr	
OSCPUUsage	OSStatTaskCPUUsage	(1)
OSIdleCtr	OSIdleTaskCtr	
OSIdleCtrMax	OSIdleTaskCtrMax	
OSIntNesting	OSIntNestingCtr	(2)
OSPrioCur	OSPrioCur	
OSPrioHighRdy	OSPrioHighRdy	
OSRunning	OSRunning	
OSSchedNesting	OSSchedLockNestingCtr	(3)
	OSSchedLockTimeMax	
OSTaskCtr	OSTaskQty	
OSTCBCur	OSTCBCurPtr	(4)
OSTCBHighRdy	OSTCBHighRdyPtr	(4)
OSTime	OSTickCtr	(5)
OSTmrTime	OSTmrTickCtr	

Table C-6 **Changes in variable naming**

TC-6(1) In µC/OS-II, **OSCPUUsage** contains the total CPU utilization in percentage format. If the CPU is busy 12% of the time, **OSCPUUsage** has the value 12. In µC/OS-III, the same information is provided in **OSStatTaskCPUUsage**.

TC-6(2) In µC/OS-II, **OSIntNesting** keeps track of the number of interrupts nesting. µC/OS-III uses **OSIntNestingCtr**. The "**Ctr**" has been added to indicate that this variable is a counter.

TC-6(3)   OSSchedNesting represents the number of times OSSchedLock() is called. µC/OS-III renames this variable to OSSchedLockNestingCtr to better represent the variable's meaning.

TC-6(4)   In µC/OS-II, OSTCBCur and OSTCBHighRdy are pointers to the OS_TCB of the current task, and to the OS_TCB of the highest-priority task that is ready to run. In µC/OS-III, these are renamed by adding the "Ptr" to indicate that they are pointers.

TC-6(5)   The internal counter of the number of ticks since power up, or the last time the variable was changed through OSTimeSet(), has been renamed to better reflect its function.

C-4 API CHANGES

The most significant change from µC/OS-II to µC/OS-III occurs in the API. In order to port a µC/OS-II-based application to µC/OS-III, it is necessary to change the way services are invoked.

Table C-7 shows changes in the way critical sections in µC/OS-III are handled. Specifically, µC/OS-II defines macros to disable interrupts, and they are moved to µC/CPU since they are CPU specific functions.

µC/OS-II (OS_CPU.H)	µC/CPU (CPU.H)	Note
OS_ENTER_CRITICAL()	CPU_CRITICAL_ENTER()	
OS_EXIT_CRITICAL()	CPU_CRITICAL_EXIT()	

Table C-7 **Changes in variable naming**

One of the biggest changes in the µC/OS-III API is its consistency. In fact, based on the function performed, it is possible to guess which arguments are needed, and in what order. For example, "*p_err" is a pointer to an error-returned variable. When present, "*p_err" is always the last argument of a function. In µC/OS-II, error-returned values are at times returned as a "*perr," and at other times as the return value of the function.

C-4-1 EVENT FLAGS

Table C-8 shows the API for event-flag management.

µC/OS-II (OS_FLAG.C)	µC/OS-III (OS_FLAG.C)	Note

`OS_FLAGS`
`OSFlagAccept(`
    `OS_FLAG_GRP  *pgrp,`
    `OS_FLAGS     flags,`
    `INT8U        wait_type,`
    `INT8U        *perr);`
		(1)

`OS_FLAG_GRP *`
`OSFlagCreate(`
    `OS_FLAGS     flags,`
    `INT8U        *perr);`
	`void`
	`OSFlagCreate(`
	    `OS_FLAG_GRP  *p_grp,`
	    `CPU_CHAR     *p_name,`
	    `OS_FLAGS     flags,`
	    `OS_ERR       *p_err);`
		(2)

`OS_FLAG_GRP *`
`OSFlagDel(`
    `OS_FLAG_GRP  *pgrp,`
    `INT8U        opt,`
    `INT8U        *perr);`
	`OS_OBJ_QTY`
	`OSFlagDel(`
	    `OS_FLAG_GRP  *p_grp,`
	    `OS_OPT       opt,`
	    `OS_ERR       *p_err);`	

`INT8U`
`OSFlagNameGet(`
    `OS_FLAG_GRP  *pgrp,`
    `INT8U        **pname,`
    `INT8U        *perr);`		

`void`
`OSFlagNameSet(`
    `OS_FLAG_GRP  *pgrp,`
    `INT8U        *pname,`
    `INT8U        *perr);`
		(3)

`OS_FLAGS`
`OSFlagPend(`
    `OS_FLAG_GRP  *pgrp,`
    `OS_FLAGS     flags,`
    `INT8U        wait_type,`
    `INT32U       timeout,`
    `INT8U        *perr);`
	`OS_FLAGS`
	`OSFlagPend(`
	    `OS_FLAG_GRP  *p_grp,`
	    `OS_FLAGS     flags,`
	    `OS_TICK      timeout,`
	    `OS_OPT       opt,`
	    `OS_TS        *p_ts,`
	    `OS_ERR       *p_err);`	

µC/OS-II (`OS_FLAG.C`)	µC/OS-III (`OS_FLAG.C`)	Note

OS_FLAGS
OSFlagPendGetFlagsRdy(
    void);
	OS_FLAGS
	OSFlagPendGetFlagsRdy(
	    OS_ERR *p_err);	

OS_FLAGS
OSFlagPost(
    OS_FLAG_GRP *pgrp,
    OS_FLAGS   flags,
    INT8U   opt,
    INT8U   *perr);
	OS_FLAGS
	OSFlagPost(
	    OS_FLAG_GRP *p_grp,
	    OS_FLAGS flags,
	    OS_OPT opt,
	    OS_ERR *p_err);	

OS_FLAGS
OSFlagQuery(
    OS_FLAG_GRP *pgrp,
    INT8U   *perr);
		(4)

Table C-8 **Event Flags API**

TC-8(1)   In µC/OS-III, there is no "accept" API. This feature is actually built-in the `OSFlagPend()` by specifying the `OS_OPT_PEND_NON_BLOCKING` option.

TC-8(2)   In µC/OS-II, `OSFlagCreate()` returns the address of an `OS_FLAG_GRP`, which is used as the "handle" to the event-flag group. In µC/OS-III, the application must allocate storage for an `OS_FLAG_GRP`, which serves the same purpose as the `OS_EVENT`. The benefit in µC/OS-III is that it is not necessary to predetermine the number of event flags at compile time.

TC-8(3)   In µC/OS-II, the user may assign a name to an event-flag group after the group is created. This functionality is built-into `OSFlagCreate()` for µC/OS-III.

TC-8(4)   µC/OS-III does not provide query services, as they are typically rarely used.

C-4-2 MESSAGE MAILBOXES

Table C-9 shows the API for message mailbox management. Note that µC/OS-III does not directly provide services for managing message mailboxes. Given that a message mailbox is a message queue of size one, µC/OS-III can easily emulate message mailboxes.

µC/OS-II (OS_MBOX.C)	µC/OS-III (OS_Q.C)	Note
void * OSMboxAccept(OS_EVENT *pevent);		(1)

OS_EVENT *
OSMboxCreate(
    void   *pmsg);
	void
	OSQCreate(
	    OS_Q *p_q,
	    CPU_CHAR *p_name,
	    OS_MSG_QTY max_qty,
	    OS_ERR *p_err);
		(2)

void *
OSMboxDel(
    OS_EVENT   *pevent,
    INT8U   opt,
    INT8U   *perr);
	OS_OBJ_QTY,
	OSQDel(
	    OS_Q *p_q,
	    OS_OPT opt,
	    OS_ERR *p_err);	

void *
OSMboxPend(
    OS_EVENT   *pevent,
    INT32U   timeout,
    INT8U   *perr);
	void *
	OSQPend(
	    OS_Q *p_q,
	    OS_TICK timeout,
	    OS_OPT opt,
	    OS_MSG_SIZE *p_msg_size,
	    CPU_TS *p_ts,
	    OS_ERR *p_err);
		(3)

INT8U
OSMBoxPendAbort(
    OS_EVENT   *pevent,
    INT8U   opt,
    INT8U   *perr);
	OS_OBJ_QTY
	OSQPendAbort(
	    OS_Q *p_q,
	    OS_OPT opt
	    OS_ERR *p_err);	

µC/OS-II (OS_MBOX.C)	µC/OS-III (OS_Q.C)	Note

INT8U
OSMboxPost(
    OS_EVENT   *pevent,
    void   *pmsg);
	void
	OSQPost(
	    OS_Q *p_q,
	    Void *p_void,
	    OS_MSG_SIZE msg_size,
	    OS_OPT opt,
	    OS_ERR *p_err);
		(4)

INT8U
OSMboxPostOpt(
    OS_EVENT   *pevent,
    void   *pmsg,
    INT8U   opt);
		(4)

INT8U
OSMboxQuery(
    OS_EVENT   *pevent,
    OS_MBOX_DATA *p_mbox_data);
		(5)

Table C-9 **Message Mailbox API**

TC-9(1)   In µC/OS-III, there is no "accept" API since this feature is built into the **OSQPend()** by specifying the **OS_OPT_PEND_NON_BLOCKING** option.

TC-9(2)   In µC/OS-II, **OSMboxCreate()** returns the address of an **OS_EVENT**, which is used as the "handle" to the message mailbox. In µC/OS-III, the application must allocate storage for an **OS_Q**, which serves the same purpose as the **OS_EVENT**. The benefit in µC/OS-III is that it is not necessary to predetermine the number of message queues at compile time.

TC-9(3)   µC/OS-III returns additional information about the message received. Specifically, the sender specifies the size of the message as a snapshot of the current timestamp is taken and stored as part of the message. The receiver of the message therefore knows when the message was sent.

TC-9(4)   In µC/OS-III, **OSQPost()** offers a number of options that replaces the two post functions provided in µC/OS-II.

TC-9(5)   µC/OS-III does not provide query services, as they were rarely used.

C-4-3 MEMORY MANAGEMENT

Table C-10 shows the difference in API for memory management.

µC/OS-II (OS_MEM.C)	µC/OS-III (OS_MEM.C)	Note

OS_MEM *
 OSMemCreate(
     void   *addr,
     INT32U   nblks,
     INT32U   blksize,
     INT8U   *perr);
	void
	 OSMemCreate(
	     OS_MEM *p_mem,
	     CPU_CHAR *p_name,
	     void *p_addr,
	     OS_MEM_QTY n_blks,
	     OS_MEM_SIZE blk_size,
	     OS_ERR *p_err);
		(1)

void *
 OSMemGet(
     OS_MEM   *pmem,
     INT8U   *perr);
	void *
	 OSMemGet(
	     OS_MEM *p_mem,
	     OS_ERR *p_err);	

INT8U
 OSMemNameGet(
     OS_MEM   *pmem,
     INT8U   **pname,
     INT8U *perr);		

void
 OSMemNameSet(
     OS_MEM   *pmem,
     INT8U   *pname,
     INT8U   *perr);
	void
	 OSMemPut(
	     OS_MEM *p_mem,
	     void *p_blk,
	     OS_ERR *p_err);
		(2)

INT8U
 OSMemPut(
     OS_MEM   *pmem,
     void   *pblk);
		(3)

INT8U
 OSMemQuery(
     OS_MEM   *pmem,
     OS_MEM_DATA *p_mem_data);		

Table C-10 **Memory Management API**

TC-10(1)   In µC/OS-II, **OSMemCreate()** returns the address of an **OS_MEM** object, which is used as the "handle" to the newly created memory partition. In µC/OS-III, the application must allocate storage for an **OS_MEM**, which serves the same purpose. The benefit in µC/OS-III is that it is not necessary to predetermine the number of memory partitions at compile time.

623

TC-10(2)   µC/OS-III does not need an **OSMemNameSet()** since the name of the memory partition is passed as an argument to **OSMemCreate()**.

TC-10(3)   µC/OS-III does not support query calls.

C-4-4 MUTUAL EXCLUSION SEMAPHORES

Table C-11 shows the difference in API for mutual exclusion semaphore management.

µC/OS-II (OS_MUTEX.C)		µC/OS-III (OS_MUTEX.C)		Note

BOOLEAN
OSMutexAccept(
    OS_EVENT   *pevent,
    INT8U   *perr);
				(1)

OS_EVENT *
OSMutexCreate(
    INT8U   prio,
    INT8U   *perr);
		void
		OSMutexCreate(
		    OS_MUTEX *p_mutex,
		    CPU_CHAR *p_name,
		    OS_ERR *p_err);
				(2)

OS_EVENT *
OSMutexDel(
    OS_EVENT   *pevent,
    INT8U   opt,
    INT8U   *perr);
		void
		OSMutexDel(
		    OS_MUTEX *p_mutex,
		    OS_OPT opt,
		    OS_ERR *p_err);		

void
OSMutexPend(
    OS_EVENT   *pevent,
    INT32U   timeout,
    INT8U   *perr);
		void
		OSMutexPend(
		    OS_MUTEX *p_mutex,
		    OS_TICK timeout,
		    OS_OPT opt,
		    CPU_TS *p_ts,
		    OS_ERR *p_err);
				(3)

		OS_OBJ_QTY
		OSMutexPendAbort(
		    OS_MUTEX *p_mutex,
		    OS_OPT opt,
		    OS_ERR *p_err);		

µC/OS-II (OS_MUTEX.C)	µC/OS-III (OS_MUTEX.C)	Note

INT8U
OSMutexPost(
    OS_EVENT   *pevent);
	void
	OSMutexPost(
	    OS_MUTEX *p_mutex,
	    OS_OPT opt,
	    OS_ERR *p_err);	

INT8U
OSMutexQuery(
    OS_EVENT   *pevent,
    OS_MUTEX_DATA *p_mutex_data);		

Table C-11 **Mutual Exclusion Semaphore Management API**

TC-11(1)   In µC/OS-III, there is no "accept" API, since this feature is built into the **OSMutexPend()** by specifying the **OS_OPT_PEND_NON_BLOCKING** option.

TC-11(2)   In µC/OS-II, **OSMutexCreate()** returns the address of an **OS_EVENT**, which is used as the "handle" to the message mailbox. In µC/OS-III, the application must allocate storage for an **OS_MUTEX**, which serves the same purpose as the **OS_EVENT**. The benefit in µC/OS-III is that it is not necessary to predetermine the number of mutual-exclusion semaphores at compile time.

TC-11(3)   µC/OS-III returns additional information when a mutex is released. The releaser takes a snapshot of the current time stamp and stores it in the **OS_MUTEX**. The new owner of the mutex therefore knows when the mutex was released.

TC-11(4)   µC/OS-III does not provide query services as they were rarely used.

C-4-5 MESSAGE QUEUES

Table C-12 shows the difference in API for message-queue management.

µC/OS-II (os_q.c)	µC/OS-III (os_q.c)	Note
``void *
OSQAccept(
OS_EVENT   *pevent,
INT8U *perr);```		(1)
``OS_EVENT *
OSQCreate(
void   **start,
INT16U size);```	```void
OSQCreate(
OS_Q   *p_q,
CPU_CHAR   *p_name,
OS_MSG_QTY max_qty,
OS_ERR *p_err);```	(2)
``OS_EVENT *
OSQDel(
OS_EVENT   *pevent,
INT8U   opt,
INT8U *perr);```	```OS_OBJ_QTY,
OSQDel(
OS_Q   *p_q,
OS_OPT   opt,
OS_ERR *p_err);```	
``INT8U
OSQFlush(
OS_EVENT *pevent);```	```OS_MSG_QTY
OSQFlush(
OS_Q   *p_q,
OS_ERR *p_err);```	
``void *
OSQPend(
OS_EVENT   *pevent,
INT32U   timeout,
INT8U *perr);```	```void *
OSQPend(
OS_Q   *p_q,
OS_MSG_SIZE *p_msg_size,
OS_TICK   timeout,
OS_OPT   opt,
CPU_TS   *p_ts,
OS_ERR *p_err);```	(3)
``INT8U
OSQPendAbort(
OS_EVENT   *pevent,
INT8U   opt,
INT8U *perr);```	```OS_OBJ_QTY
OSQPendAbort(
OS_Q   *p_q,
OS_OPT   opt,
OS_ERR *p_err);```	
``INT8U
OSQPost(
OS_EVENT   *pevent,
void *pmsg);```	```void
OSQPost(
OS_Q   *p_q,
void   *p_void,
OS_MSG_SIZE msg_size,
OS_OPT   opt,
OS_ERR *p_err);```	(4)

µC/OS-II (os_q.c)	µC/OS-III (os_q.c)	Note

INT8U
OSQPostFront(
    OS_EVENT *pevent,
    void *pmsg);		

INT8U
OSQPostOpt(
    OS_EVENT *pevent,
    void   *pmsg,
    INT8U   opt);
		(4)

INT8U
OSQQuery(
    OS_EVENT *pevent,
    OS_Q_DATA *p_q_data);
		(5)

Table C-12 **Message Queue Management API**

TC-12(1)   In µC/OS-III, there is no "accept" API as this feature is built into the OSQPend()
by specifying the OS_OPT_PEND_NON_BLOCKING option.

TC-12(2)   In µC/OS-II, OSQCreate() returns the address of an OS_EVENT, which is used
as the "handle" to the message queue. In µC/OS-III, the application must
allocate storage for an OS_Q object, which serves the same purpose as the
OS_EVENT. The benefit in µC/OS-III is that it is not necessary to predetermine at
compile time, the number of message queues.

TC-12(3)   µC/OS-III returns additional information when a message queue is posted.
Specifically, the sender includes the size of the message and takes a snapshot
of the current timestamp and stores it in the message. The receiver of the
message therefore knows when the message was posted.

TC-12(4)   In µC/OS-III, OSQPost() offers a number of options that replaces the three
post functions provided in µC/OS-II.

TC-12(5)   µC/OS-III does not provide query services as they were rarely used.

C-4-6 SEMAPHORES

Table C-13 shows the difference in API for semaphore management.

µC/OS-II (os_sem.c)	µC/OS-III (os_sem.c)	Note
INT16U OSSemAccept(OS_EVENT *pevent);		(1)

OS_EVENT *
OSSemCreate(
    INT16U   cnt);
	void
	OSSemCreate(
	    OS_SEM *p_sem,
	    CPU_CHAR *p_name,
	    OS_SEM_CTR cnt,
	    OS_ERR *p_err);
		(2)

OS_EVENT *
OSSemDel(
    OS_EVENT   *pevent,
    INT8U   opt,
    INT8U   *perr);
	OS_OBJ_QTY,
	OSSemDel(
	    OS_SEM *p_sem,
	    OS_OPT opt,
	    OS_ERR *p_err);	

void
OSSemPend(
    OS_EVENT   *pevent,
    INT32U   timeout,
    INT8U   *perr);
	OS_SEM_CTR
	OSSemPend(
	    OS_SEM *p_sem,
	    OS_TICK timeout,
	    OS_OPT opt,
	    CPU_TS *p_ts,
	    OS_ERR *p_err);
		(3)

INT8U
OSSemPendAbort(
    OS_EVENT   *pevent,
    INT8U   opt,
    INT8U   *perr);
	OS_OBJ_QTY
	OSSemPendAbort(
	    OS_SEM *p_sem,
	    OS_OPT opt,
	    OS_ERR *p_err);	

void
OSSemPost(
    OS_EVENT   *pevent);
	void
	OSSemPost(
	    OS_SEM *p_sem,
	    OS_OPT opt,
	    OS_ERR *p_err);	

INT8U
OSSemQuery(
    OS_EVENT   *pevent,
    OS_SEM_DATA *p_sem_data);
		(4)

µC/OS-II (OS_SEM.C)	µC/OS-III (OS_SEM.C)	Note
| ```
void
OSSemSet(
    OS_EVENT    *pevent,
    INT16U      cnt,
    INT8U       *perr);
``` | ```
void
OSSemSet(
    OS_SEM      *p_sem,
    OS_SEM_CTR  cnt,
    OS_ERR      *p_err);
``` |  |

Table C-13 **Semaphore Management API**

TC-13(1)   In µC/OS-III, there is no "accept" API since this feature is built into the **OSSemPend()** by specifying the **OS_OPT_PEND_NON_BLOCKING** option.

TC-13(2)   In µC/OS-II, **OSSemCreate()** returns the address of an **OS_EVENT**, which is used as the "handle" to the semaphore. In µC/OS-III, the application must allocate storage for an **OS_SEM** object, which serves the same purpose as the **OS_EVENT**. The benefit in µC/OS-III is that it is not necessary to predetermine the number of semaphores at compile time.

TC-13(3)   µC/OS-III returns additional information when a semaphore is signaled. The ISR or task that signals the semaphore takes a snapshot of the current timestamp and stores this in the **OS_SEM** object signaled. The receiver of the signal therefore knows when the signal was sent.

TC-13(5)   µC/OS-III does not provide query services, as they were rarely used.

C-4-7 TASK MANAGEMENT

Table C-14 shows the difference in API for task-management services.

µC/OS-II (os_task.c)	µC/OS-III (os_task.c)	Note

INT8U
OSTaskChangePrio(
    INT8U   oldprio,
    INT8U   newprio);
	void
	OSTaskChangePrio(
	    OS_TCB *p_tcb,
	    OS_PRIO prio,
	    OS_ERR *p_err);
		(1)

INT8U
OSTaskCreate(
    void   (*task)(void *p_arg),
    void   *p_arg,
    OS_STK   *ptos,
    INT8U   prio);
	void
	OSTaskCreate(
	    OS_TCB *p_tcb,
	    CPU_CHAR *p_name,
	    OS_TASK_PTR *p_task,
	    void *p_arg,
	    OS_PRIO prio,
	    CPU_STK *p_stk_base,
	    CPU_STK_SIZE stk_limit,
	    CPU_STK_SIZE stk_size,
	    OS_MSG_QTY q_size,
	    OS_TICK time_quanta,
	    void *p_ext,
	    OS_OPT opt,
	    OS_ERR *p_err);
		(2)

INT8U
OSTaskCreateExt(
    void   (*task)(void *p_arg),
    void   *p_arg,
    OS_STK   *ptos,
    INT8U   prio,
    INT16U   id,
    OS_STK   *pbos,
    INT32U   stk_size,
    void   *pext,
    INT16U   opt);
	void
	OSTaskCreate(
	    OS_TCB *p_tcb,
	    CPU_CHAR *p_name,
	    OS_TASK_PTR *p_task,
	    void *p_arg,
	    OS_PRIO prio,
	    CPU_STK *p_stk_base,
	    CPU_STK_SIZE stk_limit,
	    CPU_STK_SIZE stk_size,
	    OS_MSG_QTY q_size,
	    OS_TICK time_quanta,
	    void *p_ext,
	    OS_OPT opt,
	    OS_ERR *p_err);
		(2)

INT8U
OSTaskDel(
    INT8U   prio);
	void
	OSTaskDel(
	    OS_TCB *p_tcb,
	    OS_ERR *p_err);	

µC/OS-II (OS_TASK.C)	µC/OS-III (OS_TASK.C)	Note
INT8U OSTaskDelReq(INT8U prio);		

INT8U
OSTaskNameGet(
    INT8U   prio,
    INT8U   **pname,
    INT8U *perr);		

void
OSTaskNameSet(
    INT8U   prio,
    INT8U   *pname,
    INT8U   *perr);
		(3)

	OS_MSG_QTY
	OSTaskQFlush(
	    OS_TCB *p_tcb,
	    OS_ERR *p_err);
		(4)

	void *
	OSTaskQPend(
	    OS_TICK timeout,
	    OS_OPT opt,
	    OS_MSG_SIZE *p_msg_size,
	    CPU_TS *p_ts,
	    OS_ERR *p_err);
		(4)

	CPU_BOOLEAN
	OSTaskQPendAbort(
	    OS_TCB *p_tcb,
	    OS_OPT opt,
	    OS_ERR *p_err);
		(4)

	void
	OSTaskQPost(
	    OS_TCB *p_tcb,
	    void *p_void,
	    OS_MSG_SIZE msg_size,
	    OS_OPT opt,
	    OS_ERR *p_err);
		(4)

INT32U
OSTaskRegGet(
    INT8U   prio,
    INT8U   id,
    INT8U   *perr);
	OS_REG
	OSTaskRegGet(
	    OS_TCB *p_tcb,
	    OS_REG_ID id,
	    OS_ERR *p_err);	

µC/OS-II (`OS_TASK.C`)	µC/OS-III (`OS_TASK.C`)	Note

`void`
`OSTaskRegSet(`
    `INT8U     prio,`
    `INT8U     id,`
    `INT32U    value,`
    `INT8U     *perr);`
	`void`
	`OSTaskRegGet(`
	    `OS_TCB     *p_tcb,`
	    `OS_REG_ID  id,`
	    `OS_REG     value,`
	    `OS_ERR     *p_err);`	

`INT8U`
`OSTaskResume(`
    `INT8U     prio);`
	`void`
	`OSTaskResume(`
	    `OS_TCB     *p_tcb,`
	    `OS_ERR     *p_err);`	

	`OS_SEM_CTR`
	`OSTaskSemPend(`
	    `OS_TICK    timeout,`
	    `OS_OPT     opt,`
	    `CPU_TS     *p_ts,`
	    `OS_ERR     *p_err);`
		(5)

	`CPU_BOOLEAN`
	`OSTaskSemPendAbort(`
	    `OS_TCB     *p_tcb,`
	    `OS_OPT     opt,`
	    `OS_ERR     *p_err);`
		(5)

	`CPU_BOOLEAN`
	`OSTaskSemPendAbort(`
	    `OS_TCB     *p_tcb,`
	    `OS_OPT     opt,`
	    `OS_ERR     *p_err);`
		(5)

	`OS_SEM_CTR`
	`OSTaskSemPost(`
	    `OS_TCB     *p_tcb,`
	    `OS_OPT     opt,`
	    `OS_ERR     *p_err);`
		(5)

	`OS_SEM_CTR`
	`OSTaskSemSet(`
	    `OS_TCB     *p_tcb,`
	    `OS_SEM_CTR cnt,`
	    `OS_ERR     *p_err);`
		(5)

`INT8U`
`OSTaskSuspend(`
    `INT8U     prio);`
	`void`
	`OSTaskSuspend(`
	    `OS_TCB     *p_tcb,`
	    `OS_ERR     *p_err);`	

μC/OS-II (OS_TASK.C)	μC/OS-III (OS_TASK.C)	Note
```INT8U OSTaskStkChk(INT8U prio, OS_STK_DATA *p_stk_data);```	```void OSTaskStkChk(OS_TCB *p_tcb, CPU_STK_SIZE *p_free, CPU_STK_SIZE *p_used, OS_ERR *p_err);```	(6)
	```void OSTaskTimeQuantaSet(OS_TCB *p_tcb, OS_TICK time_quanta, OS_ERR *p_err);```	(7)
```INT8U OSTaskQuery(INT8U prio, OS_TCB *p_task_data);```		(8)

Table C-14 **Task Management API**

TC-14(1) In μC/OS-II, each task must have a unique priority. The priority of a task can be changed at run-time, however it can only be changed to an unused priority. This is generally not a problem since μC/OS-II supports up to 255 different priority levels and is rare for an application to require all levels. Since μC/OS-III supports an unlimited number of tasks at each priority, the user can change the priority of a task to any available level.

TC-14(2) μC/OS-II provides two functions to create a task: **OSTaskCreate()** and **OSTaskCreateExt()**. **OSTaskCreateExt()** is recommended since it offers more flexibility. In μC/OS-III, only one API is used to create a task, **OSTaskCreate()**, which offers similar features to **OSTaskCreateExt()** and provides additional ones.

TC-14(3) μC/OS-III does not need an **OSTaskNameSet()** since an ASCII name for the task is passed as an argument to **OSTaskCreate()**.

TC-14(4) μC/OS-III allows tasks or ISRs to send messages directly to a task instead of having to pass through a mailbox or a message queue as does μC/OS-II.

TC-14(5) μC/OS-III allows tasks or ISRs to directly signal a task instead of having to pass through a semaphore as does μC/OS-II.

TC-14(6)   In µC/OS-II, the user must allocate storage for a special data structure called **OS_STK_DATA**, which is used to place the result of a stack check of a task. This data structure contains only two fields: **.OSFree** and **.OSUsed**. In µC/OS-III, it is required that the caller pass pointers to destination variables where those values will be placed.

TC-14(7)   µC/OS-III allows users to specify the time quanta of each task on a per-task basis. This is available since µC/OS-III supports multiple tasks at the same priority, and allows for round robin scheduling. The time quanta for a task is specified when the task is created, but it can be changed by the API at run time.

TC-14(8)   µC/OS-III does not provide query services as they were rarely used.

C-4-8 TIME MANAGEMENT

Table C-15 shows the difference in API for time-management services.

µC/OS-II (OS_TIME.C)	µC/OS-III (OS_TIME.C)	Note

`void`
`OSTimeDly(`
   `INT32U     ticks);`
	`void`
	`OSTimeDly(`
	   `OS_TICK    dly,`
	   `OS_OPT     opt,`
	   `OS_ERR     *p_err);`
		(1)

`INT8U`
`OSTimeDlyHMSM(`
   `INT8U     hours,`
   `INT8U     minutes,`
   `INT8U     seconds,`
   `INT16U    ms);`
	`void`
	`OSTimeDlyHMSM(`
	   `CPU_INT16U  hours,`
	   `CPU_INT16U  minutes,`
	   `CPU_INT16U  seconds`
	   `CPU_INT32U  milli,`
	   `OS_OPT      opt,`
	   `OS_ERR      *p_err);`
		(2)

`INT8U`
`OSTimeDlyResume(`
   `INT8U     prio);`
	`void`
	`OSTimeDlyResume(`
	   `OS_TCB    *p_tcb,`
	   `OS_ERR    *p_err);`	

`INT32U`
`OSTimeGet(void);`
	`OS_TICK`
	`OSTimeGet(`
	   `OS_ERR    *p_err);`	

µC/OS-II (OS_TIME.C)	µC/OS-III (OS_TIME.C)	Note

void
OSTimeSet(
    INT32U   ticks);
	void
	OSTimeSet(
	    OS_TICK ticks,
	    OS_ERR *p_err);	

void OSTimeTick(void)	void OSTimeTick(void)	

Table C-15 **Time Management API**

TC-15(1)   µC/OS-III includes an option argument, which allows the user to delay a task for a certain number of ticks, or wait until the tick counter reaches a certain value. In µC/OS-II, only the former is available.

TC-15(2)   OSTimeDlyHMSM() in µC/OS-III is more flexible as it allows a user to specify whether to be "strict" about the ranges of hours (0 to 999), minutes (0 to 59), seconds (0 to 59), and milliseconds (0 to 999), or whether to allow any values such as 200 minutes, 75 seconds, or 20,000 milliseconds.

C-4-9 TIMER MANAGEMENT

Table C-16 shows the difference in API for timer-management services. The timer management in µC/OS-III is similar to that of µC/OS-II except for minor changes in arguments in OSTmrCreate().

µC/OS-II (OS_TMR.C)	µC/OS-III (OS_TMR.C)	Note

OS_TMR *
OSTmrCreate(
    INT32U   dly,
    INT32U   period,
    INT8U   opt,
    OS_TMR_CALLBACK callback,
    void   *callback_arg,
    INT8U   *pname,
    INT8U   *perr);
	void
	OSTmrCreate(
	    OS_TMR *p_tmr,
	    CPU_CHAR *p_name,
	    OS_TICK dly,
	    OS_TICK period,
	    OS_OPT opt,
	    OS_TMR_CALLBACK_PTR *p_callback,
	    void *p_callback_arg,
	    OS_ERR *p_err);	

µC/OS-II (OS_TMR.C)		µC/OS-III (OS_TMR.C)		Note

BOOLEAN
OSTmrDel(
    OS_TMR   *ptmr,
    INT8U   *perr);
		CPU_BOOLEAN
		OSTmrDel(
		    OS_TMR *p_tmr,
		    OS_ERR *p_err);		

INT8U
OSTmrNameGet(
    OS_TMR   *ptmr,
    INT8U   **pdest,
    INT8U *perr);				

INT32U
OSTmrRemainGet(
    OS_TMR   *ptmr,
    INT8U   *perr);
		OS_TICK
		OSTmrRemainGet(
		    OS_TMR *p_tmr,
		    OS_ERR *p_err);		

INT8U
OSTmrStateGet(
    OS_TMR   *ptmr,
    INT8U   *perr);
		OS_STATE
		OSTmrStateGet(
		    OS_TMR *p_tmr,
		    OS_ERR *p_err);		

BOOLEAN
OSTmrStart(
    OS_TMR   *ptmr,
    INT8U   *perr);
		CPU_BOOLEAN
		OSTmrStart(
		    OS_TMR *p_tmr,
		    OS_ERR *p_err);		

BOOLEAN
OSTmrStop(
    OS_TMR   *ptmr,
    INT8U   opt,
    void   *callback_arg,
    INT8U   *perr);
		CPU_BOOLEAN
		OSTmrStop(
		    OS_TMR *p_tmr,
		    OS_OPT opt,
		    void *p_callback_arg,
		    OS_ERR *p_err);		

INT8U OSTmrSignal(void);				

Table C-16 **Timer Management API**

C-4-10 MISCELLANEOUS

Table C-17 shows the difference in API for miscellaneous services.

µC/OS-II (OS_CORE.C)	µC/OS-III (OS_CORE.C)	Note

INT8U
OSEventNameGet(
    OS_EVENT   *pevent,
    INT8U   **pname,
    INT8U *perr);		

void
OSEventNameSet(
    OS_EVENT   *pevent,
    INT8U   *pname,
    INT8U   *perr);
		(1)

INT16U
OSEventPendMulti(
    OS_EVENT **pevent_pend,
    OS_EVENT **pevent_rdy,
    void   **pmsgs_rdy,
    INT32U   timeout,
    INT8U   *perr);
	OS_OBJ_QTY
	OSPendMulti(
	    OS_PEND_DATA *p_pend_data_tbl,
	    OS_OBJ_QTY tbl_size,
	    OS_TICK timeout,
	    OS_OPT opt,
	    OS_ERR *p_err);
		(2)

void OSInit(void)	void OSInit(OS_ERR *p_err);	(3)
void OSIntEnter(void)	void OSIntEnter(void);	
void OSIntExit(void)	void OSIntExit(void)	
	void OSSched(void);	
void OSSchedLock(void)	void OSSchedLock(OS_ERR *p_err);	(4)

	void
	OSSchedRoundRobinCfg(
	    CPU_BOOLEAN en,
	    OS_TICK dflt_time_quanta,
	    OS_ERR *p_err);
		(5)

	void OSSchedRoundRobinYield(OS_ERR *p_err);	(6)

637

µC/OS-II (OS_CORE.C)	µC/OS-III (OS_CORE.C)	Note

`void`
`OSSchedUnlock(void)`
	`void`
	`OSSchedUnlock(`
	    `OS_ERR        *p_err);`
		(7)

`void` `OSStart(void)`	`void` `OSStart(void);`	

`void`
`OSStatInit(void)`
	`void`
	`OSStatTaskCPUUsageInit(`
	    `OS_ERR        *p_err);`
		(8)

`INT16U`
`OSVersion(void)`
	`CPU_INT16U`
	`OSVersion(`
	    `OS_ERR        *p_err);`
		(9)

Table C-17 **Miscellaneous API**

TC-17(1)   Objects in µC/OS-III are named when they are created and these functions are not required in µC/OS-III.

TC-17(2)   The implementation of the multi-pend functionality is changed from µC/OS-II. However, the purpose of multi-pend is the same, to allow a task to pend (or wait) on multiple objects. In µC/OS-III, however, it is possible to only multi-pend on semaphores and message queues and not event flags and mutexes.

TC-17(3)   An error code is returned in µC/OS-III for this function. Initialization is successful if **OS_ERR_NONE** is received back from **OSInit()**. In µC/OS-II, there is no way of knowing whether there is an error in the configuration that caused **OSInit()** to fail.

TC-17(4)   An error code is returned in µC/OS-III for this function.

TC-17(5)   Enable or disable µC/OS-III's round-robin scheduling at run time, as well as change the default time quanta.

TC-17(6)   A task that completes its work before its time quanta expires may yield the CPU to another task at the same priority.

TC-17(7)   An error code is returned in µC/OS-III for this function.

TC-17(8)   Note the change in name for the function that computes the "capacity" of the CPU for the purpose of computing CPU usage at run-time.

TC-17(9)   An error code is returned in µC/OS-III for this function.

C-4-11 HOOKS AND PORT

Table C-18 shows the difference in APIs used to port µC/OS-II to µC/OS-III.

µC/OS-II (OS_CPU*.C/H)	µC/OS-III (OS_CPU*.C/H)	Note
	OS_TS OSGetTS(void);	(1)
void OSInitHookBegin(void);	void OSInitHook(void);	
void OSInitHookEnd(void);		

void
OSTaskCreateHook(
    OS_TCB   *ptcb);
	void
	OSTaskCreateHook(
	    OS_TCB *p_tcb);	

void
OSTaskDelHook(
    OS_TCB   *ptcb);
	void
	OSTaskDelHook(
	    OS_TCB *p_tcb);	

void OSTaskIdleHook(void);	void OSIdleTaskHook(void);	
	void OSTaskReturnHook(OS_TCB *p_tcb);	(2)
void OSTaskStatHook(void)	void OSStatTaskHook(void);	

void
OSTaskStkInit(
    void   (*task)(void *p_arg),
    void   *p_arg,
    OS_STK   *ptos,
    INT16U   opt);
	CPU_STK *
	OSTaskStkInit(
	    OS_TASK_PTR p_task,
	    void *p_arg,
	    CPU_STK *p_stk_base,
	    CPU_STK *p_stk_limit,
	    CPU_STK_SIZE size,
	    OS_OPT opt);
		(3)

void OSTaskSwHook(void)	void OSTaskSwHook(void);	

µC/OS-II (OS_CPU*.C/H)	µC/OS-III (OS_CPU*.C/H)	Note
```void OSTCBInitHook(OS_TCB *ptcb); ```		(4)
```void OSTimeTickHook(void); ```	```void OSTimeTickHook(void); ```	
```void OSStartHighRdy(void); ```	```void OSStartHighRdy(void); ```	(5)
```void OSIntCtxSw(void); ```	```void OSIntCtxSw(void); ```	(5)
```void OSCtxSw(void); ```	```void OSCtxSw(void); ```	(5)

Table C-18 **Hooks and Port API**

TC-18(1)   µC/OS-III requires that the Board Support Package (BSP) provide a 32-bit free-running counter (from **0x00000000** to **0xFFFFFFFF** and rolls back to **0x00000000**) for the purpose of performing time measurements. When a signal is sent, or a message is posted, this counter is read and sent to the recipient. This allows the recipient to know when the message was sent. If a 32-bit free-running counter is not available, simulate one using a 16-bit counter.

TC-18(2)   µC/OS-III is able to terminate a task that returns. Recall that tasks should not return since they should be either implemented as an infinite loop, or deleted if implemented as run once.

TC-18(3)   The code for **OSTaskStkInit()** must be changed slightly in µC/OS-III since several arguments passed to this function are different than in µC/OS-II. Instead of passing the top-of-stack as in µC/OS-II, **OSTaskStkInit()** is passed the base address of the task stack, as well as the size of the stack.

TC-18(4)   This function is not needed in µC/OS-III.

TC-18(5)   These functions are a part of **OS_CPU_A.ASM**, and should only require name changes for the following variables:

µC/OS-II variable changes to ...	... in µC/OS-III
OSIntNesting	OSIntNestingCtr
OSTCBCur	OSTCBCurPtr
OSTCBHighRdy	OSTCBHighRdyPtr

MISRA-C:2004 and µC/OS-III

MISRA C is a software development standard for the C programming language developed by the Motor Industry Software Reliability Association (MISRA). Its aims are to facilitate code safety, portability, and reliability in the context of embedded systems, specifically those systems programmed in ANSI C. There is also a set of guidelines for MISRA C++.

There are now more MISRA users outside of the automotive industry than within it. MISRA has evolved into a widely accepted model of best practices by leading developers in such sectors as aerospace, telecom, medical devices, defense, railway, and others.

The first edition of the MISRA C standard, "Guidelines for the use of the C language in vehicle based software," was produced in 1998 and is officially known as MISRA-C:1998. MISRA-C:1998 had 127 rules, of which 93 were required and 34 advisory. The rules were numbered in sequence from 1 to 127.

In 2004, a second edition "Guidelines for the use of the C language in critical systems," or MISRA-C:2004 was produced with many substantial changes, including a complete renumbering of the rules.

The MISRA-C:2004 document contains 141 rules, of which 121 are "required" and 20 are "advisory," divided into 21 topical categories, from "Environment" to "Run-time failures."

µC/OS-III follows most of the MISRA-C:2004 except that five (5) of the required rules were suppressed. The reasoning behind this is discussed within this appendix.

IAR Embedded Workbench for ARM (EWARM) V5.40 was used to verify MISRA-C:2004 compliance, which required suppressing the rules to achieve a clean build.

D

D-1 MISRA-C:2004, RULE 8.5 (REQUIRED)

Rule Description

There shall be no definitions of objects or functions in a header file.

Offending code appears as

```
OS_EXT    OS_IDLE_CTR    OSIdleTaskCtr;
```

OS_EXT allows us to declare "extern" and storage using a single declaration in OS.H but allocation of storage actually occurs in OS_VAR.C.

Rule suppressed

The method used in µC/OS-III is an improved scheme as it avoids declaring variables in multiple files. Storage for a variable must be declared in one file (such as OS_VAR.C) and another file needs to extern the variables in a separate file (such as OS.H).

Occurs in

OS.H

D-2 MISRA-C:2004, RULE 8.12 (REQUIRED)

Rule Description:

When an array is declared with external linkage, its size shall be stated explicitly or defined implicitly by initialization.

Offending code appears as

```
extern  CPU_STK        OSCfg_IdleTaskStk[];
```

µC/OS-III can be provided in object form (linkable object), but requires that the value and size of known variables and arrays be declared in application code. It is not possible to know the size of the arrays.

Rule suppressed

There is no choice other than to suppress or add a fictitious size, which would not be proper. For example, we could specify a size of 1 and the MISRA-C:2004 would pass.

Occurs in:

OS.H

D-3 MISRA-C:2004, RULE 14.7 (REQUIRED)

Rule Description

A function shall have a single point of exit at the end of the function.

Offending code appears as

```
if (argument is invalid) {
    Set error code;
    return;
}
```

Rule suppressed

We prefer to exit immediately upon finding an invalid argument rather than create nested "if" statements.

Occurs in

OS_CORE.C

OS_FLAG.C

OS_INT.C

OS_MEM.C

OS_MSG.C

OS_MUTEX.C

OS_PEND_MULTI.C

OS_PRIO.C

OS_Q.C

OS_SEM.C

OS_STAT.C

OS_TASK.C

OS_TICK.C

OS_TIME.C

OS_TMR.C

D

D-4 MISRA-C:2004, RULE 15.2 (REQUIRED)

Rule Description
An unconditional break statement shall terminate every non-empty switch clause.

Offending code appears as

```
switch (value) {
    case constant_value:
        /* Code */
        return;
}
```

Rule suppressed
The problem involves using a return statement to exit the function instead of using a break. When adding a "break" statement after the return, the compiler complains about the unreachable code of the "break" statement.

Occurs in
OS_FLAG.C
OS_MUTEX.C
OS_Q.C
OS_TMR.C

D-5 MISRA-C:2004, RULE 17.4 (REQUIRED)

Rule Description

Array indexing shall be the only allowed form of pointer arithmetic.

Offending code appears as

```
    :
p_tcb++;
    :
```

Rule suppressed

It is common practice in C to increment a pointer instead of using array indexing to accomplish the same thing. This common practice is not in agreement with this rule.

Occurs in

OS_CORE.C

OS_CPU_C.C

OS_INT.C

OS_MSG.C

OS_PEND_MULTI.C

OS_PRIO.C

OS_TASK.C

OS_TICK.C

OS_TMR.C

D

Appendix

E

Bibliography

Bal Sathe, Dhananjay. 1988. *Fast Algorithm Determines Priority*. EDN (India), September, p. 237.

Comer, Douglas. 1984. *Operating System Design, The XINU Approach*. Englewood Cliffs, New Jersey: Prentice-Hall. ISBN 0-13-637539-1.

Kernighan, Brian W. and Dennis M. Ritchie. 1988. *The C Programming Language, 2nd edition*. Englewood Cliffs, New Jersey: Prentice Hall. ISBN 0-13-110362-8.

Klein, Mark H., Thomas Ralya, Bill Pollak, Ray Harbour Obenza, and Michael Gonzlez. 1993. *A Practioner's Handbook for Real-Time Analysis: Guide to Rate Monotonic Analysis for Real-Time Systems*. Norwell, Massachusetts: Kluwer Academic Publishers Group. ISBN 0-7923-9361-9.

Labrosse, Jean J. 2002, *MicroC/OS-II, The Real-Time Kernel*, CMP Books, 2002, ISBN 1-57820-103-9.

Li, Qing. *Real-Time Concepts for Embedded Systems*, CMP Books, July 2003, ISBN 1-57820-124-1.

The Motor Industry Software Reliability Association, *MISRA-C:2004*, Guidelines for the Use of the C Language in Critical Systems, October 2004. www.misra-c.com.

E

Appendix

Licensing Policy

This book contains µC/OS-III, precompiled in linkable object form, and is accompanied by an evaluation board and tools (compiler/assembler/linker/debugger). The user may use µC/OS-III with the evaluation board that accompanied the book and it is not necessary to purchase anything else as long as the initial purchase is used for educational purposes. Once the code is used to create a commercial project/product for profit, however, it is necessary to purchase a license.

It is necessary to purchase this license when the decision to use µC/OS-III in a design is made, not when the design is ready to go to production.

If you are unsure about whether you need to obtain a license for your application, please contact Micrium and discuss the intended use with a sales representative.

Contact Micrium

Micrium
1290 Weston Road, Suite 306
Weston, FL 33326

+1 954 217 2036
+1 954 217 2037 (FAX)

E-Mail : sales@micrium.com
Website : www.micrium.com

F

µC/OS-III™
The Real-Time Kernel

and the Renesas
RX62N
32-bit MCU with FPU

Jean J. Labrosse
Fabiano Kovalski

Micriµm
📖 *Press*

Weston, FL 33326

Micriµm Press
1290 Weston Road, Suite 306
Weston, FL 33326
USA
www.micrium.com

Library of Congress Control Number: 2010922732

Library of Congress subject headings:

1. Embedded computer systems
2. Real-time data processing
3. Computer software - Development

For bulk orders, please contact Micrium Press at: +1 954 217 2036

100-uCOS-III-Renesas-RX62N-001

ISBN: 978-0-9823375-7-8

Foreword

The sophistication, capabilities, performance, and system design opportunities offered by Renesas RX™ microcontrollers are quite astounding and continue to grow. A good operating system—especially a well-proven real-time operating system (RTOS)—can shorten the time to market and help achieve the enormous solution potential of these devices.

What is needed for many applications is an RTOS with features honed to deliver the kind of fast, reliable system that takes full advantage of the microcontroller and turns them into actions and operations that make successful end products, equipment and electronic systems. Micriµm, one of our Platinum Partners, delivers this key software in the form of their popular µC/OS-III real-time kernel. And to better support this product, Jean Labrosse, president of Micriµm Inc., has written this incredibly informative book.

Academic theory for creating a real-time kernel is quite straightforward. But a world of difference exists between theory and practice. There are a myriad of practical issues related to designing, testing and implementing an RTOS that delivers all the capabilities essential for today's embedded systems, especially for those that are mission-critical or bear huge safety burdens. Moreover, of necessity, there are complexities associated with ensuring the optimum use of the features that the RTOS delivers. Mr. Labrosse's book is a tremendous body of work; an amazing investment of effort produced to make it easier for system engineers to create powerful and reliable new products for diverse global markets, while also saving valuable time in the development cycle.

Micriµm's real-time kernels are compact, portable designs used in thousands of products, including safety-critical systems. Scalable and ROM-able, they support most MISRA-C rules, are third-party certified and ensure that applications are guaranteed run-time. Among the wide range of middleware products offered by Micriµm, µC/TCP-IP, µC/USB Host and Device, µC/FS, and µC/CAN conform to applicable standards, are highly reliable, and specifically put the processing power of microcontrollers like the Renesas RX62N chip to work with high efficiency.

This package, containing Mr. Labrosse's book, the companion Renesas Demo Kit YRDKRX62N, µC/OS-III real-time kernel and the HEW integrated development environment with software tools, combines Renesas' strengths and Micriµm's strengths in a very synergistic way. Based on true out-of-the-box thinking, it is much more than just a convenient entry point for meeting the requirements of even the most challenging new design projects. It's also a valuable tutorial for getting the most out of the system implementation, as well as a valuable reference for analysis and troubleshooting.

Renesas and Micriµm had two primary goals in creating this package. We wanted to simplify and facilitate the application of RX600 series microcontrollers, and wanted to help you build the highest possible level of quality into your system designs. If we've been successful in meeting these objectives, you will enjoy using the system development resources delivered herein and be able to put them to good use easily, again and again.

Thank you for your interest in Renesas microcontrollers and advanced embedded system solutions.

Ali Sebt
Executive Vice President
Renesas Technology America, Inc.

1

Introduction

Part II of this book delivers to the reader the experience of µC/OS-III through the use of world-class tools and step-by-step instructions.

The book is packaged with the Renesas Demo Kit (RDK) YRDKRX62N, which contains a Renesas RX62N Ultra-Fast MCU (Micro Controller Unit) with Ethernet, CAN, and USB connectivity.

To build the example code provided in Part II of this book, it is necessary to download the Renesas development tools from the Renesas website, www.renesas.com/rdkrx62ninstall. The award-winning µC/Probe is used to monitor and change application variables at run time throughout all the examples in the book (see Chapter 2, Setup). µC/Probe is available for download at Micriµm's website at www.Micrium.com/probe.

The heart of the evaluation board is the Renesas RX62N, one of the highest performing cores available on the market today.

The RX62N is available at clock frequencies up to 100 MHz and contains such high performance peripherals as a 10/100 Ethernet MAC, full-speed USB-Host/Device/OTG controller, timers, UARTs, and more. The RX62N provided in the YRDKRX62N features built-in Flash memory of 512 kbytes and 96 kbytes of high-speed static RAM.

THE RENESAS YRDKRX62N

Figure 1-1 shows a picture of the Renesas Demo Kit YRDKRX62N which has the following features:

■ Low cost

■ Renesas RX62N Ultra-Fast MCU

■ 10/100 Ethernet connector using National Semiconductors IEEE1588 compatible PHY

■ USB Host, Device and On-The-Go (OTG) functionality

■ RS-232C female connector

■ CAN 2.0 circuitry including transceiver

■ SPI

■ I^2C

■ Micro Secure Digital (microSD) card socket

■ 128 MB of Phase Change Memory (PCM) from Micron

■ On-board Segger J-Link debugger, µC/Probe compatible

■ Temperature sensor

■ 12 User LEDs

■ Three-axis accelerometer

■ Audio amplifier, Microphone, Speaker and output circuitry

■ Expansion connector

The RX62N is capable of running a TCP/IP stack such as Micriµm's high-quality µC/TCP-IP. This allows an application to network with other devices, as well as access the Internet. Micriµm offers a number of application protocols such as DHCP client (to obtain an IP address), FTP client/server, HTTP server (i.e., a web server), SMTP client (to send e-mails), POP3 client (to receive e-mails), and more. µC/TCP-IP can also be used in conjunction with µC/Probe to read and write data to the embedded target.

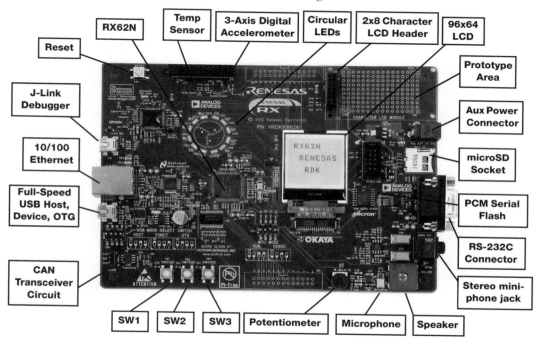

Figure 1-1 **Renesas YRDKRX62N**

The RX62N is also capable of running USB host and USB device stacks such as Micriµm's µC/USB-Host and µC/USB-Device. The USB controller can act as a host, device, or OTG, supports full-speed, and can transfer data up to 12 Mbps. As a device, the evaluation board can act as a Human Interface Device (HID) or a Mass Storage Device (MSD), especially with the on-board microSD card slot and the 128 MB of Phase Change Memory (serial flash). In other words, the YRDKRX62N can be made to appear as a disk drive to a PC. As a host, the evalution board can interface several different classes of devices connected to it: Communications Device Class (CDC), Human Interface Device (HID), Mass Storage Class (MSC), Printer Class, among others.

The included microSD connector allows applications to run a file system such as Micrium's μC/FS. A file system allows an application to store and retrieve contents to/from a microSD card. The microSD card can be used to log data to a file. This data can then be read from a PC using a USB-MSD stack, a FTP server, or the card can be removed and read using an external card reader.

The RS-232C connector allows an application to output information to a terminal (or a terminal emulator) or used to interface to μC/Probe.

ACKNOWLEDGEMENTS

I would like to thank the following people at Renesas who made part II of this book possible:

Mr. Blake Carpenter, Online Training Manager, for managing this project on Renesas' side and for making sure some of the fine details from a logistics point of view didn't get dropped.

Mr. Mark Rootz, Sr. Marketing Manager, for providing the contents for the RX architecture chapter.

Mr. Ian Hall, Systems Applications Specialist, for putting most of the example projects together. Your technical expertise, dedication and patience were again key to the success of this book and were appreciated by all of us. Working with you is a charm.

I would also like to thank my team at Micriµm:

Mr. John Paul Umana and Mr. Carlos Diaz for ever improving µC/Probe and for doing such a fine job getting µC/Probe to work with the J-Link on the YRDKRX62N.

Mr. Jim Royal for formatting and putting this book together.

Mr. Fabiano Kovalski who handled the logistics of Part II and worked diligently with the Renesas team. I was able to sleep at night knowing that you were on this team.

CO-AUTHOR BIOGRAPHY

Fabiano Kovalski is a Software Development Engineer at Micriµm. He has worked on TCP/IP, USB and RTOS development. Fabiano holds BSEE and MSEE degrees from Florida Atlantic University, USA. His technical interests, besides embedded systems, include multicore systems architecture, parallel and distributed programming, and digital signal processing.

2

The Renesas RX600 MCU

Renesas's RX600 32-bit CPU enables a new class of microcontrollers which meets many demands of today's embedded real time control applications including: high performance yet very low power consumption; the smallest possible code and data size; the lowest cost; and the need for digital signal processing.

The RX600 is an MCU/DSP hybrid, or Digital Signal Controller (DSC), producing 1.65 Dhrystone MIPS/MHz as an MCU, but it is also a very powerful signal processor because of the integrated Floating Point Unit (FPU) and Multiply-Accumulate (MAC) unit. This unified processor has 73 basic instructions, plus eight floating point and nine DSP instructions. Code for both traditional real time embedded control tasks as well as DSP algorithms are developed for the RX600 in C/C++ using a single, easy-to-use Integrated Development Environment (IDE).

DSC capability spans many applications, including energy efficient motor control in white goods and home appliances, medical patient monitoring, smart metering, factory/building/home automation, personal audio, barcode and image scanning, point-of-sale terminals, human-machine interfacing, and many more.

2-1 ORIGINS OF RX600

The design team at Renesas has combined the advantages of high-speed RISC CPU designs refined in the SuperH family with those of the flexible, code-efficient CISC designs nurtured in the H8S/H8SX and the M16C/R32C families. Specifically, to create a next-generation CPU architecture, the RX design team combined a RISC-like 32-bit general purpose register-based Modified Harvard architecture machine having a 5-stage pipeline, with a set of CISC-like variable-length instructions ranging from 8-bits to 64-bits and a rich set of addressing modes. The result, a minimum execution time of one clock-per-instruction was achieved while maintaining ultra-compact code and data size. And as a natural extension, the FPU and MAC were included from SuperH and M16C heritage to complete the DSC capability of RX600. This CPU is capable of up to 200 MHz maximum frequency producing 1.65 Dhrystone MIPS/MHz, and the core uses just 30 µA/MHz (on 90 nm flash memory technology). This clever design approach was made possible by building on decades of MCU design experience and applying a large library of accumulated IP.

2-2 RX600 SERIES DEVICES

As of June 2010, Renesas has introduced 3 major groups within the RX600 Series, the RX610, RX62N, and RX62T. All of these MCUs currently have a maximum frequency of 100 MHz, and are based on the proven 90 nm MONOS (Metal Oxide Nitride Oxide Silicon) embedded flash memory technology capable of read access up to 100 MHz with no wait-states. This means the RX600 CPU core will have full performance with no stalls due to reading code from on-chip flash memory, and no need for memory acceleration techniques.

Key attributes for each of these RX600 groups:

■ RX610 group has very large memory with flash memory up to 2 MB and SRAM of 128 kB, and fast ADCs up to 4M samples/second.

■ RX62N group enables connectivity with Ethernet, USB-FS Host/Device/OTG, and CAN, plus the ability to drive a color TFT-LCD.

■ RX62T has special timers and analog functions optimizing motor control, including embedded op-amps with programmable gain. This MCU can drive two motors at once.

Figure 2-1 shows the current RX600 Series line-up. Many more RX600 devices are coming in 2011, expanding choices for connectivity, memory size, package selection, and additional low-power modes. Please check the web for the latest offerings at www.renesas.com/rx.

1.65 DMIPS/MHz, 100 MHz max frequency
Precision 32-bit Floating Point Unit
Up to 28% less code size with CISC Instructions
No Wait-State 90 nm Flash at 100 MHz
Blazing DSP capability with 32-bit hardware MAC
Spartan use of Power at only 1mW per DMIPS

RX610 Group	RX62N Group	RX62T Group
Flash: 768KB – 2 MB SRAM: 128KB Data Flash: 32KB	Flash: 256KB — 512KB SRAM: 64KB — 96KB Data Flash: 32KB	Flash: 64KB — 256KB SRAM: 8KB — 16KB Data Flash: 8KB
1 µsec 10b ADC, 4 units External Bus	Ethernet MAC, 10/100 USB-FS Host-Dev-OTG CAN TFT-LCD, SDRAM 1 µsec 12b ADC	Special Motor Timers Programmable OpAmps Window Comparators CAN, LIN 1µsec 12b ADC
144, 176 pin packages	85, 100, 144, 145, 176 pin packages	64, 80, 100, 112 pin packages
General Purpose	**General Purpose & Connectivity**	**Motor/Inverter Control**

Figure 2-1 **RX600 MCU Series**

The new RX200 Series, which debuts in 2011, maintains the common RX CPU core and carries many of the same peripherals of the RX600 Series, but the RX200 will be based on an ultra-low leakage 130 nm flash memory process for very low-power portable applications with enhanced analog capabilities. The RX600 and RX200 Series will complement each other in applications needing the most performance and the least power consumption, as shown in Figure 2-2.

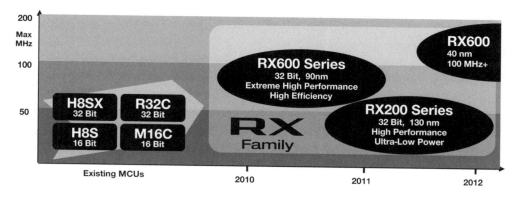

Figure 2-2 **RX Family**

2-3 RX600 FEATURES

CPU

- 32-bit Modified Harvard architecture CPU core

- 5-stage instruction pipeline

- Minimum execution time One CPU clock per instruction

- 1.65 DMIPS/MHz (Dhrystone v2.1)

- 200 MHz Maximum operating frequency

- 4-Gbyte linear address space

- CPU Register Set

  - Sixteen general 32-bit registers

  - Nine 32-bit control registers

  - One 64-bit accumulator

- Memory-protection unit (MPU)

- Single precision (32-bit) floating point unit (FPU)

  - Data types and floating-point exceptions in conformance IEEE754

- 16 x 16 + 48 → 48 bits Multiply Accumulate (MAC), single-cycle

- 32 x 32 + 80 → 80 bits Repeated Multiply Accumulate (RMPA)

- On-chip 32-bit multiplier: 32 x 32 → 64 bits

- On-chip divider: 32 / 32 → 32 bits

- Barrel shifter: 32 bits

- 73 Basic instructions including:

  - arithmetic/logic

  - data-transfer

  - relative branches to optimize for branch distances

  - bit-manipulation

- string-manipulation

- system control

■ 8 Floating-point instructions including:

  - Addition

  - Subtraction

  - Multiplication

  - Division

  - Compare

  - Integer conversion

  - Floating Point conversion

  - Rounding

■ 9 DSP instructions including:

  - Multiply Accumulate

  - Repeated Multiply Accumulate

  - Saturating math

  - Barrel Shift

  - Accumulator data rounding

■ 10 Addressing modes including:

  - Immediate

  - Register direct

  - Register indirect

  - Register relative

  - Post-increment register indirect

  - Pre-decrement register indirect

  - Indexed register indirect

  - Control register direct

- ■ PSW direct

- ■ Program counter relative

■ Data arrangement

- ■ Instructions: Little endian

- ■ Data: Selectable as little endian or big endian

2-4 CPU REGISTERS

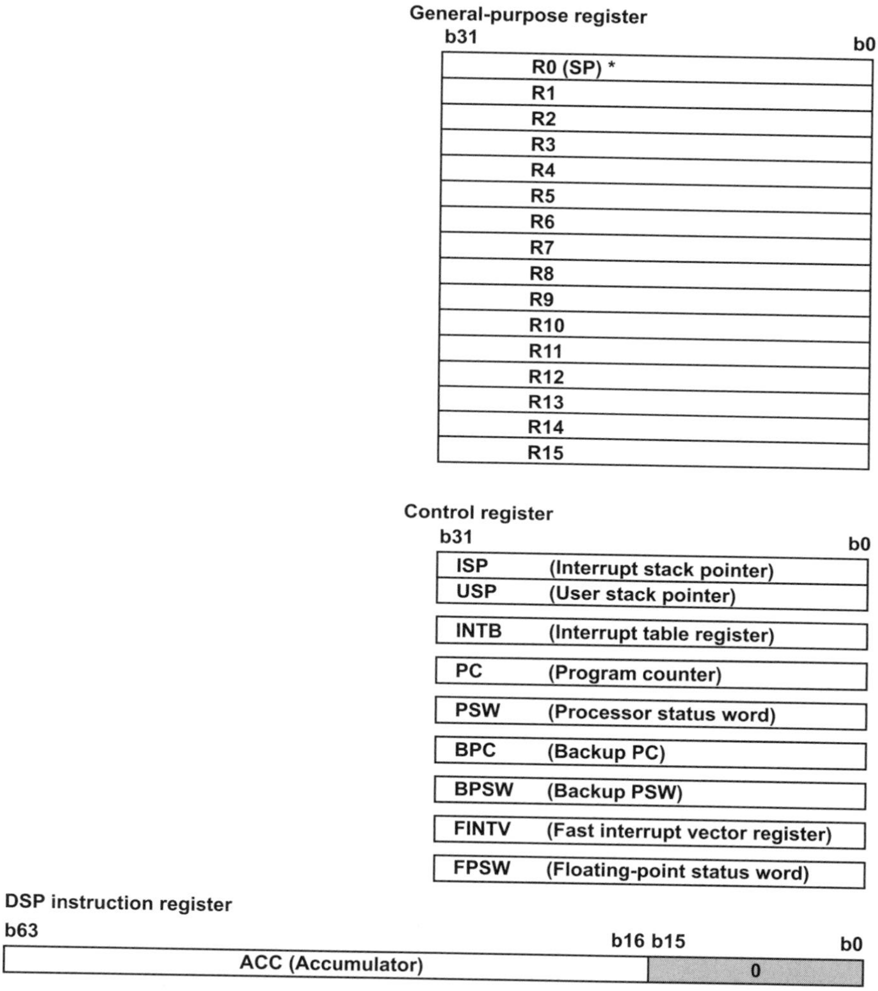

General-purpose register

b31   b0

| R0 (SP) * |
| R1 |
| R2 |
| R3 |
| R4 |
| R5 |
| R6 |
| R7 |
| R8 |
| R9 |
| R10 |
| R11 |
| R12 |
| R13 |
| R14 |
| R15 |

Control register

b31   b0

ISP	(Interrupt stack pointer)
USP	(User stack pointer)
INTB	(Interrupt table register)
PC	(Program counter)
PSW	(Processor status word)
BPC	(Backup PC)
BPSW	(Backup PSW)
FINTV	(Fast interrupt vector register)
FPSW	(Floating-point status word)

DSP instruction register

b63   b16 b15   b0

| ACC (Accumulator) | 0 |

Note: * The stack pointer (SP) can be the interrupt stack pointer (ISP) or user stack pointer (USP) according to the value of the U bit in the PSW register.

Figure 2-3 **RX600 Programmer's Model**

669

GENERAL REGISTERS R0 TO R15

This CPU has sixteen general-purpose registers (R0 to R15). R1 to R15 can be used as data register or address register. R0, a general-purpose register, also functions as the stack pointer (SP). The stack pointer is switched to operate as the interrupt stack pointer (ISP) or user stack pointer (USP) by the value of the stack pointer select bit (U) in the processor status word (PSW).

CONTROL REGISTERS

This CPU has the following nine control registers.

- Interrupt stack pointer (ISP)

- User stack pointer (USP)

- Interrupt table register (INTB)

- Program counter (PC)

- Processor status word (PSW)

- Backup PC (BPC)

- Backup PSW (BPSW)

- Fast interrupt vector register (FINTV)

- Floating-point status word (FPSW)

INTERRUPT STACK POINTER (ISP)/USER STACK POINTER (USP)

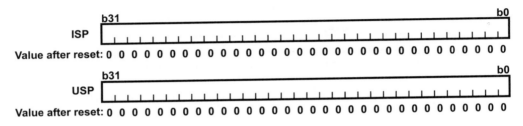

The stack pointer (SP) can be either of two types, the interrupt stack pointer (ISP) or the user stack pointer (USP). Whether the stack pointer operates as the ISP or USP depends on the value of the stack pointer select bit (U) in the processor status word (PSW).

INTERRUPT TABLE REGISTER (INTB)

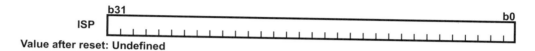

ISP

b31   **b0**

Value after reset: Undefined

The interrupt table register (INTB) specifies the address where the relocatable vector table starts.

PROGRAM COUNTER (PC)

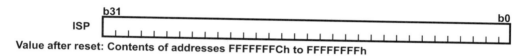

ISP

b31   **b0**

Value after reset: Contents of addresses FFFFFFFCh to FFFFFFFFh

The program counter (PC) indicates the address of the instruction being executed.

PROCESSOR STATUS WORD (PSW)

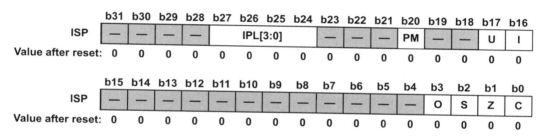

	b31	b30	b29	b28	b27	b26	b25	b24	b23	b22	b21	b20	b19	b18	b17	b16
ISP	—	—	—	—	IPL[3:0]				—	—	—	PM	—	—	U	I
Value after reset:	0	0	0	0	0	0	0	0	0	0	0	0	0	0	0	0

	b15	b14	b13	b12	b11	b10	b9	b8	b7	b6	b5	b4	b3	b2	b1	b0
ISP	—	—	—	—	—	—	—	—	—	—	—	—	O	S	Z	C
Value after reset:	0	0	0	0	0	0	0	0	0	0	0	0	0	0	0	0

Bit	Symbol	Bit Name	Description	R/W
b0	C	Carry flag	0: No carry has occurred. 1: A carry has occurred.	R/W
b1	Z	Zero flag	0: Result is non-zero. 1: Result is 0.	R/W
b2	S	Sign flag	0: Result is a positive value or 0. 1: Result is a negative value.	R/W
b3	O	Overflow flag	0: No overflow has occurred. 1: An overflow has occurred.	R/W

Bit	Symbol	Bit Name	Description	R/W
b4 to b15		(Reserved) When writing, write 0 to these bits. The value read is always 0.		R/W
b16	I	Interrupt enable bit	0: Interrupt disabled. 1: Interrupt enabled.	R/W
b17	U	Stack pointer select bit	0: Interrupt stack pointer (ISP) is selected. 1: User stack pointer (USP) is selected.	R/W
b18, b19		(Reserved) When writing, write 0 to these bits. The value read is always 0.		R/W
b20	PM	Processor mode select bit	0: Supervisor mode is selected. 1: User mode is selected.	R/W
b21 to b23		(Reserved) When writing, write 0 to these bits. The value read is always 0.		R/W
b27 to b24	IPL[3:0]	Processor interrupt priority level b27 b24 0 0 0 0: Priority level 0 (lowest) 1 0 0 0: Priority level 8 0 0 0 1: Priority level 1 1 0 0 1: Priority level 9 0 0 1 0: Priority level 2 1 0 1 0: Priority level 10 0 0 1 1: Priority level 3 1 0 1 1: Priority level 11 0 1 0 0: Priority level 4 1 1 0 0: Priority level 12 0 1 0 1: Priority level 5 1 1 0 1: Priority level 13 0 1 1 0: Priority level 6 1 1 1 0: Priority level 14 0 1 1 1: Priority level 7 1 1 1 1: Priority level 15 (highest)		R/W
b28 to b31		(Reserved) When writing, write 0 to these bits. The value read is always 0.		R/W

BACKUP PC (BPC)

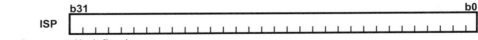

b31 ISP b0

Value after reset: Undefined

The backup PC (BPC) is provided to speed up response to interrupts. After a fast interrupt has been generated, the contents of the program counter (PC) are saved in the BPC register.

BACKUP PSW (BPSW)

ISP

Value after reset: Undefined

The backup PSW (BPSW) is provided to speed up response to interrupts. After a fast interrupt has been generated, the contents of the processor status word (PSW) are saved in the BPSW register. The allocation of bits in the BPSW register corresponds to that in the PSW register.

FAST INTERRUPT VECTOR REGISTER (FINTV)

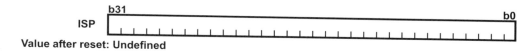

ISP

Value after reset: Undefined

The fast interrupt vector register (FINTV) is provided to speed up response to interrupts. The FINTV register specifies a branch destination address when a fast interrupt has been generated.

FLOATING POINT STATUS WORD

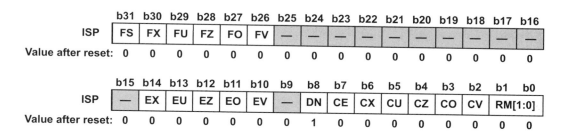

See RX600 Software Manual for detailed bit description.

ACCUMULATOR (ACC)

Accumulator (ACC)

b63	b48 b47	b32 b31	b16 b15	b0

Bits 15 to 0 contain: **0**

Value after reset: Undefined
Note: Bits 15 to 0 are always read as 0. Values written to these bits are ignored.

The accumulator (ACC) is a 48-bit register used for DSP and other instructions. The accumulator is handled as a 64-bit register in access for reading and writing. When data are read from the accumulator, the value of bits 15 to 0 is fixed to 0. The accumulator is also used for the multiply and multiply-and-accumulate instructions; EMUL, EMULU, FMUL, MUL, and RMPA, in which case the prior value in the accumulator is modified by execution of the instruction.

2-5 CPU ADDRESSING MODES

An addressing mode is the way for the processor to access the data. Table 2-1 shows the ten addressing modes available on the RX600 CPU. Of course, all of these are transparent to the C programmer but just give C compilers a lot of flexibility.

Address Mode	Assembly Language Convention	Note
Immediate	#IMM, #UIMM	1
Register Direct	Rn	2
Register Indirect	[Rn]	3
Register Relative	dsp:d[Rn]	4
Post-Increment Register Indirect	[Rn+]	5
Post-Decrement Register Indirect	[-Rn]	6
Indexed Register Indirect	[Ri,Rb]	7
Control Register Direct	PC, ISP, USP, INTB, PSW, BPC, PSW, BPSW, FINTV, FPSW	8
PSW Direct	C, Z, S, O, I, U	9
Program Counter Relative	pcdsp:d	10

Table 2-1 **RX600 Addressing Modes**

Notes:

1   Immediate is the simplest mode because the operand is the value specified by the immediate value contained within the instruction.

2   Register Direct is used by standard arithmetic and logical operations. It involves no address calculations because the operand is stored directly in the register.

3   Register Indirect uses a register as the pointer to a memory location that contains an operand.

4   Register Relative produces an effective operand address by adding the specified displacement (d) and the pointer contained in the specified register.

5   Post-Increment Register Indirect is particularly useful for consecutive accesses of array contents for popping values from a stack. In this addressing mode, the address is stored in the register and is automatically incremented after the memory access has been performed.

6   Post-Decrement Register Indirect is used for pushing values onto the stack. The address stored in the register is automatically decremented prior to the access.

7   Indexed Register Indirect uses Rb as the base address of an array or structure and Ri as an index into that array or offset into the structure.

8   Control Register Direct accesses the specified control register directly.

9   PSW Direct accesses the specified flag or bit directly.

10   Program Counter Relative produces an effective operand address by adding the specified displacement (d) to the Program Counter value.

2-6 INTERRUPT HANDLING AND EXCEPTIONS

During the execution of a program by the CPU, the occurrence of certain events may necessitate suspending execution of the main flow of the program and starting the execution of another flow. Such events are called exceptions. The RX CPU supports the seven types of exceptions listed in Figure 2-4.

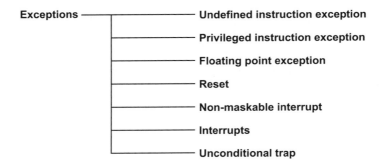

Figure 2-4 **RX600 Exceptions**

The occurrence of an exception causes the processor mode to switch to supervisor mode.

UNDEFINED INSTRUCTION EXCEPTION

An undefined instruction exception occurs when execution of an undefined instruction (an instruction not implemented) is detected.

PRIVILEGED INSTRUCTION EXCEPTION

A privileged instruction exception occurs when execution of a privileged instruction is detected while operation is in usermode. Privileged instructions can only be executed in supervisor mode.

FLOATING-POINT EXCEPTIONS

Floating-point exceptions include the five specified in the IEEE754 standard, namely overflow, underflow, inexact, division-by-zero, and invalid operation, and a further floating-point exception that is generated on the detection of unimplemented processing.

RESET

A reset through input of the reset signal to the CPU causes the exception request. This has the highest priority of any exception and is always accepted.

NON-MASKABLE INTERRUPT

The non-maskable interrupt is generated by input of the non-maskable interrupt signal to the CPU and is only used when a fatal fault is considered to have occurred in the system.

INTERRUPTS

Interrupts are generated by the input of interrupt signals to the CPU. The interrupt with the highest priority can be selected for handling as a fast interrupt.

UNCONDITIONAL TRAP

An unconditional trap is generated when the INT or BRK instruction is executed.

EXCEPTION HANDLING PROCEDURE

For exception handling, part of the processing is handled automatically by hardware and part is handled by a program (the exception handler) that has been written by the user. Figure 2-5 shows the handling procedure when an exception other than a reset is accepted.

Note that there are two types of interrupts, Normal and Fast interrupt. A Fast interrupt offers more hardware assistance than a Normal exception regarding saving and restoring CPU status. A Fast interrupt may be assigned dynamically by the firmware to various interrupt sources.

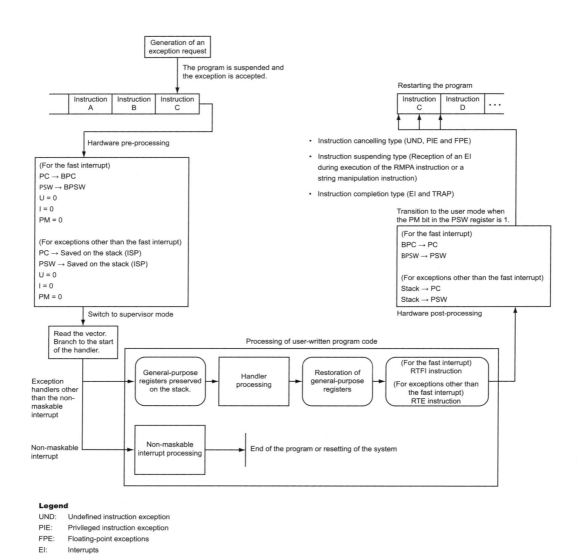

Figure 2-5 **RX600 Exception Sequence**

When an exception is accepted, hardware processing by the RX CPU is followed by vector access to acquire the address of the branch destination. A vector address is allocated to each exception. The branch destination address of the handler for the given exception is written to each vector address. The combination is referred to as a vector.

The vector addresses are stored in flash memory in two types of tables: a fixed table and a relocatable table. Each vector in each of the tables consists of four bytes and specifies the address where the corresponding exception handler starts. The fixed vector table always starts at address 0xFFFFFFFC with the Reset vector, and addresses lower from there have vector entries for non-maskable interrupt, floating point exception, undefined instruction exception, and privileged instruction exception. The relocatable vector table is a 1024-byte region capable of holding up to 256 exception handler addresses. The base address of this table (IntBase) is specified by the initialization firmware, or startup code. The BRK instruction vector is always allocated to the first entry of this relocatable table, and the remaining 255 entries are allocated to all other exceptions as defined on a per-product basis.

Hardware pre-processing by the RX CPU handles saving of the contents of the program counter (PC) and processor status word (PSW). In the case of the Fast interrupt, the contents are saved in the backup PC (BPC) and the backup PSW (BPSW), respectively. In the case of other Normal exceptions, the contents are preserved in the stack area.

General purpose registers and control registers other than the PC and PSW that are to be used within the exception handler must be preserved on the stack by user program code at the start of the exception handler.

A technique can be used to reduce interrupt latency by configuring the compiler to assign up to four of the 16 RX general registers (R12 through R15) for exclusive use by exception handling, no other processes may use these specific registers. This eliminates the need of preserving and restoring general registers to and from the stack during the exception handler, saving clock cycles before and after the actual exception handler tasks are executed.

On completion of processing by most exception processing handlers, registers preserved under program control are restored and the RTE instruction is executed to restore execution from the exception handler to the original program.

For return from the Fast interrupt, the RTFI instruction is used instead. In the case of the non-maskable interrupt, however, end the program or reset the system without returning to the original program.

Hardware post-processing by the RX CPU handles restoration of the pre-exception contents of the PC and PSW registers. In the case of the Fast interrupt, the contents of the BPC and BPSW registers are restored to the PC and PSW registers, respectively. In the case of other Normal exceptions, the contents are restored from the stack area to the PC and PSW registers.

Exceptions are accepted with various types of handling and timing. For example, an instruction that is currently being executed by the CPU will be:

1   Cancelled immediately when an exception occurs from a reset, an undefined instruction, a privileged instruction, or a floating-point exception.

2   Suspended immediately and resumed later if an interrupt occurs and the instruction is a Repeated Multiply Accumulate (RMPA), or one of many string manipulation instructions.

3   Completed; interrupt handling will progress at the next break between instructions for instructions not listed in #2.

4   Completed; exception handling for an unconditional trap will occur at the next break for all instructions.

2-7 µC/OS-III AWARE INTERRUPT HANDLING

An interrupt service routine (ISR) can be classified as a *Kernel Aware* ISR, or a *Non Kernel Aware* ISR. A *Kernel Aware* ISR is an ISR that needs to notify a task that an event occurred by interacting with µC/OS-III. `OSTickISR()` is an example of a *Kernel Aware* ISR (see Appendix A on page 787) as it notifies µC/OS-III to process a system tick. All *Kernel Aware* ISRs should be modeled as the `OSTickISR()`.

If an ISR does not need to signal or send a message to a task, it is called a *Non Kernel Aware* ISR. Therefore, all the work that needs to be done in response to the interrupt is handle in the ISR itself. *Non Kernel Aware* interrupts are typically used when the ISR is very short, and for high rate interrupts. In other words, for interrupts that occur very often and that have little processing to do.

Whether an ISR is allowed to be kernel aware or not depends on the value of the interrupt mask used to disable interrupts. Specifically, this is determined in the µC/CPU's module 'CRITICAL SECTION CONFIGURATION' section (see CPU.H).

On the RX600, non kernel aware interrupts must be assigned a priority level higher than the interrupt mask level. For example, if the interrupt mask (using set_ipl()) is set to 12, then kernel aware interrupts must be assigned to levels 1 through 12, and non kernel aware interrupts from levels 13 and up (see section A-7 "Kernel Aware vs. Non Kernel Aware Interrupts" on page 814)

2-8 ZERO WAIT-STATE FLASH UP TO 100MHz

At the time of printing, all RX600 MCUs from Renesas are designed with high speed 90 nm flash memory that operates up to 100 MHz (10 ns) read speed. Most other MCU manufacturers use flash memory technology that has a limited read speed of around 20 to 50 MHz. A slower flash memory requires more wait states than a faster flash memory as MCU operating frequency is increased beyond the flash read speed. For every wait state addition, the CPU has to wait longer and longer to fetch instructions from the flash memory and ultimately, the MCU performance at higher frequency suffers. Figure 2-6 shows the impact of wait states on the MCU performance. To minimize the performance penalty due to slower flash, most MCU manufacturers use 64-bit or wider prefetch buffer with cache memory. This technique, however, does not completely overcome the performance penalty when the CPU executes non-sequential code, like happens so often in embedded control applications. The RX600 MCUs use a combination of a fast 100 MHz 64-bit wide flash memory and a simple 64-bit wide by 4-deep prefetch queue containing up to 32 instructions to provide a constant stream of instruction flow to the CPU at all speeds. For non-linear execution of code (a branch for example), the maximum delay in flash memory access for RX600 is only one CPU clock (10 ns) if the instruction of the branch is not already in the prefetch queue. This one CPU clock is all that it takes to reload the prefetch queue with the new instruction stream started by the branch operation. If the instruction from the branch is already in the prefetch queue, there is no extra CPU clock needed and execution progresses without delay. Therefore, the RX requires no wait states, and needs no caching methods to reduce the latency on non-linear code execution.

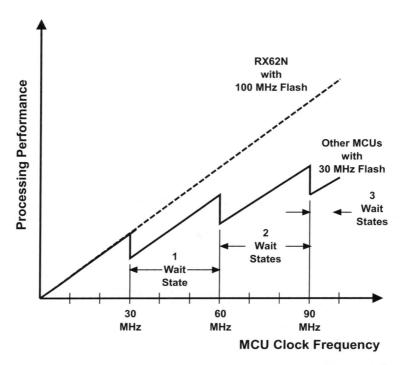

Figure 2-6 **RX62N with 100MHz on-chip flash**

2-9 THE RENESAS RX62N

The specific RX600 MCU group member used in this book for demonstration is the RX62N. This 100 MHz MCU has the RX CPU core just described, plus up to 512 kB of Zero Wait-State flash memory, up to 96 kB of SRAM, 32 kB of data flash memory, and connectivity with 10/100 Ethernet, USB-FS Host/Device/OTG, CAN, and others. The block diagram is shown in Figure 2-7.

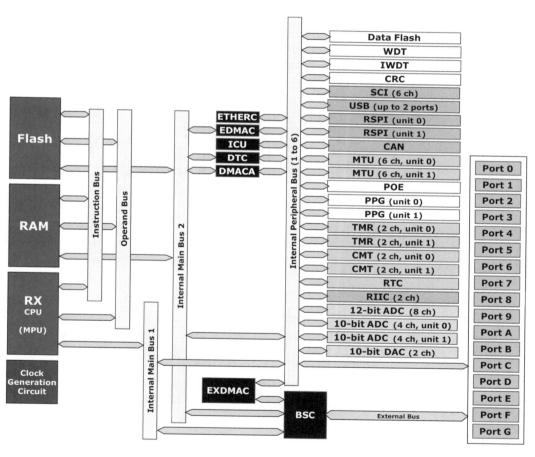

Figure 2-7 **RX62N Block Diagram**

Below is a brief description of just a few of many peripherals found on the RX62N, which significantly offload work from the CPU and enhance connectivity.

DMAC (DIRECT MEMORY ACCESS CONTROLLER)

There are four programmable DMAC channels on the RX62N to manage movement of data between peripherals and memory, memory to memory, and peripheral to peripheral, with very minimal overhead of CPU involvement. These transfers occur in the background on separate physical busses inside the RX62N, removing any restrictions on the RX CPU's immediate local busses for code and data access. The DMAC channels operate in many flexible modes, including Normal Transfer, Repeat Transfer, and Block Transfer with burst and cycle-stealing options. There is also a very useful option to automatically update the data transfer address after each transfer by incrementing, decrementing, or offset addition. The DMAC can be set to activate automatically by on-chip peripherals, including timers, serial channels, A/D Converters, as well as external interrupt pins and by software.

EXDMAC (EXTERNAL DIRECT MEMORY ACCESS CONTROLLER)

There are two EXDMAC channels on the RX62N, which are very similar to the DMACs, but instead of operating on data internal to the RX62N chip, the EXDMAC channels control movement of data outside the RX62N chip. This means the RX62N can orchestrate data movement from one external memory or device to another memory or external device, and the data never enters the RX chip. A good example of this is when the RX62N drives a TFT-LCD panel with EXDMAC. The graphic image data is stored in an external SDRAM (frame buffer), and the EXDMAC automatically moves the graphic data from the SDRAM (one external device) to the TFT-LCD panel (the other external device), refreshing the panel at a 60 Hz rate. All this happens with very little CPU overhead because the graphic data never enters the RX62N chip.

DTC (DATA TRANSFER CONTROLLER)

The DTC performs a task similar to that of a DMAC. That is, when triggered, the DTC transfers data from one memory location to another without CPU intervention. This eases the load on the CPU, freeing up processing power for applications and control tasks. It differs from the DMAC in that the configuration data for a data transfer is loaded on the fly from RAM based tables. This has the advantage of offering more transfer channels than a DMAC as the number of channels is limited only by available RAM. Data transfer activated by an on-chip peripheral module interrupt can be done independently of the CPU. The transfer mode is selectable for each interrupt source. The DTC supports multiple transfer modes: Normal mode, repeat mode, or block transfer mode. The data transfer can be specified as byte (8-bit), word (16-bit), or longword (32-bit). The interrupt that activated the DTC can also be issued to the CPU. A CPU interrupt can be requested after one data transfer is complete. Finally, a CPU interrupt can be requested after all specified data transfers are complete.

MTU2 (MULTI-FUNCTION TIMER UNIT)

The RX62N has two MTU timer units which can be used for sophisticated motor control, or for general timer/counter/PWM functions. Each one provides a maximum of 16 lines of pulse input/output and three lines of pulse input based on six channels of 16-bit timers. The MTU can be configured to provide 21 output compare and input capture registers. The pulse output modes can be set to: Toggle, PWM, and complementary PWM. The MTU allows the synchronization of multiple counters. The complementary PWM output mode allows for non-overlapping waveforms output for 3-phase inverter control, automatic dead time setting, 0% to 100% PWM duty value specifiable, A/D conversion delaying function, and interrupt skipping at crest or trough. The reset-synchronized PWM mode allows three-phase PWM waveforms in positive and negative phases and can be output with a required duty value. The phase counting mode allows for two-phase encoder pulse counting. Each MTU2 unit is supported by the DMAC and DTC units.

TMR (8-BIT TIMER)

There are two TMR channels on the RX62N, each timer unit is 8-bits and supports counting, comparing, pulse and PWM outputs. These timer units are frequently used for baud rate generation for the SCI serial interfaces. TMR channels are supported by the DTC.

CMT (COMPARE MATCH TIMER)

The RX62N provides two 16-bit compare match timers. Each CMT channel is supported by the DMAC and DTC units. These are actually used by µC/OS-III: CMT0 is used to generate the tick rate interrupt, and CMT1 is used for time measurements.

RSPI (RENESAS SERIAL PERIPHERAL INTERFACE)

There are two RSPI channels on the RX62N. Each one supports Master, Slave, and Multi-master modes up to 18 MHz clock rate. All standard SPI clock synchronous transfer modes are supported and configured at run-time, including all combinations of clock phase, clock polarity, and MSB/LSB bit ordering. Variable data length transfers are supported from 8 to 32 bits. Up to four slaves can be controlled in single master mode. Up to three slaves can be controlled in multi-master mode. Data is double-buffered for higher throughput. There is a simple interface to the RX CPU with a number of registers and four interrupts per RSPI channel. RSPI channels are supported by the DMAC and DTC units.

RIIC (RENESAS I²C BUS)

There are two RIIC channels on the RX62N. Each one supports Master, Slave, and Multi-master modes up to 1 Mbps transfer rates. There is a simple interface to the RX CPU with a number of registers and four interrupts per RIIC channel. The hardware takes care of all low-level I^2C data transfers including bus arbitration, time-outs, re-starts, handshaking, clock stretching and clock holding to adjust dissimilar speeds of master and slave devices, as well as use of the acknowledge bit. RIIC channels are supported by the DMAC and DTC units.

SERIAL COMMUNICATIONS INTERFACE (SCI)

RX62N has six SCI channels, each one capable of asynchronous and clock synchronous transfers. The SCI channels can also handle smartcard ISO/IEC 7816-3 protocol for ID cards. Various UART modes are supported, including Multi-Processor Communications (9-bit UART), and speeds over 3 Mbps. There is a simple interface to the RX CPU with a number of registers and four interrupts per SCI channel. The hardware takes care of all low-level SCI data transfers, and data is double-buffered in the transmit and receive paths for higher throughput. SCI channels are supported by the DMAC and DTC units.

USB (UNIVERSAL SERIAL BUS – HOST/DEVICE/OTG)

There are up to two USB interfaces on the RX62N, each one supports USB 2.0 full-speed mode (12 Mbps) Host, Device, or OTG operation selectable by firmware. Each interface provides 10 endpoints (EP0 to EP9) and contains on-chip transceivers for Host and Device modes (OTG needs external circuit). Standard commands are automatically processed by hardware. The USB peripheral supports four USB transfer types: control transfer, bulk transfer, isochronous transfer, and interrupt transfer. DMAC and DTC transfers are supported and the data can be automatically streamed to or from the common SRAM in the RX62N chip. There is also a 2 kB FIFO dedicated to the data transmitted and received by the USB peripheral to maximize throughput. The RX62N USB controller is supported by Micriµm's µC/USB-Host/Device/OTG.

ETHERNET CONTROLLER (MEDIA ACCESS CONTROLLER OR MAC)

The RX62N has a single Media Access Control (MAC) unit which assembles and disassembles data frames based on the IEEE-802.3 format at either 10 or 100 Mbps. The MAC contains a 2 kbytes FIFO for transmission and a separate 2 kbytes FIFO for reception. The MAC allows for full duplex and half-duplex communication. The Ethernet controller supports the MII standard (Media Independent Interface) and the RMII standard (Reduced Media Independent Interface) connection to an external PHY device. Data to and from the Ethernet controller is managed by a dedicated DMA controller, the EDMAC, to maximize data throughput. The RX62N Ethernet controller is supported by Micriµm's µC/TCP-IP and complementary protocol stacks (DHCP, DNS, FTP, HTTP, POP3, SMTP, SNTP, Telnet, etc.).

CAN (CONTROLLER AREA NETWORK)

The RX62N has a single CAN interface supporting the ISO118998-1 CAN protocol standard operating at 1 Mbps. This interface supports 32 message mailboxes, each one can be configured for transmit or receive, and up to eight of them can have FIFO support to increase throughput. There are eight acceptance filters to apply to these mailboxes to reduce overhead of the CPU in filtering which messages are destined for the RX62N on the CAN bus. An automatic time-stamp for messages is also supported. The RX62N CAN controller is supported by Micriµm's µC/CAN.

EXTERNAL BUS

The RX62N supports an external, non-multiplexed, data bus in the larger packages (144-pin and 176-pin) with up to 32 data lines and 24 address lines. Eight memory regions are available, each one with a separate chip-select signal and programmable timing. SDRAM memory is also supported.

2-10 SUMMARY

The RX CPU is a unique architecture taking an ideal blend of CISC and RISC ideas to achieve the lowest clock-per-instruction rate at the same time making the smallest memory footprint size possible. Since this RX core, at 1.65 DMIPS/MHz, is built on a platform of 100 MHz no wait-states flash memory, it provides a tremendous amount of deterministic CPU processing power to add rich capabilities to embedded systems. In addition to this, the presence of RX's hardware floating point (FPU) and multiply-accumulate (MAC) units push RX's capabilities beyond standard real-time embedded control, and into the Digital Signal Controller category.

The RX62N MCU on the Renesas Demonstration Kit that accompanies this book is one of many varieties of RX600 devices available now, with many more new varieties coming in the future. A wide range of RX600 devices is available, covering many memory and packages sizes, as well as many different communication and analog capabilies. To learn about the entire RX MCU series, visit www.renesas.com/rx.

3

Setup

This chapter walks through the set up of the environment to run µC/OS-III-based projects on the Renesas Demonstration Kit, YRDKRX62N.

It is assumed that the following elements are available:

1   A Windows™-based PC running 32- or 64-bits Windows-XP, Vista or Windows 7

2   The Renesas Demostration Kit, YRDKRX62N, and the USB cable that accompanies the RDK

3   The installation CD (or Web installer) to provide the following software development tools:

    a)   The Renesas High-performance Embedded Workshop (HEW) version 4.08 or higher

    b)   The GNURX toolchain (maintained by KPIT Cummins)

    c)   Micriµm's µC/Probe

    d)   The example code that accompanies this book

    e)   Segger J-Link Lite Debugger

The installation CD contents or Web installer for all required software can be found on the following webpage:

`http://www.renesas.com/rdkrx62ninstall`

Support for this book can be found at:

`http://www.renesasrulz.com/rdkrx62n`

3-1 DOWNLOADING "HEW"

Examples provided with this book were developed using the High-performance Embedded Workshop (HEW) version 4.08. HEW provides a GUI-based integrated development environment (IDE) for the development and debugging of embedded applications for Renesas microcontrollers. The compiler used for the examples is the KPIT Cummins GNURX compiler, since the Renesas RX compiler has an evaluation period of 60 days. Renesas provides this free of charge 'Evaluation' version of its RX compiler. During the evaluation period, the Renesas RX compilter has *no limitations*. After the evaluation period, the Renesas RX compiler limits the output of the linker to 128 kbytes in size (both Code and Data).

HEW, a powerful yet easy to use tool suite, features an industry standard user interface and is designed using a modular approach, seamlessly incorporating family-specific C/C++ compilers and the debugger elements for various debugging platforms including simulators, emulators, evaluation boards and demo kits. This provides the user with a single interface to fully exploit the advanced capabilities of the development tools for the entire development cycle from evaluation of a device through to completion of code development.

HEW enables the use of the right tool for each process. HEW supports multiple toolchain integration enabling development for any number of projects under a single user interface.

HEW eliminates the need to switch environments between coding and debugging operations or between targets as all Renesas software and hardware development tools are supported under the same single user interface.

To make it easy for the reader, everything needed to get started is located at the following link:

`www.renesas.com/rdkrx62ninstall`

A single executable file is available to download, where it installs the following tools and files once executed:

1   HEW (High Performance Embedded Workshop) – IDE

2   RX Toolchain (C/C++ compiler, assembler, linker)

3   RX Debugger/Segger J-Link Debugger

4   Micriµm Files:

    a. Example Files

    b. Port for RX62N

    c. µC/Probe

5   Manual Navigator with the following documents loaded: schematics, RX62N & RX621 Group Hardware Manual, RX Software Manual, YRDKRX62N Users Manual

Also, the individual downloads for all of these files are available at:

`www.renesas.com/rdkrx62n`

3-2 DOWNLOADING THE DOCUMENTATION

The latest RX62N hardware and software manuals can be downloaded from Renesas website:

Description	Document file name
RX62N & RX621 Group Hardware Manual	rej09b0552_rx62nhm.pdf
RX Software Manual	rej09b0435_rxsm.pdf
YRDKRX62N User's Manual	reu10b0009_yrdkrx62n_users_manual.pdf

Table 3-1 **Recommended documents available from Renesas**

3

3-3 DOWNLOADING µC/PROBE

µC/Probe is an award-winning Microsoft Windows-based application that allows users to display or change the value (at run time) of virtually any variable or memory location in a connected embedded target. See Appendix C, "µC/Probe" on page 827 for a brief introduction.

µC/Probe is used in all of the examples described in this book and allows to gain run-time visibility of the running application. There are two versions of µC/Probe:

The full version of µC/Probe is included with all µC/OS-III licenses. The full version supports, RS-232C, TCP/IP, USB, J-Link, and other interfaces. The full version allows users to display or change an unlimited number of variables.

The trial version of µC/Probe is not time limited, but allows users to display or change only up to eight application variables. However, the trial version allows users to monitor any µC/OS-III variables because µC/Probe is µC/OS-III aware.

Both versions are available from Micrium's website at:

www.Micrium.com/probe

Follow the links to download the desired version (or both). It is necessary to register on Micrium's website in order to proceed with the download. Once downloaded, execute the appropriate µC/Probe setup file:

Micrium-uC-Probe-Setup-Full.exe
Micrium-uC-Probe-Setup-Trial.exe

3-4 µC/OS-III, AND µC/TCP-IP LIBRARIES

Micriµm and Renesas teamed up to provide the necessary libraries to run the examples provided with this book.

These libraries are downloaded as part of the installation CD available from the Renesas website:

www.renesas.com/rdkrx62ninstall

3-4-1 µC/OS-III

µC/OS-III is provided in linkable library format. The library has been compiled with speed and size optimization but has limitations as listed below. However, µC/OS-III licensees will obtain the full source code for µC/OS-III and thus all these restrictions can easily be lifted.

■ The linkable library supports only 16 different priority levels (0 to 15) but allows an unlimited number of tasks at priorities 0 to 14 (15 is reserved for the idle task).

■ The library does not support round-robin scheduling.

■ The linkable library does not support the µC/OS-III multi-pend feature.

■ The library does not perform API (Application Programming Interface) argument checking, does not validate object types (a semaphore is passed to a semaphore API), and does not verify that only valid APIs are called from ISRs (Interrupt Service Routines). Disabling these features has the side benefit of improving µC/OS-III's performance.

■ The library does not allow deletion of kernel objects at run-time, does not support the OSTimeDlyResume() API, does not support software timers (OSTmr???()), does not support memory partitions (OSMem???()) and does not support task registers (OSTaskReg???()).

■ Finally, the library has been compiled assuming the 'Direct Post' mode.

3-4-2 µC/TCP-IP AND µC/DHCPc

µC/TCP-IP and µC/DHCPc are provided in linkable library format mostly to allow µC/Probe (see Appendix C, "µC/Probe" on page 827) to run using an Ethernet connection. The libraries have been compiled with speed and size optimization but also have limitations as listed below. However, µC/TCP-IP licensees will obtain the full source code for µC/TCP-IP and thus all these restrictions can easily be lifted.

■ µC/TCP-IP only supports one interface with one configured IP address

■ Loopback mode has been disabled

■ The ARP cache only contains three entries

■ Allow up to ten sockets

■ `select()` API disabled

The µC/DHCPc library provides full functionality and thus allows clients to obtain an IP address from a DHCP server or an IP address when connected directly to a PC (this is called "AutoIP" or Link-Local address assignment).

3-5 RENESAS SIGNAL PROCESSING LIBRARY (SPL)

The Renesas Signal Processing Library (SPL) is a set of routines that implement filter functions and signal processing primitives. The SPL has been optimized for performance in RX600 core based processors. This library is available free of charge to users of Renesas RX600 based MCU devices. It is distributed in object form and users are required to agree to a click-through license. The SPL implements some of the most frequently used functions in typical signal processing applications such as speech processing, digital filters, image processing to name a few. The library is accompanied by a user manual and sample workspace.

3-6 µC/OS-III PROJECTS FOR THIS BOOK

Once installed, all files available with this book are placed under the `\Micrium\Software` directory as shown in Figure 3-1.

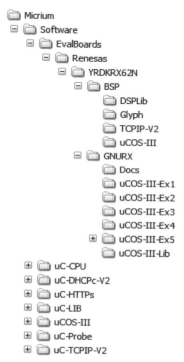

Figure 3-1 **Book Download Directories**

The contents of the `\EvalBoards` subdirectory are discussed in detail in the following section. The other subdirectories contain various Micrium's modules with their respective documentation directory.

3-6-1 \EvalBoards **DIRECTORY**

This is the standard Micrium subdirectory where all evaluation board examples are placed. This directory contains additional subdirectories organizing demo/evaluation boards by manufacturers. In this case, \Renesas is the manufacturer of the YRDKRX62N board, and projects are compiled using the HEW with the GNURX compiler. Therefore, project files are found under:

\EvalBoards\Renesas\YRDKRX62N\GNURX

\EvalBoards\Renesas\YRDKRX62N\GNURX contains the main HEW IDE workspace using the GNURX compiler, which includes all the projects provided with this book. Specifically, the file **GNURX.hws** is the workspace to open with the Renesas High-performance Embedded Workshop.

\EvalBoards\Renesas\YRDKRX62N\BSP contains Board Support Package (BSP) files used to support the peripherals found on the YRDKRX62N demo board. A BSP is a collection of functions that encapsulate access to peripherals found on the board. Specifically, functions are available to turn on or off the onboard LEDs, display characters or strings on the LCD and more. This sub-directory contains the following files:

```
bsp.c
bsp.h
bsp_adt7420.c
bsp_adt7420.h
bsp_adxl345.c
bsp_adxl345.h
bsp_glcd.c
bsp_glcd.h
bsp_tick_a.s
bsp_tick_c.c
\DSPLib
    rtadsplib.h
    SPLib_rx600_sl.a
\Glyph
\TCPIP-V2
    net_bsp.c
    net_bsp.h
```

```
    net_bsp_a.s
    net_phy_dp83640.c
    net_phy_dp83640.h
\uCOS-III
    bsp_os.c
    bsp_os.h
```

The GNURX directory contains the example projects sub-directories:

```
\uCOS-III-Ex1
\uCOS-III-Ex2
\uCOS-III-Ex3
\uCOS-III-Ex4
\uCOS-III-Ex5
\uCOS-III-Lib
```

These example projects are as follows:

\EvalBoards\Renesas\YRDKRX62N\GNURX\uCOS-III-Ex1 presents a simple project that demonstrates how to properly initialize and start a µC/OS-III based application. This project is described in Chapter 4, "Running µC/OS-III and µC/Probe on the YRDKRX62N" on page 703.

\EvalBoards\Renesas\YRDKRX62N\GNURX\uCOS-III-Ex2 demonstrates the accelerometer available in the RX62N. The inclination of the evaluation board is captured by the accelerometer to illuminate one of the LEDs in the LED circle. This project is described in Chapter 5, "PCB Tilt Direction using an Accelerometer" on page 723.

\EvalBoards\Renesas\YRDKRX62N\GNURX\uCOS-III-Ex3 presents a project that measures some performance metrics on µC/OS-III. This project is described in Chapter 6, "Customizable Performance Measurements" on page 737.

\EvalBoards\Renesas\YRDKRX62N\GNURX\uCOS-III-Ex4 presents a simulation of a Variable Frequency Drive (VFD) motor control using Pulse Width Modulation (PWM). For the simulation, a single PWM output is used and this output is filtered to produce a sine wave with frequency between 50 and 200 Hz. The generated sine wave is sampled back using an ADC and a Fast Fourier Transform (FFT) is performed on the sampled signal. The measured frequency is then used to alter the rotating frequency of the 12 LEDs mounted on the YRDKRX62N. This project is described in Chapter 7, "Motor Drive Simulation" on page 751.

\EvalBoards\Renesas\YRDKRX62N\GNURX\uCOS-III-Ex5 presents a project with a web server. This project combines µC/OS-III, µC/TCP-IP, µC/DHCPc, and µC/HTTPs to provide a web interface to the YRDKRX62N evaluation board's temperature sensor and LEDs. This project is described in Chapter 8, "Web Server Example" on page 765.

\EvalBoards\Renesas\YRDKRX62N\GNURX\uCOS-III-Lib is the directory where all the libraries can be found. This directory also contains the header files used to configure these libraries. These libraries are compiled for the RX62N to run the examples provided with this book, and possibly run examples created or modified by the reader. These libraries are:

- **uC-CPU.a** is a linkable object file containing code for the µC/CPU module. µC/CPU contains CPU specific typedefs, #defines, macros and functions. See Appendix B, "µC/CPU Port to the RX62N" on page 817 for additional details.

- **uC-DHCPc-V2.a** is a linkable object file containing code for the µC/DHCPc module which is used by the TCP/IP stack to obtain the IP address from a router or, a Windows based PC using AutoIP or Link-Local address assignment.

- **uC-HTTPs.a** is a linkable object file containing code for the µC/HTTPs module which is used by the Web Server example.

- **uC-LIB.a** is a linkable object file containing code for the µC/LIB module which is used by the µC/TCP-IP stack.

- **uCOS-III.a** is a linkable object file containing code for µC/OS-III.

- **uC-TCPIP-V2.a** is a linkable object file containing code for the µC/TCP-IP stack which is used to run µC/Probe.

3-7 CONNECTING THE YRDKRX62N TO A PC

There are three ways to connect the YRDKRX62N to the PC. It is assumed the PC runs Microsoft Windows XP, Windows Vista, or Windows 7.

1   Using an RS-232C connection for μC/Probe

2   Using an Ethernet cable connected directly to the PC

3   Using an Ethernet cable connected through a router

3-7-1 CONNECTING THE YRDKRX62N (RS-232C)

Figure 3-2 shows a simple block diagram of how to connect the YRDKRX62N to a PC using an RS-232C cable in order to use μC/Probe with this type of interface.

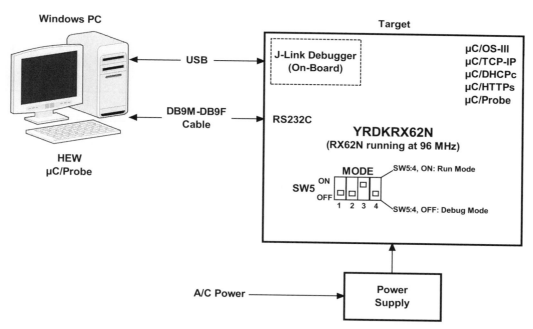

Figure 3-2 **YRDKRX62N setup with RS-232C for μC/Probe**

3-7-2 CONNECTING THE YRDKRX62N (ETHERNET – AUTO IP)

Figure 3-3 shows a simple block diagram of how to connect the YRDKRX62N to a PC using an Ethernet cable for µC/Probe without requiring a router.

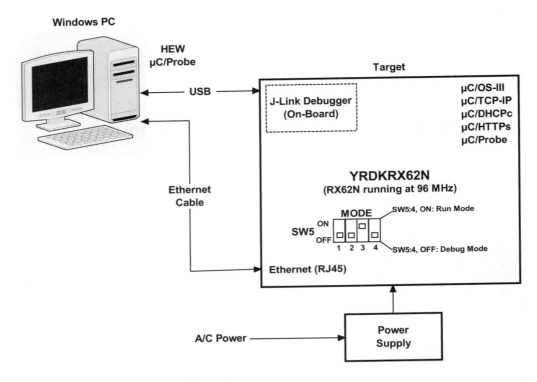

Figure 3-3 **YRDKRX62N setup with Ethernet for µC/Probe (no router)**

3-7-3 CONNECTING THE YRDKRX62N (ETHERNET & ROUTER)

Figure 3-4 shows a simple block diagram of how to connect the YRDKRX62N to a PC using an Ethernet cable for µC/Probe, but using a router to obtain an IP address.

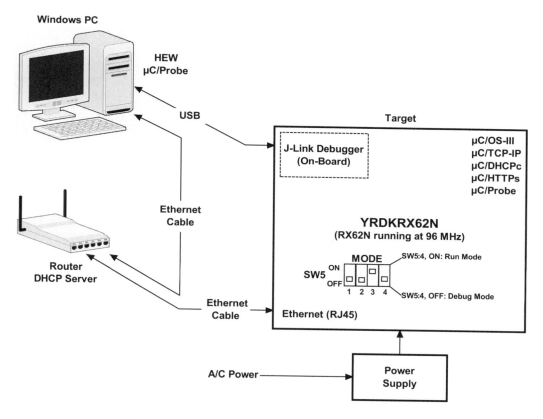

Figure 3-4 **YRDKRX62N setup with Ethernet for µC/Probe (using a router to obtain an IP address)**

4

Running µC/OS-III and µC/Probe on the YRDKRX62N

This chapter demostrates how easy it is to put together a µC/OS-III-based application using the Renesas HEW. The Renesas Demonstration Kit YRDKRX62N is shown in Figure 4-1 and it is the basis of the example.

Figure 4-1 **Renesas YRDKRX62N**

This first project presents a simple project that demonstrates how to properly initialize and start a µC/OS-III based application. This example allows all the necessary pieces to be put together for the more advanced examples. It is assumed the setup shown in Chapter 3, on page 701, where the PC interface with the YRDKRX62N using an Ethernet connection through a router.

4

Before proceeding, the High-performance Embedded Workshop (HEW) must be properly installed. Use a USB cable to connect the YRDKRX62N demonstration board **J-Link Debugger** to a USB port on the PC. The debugger connector is labeled **J-Link USB** on the demonstration board. The debugger also provides power to the board, therefore while debugging, there is no need to connect a power supply.

As HEW starts, a "Welcome!" dialog box is displayed. Select "Browse to another project workspace", and in the Open Workspace dialog box, navigate to open the `GNURX.hws` file from the following path:

`\Micrium\Software\EvalBoards\Renesas\YRDKRX62N\GNURX\GNURX.hws`

The dialog box in Figure 4-2 shows the directory where `GNURX.hws` is located.

Figure 4-2 **Opening the HEW workspace**

The workspace has the project uCOS-III-Ex1 saved as the last active project. This Example #1 project has been saved in the DefaultSession configuration. To allow the target to be debugged, the J-Link configuration needs to be selected for the debug session. In the upper right corner of the HEW application window, a pull down box is labeled DefaultSession. Click on the pull down box and select JLink as the debug target. A message box shows up to save the modifications to the current debug session. Click on the "Yes" button to confirm.

4-1 CONNECTING TO THE TARGET

HEW tries to connect to the YRDKRX62N on-board J-Link. A series of dialog windows are presented during this connection procedure. The first dialog window is shown in Figure 4-3. The first available emulator is selected as the communication interface to the evaluation board. The emulator serial number, found in the emulator case, can be used to differentiate between more than one evaluation board connected to the PC. Once the correct emulator is selected, click the OK button to accept the settings.

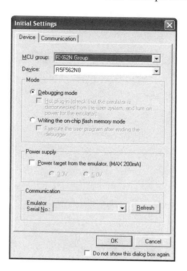

Figure 4-3 **Selecting the Emulator Mode**

HEW then attempts to connect to the target and displays the dialog box shown in Figure 4-4. There is no interaction with the evaluation board during this step of the process. The dialog box automatically closes when this part of the process completes.

Figure 4-4 **Connecting to the YRDKRX62N**

4

After the connecting dialog box, a configuration properties dialog window appears, as shown in Figure 4-5. This dialog is reponsible for setting the input clock frequency. The frequency of the crystal used on the YRDKRX62N is 12 MHz. The value in the input clock field in the dialog window must match the crystal frequency. Once this value is correctly input, click on the OK button to accept the settings.

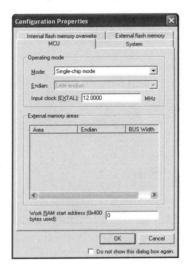

Figure 4-5 **Setting the Configuration Properties**

Finally, the upper left corner of HEW window should look similar to Figure 4-6, the first time the examples workspace is opened. The project labelled **uCOS-III-Ex1** is bold compared to the other projects, this indicates the active project in the workspace.

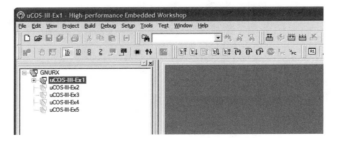

Figure 4-6 **µC/OS-III Project Workspace under the HEW**

4-2 RUNNING THE PROJECT

Before running the project, it must be built. This task can be accomplished by clicking on menu Build\Build, or the shortcut by pressing the 'F7' key.

To visualize the files in the project, the projects can be expanded by clicking on the "+" sign next to their labels. The group contents can be expanded in a similar fashion. To expand or collapse all groups and subgroups within a project, a right-click in the project label would show the context-menu "Expand/Collapse" to perform this task. The files in the "uCOS-III-Ex1" project are shown in Figure 4-7.

Figure 4-7 **Expanded Example #1 Project**

Once the project is built, the executable needs to download into the evalution board. This step can be set to be done automatically after the build process, or can be manually done by double-clicking on the file "**uCOS-III-Ex1.x — 00000000**" under "Download modules" (as shown in Figure 4-7). Besides the double-click, a right-click in the file label brings the context-menu with the option "Download", which performs the same operation. In order to configure this process to be done automatically, the debug settings must be changed. The menu "Debug\Debug Settings...", opens the debug settings dialog window. In the options tab, the checkbox "Download modules after build" must be checked, as shown in Figure 4-8.

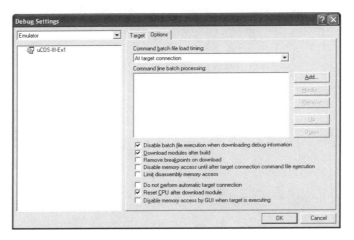

Figure 4-8 **Debug Settings**

Once the executable file (i.e., **uCOS-III-Ex1.x**) has been downloaded to the target, the target must be reset in order to run the application. The menu "Debug\Reset Go," or the toolbar icon shown in Figure 4-9, performs this operation.

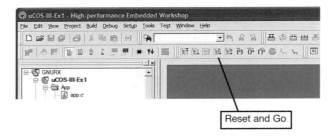

Figure 4-9 **Reset and Go to start running Example #1 on the YRDKRX62N**

This example application blinks the user LEDs in a few different sequences.

4-3 RUNNING µC/PROBE

The trial version of µC/Probe is a part of the "Master Install" of the tools and examples provided.

Start µC/Probe by locating the µC/Probe icon on the PC, as shown in Figure 4-10. The icon, by the way, represents a "box" and the "eye" sees inside the box (which corresponds to the embedded system). In fact, at Micriµm, we like to say, "Think outside the box, but see inside with µC/Probe!"

Figure 4-10 **µC/Probe icon**

Figure 4-11 shows the initial screen when µC/Probe is first started.

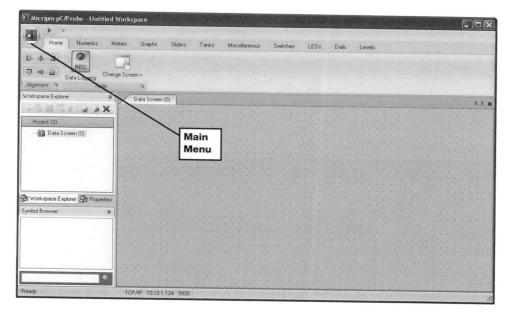

Figure 4-11 **µC/Probe Startup Screen**

Click on the "Main Menu" icon to open up the main menu, as shown in Figure 4-12. First, click on "**uCOS-III-Ex1-Probe.wsp**" in the list of previous projects to load the workspace created for this example. In case the workspace is not displayed in the previous projects list, the workspace needs to be located by clicking on the "Open" icon and navigating the file browser to the following directory:

\Micrium\Software\EvalBoards\Renesas\YRDKRX62N\GNURX\uCOS-III-Ex1

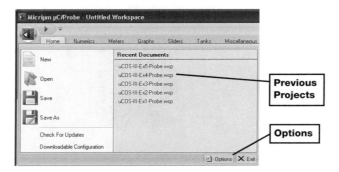

Figure 4-12 **µC/Probe's Main Menu**

The µC/Probe workspace created to demostrate this first example is shown in Figure 4-13.

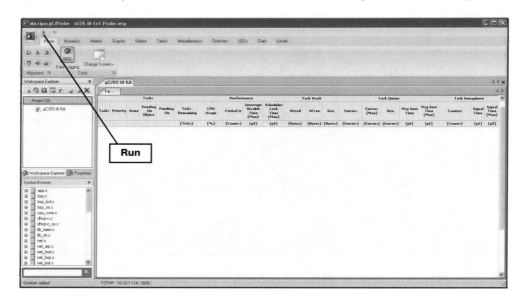

Figure 4-13 **µC/Probe's Workspace for Example #1**

In order to communicate with the target, µC/Probe communication protocol needs to be configured to match the communication protocol in the target. Click again on the "Main Menu" icon to open up the main menu. The "Options" button opens the dialog window to configure this setting. The Options dialog window is shown in Figure 4-14.

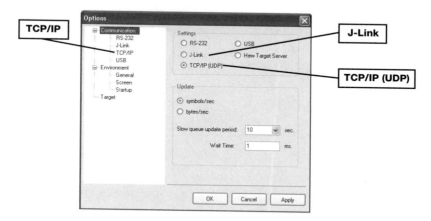

Figure 4-14 **µC/Probe's Options**

Select TCP/IP in the "Settings" group panel, on the right of the options dialog window. Now click on the TCP/IP communications protocol in the "Communication" category. Figure 4-15 shows the TCP/IP parameters that are allowed to be modified. On the test setup, the IP address that the DHCP server assigned to the YRDKRX62N board is `10.10.1.124` (the Remote Host). The IP address the DHCP server assigns can vary. Therefore, a different IP address may need to be entered in the "Remote Host" field. The "Remote Port" field does not require any change, since the µC/Probe server code on the YRDKRX62N is set to `9930` by default. Click "OK" to accept the changes.

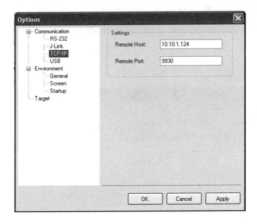

Figure 4-15 **TCP/IP IP address and port number of Target**

Besides the TCP/IP communication protocol, µC/Probe also supports communicating with the YRDKRX62N through the on-board J-Link Debugger. The advantage of using µC/Probe over the J-Link Debugger is that the µC/Probe target side code is not required. In order to communicate with the target using the J-Link, the configuration process must be repeated. Click again on the "Main Menu" icon to open up the main menu. The "Options" button opens the dialog window to configure this setting. The Options dialog window is shown in Figure 4-14. Select J-Link in the "Settings" group panel, on the right of the options dialog window. Now click on the J-Link communications protocol in the "Communication" category. Figure 4-16 shows the J-Link parameters that are allowed to be modified. To communicate with the YRDKRX62N, the J-Link interface mode *must* be set to JTAG.

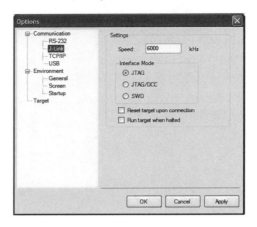

Figure 4-16 **J-Link Interface Settings**

Finally, click on the "Run" icon (see Figure 4-13) to have µC/Probe start collecting task information from the target and display it on the µC/Probe Kernel Awareness screen, as shown in Figure 4-17.

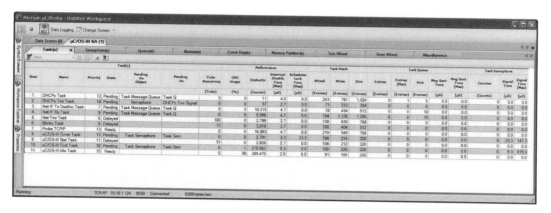

Figure 4-17 **µC/Probe's µC/OS-III Kernel Awareness**

F4-17(1)   The first column shows the item number (1 to the total number of tasks).

F4-17(2)   The second column displays the name of each task. The name of a task is assigned when the task is created in the application.

F4-17(3)   The priority of each task is displayed in the third column. The `uCOS-III-Lib.a` library is configured to have up to 16 priority levels (0 to 15). The idle task is always assigned the lowest priority (i.e., 15).

F4-17(4)   The next column indicates the state of each task. A task can be in one of eight states as described in Chapter 5, "Task Management" on page 81 in Part I of this book. The idle task is always shown as a ready task. The tick and timer tasks either are ready or pending, because both tasks wait (i.e., pend) on their internal task semaphore. The statistics task is shown as delayed, because it calls `OSTimeDly()` every 1/10th of a second.

F4-17(5)   The CPU Usage column indicates the CPU usage of each task relative to the system. The `OSStatTaskCPUUsage` indicates how much total CPU usage the application consumes.

4

F4-17(6)   The "**CtxSwCtr**" column indicates the number of times the task executed. In other words, the number of times it has been context switched to.

F4-17(7)   The "Interrupt Disable Time" column indicates the maximum amount of time interrupts were disabled when running the corresponding task.

F4-17(8)   The "Scheduler Lock Time" column indicates the maximum amount of time the scheduler was locked when running the corresponding task.

F4-17(9)   The next three columns indicate the stack usage of each task. This information is collected by the statistics task 10 times per second. These numbers represent the number of stack entries. Specifically, on the RX architecture, each entry corresponds to 4 bytes.

F4-17(10)   These next five columns provide statistics about each task's internal message queue. If a task does not make use of its task message queue, all its entries are zero.

F4-17(11)   The last three columns provide run-time statistics for each task's internal semaphore.

4-4 HOW THE EXAMPLE CODE WORKS

The code for **main()** is shown in Listing 4-1, where the system is initialized and the application task is created:

```
void  main (void)
{
    OS_ERR   err;


    CPU_IntDis();                                                      (1)
    OSInit(&err);                                                      (2)
    App_OS_SetAllHooks();                                              (3)
    OSTaskCreate((OS_TCB      *)&AppTaskStartTCB,                      (4)
                 (CPU_CHAR    *)"App Task Start",
                 (OS_TASK_PTR ) AppTaskStart,
                 (void        *) 0,
                 (OS_PRIO     ) APP_TASK_START_PRIO,
                 (CPU_STK     *)&AppTaskStartStk[0],
                 (CPU_STK_SIZE) APP_TASK_START_STK_SIZE / 10u,
                 (CPU_STK_SIZE) APP_TASK_START_STK_SIZE,
                 (OS_MSG_QTY  ) 0u,
                 (OS_TICK     ) 0u,
                 (void        *) 0,
                 (OS_OPT      )(OS_OPT_TASK_STK_CHK | OS_OPT_TASK_STK_CLR),
                 (OS_ERR      *)&err);

    OSStart(&err);                                                     (5)

    while (1) {                                                        (6)
        ;
    }
}
```

Listing 4-1 **main()**

L4-1(1)   **main()** starts by calling **CPU_IntDis()** which ensures that CPU interrupts are disabled (see Appendix B, "µC/CPU Port to the RX62N" on page 817).

4

L4-1(2)   **OSInit()** is then called to initialize µC/OS-III. Ideally, the application should verify that **OSInit()** returns without error, by verifying that 'err' contains **OS_ERR_NONE** (i.e., the value 0). Alternatively, this can be performed with the debugger by single stepping through the code (step over) and stop after **OSInit()** returns.

Depending on selected configuration options, **OSInit()** creates up to five internal tasks: the idle task, the tick task, the interrupt queue handler task, the timer task, and the statistic task.

L4-1(3)   Set all application hooks. The application hooks are defined on **OS_APP_HOOKS.C**.

L4-1(4)   **OSTaskCreate()** creates the application task called **AppTaskStart()**. **OSTaskCreate()** contains 13 arguments as described in Appendix A, "µC/OS-III API Reference Manual" on page 381 in Part I of this book.

AppTaskStartTCB is the **OS_TCB** used by the task. This variable is declared in the "Local Variables" section of the **APP.C**.

AppTaskStartStk[] is an array of **CPU_STK**'s used to declare the stack for the task. In µC/OS-III, each task requires its own stack space. The size of the stack greatly depends on the application. In this example, the stack size is declared through **APP_TASK_START_STK_SIZE**, which is defined in **APP_CFG.H**.

APP_TASK_START_PRIO determines the priority of the start task and is also defined in **APP_CFG.H**.

The application should check the error code 'err' to ensure that the call was successful. Alternatively, this can be performed with the debugger by single stepping through the code (step over) and stop after **OSTaskCreate()** returns. The error code returned by **OSTaskCreate()** can be examined and compared with the list of errors on **OS.H** (see **OS_ERR_????**) to determine the cause of the error.

L4-1(5)   **OSStart()** starts the multitasking process. With the application task, µC/OS-III manages up to six tasks in this example. However, **OSStart()** starts the highest priority of the tasks created. In this example, the highest priority task is **AppTaskStart()**.

L4-1(6)   **OSStart()** is not supposed to return under normal conditions. However, if **OSStart()** does return, the **while (1)** allows a breakpoint to be added during debugging. Therefore, the error code returned by **OSStart()** can be examined to determine the cause of the error (see **OS_ERR_????** in **OS.H**).

Listing 4-2 shows the code for **AppTaskStart()** which is the first task that µC/OS-III starts, once **main()** calls **OSStart()**.

```
static   void AppTaskStart (void  *p_arg)
{
    OS_ERR   err;
#if (APP_CFG_TCPIP_MODULE_EN > 0u)
    NET_ERR  net_err;
#endif


    (void)&p_arg;

    BSP_Init();                                              (1)
    CPU_Init();                                              (2)
    OS_CPU_TickInit();                                       (3)

#if OS_CFG_STAT_TASK_EN > 0
    OSStatTaskCPUUsageInit(&err);                            (4)
#endif

    Mem_Init();                                              (5)

#if APP_CFG_PROBE_COM_MODULE_EN > 0
    AppProbe_Init(&err);                                     (6)
#endif
```

```
    OSTaskCreate((OS_TCB     *)&AppBlinkyTaskTCB,                        (7)
                 (CPU_CHAR   *)"Blinky Task",
                 (OS_TASK_PTR ) AppBlinkyTask,
                 (void       *) 0,
                 (OS_PRIO     ) BLINKY_TASK_PRIO,
                 (CPU_STK    *)&AppBlinkyTaskStk[0],
                 (CPU_STK_SIZE) BLINKY_TASK_STK_SIZE / 10u,
                 (CPU_STK_SIZE) BLINKY_TASK_STK_SIZE,
                 (OS_MSG_QTY ) 0u,
                 (OS_TICK    ) 0u,
                 (void       *) 0,
                 (OS_OPT      )(OS_OPT_TASK_STK_CHK | OS_OPT_TASK_STK_CLR),
                 (OS_ERR     *)&err);


    BSP_GraphLCD_Init();                                                 (8)
    AppGraphLCD_Hdr();                                                   (9)

#if (APP_CFG_TCPIP_MODULE_EN > 0u)
    AppTCPIP_Init(&net_err);                                           (10)
#endif

#ifdef CPU_CFG_INT_DIS_MEAS_EN
    CPU_IntDisMeasMaxCurReset();                                       (11)
#endif

    AppTCPIP_Cfg = DEF_TRUE;

    OSTaskDel(&AppTaskStartTCB,                                        (12)
             &err);

    while (DEF_ON) {                                                   (13)
        ;
    }
}
```

Listing 4-2 **AppTaskStart()**

L4-2(1) **AppTaskStart()** starts by calling **BSP_Init()** (see **BSP.C**) to initialize peripherals used on the YRDKRX62N. BSP stands for Board Support Package, and it is a collection of functions that are provided to interface to common peripherals such as LEDs, ADCs, DACs, UARTs and more. In other words, BSP functions make it easy to use these peripherals.

BSP_Init() then calls LED_Init() which initializes the I/O ports that are driving the LEDs on the evaluation board. Once the I/Os are initialized, LED_Init() turns off all the LEDs.

L4-2(2)   CPU_Init() is called to initialize the CPU services provided by the µC/CPU module.

L4-2(3)   OS_CPU_TickInit() which is found in BSP_TICK_C.C is called to setup the µC/OS-III tick interrupt. The tick interrupt uses CMT0.

L4-2(4)   OSStatTaskCPUUsageInit() is called to determine the "capacity" of the CPU. µC/OS-III runs "only" its internal tasks for 1/10 of a second and determines the maximum amount of time the idle task loops. The number of loops is counted and placed in the variable OSStatTaskCtr. This value is saved in OSStatTaskCtrMax just before OSStatTaskCPUUsageInit() returns. OSStatTaskCtrMax is used to determine the CPU usage when other tasks are added. Specifically, as tasks are added to the application, OSStatTaskCtr (which is reset every 1/10 of a second) is incremented less by the idle task because other tasks consume CPU cycles. CPU usage is determined by the following equation:

$$OSStatTaskCPUUsage_{(\%)} = (100 - \frac{100 \times OSStatTaskCtr}{OSStatTaskCtrMax})$$

The value of OSStatTaskCPUUsage can be displayed at run-time by µC/Probe by using a circular gauge or other display object.

L4-2(5)   The µC/LIB memory management services are initialized. This functionality is used by the TCP/IP stack.

L4-2(6)   AppProbe_Init() (see APP_PROBE.C) is called to initialize µC/Probe to be used either via RS-232C or TCP/IP. In addition, µC/Probe can be used with the RX through the J-Link interface. The J-Link interface can be used simultaneously by µC/Probe and the HEW debugger. In other words, µC/Probe can interface with the YRDKRX62N with either RS-232C, TCP/IP or the debug port through the J-Link. The benefit of using the J-Link port is that, unlike RS-232C or TCP/IP, the µC/Probe target resident software is not required.

L4-2(7)   The 'blinky' task (AppBlinkyTask()) is created.

L4-2(8)   The OKAYA 96x64 graphics LCD is initialized by calling **BSP_GraphLCD_Init()** (see **BSP_GLCD.C**).

L4-2(9)   The graphics display shows the word "**Micrium**" in bold followed by "uC/OS-III" and "uC/TCP-IP" on the next two lines as shown below.

     " **Micrium** "
     "uC/OS-III"
     "uC/TCP-IP"

L4-2(10)   **AppTCPIP_Init()** is called to initialize all the necessary TCP/IP stack services needed by this application. Specifically, the µC/TCP-IP stack is used in conjunction with µC/DHCPc in order to use µC/Probe through this interface. More details on TCP/IP stack services are described in the subsequent chapters.

L4-2(11)   **CPU_IntDisMeasMaxCurReset()** is called to reset the interrupt disable time measurement feature of the µC/CPU module. This is done to not consider initialization code in the measurement of maximum interrupt disable time.

L4-2(12)   The start task then gets deleted as it is no longer needed.

L4-2(13)   The while loop is actually not necessary because **OSTaskDel()** should not return.

4-5 SUMMARY

The Renesas HEW is a powerful tool that allows developers to edit, compile, assemble, link and debug embedded applications.

μC/Probe is a powerful tool that allows target variables to be displayed and changed at run-time. The Trial version is limited to displaying and/or changing up to eight application variables at a time. However, because μC/OS-III kernel awareness is built-into μC/Probe, there is no limitation on the display of the important run-time information about μC/OS-III (task status, semaphores, queues, etc.).

The display screens in μC/Probe only show μC/OS-III variables. However, μC/Probe allows any variable in the target to be monitored, as long as the variable is declared global or static. In fact, it is fairly easy to add the application task to the task list.

Variables are updated on the μC/Probe data screen as quickly as the interface permits it. μC/Probe is demonstrated using a TCP/IP connection over an Ethernet port. μC/Probe can also interface through the serial port (RS-232C), and the J-Link Debugger. With RS-232C and TCP/IP, target resident code is required to allow the communication with μC/Probe. For this reason, μC/Probe would only be able to update the workspace when the target is running. When μC/Probe is communicating through the J-Link debug interface, target resident code is not required.

Chapter

5

PCB Tilt Direction using an Accelerometer

This example builds on the first example and demonstrates the following:

1   Use of an accelerometer to determine the tilt of the evaluation board

2   Use of a mutex in the I^{2}C driver to provide exclusive access to this resource

3   Use of the µC/OS-III delay function

In this demo, channel 0 of the RX62N's RIIC (Renesas I^{2}C Bus Interface) is used to communicate with an Analog Devices ADXL345 accelerometer. The accelerometer measures the acceleration of gravity for three axes, two of which are used to determine the inclination of the board. The direction of inclination is displayed by illuminating one of the 12 LEDs laid out in a circular pattern. By careful rolling of the board, it is possible to "roll" the illuminated LED round the circle. All the LEDs turn back on if the board is put back on a flat surface (or the original angled surface).

Start HEW and open the following workspace:

`\Micrium\Software\EvalBoards\Renesas\YRDKRX62N\GNURX\GNURX.hws`

Right-click on the "**uCOS-III-Ex2**" tab on the top-left of the HEW workspace as shown on Figure 5-1 and select "Set as Current Project". A message box asks to save the modifications in the session settings. Click "No" to dismiss the message box. HEW tries to connect to the YRDKRX62N on-board J-Link, as described on Chapter 4, "Connecting to the Target" on page 704. After connecting to the target, press the 'F7' key to ensure the project is built. Click "Yes" to confirm the download of the module, after the project is built. If a dialog box requests files to be located, click "Cancel" to dismiss it.

Figure 5-1 **Selecting Example #2**

5-1 RUNNING THE PROJECT

The workspace project is configured to automatically download the Example #2 module to the YRDKRX62N evaluation board after every build. To manually force the download of the module to the target, double click on the "**uCOS III Ex2.x**" file under the Download modules in the workspace window. To locate the module file, expand the project by clicking on the "+" sign next to uCOS-III-Ex2, then expand the Download module folder.

To run µC/Probe over Ethernet, an Ethernet cable should be connected to the YRDKRX62N. µC/Probe also supports the J-Link interface. Finally, click on the Reset/Go button in HEW as shown in Figure 5-2., or press the "Shift"+'F5' key.

Figure 5-2 **Running the Example**

As the TCP/IP stack is being initialized, the LEDs are lit in the pattern shown on the left side of Figure 5-3 (half the LEDs are on). Once the TCP/IP stack is initialized, all LEDs are turned on, as shown on the right side of Figure 5-3. The numbers in the LEDs correspond to the LED numbers on the YRDKRX62N demonstration board.

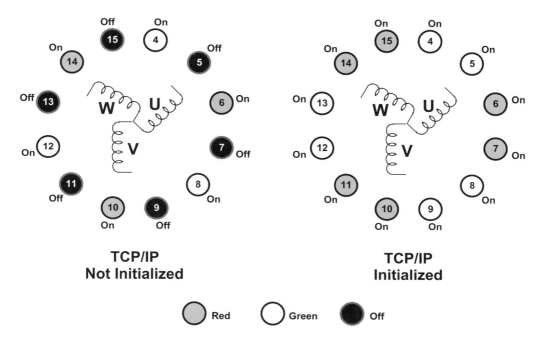

Figure 5-3 **Circular LEDs during Initialization**

At any time, the YRDKRX62N evaluation board can be pickup and rotated around. At this point, only one of the LEDs is lit and appear as if the LED was pulled by 'gravity'. Rotating the board around, one of the LEDs follows the direction of the tilt. By careful rolling the board, it is possible to "roll" the illuminated LED round the circle. All the LEDs turn back on if the board is put back on a flat surface (or the original angled surface).

5-2 HOW THE EXAMPLE CODE WORKS

Most of the code for this example is found in APP.C, BSP.C, BSP_ADXL345.C and BSP_ADT7420.C. main() is identical to main() shown in the previous example. Figure 5-4 shows a block diagram of the code for this example.

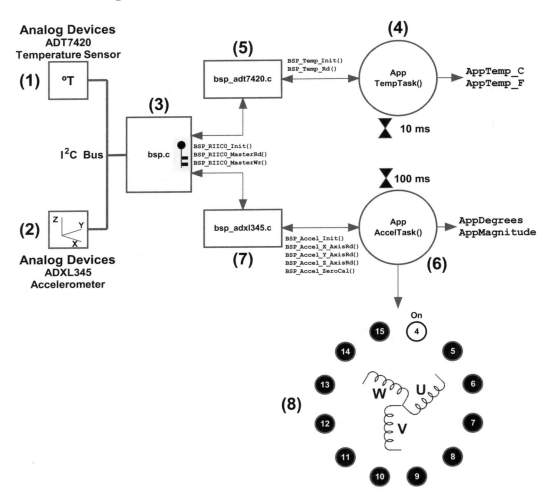

Figure 5-4 **Block Diagram of Example Code**

F5-4(1)   The temperature surrounding the YRDKRX62N is measured by an Analog Devices ADT7420 temperature sensor.

F5-4(2)   An Analog Devices ADXL345 digital accelerometer is used to measure the g-forces on the evaluation board. The accelerometer is configured to operate in +/-16g full resolution mode, resulting in a 4 mg/LSB scaling factor. The accelerometer is capable of measuring static acceleration of gravity in tilt-sensing applications, as well as dynamic acceleration due to motion or shock. This is the type of device used in laptop hard disk drives to enable them to sense if they are being dropped, and, in this case, made to quickly move the heads to a safe part of the disk before impact. Other uses include game controllers, mobile phones and instrumentation devices. This particular accelerometer features single and double tap detection and a 32 level FIFO.

F5-4(3)   Both the temperature sensor and accelerometer are connected to an I^2C bus. Access to the I^2C bus is done via the BSP functions **BSP_RIIC0_MasterRd()** and **BSP_RIIC0_MasterWr()**, which are found in **BSP.C**. A mutual exclusion semaphore (mutex) is used to ensure that only one task accesses the bus at any given time. The mutex is encapsulated in the above two BSP functions so the caller does not have to implement similar resource protection.

F5-4(4)   **AppTempTask()** is a task that runs every 10 milliseconds to read the current temperature. The temperature is not actually used for any purpose in this example, except to demonstrate the proper use of a mutex to guard the access to a shared resource (the I^2C bus). **AppTempTask()** outputs the value of the temperature in degrees Fahrenheit and degrees Celsius through the variables **AppTemp_F** and **AppTemp_C**, respectively. These values can be easily displayed using µC/Probe.

F5-4(5)   **AppTempTask()** calls **BSP_Temp_Rd()** (found in **BSP_ADT7420.C**) when it needs to read the current temperature from the ADT7420. **BSP_Temp_Rd()** in turn calls **BSP_RIIC0_MasterRd()** and **BSP_RIIC0_MasterWr()** as needed.

F5-4(6)   **AppAccelTask()** is a task that runs every 100 milliseconds to obtain the current acceleration on the X and Y axis of the accelerometer. The Z axis is not used for the purpose of this example, but can just as easily be read if needed for other applications. The code for **AppAccelTask()** is further described below.

5

F5-4(7)   The accelerometer is read by calling BSP functions found in the file **BSP_ADXL345.C**. There is a dedicated function to read each of the three axis: **BSP_Accel_X_AxisRd()**, **BSP_Accel_Y_AxisRd()** and **BSP_Accel_Z_AxisRd()**. As with the temperature sensor, these functions in turn call the **BSP.C** functions **BSP_RIIC0_MasterRd()** and **BSP_RIIC0_MasterWr()** functions to access the I²C bus.

F5-4(8)   **AppAccelTask()** updates the LEDs as described in the introduction of this chapter.

The code for **AppAccelTask()** is shown in Listing 5-1 and is split into two parts.

```
static  void  AppAccelTask (void  *p_arg)
{
    OS_ERR      err;
    CPU_FP32    angle_radians;
    CPU_FP32    angle_degrees;
    CPU_INT16S  accel_x_axis;
    CPU_INT16S  accel_y_axis;
    CPU_INT16S  accel_z_axis;
    CPU_FP32    x;
    CPU_FP32    x2;
    CPU_FP32    y;
    CPU_FP32    y2;
    CPU_FP32    sum_x2_y2;


    (void)&p_arg;

    angle_radians = 0.0f;
    angle_degrees = 0.0f;

    BSP_Accel_Init();                                           (1)
    BSP_Accel_ZeroCal();                                        (2)

    LED_Off(0);                                                 (3)


    while (DEF_ON) {                                            (4)
        OSTimeDlyHMSM(0u, 0u, 0u, 100u,                         (5)
                      OS_OPT_TIME_HMSM_STRICT,
                      &err);

        accel_x_axis = BSP_Accel_X_AxisRd();                   (6)
        accel_y_axis = BSP_Accel_Y_AxisRd();
```

```
    if ((APP_ACCEL_ZERO(accel_x_axis, BSP_Accel_X_Zero)) &&          (7)
        (APP_ACCEL_ZERO(accel_y_axis, BSP_Accel_Y_Zero))) {
        AppQuadrant = 5;

    } else if ((APP_ACCEL_NEG (accel_y_axis, BSP_Accel_Y_Zero)) &&
               (APP_ACCEL_ZERO(accel_x_axis, BSP_Accel_X_Zero))) {
        AppQuadrant = 6;

    } else if ((APP_ACCEL_POS (accel_y_axis, BSP_Accel_Y_Zero)) &&
               (APP_ACCEL_ZERO(accel_x_axis, BSP_Accel_X_Zero))) {
        AppQuadrant = 7;

    } else if ((APP_ACCEL_POS (accel_x_axis, BSP_Accel_X_Zero)) &&
               (APP_ACCEL_ZERO(accel_y_axis, BSP_Accel_Y_Zero))) {
        AppQuadrant = 8;

    } else if ((APP_ACCEL_NEG (accel_x_axis, BSP_Accel_X_Zero)) &&
               (APP_ACCEL_ZERO(accel_y_axis, BSP_Accel_Y_Zero))) {
        AppQuadrant = 9;

    } else if ((APP_ACCEL_POS(accel_x_axis, BSP_Accel_X_Zero)) &&
               (APP_ACCEL_POS(accel_y_axis, BSP_Accel_Y_Zero))) {
        AppQuadrant = 3;

    } else if ((APP_ACCEL_POS(accel_x_axis, BSP_Accel_X_Zero)) &&
               (APP_ACCEL_NEG(accel_y_axis, BSP_Accel_Y_Zero))) {
        AppQuadrant = 4;

    } else if ((APP_ACCEL_NEG(accel_x_axis, BSP_Accel_X_Zero)) &&
               (APP_ACCEL_POS(accel_y_axis, BSP_Accel_Y_Zero))) {
        AppQuadrant = 2;

    } else if ((APP_ACCEL_NEG(accel_x_axis, BSP_Accel_X_Zero)) &&
               (APP_ACCEL_NEG(accel_y_axis, BSP_Accel_Y_Zero))) {
        AppQuadrant = 1;
    }
```

Listing 5-1 **AppAccelTask(), Part 1**

L5-1(1)   The task starts by initializing the ADXL345 accelerometer.

L5-1(2)   The current resting position of the board is considered as the flat position. Most likely, the YRDKRX62N evaluation board is laying flat, electronic components facing up.

L5-1(3)   The 12 LEDs are turned off. The BSP `LED_Off()` function assumes a single argument. Specifying 0 indicates to turn off all the LEDs. A non-zero value specifies which LED to turn on. The LED functions are located in `BSP.C`.

L5-1(4)   A typical µC/OS-III task is implemented as an infinite loop. `DEF_ON` is declared as a non-zero value in `LIB_DEF.H`.

L5-1(5)   The infinite loop starts by calling the µC/OS-III `OSTimeDlyHMSM()` function. This allows the task to suspend for a specified amount of hours, minutes, seconds and milliseconds. In this example, the task is suspended for 100 milliseconds.

L5-1(6)   The X and Y accelerometer axis are read into local variables.

L5-1(7)   This code determines the quadrant of the LED to turn on based on the tilt. The different quadrants are shown in Figure 5-5 (1 through 9). It is assumed the board is oriented such that the Ethernet connector is on the left (Left Side of Board), and the audio connector is to the right (Right Side of Board).

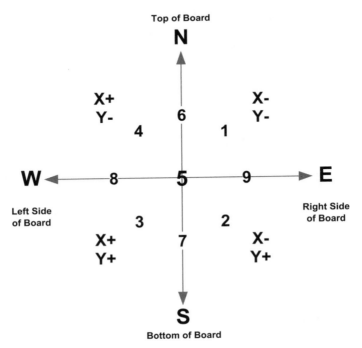

Figure 5-5 **Determining the Quadrant Based on the Tilt.**

The numbers in Figure 5-5 are the quadrant numbers used in the software. Quadrants 1, 2, 3 and 4 are when both X and Y accelerometer values are non-zero. Quadrant 6 and 7 occurs when the accelerometer X-axis is zero and Quadrants 8 and 9 occur when the accelerometer Y-axis is zero.

Quadrant 5 is used to indicate that both the X-axis and Y-axis values are zero, and so the board is laying flat or, rather in the orientation it was when **BSP_Accel_ZeroCal()** was called. In this case, all the LEDs are turned on.

If the board is tilted such that the bottom left of the board is lower than the rest of the board, then the LED that is turned on is in Quadrant 3. The exact LED depends on the tilt angle. In this case, both accelerometer X-axis and Y-axis have positive values.

If the board is tilted such that the bottom edge is horizontal and lower than the rest of the board, then the board is considered being in Quadrant 7 (X = 0).

```
x           = accel_x_axis;                                      (8)
y           = accel_y_axis;
x          -= BSP_Accel_X_Zero;
y          -= BSP_Accel_Y_Zero;

x2          = x * x;
y2          = y * y;
sum_x2_y2   = x2 + y2;
AppMagnitude = sqrt(sum_x2_y2 / 2.0f);

if ((fabs(x) > 0.5f) &&                                          (9)
    (fabs(y) > 0.5f)) {
    angle_radians = atan2(fabs(x), fabs(y));
    angle_degrees = (angle_radians * 180.0f) / 3.1415926535897932f;
}

if (AppQuadrant == 5) {                                          (10)
    AppDegrees = 0.0f;
    if (AppTCPIP_Cfg == DEF_TRUE) {
        LED_On( 4);
        LED_On( 5);
        LED_On( 6);
        LED_On( 7);
        LED_On( 8);
        LED_On( 9);
```

```
            LED_On(10);
            LED_On(11);
            LED_On(12);
            LED_On(13);
            LED_On(14);
            LED_On(15);
        } else {
            LED_On ( 4);
            LED_Off( 5);
            LED_On ( 6);
            LED_Off( 7);
            LED_On ( 8);
            LED_Off( 9);
            LED_On (10);
            LED_Off(11);
            LED_On (12);
            LED_Off(13);
            LED_On (14);
            LED_Off(15);
        }

    } else {

        LED_Off(0);
        switch (AppQuadrant) {
            case 1:
                AppDegrees = angle_degrees;
                if (angle_degrees < 30.0f) {
                    LED_On(4);
                } else if (angle_degrees < 60.0f) {
                    LED_On(5);
                } else {
                    LED_On(6);
                }
                break;

            case 2:
                AppDegrees = 180.0f - angle_degrees;
                if (angle_degrees < 30.0f) {
                    LED_On(9);
                } else if (angle_degrees < 60.0f) {
                    LED_On(8);
                } else {
                    LED_On(7);
                }
                break;
```

(11)

```
        case 3:
            AppDegrees = angle_degrees + 180.0f;
            if (angle_degrees < 30.0f) {
                LED_On(10);
            } else if( angle_degrees < 60.0f) {
                LED_On(11);
            } else {
                LED_On(12);
            }
            break;

        case 4:
            AppDegrees = 360.0f - angle_degrees;
            if (angle_degrees < 30.0f) {
                LED_On(15);
            } else if (angle_degrees < 60.0f) {
                LED_On(14);
            } else {
                LED_On(13);
            }
            break;

        case 6:
            AppDegrees =   0.0f;
            LED_On(4);
            break;

        case 7:
            AppDegrees = 180.0f;
            LED_On(10);
            break;

        case 8:
            AppDegrees = 270.0f;
            LED_On(13);
            break;

        case 9:
            AppDegrees =  90.0f;
            LED_On(7);
            break;
        }
      }
    }
  }
}
```

Listing 5-1 **AppAccelTask(), Part 2**

5

L5-1(8) This code determines the magnitude of the resultant accelerometer value and is obtained by computing the following equation:

$$AppMagnitude = \sqrt{\frac{x^2 + y^2}{2}}$$

The magnitude is not actually used to determine which LED is turned on, but can be displayed using µC/Probe. There is very little performance impact to use floating-point math on the RX62N because of its built-in floating-point hardware.

L5-1(9) The tilt angle is computed in order to determine which of the 3 LEDs within a quadrant is turned on. The angle uses the same coordinate system as a compass, where 0 degrees corresponds to north as shown in Figure 5-6. Additionally the tilt direction from 0 to 360 degrees is calculated and written to the variable **AppDegrees**.

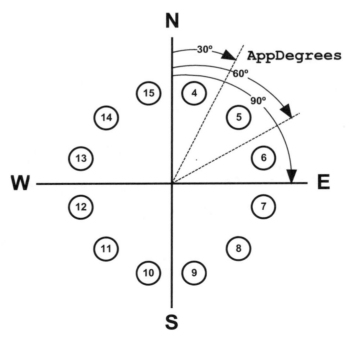

Figure 5-6 **Determining the Tilt Angle**

L5-1(10)   If the board is laying flat, then the LED pattern depends on whether the TCP/IP stack has been initialized or not. When the application starts, the TCP/IP stack determines its IP address using a DHCP client. Half of the LEDs in the ring are lit until the DHCP assigns the IP address. Once the TCP/IP initialization completes, a board laying 'flat' is indicated by all LEDs lit. This scheme allows the user to know when the µC/Probe interface to the target board is ready to be connected.

L5-1(11)   If the board is tilted then the exact LED to be lit is determined by the tilt angle and the quadrant.

5-3 SUMMARY

This simple example demonstrated how the on-board 3-axis accelerometer and temperature sensor of the YRDKRX62N are used. Floating-point math operations are used in the calculation of the 'magnitude' as well as the tilt angle of the board. The RX62N has built-in hardware floating-point capabilities making it well suited for this type of application, without any performance penalty.

The use of a mutual exclusion semaphore ensures exclusive access to the I^2C bus, making sure that only one task can use the I^2C bus at any given time. A task running on a periodic interval is demonstrated by using µC/OS-III's `OSTimeDlyHMSM()` function.

µC/Probe can be used to display the values of the application variables related to the tilt computation and temperature: `AppMagnitude`, `AppDegrees`, `AppQuadrant`, `AppTemp_C` and `AppTemp_F`. This is left as an exercise to the reader.

5

6

Customizable Performance Measurements

The example described in this chapter demostrates μC/OS-III performance measurements. Specifically, the built-in time measurement features of μC/OS-III are covered, as well as methods to compute post-to-pend times for various kernel objects. The built-in performance measurement feature of μC/OS-III is also capable of measuring the maximum interrupt disable time, and the maximum amount of time the scheduler is locked.

To setup the example demostrated in this chapter, the HEW toolchain and μC/Probe must be installed. Additionally, the YRDKRX62N demonstration board must be connected to the PC.

Start HEW and open the following workspace:

`\Micrium\Software\EvalBoards\Renesas\YRDKRX62N\GNURX\GNURX.hws`

Right click on "uCOS-III-Ex3" on the top-left of the HEW workspace as shown on Figure 6-1 and select "Set as Current Project". A message box asks to save the modifications in the session settings. Click "No" to dismiss the message box. HEW tries to connect to the YRDKRX62N on-board J-Link, as described on Chapter 4, "Connecting to the Target" on

6

page 704. After connecting to the target, press the 'F7' key to ensure the project is built. Click "Yes" to confirm the download of the module, after the project is built. If a dialog box requests files to be located, click "Cancel" to dismiss it.

Figure 6-1 **Selecting Example #3**

6-1 RUNNING THE PROJECT

The workspace project is configured to automatically download the Example #3 module to the YRDKRX62N evaluation board after every build. To manually force the download of the module to the target, double click on the "**uCOS III Ex3.x**" file under the Download modules in the workspace window. To locate the module file, expand the project by clicking on the "+" sign next to uCOS-III-Ex3, then expand the Download module folder.

Finally, click on the Reset/Go button in HEW or press the "Shift"+'F5' key.

6-2 EXAMINING PERFORMANCE TEST RESULTS WITH µC/PROBE

Start µC/Probe and open the **uCOS-III-Ex3-Probe.wsp** workspace found in the following directory:

\Micrium\Software\EvalBoards\Renesas\YRDKRX62N\GNURX\uCOS-III-Ex3

Select the "Application" tab and click on the μC/Probe "Run" button. The screen should appear as shown in Figure 6-2 (the dial is rotated to position 16). The dial acts as a rotary switch selecting one of 21 values of "Test #". The resulting execution time of the selected test is displayed in the "Execution Time (μs)" display.

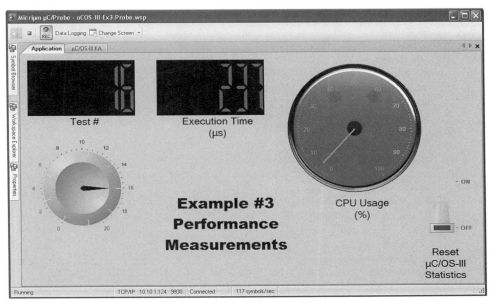

Figure 6-2 **Selecting test results using μC/Probe**

With the mouse, "grab" the dial and rotate it. The number on the "Test #" indicator reflects the position on the dial. As the dial rotates, the "Execution Time (μs)" indicator displays the execution time for the test being performed. The "Reset Statistics" toggle switch allows the "reset" of the "maximum" values reported in tests #15 through #20 (see table below).

6

Example #3 creates two additional tasks (compared to example #1) used to perform a series of 21 performance measurements. One of the tasks signals or sends messages to the other task, which waits for these signals or messages. The receiving task has a higher priority than the sender. Table 6-1 summarizes the results.

Test #	Description	Execution Time (µs)
0	**Semaphore** Rx task waits on a semaphore Context Switch to Tx task **Start time measurement** Tx task signals the semaphore Context Switch to Rx task Rx task returns from wait **Stop time measurement**	11.3
1	**Semaphore** **Start time measurement** Rx task signals a semaphore Rx task waits for the semaphore Rx task returns from wait **Stop time measurement** No context switch	5.3
2	**Task Semaphore** Rx task waits on its internal task semaphore Context Switch to Tx task **Start time measurement** Tx task signals the task semaphore of the Rx task Context Switch to Rx task Rx task returns from wait **Stop time measurement**	11.3
3	**Task Semaphore** **Start time measurement** Rx task signals its own task semaphore Rx task waits for its task semaphore Rx task returns from wait **Stop time measurement** No context switch	6.0

Test #	Description	Execution Time (µs)
4	**Message Queue** Rx task waits on a message queue Context Switch to Tx task **Start time measurement** Tx task sends a message to the message queue Context Switch to Rx task Rx task returns from wait **Stop time measurement**	11.3
5	**Message Queue** **Start time measurement** Rx task sends a message to the message queue Rx task waits on the message queue Rx task returns from wait **Stop time measurement** No context switch	6.0
6	**Task Message Queue** Rx task waits on its internal task message queue Context Switch to Tx task **Start time measurement** Tx task sends a message to the Rx task's internal message queue Context Switch to Rx task Rx task returns from wait **Stop time measurement**	11.3
7	**Task Message Queue** **Start time measurement** Rx task sends a message to its own task message queue Rx task waits on its task message queue Rx task returns from wait **Stop time measurement** No context switch	7.3
8	**Mutual Exclusion Semaphore** **Start time measurement** Rx task waits on a mutex (mutex is available) Rx task releases the mutex **Stop time measurement** No context switch	4.7

6

Test #	Description	Execution Time (µs)
9	**Event Flags** Rx task waits on an event flag group Context Switch to Tx task **Start time measurement** Tx task sets event flag group bits Context Switch to Rx task Rx task returns from wait **Stop time measurement**	11.3
10	**Event Flags** **Start time measurement** Rx task sets event flag group bits Rx task waits on the event flag group Rx task returns from wait **Stop time measurement** No context switch	5.3
11	Spare	0
12	Spare	0
13	Spare	0
14	Spare	0
15	**Maximum execution time of Interrupt Handler Queue task** (assuming OS_CFG_ISR_POST_DEFERRED_EN is set to 1)	0
16	**Maximum execution time of the Statistic task** (assuming OS_CFG_STAT_TASK_EN is set to 1)	478.7
17	**Maximum execution time of the Tick task**	4.7
18	**Maximum execution time of the Timer task** (assuming OS_CFG_TMR_EN is set to 1)	8.0
19	**Maximum interrupt disable time**	10.7
20	**Maximum scheduler lock time**	10.7

Table 6-1 µC/Probe **Test Results**

6-3 HOW THE EXAMPLE CODE WORKS

APP.C contains most of the code for this example. **main()** is identical to **main()** shown in the previous examples.

AppTaskStart() is also nearly identical to the previous examples, except for a call to the function **AppObjCreate()**. This function initializes kernel objects that are used in this example. The code for **AppObjCreate()** is shown in Listing 6-1.

```
static void AppObjCreate (void)
{
    OS_ERR   err;


    OSSemCreate  ((OS_SEM      *)&AppSem,
                  (CPU_CHAR     *)"App Sem",
                  (OS_SEM_CTR   )0,
                  (OS_ERR       *)&err);
    OSFlagCreate ((OS_FLAG_GRP *)&AppFlagGrp,
                  (CPU_CHAR     *)"App Flag Group",
                  (OS_FLAGS     )0,
                  (OS_ERR       *)&err);
    OSQCreate    ((OS_Q        *)&AppQ,
                  (CPU_CHAR     *)"App Queue",
                  (OS_MSG_QTY   )20,
                  (OS_ERR       *)&err);
    OSMutexCreate((OS_MUTEX    *)&AppMutex,
                  (CPU_CHAR     *)"App Mutex",
                  (OS_ERR       *)&err);
}
```

Listing 6-1 **AppObjCreate()**

AppTaskCreate() creates two tasks called: **AppTaskRx()** and **AppTaskTx()**. These tasks are used in the post-to-pend performance measurements. **AppTaskRx()** has a higher priority than **AppTaskTx()**. **AppTaskRx()** receives signals or messages from **AppTaskTx()**.

Figure 6-3 shows how the two tasks interact to perform the tests.

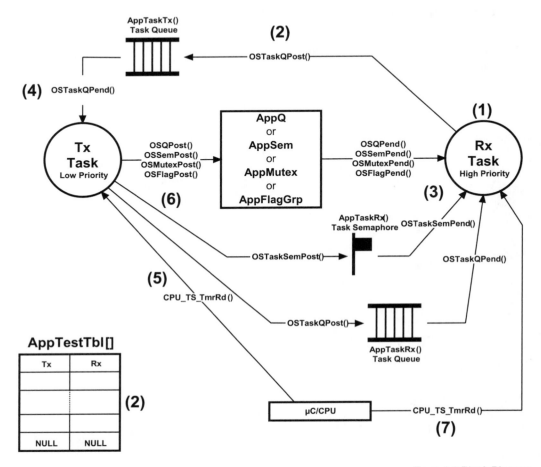

Figure 6-3 **Block Diagram**

F6-3(1)   AppTaskRx() executes first, since it has a higher priority than AppTaskTx().

F6-3(2)   AppTaskRx() reads the table AppTestTbl[], which contains pointers to functions that need to be executed by both AppTaskTx() and AppTaskRx(). Each entry contains one test to perform. AppTaskRx() posts the address of the current entry of AppTestTbl[] to AppTaskTx(), so that it can perform its test function.

F6-3(3)   **AppTaskRx()** then executes its "Rx" test as directed by the current table entry. In most cases, this corresponds to pending on one of the four kernel objects created or, **AppTaskRx()**'s internal task semaphore or message queue. Since no posts have been performed yet, **AppTaskRx()** blocks waiting for **AppTaskTx()** to send a signal or a message.

F6-3(4)   **AppTaskTx()** executes and immediately waits on its internal message queue.

F6-3(5)   **AppTaskTx()** reads the current timestamp by calling **CPU_TS_TmrRd()**. The value returned is stored in an array called **AppTS_Start[]** using the index of **AppTestTbl[]** as the index to **AppTS_Start[]**.

F6-3(6)   Since **AppTaskRx()** sent the address of the current **AppTestTbl[]** entry to **AppTaskTx()**, **AppTaskTx()** executes its "Tx" function from the table. This will most likely correspond to either sending a signal or a message to **AppTaskRx()**, based on the test function being executed.

F6-3(7)   Since **AppTaskRx()** has a higher priority, a context switch occurs and **AppTaskRx()** resumes execution. Then, **AppTaskRx()** reads the current timestamp from the µC/CPU module and store the value in another array, **AppTS_End[]**. The difference between the start and end time is computed and it is saved in **AppTS_Delta[]**. All the values in these arrays are in **CPU_TS_TMR** units.

For the YRDKRX62N, a timestamp is obtained by calling **CPU_TS_TmrRd()**, which counts at a rate of 1.5 MHz (48 MHz peripheral clock / 32) for this evaluation board. Execution time in microseconds simply requires a multiplication by 0.666667 of the **AppTS_Delta[]** entry.

745

6

The code for **AppTaskRx( )** is shown in Listing 6-2.

```
static  void  AppTaskRx (void *p_arg)
{
    OS_ERR      err;
    CPU_INT08U  i;
    APP_TEST    *p_test;


    (void)&p_arg;

    i            = 0;
    p_test       = &AppTestTbl[0];
    AppTestSel   = 0;
    App_TS_to_us = (CPU_FP32)1000000.0f / (CPU_FP32)CPU_TS_TmrFreqGet();        (1)


    for (i = 0; i < APP_TEST_MAX; i++) {                                        (2)
        AppTS_Delta[i] = (CPU_TS_TMR)0;
    }

    while (DEF_ON) {
        LED_Toggle(14);
        OSTimeDlyHMSM(0, 0, 0, 50u,                                            (3)
                      OS_OPT_TIME_HMSM_STRICT,
                      &err);
        if ((void *)p_test->Tx != (void *)0) {                                 (4)
            OSTaskQPost((OS_TCB     *)&AppTaskTxTCB,                            (5)
                        (void       *) p_test,
                        (OS_MSG_SIZE) i,
                        (OS_OPT     ) OS_OPT_POST_FIFO,
                        (OS_ERR     *)&err);
            (*(p_test->Rx))(i);                                                (6)
            i++;
            p_test++;
        } else {
            i       = 0;
            p_test = &AppTestTbl[0];
        }
```

```
#if OS_CFG_ISR_POST_DEFERRED_EN > 0u
        AppTS_Delta[15] = (CPU_TS_TMR)OSIntQTaskTimeMax;              (7)
#endif
#if OS_CFG_STAT_TASK_EN > 0u
        AppTS_Delta[16] = (CPU_TS_TMR)OSStatTaskTimeMax;
#endif
        AppTS_Delta[17] = (CPU_TS_TMR)OSTickTaskTimeMax;
#if OS_CFG_TMR_EN > 0u
        AppTS_Delta[18] = (CPU_TS_TMR)OSTmrTaskTimeMax;
#endif
        AppTS_Delta[19] = (CPU_TS_TMR)OSIntDisTimeMax;
        AppTS_Delta[20] = (CPU_TS_TMR)OSSchedLockTimeMax;

        AppTestTime_us  = (CPU_INT16U)((CPU_FP32)AppTS_Delta[AppTestSel] * App_TS_to_us); (8)
    }
}
```

Listing 6-2 **AppTaskRx()**

L6-2(1)   The conversion factor from **CPU_TS_TMR** to microseconds is computed to avoid doing the division in the loop where all the tests are performed. The value is computed in floating-point because the frequency is not an integer multiple.

L6-2(2)   The table containing the execution times is cleared (i.e., initialized).

L6-2(3)   **AppTaskRx()** executes a test every 50 milliseconds, or 20 tests per second.

L6-2(4)   **AppTaskRx()** goes through **AppTestTbl[]** until all tests have been performed, and continuously restarts the tests from the beginning.

L6-2(5)   **AppTaskRx()** sends the address of the current **AppTestTbl[]** entry to **AppTaskTx()**. The index into **AppTestTbl[]** is sent as the message size.

L6-2(6)   **AppTaskRx()** then executes the "Rx" function provided in **AppTestTbl[]** at the current entry.

L6-2(7)   The execution times (in **CPU_TS_TMR** units) are copied to their appropriate slot in the **AppTS_Delta[]** array.

6

L6-2(8)   The execution time of the test is computed (in microseconds) so that it can be displayed by µC/Probe. **AppTestSel** corresponds to the value of the "dial" on the µC/Probe application data screen.

The code for **AppTaskTx()** is shown in Listing 6-3.

```
static  void  AppTaskTx (void *p_arg)
{
    OS_ERR         err;
    OS_MSG_SIZE    msg_size;
    CPU_TS         ts;
    APP_TEST       *p_test;


    (void)p_arg;

    while (DEF_ON) {
        LED_Toggle(5);
        p_test = (APP_TEST *)OSTaskQPend((OS_TICK       )0,                      (1)
                                         (OS_OPT        )OS_OPT_PEND_BLOCKING,
                                         (OS_MSG_SIZE *)&msg_size,
                                         (CPU_TS       *)&ts,
                                         (OS_ERR       *)&err);
        (*p_test->Tx)((CPU_INT08U)msg_size);                                    (2)
    }
}
```

Listing 6-3 **AppTaskTx()**

L6-3(1)   **AppTaskTx()** waits for a message to be sent by **AppTaskRx()**.

L6-3(2)   Once the message is received, **AppTaskTx()** executes the function at the current entry in **AppTestTbl[]**. The "Tx" function expects the index into **AppTS_Start[]**, **AppTS_End[]**, and **AppTS_Delta[]**, where the measurement results are saved.

6-4 SUMMARY

This example shows only a fraction of the performance measurements performed by µC/OS-III.

Four spare slots (**AppTS_Delta[11]** to **AppTS_Delta[14]**) have been reserved to extend the example with additional performance measurements. This array assumes values placed in **CPU_TS_TMR** units.

With µC/Probe, it is possible to show the performance data of the application tasks. However, the Trial Version of µC/Probe limits the display of only eight application variables at one time. There is no limitations for µC/OS-III variables, since µC/Probe is µC/OS-III aware. µC/OS-III licensees receive one free license of the full version of µC/Probe to utilize all the features available without any limitation.

6

Motor Drive Simulation

This chapter demostrates a simulation of a variable frequency drive (VFD) motor controlled by PWM signals, using specialized timers and fast fourier transform (FFT) of the output signal. For the simulation, a single PWM output is used and this output is filtered to produce a sine wave having a frequency between 50 and 200 Hz. The frequency of the sine wave is adjusted using either the potentiometer on the YRDKRX62N or a slider object in µC/Probe. The sine wave is then fed into an ADC. The ADC is sampled, and the frequency is calculated using a FFT. The measured frequency is then used to alter the rotating frequency of the 12 LEDs mounted on the YRDKRX62N. The measured frequency is also displayed using µC/Probe and on the on-board LCD.

This example demonstrates the following features:

1   Motor drive capability of the RX62N

2   FPU intensive processing

3   RX62N fast, non-kernel aware ISR

4   µC/OS-III's built-in task semaphore

5   µC/Probe writing to a variable using a slider

6   The use of Renesas's Signal Processing Library (SPL)

7-1 AC MOTOR CONTROL THEORY

The demostrated example is based on motor control theory: variable frequency drive (VFD). An AC motor is driven by an AC supply where the speed of the motor is controlled by the frequency of the supply. By altering the supply frequency, the speed of the motor can be controlled, and such a drive control system is called a variable frequency drive. In order to control the generated torque, the voltage supplied to the drive is also controlled.

In VFD applications, the AC supply is generated and supplied to the motor via a bridge circuit consisting of high current drivers such as MOSFETs (Metal Oxide Semiconductor Field Effect Transistor) or IGBTs (Insulated Gate Bipolar Transistors). Typically an AC motor is driven by a 3-phase AC signal with each phase having a pair of drivers. Therefore, a three-phase system has a total of six high current drivers, as shown in Figure 7-1.

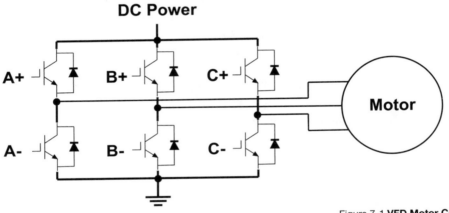

Figure 7-1 **VFD Motor Control**

Each phase of the motor has a pair of transistors. One for the positive side of the signal (A+, B+ and C+) and one for the negative side (A-, B- and C-). It is very important that both transistors in a pair (*e.g.*, A+ and A-) are not enabled at the same time, otherwise it creates a short circuit between the power rails and will certainly result in a failure of the bridge. As transistors usually do not switch on and off at the same speed, it is necessary to insert some deadtime between one transistor turning off and the next turning on, in a pair. During this deadtime neither transistor is switched on.

The AC waveform required by the motor is generated in a microcontroller using pulse width modulation (PWM). Renesas RX microcontrollers are particularly well suited to motor drive applications due to peripherals such as the MTU2, which is able to generate the three phase complimentary PWM signals consisting of a total of six outputs. The PWMs produce three sine waves (as seen by the motor as it acts like a filter) 120 degrees apart. The MTU2 can automatically insert deadtime and can also measure this deadtime so it can be adjusted during operation to ensure the safe and efficient operation of the system. The MTU2 timer compare match registers are buffered which can relax interrupt response time of the CPU in order to update the compare match value. Renesas RX microcontrollers also offer a POE (port output enable) peripheral which can turn off the 3-phase signals when triggered from an external source. Therefore, an external circuit can monitor the current flow in the motor and should a problem occur, switch off the MTU2 outputs without the need to go through software such as an ISR to achieve this.

The MTU2 PWM outputs are used to generate sine waves. The frequency of these sine waves control the synchronous speed of an AC motor. The synchronous speed of a VFD motor is basically dependent upon the input frequency, and the number of stator poles according to the equation below.

$$RPM = \frac{120 \times f}{p}$$

Where, "RPM" is the motor speed in revolutions per minute (RPM), "f" is the AC supply frequency in Hz and "p" is the number of stator winding poles. Therefore, a 4-pole motor (p) with a variable frequency supply of 50Hz to 200Hz (f) would run at speeds between 1500 and 6000 RPM.

7-2 RUNNING THE PROJECT

Start HEW and open the following workspace:

`\Micrium\Software\EvalBoards\Renesas\YRDKRX62N\GNURX\GNURX.hws`

Right click on "uCOS-III-Ex4" on the top-left of the HEW workspace as shown on Figure 7-2 and select "Set as Current Project". A message box asks to save the modifications in the session settings. Click "No" to dismiss the message box. HEW tries to connect to the YRDKRX62N on-board J-Link, as described on Chapter 4, "Connecting to the Target" on page 704. After connecting to the target, press the 'F7' key to ensure the project is built. Click "Yes" to confirm the download of the module, after the project is built. If a dialog box requests files to be located, click "Cancel" to dismiss it.

Figure 7-2 **Selecting Example #4 in HEW**

The workspace project is configured to automatically download the Example #4 module to the YRDKRX62N evaluation board after every build. To manually force the download of the module to the target, double click on the "**uCOS III Ex4.x**" file under the Download modules in the workspace window. To locate the module file, expand the project by clicking on the "+" sign next to uCOS-III-Ex4, then expand the Download module folder.

Finally, click on the Reset/Go button in HEW or press the "Shift"+'F5' key.

Start µC/Probe and open the uCOS-III-Ex4-Probe.wsp workspace found in the following directory:

`\Micrium\Software\EvalBoards\Renesas\YRDKRX62N\GNURX\uCOS-III-Ex4`

Select the "Application" tab and click on the µC/Probe "Run" button. The screen should appear as shown in Figure 7-3.

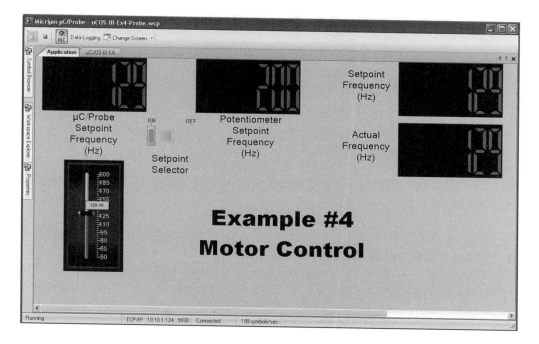

Figure 7-3 **µC/Probe Motor Control Panel**

F7-3(1)   This slider determines the frequency of the sine wave generated by the PWM.

F7-3(2)   The slider value is also shown using a numeric indicator.

F7-3(3)   This switch determines whether the sine wave frequency is selected by the slider on this screen or, the potentiometer on-board the YRDKRX62N.

F7-3(4)   This numeric indicator displays the setpoint frequency as determined by the potentiometer on the YRDKRX62N. As the potentiometer is rotated, this indicator changes accordingly.

F7-3(5)   These two indicators are similar to the LCD display on the YRDKRX62N. The top value indicates the sine wave frequency setpoint as determined by either the slider or the potentiometer. The value chosen depends on the position of the switch.

The bottom numeric indicator displays the actual frequency which is determined by doing an FFT on the generated sine wave.

7-3 HOW THE EXAMPLE CODE WORKS

As with the other examples, **APP.C** contains most of the code for this example. **main()** is identical to **main()** shown in the previous examples.

AppTaskStart() is also nearly identical to the previous examples except that another task is created, **AppFFT_Task()**. Once this second task is created, **AppTaskStart()** monitors the value of the variable **AppStatReset** which is expected to be changed by a switch in µC/Probe. When the switch is toggled on, the µC/OS-III statistics are reset by calling **OSStatReset()**. **AppTaskStart()** also writes the desired and actual sine wave frequency information to the LCD.

7-4 GENERATING A SINE WAVE

The sine wave is generated using an MTU2 channel operating in complementary PWM mode. Such sine wave generation is used in AC motor control, which the RX microcontroller is particularly well suited for.

Figure 7-4 is a block diagram of the pieces involved in the generation of the sine wave. The sine wave generation is interrupt driven and is handled by the **AppPWM_ISR()** function found in **APP.C**.

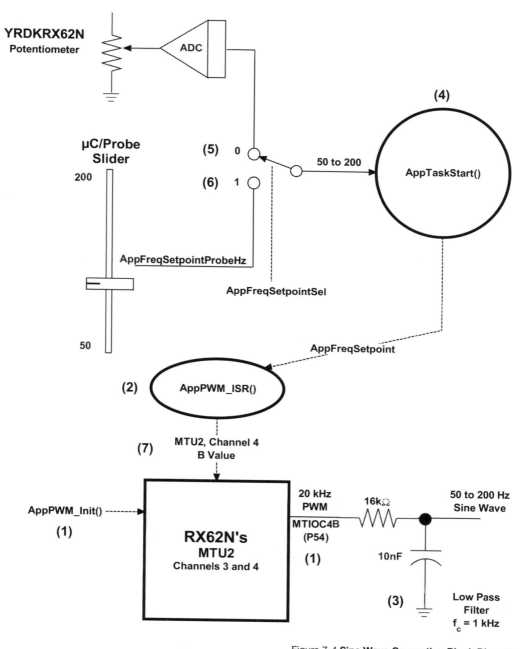

Figure 7-4 **Sine Wave Generation Block Diagram**

F7-4(1)   **AppPWM_Init()** initializes MTU2, channels 3 & 4, which are used to generate the PWM signal that is filtered into a sine wave. **AppPWM_Init()** is called by **AppFFT_Task()** and sets the PWM carrier frequency to 20 kHz. This frequency was chosen as in most motor drive systems; the period of the PWM is set above that which can be heard by humans. In some systems, the period is modulated with a random seed to eliminate any sort of repetitive noise. The PWM output can be monitored using an oscilloscope by probing the output from the filter on C82, which is assigned to **MTIOC4B** by **AppPWM_Init()**.

F7-4(2)   **AppPWM_ISR()** services the PWM interrupts which occur every 50 µs. Normally, such a fast interrupt rate would impose a huge overhead in a kernel-based application. However, the RX62N can handle very fast interrupts with non-kernel aware interrupt handlers.

   AppPWM_ISR() is independent of the kernel and thus does not need to communicate anything to other tasks. In other words, the ISR makes no kernel API calls, which classifies it as a non-kernel aware interrupt. The priority level of this interrupt is higher than that of the kernel. In fact, **AppPWM_ISR()** has an interrupt priority of 13, whereas all kernel aware interrupts need to be set to level 12, or lower.

F7-4(3)   The sine wave is actually obtained by passing the PWM signal through a simple 1st order low pass filter, consisting of a resistor and a capacitor. The filter cutoff frequency is set to 1 kHz.

   The frequency of the output sine wave is controlled by how many "steps" make up the sine wave. Since the timer interrupt occurs at 20 kHz, a 100 step sine wave is used (that is, a sine wave made up of 100 values, each every 1/20,000 seconds = 50 µs apart) to produce a sine wave frequency of 200 Hz. If a 400 step sine wave is output, its frequency would be 50 Hz. The "step" increment is calculated from the setpoint frequency (**AppFreqSetpointHz**).

   Each step in the sine wave is calculated within the ISR each time the ISR occurs and the value is loaded into **TGRD** of MTU2, channel 4. Normally loading small compare match values into the compare match registers would cause problems as the time taken to calculate the value is longer than the time for the compare match to occur, and therefore resulting in the event being missed. The MTU2 eliminates this problem using **TGRD** as a buffer register for **TGRB**. The contents of **TGRD** are copied to **TGRB** once per PWM period.

As the sine wave generation is independent of the RTOS and is interrupt driven, it will continue to output the sine wave while the program is running.

F7-4(4)   The sine wave frequency is determined by either the position of the potentiometer on the YRDKRX62N or, by a "slider" object in µC/Probe. **AppFreqSetpointSel** is a variable that is mapped to a "switch" object in µC/Probe. **AppFreqSetpointHz** is determined by **AppTaskStart()**, which runs 4 times per second.

F7-4(5)   When **AppFreqSetpointSel** is set to 0 (the default value), the sine wave frequency is determined by the position of the potentiometer on the YRDKRX62N. The position of the potentiometer is actually read using one of the ADC channels of the RX62N. The ADC value is scaled in **AppTaskStart()**.

F7-4(6)   When **AppFreqSetpointSel** is set to 1, the sine wave frequency is determined by a slider object in µC/Probe. The slider object is mapped to **AppFreqSetpointProbeHz** which then gets copied to **AppFreqSetpointHz**.

F7-4(7)   **AppPWM_ISR()** computes the new value to load into the "B" register of the MTU2 channel 2. The "B" register establishes the duty cycle of the PWM.

7-5 COMPUTING THE FFT OF THE SINE WAVE

Figure 7-5 shows a block diagram of the operations performed to determine the dominant frequency of the sampled sine wave.

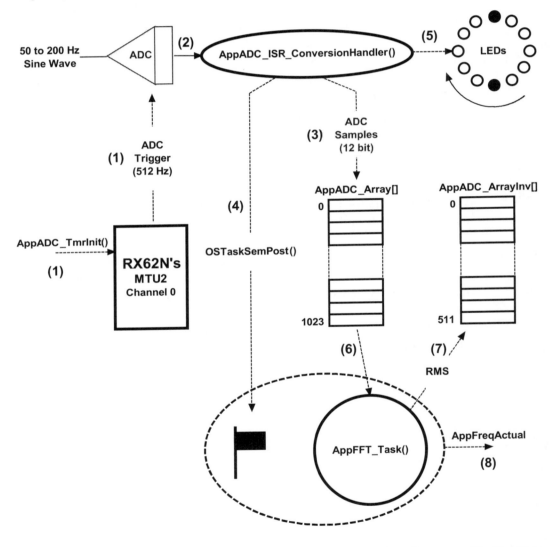

Figure 7-5 **Determining the Dominant Frequency of the Sine Wave**

F7-5(1)   **AppADC_TmrInit()** initializes MTU2 channel 0 to generate a frequency of 512 Hz which is used to trigger an ADC conversion of the generated sine wave. By using the timer to trigger the ADC, accurate periodic samples can be achieved which is important when the data is being used with an FFT function. The sampling frequency satisfies the Nyquist criterion of sampling an analog signal at at least twice the highest frequency being read in order to avoid aliasing.

F7-5(2)   The ADC interrupts the CPU and this time, the ISR is kernel aware.

F7-5(3)   The data is copied to the next even (real data) element of the **AppADC_Array[]** array while the odd (imaginary data) element is filled with zero.

F7-5(4)   When the required number of conversions (**APP_FFT_N_POINTS**) have been transferred, the ISR signals the FFT task (**AppFFT_Task()**) to indicate that an FFT needs to be performed. The signal is performed by signaling **AppFFT_Task()**'s built-in task semaphore. Before signaling the semaphore, ADC interrupts are suspended allowing the FFT task to perform its computations on the sampled data.

F7-5(5)   **AppADC_ISR_ConversionHandler()** rotates the LED wheel of the YRDKRX62N at a rate of roughly 10 times slower than the actual sine wave frequency. In other words, a 200 Hz sine wave causes the display to change LEDs 20 times per second.

Two LEDs are "rotated" at the same time to simulate the control signals of a VFD. The LED code is placed in **AppADC_ISR_ConversionHandler()** since the ISR is synchronous with the sine wave sampling and occurs fast enough to provide a suitable range of "rotation" speeds.

F7-5(6)   **AppFFT_Task()** performs a complex FFT on the sampled ADC data (sampled at 512 Hz) to transform it from the time domain to frequency domain. Input data is made of complex pairs where the real element of each pair is the ADC value and the complex element is zero. FFT library function supplied by Renesas Electronics America (REA) normally requires a license for use, which is free and obtainable from Renesas. The execution time of the FFT is measured and placed in a variable called **AppFFT_FFT_Time_us**, which can be displayed using µC/Probe.

F7-5(7)   The outputs from the FFT are complex pairs. **AppFFT_Task()** performs a root mean square (RMS) operation to convert the real and imaginary values into a single magnitude. There are half as many data RMS elements as a result of this operation. The execution time of the RMS calculation is measured and placed in a variable called **AppFFT_RMS_Time_us**, which can be displayed using µC/Probe.

F7-5(8)   The array of frequency magnitude data (i.e., **AppADC_ArrayRMS[]**) is scanned to find the largest value. This represents the dominant frequency in the input data. As the data is sampled at 512 Hz and there are 512 data values, each element in the array represents 1 Hz. Therefore, the array index equals the frequency. This value is written to variable **AppFreqActual**. The execution time to determine the sine wave frequency is placed in a variable called **AppFFT_Freq_Time_us**, which can be displayed using µC/Probe.

Finally, the ADC is restarted to sample another 512 values.

7-5-1 DISPLAYING THE SETPOINT AND MEASURED FREQUENCY

Once the TCP/IP address information consisting of the IP address, subnet mask and gateway address have been shown on the LCD for 10 seconds, the LCD displays the setpoint frequency of the sine wave (set by the YRDKRX62N potentiometer or µC/Probe) and the actual measured frequency (**AppFreqActual**).

7-6 SUMMARY

Renesas RX microcontrollers are great general purpose microcomputers. Devices such as the RX62N are also great in application specific roles such as motor control, thanks to peripherals like the MTU2 which can generate all the complex complimentary 3-phase PWM signals, including deadtimes with minimal CPU intervention. Add the FPU unit of the RX, complex control algorithms and signal processing tasks can easily be handled. This results in plenty of CPU performance left for HMI (Human Machine Interface) tasks, communications over Ethernet, USB etc.

A great feature of µC/OS-III is the task semaphore which makes signaling a task easy. The code is minimized because there is no need to create a semaphore to signal the task.

Like Micriµm's products, Renesas' Signal Processing Library (SPL) helps to get the user up and running quickly with complex signal processing functions. The fully documented pre-built, and just as important, tested routines make integrating FFT functionality a breeze. To get the latest SPL libraries and user's manual for these libraries, go to www.renesas.com/rx.

8

Web Server Example

The following project builds on previous examples by providing a popular service in embedded systems -- a web server. Using a web browser to configure an embedded system, or to read parameters from the same system, is a trend in the industry. Graphical representation of information from or to an embedded system is definitively a handy tool.

This project is similar to Example #1, as it uses mainly the same workspace. One additional module is added: µC/HTTPs (Hypertext Transfer Protocol Server).

Start the HEW and open the following workspace:

`\Micrium\Software\EvalBoards\Renesas\YRDKRX62N\GNURX\GNURX.hws`

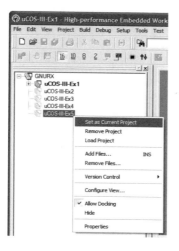

Figure 8-1 **Selecting Example #5**

8

Right-click on the "**uCOS-III-Ex5**" tab on the top-left of the HEW workspace as shown on Figure 8-1 and select "Set as Current Project". A message box asks to save the modifications in the session settings. Click "No" to dismiss the message box. HEW tries to connect to the YRDKRX62N on-board J-Link, as described on Chapter 4, "Connecting to the Target" on page 704. After connecting to the target, press the 'F7' key to ensure the project is built. Click "Yes" to confirm the download of the module, after the project is built. If a dialog box requests files to be located, click "Cancel" to dismiss it.

The μC/HTTPs user manual is part of the documentation package included for these examples (see Chapter 3, "μC/TCP-IP and μC/DHCPc" on page 694).

The workspace with the additional expanded group for μC/HTTPs and the webpage compared to Example #1 workspace is shown to the right. The μC/HTTPs group contains the header files since the μC/HTTPs object code library is linked through the project linker settings. Header files are needed since the application code requires definitions and declarations found in these files.

8-1 RUNNING THE PROJECT

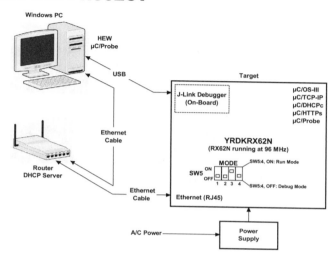

Figure 8-2 **Connecting the Evaluation Board to a Router**

Once this example application starts running, LEDs #5, #8, #11, and #14 are lit to indicate the embedded target is initializing. This project uses a DHCP client to have the IP address of the demonstration board assigned automatically. If the board is connected directly to a PC, the DHCP assigns a link-local IP address to the board. If the board is connected to a router, as shown in Figure 8-2, the router's DHCP server assigns an IP address to the board. When the TCP/IP initialization is completed, LEDs #7 to #12 are lit in sequence, and the IP address is displayed in the graphical LCD. The configured IP address can be entered in a web browser address bar to load the target's webpage. For example, if the IP address displayed is **10.10.1.65**, to connect to the target web server, **http://10.10.1.65/** should be typed in the browser address bar.

In this project, there is no file system. In fact, the webpage and the logo are placed into flash memory. This is called a static file system. To achieve this, constant tables are used to store the files. These tables are created by the **BIN2C** utility. This utility reads a binary file and converts it to a c-style array. The arrays from each converted file are placed in **WEBPAGES.H**. In the HTTP server initialization function, the tables are added to the static file system. The HTML page for this example and the **BIN2C** utility are located in the following directory:

\Micrium\Software\EvalBoards\Renesas\YRDKRX62N\GNURX\uCOS-III-Ex5\Webpages

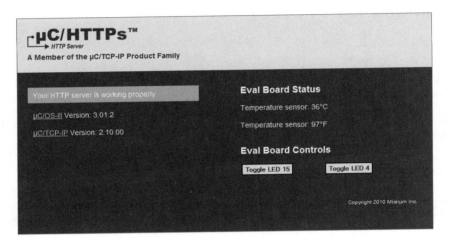

Figure 8-3 **Webpage from the Web Server on the Target**

Figure 8-3 shows a screenshot of the webpage from the HTTP server running on the embedded target. The version numbers for μC/OS-III and μC/TCP-IP are displayed on the web page. The YRDKRX62N demonstration board's temperature sensor value is also displayed on the web page, both in degrees Fahrenheit and degrees Celsius.

It is also possible for the webpage to interact with the evaluation board. The two buttons on the web page control LED #15 and LED #4 on the board. Clicking on the buttons toggles the corresponding LED.

8-2 HOW THE EXAMPLE CODE WORKS

The code from **main()** in this example is identical to Example #1. **AppTaskStart()** differs because the HTTP server must be initialized.

```
static  void  AppTaskStart (void  *p_arg)
{
    CPU_INT08U  i;
    CPU_INT08U  j;
    OS_ERR      err;
#if (APP_CFG_TCPIP_MODULE_EN > 0u)
    NET_ERR     net_err;
#endif

    (void)&p_arg;

    BSP_Init();                                             (1)
    CPU_Init();                                             (2)
    OS_CPU_TickInit();                                      (3)

#if (OS_CFG_STAT_TASK_EN > 0u)
    OSStatTaskCPUUsageInit(&err_os);                        (4)
#endif

    Mem_Init();                                             (5)

#if (APP_CFG_PROBE_COM_MODULE_EN > 0u)
    AppProbe_Init();                                        (6)
#endif


    LED_On(14);                                             (7)
    LED_On(5);
    LED_On(8);
    LED_On(11);

    BSP_GraphLCD_Init();                                    (8)
    AppGraphLCD_Hdr();                                      (9)

#if (APP_CFG_TCPIP_MODULE_EN > 0u)
    AppTCPIP_Init(&net_err);                                (10)
    if (net_err == NET_ERR_NONE) {
        AppHTTPs_Init();                                    (11)
    }
#endif

#ifdef CPU_CFG_INT_DIS_MEAS_EN
    CPU_IntDisMeasMaxCurReset();                            (12)
#endif
```

```
        LED_Off(0u);                                              (13)

        while (DEF_ON) {                                          (14)
            for (i = 7; i <= 12; i++) {
                LED_On(i);
                OSTimeDlyHMSM(0u, 0u, 0u, 100u,
                              OS_OPT_TIME_HMSM_STRICT,
                              &err);
                LED_Off(i);

            }

            for (i = 11; i > 7 ; i--) {
                LED_On(i);
                OSTimeDlyHMSM(0u, 0u, 0u, 100u,
                              OS_OPT_TIME_HMSM_STRICT,
                              &err);
                LED_Off(i);
            }
        }
    }
```

Listing 8-1 **AppTaskStart()**

L8-1(1)   **AppTaskStart()** starts by calling **BSP_Init()** (see **BSP.C**) to initialize peripherals used on the YRDKRX62N. BSP stands for "Board Support Package" and, it is a collection of functions that are provided to interface to common peripherals such as LEDs, ADCs, DACs, UARTs and more. In other words, BSP functions make it easy to use these peripherals.

BSP_Init() then calls **LED_Init()** which initializes the I/O ports that are driving the LEDs on the evaluation board. Once the I/Os are initialized, **LED_Init()** turns off all the LEDs.

L8-1(2)   **CPU_Init()** is called to initialize the CPU services provided by the µC/CPU module.

L8-1(3)   **OS_CPU_TickInit()** which is found in **BSP_TICK_C.C** is called to setup the µC/OS-III tick interrupt. The tick interrupt uses **CMT0**.

L8-1(4)   **OSStatTaskCPUUsageInit()** is called to determine the "capacity" of the CPU. µC/OS-III runs "only" its internal tasks for 1/10 of a second and determines the maximum amount of time the idle task loops. The number of loops is counted and placed in the variable **OSStatTaskCtr**. This value is saved in **OSStatTaskCtrMax** just before **OSStatTaskCPUUsageInit()** returns. **OSStatTaskCtrMax** is used to determine the CPU usage when other tasks are added. Specifically, as tasks are added to the application, **OSStatTaskCtr** (which is reset every 1/10 of a second) is incremented less by the idle task because other tasks consume CPU cycles. CPU usage is determined by the following equation:

$$OSStatTaskCPUUsage_{(\%)} = (100 - \frac{100 \times OSStatTaskCtr}{OSStatTaskCtrMax})$$

The value of **OSStatTaskCPUUsage** can be displayed at run-time by µC/Probe by using a circular gauge or other display object.

L8-1(5)   The µC/LIB memory management services are initialized. This functionality is used by the TCP/IP stack.

L8-1(6)   **AppProbe_Init()** (see **APP_PROBE.C**) is called to initialize µC/Probe to be used either via RS-232C or TCP/IP. In addition, µC/Probe can be used with the RX through the J-Link interface. The J-Link interface can be used simultaneously by µC/Probe and the HEW debugger. In other words, µC/Probe can interface with the YRDKRX62N with either RS-232C, TCP/IP or the debug port through the J-Link. The benefit of using the J-Link port is that, unlike RS-232C or TCP/IP, the µC/Probe target resident software is not required.

L8-1(7)   The LEDs #14, #5, #8 and #11 are turned on prior to TCP/IP initialization;

L8-1(8)   The OKAYA 96x64 graphics LCD is initialized by calling **BSP_GraphLCD_Init()** (see **BSP_GLCD.C**).

L8-1(9)   The graphics display shows the word "**Micrium**" in bold followed by "uC/OS-III" and "uC/TCP-IP" on the next two lines as shown below.

" **Micrium** "
"uC/OS-III"
"uC/TCP-IP"

L8-1(10)   **AppTCPIP_Init()** is called to initialize all the necessary TCP/IP stack services needed by this application. Specifically, the µC/TCP-IP stack is used in conjunction with µC/DHCPc in order to use µC/Probe through this interface. More details on TCP/IP stack services are described in the subsequent chapters.

L8-1(11)   **AppHTTPs_Init()** initializes the HTTP server. See Listing 8-4 for a description of **AppHTTPs_Init()**.

L8-1(12)   **CPU_IntDisMeasMaxCurReset()** is called to reset the interrupt disable time measurement feature of the µC/CPU module. This is done to not consider initialization code in the measurement of maximum interrupt disable time.

L8-1(13)   All LEDs are turned off;

L8-1(14)   This task turns on and off LEDs #7 to #12 in sequence, and then the sequence is reversed.

AppTaskStart() calls **AppTCPIP_Init()** to initialize and start the TCP/IP stack. This function is shown in Listing 8-2.

```
static void AppTCPIP_Init (NET_ERR *perr)
{
    NET_IF_NBR   if_nbr;
    CPU_BOOLEAN  link_state;


    *perr = Net_Init();                                           (1)
    if (*perr != NET_ERR_NONE) {
        <display error on graphical LCD>                          (2)
        return;
    }


    if_nbr = NetIF_Add((void    *)&NetIF_API_Ether,              (3)
                       (void    *)&NetDev_API_<controller>,      (4)
                       (void    *)&NetDev_BSP_<controller>,      (5)
                       (void    *)&NetDev_Cfg_<controller>,      (6)
                       (void    *)&NetPhy_API_<controller>,      (7)
                       (void    *)&NetPhy_Cfg_<controller>,      (8)
                       (NET_ERR *) perr);                        (9)
    if (*perr != NET_IF_ERR_NONE) {
        <display error on graphical LCD>
        return;
    }

#if (APP_CFG_DHCPc_MODULE_EN == 0u)
    AppTCPIP_CfgStaticAddr(if_nbr, perr);                        (10)
    if (*perr != NET_IP_ERR_NONE) {
        <display error on graphical LCD>
        return;
    }
#endif

    NetIF_Start(if_nbr, perr);                                  (11)
    if (*perr != NET_IF_ERR_NONE) {
        <display error on graphical LCD>
        return;
    }


    link_state = NetIF_LinkStateGet(if_nbr,                     (12)
                                    perr);
    if (link_state == NET_IF_LINK_DOWN) {
        <retry for 30 seconds>
    }
```

8

```
#if (APP_CFG_DHCPc_MODULE_EN == 0u)
    <display IP address on graphical LCD>                    (13)
#else
    AppDHCPc_Init(&dhcp_err);                                (14)
    if (dhcp_err != DHCPc_ERR_NONE) {
        *perr = NET_ERR_INIT_INCOMPLETE;
        <display error on graphical LCD>
        return;
    }
#endif
}
```

Listing 8-2 **AppTCPIP_Init()**

L8-2(1)   **Net_Init()** is the Network Protocol stack initialization function.

L8-2(2)   If the initialization procedure fails, an error is displayed on the graphical LCD.

L8-2(3)   **NetIF_Add()** is a Network Interface function responsible for initializing a Network Device driver. The first parameter is the address of the Ethernet API function. **if_nbr** is the interface index number returned by this function. The first interface is index number 1. If the loopback interface is configured, it has interface index number 0. In case the loopback interface is disabled on the TCP/IP stack configuration, interface index number 0 becomes reserved and it is not assigned to any added interface.

L8-2(4)   The second parameter is the address of the device API function.

L8-2(5)   The third parameter is the address of the device BSP data structure.

L8-2(6)   The third parameter is the address of the device configuration data structure.

L8-2(7)   The fourth parameter is the address of the PHY API function. If a PHY is not present, a **NULL** address is passed.

L8-2(8)   The fifth parameter is the address of the PHY configuration data structure. If a PHY is not present, a **NULL** address is passed.

L8-2(9)   The error code is used to validate the result of the function execution.

L8-2(10)   If the µC/DHCPc module is not enabled in the application, a static IP address is configured by calling the **AppTCPIP_CfgStaticAddr()**. This function is shown in Listing 8-3.

L8-2(11)   **NetIF_Start()** makes the network interface ready to receive and transmit data.

L8-2(12)   The interface link state is checked to make sure the interface is up before proceding. This is done through the **NetIF_LinkStateGet()** API call. If the link state is detected to be down, it waits for the link to become up for 30 seconds.

L8-2(13)   If the µC/DHCPc module is not enabled in the application, the configured static IP address is displayed on the graphical LCD.

L8-2(14)   If the µC/DHCPc module is enabled in the application, **AppDHCPc_Init()** initializes it.

```
static  void  AppTCPIP_CfgStaticAddr (NET_IF_NBR    if_nbr,
                                      NET_ERR      *perr)
{
    NET_IP_ADDR  ip;
    NET_IP_ADDR  msk;
    NET_IP_ADDR  gateway;
    CPU_BOOLEAN  cfg_success;


    ip          = NetASCII_Str_to_IP((CPU_CHAR *)"10.10.1.65",    perr);    (1)
    msk         = NetASCII_Str_to_IP((CPU_CHAR *)"255.255.255.0", perr);    (2)
    gateway     = NetASCII_Str_to_IP((CPU_CHAR *)"10.10.1.1",     perr);    (3)


    cfg_success = NetIP_CfgAddrAdd(if_nbr,                                  (4)
                                  ip,
                                  msk,
                                  gateway,
                                  perr);

    (void)&cfg_success;
}
```

Listing 8-3 **AppTCPIP_CfgStaticAddr()**

L8-3(1)   Definition of the IP address to be used by the network interface. **NetASCII_Str_to_IP()** converts the human readable address into the format required by the protocol stack. In this example, the **10.10.1.65** address out of the **10.10.1.0** network with a subnet mask of **255.255.255.0** is used. To run the code on a different network, this address, the subnet mask and the default gateway IP address must be customized.

L8-3(2)   This defines the subnet mask to be used by the network interface.

L8-3(3)   This defines the default gateway address to be used by the network interface.

L8-3(4)   **NetIP_CfgAddrAdd()** configures the network parameters (IP address, subnet mask and default gateway IP address) required for the interface. More than one set of network parameters can be configured per interface; in other words, an interface can have multiple IP addresses. Lines from (1) to (4) can be repeated for as many network parameter sets as are necessary to be configured for an interface. Once the code is built and loaded into the target, the target responds to ICMP Echo (ping) requests for each configured address.

`AppTaskStart()` calls the `AppHTTPs_Init()` to initialize and start the HTTP server module, if the TCP/IP stack initialization has been successful. The code for `AppHTTPs_Init()` is shown in Listing 8-4.

```
static  void  AppHTTPs_Init (void)
{
    CPU_BOOLEAN  cfg_success;


    cfg_success = HTTPs_Init();                                                 (1)
    APP_TEST_FAULT(cfg_success, DEF_OK);


    cfg_success = Apps_FS_Init();                                               (2)
    APP_TEST_FAULT(cfg_success, DEF_OK);

    cfg_success = Apps_FS_AddFile((CPU_CHAR *)&STATIC_INDEX_HTML_NAME,          (3)
                          (CPU_CHAR *)&Index_html,
                          (CPU_INT32U) STATIC_INDEX_HTML_LEN);
    APP_TEST_FAULT(cfg_success, DEF_OK);


    cfg_success = Apps_FS_AddFile((CPU_CHAR *)&STATIC_LOGO_GIF_NAME,            (4)
                          (CPU_CHAR *)&Logo_Gif,
                          (CPU_INT32U) STATIC_LOGO_GIF_LEN);
    APP_TEST_FAULT(cfg_success, DEF_OK);


    BSP_Temp_Init();                                                           (5)
    App_TempSensorUpdate();                                                    (6)
}
```

Listing 8-4 **AppHTTPs_Init()**

L8-4(1)   `HTTPs_Init()` starts the HTTP server.

L8-4(2)   `Apps_FS_Init()` initializes the file system. The HTTP server requires a file system to serve the webpages. In this example, the file system is configured to use static pages loaded into flash memory.

L8-4(3) The **INDEX.HTML** file is compiled with the example and is loaded in flash memory. **Apps_FS_AddFile()** loads this file for usage by the HTTP server. This is done to save RAM space. On this processor, as with many microcontrollers, there is generally a lot more flash memory than RAM.

L8-4(4) The **INDEX.HTML** webpage for this example uses an image called **logo.gif**, which is also compiled with the application and loaded into Flash memory. **Apps_FS_AddFile()** loads this file to be used by the HTTP server.

L8-4(5) The webpage displays the temperature from the on-board temperature sensor and therefore, the temperature sensor is initialized.

L8-4(6) The value of the temperature sensor is updated.

The webpage built for this example displays the µC/OS-III and µC/TCP-IP version numbers. Even though these two values are fixed, µC/HTTPs allows to display dynamic values. In this example, the webpage uses the temperature sensor on the YRDKRX62N board and displays the temperature in degrees Fahrenheit and degrees Celsius.

For the webpage to send and receive data from the embedded target, two additional functions need to be defined in the application. They are both located in **APP_HTTP.C**. The first function is the **HTTPs_ValReq()**. **HTTPs_ValReq()** is a callback function that *must* be implemented in the application and *should* return the value corresponding to a token inserted in the HTML page. A token is added to the HTML page under the form of **${TOKEN}**. A token is used to take variable data from the embedded target and send it to the webpage. The following listing describes this callback function.

```
CPU_BOOLEAN  HTTPs_ValReq (CPU_CHAR   *p_tok,
                           CPU_CHAR   **p_val)
{
    static  CPU_CHAR    val_buf[HTTPs_VAL_REQ_BUF_LEN];                        (1)
#if (LIB_VERSION >= 126u)
         CPU_INT32U  ver;
#elif (LIB_STR_CFG_FP_EN == DEF_ENABLED)
         CPU_FP32    ver;
#endif
         OS_TICK     os_time_tick;
#if (LIB_STR_CFG_FP_EN == DEF_ENABLED)
         CPU_FP32    os_time_sec;
#else
         CPU_INT32U  os_time_sec;
         CPU_INT32U  os_time_ms;
         CPU_SIZE_T  os_time_len;
#endif
         OS_ERR      os_err;


   (void)Str_Copy(&val_buf[0], "%%%%%%%%");
   *p_val = &buf[0];                                                          (2)


                                                /* ---- OS VALUES ---- */     (3)
   if (Str_Cmp(p_tok, "OS_VERSION") == 0) {                                   (4)
#if (LIB_VERSION >= 126u)
#if (OS_VERSION  > 300u)
      ver =  OS_VERSION / 1000;
      (void)Str_FmtNbr_Int32U(ver,   2, DEF_NBR_BASE_DEC, ' ', DEF_NO, DEF_NO,  &val_buf[0]);
      val_buf[2] = '.';

      ver = (OS_VERSION /   10) % 100;
      (void)Str_FmtNbr_Int32U(ver,   2, DEF_NBR_BASE_DEC, '0', DEF_NO, DEF_NO,  &val_buf[3]);
      val_buf[5] = '.';

      ver = (OS_VERSION /    1) %  10;
      (void)Str_FmtNbr_Int32U(ver,   1, DEF_NBR_BASE_DEC, '0', DEF_NO, DEF_YES, &val_buf[6]);
      val_buf[8] = '\0';
```

8

```
#else
        ver =  OS_VERSION /  100;
        (void)Str_FmtNbr_Int32U(ver,   2, DEF_NBR_BASE_DEC, ' ', DEF_NO, DEF_NO,  &val_buf[0]);
        val_buf[2] = '.';

        ver = (OS_VERSION /    1) % 100;
        (void)Str_FmtNbr_Int32U(ver,   2, DEF_NBR_BASE_DEC, '0', DEF_NO, DEF_YES, &val_buf[3]);
        val_buf[5] = '\0';
#endif

#elif (LIB_STR_CFG_FP_EN == DEF_ENABLED)
#if   (OS_VERSION > 300u)
        ver = (CPU_FP32)OS_VERSION / 1000;
        (void)Str_FmtNbr_32(ver, 2, 2, ' ',  DEF_NO,  &val_buf[0]);

        ver = (CPU_FP32)OS_VERSION /  10;
        (void)Str_FmtNbr_32(ver, 0, 1, '\0', DEF_YES, &val_buf[6]);

#else
        ver = (CPU_FP32)OS_VERSION / 100;
        (void)Str_FmtNbr_32(ver, 2, 2, '\0', DEF_YES, &val_buf[0]);
#endif
#endif


    } else if (Str_Cmp(p_tok, "OS_TIME") == 0) {
        os_time_tick = (OS_TICK )OSTimeGet(&os_err);
#if (LIB_STR_CFG_FP_EN == DEF_ENABLED)
        os_time_sec  = (CPU_FP32)os_time_tick / OS_CFG_TICK_RATE_HZ;
        (void)Str_FmtNbr_32(os_time_sec, 7, 3, '\0', DEF_YES, &val_buf[0]);
#else
        os_time_sec  = (CPU_INT32U)os_time_tick / OS_CFG_TICK_RATE_HZ;
        (void)Str_FmtNbr_Int32U(os_time_sec,
                                7,
                                DEF_NBR_BASE_DEC,
                                '\0',
                                DEF_NO,
                                DEF_YES,
                                &val_buf[0]);
        (void)Str_Cat(&val_buf[0], ".");
        os_time_len  =  Str_Len(&val_buf[0]);
        os_time_ms   = (CPU_INT32U)os_time_tick % OS_CFG_TICK_RATE_HZ;
        os_time_ms  *=  1000 / OS_CFG_TICK_RATE_HZ;
```

8

```
                (void)Str_FmtNbr_Int32U(os_time_ms,
                                        3,
                                        DEF_NBR_BASE_DEC,
                                        '0',
                                        DEF_NO,
                                        DEF_YES,
                                        &val_buf[os_time_len]);
#endif


                                        /* ---- NETWORK PROTOCOL SUITE VALUES ---- */      (5)
            } else if (Str_Cmp(p_tok, "NET_VERSION") == 0) {
#if (LIB_VERSION >= 126u)
#if (NET_VERSION > 205u)
                ver =  NET_VERSION / 10000;
                (void)Str_FmtNbr_Int32U(ver,  2, DEF_NBR_BASE_DEC, ' ', DEF_NO, DEF_NO,  &val_buf[0]);
                val_buf[2] = '.';

                ver = (NET_VERSION /   100) % 100;
                (void)Str_FmtNbr_Int32U(ver,  2, DEF_NBR_BASE_DEC, '0', DEF_NO, DEF_NO,  &val_buf[3]);
                val_buf[5] = '.';
                ver = (NET_VERSION /     1) % 100;
                (void)Str_FmtNbr_Int32U(ver,  2, DEF_NBR_BASE_DEC, '0', DEF_NO, DEF_YES, &val_buf[6]);
                val_buf[8] = '\0';

#else
                ver =  NET_VERSION /   100;
                (void)Str_FmtNbr_Int32U(ver,  2, DEF_NBR_BASE_DEC, ' ', DEF_NO, DEF_NO,  &val_buf[0]);
                val_buf[2] = '.';
                ver = (NET_VERSION /     1) % 100;
                (void)Str_FmtNbr_Int32U(ver,  2, DEF_NBR_BASE_DEC, '0', DEF_NO, DEF_YES, &val_buf[3]);
                val_buf[5] = '\0';
#endif

#elif (LIB_STR_CFG_FP_EN == DEF_ENABLED)
#if   (NET_VERSION > 205u)
                ver = (CPU_FP32)NET_VERSION / 10000;
                (void)Str_FmtNbr_32(ver,  2,  2, ' ',  DEF_NO,  &val_buf[0]);

                ver = (CPU_FP32)NET_VERSION /   100;
                (void)Str_FmtNbr_32(ver,  0,  2, '\0', DEF_YES, &val_buf[6]);

#else
                ver = (CPU_FP32)NET_VERSION /   100;
                (void)Str_FmtNbr_32(ver,  2,  2, '\0', DEF_YES, &val_buf[0]);
#endif
#endif
```

```
                                        /* ---- APPLICATION VALUES ---- */    (6)
  } else if (Str_Cmp(p_tok, "TEMP_C") == 0) {
     (void)Str_FmtNbr_Int32S(AppTempSensorDegC,
                             3,
                             DEF_NBR_BASE_DEC,
                             '\0',
                             DEF_NO,
                             DEF_YES,
                             &val_buf[0]);

  } else if (Str_Cmp(p_tok, "TEMP_F") == 0) {
     (void)Str_FmtNbr_Int32S(AppTempSensorDegF,
                             3,
                             DEF_NBR_BASE_DEC,
                             '\0',
                             DEF_NO,
                             DEF_YES,
                             &val_buf[0]);
  }


  if ((Str_Cmp(p_tok, "TEMP_C") == 0) ||                                      (7)
      (Str_Cmp(p_tok, "TEMP_F") == 0)) {
     App_TempSensorUpdate();
  }

  return DEF_OK;
}
```

Listing 8-5 **HTTPs_ValReq()**

L8-5(1)   Initializes the static storage location used to transfer the embedded target data to the HTTP server.

L8-5(2)   Points the pointer used as the return argument to the location of the storage area for the values requested.

L8-5(3)   The code retrieves the µC/OS-III version number and converts it into characters transferred to **&val_buf[ ]**. Upon return from this function, the HTTP server gets the characters from this location and displays them on the webpage.

L8-5(4)   The input parameter **p_tok** is used to determine which of the variables is requested by the HTTP server.

L8-5(5)   The code retrieves the µC/TCP-IP version number and converts it into characters transferred to **&val_buf[ ]**.

L8-5(6)   Based on the selection of the temperature scale by **p_tok**, the code retrieves the value of the temperature sensor on the evaluation board, and converts it into characters transferred to **&val_buf[ ]**.

L8-5(7)   If a temperature has been requested by **p_tok**, the temperature sensor value is updated on the next read.

The second function required by the HTTP server is **HTTPs_ValRx()**. This function is a callback that *must* be implemented in the application and *should* handle the POST action for every name-value pair received. This callback is used to get data from the webpage, either directly from an user input, or indirectly through other means. The following is an example of a HTML POST form, where the name LED is passed with a value of LED1:

```
<form action="index.html" method="POST">
    <p>
        <input name="LED" type="hidden" value="LED1">
        <input type="submit" value="Toggle LED 1" class="bluebutton">
    </p>
</form>
```

8

The implementation of the HTTP server callback **HTTPs_ValRx()** is described in the Listing 8-6.

```
CPU_BOOLEAN  HTTPs_ValRx (CPU_CHAR  *p_var,
                          CPU_CHAR  *p_val)
{
    CPU_INT16U   cmp_str;
    CPU_BOOLEAN  ret_val;


    ret_val = DEF_FAIL;

    cmp_str = Str_Cmp((CPU_CHAR *)p_var,                                    (1)
                      (CPU_CHAR *)HTML_LED_INPUT_NAME);
    if (cmp_str == 0) {
        cmp_str = Str_Cmp((CPU_CHAR *)p_val,             /* Toggle LED 1.  */    (2)
                          (CPU_CHAR *)HTML_LED1_TOGGLE_INPUT_VALUE);
        if (cmp_str == 0) {
            LED_Toggle(LED1);
            ret_val = DEF_OK;
        }

        cmp_str = Str_Cmp((CPU_CHAR *)p_val,             /* Toggle LED 2.  */    (3)
                          (CPU_CHAR *)HTML_LED2_TOGGLE_INPUT_VALUE);
        if (cmp_str == 0) {
            LED_Toggle(LED2);
            ret_val = DEF_OK;
        }
    }


    return (ret_val);
}
```

Listing 8-6 **HTTPs_ValRx()**

L8-6(1)   This function is written to handle multiple inputs. The first argument ***p_var** determines which type of variable is entered by checking its name. In this example, the only valid name to check is "LED".

L8-6(2)   As a second step, the value of the HTTP POST variable is determined, since each button on the webpage selects different LEDs. The possible values of **`*p_val`** are either "LED1" or "LED2". When "LED1" is selected, its corresponding LED is toggled by the **`LED_Toggle()`** function. The "LED1" corresponds to LED #15 on the evaluation board.

L8-6(3)   When "LED2" is selected, it is toggled by the **`LED_Toggle()`** function. The "LED2" corresponds to LED #4 on the evaluation board.

8-3 SUMMARY

This chapter demonstrated how easy it is to add a web server (i.e., HTTP server) to an embedded application once the TCP/IP stack is running.

A simple **`INDEX.HTML`** web page is provided as an example. Through this example, it is demonstrated how to get data to and from the embedded target.

There are a couple of important items to take away from this example:

1   HTTP is a very popular protocol and it allows embedded systems to offer a professional looking graphical user interface that can be accessed remotely. The use of a web server in an embedded system relieves the developer from having to develop a client-side application because powerful clients are already readily available: Internet Explorer, Safari, Firefox, Chrome, etc.

2   HTTP relies on the TCP (Transmission Control Protocol). TCP is a resource intensive protocol, and proper configuration and resource allocation needs to be performed to make sure the developer is able to exploit protocol benefits.

µC/OS-III Port for the RX600

This appendix describes the adaptation of µC/OS-III to the Renesas RX600 architecture (this is called a Port). This port was done by Micrium/Renesas and these files will most likely not need to be changed. The Renesas RX600 port works on all RX600 MCUs.

The port files are found in the following directory:

```
\Micrium\Software\uCOS-III\Ports\Renesas\RX600\HEW
\Micrium\Software\uCOS-III\Ports\Renesas\RX600\GNURX
```

The µC/OS-III port files for the RX600 consists of four files:

```
OS_CPU.H
OS_CPU_C.C
OS_CPU_A.INC
OS_CPU_A.SRC
```

The contents of the above port files are explained in detail in the following sections. An explanation about Kernel Aware vs. Non Kernel Aware interrupt handlers is done in section A-7 on page 814. The last section describes how to write ISRs to satisfy µC/OS-III's requirements.

The RX600 programmer's model was presented in Chapter 2, "The Renesas RX600 MCU" on page 663, and it is assumed the reader is familiar with it in this appendix.

A-1 OS_CPU.H

OS_CPU.H contains processor- and implementation- specific #defines constants, macros, and typedefs. OS_CPU.H is shown in Listing A-1.

```
#ifndef  OS_CPU_H                                              (1)
#define  OS_CPU_H
#ifdef   OS_CPU_GLOBALS                                        (2)
#define  OS_CPU_EXT
#else
#define  OS_CPU_EXT  extern
#endif


/*
*********************************************************************************************
*                                        MACROS
*********************************************************************************************
*/

#if     OS_CFG_TS_EN == 1u
#define  OS_TS_GET()            (CPU_TS)CPU_TS_Get32()          (3)
#else
#define  OS_TS_GET()            (CPU_TS)0u
#endif


/*
*********************************************************************************************
*                                      PROTOTYPES
*********************************************************************************************
*/

void  OSCtxSw        (void);                                    (4)
void  OSIntCtxSw     (void);
void  OSStartHighRdy (void);

void  OS_CPU_TickInit(void);                                    (5)

#endif
```

Listing A-1 **OS_CPU.H**

LA-1(1)   This is the typical multiple header file inclusion protection.

LA-1(2)   **OS_CPU_GLOBALS** and **OS_CPU_EXT** allows to declare global variables that are specific to this port. The RX600 port does not currently define any port specific variables.

LA-1(3)   Time stamps are obtained by calling the µC/CPU function **CPU_TS_Get32()** which returns the value of a 32-bit free-running counter even if only a 16-bit hardware timer is available (see Appendix B, µC/CPU port for the Renesas RX600).

LA-1(4)   The prototypes of mandatory µC/OS-III functions.

LA-1(5)   The prototype of the function responsible for initializing the timer used by µC/OS-III. This function is defined in the board support package (BSP).

The task level context switch is performed by a software interrupt. A software interrupt instruction behaves almost exactly as an interrupt, except that it is invoked synchronously by code. The software interrupt handler is implemented by **OSCtxSw()** in **OS_CPU_A.SRC**.

The definition of the task level context switch macro for the Renesas RX, and GNURX compilers are shown in Listing A-2.

Renesas RX Compiler

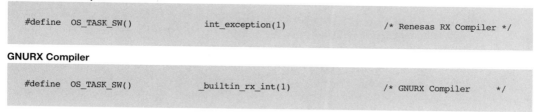

```
#define  OS_TASK_SW()              int_exception(1)              /* Renesas RX Compiler */
```

GNURX Compiler

```
#define  OS_TASK_SW()              _builtin_rx_int(1)            /* GNURX Compiler   */
```

Listing A-2 **Task Level Context Switch Macro**

A-2 OS_CPU_C.C

A µC/OS-III port requires the following functions to be defined:

```
OSIdleTaskHook()
OSInitHook()
OSStatTaskHook()
OSTaskCreateHook()
OSTaslDelHook()
OSTaskReturnHook()
OSTaskStkInit()
OSTaskSwHook()
OSTimeTickHook()
```

A-2-1 OS_CPU_C.C – OSIdleTaskHook()

The idle task hook allows the port developer to extend the functionality of the idle task. For example, it can place the processor in low power mode when no other higher priority tasks are running. This is especially useful in battery powered applications. Listing A-3 shows the RX600 code for OSIdleTaskHook().

```
void  OSIdleTaskHook (void)
{
#if OS_CFG_APP_HOOKS_EN > 0u                                    (1)
    if (OS_AppIdleTaskHookPtr != (OS_APP_HOOK_VOID)0) {         (2)
        (*OS_AppIdleTaskHookPtr)();                             (3)
    }
#endif
}
```

Listing A-3 **OS_CPU_C.C – OSIdleTaskHook()**

LA-3(1)   Application level hook functions are enabled by **OS_CFG_APP_HOOKS_EN**.

LA-3(2)   If the application developer wants a custom function to be called on every iteration of the idle task, then the developer needs to initialize the value of OS_AppIdleTaskHookPtr to point to the desired function to call. µC/OS-III initializes OS_AppIdleTaskHookPtr to NULL when OSInit() is called, and thus the application code must set this pointer only after calling OSInit().

     OSIdleTaskHook() is not called from within a critical section.

     The application hook function *must not* make any blocking calls, because the idle task must never block. In other words, it cannot call OSTimeDly(), OSTimeDlyHMSM(), OSTaskSuspend() (to suspend "self") and any of the OS???Pend() functions.

     Examples of application hooks are found in OS_APP_HOOKS.C.

LA-3(3)   The application level idle task hook is called without any argument.

A-2-2 OS_CPU_C.C – OSInitHook()

Listing A-4 shows the RX600 code for OSInitHook(). There is no application level hook for OSInitHook(). OSInitHook() is useful for port developers who want to add port-specific initialization. OSInitHook() is called by OSInit() at the beginning of OSInit().

```
void  OSInitHook (void)
{
}
```

Listing A-4 **OS_CPU_C.C – OSInitHook()**

A-2-3 OS_CPU_C.C – OSStatTaskHook()

OSTaskStatHook() allows the port developer to extend the functionality of the statistic task by allowing the inclusion of additional statistics. OSStatTaskHook() is called after computing the total CPU usage (see OS_StatTask() in OS_STAT.C). Listing A-5 shows the RX600 code for OSStatTaskHook().

```
void  OSStatTaskHook (void)
{
#if OS_CFG_APP_HOOKS_EN > 0u
    if (OS_AppStatTaskHookPtr != (OS_APP_HOOK_VOID)0) {        (1)
        (*OS_AppStatTaskHookPtr)();                            (2)
    }
#endif
}
```

Listing A-5 **OS_CPU_C.C – OSStatTaskHook()**

LA-5(1)   If the application developer wants µC/OS-III's statistic task (i.e., OS_StatTask()) to call a custom function from the application, then the developer must initialize the value of OS_AppStatTaskHookPtr to point to the desired function. µC/OS-III initializes OS_AppStatTaskHookPtr to NULL when OSInit() is called, and thus the application code must set this pointer only after calling OSInit().

OSStatTaskHook() is not called from within a critical section.

The application hook function *must not* make any blocking calls because it would affect the behavior of the statistic task.

Examples of application hooks are found in OS_APP_HOOKS.C.

LA-5(2)   The application level statistic task hook is called without any argument.

A-2-4 OS_CPU_C.C – OSTaskCreateHook()

OSTaskCreateHook() gives the port developer the opportunity to add code specific to the port when a task is created. OSTaskCreateHook() is called once the OS_TCB fields have been initialized, but prior to making the task ready to run. Listing A-6 shows the RX600 code for OSTaskCreateHook().

```
void  OSTaskCreateHook (OS_TCB *p_tcb)
{
#if OS_CFG_APP_HOOKS_EN > 0u
    if (OS_AppTaskCreateHookPtr != (OS_APP_HOOK_TCB)0) {        (1)
        (*OS_AppTaskCreateHookPtr)(p_tcb);                     (2)
    }
#else
    (void)&p_tcb;        /* Prevent compiler warning */
#endif
}
```

Listing A-6 **OS_CPU_C.C – OSTaskCreateHook()**

LA-6(1)   If the application developer wants a custom function to be called when a task is created, then the developer needs to initialize the value of OS_AppTaskCreateHookPtr to point to the desired function to call. μC/OS-III initializes OS_AppTaskCreateHookPtr to NULL when OSInit() is called, and thus the application code must set this pointer only after calling OSInit().

The application hook function *must not* make any blocking calls and should perform its function as quickly as possible.

OSTaskCreateHook() is not called from within a critical section.

Examples of application hooks are found in OS_APP_HOOKS.C.

LA-6(2)   The application level task create hook is passed the address of the OS_TCB of the task being created.

A-2-5 OS_CPU_C.C – OSTaskDelHook()

OSTaskDelHook() gives the port developer the opportunity to add code specific to the port when a task is deleted. OSTaskDelHook() is called once the task has been removed from all lists (the ready list, the tick list or a pend list). Listing A-7 shows the RX600 code for OSTaskDelHook().

```
void  OSTaskDelHook (OS_TCB *p_tcb)
{
#if OS_CFG_APP_HOOKS_EN > 0u
    if (OS_AppTaskDelHookPtr != (OS_APP_HOOK_TCB)0) {        (1)
        (*OS_AppTaskDelHookPtr)(p_tcb);                      (2)
    }
#else
    (void)&p_tcb;          /* Prevent compiler warning */
#endif
}
```

Listing A-7 **OS_CPU_C.C – OSTaskDelHook()**

LA-7(1)   If the application developer wants a custom function to be called when a task is deleted, then the developer needs to initialize the value of OS_AppTaskDelHookPtr to point to the desired function to call. µC/OS-III initializes OS_AppTaskDelHookPtr to NULL when OSInit() is called, and thus the application code must set this pointer only after calling OSInit().

The application hook function *must not* make any blocking calls and should perform its function as quickly as possible.

OSTaskDelHook() is called from within a critical section.

Examples of application hooks are found in OS_APP_HOOKS.C.

LA-7(2)   The application level task delete hook is passed the address of the OS_TCB of the task being deleted.

A-2-6 OS_CPU_C.C – OSTaskReturnHook()

With µC/OS-III, a task is never allowed to return. However, if this happens "accidentally", µC/OS-III will catch this and delete the offending task. However, `OSTaskDelHook()` will be called before the task is deleted. Listing A-8 shows the RX600 code for `OSTaskReturnHook()`.

```
void  OSTaskReturnHook (OS_TCB *p_tcb)
{
#if OS_CFG_APP_HOOKS_EN > 0u
    if (OS_AppTaskReturnHookPtr != (OS_APP_HOOK_TCB)0) {        (1)
        (*OS_AppTaskReturnHookPtr)(p_tcb);                      (2)
    }
#else
    (void)&p_tcb;              /* Prevent compiler warning */
#endif
}
```

Listing A-8 **OS_CPU_C.C – OSTaskReturnHook()**

LA-8(1) If the application developer wants a custom function to be called when a task returns then, the developer needs to initialize the value of `OS_AppTaskReturnHookPtr` to point to the desired function to call. µC/OS-III initializes `OS_AppTaskReturnHookPtr` to NULL when `OSInit()` is called, and thus the application code must set this pointer only after calling `OSInit()`.

The application hook function *must not* make any blocking calls and should perform its function as quickly as possible.

`OSTaskReturnHook()` is not called within a critical section.

Examples of application hooks are found in `OS_APP_HOOKS.C`.

LA-8(2) The application level task return hook is passed the address of the `OS_TCB` of the task returning.

A-2-7 OS_CPU_C.C – OSTaskStkInit()

This function initializes the stack frame of a task being created. When μC/OS-III creates a task, it makes its stack look as if an interrupt just occurred and simulates pushing the context of the task onto the task's stack. OSTaskStkInit() is called by OSTaskCreate().

Listing A-9 shows the RX600 code for OSTaskStkInit(). OSTaskStkInit() is not called within a critical section.

```
CPU_STK *OSTaskStkInit (OS_TASK_PTR   p_task,                                   (1)
                        void          *p_arg,
                        CPU_STK       *p_stk_base,
                        CPU_STK       *p_stk_limit,
                        OS_STK_SIZE   stk_size,
                        OS_OPT        opt)
{
    CPU_STK  *p_stk;

    (void)&p_stk_limit;                         /* prevent compiler warning   */   (2)
    (void)&opt;

    p_stk   = &p_stk_base[stk_size];            /* load stack pointer         */   (3)
    *--p_stk = (CPU_STK)PSW_INIT;               /* PSW                        */   (4)
    *--p_stk = (CPU_STK)p_task;                 /* PC of task                 */   (5)
    *--p_stk = 0x00000100u;                     /* FPSW                       */   (6)
    *--p_stk = 0x15151515u;                     /* R15                        */   (7)
    *--p_stk = 0x14141414u;                     /* R14                        */
    *--p_stk = 0x13131313u;                     /* R13                        */
    *--p_stk = 0x12121212u;                     /* R12                        */
    *--p_stk = 0x11111111u;                     /* R11                        */
    *--p_stk = 0x10101010u;                     /* R10                        */
    *--p_stk = 0x09090909u;                     /* R9                         */
    *--p_stk = 0x08080808u;                     /* R8                         */
    *--p_stk = 0x07070707u;                     /* R7                         */
    *--p_stk = 0x06060606u;                     /* R6                         */
    *--p_stk = 0x05050505u;                     /* R5                         */
    *--p_stk = 0x04040404u;                     /* R4                         */
    *--p_stk = 0x03030303u;                     /* R3                         */
    *--p_stk = 0x02020202u;                     /* R2                         */
    *--p_stk = (CPU_STK)p_arg;                  /* pass p_arg in R1           */   (8)
    *--p_stk = 0x00009ABCu;                     /* ACC (mid, lower word)      */   (9)
    *--p_stk = 0x12345678u;                     /* ACC (high)                 */

    return (p_stk);                                                               (10)
}
```

Listing A-9 **OS_CPU_C.C – OSTaskStkInit()**

LA-9(1)   OSTaskStkInit() is called by OSTaskCreate() and five arguments are passed:

The task's entry point (i.e., the address of the task).

A pointer to an argument that will be passed to the task when the task starts (i.e., **p_arg**).

The base address of the storage area in RAM of the stack. Typically, a stack is declared as an array of CPU_STKs as shown below.

```
CPU_STK MyTaskStk[stk_size];
```

In this case, the base address is simply **&MyTaskStk[0]**.

The address indicating the stack limit. The RX600 does not provide hardware stack checking and thus this argument is ignored.

The size of the stack is also passed to OSTaskStkInit().

Finally, the "**opt**" argument of OSTaskCreate() is passed to OSTaskStkInit() in case any of those are needed by OSTaskStkInit() for special options. This is not used in the RX600 port.

LA-9(2)   These two arguments are not used in the RX600 port. This notation is used to avoid compiler warnings. The compiler should not generate any code.

LA-9(3)   A local pointer is initialized with the address of the top-of-stack to initialize. The pointer is initialized outside the stack area. This is valid since "**p_stk**" is pre-decremented prior to placing the first value on the stack. In the case of the RX600, the stack grows from high memory to low memory, and thus the initial top of stack is at the highest address of the stack storage area.

LA-9(4)   The RX600's Program Status Word (PSW) register is initialized. The initial value allows all interrupts. In other words, when a task starts it allows the MCU to accept interrupts.

LA-9(5)   This register corresponds to the program counter. This register is initialized to the address of the task entry point.

LA-9(6)   The RX600's Floating-Point Status Word (FPSW) is initialized.

LA-9(7)   The general purpose registers are placed on the stack. Each register is initialized to make it easy to identify them on a memory dump or to examine their contents using the HEW debugger immediately after creating the task.

LA-9(8)   R1 contains the address of "**p_arg**", since this is the register used during a procedure call to pass the first argument for the HEW toolchain.

LA-9(9)   The 64-bit accumulator register (ACC) is initialized. Only the higher 48-bits of the accumulator register is initialized and preserved between context switch.

LA-9(10)   **OSTaskStkInit()** returns the new top of stack pointer to **OSTaskCreate()**. This value is saved in the **.StkPtr** field of the task's **OS_TCB**. The "**p_stk**" points to the last element pushed onto the stack (i.e., **R1**).

The stack frame of the task being created is shown in Figure A-1 and uses up to 20 32-bit values on the task's stack, or 80 bytes. It is thus recommended that **OS_CFG_STK_SIZE_MIN** in **OS_CFG.H** be set to at least 32 (128 bytes).

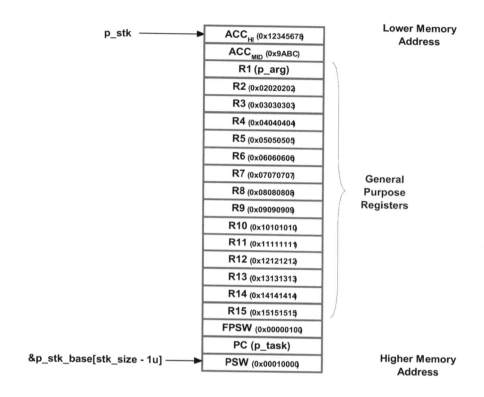

Figure A-1 **Stack frame of task being created.**

A-2-8 OS_CPU_C.C – OSTaskSwHook()

OSTaskSwHook() is called when μC/OS-III performs a context switch. In fact, OSTaskSwHook() is called immediately after saving the context of the task being suspended. The OSTaskSwHook() is called with interrupts disabled.

Listing A-10 shows the code for OSTaskSwHook(). This function is fairly complex and contains a lot of conditional compilation.

```
void  OSTaskSwHook (void)
{
#if OS_CFG_TASK_PROFILE_EN > 0u
    CPU_TS  ts;
#ifdef  CPU_CFG_INT_DIS_MEAS_EN
    CPU_TS  int_dis_time;
#endif
#endif


#if OS_CFG_APP_HOOKS_EN > 0u
    if (OS_AppTaskSwHookPtr != (OS_APP_HOOK_VOID)0) {              (1)
        (*OS_AppTaskSwHookPtr)();                                 (2)
    }
#endif

#if OS_CFG_TASK_PROFILE_EN > 0u
    ts = OS_TS_GET();                                             (3)
    if (OSTCBCurPtr != OSTCBHighRdyPtr) {
        OSTCBCurPtr->CyclesDelta  = ts - OSTCBCurPtr->CyclesStart;
        OSTCBCurPtr->CyclesTotal += (OS_CYCLES)OSTCBCurPtr->CyclesDelta;
    }
    OSTCBHighRdyPtr->CyclesStart  = ts;                           (4)
#endif

#ifdef  CPU_CFG_INT_DIS_MEAS_EN
    int_dis_time = CPU_IntDisMeasMaxCurReset();                   (5)
    if (OSTCBCurPtr->IntDisTimeMax < int_dis_time) {
        OSTCBCurPtr->IntDisTimeMax = int_dis_time;
    }
#endif
```

```
#if OS_CFG_SCHED_LOCK_TIME_MEAS_EN > 0u
    if (OSTCBCurPtr->SchedLockTimeMax < OSSchedLockTimeMaxCur) {          (6)
        OSTCBCurPtr->SchedLockTimeMax = OSSchedLockTimeMaxCur;
    }
    OSSchedLockTimeMaxCur = (CPU_TS)0;
#endif
}
```

Listing A-10 **OS_CPU_C.C – OSTaskSwHook()**

LA-10(1)   If the application developer wants a custom function to be called when a context switch occurs, then the developer needs to initialize the value of **OS_AppTaskSwHookPtr** to point to the desired function to call. μC/OS-III initializes **OS_AppTaskSwHookPtr** to NULL when **OSInit()** is called, and thus the application code must set this pointer only after calling **OSInit()**.

The application hook function *must not* make any blocking calls and should perform its function as quickly as possible.

OSTaskSwHook() is called from within a critical section.

Examples of application hooks are found in **OS_APP_HOOKS.C**.

LA-10(2)   The application level task switch hook is not passed any arguments. However, the global μC/OS-III variables **OSTCBCurPtr** and **OSTCBHighRdyPtr** will point to the **OS_TCB** of the task being switched out and the **OS_TCB** of the task being switched in, respectively.

LA-10(3)   This code measures the execution time (in **CPU_TS** units) of each task. This will be used by the statistic task to compute the relative CPU usage (in percentage) that each task uses.

This code checks if **OSTaskSwHook()** is not called from **OSStartHighRdy()** by verifying that **OSTCBCurPtr** is different than **OSTCBHighRdyPtr**.

If task profiling is enabled (i.e., **OS_CFG_TASK_PROFILE_EN** is set to 1), then the current time stamp is obtained. If a new task is being switched in, the period of execution of the task being switched out is computed. This value is accumulated in the **.CyclesTotal** field (a 64-bit value) of the **OS_TCB** for that task.

LA-10(4) OSTaskSwHook() then stores the time stamp read as the time of the beginning of the next execution cycle of the new task being switched in.

The execution time of each task also includes the execution time of any interrupt that occurred while the task was executing. It would be possible to exclude this but would require more overhead on the CPU.

LA-10(5) If CPU_CFG_INT_DIS_MEAS_EN is set to 1, μC/CPU measures the interrupt disable time on a per task basis. This code block simply detects the maximum amount of interrupt disable time (in CPU_TS units) for each task and stores this in the .IntDisTimeMax field of the OS_TCB for the task being switched out.

LA-10(6) If OS_CFG_SCHED_LOCK_TIME_MEAS_EN is set to 1, μC/OS-III keeps track of the maximum amount of time (in CPU_TS units) a task will have the scheduler locked for critical sections. This value is saved in the .SchedLockTimeMax field of the OS_TCB of the task being switched out.

A-2-9 OS_CPU_C.C – OSTimeTickHook()

OSTimeTickHook() gives the port developer the opportunity to add code that will be called by OSTimeTick(). OSTimeTickHook() is called from the tick ISR and must not make any blocking calls (it would not be allowed to anyway) and must execute as quickly as possible.

Listing A-11 shows the RX600 code for OSTimeTickHook().

```
void  OSTimeTickHook (void)
{
#if OS_CFG_APP_HOOKS_EN > 0u
    if (OS_AppTimeTickHookPtr != (OS_APP_HOOK_VOID)0) {        (1)
        (*OS_AppTimeTickHookPtr)();                            (2)
    }
#endif
#if (CPU_CFG_TS_EN == DEF_ENABLED)
    CPU_TS_Update();                                           (3)
#endif
}
```

Listing A-11 **OS_CPU_C.C – OSTimeTickHook()**

LA-11(1)   If the application developer wants a custom function to be called when a tick interrupt occurs, then the developer needs to initialize the value of **OS_AppTimeTickHookPtr** to point to the desired function to call. µC/OS-III initializes **OS_AppTimeTickHookPtr** to NULL when **OSInit()** is called, and thus the application code must set this pointer only after calling **OSInit()**.

The application hook function *must not* make any blocking calls and should perform its function as quickly as possible.

OSTimeTickHook() is typically called from an ISR with interrupts disabled.

Examples of application hooks are found in **OS_APP_HOOKS.C**.

LA-11(2)   The application level time tick hook is not passed any arguments.

LA-11(3)   **CPU_TS_Update()** is called in **OSTimeTickHook()** so that timestamp accumulation is updated faster than the overflow rate of the timer used for timestamps. This is especially true for the RX600 because of its 16-bit timer.

A-3 OS_CPU_A.SRC

OS_CPU_A.SRC contains processor-specific code for three functions that must be written in assembly language:

```
OSStartHighRdy()
OSCtxSw()
OSIntCtxSw()
```

A-3-1 OS_CPU_A.SRC – OSStartHighRdy()

OSStartHighRdy() is called by OSStart() to start the process of multitasking. µC/OS-III switches to the highest priority task that is ready to run.

Listing A-12 shows the RX600 code for OSStartHighRdy().

```
_OSStartHighRdy:
        MOV.L   #_OSTaskSwHook, R5      ; OSTaskSwHook();                    (1)
        JSR     R5

        MOV.L   #_OSTCBHighRdyPtr, R5   ; SP = OSTCBHighRdyPtr->StkPtr;      (2)
        MOV.L   [R5], R2
        MOV.L   [R2], SP

        OS_CTX_RESTORE                  ; Restore CPU registers             (3)
        RTE                             ; Return from interrupt/exception   (4)
```

Listing A-12 **OS_CPU_A.SRC – OSStartHighRdy()**

LA-12(1)   OSStartHighRdy() starts by calling the task switch hook, OSTaskSwHook(). In this case, OSTCBCurPtr and OSTCBHighRdyPtr point to the same OS_TCB indicating to OSTaskSwHook() that it is called by OSStartHighRdy().

LA-12(2)   OSStartHighRdy() then loads the CPU stack pointer from the OS_TCB of the highest priority task being started.

LA-12(3)   The CPU registers are restored from the new task's stack. This is performed by the macro OS_CTX_RESTORE (see OS_CPU_A.INC). The task's stack is initialized by OSTaskStkInit() (see OS_CPU_C.C).

LA-12(4)   The first task to run under µC/OS-III's control will start executing upon returning from the exception. The PC and PSW are loaded automatically by this instruction.

A-3-2 OS_CPU_A.SRC – OSCtxSw()

OSCtxSw() is called by OSSched() and OS_Sched0() to perform a context switch from a task. OSCtxSw() is invoked by the macro OS_TASK_SW(), which on the RX600 is implemented as a software interrupt. Listing A-13 contains the code for OSCtxSw(), but it is shown in pseudo-code for simplicity.

```
_OSCtxSw:                                             (1)
    Save the CPU registers;                           (2)
    OSTCBCurPtr->StkPtr = SP;                          (3)
    OSTaskSwHook();                                    (4)
    OSTCBCurPtr         = OSTCBHighRdy;                (5)
    OSPrioCur           = OSPrioHighRdy;               (6)
    SP                  = OSTCBHighRdy->StkPtr;        (7)
    Restore the CPU registers;                         (8)
    Return from interrupt/exception;                   (9)
```

Listing A-13 **OS_CPU_A.SRC – OSCtxSw()**

LA-13(1)   The software interrupt instruction causes the PSW and PC to be saved onto the current task's stack and forces the MCU to vector to OSCtxSw().

LA-13(2)   OSCtxSw() then saves the remaining CPU registers onto the current task's stack. This is done by the OS_CTX_SAVE macro (see OS_CPU_A.INC).

LA-13(3)   The new top-of-stack is then saved into the OS_TCB of the current task. This will allow the task to be resumed when it again becomes the highest priority task ready-to-run.

LA-13(4)   OSCtxSw() then calls the task switch hook (see section A-2-8 "OS_CPU_C.C – OSTaskSwHook()" on page 800).

LA-13(5)   The current task will now be the highest priority task which is pointed to by OSTCBHighRdyPtr.

LA-13(6)   The new priority is copied to the current priority.

LA-13(7)   OSCtxSw() then loads the stack pointer with the new top-of-stack, which is found in the OS_TCB of the new highest priority task.

LA-13(8) The CPU registers of the new task are restored into the CPU by the OS_CTX_RESTORE macro.

LA-13(9) The new task is resumed by performing a return from exception.

A-3-3 OS_CPU_A.SRC – OSIntCtxSw()

OSIntCtxSw() is called by OSIntExit() to perform a context switch at the completion of the last nested ISR. OSIntCtxSw() is called directly by OSIntExit(). Listing A-14 shows the code for OSIntCtxSw(), which is also shown in pseudo-code for simplicity.

```
_OSIntCtxSw:
    OSTaskSwHook();                        (1)
    OSTCBCurPtr = OSTCBHighRdy;            (2)
    OSPrioCur  = OSPrioHighRdy;            (3)
    SP         = OSTCBHighRdy->StkPtr;     (4)
    Restore the CPU registers;             (5)
    Return from interrupt/exception;       (6)
```

Listing A-14 **OS_CPU_A.SRC – OSIntCtxSw()**

LA-14(1) OSIntCtxSw() starts by calling the task switch hook (see section A-2-8 on page 800). The OSIntCtxSw() does not need to save the CPU registers of the interrupted task, because they are assumed to have already been saved by the ISR entry code.

LA-14(2) The current task will now be the highest priority task, which is pointed to by OSTCBHighRdyPtr.

LA-14(3) The new priority is copied to the current priority.

LA-14(4) OSIntCtxSw() then loads the stack pointer with the new top-of-stack, which is found in the OS_TCB of the new highest priority task.

LA-14(5) The CPU registers of the new task are restored into the CPU by the OS_CTX_RESTORE macro.

LA-14(6) The new task is resumed by performing a return from exception.

A-4 OS_CPU_A.INC

OS_CPU_A.INC contains the definition of four assembly language macros: OS_CTX_SAVE, OS_CTX_RESTORE, and OS_ISR_ENTER and OS_ISR_EXIT. OS_CPU_A.INC should be included by application ISR code files, which are typically written in assembly language:

```
.INCLUDE    "os_cpu_a.inc"
```

Listing A-15 **OS_CPU_A.INC – including directive**

LA-15(1)   This include directive must be present in application assembly files that define ISR handlers. The location of this file must also be added to the compiler's include file directory list.

A-4-1 OS_CPU_A.INC – OS_CTX_SAVE

The OS_CTX_SAVE macro is used to save the CPU registers into the stack. It saves the Floating-Point Status Word (FPSW), the accumulator register, and general-purpose registers R1-R15.

Listing A-16 shows the RX600 code for **OS_CTX_SAVE** for the Renesas RX and GNURX Assemblers.

Renesas RX Assembler

```
OS_CTX_SAVE     .MACRO                                ; Renesas RX Assembler
                PUSHC   FPSW
                PUSHM   R1-R15
                MVFACHI R1
                MVFACMI R2
                PUSHM   R1-R2
                .ENDM
```

GNURX Assembler

```
.macro          OS_CTX_SAVE                           ; GNURX Assembler
                PUSHC   FPSW
                PUSHM   R1-R15
                MVFACHI R1
                MVFACMI R2
                PUSHM   R1-R2
.endm
```

Listing A-16 **OS_CPU_A.INC – OS_CTX_SAVE macro**

A-4-2 OS_CPU_A.INC – OS_CTX_RESTORE

The **OS_CTX_RESTORE** macro is used to restore the CPU registers from the stack. It restores the Floating-Point Status Word (FPSW), the accumulator register, and general-purpose registers **R1-R15**.

Listing A-17 shows the RX600 code for **OS_CTX_RESTORE** for the Renesas RX and GNURX Assemblers.

Renesas RX Assembler

```
OS_CTX_RESTORE .MACRO                                  ; Renesas RX Assembler
               POPM    R1-R2
               SHLL    #16, R2
               MVTACLO R2
               MVTACHI R1
               POPM    R1-R15
               POPC    FPSW
               .ENDM
```

GNURX Assembler

```
.macro         OS_CTX_RESTORE                          ; GNURX Assembler
               POPM    R1-R2
               SHLL    #16, R2
               MVTACLO R2
               MVTACHI R1
               POPM    R1-R15
               POPC    FPSW
.endm
```

Listing A-17 **OS_CPU_A.INC – OS_CTX_RESTORE macro**

A-4-3 OS_CPU_A.INC – OS_ISR_ENTER

The OS_ISR_ENTER macro is used to perform the prologue for kernel aware interrupt service routines. It saves the CPU registers into the stack, notifies µC/OS-III about the ISR, and saves the stack pointer of the interrupted task, if it is the first level of interrupt nesting.

Listing A-18 shows the RX600 code for OS_ISR_ENTER for the Renesas RX and GNURX Assemblers.

Renesas RX Assembler

```
OS_ISR_ENTER   .MACRO                                ; Renesas RX Assembler
               OS_CTX_SAVE                           ; Save processor registers on the stack   (1)

               MOV.L   #_OSIntNestingCtr, R5         ; Notify uC/OS-III about ISR               (2)
               MOV.B   [R5], R3
               ADD     #1, R3
               MOV.B   R3, [R5]

               CMP     #1, R3                        ; if (OSNestingCtr == 1)                   (3)
               BNE     ?+
               MOV.L   #_OSTCBCurPtr, R5             ; Save current task's SP into its TCB
               MOV.L   [R5], R3
               MOV.L   SP, [R3]
?:
               .ENDM
```

GNURX Assembler

```
.macro         OS_ISR_ENTER                          ; GNURX Assembler
               OS_CTX_SAVE                           ; Save processor registers on the stack   (1)

               MOV.L   #_OSIntNestingCtr, R5         ; Notify uC/OS-III about ISR               (2)
               MOV.B   [R5], R3
               ADD     #1, R3
               MOV.B   R3, [R5]

               CMP     #1, R3                        ; if (OSNestingCtr == 1)                   (3)
               BNE     ?+
               MOV.L   #_OSTCBCurPtr, R5             ; Save current task's SP into its TCB
               MOV.L   [R5], R3
               MOV.L   SP, [R3]
?:
.endm
```

Listing A-18 **OS_CPU_A.INC – OS_ISR_ENTER macro**

LA-18(1)   The ISR needs to save all the CPU registers onto the interrupted task's stack. This is done by the **OS_CTX_SAVE** macro.

LA-18(2)   The ISR then needs to increment **OSIntNestingCtr**. All ISRs that are kernel aware must increment **OSIntNestingCtr** so that µC/OS-III services know that they are called from an interrupt as opposed to a task.

LA-18(3)   The ISR saves the current top of stack into the **OS_TCB** of the interrupted task, if it is the first level of interrupt nesting.

A-4-4 OS_CPU_A.INC – OS_ISR_EXIT

The **OS_ISR_EXIT** macro is used to perform the epilogue for kernel aware interrupt service routines. It notifies µC/OS-III about the end of the ISR, and restores the CPU registers from the stack of the interrupted task.

Listing A-19 shows the RX600 code for **OS_ISR_EXIT** for the Renesas RX and GNURX Assemblers.

Renesas RX Assembler

```
OS_ISR_EXIT   .MACRO                          ; Renesas RX Assembler
              MOV.L   #_OSIntExit, R5         ; Notify uC/OS-III about end of ISR     (1)
              JSR     R5

              OS_CTX_RESTORE                  ; Restore processor registers from stack (2)

              RTE                                                                      (3)
              .ENDM
```

GNURX Assembler

```
.macro        OS_ISR_EXIT                     ; GNURX Assembler
              MOV.L   #_OSIntExit, R5         ; Notify uC/OS-III about end of ISR     (1)
              JSR     R5

              OS_CTX_RESTORE                  ; Restore processor registers from stack (2)

              RTE                                                                      (3)
.endm
```

Listing A-19 **OS_CPU_A.INC – OS_ISR_EXIT macro**

LA-19(1)   Every ISR needs to call **OSIntExit()** prior to restoring the CPU registers. This allows µC/OS-III to switch to a higher priority task, if the tick or other nested ISRs have made a more important task (than the interrupted task) ready to run.

LA-19(2)   The ISR restores all the CPU registers which were pushed onto the interrupted task's stack.

LA-19(3)   Finally, the ISR performs a return from interrupt to resume the interrupted code.

A-5 BSP_TICK_C.C

A µC/OS-III port requires a periodic interrupt source to generate the system tick. This is commonly achieved by using a timer that generates an interrupt at a rate between 10 and 1000 Hz. The higher the tick rate, the more overhead µC/OS-III imposes on the application. The tick rate should be set at 10 Hz if timeouts and time delays need to have a resolution of 1/10 of a second. If higher resolution is required, then the higher the tick rate must be. With a fast processor like the RX600, it is reasonable to have a higher tick rate.

A-5-1 BSP_TICK_C.C – OS_CPU_TickInit()

For the RX600 port, the CMT0 is used to generate this interrupt and set the tick rate at 1000 Hz. If control loops need to run periodically at high rates, it is recommend to use one of the other RX600 timers. In other words, avoid using the tick rate for such applications; it is not meant for that.

Listing A-20 shows the RX600 code for **OS_CPU_TickInit()**.

```
void  OS_CPU_TickInit (void)
{
    CPU_INT16U  cmcor;


    cmcor = BSP_CPU_PerClkFreq() / (32u * OSCfg_TickRate_Hz);            (1)

    MSTP(CMT0)            = 0;             /* Enable CMT0 module.       */

    CMT.CMSTR0.BIT.STR0 = 0;              /* Stop timer channel 0.     */
    CMT0.CMCR.BIT.CKS   = 1;              /* Set peripheral clock divider. */

    CMT0.CMCOR           = cmcor - 1u;    /* Set compare-match value.  */
    CMT0.CMCNT           = 0;             /* Clear counter register.   */

    IR(CMT0, CMI0)       = 0;             /* Clear any pending ISR.    */
    IPR(CMT0,)           = 3;             /* Set interrupt priority.   */
    IEN(CMT0, CMI0)      = 1;             /* Enable interrupt source.  */

    CMT0.CMCR.BIT.CMIE  = 1;              /* Enable interrupt.         */

    CMT.CMSTR0.BIT.STR0 = 1;              /* Start timer.              */
}
```

Listing A-20 **OS_TICK_C.C – OS_CPU_TickInit()**

LA-20(1) **CMT0** is initialized as an auto-reload compare-match source with interrupts enabled. The peripheral clock on the YRDKRX62N evaluation board available with this book is set to 48 MHz, since this frequency is convenient for other peripherals.

A-6 BSP_TICK_A.SRC

BSP_TICK_A.SRC contains the code for the ISR handler: OSTickISR(). In fact, the application programmer should model any interrupt handler from OSTickISR(), as explained in section A-6-1 on page 814.

A-6-1 BSP_TICK_A.SRC – OSTickISR()

The full code for the tick ISR is shown in Listing A-21. Other ISRs in the application can refer to this code as a template.

```
_OSTickISR:
        OS_ISR_ENTER                    ; Save processor registers on the stack & ... (1)
                                        ; ... Notify uC/OS-III about ISR


        MOV.L   #_OSTimeTick, R5                                              (2)
        JSR     R5


        OS_ISR_EXIT                     ; Notify uC/OS-III about end of ISR & ...   (3)
                                        ; ... Restore processor registers from stack
```

Listing A-21 **BSP_TICK_A.SRC – OSTickISR()**

LA-21(1)   The handler needs to save all the CPU registers onto the interrupted task's stack, and notify µC/OS-III about the ISR. This is done by the **OS_ISR_ENTER** macro.

LA-21(2)   **OSTickISR()** then calls **OSTimeTick()**, which is a function provided by µC/OS-III to process system tick. The tick processing is actually performed in the µC/OS-III tick task (**OS_TickTask()**), where **OSTimeTick()** simply signals that task.

LA-21(3)   The handler must notify µC/OS-III about the end of the ISR. This allows µC/OS-III to switch to a higher priority task if the tick or other nested ISRs have made a more important task (than the interrupted task) ready to run. If the execution flow returns to the interrupted task, all CPU registers are restored prior to return from the interrupt.

A-7 KERNEL AWARE VS. NON KERNEL AWARE INTERRUPTS

The tick interrupt is known as a kernel aware interrupt because it notifies a µC/OS-III task about the need to process a clock tick. The application may have other ISRs that need to signal tasks for further processing. These ISRs are called *Kernel Aware* ISRs because they need to work with µC/OS-III. **OSTickISR()** is an example of a Kernel Aware ISR and thus, all Kernel Aware ISRs should be modeled as the **OSTickISR()**.

If an ISR does not need to signal or send a message to a task, it is called a *Non Kernel Aware* ISR. In other words, all the work that needs to be done in response to the interrupt is handle in the ISR itself.

Listing A-22 shows an example of a non kernel aware ISR.

```
MyNonKernelAwareISR:
        PUSHM   R??-R??                 ; save the registers on the stack        (1)

        MOV.L   #_MyNonKernelISR_Handler, R5
        JSR     R5                      ; MyNonKernelAwareISR_Handler();         (2)

        POPM    R??-R??                 ; restore registers from stack           (3)

        RTE                                                                      (4)
```

Listing A-22 **Non Kernel Aware ISR**

LA-22(1)   The ISR needs to save all the CPU registers onto the interrupted task's stack. The question marks indicate that only modified registers need to be saved by the ISR itself.

LA-22(2)   The ISR can then handle the interrupting device directly in assembly language, or call a C function to handle the interrupting device. The handler should clear the interrupt source as needed by the interrupting device.

LA-22(3)   The ISR restores all the CPU registers which were pushed onto the interrupted task's stack. This must be the same registers and in the same order as those that were pushed at the beginning of the ISR.

LA-22(4)   Finally, the ISR performs a return from interrupt to resume the interrupted code.

Non kernel aware interrupts are typically used when the ISR is very short, and for high rate interrupts. In other words, for interrupts that occur very often and that have little processing to do.

On the RX600, non kernel aware interrupts must be assigned a priority level higher than the interrupt mask level. For example, if the interrupt mask (using **set_ipl()**) is set to 12 (see **CPU_CRITICAL_ENTER()** in **CPU.H**, Appendix B), then kernel aware interrupts must be assigned to levels 1 through 12, and non kernel aware interrupts from levels 13 and up. This interrupt priority assignment is shown in Figure A-2.

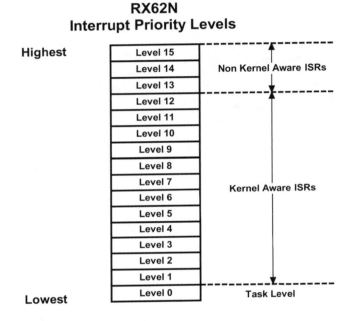

Figure A-2 **Kernel Aware VS Non-Kernel Aware Interrupt Priorities**

Appendix

B

μC/CPU Port to the RX62N

μC/CPU consists of files that encapsulate common CPU-specific functionality and CPU compiler specific data types. This appendix describes the adaptation of μC/CPU to the Renesas RX62N as it relates to μC/OS-III. This port was done by Micriμm/Renesas and these files will most likely not need to be changed. This port is specific to the Renesas RX62N MCUs. For the Renesas RX610 family, the μC/CPU RX610 port must be used.

In μC/CPU, each variable, function, #define constant, or macro is prefixed with **CPU_**. This makes it easier to identify them as belonging to the μC/CPU module when invoked by other modules, or application code.

The μC/CPU files are found in the following three directories:

\Micrium\Software\uC-CPU**CPU_CORE.C**
\Micrium\Software\uC-CPU**CPU_CORE.H**
\Micrium\Software\uC-CPU**CPU_DEF.H**
\Micrium\Software\uC-CPU\Cfg\Template**CPU_CFG.H**
\Micrium\Software\uC-CPU\RX62N\HEW**CPU.H**
\Micrium\Software\uC-CPU\RX62N\GNURX**CPU.H**

B-1 CPU_CORE.C

CPU_CORE.C contains C code that is common to all CPU architectures and this file must not be changed. Specifically, **CPU_CORE.C** contains functions to allow μC/OS-III and the application to obtain time stamps, measure the interrupt disable time of the **CPU_CRITICAL_ENTER()** and **CPU_CRITICAL_EXIT()** macros, a function that emulates a count leading zeros instruction (since the RX does not have that instruction built-in) and a few other functions.

The application code must call **CPU_Init()** before it can call any other μC/CPU function. This call should be placed in **main()**, before calling μC/OS-III's **OSInit()**.

B-2 CPU_CORE.H

CPU_CORE.H contains function prototypes for the functions provided in CPU_CORE.C and allocation of the variables used by the module to measure interrupt disable time. This file must not be modified.

B-3 CPU_DEF.H

CPU_DEF.H contains miscellaneous #define constants used by the µC/CPU module. This file must not be modified.

B-4 CPU_CFG.H

CPU_CFG.H contains a template to configure µC/CPU for the actual project. CPU_CFG.H determines whether to enable measurement of the interrupt disable time, whether the CPU implements a count leading zeros instruction in assembly language, or whether it will be emulated in C, and more.

The file CPU_CFG.H should be copied to the application directory of the project and modified as necessary. In other words, the original CPU_CFG.H file that comes with the distribution should not be modified.

Listing B-1 shows the recommended values for the Renesas RX62N.

```
#define   CPU_CFG_NAME_EN                 DEF_ENABLED          (1)
#define   CPU_CFG_NAME_SIZE                          32u       (2)
#define   CPU_CFG_TS_32_EN                DEF_ENABLED          (3)
#define   CPU_CFG_TS_64_EN                DEF_ENABLED
#define   CPU_CFG_TS_TMR_SIZE             CPU_WORD_SIZE_32     (4)
#if DEF_ENABLED
#define   CPU_CFG_INT_DIS_MEAS_EN                              (5)
#endif
#define   CPU_CFG_INT_DIS_MEAS_OVRHD_NBR            1u         (6)
#if 0
#define   CPU_CFG_LEAD_ZEROS_ASM_PRESENT                       (7)
#endif
```

Listing B-1 **CPU_CFG.H recommended values**

LB-1(1)   An ASCII name can be assigned to the CPU by calling **CPU_NameSet()**. This could be useful for debugging purposes. It is recommended to use the following name: "Renesas RX62N". The following is an example of usage of the **CPU_NameSet()** function.

```
CPU_ERR   err;


void  main (void)
{
    :
    CPU_Init();
    CPU_NameSet("Renesas RX62N", &err);
    :
}
```

LB-1(2)   The name of the CPU should be limited to 31 characters plus a NUL, unless this value is changed.

LB-1(3)   These #defines enable the code that is used to measure time stamps. The application can obtain a 32-bit timestamp by calling **CPU_TS_Get32()** and a 64-bit timestamp by calling **CPU_TS_Get64()**. Either function must be called more often than the overflow rate of the timer used to make timestamp measurements. On the RX62N, a 16-bit timer running at 48 MHz / 32 (or 1.5 MHz) is used and thus, if either of these functions are used, they must be called at least within 43.69 milliseconds. To make sure this happens, a call to **CPU_TS_Update()** is added in **OSTimeTickHook()**, which is called every one millisecond. **CPU_TS_Update()** calls both **CPU_TS_Get32()** and **CPU_TS_Get64()** internally.

LB-1(4)   This **#define** determines the size of the CPU timestamp timer's word. If the size of the CPU timestamp timer is not a binary multiple of 8-bit octets (*e.g.*, 20-bits or even 24-bits), then the next lower, binary-multiple octet word size *should* be configured (*e.g.*, to 16-bits). However, the minimum supported word size for CPU timestamp timers is 8-bits.

LB-1(5)   This **#define** determines whether interrupt disable time will be measured. This is a useful feature during development, but should be turned off when deploying the system, because measuring interrupt disable time adds measurement artifacts.

LB-1(6)   This **#define** determines how many iterations will be performed when determining the overhead involved in measuring interrupt disable time. For the Renesas RX62N, the recommended value is 1.

LB-1(7)   The Renesas RX62N instruction set does not contain a Count Leading Zeros (CLZ) instruction and thus this feature is emulated in C by the function **CPU_CntLeadZeros()** (see **CPU_CORE.C**).

B-5 µC/CPU FUNCTIONS IN BSP.C

µC/CPU requires two Board Support Package (BSP) specific functions:

CPU_TS_TmrInit()
CPU_TS_TmrRd()

These functions are typically implemented in **BSP.C** of the evaluation or target board.

The Renesas RX62N processor contains only 16-bit and 8-bit timers. Since there is no support for 32-bit timer, µC/CPU functions are used to extend the precision in software. If the application code uses the µC/CPU functions **CPU_TS_Get32()** or **CPU_TS_Get64()**, these functions must be called more often than the overflow rate of the timer. In other words, if the timer is being incremented at 1.5 MHz, then **CPU_TS_Get32()** or **CPU_TS_Get64()** must be called within 43.69 milliseconds. As mentioned in section B-4 on page 818, **CPU_TS_Update()** is called by **OSTimeTickHook()** every one millisecond to avoid the application code to maintain this update.

B-5-1 µC/CPU FUNCTIONS IN BSP.C, CPU_TS_TmrInit()

For the RX62N, the **CMT1** is used for time stamping purposes, where the RX62N's more powerful and flexible timers are saved for user applications. Listing B-2 shows how to initialize the **CMT1**.

```
#if (CPU_CFG_TS_TMR_EN == DEF_ENABLED)
void  CPU_TS_TmrInit (void)
{
    CPU_INT08U  cks;
    CPU_INT16U  n;
    CPU_INT32U  freq;


    MSTP(CMT1)            = 0;          /* enable the timer in the module stop register   */ (1)
    CMT.CMSTR0.BIT.STR1 = 0;           /* stop timer                                     */
    cks                  = 1;          /* set clock source select as follows:            */
    CMT1.CMCR.BIT.CKS  = cks;          /*    0  sets divider by   8                       */
                                       /*    1  sets divider by  32                       */
                                       /*    2  sets divider by 128                       */
                                       /*    3  sets divider by 512                       */
    CMT1.CMCOR           = 0xFFFF;     /* compare match not used                          */
    CMT1.CMCNT           = 0;          /* clear counter register                          */
    CMT1.CMCR.BIT.CMIE = 0;            /* disable compare match interrupt                 */
    CMT.CMSTR0.BIT.STR1 = 1;           /* start timer                                     */

    n    = 3 + ((cks & 3) << 1);       /* Set the count rate of the timestamp timer       */
    freq = BSP_CPU_PerClkFreq() >> n;

    CPU_TS_TmrFreqSet(freq);
}
#endif
```

Listing B-2 **BSP.C, CPU_TS_TmrInit()**

LB-2(1)   **CMT1** is initialized as a free-running counter that does not cause any interrupts. The peripheral clock on the YRDKRX62N evaluation board available with this book is set to 48 MHz, since this frequency is convenient for other peripherals. With a divider of 32, **CMT1** will increment at a 1.5 MHz rate and thus, will overflow every 43.69 milliseconds. For accurate time stamp measurements, **CMT1** needs to be read more often than this overflow rate.

B-5-2 µC/CPU FUNCTIONS IN BSP.C, CPU_TS_TmrRd()

The current value of the RX62N timer used for time stamping is read by calling CPU_TS_TmrRd(). CMT1 is an "up counter" which is the requirement of CPU_TS_TmrRd(). This function is implemented as shown in Listing B-3 by using CMT1.

```
#if (CPU_CFG_TS_TMR_EN == DEF_ENABLED)
CPU_TS_TMR  CPU_TS_TmrRd (void)
{
    CPU_TS_TMR  ts_tmr_cnts;


    ts_tmr_cnts = (CPU_TS_TMR)CMT1.CMCNT;
    return (ts_tmr_cnts);
}
#endif
```

Listing B-3 **BSP.C, CPU_TS_TmrRd()**

B-6 CPU.H

CPU.H contains processor- and implementation- specific #defines constants, macros and typedefs.

B-6-1 CPU.H – #DEFINES

CPU.H declares a number of processor specific #define constants and macros. The most important ones related to µC/OS-III are shown in Listing B-4.

```
#define  CPU_CFG_STK_GROWTH          CPU_STK_GROWTH_HI_TO_LO              (1)
#define  CPU_SR_ALLOC()              CPU_SR  cpu_sr = (CPU_SR)0           (2)
#define  CPU_CRITICAL_ENTER()   do { cpu_sr = get_ipl(); \               (3)
                                     set_ipl(12);        } while (0)
#define  CPU_CRITICAL_EXIT()    do { set_ipl(cpu_sr);    } while (0)      (4)
```

Listing B-4 **CPU.H, #defines**

LB-4(1)   This **#define** specifies that the RX62N stack grows from high memory to lower memory addresses.

LB-4(2)   The macro is used to allocate a local variable in a function that needs to protect a critical section by disabling interrupts. µC/OS-III uses **CPU_SR_ALLOC()** as follows:

```
void  SomeFunction (void)
{
    CPU_SR_ALLOC();


    :

    CPU_CRITICAL_ENTER();
    /* Code protected by critical section */
    CPU_CRITICAL_EXIT();

    :

}
```

The macro might not appear necessary if a single variable is declared, but the actual code in **CPU.H** is actually slightly more complex, and thus the macro hides this complexity from the user.

LB-4(3)   **CPU_CRITICAL_ENTER()** is invoked by µC/OS-III to disable interrupts. This macro calls **get_ipl()** to get the current value of the interrupt priority level from the RX62N's Processor Status Word (PSW), and then disables all interrupts by calling **set_ipl(12)**. **get_ipl()** and **set_ipl()** are functions provided by Renesas to avoid implementing these in assembly language. The actual code in **CPU.H** is slightly more complex than what is shown here, but this gives the overall logic of what is happening.

LB-4(4)   **CPU_CRITICAL_EXIT()** calls the function **set_ipl()** to restore the previously saved interrupt priority level. The reason the interrupt priority level was saved in the first place is because interrupts might already have been disabled prior to invoking **CPU_CRITICAL_ENTER()**, and thus prevents interrupts being inadvertently enabled when exiting the critical section. If interrupts were enabled before calling **CPU_CRITICAL_ENTER()**, they will be re-enabled by **CPU_CRITICAL_EXIT()**.

B-6-2 CPU.H – DATA TYPES

Micriµm does not make use of the standard C data types. Instead, the declared data types are both highly portable and intuitive. In addition, all data types are always declared in upper case, which follows Micriµm's coding standard.

Listing B-5 shows the data types used by Micriµm and specific to the RX62N.

```
typedef              void      CPU_VOID;
typedef              char      CPU_CHAR;              /*  8-bit character           */ (1)
typedef   unsigned   char      CPU_BOOLEAN;          /*  8-bit boolean or logical   */ (2)
typedef   unsigned   char      CPU_INT08U;           /*  8-bit unsigned integer     */ (3)
typedef     signed   char      CPU_INT08S;           /*  8-bit   signed integer     */
typedef   unsigned   short     CPU_INT16U;           /* 16-bit unsigned integer     */
typedef     signed   short     CPU_INT16S;           /* 16-bit   signed integer     */
typedef   unsigned   long      CPU_INT32U;           /* 32-bit unsigned integer     */
typedef     signed   long      CPU_INT32S;           /* 32-bit   signed integer     */
typedef   unsigned   long long CPU_INT64U;           /* 64-bit unsigned integer     */ (4)
typedef     signed   long long CPU_INT64S;           /* 64-bit   signed integer     */
typedef              float     CPU_FP32;             /* 32-bit floating point       */ (5)
typedef              double    CPU_FP64;             /* 64-bit floating point       */
typedef   volatile   CPU_INT08U CPU_REG08;           /*  8-bit register             */
typedef   volatile   CPU_INT16U CPU_REG16;           /* 16-bit register             */
typedef   volatile   CPU_INT32U CPU_REG32;           /* 32-bit register             */
typedef   volatile   CPU_INT64U CPU_REG64;           /* 64-bit register             */
typedef              void      (*CPU_FNCT_VOID)(void);
typedef              void      (*CPU_FNCT_PTR )(void *p_obj);
```

Listing B-5 **CPU.H, Data Types**

LB-5(1)   Characters are assumed to be 8-bit quantities on the RX62N.

LB-5(2)   It is often convenient to declare Boolean variables. However, even though a Boolean represents either 1 or 0, a whole byte is used. This is done because ANSI C does not define single bit variables.

LB-5(3)   The signed and unsigned integer data types are declared for 8, 16 and 32 bit quantities.

LB-5(4)   µC/OS-III requires that the compiler defines 64 bit data types. These are used when computing CPU usage on a per-task basis. The 64-bit data types are used when declaring **OS_CYCLES** in **OS_TYPE.H**.

LB-5(5)   Most of Micriµm's software components do not use floating point values. However, the floating point capabilities will most likely be used by the application programmer.

```
#define  CPU_CFG_ADDR_SIZE      CPU_WORD_SIZE_32                    (6)
#define  CPU_CFG_DATA_SIZE      CPU_WORD_SIZE_32
#if      (CPU_CFG_ADDR_SIZE == CPU_WORD_SIZE_32)
typedef  CPU_INT32U            CPU_ADDR;
#elif    (CPU_CFG_ADDR_SIZE == CPU_WORD_SIZE_16)
typedef  CPU_INT16U            CPU_ADDR;
#else
typedef  CPU_INT08U            CPU_ADDR;
#endif
#if      (CPU_CFG_DATA_SIZE == CPU_WORD_SIZE_32)
typedef  CPU_INT32U            CPU_DATA;
#elif    (CPU_CFG_DATA_SIZE == CPU_WORD_SIZE_16)
typedef  CPU_INT16U            CPU_DATA;
#else
typedef  CPU_INT08U            CPU_DATA;
#endif
typedef  CPU_DATA             CPU_ALIGN;
typedef  CPU_ADDR             CPU_SIZE_T;
typedef  CPU_INT32U           CPU_STK;                             (7)
typedef  CPU_ADDR             CPU_STK_SIZE;
typedef  CPU_INT08U           CPU_SR;                              (8)
```

Listing B-6 **CPU.H, Data Type (Continued)**

LB-6(6)   Miscellaneous types are declared.

LB-6(7)   **CPU_STK** declares the width of a CPU stack entry and these are 32-bit wide on the RX62N. µC/OS-III stacks must be declared using **CPU_STK**. **CPU_STK_SIZE** is a data type used to represent the size (in **CPU_STK** elements) of stacks.

LB-6(8)   µC/CPU provides code to protect critical sections by disabling interrupts. This is implemented by **CPU_CRITICAL_ENTER( )** and **CPU_CRITICAL_EXIT( )**, as previously shown. When **CPU_CRITICAL_ENTER( )** is invoked, the current interrupt priority level is saved in a local variable so that it can be restored when **CPU_CRITICAL_EXIT( )** is invoked. The local variable that holds the saved interrupt priority level is declared as a **CPU_SR**.

µC/Probe

µC/Probe is an award-winning Microsoft Windows™-based application that allows a user to display or change the value (at run time) of virtually any variable or memory location on a connected embedded target. The user simply populates µC/Probe's graphical environment with gauges, numeric indicators, tables, graphs, virtual LEDs, bar graphs, sliders, switches, push buttons, and other components, and associates each of these to a variable or memory location.

With µC/Probe, it is not necessary to instrument the target code in order to display or change variables at run time. In fact, there is no need to add **printf()** statements, hardware such as Light Emitting Diodes (LEDs), Liquid Crystal Displays (LCDs), or use any other means to get visibility inside an embedded target at run time.

Two versions of µC/Probe are available from Micriµm (see section 3-3 "Downloading µC/Probe" on page 692).

µC/OS-III licensees receive one free license of the full version of µC/Probe. This full version supports RS-232C, TCP/IP, USB, J-Link, and other interfaces, and allows to display or change an unlimited number of variables. The trial version only allows to display or change up to eight application variables. However, it allows to monitor any µC/OS-III variables since µC/Probe is µC/OS-III aware.

The examples provided with this book assume that one of these two versions of µC/Probe have been downloaded and is installed on the PC.

This appendix provides a brief introduction to µC/Probe.

Figure C-1 shows a block diagram of a typical development environment with the addition of µC/Probe as used with the RX62N, available with this book.

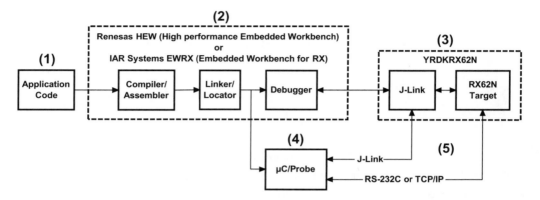

Figure C-1 **Development environment using the YRDKRX62N**

FC-1(1)   This is the application code being developed. It is assumed that µC/OS-III provided with this book is used. However, µC/Probe does not require an RTOS and can work with or without an RTOS.

FC-1(2)   The examples provided with this book assumes the Renesas High performance Embedded Workbench (HEW) or IAR Systems Embedded Workbench for the RX (EWRX), but µC/Probe works with any toolchain as long as the linker/locator is able to produce an .ELF or .IEEE695 output file.

FC-1(3)   The YRDKRX62N evaluation board available with this book contains an onboard J-Link debugger. The J-Link allows the debugger to download Flash code onto the on-board RX62N Micro Controller Unit (MCU). The J-Link also allows to debug the application code.

FC-1(4)   µC/Probe reads the exact same .ELF or .IEEE695 output file produced by the linker/locator. From this file, µC/Probe is able to extract names, data types and addresses of all the global variables of the application code. This information allows µC/Probe to display any of the values of the variables using the available display objects (gauges, meters, virtual LEDs, bar graphs, numeric indicators, graphs, and more).

FC-1(5)   µC/Probe can interface to the YRDKRX62N board using the on-board J-Link, RS-232C or Ethernet (using TCP/IP) interface (see section C-3 "Configuring the µC/Probe Interfaces" on page 832).

C-1 µC/PROBE IS A WINDOWS™-BASED APPLICATION

As previously mentioned, µC/Probe is a Microsoft Windows-based application. When opening µC/Probe, an empty workspace is loaded by default as shown in Figure C-2.

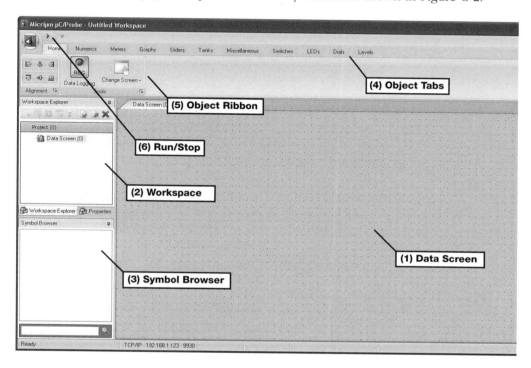

Figure C-2 **Empty µC/Probe Workspace**

FC-2(1)   µC/Probe's main focus is the Data Screen. This is where Objects are dragged and dropped. µC/Probe has a vast array of visual objects, such as gauges, meters, graphs, virtual LEDs, sliders, switches, among others, which are used to display or change the value of target variables at run time. µC/Probe allows to define any number of Data Screens and each Data Screen can be assigned a name. Each data screen is selected by using a Tab at the top of the data screen area.

FC-2(2)   When data screens are created, their names also appear in the Workspace area. The Workspace defines the structure of the µC/Probe project. Data screens can be imported from other projects, and can also be exported.

FC-2(3)   The Symbol Browser contains a list of all the variables that can be displayed or changed in the target by µC/Probe. The variables are organized alphabetically by compile modules (i.e., source files). These groups can be expanded to view all the variables defined in that module. Symbols can be searched by using the search box.

FC-2(4)   The Object Ribbon is where to find the objects (gauges, meters, numeric indicators, sliders, graphs, etc.) to drag and drop onto the data screen.

FC-2(5)   Similar objects are grouped together. Each group is selected by clicking on the appropriate tab. Drag and drop any object onto one of the available data screens, and associate a variable to the instantiated object. Some objects even allow association of multiple variables.

FC-2(6)   µC/Probe supports two modes: Run and Stop. Stop mode is used to change or edit data screens. Run mode is used to display or change the current value of target variables at run time.

Figure C-3 shows a group of Meter objects and Figure C-4 shows a group of Level objects.

Figure C-3 µC/Probe **Meter Objects**

Figure C-4 µC/Probe **Level Objects**

Figure C-5 shows a group of Slider objects, which can be used to modify target variables.

Figure C-5 µC/Probe **Slider Objects**

C-2 ASSIGNING A VARIABLE TO AN OBJECT

Assigning a variable to an object is quite simple as illustrated in Figure C-6. It is assumed that the code has been downloaded to the target and the target is running.

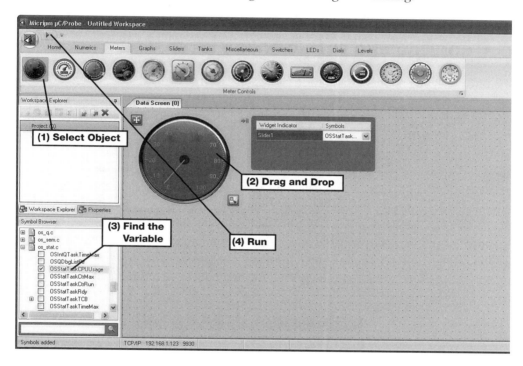

Figure C-6 **Assigning a Variable to an Object**

FC-6(1)   First, select the object that allows the best visualization of the variable (meter, thermometer, LED, etc.).

FC-6(2)   Then, drag and drop the object onto the data screen.

FC-6(3)   Now, find the variable in the symbol browser. Simply type the first few letters of the variable and µC/Probe narrows down the search. Click on the small box to the left of the variable name.

FC-6(4)   To see the value of the variable, simply click on the "Run/Stop" button on the upper left corner.

If the "full version" has been purchased, there is no limitations on the number of objects and the number of data screens a workspace can have. However, the trial-version of μC/Probe only allows to have a total of eight application variables, but enables the display of any μC/OS-III variable.

C-3 CONFIGURING THE μC/PROBE INTERFACES

As previously mentioned, μC/Probe allows to interface the target using a number of different communication interfaces such as J-Link, RS-232C, TCP/IP (Ethernet), USB and others. The example code provided with this book allows to interface either using J-Link, RS-232C or TCP/IP.

Target resident code must be added when using RS-232C. This code is however provided and included by Micriμm in the examples that are provided with the book. With RS-232C, the target data can only be displayed or changed by μC/Probe when the target is running. μC/Probe also needs to know which COM port on the computer is connected to the YRDKR62N, as well as the baud rate. This is configured in the μC/Probe "Options" as shown in Figure C-7. The example projects assume a baud rate of 38,400. However, μC/Probe supports other baud rates. The selected baud rate must match the baud rate the target is configured.

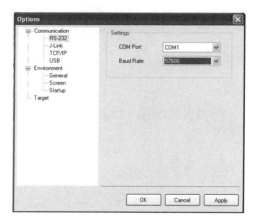

Figure C-7 **RS-232C Configuration**

Target resident code is also required if µC/Probe is communicating over the Ethernet port on the YRDKRX62N board. In fact, Micriµm's µC/TCP-IP is provided in linkable library format allowing to experience µC/Probe using TCP/IP communication. The IP address of the YRDKRX62N is displayed on the YRDKRX62N's graphical LCD display and must be configured into µC/Probe along with the default port number, 9930. This is configured in the µC/Probe "Options" as shown in Figure C-8. Similarly to RS-232C, data can only be displayed and changed when the target is running. However, the Ethernet interface provides the best throughput and data update rates for µC/Probe.

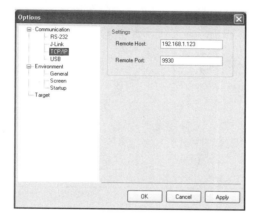

Figure C-8 **TCP/IP Configuration**

Target resident code is not required when using the J-Link to interface with µC/Probe. The J-Link, which is built-into the YRDKRX62N, uses the debug DMA feature of the RX and can thus access target memory without CPU intervention. To use this interface, the J-Link option needs to be selected in the communication settings, and in the J-Link "Communication" category, the JTAG option *must* be selected to communicate with the YRDKRX62N, as shown in Figure C-9. With the J-Link interface, data can be displayed and changed when the target is either stopped at a breakpoint or running.

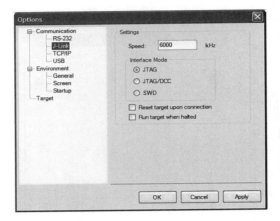

Figure C-9 **J-Link Configuration**

This appendix contains the schematic diagrams for the Renesas YRDKRX62N demostration board that is available separately for use with this book. The YRDKRX62N is shown in Figure D-1.

Figure D-1 **YRDKRX62N**

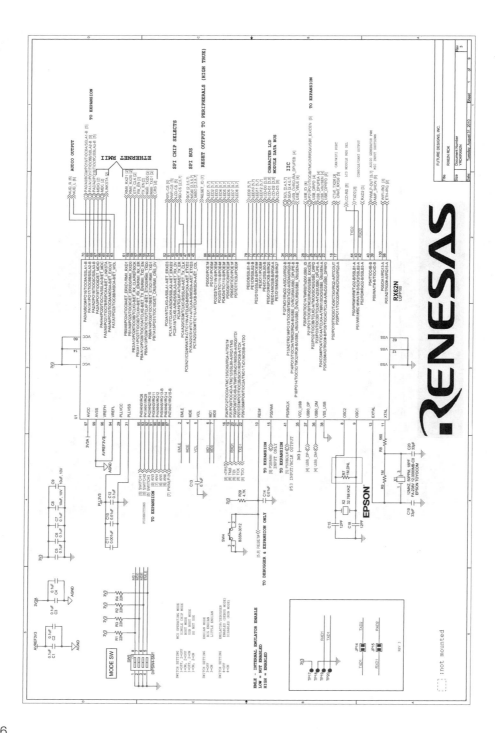

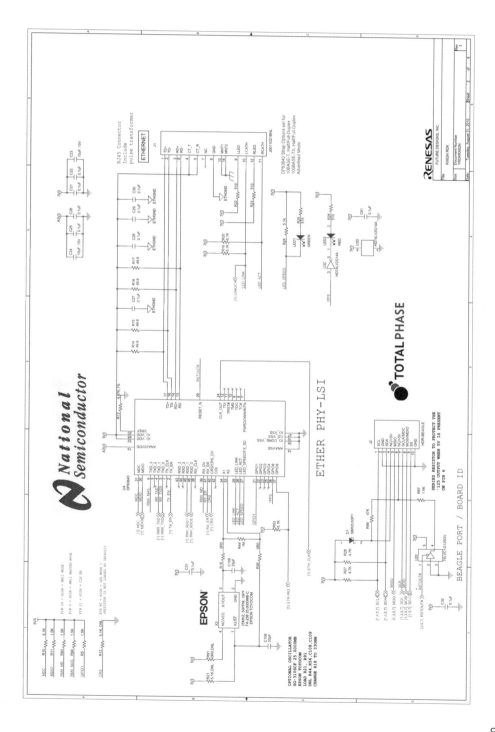

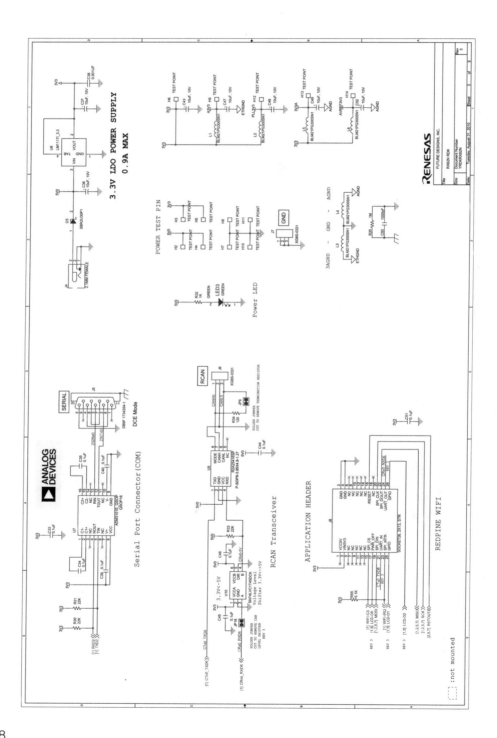

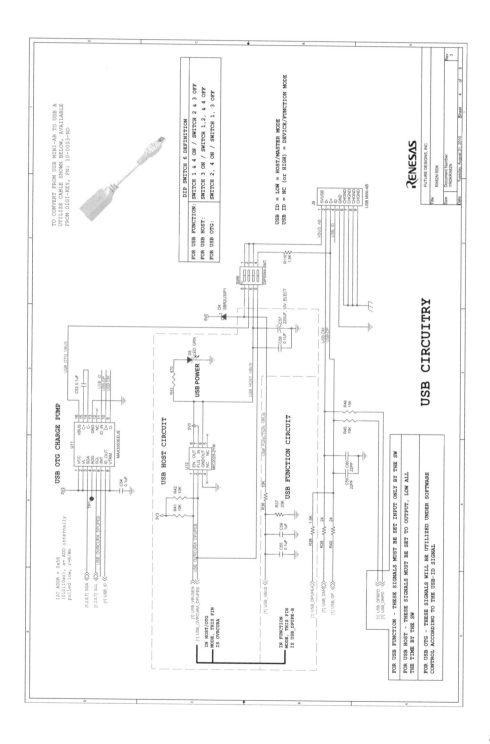

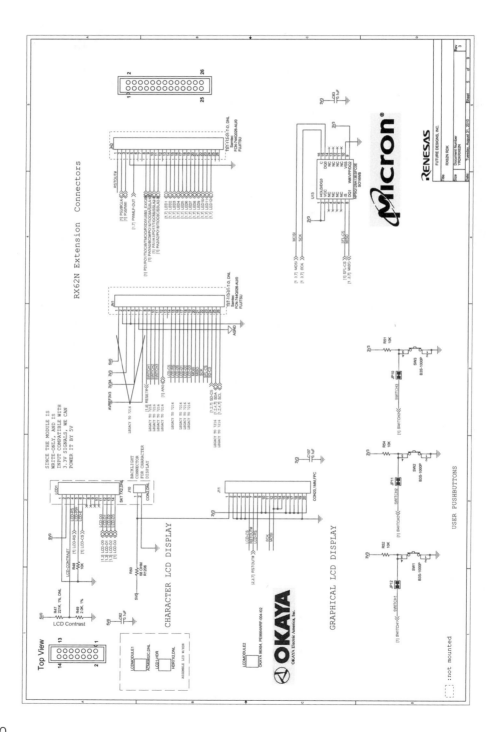

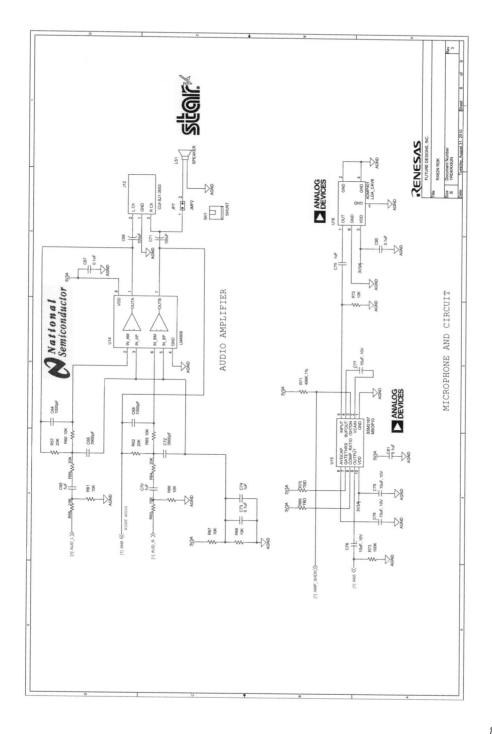

AUDIO AMPLIFIER

MICROPHONE AND CIRCUIT

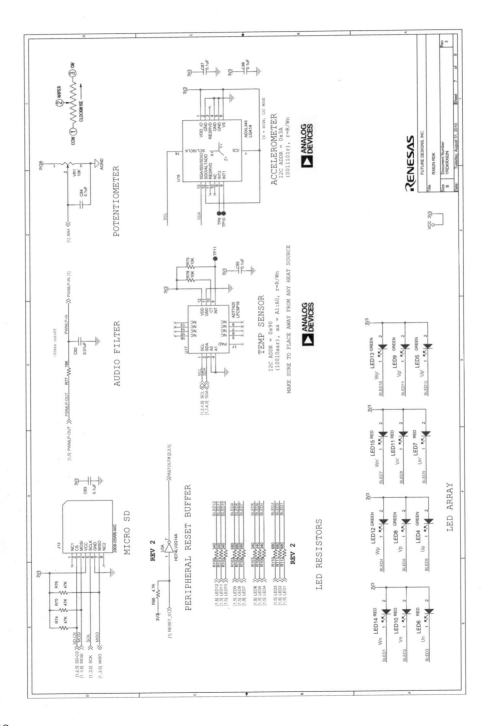

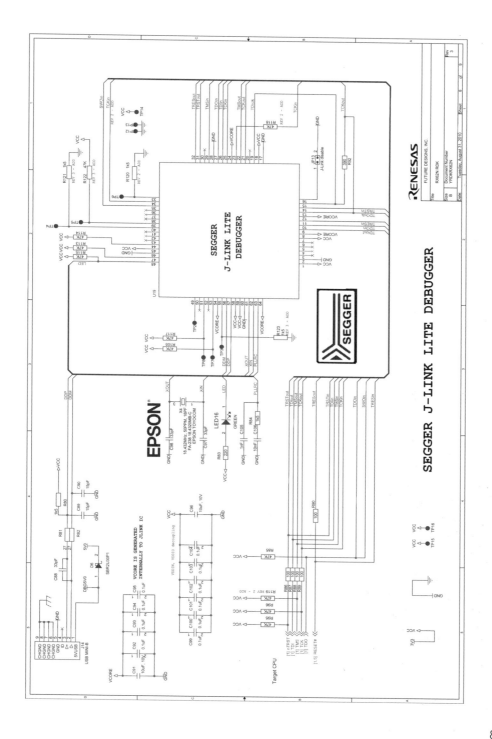

SEGGER J-LINK LITE DEBUGGER

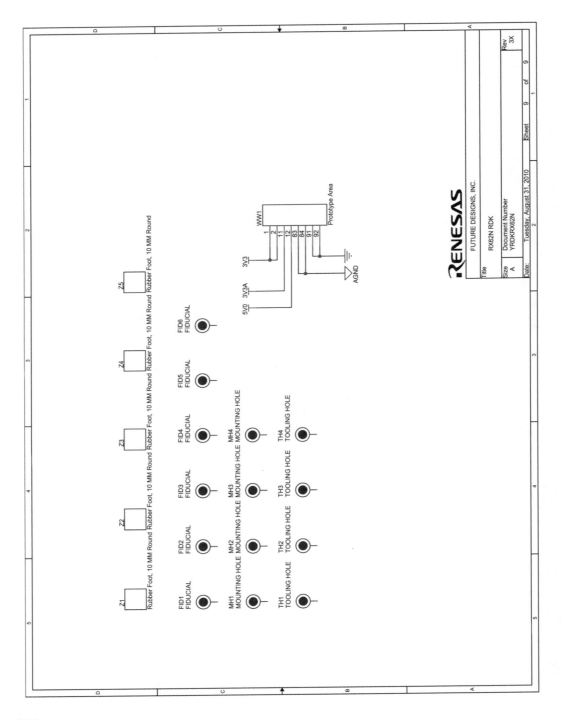

Renesas Electronics. *RX Family Software Manual*,
Document REJ09B0435-xxxx, www.renesas.com/rx.

Renesas Electronics. *RX62N Group & RX621 Group Hardware Manual*,
Document R01UH0033EJ-xxxx, www.renesas.com/rx.

Appendix

F

Licensing

This book comes with µC/OS-III precompiled in linkable object form, an evaluation board and tools (compiler/assembler/linker/debugger). You are allowed to use µC/OS-III for free as long as it is only used with the evaluation board that came with this book. In other words, you will need to purchase a license if you intend to use this code in a commercial project where you have the intent to make a profit. You don't have to pay anything else beyond the book, evaluation board and tools as long as they are used for educational purposes.

You will need to license the use of µC/OS-III if you intend to use µC/OS-III in a commercial product where you intend to make a profit. You need to purchase this license when you make the decision to use µC/OS-III in your design, not when you are ready to go to production.

If you are unsure about whether you need to obtain a license for your application, please contact Micriµm and discuss your use with a sales representative.

CONTACTING MICRIUM

Micriµm
1290 Weston Road, Suite 306
Weston, FL 33326

+1 954 217 2036
+1 954 217 2037 (FAX)

e-mail   : sales@micrium.com
website : www.micrium.com

F-1 RENESAS SIGNAL PROCESSING LIBRARY (SPL)

The Renesas Signal Processing Library (SPL) is a set of routines that implement filter functions and signal processing primitives. The SPL has been optimized for performance in RX600 core based processors. This library is available free of charge to users of Renesas RX600 series based MCU devices. It is distributed in object form and users are required to agree to a click-through license. The SPL implements some of the most frequently used functions in typical signal processing applications such as speech processing, digital filters, and image processing, to name a few. The library is accompanied by a user manual and sample workspace.

G

Bill of Materials

The following pages contain a full list of the components of the Renesas Demo Kit YRDKRX62N

G-1 BILL OF MATERIALS

Qty	Description	Location	Mfg	Mfg Part Number
1	RX62N, LQFP100	U1	RENESAS	R5F56218BDFPU
1	HD74LV2G14A, TTP-8DBV-PBF	U3	TI	SN74LVC3G14DCUR
1	DP83640, LQFP48-SOT313-2	U4	NATIONAL SEMI	DP83640TVVX/NOPB
1	LM1117I_3.3, SOT223	U6	NATIONAL	LM1117IMPX-3.3
1	ADM3101E_QSOP16	U7	ANALOG DEVICE	ADM3101EARQZ
1	R2A25416SP, P-SOP8-3.95X4.9-1.27	U9	RENESAS	R2A25416SP
1	SN74LVC1T45DCK, SC70	U10	TI	SN74LVC1T45DCK
1	MAX3353EEUE, TSSOP16	U11	MAXIM	MAX3353EEUE+
1	MIC2025-2YM, SO8NB	U12	MICREL	MIC2025-2YM
1	NP5Q128A13ESFC0E, SO16WB	U13	NUMONYX	NP5Q128A13ESFC0E
1	LM4808, SO8-SOT96-1	U14	NATIONAL SEMI	LM4808M/NOPB
1	SSM2167, MSOP10	U15	ANALOG DEVICES	SSM2167-1RMZ-REEL
1	ADMP401, LGA_CAV6	U16	ANALOG DEVICES	ADMP401XACEZ-RL7
1	ADT7420, LFCSP16	U17	ANALOG DEVICES	ADT7420
1	ADXL345, LGA14	U18	ANALOG DEVICES	ADXL345BCCZ-RL
1	Segger J-Link Debugger	U19	SEGGER	

850

Qty	Description	Location	Mfg	Mfg Part Number
1	74LVC1G125GV, SOT23-5	U20	NXP	74LVC1G125GV,125
1	LCD OKAYA 96X64	LCDMODULE1	Okaya	SE9664WRF-004-I02Q
0	LCD_AZ_ACM0802C	(LCDMODULE1)	AZ Displays	ACM0802C-RN-GBS
1	12MHZ, 50ppm, 18pf, FA-238V, XTAL	X1	EPSON TOYOCOM	FA-238V 12.0000MB-C0
1	32.768 KHZ, JTX410, 12.5pf, XTAL	X2	EPSON TOYOCOM	FC-135 32.7680KA-A3
1	25MHZ, 50ppm, 18pf, FA-238, XTAL	X3	EPSON TOYOCOM	FA-238 25.0000MB-C
1	18.432MHz, 50ppm, 18pf FA-238, XTAL	X4	EPSON TOYOCOM	FA-238 18.4320MB-C
4	B3S-1000P, SW, 6MM, 160GF	SW1,SW2,SW3,SW4	OMRON	B3S-1000P
2	A6S-4104	SW5,SW6	CTS	219-4MSTR
1	SPEAKER	LS1	Star Micronics	NDT-03C
9	LED SMARTLED GREEN, 0603	LED1,LED3,LED4,LED5,LED8,LED9,LED12,LED13,LED16	OSRAM	LG L29K-G2J1-24-Z
7	LED SMARTLED, RED, 0603	LED2,LED6,LED7,LED10,LED11,LED14,LED15	OSRAM	LS L29K-G1J2-1-0-2-R18-Z
1	LED, GRN, 1206	D5	AVAGO	HSMG-C150
4	SBR2U30P1	D1,D3,D4,D6	DIODES INC	SBR2U30P1
1	SHUNT	SH1-JP7 - SHUNT	Shunt	

Qty	Description	Location	Mfg	Mfg Part Number
55	0.1UF, X7R, 10%, 25V,0603	C1-C7,C12,C13,C21,C22,C25-C35,C39, C40,C44-C46,C51,C53-C55,C58,C61-C6 3,C67,C73,C80,C81,C83-C87,C92-C95, C99-C104,C107	KEMET	C0603C104K4RACTU
17	10UF, 10V, X7R, 10%,0805	C8,C9,C23,C24,C36,C37,C43,C47-C49, C52,C76-C79,C91,C96	MURATA	GRM21BR71A106KE51L
4	0.01uF, 50V, X7R, 10%, 0603	C10,C14,C82,C106	PANASONIC	ECJ-1VB1H103K
2	12PF, 5%, 0603	C15,C18	PANASONIC	ECU-V1H120JCV
6	0.001UF/1000pf, 0603	C38,C50,C64,C68,C11,C105	YAGEO	C0603KRX7R9BB102
5	1uF, 16V, 10%, X5R,0603	C56,C65,C70,C74,C75	AVX	0603YD105KAT2A
1	220UF, 10V, ELECT	C57	PANASONIC	ECE-V1AA221P
2	22PF, 5%, 0603	C59,C60	PANASONIC	ECJ-1VC2A220J
2	3900pF,5%, 25V, 0603	C66,C72	TDK	C1608COG1E392J
2	100uF,10V, TANT D	C69,C71	PANASONIC	ECS-T1AD107R
7	33pF, 50V, 5%, 0603	C88,C19,C20,C97,C98,C108,C109	MURATA	GRM1885C1H330JA01D
2	15pF, 50V, 5%, 0603	C89,C90	MURATA	GRM1885C1H150JA01D
6	BLM21PG300SN1, 0805	L1,L2,L3,L4,L5,L6	MURATA	BLM21PG300SN1
1	10K, POT 3352T	VR1	Bourns	3352T-1-103LF
7	22K, 5%,0603	R1,R2,R3,R4,R30,R31,R33	PANASONIC	ERJ-3GEYJ223V

G

Qty	Description	Location	Mfg	Mfg Part Number
10	1.5K, 5%, 0603	R5,R11,R38,R93,R94,R97,R80,R84,R116,R120	PANASONIC	ERJ-3GEYJ152V
3	1M, 5%, 0603	(R7), R9,R35,R44	PANASONIC	ERJ-3GEYJ105V
1	560, 5%,0603	R8	YAGEO	RC0603JR-07560RL
6	5.1K, 5%, 0603	R10,R19,R20,(R21),R24,R53,(R12),R55	PANASONIC	ERJ-3GEYJ512V
1	4.87K,1%, 0603	R13	STACKPOLE	RMCF1/164.87K1%R
4	49.9, 1%, 0603	R14,R15,R16,R17	PANASONIC	ERJ-3EKF49R9V
4	510, 5%, 0603	R22,R23,R25,R26	PANASONIC	ERJ-3GEYJ511V
4	4.7K, 5%, 0603	R27,R28,R29,R98	PANASONIC	ERJ-3GEYJ472V
1	1K, 5%, 0603	R32	PANASONIC	ERJ-3GEYJ102V
1	120, 5%, 0603	R34	PANASONIC	ERJ-3GEYJ121V
18	10K, 5%, 0603	R36,R41,R42,R48,R51,R52,R54,R58,R60,R61,R63,R65-R68,R72,R78,R79	PANASONIC	ERJ-3GEYJ103V
5	20K, 5%, 0603	R37,R57,R59,R62,R64	PANASONIC	ERJ-3GEYJ203V
2	24, 5%, 0603	R39,R40	DALE	CRCW0603240JRT1
1	470, 5%, 0603	R43	PANASONIC	ERJ-3GEYJ471V
2	15K, 5%, 0603	R45,R46	YAGEO	RC0603JR-0715KL
0	221K, 1%, 0603	(R47)	YAGEO	RC0603FR-07221KL

Qty	Description	Location	Mfg	Mfg Part Number
1	2.0K, 1%, 0603	R49	PANASONIC	ERJ-3EKF2001V
1	68, 5%, 1206	R50	STACKPOLE	RMCF1/8685%R
0	TBD, 0603	(R69,R70)		
1	499K, 1%,0603	R71	PANASONIC	ERJ-3EKF4993V
1	100K, 5%, 0603	R73	PANASONIC	ERJ-3GEYJ104V
14	47K, 5%, 0603	R74-R76,R85,R95,R96,R99,R105,R113-R115,R117-R119	PANASONIC	ERJ-3GEYJ473V
1	16K, 5%, 0603	R77	YAGEO	RC0603JR-0716KL
2	27, 5%,0603	R81,R82	PANASONIC	ERJ-3GEYJ270V
1	220, 5%, 0603	R83	PANASONIC	ERJ-3GEYJ221V
5	100, 5%, 0603	R86,R87,R88,R89,R90	PANASONIC	ERJ-3GEYJ101V
1	390, 5%, 0603	R92	PANASONIC	ERJ-3GEYJ391V
2	0, 5%, 0603	(R91),R18,R56	VISHAY	CRCW06030000Z0EA
6	340, 1%, 0603	R100,R101,R102,R107,R108,R109	YAGEO	RC0603FR-07340RL
6	680, 5%, 0603	R103,R104,R106,R110,R111,R112	STACKPOLE	RMCF1/166805%R
0	CON26_SAM_TST-113-01-T-D	(JN1,JN2)	SAMTEC	TST-113-01-T-D
2	SIP-2P, 1X2	JP7,(J10),JP13	Break Away HDR	Break to Fit
0	JUMPER SOLDER, 0805	(JP9,JP10,JP11,JP12)		

Qty	Description	Location	Mfg	Mfg Part Number
1	CON8_RJ45_PUL_J0011D21BNL	J1	PULSE	J0011D21BNL
1	HDR_10_AMP_5103308-1	J2	AMP	5103308-1
1	Female 2.1MM, PWR_JACK	J4	Switchcraft	RAPC722X
1	CON-DB9F-747844-4	J5	TYCO	5747844-4
2	SIP-3P, 3x1	J6,J7	Break Away HDR	Break to Fit
1	HEADER26, REDPINE WIFI, 26 pin Female Socket, Gold Flash, PTH	J8	Sullins	PPPC132LFBN-RC
1	CONN USB MINI B JAE DX2R005HN2E700	J14	JAE	DX2R005HN2E700
1	CONN USB MINI AB 5POS R/A (OTG)	J9	JAE	DX3R005HN2E700
1	CON20_FCI_SFW20R-4STE1LF	J11	FCI	SFW20R-4STE1LF
1	CUI-SJ1-3553B	J12	CUI	SJ1-3553NG
1	CON8_MICROSD_MLX_500873-0801	J13	3M	2908-05WB-MG
0	7X2 HDR	(LCD1)		
0	CONN, HDR, FEMALE, 7X2	(LCD1 / AZ DISPLAY TO HDR)	Sullins	PPPC072LFBN-RC
5	RUBBER FEET, 0.44"x0.20: (11.8mmx5.08mm) ROUND	Z1,Z2,Z3,Z4,Z5	3M	SJ-5003(BLACK)
1	PCB, 4L, 130mm X 175 mm (5.118" X 6.890 ")	PCB; 1UP w rails ; (5.901" X 6.890 ")		

G

Index

857

859

863

Index

Analog Devices Products Featured in the Renesas Demonstration Kit

ADXL345 Low Power, 3-Axis Digital *i*MEMS Accelerometer
- ±2 g, ±4 g, ±8 g, and ±16 g ranges
- Ultralow power
  - From 30 μA to 140 μA in full measurement mode
  - 0.1 μA in standby mode at VS = 2.5 V (typ)
- Supply Voltage: 2.0 V to 3.6 V
- 10-bit to 13-bit / 4mg resolution
- SPI and I²C digital interfaces
- Temp range: −40°C to +85°C
- 3 mm × 5 mm × 1 mm LGA package

ADMP401 Analog Output, Omni-Directional *i*MEMS Microphone
- SNR: 62 dBA
- Flat Frequency Response: 100 Hz to 15 kHz
- PSRR: 70 dBV
- Sensitivity: -42 dBV
- Current Consumption: < 250 μA
- 4.72 mm × 3.76 mm × 1.00 mm SMT package

SSM2167 Low Power Microphone Preamp
- Low shutdown current < 2 μA
- Adjustable compression ratio and noise gate threshold
- Low noise and distortion: 0.2% THD + N
- 20 kHz bandwidth
- Single 3 V operation

ADT7420 High Accuracy, 16-Bit Digital Temp Sensor
- ±0.25°C temp accuracy from −20°C to +105°C
- I²C-compatible interface
- Supply voltages: 2.7 V to 5.5 V
- Operating temperature: −40°C to +150°C
- LFCSP package

ADM3101 ±15 kV ESD Protected, Single-Channel RS-232 Line Driver/Receiver
- Conforms to EIA/TIA-232E and CCITT V.28 Specifications
- Data Rate: 460 kbps
- 0.1 μF charge pump capacitors
- Contact discharge: ±8 kV ap discharge: ±15 kV

www.analog.com

Omneo™ P5Q

Phase Change Memory

128Mb, 90nm, Serial Interface

Phase change memory (PCM) is today's technology breakthrough. Like Flash memory, PCM is a nonvolatile memory that can store bits even without a power supply. But unlike Flash, data can be read at rates comparable to DRAM and SRAM. PCM blends together the best attributes of NOR Flash, NAND Flash, EEPROM, and RAM.

The Omneo™ P5Q product family is serial PCM with multiple I/O capability and compatibility with familiar SPI NOR interfaces. Omneo PCM products are built to meet the memory requirements of embedded systems.

Omneo P5Q improves overall system performance and enables software simplification using byte-alterability (or over-write capability) because no erase is required. It also increases system level reliability by delivering 1 million WRITE cycle endurance (compared to 100,000 for NOR Flash).

Omneo P5Q Features

- Byte-alterability (over-write capability)
- 1 million WRITE cycle endurance
- I/O bus width:
  - Quad – 50 MHz (MAX)
  - Single/Dual – 66 MHz (MAX)
- Single supply voltage: 2.7– 3.6V
- Programming time: 0.7 MB/s
- Temperature range: 0°C to +70°C

Applications

- EEPROM and SPI NOR consolidation
- Battery-backed SRAM replacement
- Software simplification
- High endurance

EEPROM + SPI NOR → Omneo P5Q

Learn how this new technology can improve the system performance of your next design. Order design samples today or visit the online toolkit at **micron**.com/pcm.

Micron®

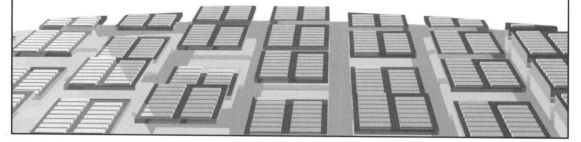

National Semiconductor
10/100 PHYTER®

DP83640

The IEEE 1588 Precision Time Protocol (PTP) is an important improvement to Ethernet systems that provides precise time synchronization for applications such as test and measurement, factory automation, and telecommunications. National Semiconductor's DP83640 Precision PHYTER transceiver is the industry's first to add the IEEE 1588 PTP functionality to a fully-featured, 10/100 Mbps Ethernet PHY.

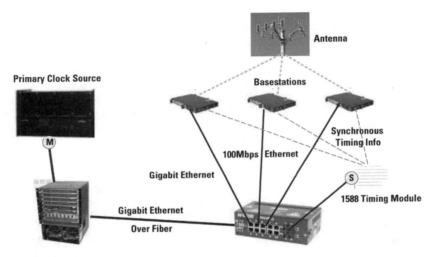

Wireless BTS Timing Sync Using IEEE 1588

High-Speed Industrial Ethernet

Product ID	Temp Range (°C)	Number of Ports	Interface	Typ Power (mW)	Package
DP83640*	-40 to 85	10/100 Single	MII/RMII	280	LQFP-48
DP83848I	-40 to 85	10/100 Single	MII/RMII/SNI	265	LQFP-48
DP83848VYB	-40 to 105	10/100 Single	MII/RMII/SNI	265	LQFP-48
DP83848J	-40 to 85	10/100 Single	MII/RMII	265	LLP-40
DP83849I	-40 to 85	10/100 Dual	MII/RMII	300/Port	TQFP-80

*IEEE 1588

national.com/ethernet

National Semiconductor

OKAYA

Color TFT LCDs

- Size (Diagonal) : 3.5" - 7"
- Resolution: QVGA – WVGA
- Backlight: LED
- Interface: 18 bit TTL RGB
- Touch Panel: Resistive, capacitive, projected capacitive
- Daylight readable options

Chip On Glass (COG)

- Custom and Standard
- No PCB, light weight, low cost
- Minimum external components
- Text, graphic and segment type
- High resolution/duty displays
- RGB or white LED backlight

Custom LCDs

- Full or semi custom
- Color, graphic, COG, panels
- Ruggedized displays
- System on display
- Tailor made form factor

Okaya
Graphic LCD

Display Device for Technology

Graphic LCDs

- Wide range of size & resolutions
- TAB, COG, COB ICs
- Yellow green, blue , white, LED backlights
- Extended and wide operating temp range
- Semi and full custom options
- Touch panels available
- TN, STN, FSTN, ASTN technology

Alpahnumeric/Text LCDs

- 8 character x 1 line to 40 character x 4 lines
- COG, COB ICs
- Yellow green, blue, white LED backlights
- TAB, COG, COB ICs
- Extended and wide operating temp range
- Semi and full custom options
- TN, STN, FSTN, ASTN technology

---

800 852 0122   www.okaya.com   lcdsales@okaya.com

SEGGER J-Link Debug Probe line now supports the Renesas RX.

- **EXTREMELY FAST**
  (2-6 times faster than E1)

- **FLASH BREAKPOINTS**

- **SDK AVAILABLE**

- **J-FLASH AVAILABLE**
  (Flash programming utility)

Support for the Renesas RX does not stop at our extremely fast and sophisticated J-Link debug probe line; it carries through to our production flash programming utility and other products. We are here to assist from development to production.

SEGGER Flash Programmer for Renesas RX

Our flash programming utility (Flasher RX) is a superset of our J-Link described above. It contains all of the debug probe features, while being designed for use in a production environment. The Flasher RX has onboard memory to store your binary image permitting simple standalone flash programming.

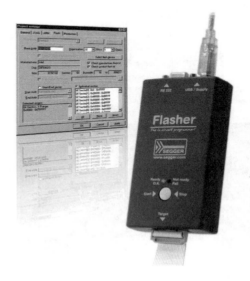

(Email) info@segger.com   (U.S.) 978.874.0299   (International) +49.2103.2878.0

NDT-03C: Small Surface Mount Speaker Solution

The NDT-03C dynamic speaker from Star Micronics is the ideal small surface mount solution for automotive telematics, handheld devices, medical, and many other applications.

With its unique design, high SPL rating, and flat frequency response, the NDT-03C delivers clear sound in a variety of tones. The NDT-03C is perfect for applications with audio outputs including polyphonic tones, voice and music. The NDT-03C features a top sound port and is reflowable. With availability in tape and reel packaging, NDT-03C speaker is ideal for automatic mounting in high volume applications.

NDT-03C Features include:

- *Top Sound Port*
- *Reflowable (Conforms to EIAJ ED-4702)*
- *Flat Frequency response with a high sound level*
- *Excellent Durability in Severe Environments*
- *Compact 15 x 15 x 4 mm size*

Always Leading - Always Innovating

Star Micronics America, Inc.
1150 King Georges Post Rd.
Edison, NJ 08837
800-782-7636 ext. 986
www.starmicronics.com/NDT-03C